Śrī Caitanya-caritāmṛta

BOOKS by
His Divine Grace A.C. Bhaktivedanta Swami Prabhupāda

Bhagavad-gītā As It Is
Śrīmad-Bhāgavatam, Cantos 1-5 (15 Vols.)
Śrī Caitanya-caritāmṛta (17 Vols.)
Teachings of Lord Caitanya
The Nectar of Devotion
Śrī Īśopaniṣad
Easy Journey to Other Planets
Kṛṣṇa Consciousness: The Topmost Yoga System
Kṛṣṇa, The Supreme Personality of Godhead (3 Vols.)
Transcendental Teachings of Prahlād Mahārāja
Kṛṣṇa, the Reservoir of Pleasure
The Perfection of Yoga
Beyond Birth and Death
On the Way to Kṛṣṇa
Rāja-vidyā: The King of Knowledge
Elevation to Kṛṣṇa Consciousness
Kṛṣṇa Consciousness: The Matchless Gift
Back to Godhead Magazine (Founder)

A complete catalogue is available upon request

International Society for Krishna Consciousness
3764 Watseka Avenue
Los Angeles, California 90034

All Glory to Śrī Guru and Gaurāṅga

ŚRĪ CAITANYA-CARITĀMṚTA

of Kṛṣṇadāsa Kavirāja Gosvāmī

Madhya-līlā
Volume Seven

"The Lord Enters Śrī Vṛndāvana"

with the original Bengali text, Roman transliterations, synonyms, translation and elaborate purports

by

HIS DIVINE GRACE
A.C. Bhaktivedanta Swami Prabhupāda
Founder-Ācārya of the International Society for Krishna Consciousness

THE BHAKTIVEDANTA BOOK TRUST
New York · Los Angeles · London · Bombay

Readers interested in the subject matter of this book
are invited by the International Society for Krishna Consciousness
to correspond with its Secretary.

International Society for Krishna Consciousness
3764 Watseka Avenue
Los Angeles, California 90034

Library of Congress Catalogue Card Number: 73-93206
International Standard Book Number: 0-912776-69-2

First printing, 1975: 20,000 copies

Printed in the United States of America

Contents

Introduction

Śrī Caitanya-caritāmṛta is the principal work on the life and teachings of Śrī Kṛṣṇa Caitanya. Śrī Caitanya is the pioneer of a great social and religious movement which began in India a little less than five hundred years ago and which has directly and indirectly influenced the subsequent course of religious and philosophical thinking not only in India but in the recent West as well.

Caitanya Mahāprabhu is regarded as a figure of great historical significance. However, our conventional method of historical analysis—that of seeing a man as a product of his times—fails here. Śrī Caitanya is a personality who transcends the limited scope of historical settings.

At a time when, in the West, man was directing his explorative spirit toward studying the structure of the physical universe and circumnavigating the world in search of new oceans and continents, Śrī Kṛṣṇa Caitanya, in the East, was inaugurating and masterminding a revolution directed inward, toward a scientific understanding of the highest knowledge of man's spiritual nature.

The chief historical sources for the life of Śrī Kṛṣṇa Caitanya are the *kaḍacās* (diaries) kept by Murāri Gupta and Svarūpa Dāmodara Gosvāmī. Murāri Gupta, a physician and close associate of Śrī Caitanya's, recorded extensive notes on the first twenty-four years of Śrī Caitanya's life, culminating in his initiation into the renounced order, *sannyāsa*. The events of the rest of Caitanya Mahāprabhu's forty-eight years are recorded in the diary of Svarūpa Dāmodora Gosvāmī, another of Caitanya Mahāprabhu's intimate associates.

Śrī Caitanya-caritāmṛta is divided into three sections called *līlās,* which literally means "pastimes"—*Ādi-līlā* (the early period), *Madhya-līlā* (the middle period) and *Antya-līlā* (the final period). The notes of Murāri Gupta form the basis of the *Ādi-līlā,* and Svarūpa Dāmodara's diary provides the details for the *Madhya-* and *Antya-līlās.*

The first twelve of the seventeen chapters of *Ādi-līlā* constitute the preface for the entire work. By referring to Vedic scriptural evidence, this preface establishes Śrī Caitanya as the *avatāra* (incarnation) of Kṛṣṇa (God) for the age of Kali—the current epoch, beginning five thousand years ago and characterized by materialism, hypocrisy and dissension. In these descriptions, Caitanya Mahāprabhu, who is identical with Lord Kṛṣṇa, descends to liberally grant pure love of God to the fallen souls of this degraded age by propagating *saṅkīrtana*—literally, "congregational glorification of God"—especially by organizing massive public chanting of the *mahā-mantra* (Great Chant for Deliverance). The esoteric purpose of Lord Caitanya's appearance in the world is revealed, his co-*avatāras* and principal devotees are described and his teachings are summarized. The remaining portion of *Ādi-līlā,* chapters thirteen through seventeen, briefly recounts his divine birth and his life until he accepted the renounced order. This includes his childhood miracles, schooling, marriage and early philosophical confrontations, as well as his organization of a widespread *saṅkīrtana* movement and his civil disobedience against the repression of the Mohammedan government.

The subject of *Madhya-līlā,* the longest of the three divisions, is a detailed narration of Lord Caitanya's extensive and eventful travels throughout India as a renounced mendicant, teacher, philosopher, spiritual preceptor and mystic. During this period of six years, Śrī Caitanya transmits his teachings to his principal disciples. He debates and converts many of the most renowned philosophers and theologians of his time, including Śaṅkarites, Buddhists and Muslims, and incorporates their many thousands of followers and disciples into his own burgeoning numbers. A dramatic account of Caitanya Mahāprabhu's miraculous activities at the giant Jagannātha Cart Festival in Orissa is also included in this section.

Antya-līlā concerns the last eighteen years of Śrī Caitanya's manifest presence, spent in semiseclusion near the famous Jagannātha temple at Jagannātha Purī in Orissa. During these final years, Śrī Caitanya drifted deeper and deeper into trances of spiritual ecstasy unparalleled in all of religious and literary history, Eastern or Western. Śrī Caitanya's perpetual and ever-increasing religious beatitude, graphically described in the eyewitness accounts of Svarūpa Dāmodara Gosvāmī, his constant companion during this period, clearly defy the investigative and descriptive abilities of modern psychologists and phenomenologists of religious experience.

The author of this great classic, Kṛṣṇadāsa Kavirāja Gosvāmī, born in the year 1507, was a disciple of Raghunātha dāsa Gosvāmī, a confidential follower of Caitanya Mahāprabhu. Raghunātha dāsa, a renowned ascetic saint, heard and memorized all the activities of Caitanya Mahāprabhu told to him by Svarūpa Dāmodara. After the passing away of Śrī Caitanya and Svarūpa Dāmodara, Raghunātha dāsa, unable to bear the pain of separation from these objects of his complete devotion, traveled to Vṛndāvana, intending to commit suicide by jumping from Govardhana Hill. In Vṛndāvana, however, he encountered Rūpa Gosvāmī and Sanātana Gosvāmī, the most confidential disciples of Caitanya Mahāprabhu. They convinced him to give up his plan of suicide and impelled him to reveal to them the spiritually inspiring events of Lord Caitanya's later life. Kṛṣṇadāsa Kavirāja Gosvāmī was also residing in Vṛndāvana at this time, and Raghunātha dāsa Gosvāmī endowed him with a full comprehension of the transcendental life of Śrī Caitanya.

By this time, several biographical works had already been written on the life of Śrī Caitanya by contemporary and near-contemporary scholars and devotees. These included *Śrī Caitanya-carita* by Murāri Gupta, *Caitanya-maṅgala* by Locana dāsa Ṭhākura and *Caitanya-bhāgavata.* This latter text, a work by Vṛndāvana dāsa Ṭhākura, who was then considered the principal authority on Śrī Caitanya's life, was highly revered. While composing his important work, Vṛndāvana dāsa, fearing that it would become too voluminous, avoided elaborately describing many of the events of Śrī Caitanya's life, particulary the later ones. Anxious to hear of these later pastimes, the devotees of Vṛndāvana requested Kṛṣṇadāsa Kavirāja Gosvāmī, whom they respected as a great saint, to compose a book to narrate these episodes in detail. Upon this request, and with the permission and blessings of the Madana-mohana Deity of Vṛndāvana, he began compiling *Śrī Caitanya-caritāmṛta,* which, due to its biographical excellence and thorough exposition of Lord Caitanya's profound philosophy and teachings, is regarded as the most significant of biographical works on Śrī Caitanya.

He commenced work on the text while in his late nineties and in failing health, as he vividly describes in the text itself: "I have now become too old and disturbed in invalidity. While writing, my hands tremble. I cannot remember anything, nor can I see or hear properly. Still I write, and this is a great wonder." That he nevertheless completed, under such debilitating conditions, the greatest literary gem of medieval India is surely one of the wonders of literary history.

This English translation and commentary is the work of His Divine Grace A. C. Bhaktivedanta Swami Prabhupāda, the world's most distinguished teacher of Indian religious and philosophical thought. His commentary is based upon two Bengali commentaries, one by his teacher Śrīla Bhaktisiddhānta Sarasvatī Gosvāmī, the eminent Vedic scholar who predicted, "The time will come when the people of the world will learn Bengali to read *Śrī Caitanya-caritāmṛta,*" and the other by Śrīla Bhaktisiddhānta's father, Bhaktivinoda Ṭhākura.

His Divine Grace A. C. Bhaktivedanta Swami Prabhupāda is himself a disciplic descendant of Śrī Caitanya Mahāprabhu, and he is the first scholar to execute systematic English translations of the major works of Śrī Caitanya's followers. His consummate Bengali and Sanskrit scholarship and intimate familiarity with the precepts of Śrī Kṛṣṇa Caitanya are a fitting combination that eminently qualifies him to present this important classic to the English-speaking world. The ease and clarity with which he expounds upon difficult philosophical concepts lures even a reader totally unfamiliar with Indian religious tradition into a genuine understanding and appreciation of this profound and monumental work.

The entire text, with commentary, presented in seventeen lavishly illustrated volumes by the Bhaktivedanta Book Trust, represents a contribution of major importance to the intellectual, cultural and spiritual life of contemporary man.

—The Publishers

His Divine Grace
A. C. Bhaktivedanta Swami Prabhupāda
Founder-Ācārya of the International Society for Krishna Consciousness

PLATE ONE

"When the Lord passed through the jungle in great ecstasy, packs of tigers, elephants, rhinoceros and boars came, and the Lord passed right through them. Balabhadra Bhaṭṭācārya was very much afraid to see them, but by Śrī Caitanya Mahāprabhu's influence, all the animals stood to one side. The elephants whose bodies were touched by the water splashed by the Lord began to chant, 'Kṛṣṇa! Kṛṣṇa!' and dance and sing in ecstasy. Some of the elephants fell to the ground, and some screamed in ecstasy. Seeing this, Balabhadra Bhaṭṭācārya was completely astonished. Sometimes Śrī Caitanya Mahāprabhu chanted very loudly while passing through the jungle. Hearing His sweet voice, all the does came near Him. While Śrī Caitanya Mahāprabhu was passing through the jungle, five or seven tigers came. Joining the deer, the tigers began to follow the Lord. When Śrī Caitanya Mahāprabhu said, 'Chant Kṛṣṇa! Kṛṣṇa!' the tigers and deer began to chant, 'Kṛṣṇa!' When all the tigers and does danced and jumped, Balabhadra Bhaṭṭācārya saw them and was struck with wonder. Indeed, the tigers and deer began to embrace one another, and, touching mouths, they began to kiss. When Śrī Caitanya Mahāprabhu saw all this fun, He began to smile." (*pp.13-22*)

PLATE TWO

"When Śrī Caitanya Mahāprabhu passed through Vṛndāvana, herds of grazing cows saw Him pass and, immediately surrounding Him, began to moo very loudly. Seeing the herds approach Him, the Lord was stunned with ecstatic love. The cows then began to lick His body in great affection. Becoming pacified, Śrī Caitanya Mahāprabhu began to caress the cows, and the cows, being unable to give up His company, went with Him. Then when the Lord chanted, all the deer heard His sweet voice and approached Him. When the does and bucks came and saw the Lord's face, they began to lick His body. Not being at all afraid of Him, they accompanied Him along the path. Bumblebees and birds like the parrot and cuckoo all began to sing loudly on the fifth note, and the peacocks began to dance in front of the Lord. Upon seeing Śrī Caitanya Mahāprabhu, the trees and creepers, overloaded with fruits and flowers, fell down at the lotus feet of the Lord and greeted Him with various presentations as if they were friends. Thus all the moving and nonmoving living entities of Vṛndāvana became very jubilant to see the Lord." (*pp.110-113*)

PLATE THREE

"Śrī Caitanya Mahāprabhu traveled all over Vṛndāvana and pleased all living entities, moving and nonmoving, with His glances. The Lord took much personal pleasure in seeing everyone. In this way Lord Gaurāṅga traveled in Vṛndāvana. From Rādhā-kuṇḍa, Śrī Caitanya Mahāprabhu went to Sumanah Lake. When He saw Govardhana Hill from there, He was overwhelmed by joy. When the Lord saw Govardhana Hill, He immediately offered obeisances, falling down on the ground like a rod. He embraced one piece of rock from Govardhana Hill and became mad." (*pp.130-138*)

PLATE FOUR

"Śrī Caitanya Mahāprabhu then took His bath in a lake called Govinda-kuṇḍa, and while He was there, He heard that the Deity Gopāla had already gone to Gāṅṭhuli-grāma. Śrī Caitanya Mahāprabhu then went to the village of Gāṅṭhuli-grāma and saw the Lord Gopāla Deity. Overwhelmed by ecstatic love, He began to chant and dance. As soon as the Lord saw the beauty of the Gopāla Deity, He was immediately overwhelmed by ecstatic love, and He recited the following verse. He then chanted and danced until the day ended. Śrī Caitanya Mahāprabhu said, 'May the left arm of Śrī Kṛṣṇa, whose eyes are like the petals of a lotus flower, always protect you. With His left arm He raised Govardhana Hill as if it were a toy.' " (*pp.147-149*)

PLATE FIVE

"Śrī Caitanya Mahāprabhu bathed in all the celebrated lakes, beginning with Lake Pāvana. Thereafter He climbed a hill and spoke to the people. Śrī Caitanya Mahāprabhu asked, 'Are there any deities on top of this hill?' The local people replied, 'There are deities on this hill, but they are located within a cave. There is a father and mother with well-built bodies, and between them is a very beautiful child who is curved in three places.' Hearing this, Śrī Caitanya Mahāprabhu became very happy. After excavating the cave, He saw the three deities. Śrī Caitanya Mahāprabhu offered His respects to Nanda Mahārāja and mother Yaśodā, and with great ecstatic love He touched the body of Lord Kṛṣṇa." *(pp.160-162)*

PLATE SIX

"While walking, Śrī Caitanya Mahāprabhu, understanding that the others were fatigued, took them all beneath a tree and sat down. There were many cows grazing near the tree, and the Lord was very pleased to see them. Suddenly a cowherd boy blew on his flute, and immediately the Lord was struck with ecstatic love. Filled with ecstatic love, the Lord fell unconscious to the ground. He foamed at the mouth, and His breathing stopped. While the Lord was unconscious, ten cavalry soldiers belonging to the Mohammedan Pāṭhāna military order rode up and dismounted. Seeing the Lord unconscious, the soldiers thought, 'This *sannyāsī* must have possessed a large quantity of gold. These four rogues here must have taken away the *sannyāsī's* riches after killing Him by making Him take the poison *dhuturā.*' Thinking this, the Pāṭhāna soldiers arrested the four persons and decided to kill them. Because of this, the two Bengalis began to tremble." (*pp.211-214*)

PLATE SEVEN

"On the pretext of bad health, Sanātana Gosvāmī remained home. Thus he gave up government service and did not go to the royal court. The greedy masters of his clerical and secretarial staff performed the government duties while Sanātana personally remained home and discussed the revealed scriptures. Śrī Sanātana Gosvāmī used to discuss *Śrīmad-Bhāgavatam* in an assembly of twenty or thirty learned *brāhmaṇa* scholars. While Sanātana Gosvāmī was studying *Śrīmad-Bhāgavatam* in the assembly of learned *brāhmaṇas,* one day the Nawab of Bengal and another person suddenly appeared. As soon as all the *brāhmaṇas* and Sanātana Gosvāmī saw the Nawab appear, they all stood up and respectfully gave him a sitting place to honor him. The Nawab said, 'I sent my physician to you, and he has reported that you are not diseased. As far as he could see, you are completely healthy. I am depending on you to carry out so many of my activities, but you have given up your governmental duties to sit here at home. You have spoiled all my activities. What is your intention? Please tell me frankly.' " (*pp.252-258*)

PLATE EIGHT

"While crossing the River Yamunā, Śrī Caitanya Mahāprabhu saw the glossy black water and was immediately bewildered with ecstatic love. Indeed, as soon as Śrī Caitanya Mahāprabhu saw the River Yamunā, He immediately made a great sound and jumped into the water. Everyone was filled with fear and trembling to see this. They all hastily grabbed Śrī Caitanya Mahāprabhu and pulled Him out of the water. Once on the boat's platform, the Lord began to dance. Due to the Lord's heavy weight, the boat began to tilt. It began filling up with water and was on the verge of sinking. Śrī Caitanya Mahāprabhu tried to restrain Himself as far as possible before Vallabhācārya, but although He tried to keep calm, His ecstatic love could not be checked." (*pp.286-288*)

PLATE NINE

"'Although Kṛṣṇa is beyond sense perception and is unmanifest to human beings, He takes up the guise of a human being with a material body. Thus mother Yaśodā thought Him to be her son, and she bound Lord Kṛṣṇa with a rope to a wooden mortar, as if He were an ordinary child.' When Lord Kṛṣṇa exhibited Himself like an ordinary child before mother Yaśodā, He was playing like a naughty boy stealing butter and breaking butter pots. Mother Yaśodā became disturbed and wanted to bind the Lord to a mortar used for pounding spices. In other words, she considered the Supreme Personality of Godhead an ordinary child." (*p.379*)

PLATE TEN

"When all the cowherd boys were playing in the forest of Vṛndāvana, the demon Pralambāsura appeared to kidnap Kṛṣṇa and Balarāma. The *asura* appeared disguised as a cowherd boy, but Kṛṣṇa could understand his trick. Kṛṣṇa therefore divided all the cowherd boys into two parties. One party belonged to Balarāma, and the other party belonged to Kṛṣṇa Himself. Ultimately Kṛṣṇa was defeated in this play, and according to the wager, the defeated party had to carry the victorious party on their shoulders. Kṛṣṇa had to carry Śrīdāma on His shoulders, and Bhadrasena had to carry Vṛṣabha. The demon Pralambāsura had to carry Balarāma, and when Balarāma mounted his shoulders, the demon ran far away. Finally the demon began to expand his body to a gigantic size, and Balarāma understood that he intended to kill Him. Balarāma immediately struck the demon's head with His strong fist, and the demon fell down dead as if he were a snake whose head had been smashed." (*p.380*)

PLATE ELEVEN

"The next morning, when Śrī Caitanya Mahāprabhu arose and prepared to leave for Vārāṇasī (Benares), Śrīla Rūpa Gosvāmī made the following statement at the Lord's lotus feet: 'If You give me permission, I shall go with Your Lordship. It is not possible for me to tolerate the waves of separation.' Śrī Caitanya Mahāprabhu replied, 'Your duty is to carry out My order. You have come near Vṛndāvana. Now you should go there. Later, you can go from Vṛndāvana to Jagannātha Purī through Bengal (Gauḍa-deśa). There you will meet Me again.' After embracing Rūpa Gosvāmī, Śrī Caitanya Mahāprabhu got into a boat. Rūpa Gosvāmī fainted and fell down on the spot." (*pp.398-399*)

CHAPTER 17

The Lord Travels to Vṛndāvana

The following summary of the Seventeenth Chapter is given by Bhaktivinoda Ṭhākura in his *Amṛta-pravāha-bhāṣya.* After attending the Ratha-yātrā ceremony of Śrī Jagannātha, Śrī Caitanya Mahāprabhu decided to start for Vṛndāvana. Śrī Rāmānanda Rāya and Svarūpa Dāmodara Gosvāmī selected a *brāhmaṇa* named Balabhadra Bhaṭṭācārya to personally assist Śrī Caitanya Mahāprabhu. Early in the morning before sunrise, the Lord started for the town of Kaṭaka. North of Kaṭaka, He penetrated a dense forest and visited many tigers and elephants, whom He engaged in chanting the Hare Kṛṣṇa *mahā-mantra.* Whenever He had a chance to visit a village, He would beg alms and acquire some rice and vegetables. If there were no village, He would cook whatever rice remained and collect some spinach from the forest to eat. Śrī Caitanya Mahāprabhu was very pleased with the behavior of Balabhadra Bhaṭṭācārya.

In this way the Lord passed through the jungle of Jhārikhaṇḍa and finally reached Vārāṇasī. After taking His bath at the Maṇikarṇikā-ghāṭa at Vārāṇasī, He met Tapana Miśra, who took the Lord to his place and respectfully gave Him a comfortable residence. At Vārāṇasī, Vaidya Candraśekhara, Śrī Caitanya Mahāprabhu's old friend, also rendered service unto Him. Seeing the behavior of Śrī Caitanya Mahāprabhu, one Mahārāṣṭrīya *brāhmaṇa* informed Prakāśānanda Sarasvatī, the leader of the Māyāvādī *sannyāsīs.* Prakāśānanda made various accusations against the Lord. The Mahārāṣṭrīya *brāhmaṇa* was very sorry about this, and he brought the news to Śrī Caitanya Mahāprabhu, inquiring from Him why the Māyāvādī *sannyāsīs* did not utter the holy name of Kṛṣṇa. In reply, Śrī Caitanya Mahāprabhu said that they were offenders and that one should not associate with them. In this way the Lord bestowed His blessings upon the *brāhmaṇa.*

Śrī Caitanya Mahāprabhu next passed through Prayāga and Mathurā and then took His lunch at the home of a Sānoḍiyā *brāhmaṇa,* a disciple of Mādhavendra Purī. He bestowed His blessings upon the *brāhmaṇa* by accepting lunch at his place. Thereafter the Lord visited the twelve forests of Vṛndāvana and was filled with great ecstatic love. As He toured the Vṛndāvana forests, He heard the chirping of parrots and other birds.

TEXT 1

গচ্ছন্ বৃন্দাবনং গৌরো ব্যাঘ্রেভৈণখগান্ বনে ।
প্রেমোন্মত্তান্ সহোন্নৃত্যান্ বিদধে কৃষ্ণজল্পিনঃ ॥ ১ ॥

gacchan vṛndāvanaṁ gauro
vyāghrebhaiṇa-khagān vane
premonmattān sahonnṛtyān
vidadhe kṛṣṇa-jalpinaḥ

SYNONYMS

gacchan—going; *vṛndāvanam*—to Vṛndāvana-dhāma; *gauraḥ*—Śrī Caitanya Mahāprabhu; *vyāghra*—tigers; *ibha*—elephants; *eṇa*—deer; *khagān*—and birds; *vane*—in the forest; *prema-unmattān*—maddened by ecstatic love; *saha*—with; *unnṛtyān*—dancing; *vidadhe*—made; *kṛṣṇa*—Lord Kṛṣṇa's name; *jalpinaḥ*—chanting.

TRANSLATION

On His way to Vṛndāvana, Lord Śrī Caitanya Mahāprabhu passed through the forest of Jhārikhaṇḍa and made all the tigers, elephants, deer and birds dance and chant the Hare Kṛṣṇa mahā-mantra. Thus all these animals were overwhelmed by ecstatic love.

TEXT 2

জয় জয় গৌরচন্দ্র জয় নিত্যানন্দ ।
জয়াদ্বৈতচন্দ্র জয় গৌরভক্তবৃন্দ ॥ ২ ॥

jaya jaya gauracandra jaya nityānanda
jayādvaita-candra jaya gaura-bhakta-vṛnda

SYNONYMS

jaya jaya—all glories; *gauracandra*—to Śrī Caitanya Mahāprabhu; *jaya*—all glories; *nityānanda*—to Nityānanda Prabhu; *jaya*—all glories; *advaita-candra*—to Advaita Ācārya; *jaya*—all glories; *gaura-bhakta-vṛnda*—to the devotees of Lord Caitanya.

TRANSLATION

All glories to Śrī Caitanya Mahāprabhu! All glories to Lord Nityānanda! All glories to Advaitacandra! All glories to all the devotees of the Lord!

TEXT 3

শরৎকাল হৈল, প্রভুর চলিতে হৈল মতি ।
রামানন্দ-স্বরূপ-সঙ্গে নিভৃতে যুকতি ॥ ৩ ॥

śarat-kāla haila, prabhura calite haila mati
rāmānanda-svarūpa-saṅge nibhṛte yukati

SYNONYMS

śarat-kāla haila—autumn arrived; *prabhura*—of Lord Śrī Caitanya Mahāprabhu; *calite*—to travel; *haila*—was; *mati*—desire; *rāmānanda*—Rāmānanda Rāya; *svarūpa*—Svarūpa Dāmodara; *saṅge*—with; *nibhṛte*—solitary; *yukati*—consultation.

TRANSLATION

When autumn arrived, Śrī Caitanya Mahāprabhu decided to go to Vṛndāvana. In a solitary place, He consulted with Rāmānanda Rāya and Svarūpa Dāmodara Gosvāmī.

TEXT 4

“মোর সহায় কর যদি, তুমি-দুই জন।
তবে আমি যাঞা দেখি শ্রীবৃন্দাবন ॥ ৪ ॥

"mora sahāya kara yadi, tumi-dui jana
tabe āmi yāñā dekhi śrī-vṛndāvana

SYNONYMS

mora—of Me; *sahāya*—help; *kara*—you do; *yadi*—if; *tumi*—you; *dui jana*—two persons; *tabe*—then; *āmi*—I; *yāñā*—going; *dekhi*—shall see; *śrī-vṛndāvana*—Śrī Vṛndāvana-dhāma.

TRANSLATION

The Lord requested Rāmānanda Rāya and Svarūpa Dāmodara Gosvāmī to help Him go to Vṛndāvana.

TEXT 5

রাত্র্যে উঠি' বনপথে পলাঞা যাব।
একাকী যাইব, কাহোঁ সঙ্গে না লইব ॥ ৫ ॥

rātrye uṭhi' vana-pathe palāñā yāba
ekākī yāiba, kāhoṅ saṅge nā la-iba

SYNONYMS

rātrye uṭhi'—rising at night; *vana-pathe*—on the road to the forest; *palāñā yāba*—I shall go away secretly; *ekākī yāiba*—I shall go alone; *kāhoṅ*—anyone; *saṅge*—with Me; *nā la-iba*—I shall not take.

TRANSLATION

Śrī Caitanya Mahāprabhu said, "I shall leave early in the morning and go incognito, taking the road to the forest. I shall go alone and not take anyone with Me.

TEXT 6

কেহ যদি সঙ্গ লইতে পাছে উঠি' ধায় ।
সবারে রাখিবা, যেন কেহ নাহি যায় ॥ ৬ ॥

keha yadi saṅga la-ite pāche uṭhi' dhāya
sabāre rākhibā, yena keha nāhi yāya

SYNONYMS

keha—someone; *yadi*—if; *saṅga la-ite*—to take company; *pāche*—behind; *uṭhi'*—getting up; *dhāya*—runs; *sabāre*—everyone; *rākhibā*—please stop; *yena*—so that; *keha*—anyone; *nāhi yāya*—does not go.

TRANSLATION

"If someone wants to follow Me, please stop him. I don't want anyone to go with Me.

TEXT 7

প্রসন্ন হঞা আজ্ঞা দিবা, না মানিবা 'দুঃখ' ।
তোমা-সবার 'সুখে' পথে হবে মোর 'সুখ' ॥" ৭ ॥

prasanna hañā ājñā dibā, nā mānibā 'duḥkha'
tomā-sabāra 'sukhe' pathe habe mora 'sukha' "

SYNONYMS

prasanna hañā—being pleased; *ājñā dibā*—give permission; *nā*—do not; *mānibā duḥkha*—become unhappy; *tomā-sabāra*—of all of you; *sukhe*—by the happiness; *pathe*—on the road; *habe*—there will be; *mora*—My; *sukha*—happiness.

TRANSLATION

"Please give Me your permission with great pleasure and do not be unhappy. If you are happy, I shall be happy on My way to Vṛndāvana."

TEXT 8

দুইজন কহে,—'তুমি ঈশ্বর 'স্বতন্ত্র' ।
যেই ইচ্ছা, সেই করিবা, নহ 'পরতন্ত্র' ॥ ৮ ॥

dui-jana kahe,——'tumi īśvara 'svatantra'
yei icchā, sei karibā, naha 'paratantra'

SYNONYMS

dui-jana kahe—the two persons replied; *tumi*—You; *īśvara*—the Supreme Personality of Godhead; *svatantra*—completely independent; *yei icchā*—whatever You desire; *sei*—that; *karibā*—You will do; *naha*—You are not; *para-tantra*—dependent on anyone.

TRANSLATION

Upon hearing this, Rāmānanda Rāya and Svarūpa Dāmodara Gosvāmī replied, "Dear Lord, You are completely independent. Since You are not dependent on anyone, You do whatever You desire.

TEXT 9

কিন্তু আমা-দুঁহার শুন এক নিবেদনে ।
'তোমার সুখে আমার সুখ'— কহিলা আপনে ॥ ৯ ॥

kintu āmā-duṅhāra śuna eka nivedane
'tomāra sukhe āmāra sukha'——kahilā āpane

SYNONYMS

kintu—but; *āmā-duṅhāra*—of both of us; *śuna*—please hear; *eka nivedane*—one submission; *tomāra sukhe*—by your happiness; *āmāra sukha*—our happiness; *kahilā*—You have already stated; *āpane*—personally.

TRANSLATION

"Dear Lord, kindly hear our one petition. You have already said that You will derive happiness from our happiness. This is Your own statement.

TEXT 10

আমা-দুঁহার মনে তবে বড় 'সুখ' হয় ।
এক নিবেদন যদি ধর, দয়াময় ॥ ১০ ॥

āmā-duṅhāra mane tabe baḍa 'sukha' haya
eka nivedana yadi dhara, dayāmaya

SYNONYMS

āmā-duṅhāra—of us two; *mane*—in the mind; *tabe*—therefore; *baḍa*—very much; *sukha haya*—there is happiness; *eka nivedana*—one request; *yadi*—if; *dhara*—You accept; *dayā-maya*—merciful.

TRANSLATION

"If You will please accept just one request, we shall be very, very happy.

TEXT 11

'উত্তম ব্রাহ্মণ' এক সঙ্গে অবশ্য চাহি।
ভিক্ষা করি' ভিক্ষা দিবে, যাবে পাত্র বহি' ॥ ১১ ॥

'uttama brāhmaṇa' eka saṅge avaśya cāhi
bhikṣā kari' bhikṣā dibe, yābe pātra vahi'

SYNONYMS

uttama brāhmaṇa—a high-class *brāhmaṇa; eka*—one; *saṅge*—along; *avaśya*—certainly; *cāhi*—we want; *bhikṣā kari'*—collecting alms; *bhikṣā dibe*—will give You food; *yābe*—will go; *pātra vahi'*—bearing Your waterpot.

TRANSLATION

"Our Lord, please take one very nice brāhmaṇa with You. He will collect alms for You, cook for You, give You prasāda, and carry Your waterpot while traveling.

TEXT 12

বনপথে যাইতে নাহি 'ভোজ্যান্ন'-ব্রাহ্মণ।
আজ্ঞা কর,—সঙ্গে চলুক বিপ্র একজন ॥' ১২ ॥

vana-pathe yāite nāhi 'bhojyānna'-brāhmaṇa
ājñā kara,——saṅge caluka vipra eka-jana'

SYNONYMS

vana-pathe—on the forest path; *yāite*—going; *nāhi*—there is not; *bhojya-anna-brāhmaṇa*—a *brāhmaṇa* whose food can be accepted; *ājñā kara*—please give permission; *saṅge*—along; *caluka*—may go; *vipra*—*brāhmaṇa; eka-jana*—one person.

TRANSLATION

"When You go through the jungle, there will be no brāhmaṇa available from whom You can accept lunch. Therefore please give permission for at least one pure brāhmaṇa to accompany You."

TEXT 13

প্রভু কহে,—নিজ-সঙ্গী কাঁহো না লইব।
একজনে নিলে, আনের মনে দুঃখ হইব ॥ ১৩ ॥

prabhu kahe,——nija-saṅgī kāṅho nā la-iba
eka-jane nile, ānera mane duḥkha ha-iba

SYNONYMS

prabhu kahe—Śrī Caitanya Mahāprabhu replied; *nija-saṅgī*—of My associates; *kāṅho*—anyone; *nā*—not; *la-iba*—I shall take; *eka-jane nile*—if I take someone; *ānera mane*—in the mind of others; *duḥkha ha-iba*—there will be unhappiness.

TRANSLATION

Śrī Caitanya Mahāprabhu said, "I shall not take any of My associates with Me because if I choose someone, all the others will be unhappy.

TEXT 14

নূতন সঙ্গী হইবেক,—স্নিগ্ধ যাঁর মন।
ঐছে যবে পাই, তবে লই 'এক' জন ॥ ১৪ ॥

nūtana saṅgī ha-ibeka,——snigdha yāṅra mana
aiche yabe pāi, tabe la-i 'eka' jana

SYNONYMS

nūtana—new; *saṅgī*—associate; *ha-ibeka*—must be; *snigdha*—very peaceful; *yāṅra*—whose; *mana*—mind; *aiche*—such; *yabe*—if; *pāi*—I get; *tabe*—then; *la-i*—I take; *eka jana*—one person.

TRANSLATION

"Such a person must be a new man, and he must have a peaceful mind. If I can obtain such a man, I shall agree to take him with Me."

PURPORT

When Śrī Caitanya Mahāprabhu formerly went to South India, a *brāhmaṇa* named Kālā Kṛṣṇadāsa went with Him. It was Kālā Kṛṣṇadāsa who fell victim to a woman, and Śrī Caitanya Mahāprabhu had to take the trouble to free him from the clutches of the gypsies. Therefore the Lord here says that He wants a new man who is peaceful in mind. One whose mind is not peaceful is agitated by certain drives, especially sex desire, even though he be in the company of Caitanya Mahāprabhu. Such a man will become a victim of women and will fall down even in the company of the Supreme Personality of Godhead. *Māyā* is so strong that unless one is determined not to fall victim, even the Supreme Personality of Godhead cannot give protection. The Supreme Lord and His representative always want to give protection, but a person must take advantage of their personal contact. If one thinks that the Supreme Personality of Godhead or His representative is an ordinary man, he will certainly fall down. Thus Śrī Caitanya Mahāprabhu did not want a person like Kālā Kṛṣṇadāsa to accompany Him. He wanted someone who was determined, who had a peaceful mind and who was not agitated by ulterior motives.

TEXT 15

স্বরূপ কহে,—এই বলভদ্র-ভট্টাচার্য।
তোমাতে সুস্নিগ্ধ বড়, পণ্ডিত, সাধু, আর্য ॥ ১৫ ॥

svarūpa kahe,——ei balabhadra-bhaṭṭācārya
tomāte susnigdha baḍa, paṇḍita, sādhu, ārya

SYNONYMS

svarūpa kahe—Svarūpa Dāmodara Gosvāmī said; *ei*—this; *balabhadra-bhaṭṭācārya*—Balabhadra Bhaṭṭācārya; *tomāte*—unto You; *su-snigdha*—affectionate; *baḍa*—very; *paṇḍita*—educated; *sādhu*—honest; *ārya*—advanced in spiritual consciousness.

TRANSLATION

Svarūpa Dāmodara then said, "Here is Balabhadra Bhaṭṭācārya, who has great love for You. He is an honest, learned scholar, and he is advanced in spiritual consciousness.

PURPORT

Śrī Caitanya Mahāprabhu wanted a new man, not a person like Kālā Kṛṣṇadāsa who would fall for women. Svarūpa Dāmodara therefore immediately pointed out a new *brāhmaṇa* named Balabhadra Bhaṭṭācārya. Śrī Svarūpa Dāmodara Gosvāmī had studied this person very thoroughly and had seen that he had great love for Śrī Caitanya Mahāprabhu. Not only did he love the Lord, but he was also learned and honest. He was not duplicitous, and he was advanced in Kṛṣṇa consciousness. According to a Bengali proverb, *ati bhakti corera lakṣaṇa:* "Too much devotion is a symptom of a thief." A person who assumes himself to be a great devotee but mentally is thinking of something else is duplicitous. One who is not duplicitous is called *sādhu.* Svarūpa Dāmodara immediately pointed out that Balabhadra Bhaṭṭācārya was quite fit to accompany the Lord because he was a learned scholar and was simple and had great love for Śrī Kṛṣṇa Caitanya Mahāprabhu. He was also advanced in Kṛṣṇa consciousness; therefore he was considered appropriate to accompany the Lord as a personal servant.

The word *snigdha* (very peaceful) and the word *su-snigdha* (affectionate) are used in verses fourteen and fifteen, and they are also found in *Śrīmad-Bhāgavatam* (1.1.8): *brūyuḥ snigdhasya śiṣyasya guravo guhyam apy uta.* "A disciple who has actual love for his spiritual master is endowed, by the blessings of the spiritual master, with all confidential knowledge." Śrīla Śrīdhara Svāmī has commented that the word *snigdhasya* means *prema-vataḥ.*The word *prema-vataḥ* indicates that one has great love for his spiritual master.

TEXT 16

প্রথমেই তোমা-সঙ্গে আইলা গৌড় হৈতে।
ইঁহার ইচ্ছা আছে 'সর্বতীর্থ' করিতে ॥ ১৬ ॥

prathamei tomā-saṅge āilā gauḍa haite
iṅhāra icchā āche 'sarva-tīrtha' karite

SYNONYMS

prathamei—in the beginning; *tomā-saṅge*—with You; *āilā*—came; *gauḍa haite*—from Bengal; *iṅhāra icchā*—his desire; *āche*—is; *sarva-tīrtha*—all places of pilgrimage; *karite*—to go see.

TRANSLATION

"In the beginning, he came with You from Bengal. It is his desire to see and visit all the holy places of pilgrimage.

TEXT 17

ইঁহার সঙ্গে আছে বিপ্র এক 'ভৃত্য'।
ইঁহো পথে করিবেন সেবা-ভিক্ষা-কৃত্য ॥ ১৭ ॥

iṅhāra saṅge āche vipra eka 'bhṛtya'
iṅho pathe karibena sevā-bhikṣā-kṛtya

SYNONYMS

iṅhāra saṅge—with him; *āche*—is; *vipra*—*brāhmaṇa;* *eka*—one; *bhṛtya*—servant; *iṅho*—this man; *pathe*—on the way; *karibena*—will do; *sevā*—service; *bhikṣā-kṛtya*—and arrangements for cooking.

TRANSLATION

"In addition, You may take another brāhmaṇa who would act as a servant en route and make arrangements for Your food.

TEXT 18

ইঁহারে সঙ্গে লহ যদি, সবার হয় 'সুখ'।
বন-পথে যাইতে তোমার নহিবে কোন 'দুঃখ' ॥১৮॥

iṅhāre saṅge laha yadi, sabāra haya 'sukha'
vana-pathe yāite tomāra nahibe kona 'duḥkha'

SYNONYMS

iṅhāre—him; *saṅge*—along; *laha*—You accept; *yadi*—if; *sabāra haya sukha*—everyone will be happy; *vana-pathe*—on the path through the jungle; *yāite*—going; *tomāra*—Your; *nahibe*—there will not be; *kona*—any; *duḥkha*—difficulty.

TRANSLATION

"If You can also take him with You, we will be very happy. If two people go with You through the jungle, there will certainly be no difficulty or inconvenience.

TEXT 19

সেই বিপ্র বহি' নিবে বস্ত্রাম্বুভাজন।
ভট্টাচার্য ভিক্ষা দিবে করি' ভিক্ষাটন ॥ ১৯ ॥

sei vipra vahi' nibe vastrāmbu-bhājana
bhaṭṭācārya bhikṣā dibe kari' bhikṣāṭana

SYNONYMS

sei vipra—the other *brāhmaṇa; vahi' nibe*—will carry; *vastra-ambu-bhājana*—the cloth and waterpot; *bhaṭṭācārya*—Balabhadra Bhaṭṭācārya; *bhikṣā dibe*—will arrange for cooking; *kari'*—performing; *bhikṣā-aṭana*—collecting alms.

TRANSLATION

"The other brāhmaṇa can carry Your cloth and waterpot, and Balabhadra Bhaṭṭācārya will collect alms and cook for You."

TEXT 20

তাঁহার বচন প্রভু অঙ্গীকার কৈল।
বলভদ্র-ভট্টাচার্যে সঙ্গে করি' নিল ॥ ২০ ॥

tāṅhāra vacana prabhu aṅgīkāra kaila
balabhadra-bhaṭṭācārye saṅge kari' nila

SYNONYMS

tāṅhāra vacana—his words; *prabhu*—Śrī Caitanya Mahāprabhu; *aṅgīkāra kaila*—accepted; *balabhadra-bhaṭṭācārye*—Balabhadra Bhaṭṭācārya; *saṅge kari' nila*—took with Him.

TRANSLATION

Thus Śrī Caitanya Mahāprabhu accepted the request of Svarūpa Dāmodara Paṇḍita and agreed to take Balabhadra Bhaṭṭācārya with Him.

TEXT 21

পূর্বরাত্র্যে জগন্নাথ দেখি' 'আজ্ঞা' লঞা।
শেষ-রাত্রে উঠি' প্রভু চলিলা লুকাঞা ॥ ২১ ॥

pūrva-rātrye jagannātha dekhi' 'ājñā' lañā
śeṣa-rātre uṭhi' prabhu calilā lukāñā

SYNONYMS

pūrva-rātrye—on the previous night; *jagannātha dekhi'*—seeing Lord Jagannātha; *ājñā lañā*—taking permission; *śeṣa-rātre*—near the end of night; *uṭhi'*—rising; *prabhu*—Śrī Caitanya Mahāprabhu; *calilā*—started; *lukāñā*—without being seen.

TRANSLATION

On the previous night, Śrī Caitanya Mahāprabhu had visited Lord Jagannātha and taken His permission. Now, near the end of night, the Lord got up and started immediately. He was not seen by others.

TEXT 22

প্রাতঃকালে ভক্তগণ প্রভু না দেখিয়া।
অন্বেষণ করি' ফিরে ব্যাকুল হঞা ॥ ২২ ॥

prātaḥ-kāle bhakta-gaṇa prabhu nā dekhiyā
anveṣaṇa kari' phire vyākula hañā

SYNONYMS

prātaḥ-kāle—early in the morning; *bhakta-gaṇa*—all the devotees; *prabhu*—Lord Śrī Caitanya Mahāprabhu; *nā dekhiyā*—not seeing; *anveṣaṇa kari'*—searching; *phire*—wander; *vyākula hañā*—becoming very anxious.

TRANSLATION

Because the Lord had departed, the devotees, unable to see Him early in the morning, began to search for Him with great anxiety.

TEXT 23

স্বরূপ-গোসাঞি সবায় কৈল নিবারণ ।
নিবৃত্ত হঞা রহে সবে জানি' প্রভুর মন ॥ ২৩ ॥

svarūpa-gosāñi sabāya kaila nivāraṇa
nivṛtta hañā rahe sabe jāni' prabhura mana

SYNONYMS

svarūpa-gosāñi—Svarūpa Dāmodara Gosvāmī; *sabāya*—unto everyone; *kaila*—did; *nivāraṇa*—forbidding; *nivṛtta hañā*—being restrained; *rahe*—remain; *sabe*—all; *jāni'*—knowing; *prabhura mana*—the mind of Śrī Caitanya Mahāprabhu.

TRANSLATION

While all the devotees were searching for the Lord, Svarūpa Dāmodara restrained them. Then everyone fell silent, knowing the mind of Śrī Caitanya Mahāprabhu.

TEXT 24

প্রসিদ্ধ পথ ছাড়ি' প্রভু উপপথে চলিলা ।
'কটক' ডাহিনে করি' বনে প্রবেশিলা ॥ ২৪ ॥

prasiddha patha chāḍi' prabhu upapathe calilā
'kaṭaka' ḍāhine kari' vane praveśilā

SYNONYMS

prasiddha—well-known; *patha*—public way; *chāḍi'*—giving up; *prabhu*—Śrī Caitanya Mahāprabhu; *upapathe*—through a bypass; *calilā*—began to walk;

kaṭaka—the city of Kaṭaka; *ḍāhine*—on the right side; *kari'*—keeping; *vane*—within the forest; *praveśilā*—entered.

TRANSLATION

The Lord abandoned walking on the well-known public road and went instead along a bypass. He thus kept the city of Kaṭaka on His right as He entered the forest.

TEXT 25

নির্জন-বনে চলে প্রভু কৃষ্ণনাম লঞা ।
হস্তি-ব্যাঘ্র পথ ছাড়ে প্রভুরে দেখিয়া ॥ ২৫ ॥

nirjana-vane cale prabhu kṛṣṇa-nāma lañā
hasti-vyāghra patha chāḍe prabhure dekhiyā

SYNONYMS

nirjana-vane—in a solitary forest; *cale*—walks; *prabhu*—Śrī Caitanya Mahāprabhu; *kṛṣṇa-nāma lañā*—chanting the holy name of Kṛṣṇa; *hasti*—elephants; *vyāghra*—tigers; *patha chāḍe*—leave the path; *prabhure*—Śrī Caitanya Mahāprabhu; *dekhiyā*—seeing.

TRANSLATION

When the Lord passed through the solitary forest chanting the holy name of Kṛṣṇa, the tigers and elephants, seeing Him, gave way.

TEXT 26

পালে-পালে ব্যাঘ্র, হস্তী, গণ্ডার, শূকরগণ ।
তার মধ্যে আবেশে প্রভু করিলা গমন ॥ ২৬ ॥

pāle-pāle vyāghra, hastī, gaṇḍāra, śūkara-gaṇa
tāra madhye āveśe prabhu karilā gamana

SYNONYMS

pāle-pāle—in flocks; *vyāghra*—tigers; *hastī*—elephants; *gaṇḍāra*—rhinoceros; *śūkara-gaṇa*—boars; *tāra madhye*—through them; *āveśe*—in ecstasy; *prabhu*—Śrī Caitanya Mahāprabhu; *karilā gamana*—passed.

TRANSLATION

When the Lord passed through the jungle in great ecstasy, packs of tigers, elephants, rhinoceros and boars came, and the Lord passed right through them.

TEXT 27

দেখি' ভট্টাচার্যের মনে হয় মহাভয় ।
প্রভুর প্রতাপে তারা এক পাশ হয় ॥ ২৭ ॥

dekhi' bhaṭṭācāryera mane haya mahā-bhaya
prabhura pratāpe tārā eka pāśa haya

SYNONYMS

dekhi'—seeing; *bhaṭṭācāryera*—of Bhaṭṭācārya; *mane*—in the mind; *haya*—there was; *mahā-bhaya*—great fear; *prabhura pratāpe*—by the influence of Lord Caitanya Mahāprabhu; *tārā*—they; *eka pāśa haya*—stand to one side.

TRANSLATION

Balabhadra Bhaṭṭācārya was very much afraid to see them, but by Śrī Caitanya Mahāprabhu's influence, all the animals stood to one side.

TEXT 28

একদিন পথে ব্যাঘ্র করিয়াছে শয়ন ।
আবেশে তার গায়ে প্রভুর লাগিল চরণ ॥ ২৮ ॥

eka-dina pathe vyāghra kariyāche śayana
āveśe tāra gāye prabhura lāgila caraṇa

SYNONYMS

eka-dina—one day; *pathe*—on the path; *vyāghra*—a tiger; *kariyāche śayana*—was lying down; *āveśe*—in ecstatic love; *tāra gāye*—on his body; *prabhura*—of Lord Śrī Caitanya Mahāprabhu; *lāgila*—touched; *caraṇa*—lotus feet.

TRANSLATION

One day a tiger was lying on the path, and Śrī Caitanya Mahāprabhu, walking along the path in ecstatic love, touched the tiger with His feet.

TEXT 29

প্রভু কহে,—কহ 'কৃষ্ণ', ব্যাঘ্র উঠিল ।
'কৃষ্ণ' 'কৃষ্ণ' কহি' ব্যাঘ্র নাচিতে লাগিল ॥ ২৯ ॥

prabhu kahe,—kaha 'kṛṣṇa', vyāghra uṭhila
'kṛṣṇa' 'kṛṣṇa' kahi' vyāghra nācite lāgila

SYNONYMS

prabhu kahe—Śrī Caitanya Mahāprabhu said; *kaha kṛṣṇa*—please chant Hare Kṛṣṇa; *vyāghra uṭhila*—the tiger got up; *kṛṣṇa kṛṣṇa kahi'*—chanting the holy name of Kṛṣṇa; *vyāghra*—the tiger; *nācite*—to dance; *lāgila*—began.

TRANSLATION

The Lord said, "Chant the holy name of Kṛṣṇa!" The tiger immediately got up and began to dance and chant, "Kṛṣṇa! Kṛṣṇa!"

TEXT 30

আর দিনে মহাপ্রভু করে নদী স্নান ।
মত্তহস্তিযূথ আইল করিতে জলপান ॥ ৩০ ॥

āra dine mahāprabhu kare nadī snāna
matta-hasti-yūtha āila karite jala-pāna

SYNONYMS

āra dine—another day; *mahāprabhu*—Śrī Caitanya Mahāprabhu; *kare*—does; *nadī snāna*—bathing in the river; *matta-hasti-yūtha*—a herd of maddened elephants; *āila*—came; *karite*—to do; *jala-pāna*—drinking water.

TRANSLATION

Another day, while Śrī Caitanya Mahāprabhu was bathing in a river, a herd of maddened elephants came there to drink water.

TEXT 31

প্রভু জল-কৃত্য করে, আগে হস্তী আইলা ।
'কৃষ্ণ কহ' বলি' প্রভু জল ফেলি' মারিলা ॥ ৩১ ॥

prabhu jala-kṛtya kare, āge hastī āilā
'kṛṣṇa kaha' bali' prabhu jala pheli' mārilā

SYNONYMS

prabhu—Lord Śrī Caitanya Mahāprabhu; *jala-kṛtya kare*—bathed and was chanting the Gāyatrī *mantra* within the water; *āge*—in front; *hastī*—the elephants; *āilā*—came; *kṛṣṇa kaha*—chant Hare Kṛṣṇa; *bali'*—saying; *prabhu*—Lord Śrī Caitanya Mahāprabhu; *jala pheli'*—throwing water; *mārilā*—struck.

TRANSLATION

While the Lord was bathing and murmuring the Gāyatrī mantra, the elephants came before Him. The Lord immediately splashed some water on the elephants and asked them to chant the name of Kṛṣṇa.

PURPORT

Śrī Caitanya Mahāprabhu was the Supreme Personality of Godhead playing the part of a very great advanced devotee. On the *mahā-bhāgavata* platform, the devotee makes no distinction between friends and enemies. On that platform he sees everyone as a servant of Kṛṣṇa. As stated in *Bhagavad-gītā:*

vidyā-vinaya-sampanne
brāhmaṇe gavi hastini
śuni caiva śvapāke ca
paṇḍitāḥ sama-darśinaḥ

"The humble sage, by virtue of true knowledge, sees with equal vision a learned and gentle *brāhmaṇa,* a cow, an elephant, a dog, and a dog-eater [outcaste]." (Bg. 5.18)

A *mahā-bhāgavata,* being learned and advanced in spiritual consciousness, sees no difference between a tiger, an elephant or a learned scholar. The test of advanced spiritual consciousness is that one becomes fearless. He envies no one, and he is always engaged in the Lord's service. He sees every living entity as an eternal part and parcel of the Lord, rendering service according to his capacity by the will of the Supreme Lord. As *Bhagavad-gītā* confirms:

sarvasya cāhaṁ hṛdi sanniviṣṭo
mattaḥ smṛtir jñānam apohanaṁ ca

"I am seated in everyone's heart, and from Me come remembrance, knowledge and forgetfulness." (Bg. 15.15)

The *mahā-bhāgavata* knows that Kṛṣṇa is in everyone's heart. Kṛṣṇa is dictating, and the living entity is following His dictations. Kṛṣṇa is within the heart of the tiger, elephant and boar. Therefore Kṛṣṇa tells them, "Here is a *mahā-bhāgavata.* Please do not disturb him." Why, then, should the animals be envious of such a great personality? Those who are neophytes or even a little progressed in devotional service should not try to imitate the *mahā-bhāgavata.* Rather, they should only follow in their footsteps. The word *anukara* means "imitating," and *anusara* means "trying to follow in the footsteps." We should not try to imitate the activities of a *mahā-bhāgavata* or Śrī Caitanya Mahāprabhu. Our best efforts should be exerted in trying to follow them according to our ability. The *mahā-bhāgavata's* heart is completely freed from material contamination, and he can become very dear even to fierce animals like tigers and elephants. Indeed, the *mahā-bhāgavata* treats them as his very intimate friends. On this platform there is no question of envy. When the Lord was passing through the forest, He was in ecstasy, thinking the forest to be Vṛndāvana. He was simply searching for Kṛṣṇa.

TEXT 32

সেই জল-বিন্দু-কণা লাগে যার গায় ।
সেই 'কৃষ্ণ' 'কৃষ্ণ' কহে, প্রেমে নাচে, গায় ॥ ৩২ ॥

sei jala-bindu-kaṇā lāge yāra gāya
sei 'kṛṣṇa' 'kṛṣṇa' kahe, preme nāce, gāya

SYNONYMS

sei—those; *jala*—of water; *bindu*—drops; *kaṇā*—particles; *lāge*—touch; *yāra*—whose; *gāya*—body; *sei*—they; *kṛṣṇa kṛṣṇa*—Kṛṣṇa, Kṛṣṇa; *kahe*—say; *preme*—in ecstasy; *nāce*—dance; *gāya*—sing.

TRANSLATION

The elephants whose bodies were touched by the water splashed by the Lord began to chant, "Kṛṣṇa! Kṛṣṇa!" and dance and sing in ecstasy.

TEXT 33

কেহ ভূমে পড়ে, কেহ করয়ে চিৎকার ।
দেখি' ভট্টাচার্যের মনে হয় চমৎকার ॥ ৩৩ ॥

keha bhūme paḍe, keha karaye citkāra
dekhi' bhaṭṭācāryera mane haya camatkāra

SYNONYMS

keha—some of them; *bhūme*—on the ground; *paḍe*—fall down; *keha*—some of them; *karaye*—perform; *cit-kāra*—screaming; *dekhi'*—seeing; *bhaṭṭācāryera*—of Bhaṭṭācārya; *mane*—in the mind; *haya*—there was; *camatkāra*—astonishment.

TRANSLATION

Some of the elephants fell to the ground, and some screamed in ecstasy. Seeing this, Balabhadra Bhaṭṭācārya was completely astonished.

TEXT 34

পথে যাইতে করে প্রভু উচ্চ সংকীর্তন ।
মধুর কণ্ঠধ্বনি শুনি' আইসে মৃগীগণ ॥ ৩৪ ॥

pathe yāite kare prabhu ucca saṅkīrtana
madhura kaṇṭha-dhvani śuni' āise mṛgī-gaṇa

SYNONYMS

pathe yāite—while passing on the path; *kare*—does; *prabhu*—Śrī Caitanya Mahāprabhu; *ucca*—loud; *saṅkīrtana*—chanting of Hare Kṛṣṇa; *madhura*—sweet; *kaṇṭha-dhvani*—the voice from His throat; *śuni'*—hearing; *āise*—came; *mṛgī-gaṇa*—she-deer.

TRANSLATION

Sometimes Śrī Caitanya Mahāprabhu chanted very loudly while passing through the jungle. Hearing His sweet voice, all the does came near Him.

TEXT 35

ডাহিনে-বামে ধ্বনি শুনি' যায় প্রভু-সঙ্গে ।
প্রভু তার অঙ্গ মুছে, শ্লোক পড়ে রঙ্গে ॥ ৩৫ ॥

ḍāhine-vāme dhvani śuni' yāya prabhu-saṅge
prabhu tāra aṅga muche, śloka paḍe raṅge

SYNONYMS

ḍāhine-vāme—right and left; *dhvani*—vibration; *śuni'*—hearing; *yāya*—they follow; *prabhu-saṅge*—with the Lord; *prabhu*—Śrī Caitanya Mahāprabhu; *tāra*—their; *aṅga*—bodies; *muche*—pats; *śloka*—verse; *paḍe*—recites; *raṅge*—in great curiosity.

TRANSLATION

Hearing the Lord's great vibration, all the does followed Him left and right. While reciting a verse with great curiosity, the Lord patted them.

TEXT 36

ধন্যাঃ স্ম মূঢ়মতয়োঽপি হরিণ্য এতা
যা নন্দনন্দনমুপাত্ত-বিচিত্রবেশম্ ।
আকর্ণ্য বেণুরণিতং সহকৃষ্ণসারাঃ
পূজাং দধুর্বিরচিতাং প্রণয়াবলোকৈঃ ॥ ৩৬ ॥

dhanyāḥ sma mūḍha-matayo 'pi hariṇya etā
yā nanda-nandanam upātta-vicitra-veśam
ākarṇya veṇu-raṇitaṁ saha-kṛṣṇa-sārāḥ
pūjāṁ dadhur viracitāṁ praṇayāvalokaiḥ

SYNONYMS

dhanyāḥ—fortunate, blessed; *sma*—certainly; *mūḍha-matayaḥ*—foolish, without good sense; *api*—although; *hariṇyaḥ*—she-deer; *etāḥ*—these; *yāḥ*—who; *nanda-nandanam*—the son of Mahārāja Nanda; *upātta-vicitra-veśam*—dressed very attractively; *ākarṇya*—hearing; *veṇu-raṇitam*—the sound of His flute; *saha-kṛṣṇa-sārāḥ*—accompanied by the black deer (their husbands); *pūjām dadhuḥ*—they worshiped; *viracitām*—performed; *praṇaya-avalokaiḥ*—by their affectionate glances.

TRANSLATION

"Blessed are all these foolish deer because they have approached the son of Mahārāja Nanda, who is gorgeously dressed and is playing on His flute. Indeed, both the does and the bucks worship the Lord with looks of love and affection."

PURPORT

This is a verse from *Śrīmad-Bhāgavatam* (10.21.11) spoken by the *gopīs* of Vṛndāvana.

TEXT 37

হেনকালে ব্যাঘ্র তথা আইল পাঁচ-সাত ।
ব্যাঘ্র-মৃগী মিলি' চলে মহাপ্রভুর সাথ ॥ ৩৭ ॥

hena-kāle vyāghra tathā āila pāṅca-sāta
vyāghra-mṛgī mili' cale mahāprabhura sātha

SYNONYMS

hena-kāle—at this time; *vyāghra*—tigers; *tathā*—there; *āila*—came; *pāṅca-sāta*—five to seven; *vyāghra-mṛgī*—the tigers and deer; *mili'*—coming together; *cale*—go; *mahāprabhura sātha*—with Śrī Caitanya Mahāprabhu.

TRANSLATION

While Śrī Caitanya Mahāprabhu was passing through the jungle, five or seven tigers came. Joining the deer, the tigers began to follow the Lord.

TEXT 38

দেখি' মহাপ্রভুর 'বৃন্দাবন'-স্মৃতি হৈল ।
বৃন্দাবন-গুণ-বর্ণন শ্লোক পড়িল ॥ ৩৮ ॥

dekhi' mahāprabhura 'vṛndāvana'-smṛti haila
vṛndāvana-guṇa-varṇana śloka paḍila

SYNONYMS

dekhi'—seeing; *mahāprabhura*—of Śrī Caitanya Mahāprabhu; *vṛndāvana*—of the holy land of Vṛndāvana; *smṛti haila*—there was remembrance; *vṛndāvana*—of Śrī Vṛndāvana; *guṇa*—of the qualities; *varṇana*—description; *śloka*—verse; *paḍila*—recited.

TRANSLATION

Seeing the tigers and deer following Him, Śrī Caitanya Mahāprabhu immediately remembered the land of Vṛndāvana. He then began to recite a verse describing the transcendental qualitity of Vṛndāvana.

TEXT 39

যত্র নৈসর্গদুর্বৈরাঃ সহাসন্ নৃ-মৃগাদয়ঃ ।
মিত্রাণীবাজিতাবাস-দ্রুত-রুট্-তর্ষণাদিকম্ ॥ ৩৯ ॥

yatra naisarga-durvairāḥ
sahāsan nṛ-mṛgādayaḥ
mitrāṇīvājitāvāsa-
druta-ruṭ-tarṣaṇādikam

SYNONYMS

yatra—where; *naisarga*—by nature; *durvairāḥ*—living in enmity; *saha-āsan*—live together; *nṛ*—human beings; *mṛga-ādayaḥ*—and animals; *mitrāṇi*—friends; *iva*—like; *ajita*—of Lord Śrī Kṛṣṇa; *āvāsa*—residence; *druta*—gone away; *ruj*—anger; *tarṣaṇa-ādikam*—thirst and so on.

TRANSLATION

"Vṛndāvana is the transcendental abode of the Lord. There is no hunger, anger or thirst there. Though naturally inimical, both human beings and fierce animals live together there in transcendental friendship."

PURPORT

This is a statement from *Śrīmad-Bhāgavatam* (10.13.60). After stealing the cowherd boys, calves and cows of Śrī Kṛṣṇa, Lord Brahmā kept them asleep and hid them. After a moment, Brahmā returned to see Kṛṣṇa's condition. When he saw that Kṛṣṇa was still busy with His cowherd boyfriends and animals and was not disturbed, Lord Brahmā appreciated the transcendental opulence of Vṛndāvana.

TEXT 40

'কৃষ্ণ কৃষ্ণ কহ' করি' প্রভু যবে বলিল ।
'কৃষ্ণ' কহি' ব্যাঘ্র-মৃগ নাচিতে লাগিল ॥ ৪০ ॥

'kṛṣṇa kṛṣṇa kaha' kari' prabhu yabe balila
'kṛṣṇa' kahi' vyāghra-mṛga nācite lāgila

SYNONYMS

kṛṣṇa kṛṣṇa kaha—chant Kṛṣṇa, Kṛṣṇa; *kari'*—in this way; *prabhu*—Śrī Caitanya Mahāprabhu; *yabe*—when; *balila*—uttered; *kṛṣṇa kahi'*—chanting the holy name of Kṛṣṇa; *vyāghra-mṛga*—the tigers and deer; *nācite lāgila*—began to dance.

TRANSLATION

When Śrī Caitanya Mahāprabhu said, "Chant Kṛṣṇa! Kṛṣṇa!" the tigers and deer began to dance and chant, "Kṛṣṇa!"

TEXT 41

নাচে, কুন্দে ব্যাঘ্রগণ মৃগীগণ-সঙ্গে ।
বলভদ্র-ভট্টাচার্য দেখে অপূর্ব-রঙ্গে ॥ ৪১ ॥

nāce, kunde vyāghra-gaṇa mṛgī-gaṇa-saṅge
balabhadra-bhaṭṭācārya dekhe apūrva-raṅge

SYNONYMS

nāce—dance; *kunde*—jump; *vyāghra-gaṇa*—the tigers; *mṛgī-gaṇa-saṅge*—with the does; *balabhadra-bhaṭṭācārya*—Balabhadra Bhaṭṭācārya; *dekhe*—sees; *apūrva-raṅge*—with great wonder.

TRANSLATION

When all the tigers and does danced and jumped, Balabhadra Bhaṭṭācārya saw them and was struck with wonder.

TEXT 42

**ব্যাঘ্র-মৃগ অন্যোন্যে করে আলিঙ্গন ।
মুখে মুখ দিয়া করে অন্যোন্যে চুম্বন ॥ ৪২ ॥**

vyāghra-mṛga anyonye kare āliṅgana
mukhe mukha diyā kare anyonye cumbana

SYNONYMS

vyāghra-mṛga—the tigers and deer; *anyonye*—one another; *kare*—do; *āliṅgana*—embracing; *mukhe mukha diyā*—touching one anothers' mouths; *kare*—do; *anyonye cumbana*—kissing one another.

TRANSLATION

Indeed, the tigers and deer began to embrace one another, and, touching mouths, they began to kiss.

TEXT 43

**কৌতুক দেখিয়া প্রভু হাসিতে লাগিলা ।
তা-সবাকে তাহাঁ ছাড়ি' আগে চলি' গেলা ॥ ৪৩ ॥**

kautuka dekhiyā prabhu hāsite lāgilā
tā-sabāke tāhāṅ chāḍi' āge cali' gelā

SYNONYMS

kautuka dekhiyā—seeing this fun; *prabhu*—Śrī Caitanya Mahāprabhu; *hāsite lāgilā*—began to smile; *tā-sabāke*—all of them; *tāhāṅ chāḍi'*—leaving there; *āge*—forward; *cali' gelā*—advanced.

TRANSLATION

When Śrī Caitanya Mahāprabhu saw all this fun, He began to smile. Finally He left the animals and continued on His way.

TEXT 44

**ময়ূরাদি পক্ষিগণ প্রভুরে দেখিয়া ।
সঙ্গে চলে, 'কৃষ্ণ' বলি' নাচে মত্ত হঞা ॥ ৪৪ ॥**

mayūrādi pakṣi-gaṇa prabhure dekhiyā
saṅge cale, 'kṛṣṇa' bali' nāce matta hañā

SYNONYMS

mayūra-ādi—beginning with peacocks; *pakṣi-gaṇa*—different types of birds; *prabhure*—Śrī Caitanya Mahāprabhu; *dekhiyā*—seeing; *saṅge cale*—go with Him; *kṛṣṇa bali'*—chanting the holy name of Kṛṣṇa; *nāce*—dance; *matta hañā*—becoming mad.

TRANSLATION

Various birds, including the peacock, saw Śrī Caitanya Mahāprabhu and began to follow Him, chanting and dancing. They were all maddened by the holy name of Kṛṣṇa.

TEXT 45

'হরিবোল' বলি' প্রভু করে উচ্চধ্বনি ।
বৃক্ষলতা—প্রফুল্লিত, সেই ধ্বনি শুনি' ॥ ৪৫ ॥

'hari-bola' bali' prabhu kare ucca-dhvani
vṛkṣa-latā——praphullita, sei dhvani śuni'

SYNONYMS

hari-bola—the vibration of Hari-bol; *bali'*—chanting; *prabhu*—Śrī Caitanya Mahāprabhu; *kare*—makes; *ucca-dhvani*—a loud sound; *vṛkṣa-latā*—the trees and creepers; *praphullita*—very jubilant; *sei*—that; *dhvani*—sound; *śuni'*—hearing.

TRANSLATION

When the Lord loudly chanted "Hari bol!" the trees and creepers became jubilant to hear Him.

PURPORT

The loud chanting of the Hare Kṛṣṇa *mantra* is so powerful that it can even penetrate the ears of trees and creepers—what to speak of animals and human beings. Śrī Caitanya Mahāprabhu once asked Haridāsa Ṭhākura how trees and plants could be delivered, and Haridāsa Ṭhākura replied that the loud chanting of the Hare Kṛṣṇa *mahā-mantra* would benefit not only trees and plants but insects and all other living beings. One should therefore not be disturbed by the loud chanting of Hare Kṛṣṇa, for it is beneficial not only to the chanter but to everyone who gets an opportunity to hear.

TEXT 46

'ঝারিখণ্ডে' স্থাবর-জঙ্গম আছে যত ।
কৃষ্ণনাম দিয়া কৈল প্রেমেতে উন্মত্ত ॥ ৪৬ ॥

'jhārikhaṇḍe' sthāvara-jaṅgama āche yata
kṛṣṇa-nāma diyā kaila premete unmatta

SYNONYMS

jhārikhaṇḍe—in the place known as Jhārikhaṇḍa; *sthāvara-jaṅgama*—moving and not moving; *āche*—there are; *yata*—all; *kṛṣṇa-nāma diyā*—giving them the holy name of Lord Kṛṣṇa; *kaila*—made; *premete*—in ecstasy; *unmatta*—mad.

TRANSLATION

Thus all living entities—some moving and some standing still in the forest of Jhārikhaṇḍa—became maddened by hearing the holy name of Lord Kṛṣṇa vibrated by Śrī Caitanya Mahāprabhu.

PURPORT

The great forest of Jhārikhaṇḍa is a great tract of land including Āṭagaḍa, Ḍheṅkānala, Āṅgula, Lāhārā, Kiyañjhaḍa, Bāmaḍā, Bonāi, Gāṅgapura, Choṭa Nāgapura, Yaśapura and Saragujā. All these places, which are covered with mountains and jungles, are known as Jhārikhaṇḍa.

TEXT 47

যেই গ্রাম দিয়া যান, যাহাঁ করেন স্থিতি ।
সে-সব গ্রামের লোকের হয় 'প্রেমভক্তি' ॥ ৪৭ ॥

yei grāma diyā yāna, yāhāṅ karena sthiti
se-saba grāmera lokera haya 'prema-bhakti'

SYNONYMS

yei grāma—which villages; *diyā yāna*—the Lord goes through; *yāhāṅ*—where; *karena*—takes; *sthiti*—rest; *se-saba*—all those; *grāmera*—of the villages; *lokera*—of the people; *haya*—there is awakening of; *prema-bhakti*—ecstatic love of God.

TRANSLATION

In all the villages through which the Lord passed and in all the places He rested on His journey, everyone was purified and awakened to ecstatic love of God.

TEXTS 48-49

কেহ যদি তাঁর মুখে শুনে কৃষ্ণনাম ।
তাঁর মুখে আন শুনে তাঁর মুখে আন ॥ ৪৮ ॥
সবে 'কৃষ্ণ' 'হরি' বলি' নাচে, কান্দে, হাসে ।
পরম্পরায় 'বৈষ্ণব' হইল সর্বদেশে ॥ ৪৯ ॥

keha yadi tāṅra mukhe śune kṛṣṇa-nāma
tāṅra mukhe āna śune tāṅra mukhe āna

sabe 'kṛṣṇa' 'hari' bali' nāce, kānde, hāse
paramparāya 'vaiṣṇava' ha-ila sarva deśe

SYNONYMS

keha—someone; *yadi*—when; *tāṅra mukhe*—from His mouth; *śune*—hears; *kṛṣṇa-nāma*—chanting of the Hare Kṛṣṇa *mantra; tāṅra mukhe*—from the mouth of such chanters; *āna śune*—someone else hears; *tāṅra mukhe*—and from his mouth; *āna*—someone else; *sabe*—all of them; *kṛṣṇa*—Lord Kṛṣṇa's holy name; *hari*—another holy name of the Lord; *bali'*—chanting; *nāce*—dance; *kānde*—cry; *hāse*—smile; *paramparāya*—by disciplic succession; *vaiṣṇava*—devotees; *ha-ila*—became; *sarva-deśe*—in all countries.

TRANSLATION

When someone heard the chanting of the holy name from the mouth of Śrī Caitanya Mahāprabhu, and someone else heard this chanting from that second person, and someone again heard this chanting from the third person, everyone in all countries became a Vaiṣṇava through such disciplic succession. Thus everyone chanted the holy name of Kṛṣṇa and Hari, and they danced, cried and smiled.

PURPORT

The transcendental power or potency of the Hare Kṛṣṇa *mahā-mantra* is herein explained. First, the holy name is vibrated by Śrī Caitanya Mahāprabhu. When someone hears from Him directly, he is purified. When another person hears from that person, he also is purified. In this way the purification process is advanced among pure devotees. Śrī Caitanya Mahāprabhu is the Supreme Personality of Godhead, and no one can claim His potency. Nonetheless, if one is a pure devotee, hundreds and thousands of men can be purified by his vibration. This potency is within every living being, provided he chants the Hare Kṛṣṇa *mahā-mantra* offenselessly and without material motives. When a pure devotee chants offenselessly, another person will become a Vaiṣṇava, and from him another Vaiṣṇava will emerge. This is the *paramparā* system.

TEXT 50

যদ্যপি প্রভু লোক-সংঘট্টের ত্রাসে ।
প্রেম 'গুপ্ত' করেন, বাহিরে না প্রকাশে ॥ ৫০ ॥

yadyapi prabhu loka-saṅghaṭṭera trāse
prema 'gupta' karena, bāhire nā prakāśe

SYNONYMS

yadyapi—although; *prabhu*—Śrī Caitanya Mahāprabhu; *loka-saṅghaṭṭera*—of crowds of people; *trāse*—being afraid; *prema*—ecstasy; *gupta karena*—keeps hidden; *bāhire*—externally; *nā*—does not; *prakāśe*—manifest.

TRANSLATION

The Lord did not always manifest His ecstasy. Being afraid of a great assembly of people, the Lord kept His ecstasy concealed.

TEXT 51

তথাপি তাঁর দর্শন-শ্রবণ-প্রভাবে ।
সকল দেশের লোক হইল 'বৈষ্ণবে' ॥ ৫১ ॥

tathāpi tāṅra darśana-śravaṇa-prabhāve
sakala deśera loka ha-ila 'vaiṣṇave'

SYNONYMS

tathāpi—still; *tāṅra*—His; *darśana*—of seeing; *śravaṇa*—of hearing; *prabhāve*—by the potency; *sakala*—all; *deśera*—of countries; *loka*—people; *ha-ila*—became; *vaiṣṇave*—pure devotees of the Lord.

TRANSLATION

Although Śrī Caitanya Mahāprabhu did not manifest His natural ecstatic love, everyone became a pure devotee simply by seeing and hearing Him.

PURPORT

Śrīla Rūpa Gosvāmī has described Śrī Caitanya Mahāprabhu as *mahā-vadānya-avatāra,* the most munificent incarnation. Although Śrī Caitanya Mahāprabhu is not physically present now, simply by chanting His holy name (*śrī-kṛṣṇa-caitanya prabhu nityānanda śrī-advaita gadādhara śrīvāsādi-gaura-bhakta-vṛnda*) people throughout the world are becoming devotees. This is due to the ecstatic chanting of the holy name of the Lord. It is said that a pure devotee can see the Lord every moment, and because of this he is empowered by the Lord. This is confirmed in *Brahma-saṁhitā: premāñjana-cchurita-bhakti-vilocanena santaḥ sadaiva hṛdayeṣu vilokayanti.* Śrī Caitanya Mahāprabhu appeared five hundred years ago, but it cannot be said that now the potency of the Hare Kṛṣṇa *mahā-mantra* is less powerful than it was in His presence. By hearing Śrī Caitanya Mahāprabhu through the *paramparā* system, one can be purified. Therefore in this verse it is said: *tathāpi tāṅra darśana-śravaṇa-prabhāve.* It is not that everyone is able to see Kṛṣṇa or Śrī Kṛṣṇa Caitanya Mahāprabhu physically, but if one hears about Him through books like *Śrī Caitanya-caritāmṛta* and through the *paramparā* system of pure Vaiṣṇavas, there is no difficulty in becoming a pure Vaiṣṇava, free from mundane desires and personal motivations.

TEXT 52

গৌড়, বঙ্গ, উৎকল, দক্ষিণ-দেশে গিয়া ।
লোকের নিস্তার কৈল আপনে ভ্রমিয়া ॥ ৫২ ॥

gauḍa, baṅga, utkala, dakṣiṇa-deśe giyā
lokera nistāra kaila āpane bhramiyā

SYNONYMS

gauḍa—Bengal; *baṅga*—East Bengal; *utkala*—Orissa; *dakṣiṇa-deśe*—southern India; *giyā*—going; *lokera*—of all the people; *nistāra*—liberation; *kaila*—did; *āpane*—personally; *bhramiyā*—touring.

TRANSLATION

In this way, Śrī Caitanya Mahāprabhu personally toured Bengal, East Bengal, Orissa and the southern countries, and He delivered all kinds of people by spreading Kṛṣṇa consciousness.

TEXT 53

মথুরা যাইবার ছলে আসেন ঝারিখণ্ড ।
ভিল্লপ্রায় লোক তাহাঁ পরম-পাষণ্ড ॥ ৫৩ ॥

mathurā yāibāra chale āsena jhārikhaṇḍa
bhilla-prāya loka tāhāṅ parama-pāṣaṇḍa

SYNONYMS

mathurā—to Mathurā; *yāibāra*—of going; *chale*—on the pretext; *āsena*—came; *jhārikhaṇḍa*—to Jhārikhaṇḍa; *bhilla-prāya*—like the Bheels, a kind of low people; *loka*—people; *tāhāṅ*—there; *parama-pāṣaṇḍa*—without God consciousness.

TRANSLATION

When Śrī Caitanya Mahāprabhu came to Jhārikhaṇḍa on His way to Mathurā, He found that the people there were almost uncivilized and were devoid of God consciousness.

PURPORT

The word *bhilla* refers to a class of men belonging to the Bheels. The Bheels are like Black Africans, and they are lower than *śūdras.* Such people generally live in the jungle, and Śrī Caitanya Mahāprabhu had to meet them.

TEXT 54

নাম-প্রেম দিয়া কৈল সবার নিস্তার ।
চৈতন্যের গূঢ়লীলা বুঝিতে শক্তি কার ॥ ৫৪ ॥

nāma-prema diyā kaila sabāra nistāra
caitanyera gūḍha-līlā bujhite śakti kāra

SYNONYMS

nāma-prema diyā—bestowing upon them ecstatic love and the holy name; *kaila*—did; *sabāra nistāra*—liberation of all of them; *caitanyera*—of Śrī Caitanya Mahāprabhu; *gūḍha-līlā*—confidential pastimes; *bujhite*—to understand; *śakti*—the power; *kāra*—who has.

TRANSLATION

Śrī Caitanya Mahāprabhu gave even the Bheels an opportunity to chant the holy name and come to the platform of ecstatic love. Thus He delivered all of them. Who has the power to understand the transcendental pastimes of the Lord?

PURPORT

As evidence of Śrī Caitanya Mahāprabhu's mercy, we are experiencing that the people of Africa are taking to Kṛṣṇa consciousness, chanting and dancing and taking *prasāda* like other Vaiṣṇavas. This is all due to the power of Śrī Caitanya Mahāprabhu. Who can understand how His potency is working all over the world?

TEXT 55

বন দেখি' ভ্রম হয়—এই 'বৃন্দাবন' ।
শৈল দেখি' মনে হয়—এই 'গোবর্ধন' ॥ ৫৫ ॥

vana dekhi' bhrama haya——ei 'vṛndāvana'
śaila dekhi' mane haya——ei 'govardhana'

SYNONYMS

vana dekhi'—seeing the forest; *bhrama haya*—there is illusion; *ei*—this; *vṛndāvana*—Vṛndāvana forest; *śaila dekhi'*—seeing a hill; *mane haya*—considers; *ei govardhana*—this is Govardhana Hill.

TRANSLATION

When Śrī Caitanya Mahāprabhu passed through the Jhārikhaṇḍa forest, He took it for granted that it was Vṛndāvana. When He passed over the hills, He took it for granted that they were Govardhana.

TEXT 56

যাহাঁ নদী দেখে তাহাঁ মানয়ে—'কালিন্দী' ।
মহাপ্রেমাবেশে নাচে প্রভু পড়ে কান্দি' ॥ ৫৬ ॥

yāhāṅ nadī dekhe tāhāṅ mānaye——'kālindī'
mahā-premāveśe nāce prabhu paḍe kāndi'

SYNONYMS

yāhāṅ—wherever; *nadī*—river; *dekhe*—sees; *tāhāṅ*—there; *mānaye*—considers; *kālindī*—the River Yamunā; *mahā-prema-āveśe*—in great ecstatic love; *nāce*—dances; *prabhu*—Śrī Caitanya Mahāprabhu; *paḍe*—falls down; *kāndi'*—crying.

TRANSLATION

Similarly, whenever Śrī Caitanya Mahāprabhu saw a river, He immediately accepted it as the River Yamunā. Thus while in the forest He was filled with great ecstatic love, and He danced and fell down crying.

TEXT 57

পথে যাইতে ভট্টাচার্য শাক-মূল-ফল ।
যাহাঁ যেই পায়েন তাহাঁ লয়েন সকল ॥ ৫৭ ॥

pathe yāite bhaṭṭācārya śāka-mūla-phala
yāhāṅ yei pāyena tāhāṅ layena sakala

SYNONYMS

pathe yāite—while passing on the way; *bhaṭṭācārya*—Balabhadra Bhaṭṭācārya; *śāka*—spinach; *mūla*—roots; *phala*—fruits; *yāhāṅ*—wherever; *yei*—whatever; *pāyena*—he gets; *tāhāṅ*—there; *layena*—he takes; *sakala*—all.

TRANSLATION

Along the way, Balabhadra Bhaṭṭācārya collected all kinds of spinach, roots and fruit whenever possible.

TEXT 58

যে-গ্রামে রহেন প্রভু, তথায় ব্রাহ্মণ ।
পাঁচ-সাত জন আসি' করে নিমন্ত্রণ ॥ ৫৮ ॥

ye-grāme rahena prabhu, tathāya brāhmaṇa
pāṅca-sāta jana āsi' kare nimantraṇa

SYNONYMS

ye-grāme—in whatever village; *rahena*—stays; *prabhu*—Śrī Caitanya Mahāprabhu; *tathāya*—there; *brāhmaṇa*—*brāhmaṇas; pāṅca-sāta jana*—five or seven persons; *āsi'*—coming; *kare*—do; *nimantraṇa*—invitation.

TRANSLATION

Whenever Śrī Caitanya Mahāprabhu visited a village, a few brāhmaṇas—five or seven—would come and extend invitations to the Lord.

TEXT 59

কেহ অন্ন আনি' দেয় ভট্টাচার্য-স্থানে ।
কেহ দুগ্ধ, দধি, কেহ ঘৃত, খণ্ড আনে ॥ ৫৯ ॥

keha anna āni' deya bhaṭṭācārya-sthāne
keha dugdha, dadhi, keha ghṛta, khaṇḍa āne

SYNONYMS

keha—someone; *anna*—grains; *āni'*—bringing; *deya*—delivers; *bhaṭṭācārya-sthāne*—before Balabhadra Bhaṭṭācārya; *keha*—someone; *dugdha*—milk; *dadhi*—yogurt; *keha*—someone; *ghṛta*—ghee; *khaṇḍa*—sugar; *āne*—brings.

TRANSLATION

Some people would bring grains and deliver them to Balabhadra Bhaṭṭācārya. Others would bring milk and yogurt, and still others would bring ghee and sugar.

TEXT 60

যাহাঁ বিপ্র নাহি তাহাঁ 'শূদ্রমহাজন' ।
আসি' সবে ভট্টাচার্যে করে নিমন্ত্রণ ॥ ৬০ ॥

yāhāṅ vipra nāhi tāhāṅ 'śūdra-mahājana'
āsi' sabe bhaṭṭācārye kare nimantraṇa

SYNONYMS

yāhāṅ—wherever; *vipra*—*brāhmaṇa; nāhi*—there is not; *tāhāṅ*—there; *śūdra-mahā-jana*—devotees born in families other than *brāhmaṇa; āsi'*—coming; *sabe*—all of them; *bhaṭṭācārye*—to Balabhadra Bhaṭṭācārya; *kare nimantraṇa*—make invitation.

TRANSLATION

In some villages there were no brāhmaṇas; nonetheless, devotees born in non-brāhmaṇa families came and extended invitations to Balabhadra Bhaṭṭācārya.

PURPORT

Actually a *sannyāsī* or a *brāhmaṇa* will not accept an invitation extended by a person born in a lower family. However, there are many devotees who are raised to the platform of *brāhmaṇa* by their initiation. These people are called *śūdra-mahājana.* This indicates that one who is born in a non-*brāhmaṇa* family has accepted the *brāhmaṇa* status by initiation. Such devotees extended invitations to Balabhadra Bhaṭṭācārya. A Māyāvādī *sannyāsī* will accept an invitation only from a *brāhmaṇa* family, but a Vaiṣṇava does not accept an invitation from a *brāhmaṇa* if he does not belong to the Vaiṣṇava sect. However, a Vaiṣṇava will accept an invitation from a *brāhmaṇa* or *śūdra-mahājana* if that person is an initiated Vaiṣṇava. Śrī Caitanya Mahāprabhu Himself accepted invitations from *śūdra-mahājanas,* and this confirms the fact that anyone initiated by a Vaiṣṇava *mantra* can be accepted as a *brāhmaṇa.* One can accept an invitation from such a person.

TEXT 61

ভট্টাচার্য পাক করে বন্য-ব্যঞ্জন ।
বন্য-ব্যঞ্জনে প্রভুর আনন্দিত মন ॥ ৬১ ॥

bhaṭṭācārya pāka kare vanya-vyañjana
vanya-vyañjane prabhura ānandita mana

SYNONYMS

bhaṭṭācārya—Balabhadra Bhaṭṭācārya; *pāka kare*—cooks; *vanya-vyañjana*—all varieties of forest vegetables; *vanya-vyañjane*—by such forest vegetables; *prabhura*—of Śrī Caitanya Mahāprabhu; *ānandita mana*—the mind is very happy.

TRANSLATION

Balabhadra Bhaṭṭācārya used to cook all kinds of vegetables gathered from the forest, and Śrī Caitanya Mahāprabhu was very pleased to accept these preparations.

TEXTS 62-63

দুই-চারি দিনের অন্ন রাখেন সংহতি ।
যাহাঁ শূন্য বন, লোকের নাহিক বসতি ॥ ৬২ ॥
তাহাঁ সেই অন্ন ভট্টাচার্য করে পাক ।
ফল-মূলে ব্যঞ্জন করে, বন্য নানা শাক ॥ ৬৩ ॥

dui-cāri dinera anna rākheṇa saṁhati
yāhāṅ śūnya vana, lokera nāhika vasati

tāhāṅ sei anna bhaṭṭācārya kare pāka
phala-mūle vyañjana kare, vanya nānā śāka

SYNONYMS

dui-cāri—two to four; *dinera*—of days; *anna*—food grains; *rākhena*—keeps; *saṁhati*—in stock; *yāhāṅ*—wherever; *śūnya vana*—the solitary forest; *lokera*—of people; *nāhika*—there is not; *vasati*—habitation; *tāhāṅ*—there; *sei*—those; *anna*—food grains; *bhaṭṭācārya*—Balabhadra Bhaṭṭācārya; *kare pāka*—cooks; *phala-mūle*—with roots and fruits; *vyañjana kare*—he prepares vegetables; *vanya*—from the forest; *nānā śāka*—many kinds of spinach.

TRANSLATION

Balabhadra Bhaṭṭācārya used to keep a stock of food grains that would last from two to four days. Where there were no people, he would cook the grains and prepare vegetables, spinach, roots and fruits collected from the forest.

TEXT 64

পরম সন্তোষ প্রভুর বন্য-ভোজনে ।
মহাসুখ পান, যে দিন রহেন নির্জনে ॥ ৬৪ ॥

parama santoṣa prabhura vanya-bhojane
mahā-sukha pāna, ye dina rahena nirjane

SYNONYMS

parama—very much; *santoṣa*—satisfaction; *prabhura*—of the Lord; *vanya-bhojane*—in eating vegetables collected from the forest; *mahā-sukha pāna*—gets great happiness; *ye dina*—on which day; *rahena*—stays; *nirjane*—in a solitary place.

TRANSLATION

The Lord was always very happy to eat these forest vegetables, and He was even happier when He had an opportunity to stay in a solitary place.

TEXT 65

ভট্টাচার্য সেবা করে, স্নেহে যৈছে 'দাস' ।
তাঁর বিপ্র বহে জলপাত্র-বহির্বাস ॥ ৬৫ ॥

bhaṭṭācārya sevā kare, snehe yaiche 'dāsa'
tāṅra vipra vahe jala-pātra-bahirvāsa

SYNONYMS

bhaṭṭācārya—Balabhadra Bhaṭṭācārya; *sevā kare*—renders service; *snehe*—in great affection; *yaiche*—exactly like; *dāsa*—a servant; *tāṅra vipra*—his *brāhmaṇa* assistant; *vahe*—carries; *jala-pātra*—the waterpot; *bahirvāsa*—and garments.

TRANSLATION

Balabhadra Bhaṭṭācārya was so affectionate to the Lord that he was rendering service just like a menial servant. His assistant brāhmaṇa carried the waterpot and garments.

TEXT 66

নির্ঝরেতে উষ্ণোদকে স্নান তিনবার ।
দুইসন্ধ্যা অগ্নিতাপ কাষ্ঠের অপার ॥ ৬৬ ॥

nirjharete uṣṇodake snāna tina-bāra
dui-sandhyā agni-tāpa kāṣṭhera apāra

SYNONYMS

nirjharete—in the waterfalls; *uṣṇa-udake*—in warm water; *snāna*—bath; *tina-bāra*—thrice; *dui-sandhyā*—morning and evening; *agni-tāpa*—heating by a fire; *kāṣṭhera*—of wood; *apāra*—without limit.

TRANSLATION

The Lord used to bathe three times a day in the warm water of the waterfalls. He also used to heat Himself morning and evening with a fire made of the limitless wood.

TEXT 67

নিরন্তর প্রেমাবেশে নির্জনে গমন ।
সুখ অনুভবি' প্রভু কহেন বচন ॥ ৬৭ ॥

nirantara premāveśe nirjane gamana
sukha anubhavi' prabhu kahena vacana

SYNONYMS

nirantara—always; *prema-āveśe*—in ecstatic love; *nirjane*—in a solitary place; *gamana*—going; *sukha anubhavi'*—feeling happiness; *prabhu*—Śrī Caitanya Mahāprabhu; *kahena*—says; *vacana*—statement.

TRANSLATION

While traveling in this secluded forest and feeling very happy, Śrī Caitanya Mahāprabhu made the following statement.

TEXT 68

শুন, ভট্টাচার্য,—"আমি গেলাঙ বহু-দেশ ।
বনপথে দুঃখের কাহাঁ নাহি পাই লেশ ॥ ৬৮ ॥

śuna, bhaṭṭācārya,—"āmi gelāṅa bahu-deśa
vana-pathe duḥkhera kāhāṅ nāhi pāi leśa

SYNONYMS

śuna—please hear; *bhaṭṭācārya*—My dear Bhaṭṭācārya; *āmi*—I; *gelāṅa*—traveled; *bahu-deśa*—many countries; *vana-pathe*—through the forest path;

duḥkhera—of unhappiness; *kāhāṅ*—anywhere; *nāhi pāi*—I do not get; *leśa*—even a trace.

TRANSLATION

"My dear Bhaṭṭācārya, I have traveled very far through the forest, and I have not even slightly received any trouble.

TEXT 69

কৃষ্ণ—কৃপালু, আমায় বহুত কৃপা কৈলা ।
বনপথে আনি' আমায় বড় সুখ দিলা ॥ ৬৯ ॥

kṛṣṇa——kṛpālu, āmāya bahuta kṛpā kailā
vana-pathe āni' āmāya baḍa sukha dilā

SYNONYMS

kṛṣṇa—Lord Kṛṣṇa; *kṛpālu*—very kind; *āmāya*—upon Me; *bahuta*—greatly; *kṛpā*—mercy; *kailā*—showed; *vana-pathe*—on the path in the forest; *āni'*—bringing; *āmāya*—unto Me; *baḍa*—very much; *sukha*—happiness; *dilā*—gave.

TRANSLATION

"Kṛṣṇa is very merciful, especially to Me. He has shown His mercy by bringing Me on this path through the forest. Thus He has given Me great pleasure.

TEXT 70

পূর্বে বৃন্দাবন যাইতে করিলাঙ বিচার ।
মাতা, গঙ্গা, ভক্তগণে দেখিব একবার ॥ ৭০ ॥

pūrve vṛndāvana yāite karilāṅa vicāra
mātā, gaṅgā, bhakta-gaṇe dekhiba eka-bāra

SYNONYMS

pūrve—formerly; *vṛndāvana*—to the holy place of Vṛndāvana; *yāite*—to go; *karilāṅa*—I did; *vicāra*—consideration; *mātā*—mother; *gaṅgā*—the Ganges; *bhakta-gaṇe*—and devotees; *dekhiba*—I shall see; *eka-bāra*—once.

TRANSLATION

"Before this, I decided to go to Vṛndāvana and on the way see My mother, the River Ganges and other devotees once again.

TEXT 71

ভক্তগণ-সঙ্গে অবশ্য করিব মিলন।
ভক্তগণে সঙ্গে লঞা যাব 'বৃন্দাবন'॥ ৭১॥

bhakta-gaṇa-saṅge avaśya kariba milana
bhakta-gaṇe saṅge lañā yāba 'vṛndāvana'

SYNONYMS

bhakta-gaṇa-saṅge—with all My devotees; *avaśya*—certainly; *kariba*—shall do; *milana*—meeting; *bhakta-gaṇe*—all the devotees; *saṅge*—along with Me; *lañā*—taking; *yāba*—I shall go; *vṛndāvana*—to Vṛndāvana-dhāma.

TRANSLATION

"I thought that once again I would see and meet all the devotees and take them with Me to Vṛndāvana.

TEXT 72

এত ভাবি' গৌড়দেশে করিলুঁ গমন।
মাতা, গঙ্গা ভক্তে দেখি' সুখী হৈল মন॥ ৭২॥

eta bhāvi' gauḍa-deśe kariluṅ gamana
mātā, gaṅgā bhakte dekhi' sukhī haila mana

SYNONYMS

eta bhāvi'—thinking like this; *gauḍa-deśe*—to Bengal; *kariluṅ gamana*—I went; *mātā*—My mother; *gaṅgā*—the Ganges; *bhakte*—devotees; *dekhi'*—seeing; *sukhī*—happy; *haila*—became; *mana*—My mind.

TRANSLATION

"Thus I went to Bengal, and I was very happy to see My mother, the River Ganges and the devotees.

TEXT 73

ভক্তগণে লঞা তবে চলিলাঙ রঙ্গে।
লক্ষকোটি লোক তাহাঁ হৈল আমা-সঙ্গে॥ ৭৩॥

bhakta-gaṇe lañā tabe calilāṅa raṅge
lakṣa-koṭi loka tāhāṅ haila āmā-saṅge

SYNONYMS

bhakta-gaṇe—all the devotees; *lañā*—taking; *tabe*—then; *calilāṅa raṅge*—I started with great pleasure; *lakṣa-koṭi*—many thousands and millions; *loka*—people; *tāhāṅ*—there; *haila*—became; *āmā-saṅge*—My companions.

TRANSLATION

"However, when I started for Vṛndāvana, many thousands and millions of people gathered and began to go with Me.

TEXT 74

সনাতন-মুখে কৃষ্ণ আমা শিখাইলা ।
তাহা বিঘ্ন করি' বনপথে লঞা আইলা ॥ ৭৪ ॥

sanātana-mukhe kṛṣṇa āmā śikhāilā
tāhā vighna kari' vana-pathe lañā āilā

SYNONYMS

sanātana-mukhe—from the mouth of Sanātana; *kṛṣṇa*—Lord Kṛṣṇa; *āmā*—unto Me; *śikhāilā*—gave instructions; *tāhā*—that; *vighna kari'*—making a hindrance; *vana-pathe*—on the path through the forest; *lañā*—taking; *āilā*—came.

TRANSLATION

"Thus I was going to Vṛndāvana with a big crowd, but through the mouth of Sanātana, Kṛṣṇa taught Me a lesson. Thus by making some impediment, He has brought Me on a path through the forest to Vṛndāvana.

TEXT 75

কৃপার সমুদ্র, দীন-হীনে দয়াময় ।
কৃষ্ণকৃপা বিনা কোন 'সুখ' নাহি হয় ॥" ৭৫ ॥

kṛpāra samudra, dīna-hīne dayāmaya
kṛṣṇa-kṛpā vinā kona 'sukha' nāhi haya"

SYNONYMS

kṛpāra samudra—ocean of mercy; *dīna-hīne*—unto the poor and fallen; *dayā-maya*—very merciful; *kṛṣṇa-kṛpā*—the mercy of Kṛṣṇa; *vinā*—without; *kona*—any; *sukha*—happiness; *nāhi haya*—there is not.

TRANSLATION

"Kṛṣṇa is an ocean of mercy. He is especially merciful to the poor and fallen. Without His mercy, there is no possibility of happiness."

TEXT 76

ভট্টাচার্যে আলিঙ্গিয়া তাঁহারে কহিল ।
'তোমার প্রসাদে আমি এত সুখ পাইল' ॥ ৭৬ ॥

bhaṭṭācārye āliṅgiyā tāṅhāre kahila
'tomāra prasāde āmi eta sukha pāila'

SYNONYMS

bhaṭṭācārye—Balabhadra Bhaṭṭācārya; *āliṅgiyā*—embracing; *tāṅhāre*—unto him; *kahila*—said; *tomāra prasāde*—by your kindness; *āmi*—I; *eta*—so much; *sukha*—happiness; *pāila*—got.

TRANSLATION

Śrī Caitanya Mahāprabhu then embraced Balabhadra Bhaṭṭācārya and told him, "It is only by your kindness that I am now so happy."

TEXT 77

তেঁহো কহেন,—"তুমি 'কৃষ্ণ', তুমি 'দয়াময়' ।
অধম জীব মুঞি, মোরে হইলা সদয় ॥ ৭৭ ॥

teṅho kahena,——"tumi 'kṛṣṇa', tumi 'dayāmaya'
adhama jīva muñi, more ha-ilā sadaya

SYNONYMS

teṅho kahena—Bhaṭṭācārya said; *tumi kṛṣṇa*—You are Kṛṣṇa Himself; *tumi*—You; *dayā-maya*—merciful; *adhama*—the lowest of the low; *jīva*—living entity; *muñi*—I; *more*—unto me; *ha-ilā*—You have been; *sa-daya*—favorable.

TRANSLATION

Balabhadra Bhaṭṭācārya replied, "My dear Lord, You are Kṛṣṇa Himself, and therefore You are merciful. I am a fallen living entity, but You have bestowed a great favor upon me.

TEXT 78

মুঞি ছার, মোরে তুমি সঙ্গে লঞা আইলা ।
কৃপা করি' মোর হাতে 'প্রভু' ভিক্ষা কৈলা ॥ ৭৮ ॥

muñi chāra, more tumi saṅge lañā āilā
kṛpā kari' mora hāte 'prabhu' bhikṣā kailā

SYNONYMS

muñi—I; *chāra*—most fallen; *more*—me; *tumi*—You; *saṅge*—with; *lañā*—taking; *āilā*—have come; *kṛpā kari'*—showing great mercy; *mora hāte*—from my hand; *prabhu*—my Lord; *bhikṣā kailā*—You accepted food.

TRANSLATION

"Sir, I am most fallen, yet You have brought me with You. Showing great mercy, You have accepted food prepared by me.

TEXT 79

অধম-কাকেরে কৈলা গরুড়-সমান ।
'স্বতন্ত্র ঈশ্বর' তুমি—স্বয়ং ভগবান্ ॥" ৭৯ ॥

adhama-kākere kailā garuḍa-samāna
'svatantra īśvara' tumi——svayaṁ bhagavān"

SYNONYMS

adhama-kākere—the most condemned crow; *kailā*—You have made; *garuḍa-samāna*—like Garuḍa; *svatantra*—independent; *īśvara*—Supreme Personality of Godhead; *tumi*—You; *svayam bhagavān*—the original Personality of Godhead.

TRANSLATION

"You have made me Your carrier Garuḍa, although I am no better than a condemned crow. Thus You are the independent Personality of Godhead, the original Lord.

TEXT 80

মূকং করোতি বাচালং পঙ্গুং লঙ্ঘয়তে গিরিম্ ।
যৎকৃপা তমহং বন্দে পরমানন্দ-মাধবম্ ॥ ৮০ ॥

mūkaṁ karoti vācālaṁ
paṅguṁ laṅghayate girim
yat-kṛpā tam ahaṁ vande
paramānanda-mādhavam

SYNONYMS

mūkam—a person who cannot speak; *karoti*—makes; *vācālam*—an eloquent speaker; *paṅgum*—a person who cannot even walk; *laṅghayate*—causes to cross over; *girim*—the mountain; *yat-kṛpā*—whose mercy; *tam*—unto Him; *aham*—I; *vande*—offer obeisances; *parama-ānanda*—the transcendentally blissful; *mādhavam*—Supreme Personality of Godhead.

TRANSLATION

" 'The Supreme Personality of Godhead has the form of sac-cid-ānanda-vigraha, transcendental bliss, knowledge and eternity. I offer my respectful obeisances unto He who turns the dumb into eloquent speakers and enables the lame to cross mountains. Such is the mercy of the Lord.' "

PURPORT

This is a quotation from the *Bhāvārtha-dīpikā* commentary on *Śrīmad-Bhāgavatam* (1.1.1).

TEXT 81

এইমত বলভদ্র করেন স্তবন ।
প্রেমসেবা করি' তুষ্ট কৈল প্রভুর মন ॥ ৮১ ॥

ei-mata balabhadra karena stavana
prema-sevā kari' tuṣṭa kaila prabhura mana

SYNONYMS

ei-mata—in this way; *balabhadra*—Balabhadra Bhaṭṭācārya; *karena*—offers; *stavana*—prayers; *prema-sevā kari'*—rendering service in love; *tuṣṭa*—pacified; *kaila*—made; *prabhura*—of Śrī Caitanya Mahāprabhu; *mana*—the mind.

TRANSLATION

In this way Balabhadra Bhaṭṭācārya offered his prayers to the Lord. By rendering service unto Him in ecstatic love, He pacified the Lord's mind.

TEXT 82

এইমত নানা-সুখে প্রভু আইলা 'কাশী'।
মধ্যাহ্ন-স্নান কৈল মণিকর্ণিকায় আসি' ॥ ৮২ ॥

ei-mata nānā-sukhe prabhu āilā 'kāśī'
madhyāhna-snāna kaila maṇikarṇikāya āsi'

SYNONYMS

ei-mata—in this way; *nānā-sukhe*—in great happiness; *prabhu*—Śrī Caitanya Mahāprabhu; *āilā*—came; *kāśī*—to the holy place named Kāśī; *madhyāhna-snāna*—afternoon bath; *kaila*—took; *maṇikarṇikāya*—to the bathing place known as Maṇikarṇikā; *āsi'*—coming.

TRANSLATION

Finally the Lord with great happiness arrived at the holy place called Kāśī. There He took His bath in the bathing ghat known as Maṇikarṇikā.

PURPORT

Kāśī is another name for Vārāṇasī (Benares). It has been a place of pilgrimage since time immemorial. Two rivers named Asiḥ and Varuṇā merge there. Maṇikarṇikā is famous because, according to the opinion of great personalities, a bejeweled earring fell there from the ear of Lord Viṣṇu. According to some, it fell from the ear of Lord Śiva. The word *maṇi* means "jewel," and *karṇika* means "from the ear." According to some, Lord Viśvanātha is the great physician who cures the disease of material existence by delivering a person through the ear, which receives the vibration of the holy name of Lord Rāma. Because of this, this holy place is called Maṇi-karṇikā. It is said that there is no better place than where the River Ganges flows, and the bathing ghat known as Maṇikarṇikā is especially sanctified because it is very dear to Lord Viśvanātha. In the *Kāśī-khaṇḍa* it is said: *saṁsāri-cintāmaṇir atra yasmāt tārakaṁ sajjana-karṇikāyām. śivo 'bhidhatte saha-sānta-kāle tad gīyate 'sau maṇi-karṇiketi. mukti-lakṣmī mahā-pīṭha-maṇis tac-caraṇābjayoḥ. karṇikeyaṁ tataḥ prāhur yāṁ janā maṇi-karṇikām.* According to the *Kāśī-khaṇḍa,* if one gives up his body at Maṇikarṇikā, he is liberated simply by remembering Lord Śiva's name.

TEXT 83

সেইকালে তপনমিশ্র করে গঙ্গাস্নান।
প্রভু দেখি' হৈল তাঁর কিছু বিস্ময় জ্ঞান ॥ ৮৩ ॥

sei-kāle tapana-miśra kare gaṅgā-snāna
prabhu dekhi' haila tāṅra kichu vismaya jñāna

SYNONYMS

sei-kāle—at that time; *tapana-miśra*—a *brāhmaṇa* named Tapana Miśra; *kare gaṅgā-snāna*—was taking his bath in the Ganges; *prabhu dekhi'*—seeing the Lord; *haila*—there was; *tāṅra*—his; *kichu*—some; *vismaya jñāna*—astonishment.

TRANSLATION

At that time, Tapana Miśra was taking his bath in the Ganges, and he was astonished to see the Lord there.

TEXT 84

‘পূর্বে শুনিয়াছি প্রভু কর্য়াছেন সন্ন্যাস’।
নিশ্চয় করিয়া হৈল হৃদয়ে উল্লাস ॥ ৮৪ ॥

'pūrve śuniyāchi prabhu karyāchena sannyāsa'
niścaya kariyā haila hṛdaye ullāsa

SYNONYMS

pūrve—formerly; *śuniyāchi*—I have heard; *prabhu*—Lord Śrī Caitanya Mahāprabhu; *karyāchena sannyāsa*—has accepted the renounced order of life; *niścaya kariyā*—ascertaining that; *haila*—there was; *hṛdaye*—within the heart; *ullāsa*—great jubilation.

TRANSLATION

Tapana Miśra then began to think, "I have heard that Śrī Caitanya Mahāprabhu has accepted the renounced order." Thinking this, Tapana Miśra became very jubilant within his heart.

TEXT 85

প্রভুর চরণ ধরি করেন রোদন।
প্রভু তারে উঠাঞা কৈল আলিঙ্গন ॥ ৮৫ ॥

prabhura caraṇa dhari' karena rodana
prabhu tāre uṭhāñā kaila āliṅgana

SYNONYMS

prabhura—of Śrī Caitanya Mahāprabhu; *caraṇa*—lotus feet; *dhari'*—touching; *karena*—does; *rodana*—crying; *prabhu*—Śrī Caitanya Mahāprabhu; *tāre*—him; *uṭhāñā*—raising; *kaila*—did; *āliṅgana*—embracing.

TRANSLATION

He then clasped the lotus feet of Śrī Caitanya Mahāprabhu and began to cry. The Lord raised him up and embraced him.

TEXT 86

প্রভু লঞা গেলা বিশ্বেশ্বর-দরশনে ।
তবে আসি' দেখে বিন্দুমাধব-চরণে ॥ ৮৬ ॥

prabhu lañā gelā viśveśvara-daraśane
tabe āsi' dekhe bindu-mādhava-caraṇe

SYNONYMS

prabhu lañā—taking the Lord; *gelā*—he went; *viśveśvara-daraśane*—to visit the temple of Viśveśvara; *tabe*—thereafter; *āsi'*—coming; *dekhe*—see; *bindu-mādhava-caraṇe*—the lotus feet of Bindu Mādhava.

TRANSLATION

Tapana Miśra then took Śrī Caitanya Mahāprabhu to visit the temple of Viśveśvara. Coming from there, they saw the lotus feet of Lord Bindu Mādhava.

PURPORT

This Bindu Mādhava is the oldest Viṣṇu temple in Vārāṇasī. Presently this temple is known as Veṇī Mādhava, and it is situated on the banks of the Ganges. Formerly five rivers converged there, and they were named Dhūtapāpā, Kiraṇā, Sarasvatī, Gaṅgā and Yamunā. Now only the River Ganges is visible. The old temple of Bindu Mādhava, which was visited by Śrī Caitanya Mahāprabhu, was later dismantled by Aurangzeb, the great Hindu-hating emperor of the Mogul dynasty. In the place of this temple, he constructed a big *majīda,* or mosque. Later, another temple was constructed by the side of the mosque, and this temple is still existing. In the temple of Bindu Mādhava there are Deities of four-handed Nārāyaṇa and the goddess Lakṣmī. In front of these Deities is a column of Śrī Garuḍa, and along the side are deities of Lord Rāma, Sītā, Lakṣmaṇa and Śrī Hanumānjī.

In the province of Mahārāṣṭra is a state known as Sātārā. During the time of Bhaktisiddhānta Sarasvatī Ṭhākura, the native prince belonged to the Vaiṣṇava cult. Being a *brāhmaṇa,* he took charge of worshiping the Deity. He was known as Śrīmanta Bālāsāheba Pantha Mahārāja. The state still bears the expenditure for temple maintenance. The first king in this dynasty to take charge of worship in the temple, two hundred years ago, was Mahārāja Jagatjīvana Rāo Sāheba.

TEXT 87

ঘরে লঞা আইলা প্রভুকে আনন্দিত হঞা ।
সেবা করি' নৃত্য করে বস্ত্র উড়াঞা ॥ ৮৭ ॥

ghare lañā āilā prabhuke ānandita hañā
sevā kari' nṛtya kare vastra uḍāñā

SYNONYMS

ghare lañā—taking to his home; *āilā*—came; *prabhuke*—Śrī Caitanya Mahāprabhu; *ānandita hañā*—in great happiness; *sevā kari'*—rendering service; *nṛtya kare*—began to dance; *vastra uḍāñā*—waving his cloth.

TRANSLATION

With great pleasure Tapana Miśra brought Śrī Caitanya Mahāprabhu to his home and rendered service unto Him. Indeed, he began to dance, waving his cloth.

TEXT 88

প্রভুর চরণোদক সবংশে কৈল পান ।
ভট্টাচার্যের পূজা কৈল করিয়া সম্মান ॥ ৮৮ ॥

prabhura caraṇodaka savaṁśe kaila pāna
bhaṭṭācāryera pūjā kaila kariyā sammāna

SYNONYMS

prabhura—of Śrī Caitanya Mahāprabhu; *caraṇa-udaka*—the water used to wash the lotus feet; *sa-vaṁśe*—with his whole family; *kaila pāna*—drank; *bhaṭṭācāryera*—of Bhaṭṭācārya; *pūjā*—worship; *kaila*—performed; *kariyā*—showing; *sammāna*—respect.

TRANSLATION

He washed the lotus feet of Śrī Caitanya Mahāprabhu, and afterwards he and his whole family drank the wash water. He also worshiped Balabhadra Bhaṭṭācārya and showed him respect.

TEXT 89

প্রভুরে নিমন্ত্রণ করি' ঘরে ভিক্ষা দিল ।
বলভদ্র-ভট্টাচার্যে পাক করাইল ॥ ৮৯ ॥

prabhure nimantraṇa kari' ghare bhikṣā dila
balabhadra-bhaṭṭācārye pāka karāila

SYNONYMS

prabhure nimantraṇa kari'—inviting the Lord; *ghare*—at home; *bhikṣā dila*—gave lunch; *balabhadra-bhaṭṭācārye*—Balabhadra Bhaṭṭācārya; *pāka karāila*—he had cook.

TRANSLATION

Tapana Miśra invited Śrī Caitanya Mahāprabhu to take lunch at his home, and he had Balabhadra Bhaṭṭācārya cook.

PURPORT

While at Vārāṇasī (Benares), Śrī Caitanya Mahāprabhu stayed at the house of Tapana Miśra. Near Tapana Miśra's house was a bathing ghat known as Pañcanadī-ghāṭa. Śrī Caitanya Mahāprabhu used to take His bath daily at this ghat, and He used to see the temple of Bindu Mādhava. Then He took His lunch at Tapana Miśra's house. Near the Bindu Mādhava temple is a big banyan tree, and it is said that after eating, Śrī Caitanya Mahāprabhu used to rest beneath the tree. That banyan tree is still known today as Caitanya-vaṭa. Gradually, due to changes in language, the name became Yatana-vaṭa. The local people still call that place Yatana-vaṭa.

Presently, beside a lane there is a tomb of Vallabhācārya, but there is no sign that Caitanya Mahāprabhu ever lived there. Vallabhācārya was also known as Mahāprabhu among his disciples. Śrī Caitanya Mahāprabhu probably lived at Yatana-vaṭa, but there is no sign of Candraśekhara's or Tapana Miśra's house, nor is there sign of the Māyāvādī *sannyāsī* Prakāśānanda Sarasvatī, with whom Śrī Caitanya Mahāprabhu discussed *Vedānta-sūtra.* A little distance from Yatana-vaṭa is a temple of Gaura-Nityānanda established by Śaśibhūṣaṇa Niyogī Mahāśaya of Calcutta. This temple is now managed by the mother-in-law of Śaśibhūṣaṇa and his brother-in-law Nārāyaṇa-candra Ghosh.

TEXT 90

ভিক্ষা করি' মহাপ্রভু করিলা শয়ন ।
মিশ্রপুত্র রঘু করে পাদ-সম্বাহন ॥ ৯০ ॥

bhikṣā kari' mahāprabhu karilā śayana
miśra-putra raghu kare pāda-saṁvāhana

SYNONYMS

bhikṣā kari'—after finishing His lunch; *mahāprabhu*—Śrī Caitanya Mahāprabhu; *karilā śayana*—took rest; *miśra-putra*—the son of Tapana Miśra; *raghu*—Raghu; *kare*—does; *pāda-saṁvāhana*—massaging the legs.

TRANSLATION

When Śrī Caitanya Mahāprabhu took His rest after lunch, the son of Tapana Miśra, named Raghu, used to massage His legs.

TEXT 91

প্রভুর 'শেষান্ন' মিশ্র সবংশে খাইল।
'প্রভু আইলা' শুনি' চন্দ্রশেখর আইল ॥ ৯১ ॥

prabhura 'śeṣānna' miśra savaṁśe khāila
'prabhu āilā' śuni' candraśekhara āila

SYNONYMS

prabhura—of Śrī Caitanya Mahāprabhu; *śeṣa-anna*—remnants of food; *miśra*—Tapana Miśra; *sa-vaṁśe*—along with his family; *khāila*—ate; *prabhu āilā*—the Lord has arrived; *śuni'*—hearing; *candraśekhara āila*—Candraśekhara came.

TRANSLATION

The remnants of food left by Śrī Caitanya Mahāprabhu were taken by the whole family of Tapana Miśra. When news spread that the Lord had come, Candraśekhara also came to see Him.

TEXT 92

মিশ্রের সখা তেঁহো প্রভুর পূর্ব দাস।
বৈদ্যজাতি, লিখনবৃত্তি, বারাণসী-বাস ॥ ৯২ ॥

miśrera sakhā teṅho prabhura pūrva dāsa
vaidya-jāti, likhana-vṛtti, vārāṇasī-vāsa

SYNONYMS

miśrera sakhā—friend of Tapana Miśra; *teṅho*—he; *prabhura*—of Śrī Caitanya Mahāprabhu; *pūrva dāsa*—former servant; *vaidya-jāti*—by caste a physician; *likhana-vṛtti*—by profession a clerk; *vārāṇasī-vāsa*—resident of Vārāṇasī.

TRANSLATION

Candraśekhara happened to be a friend of Tapana Miśra's, and he was long known to Śrī Caitanya Mahāprabhu as His servant. He was a physician by caste, and by profession he was a clerk. At the time he was living in Vārāṇasī.

TEXT 93

আসি' প্রভু-পদে পড়ি' করেন রোদন ।
প্রভু উঠি' তাঁরে কৃপায় কৈল আলিঙ্গন ॥ ৯৩ ॥

āsi' prabhu-pade paḍi' karena rodana
prabhu uṭhi' tāṅre kṛpāya kaila āliṅgana

SYNONYMS

āsi'—coming; *prabhu-pade*—at the lotus feet of Śrī Caitanya Mahāprabhu; *paḍi'*—falling down; *karena*—does; *rodana*—crying; *prabhu*—Śrī Caitanya Mahāprabhu; *uṭhi'*—standing; *tāṅre*—unto him; *kṛpāya*—out of mercy; *kaila*—did; *āliṅgana*—embracing.

TRANSLATION

When Candreśekhara came there, he fell down before the lotus feet of Śrī Caitanya Mahāprabhu and began to cry. The Lord, standing up, embraced him out of His causeless mercy.

TEXT 94

চন্দ্রশেখর কহে,—"প্রভু, বড় কৃপা কৈলা ।
আপনে আসিয়া ভৃত্যে দরশন দিলা ॥ ৯৪ ॥

candraśekhara kahe,—"prabhu, baḍa kṛpā kailā
āpane āsiyā bhṛtye daraśana dilā

SYNONYMS

candraśekhara kahe—Candraśekhara said; *prabhu*—my dear Lord; *baḍa kṛpā kailā*—You have shown Your causeless mercy; *āpane*—personally; *āsiyā*—coming; *bhṛtye*—unto Your servant; *daraśana dilā*—gave Your audience.

TRANSLATION

Candraśekhara said, "My dear Lord, You bestowed Your causeless mercy upon me because I am Your old servant. Indeed, You have come here personally to give me Your audience.

TEXT 95

আপন-প্রারব্ধে বসি' বারাণসী-স্থানে ।
'মায়া', 'ব্রহ্ম' শব্দ বিনা নাহি শুনি কাণে ॥ ৯৫ ॥

āpana-prārabdhe vasi' vārāṇasī-sthāne
'māyā', 'brahma' śabda vinā nāhi śuni kāṇe

SYNONYMS

āpana-prārabdhe—because of my past deeds; *vasi'*—staying; *vārāṇasī-sthāne*—in the place known as Vārāṇasī; *māyā*—*māyā; brahma*—and *brahma; śabda*—the words; *vinā*—except; *nāhi śuni*—I do not hear; *kāṇe*—in the ear.

TRANSLATION

"Due to my past deeds, I am residing at Vārāṇasī, but here I do not hear anything but the words māyā and Brahman."

PURPORT

The word *prārabdhe* (past deeds) is important in this verse. Since Candraśekhara was a devotee, he was always eager to hear about Kṛṣṇa and His transcendental pastimes. Most of the inhabitants of Benares were and are impersonalists, worshipers of Lord Śiva and followers of the *pañcopāsanā* method. The impersonalists imagine some form of the impersonal Brahman, and to facilitate meditation they concentrate upon the forms of Viṣṇu, Śiva, Gaṇeśa, Sūrya and goddess Durgā. Actually these *pañcopāsakas* are not devotees of anyone. As it is said, to be a servant of everyone is to be the servant of no one. Vārāṇasī, or Kāśī, is the chief holy place of pilgrimage for impersonalists, and it is not at all suitable for devotees. A Vaiṣṇava likes to live in a *viṣṇu-tīrtha,* a place where Lord Viṣṇu's temples are present. In Vārāṇasī there are many hundreds and thousands of Lord Śiva's temples, or *pañcopāsaka* temples. Consequently Candraśekhara expressed great unhappiness as he informed Lord Caitanya that he was obliged to live at Benares due to his past misdeeds. In *Bhakti-rasāmṛta-sindhu* it is also said, *durjāty-ārambhakaṁ pāpaṁ yat syāt prārabdham eva tat.* "According to one's past misdeeds, one takes birth on a lower platform." In the *Brahma-saṁhitā* (5.54) it is said: *karmāṇi nirdahati kintu ca bhakti-bhājām.* There is no *karma* attached to the past deeds or misdeeds of one in devotional service. A devotee is not subjected to *karma-phala,* the effect of fruitive activity. *Karma-phala* is applicable to *karmīs,* not *bhaktas.*

There are three kinds of devotees: those who are eternally on the transcendental platform (*nitya-siddha*), those elevated to the transcendental platform by the execution of devotional service (*sādhana-siddha*), and those who are neophytes advancing toward the perfectional platform (*sādhaka*). The *sādhakas* are gradually becoming free from fruitive reaction. *Bhakti-rasāmṛta-sindhu* (1.1.17) describes the symptoms of *bhakti-yoga* thus:

kleśa-ghnī śubhadā mokṣa-
laghutākṛt sudurlabhā
sāndrānanda-viśeṣātmā
śrī-kṛṣṇākarṣiṇī ca sā

Devotional service is *kleśa-ghnī* even for beginners. This means that it reduces or nullifies all kinds of suffering. The word *śubhadā* indicates that devotional service bestows all good fortune, and the words *kṛṣṇa-ākarṣiṇī* indicate that devotional service gradually attracts Kṛṣṇa toward the devotee. Consequently a devotee is not subject to any sinful reaction. In *Bhagavad-gītā* (18.66) Kṛṣṇa says:

sarva-dharmān parityajya
mām ekaṁ śaraṇaṁ vraja
ahaṁ tvāṁ sarva-pāpebhyo
mokṣayiṣyāmi mā śucaḥ

"Abandon all varieties of religion and just surrender unto Me. I shall deliver you from all sinful reaction. Do not fear."

Thus a fully surrendered, sincere devotee immediately receives relief from all kinds of sinful reaction. There are three stages of fructification for sinful activity. At one stage, one commits the sinful act. Before that, the seed of this act exists, and before that there is ignorance whereby one commits the sin. Suffering is involved in all three stages. However, Kṛṣṇa is merciful to His devotee, and consequently He immediately nullifies all three stages—the sin, the seed of sin and the ignorance that leads one to sin. *Padma Purāṇa* confirms this:

aprārabdha-phalaṁ pāpaṁ
kūṭaṁ bījaṁ phalonmukham
krameṇaiva pralīyeta
viṣṇu-bhakti-ratātmanām

For a further explanation of this, *The Nectar of Devotion* should be consulted.

TEXT 96

ষড়্‌দর্শন-ব্যাখ্যা বিনা কথা নাহি এথা ।
মিশ্র কৃপা করি' মোরে শুনান কৃষ্ণকথা ॥ ৯৬ ॥

ṣaḍ-darśana-vyākhyā vinā kathā nāhi ethā
miśra kṛpā kari' more śunāna kṛṣṇa-kathā

SYNONYMS

ṣaṭ-darśana—of six kinds of philosophical theses; *vyākhyā*—explanation; *vinā*—except; *kathā*—talk; *nāhi*—not; *ethā*—here; *miśra*—Tapana Miśra; *kṛpā kari'*—being very merciful; *more*—unto me; *śunāna*—explains; *kṛṣṇa-kathā*—topics of Lord Śrī Kṛṣṇa.

TRANSLATION

Candraśekhara continued, "There is no talk at Vārāṇasī other than discussions on the six philosophical theses. Nonetheless, Tapana Miśra has been very kind to me, for he speaks about topics relating to Lord Kṛṣṇa.

PURPORT

The six philosophical treatises are: (1) *vaiśeṣika,* propounded by Kaṇāda Ṛṣi, (2) *nyāya,* propounded by Gautama Ṛṣi, (3) *yoga* or mysticism, propounded by Patañjali Ṛṣi, (4) the philosophy of *sāṅkhya,* propounded by Kapila Ṛṣi, (5) the philosophy of *karma-mīmāṁsā,* propounded by Jaimini Ṛṣi, and (6) the philosophy of *brahma-mīmāṁsā,* or Vedānta, the ultimate conclusion of the Absolute Truth (*janmādy asya yataḥ*), propounded by Vedavyāsa. Actually Vedānta philosophy is meant for the devotees because in *Bhagavad-gītā* Lord Kṛṣṇa says, *vedānta-kṛd veda-vid eva cāham:* "I am the compiler of Vedānta, and I am the knower of the *Vedas."* (Bg. 15.15) Vyāsadeva is an incarnation of Kṛṣṇa, and consequently Kṛṣṇa is the compiler of Vedānta philosophy. Therefore Kṛṣṇa clearly knows the purport of Vedānta philosophy. As stated in *Bhagavad-gītā,* whoever hears Vedānta philosophy from Kṛṣṇa is actually aware of the real meaning of Vedānta. The Māyāvādīs who have called themselves Vedāntists do not at all understand the purport of Vedānta philosophy. Not being properly educated, people in general think that Vedānta means the Śaṅkarite interpretation.

TEXT 97

নিরন্তর দুঁহে চিন্তি তোমার চরণ ।
'সর্বজ্ঞ ঈশ্বর' তুমি দিলা দরশন ॥ ৯৭ ॥

nirantara duṅhe cinti tomāra caraṇa
'sarvajña īśvara' tumi dilā daraśana

SYNONYMS

nirantara—incessantly; *duṅhe*—we two; *cinti*—think of; *tomāra caraṇa*—Your lotus feet; *sarva-jña*—omniscient; *īśvara*—Supreme Personality of Godhead; *tumi*—You; *dilā daraśana*—gave Your audience.

TRANSLATION

"My dear Lord, we two think of Your lotus feet incessantly. Although You are the omniscient Supreme Personality of Godhead, You have granted us Your audience.

TEXT 98

শুনি,—'মহাপ্রভু' যাবেন শ্রীবৃন্দাবনে।
দিন কত রহি' তার' ভৃত্য দুইজনে ॥" ৯৮ ॥

śuni,——'mahāprabhu' yābena śrī-vṛndāvane
dina kata rahi' tāra' bhṛtya dui-jane"

SYNONYMS

śuni—I hear; *mahāprabhu*—Śrī Caitanya Mahāprabhu; *yābena*—will go; *śrī-vṛndāvane*—to Vṛndāvana; *dina kata*—for some days; *rahi'*—staying; *tāra'*—please deliver; *bhṛtya*—servants; *dui-jane*—two persons.

TRANSLATION

"My Lord, I have heard that You are going to Vṛndāvana. After You stay here at Vārāṇasī for some days, please deliver us, for we are Your two servants."

TEXT 99

মিশ্র কহে,—'প্রভু, যাবৎ কাশীতে রহিবা।
মোর নিমন্ত্রণ বিনা অন্য না মানিবা ॥' ৯৯ ॥

miśra kahe,——'prabhu, yāvat kāśīte rahibā
mora nimantraṇa vinā anya nā mānibā'

SYNONYMS

miśra kahe—Tapana Miśra said; *prabhu*—my Lord; *yāvat*—as long as; *kāśīte rahibā*—You will stay at Kāśī, Vārāṇasī; *mora nimantraṇa*—my invitation; *vinā*—besides; *anya*—others; *nā mānibā*—do not accept.

TRANSLATION

Tapana Miśra then said, "My dear Lord, as long as You stay at Vārāṇasī, please do not accept any invitation other than mine."

TEXT 100

এইমত মহাপ্রভু দুই ভৃত্যের বশে ।
ইচ্ছা নাহি, তবু তথা রহিলা দিন-দশে ॥ ১০০ ॥

ei-mata mahāprabhu dui bhṛtyera vaśe
icchā nāhi, tabu tathā rahilā dina-daśe

SYNONYMS

ei-mata—in this way; *mahāprabhu*—Śrī Caitanya Mahāprabhu; *dui*—two; *bhṛtyera*—by servants; *vaśe*—being obliged; *icchā nāhi*—there was no such desire; *tabu*—still; *tathā*—there; *rahilā*—remained; *dina-daśe*—for ten days.

TRANSLATION

Even though He had not made such a plan, Śrī Caitanya Mahāprabhu remained for ten days at Vārāṇasī, being obligated by the requests of His two servants.

TEXT 101

মহারাষ্ট্রীয় বিপ্র আইসে প্রভু দেখিবারে ।
প্রভুর রূপ-প্রেম দেখি' হয় চমৎকারে ॥ ১০১ ॥

mahārāṣṭrīya vipra āise prabhu dekhibāre
prabhura rūpa-prema dekhi' haya camatkāre

SYNONYMS

mahārāṣṭrīya—belonging to the Mahārāṣṭra state; *vipra*—one *brāhmaṇa; āise*—comes; *prabhu dekhibāre*—to see Lord Śrī Caitanya Mahāprabhu; *prabhura*—of Śrī Caitanya Mahāprabhu; *rūpa-prema*—beauty and ecstatic love; *dekhi'*—seeing; *haya camatkāre*—becomes astonished.

TRANSLATION

At Vārāṇasī there was a Mahārāṣṭrīyan brāhmaṇa who used to come daily to see Śrī Caitanya Mahāprabhu. This brāhmaṇa was simply astonished to see the Lord's personal beauty and ecstatic love for Kṛṣṇa.

TEXT 102

বিপ্র সব নিমন্ত্রয়, প্রভু নাহি মানে।
প্রভু কহে,—'আজি মোর হঞাছে নিমন্ত্রণে' ॥১০২॥

vipra saba nimantraya, prabhu nāhi māne
prabhu kahe,——'āji mora hañāche nimantraṇe'

SYNONYMS

vipra—the *brāhmaṇas; saba*—all; *nimantraya*—invite; *prabhu*—Lord Śrī Caitanya Mahāprabhu; *nāhi māne*—does not accept; *prabhu kahe*—the Lord replies; *āji*—today; *mora*—My; *hañāche*—has been; *nimantraṇe*—invitation.

TRANSLATION

When the brāhmaṇas of Vārāṇasī would invite Śrī Caitanya Mahāprabhu to lunch, the Lord would not accept their invitations. He would reply, "I have already been invited somewhere else."

TEXT 103

এইমত প্রতিদিন করেন বঞ্চন।
সন্ন্যাসীর সঙ্গ-ভয়ে না মানেন নিমন্ত্রণ ॥ ১০৩ ॥

ei-mata prati-dina karena vañcana
sannyāsīra saṅga-bhaye nā mānena nimantraṇa

SYNONYMS

ei-mata—in this way; *prati-dina*—daily; *karena vañcana*—denies other inviters; *sannyāsīra*—of the Māyāvādī *sannyāsīs; saṅga-bhaye*—from fear of the association; *nā mānena*—does not accept; *nimantraṇa*—invitation.

TRANSLATION

Every day Śrī Caitanya Mahāprabhu refused their invitation because He feared associating with Māyāvādī sannyāsīs.

PURPORT

A Vaiṣṇava *sannyāsī* never accepts an invitation from a party who considers Māyāvādī *sannyāsīs* and Vaiṣṇava *sannyāsīs* to be one and the same. In other words, Vaiṣṇava *sannyāsīs* do not at all like to associate with Māyāvādī *sannyāsīs,* to say nothing of eating together. This principle must be followed by the *san-*

nyāsīs of the Kṛṣṇa consciousness movement. That is the instruction of Śrī Caitanya Mahāprabhu given by His personal behavior.

TEXT 104

প্রকাশানন্দ শ্রীপাদ সভাতে বসিয়া ।
'বেদান্ত' পড়ান বহু শিষ্যগণ লঞা ॥ ১০৪ ॥

prakāśānanda śrīpāda sabhāte vasiyā
'vedānta' paḍāna bahu śiṣya-gaṇa lañā

SYNONYMS

prakāśānanda—Prakāśānanda; *śrīpāda*—a great *sannyāsī; sabhāte*—in the assembly; *vasiyā*—sitting down; *vedānta*—Vedānta philosophy; *paḍāna*—instructs; *bahu*—many; *śiṣya-gaṇa*—disciples; *lañā*—taking.

TRANSLATION

There was a great Māyāvādī sannyāsī named Prakāśānanda Sarasvatī who used to teach Vedānta philosophy to a great assembly of followers.

PURPORT

Śrīpāda Prakāśānanda Sarasvatī was a Māyāvādī *sannyāsī,* and his characteristics have been described in *Caitanya-bhāgavata* (*Madhya-khaṇḍa* Chapter Three):

'hasta', 'pada', 'mukha' mora nāhika 'locana'
veda more ei-mata kare viḍambana

kāśīte paḍāya veṭā 'prakāśa-ānanda'
sei veṭā kare mora aṅga khaṇḍa-khaṇḍa

vākhānaye veda, mora vigraha nā māne
sarvāṅge ha-ila kuṣṭha, tabu nāhi jāne

sarva-yajñamaya mora ye-aṅga——pavitra
'aja', 'bhava' ādi gāya yāṅhāra caritra

'puṇya' pavitratā pāya ye-aṅga-paraśe
tāhā 'mithyā' bale veṭā kemana sāhase

In the *Madhya-khaṇḍa,* Chapter Twenty, it is said:

sannyāsī 'prakāśānanda' vasaye kāśīte
more khaṇḍa-khaṇḍa veṭā kare bhāla-mate

paḍāya 'vedānta', mora 'vigraha' nā māne
kuṣṭha karāiluṅ aṅge, tabu nāhi jāne

'satya' mora 'līlā-karma', 'satya' mora 'sthāna'
ihā 'mithyā' bale, more kare khān-khān

Prakāśānanda Sarasvatī used to explain impersonalism, the Absolute Truth, as being without hands, legs, mouths or eyes. In this way he used to cheat the people by denying the personal form of the Lord. Such a foolish person was Prakāśānanda Sarasvatī, whose only business was to sever the limbs of the Lord by proving the Lord impersonal. Although the Lord has form, Prakāśānanda Sarasvatī was attempting to cut off the hands and legs of the Lord. This is the business of demons. The *Vedas* state that people who do not accept the Lord's form are rascals. The form of the Lord is factual, for Kṛṣṇa states in *Bhagavad-gītā* (15.15): *vedaiś ca sarvair aham eva vedyaḥ.* When Kṛṣṇa says *aham,* He says "I am," which means "I," the person. He adds the word *eva,* which is used for conclusive verification. It is by Vedānta philosophy that one has to know the Supreme Person. Whoever describes Vedic knowledge as impersonal is a demon. One becomes successful in life by worshiping the form of the Lord. The Māyāvādī *sannyāsīs* deny the form of the Lord, which delivers all fallen souls. Indeed, this form is cut to pieces by Māyāvādī demons.

The Personality of Godhead is worshiped by exalted demigods like Lord Brahmā and Lord Śiva. The original Māyāvādī *sannyāsī,* Śaṅkarācārya, also accepted the fact that the Lord's form is transcendental. *Nārāyaṇaḥ paro 'vyaktāt:* "Nārāyaṇa, the Supreme Personality of Godhead, is beyond the *avyakta,* the unmanifested material energy." *Avyaktād aṇḍa-sambhavaḥ:* "This material world is a creation of that unmanifested material energy." However, Nārāyaṇa has His own eternal form, which is not created by material energy. Simply by worshiping the form of the Lord, one is purified. However, Māyāvādī *sannyāsīs* are impersonalist philosophers, and they describe the form of the Lord as *māyā,* or false. How can one be purified by worshiping something false? Māyāvādī philosophers have no sufficient reason for being impersonalists. They blindly follow a principle that cannot be supported by reason or argument. This was the situation with Prakāśānanda Sarasvatī, the chief Māyāvādī *sannyāsī* of Benares. He was supposed to teach Vedānta philosophy, but he would not accept the form of the Lord; therefore he was attacked with leprosy. Nonetheless, he continued to commit sins by describing the Absolute Truth as impersonal. The Absolute Truth, the Supreme Personality of Godhead, always displays pastimes and activities, but Māyāvādī *sannyāsīs* claim that these activities are false.

Some people falsely claim that Prakāśānanda Sarasvatī later became known as Prabodhānanda Sarasvatī, but this is not a fact. Prabodhānanda Sarasvatī was the uncle and spiritual master of Gopāla Bhaṭṭa Gosvāmī. In his *gṛhastha* life, Prabodhānanda Sarasvatī was a resident of Śrī Raṅga-kṣetra, and he belonged to the Vaiṣṇava Rāmānuja-sampradāya. It is a mistake to consider Prakāśānanda Sarasvatī and Prabodhānanda Sarasvatī the same man.

TEXT 105

এক বিপ্র দেখি' আইলা প্রভুর ব্যবহার ।
প্রকাশানন্দ-আগে কহে চরিত্র তাঁহার ॥ ১০৫ ॥

eka vipra dekhi' āilā prabhura vyavahāra
prakāśānanda-āge kahe caritra tāṅhāra

SYNONYMS

eka vipra—one *brāhmaṇa; dekhi'*—seeing; *āilā*—came; *prabhura*—of Śrī Caitanya Mahāprabhu; *vyavahāra*—activities; *prakāśānanda-āge*—before the Māyāvādī *sannyāsī* Prakāśānanda; *kahe*—says; *caritra tāṅhāra*—His characteristics.

TRANSLATION

One brāhmaṇa who saw the wonderful behavior of Śrī Caitanya Mahāprabhu came to Prakāśānanda Sarasvatī and described the Lord's characteristics.

TEXT 106

"এক সন্ন্যাসী আইলা জগন্নাথ হৈতে ।
তাঁহার মহিমা-প্রতাপ না পারি বর্ণিতে ॥ ১০৬ ॥

"eka sannyāsī āilā jagannātha haite
tāṅhāra mahimā-pratāpa nā pāri varṇite

SYNONYMS

eka—one; *sannyāsī*—person in the renounced order of life; *āilā*—has come; *jagannātha haite*—from Jagannātha Purī; *tāṅhāra*—His; *mahimā*—glories; *pratāpa*—influence; *nā pāri varṇite*—I cannot describe.

TRANSLATION

The brāhmaṇa told Prakāśānanda Sarasvatī, "There is a sannyāsī who has come from Jagannātha Purī, and I cannot describe His wonderful influence and glories.

TEXT 107

সকল দেখিয়ে তাঁতে অদ্ভুত-কথন ।
প্রকাণ্ড-শরীর, শুদ্ধকাঞ্চন-বরণ ॥ ১০৭ ॥

sakala dekhiye tāṅte adbhuta-kathana
prakāṇḍa-śarīra, śuddha-kāñcana-varaṇa

SYNONYMS

sakala dekhiye—I see everything; *tāṅte*—in Him; *adbhuta-kathana*—wonderful description; *prakāṇḍa-śarīra*—very large body; *śuddha*—pure; *kāñcana*—gold; *varaṇa*—complexion.

TRANSLATION

"Everything is wonderful about that sannyāsī. He has a very well built and luxurious body, and His complexion is like purified gold.

TEXT 108

আজানুলম্বিত ভুজ, কমল-নয়ন ।
যত কিছু ঈশ্বরের সর্ব সল্লক্ষণ ॥ ১০৮ ॥

ājānu-lambita bhuja, kamala-nayana
yata kichu īśvarera sarva sal-lakṣaṇa

SYNONYMS

ājānu-lambita—reaching down to the knees; *bhuja*—arms; *kamala-nayana*—eyes like the petals of a lotus flower; *yata*—as many as; *kichu*—any; *īśvarera*—of the Supreme Personality of Godhead; *sarva*—all; *sat-lakṣaṇa*—transcendental symptoms.

TRANSLATION

"He has arms that extend to His knees, and His eyes are like the petals of a lotus. In His person are all the transcendental symptoms of the Supreme Personality of Godhead.

TEXT 109

তাহা দেখি' জ্ঞান হয়—'এই নারায়ণ'।
যেই তাঁরে দেখে, করে কৃষ্ণসংকীর্তন ॥ ১০৯ ॥

tāhā dekhi' jñāna haya——'ei nārāyaṇa
yei tāṅre dekhe, kare kṛṣṇa-saṅkīrtana

SYNONYMS

tāhā dekhi'—seeing that; *jñāna haya*—one comes to the conclusion; *ei nārāyaṇa*—He is the Supreme Personality of Godhead, Nārāyaṇa Himself; *yei*—anyone who; *tāṅre*—Him; *dekhe*—sees; *kare*—performs; *kṛṣṇa-saṅkīrtana*—chanting of the holy name of Kṛṣṇa.

TRANSLATION

"When one sees all these features, one takes Him to be Nārāyaṇa Himself. Whoever sees Him immediately begins to chant the holy name of Kṛṣṇa.

TEXT 110

'মহাভাগবত'-লক্ষণ শুনি ভাগবতে।
সে-সব লক্ষণ প্রকট দেখিয়ে তাঁহাতে ॥ ১১০ ॥

'mahā-bhāgavata'-lakṣaṇa śuni bhāgavate
se-saba lakṣaṇa prakaṭa dekhiye tāṅhāte

SYNONYMS

mahā-bhāgavata—of a first-class devotee; *lakṣaṇa*—symptoms; *śuni*—we hear; *bhāgavate*—in *Śrīmad-Bhāgavatam; se-saba lakṣaṇa*—all those symptoms; *prakaṭa*—manifest; *dekhiye*—I see; *tāṅhāte*—in Him.

TRANSLATION

"We have heard about the symptoms of a first-class devotee in Śrīmad-Bhāgavatam, and all those symptoms are manifest in the body of Śrī Caitanya Mahāprabhu.

TEXT 111

'নিরন্তর কৃষ্ণনাম' জিহ্বা তাঁর গায়।
দুই-নেত্রে অশ্রু বহে গঙ্গাধারা-প্রায় ॥ ১১১ ॥

'nirantara kṛṣṇa-nāma' jihvā tāṅra gāya
dui-netre aśru vahe gaṅgā-dhārā-prāya

SYNONYMS

nirantara—incessantly; *kṛṣṇa-nāma*—the holy name of the Lord; *jihvā*—tongue; *tāṅra*—His; *gāya*—chants; *dui-netre*—in the two eyes; *aśru*—tears; *vahe*—flow; *gaṅgā-dhārā-prāya*—like the flow of the Ganges.

TRANSLATION

"His tongue is always chanting the holy name of Kṛṣṇa, and from His eyes tears incessantly fall like the flowing Ganges.

TEXT 112

ক্ষণে নাচে, হাসে, গায়, করয়ে ক্রন্দন ।
ক্ষণে হুহুঙ্কার করে,—সিংহের গর্জ্জন ॥ ১১২ ॥

kṣaṇe nāce, hāse, gāya, karaye krandana
kṣaṇe huhuṅkāra kare,——siṁhera garjana

SYNONYMS

kṣaṇe—sometimes; *nāce*—dances; *hāse*—laughs; *gāya*—sings; *karaye krandana*—cries; *kṣaṇe*—sometimes; *huhuṅ-kāra*—loud vibrations; *kare*—makes; *siṁhera garjana*—the roaring of a lion.

TRANSLATION

"Sometimes He dances, laughs, sings and cries, and sometimes He roars like a lion.

TEXT 113

জগৎমঙ্গল তাঁর 'কৃষ্ণচৈতন্য'-নাম ।
নাম, রূপ, গুণ তাঁর, সব—অনুপম ॥ ১১৩ ॥

jagat-maṅgala tāṅra 'kṛṣṇa-caitanya'-nāma
nāma, rūpa, guṇa tāṅra, saba——anupama

SYNONYMS

jagat-maṅgala—all-auspicious to the whole world; *tāṅra*—His; *kṛṣṇa-caitanya*—Śrī Kṛṣṇa Caitanya; *nāma*—name; *nāma*—name; *rūpa*—form; *guṇa*—the quality; *tāṅra*—His; *saba*—all; *anupama*—unparalleled.

TRANSLATION

"His name, Kṛṣṇa Caitanya, is all-auspicious to the world. Everything about Him—His name, form, and qualities—is unparalleled.

TEXT 114

দেখিলে সে জানি তাঁর 'ঈশ্বরের রীতি'।
অলৌকিক কথা শুনি' কে করে প্রতীতি ?" ১১৪ ॥

dekhile se jāni tāṅra 'īśvarera rīti'
alaukika kathā śuni' ke kare pratīti?"

SYNONYMS

dekhile—simply by seeing; *se*—Him; *jāni*—I understand; *tāṅra*—His; *īśvarera rīti*—characteristics of the Supreme Personality of Godhead; *alaukika*—uncommon; *kathā*—story; *śuni'*—hearing; *ke*—who; *kare pratīti*—will believe.

TRANSLATION

"Simply by seeing Him, one understands that He possesses all the characteristics of the Supreme Personality of Godhead. Such characteristics are certainly uncommon. Who will believe it?"

TEXT 115

শুনিয়া প্রকাশানন্দ বহুত হাসিলা।
বিপ্রে উপহাস করি' কহিতে লাগিলা ॥ ১১৫ ॥

śuniyā prakāśānanda bahuta hāsilā
vipre upahāsa kari' kahite lāgilā

SYNONYMS

śuniyā—hearing; *prakāśānanda*—Prakāśānanda Sarasvatī; *bahuta hāsilā*—laughed very much; *vipre*—at the *brāhmaṇa; upahāsa kari'*—jokingly laughing; *kahite lāgilā*—began to speak.

TRANSLATION

Prakāśānanda Sarasvatī laughed very much to hear this description. Joking and laughing at the brāhmaṇa, he began to speak as follows.

TEXT 116

"শুনিয়াছি গৌড়দেশের সন্ন্যাসী—'ভাবুক'।
কেশব-ভারতী-শিষ্য, লোকপ্রতারক ॥ ১১৬ ॥

"śuniyāchi gauḍa-deśera sannyāsī——'bhāvuka'
keśava-bhāratī-śiṣya, loka-pratāraka

SYNONYMS

śuniyāchi—I have heard; *gauḍa-deśera sannyāsī*—the *sannyāsī* from Bengal; *bhāvuka*—sentimental; *keśava-bhāratī-śiṣya*—disciple of Keśava Bhāratī; *loka-pratāraka*—a first-class pretender.

TRANSLATION

Prakāśānanda Sarasvatī said, "Yes, I have heard about Him. He is a sannyāsī from Bengal, and He is very sentimental. I have also heard that He belongs to the Bhāratī-sampradāya, for He is a disciple of Keśava Bhāratī. However, He is only a pretender."

PURPORT

Śrī Caitanya Mahāprabhu was considered *bhāvuka* (sentimental) because He was always seen in the *bhāva* stage. That is, He always exhibited ecstatic love for Kṛṣṇa. However, foolish people considered Him sentimental. In the material world, so-called devotees sometimes exhibit emotional symptoms. Caitanya Mahāprabhu's ecstatic love cannot be compared to the imitative emotional exhibitions of pretenders. Such exhibitions do not continue for very long. They are temporary. We actually see that some emotional imitators exhibit certain symptoms, but immediately after their exhibition, they are attracted to smoking and other things. In the beginning, when Prakāśānanda Sarasvatī heard of Śrī Caitanya Mahāprabhu's activities, he considered them to be those of a pretender. Consequently he called Him a *loka-pratāraka,* a pretender. Māyāvādīs cannot understand the transcendental symptoms exhibited by a devotee; therefore when such symptoms are manifest, the Māyāvādīs equate them with temporary emotional feelings. However, Prakāśānanda Sarasvatī's statement is offensive, and consequently he should be considered an atheist (*pāṣaṇḍī*). According to Śrīla Rūpa Gosvāmī, since Prakāśānanda Sarasvatī was not engaged in the Lord's devotional service, his *sannyāsa* is to be considered *phalgu-vairāgya.* This means that since he did not know how to use things for the Lord's service, his renunciation of the world was artificial.

TEXT 117

'চৈতন্য'-নাম তাঁর, ভাবুকগণ লঞা।
দেশে দেশে গ্রামে গ্রামে বুলে নাচাঞা॥ ১১৭॥

'caitanya'-nāma tāṅra, bhāvuka-gaṇa lañā
deśe deśe grāme grāme bule nācāñā

SYNONYMS

caitanya—Caitanya; *nāma tāṅra*—His name; *bhāvuka-gaṇa lañā*—accompanied by some sentimentalists; *deśe deśe*—from country to country; *grāme grāme*—from village to village; *bule*—travels; *nācāñā*—causing to dance.

TRANSLATION

Prakāśānanda Sarasvatī continued, "I know that His name is Śrī Kṛṣṇa Caitanya and that He is accompanied by many sentimentalists. His followers dance with Him, and He tours from country to country and village to village.

TEXT 118

যেই তাঁরে দেখে, সেই ঈশ্বর করি' কহে।
ঐছে মোহন-বিদ্যা—যে দেখে সে মোহে॥ ১১৮॥

yei tāṅre dekhe, sei īśvara kari' kahe
aiche mohana-vidyā——ye dekhe se mohe

SYNONYMS

yei—anyone who; *tāṅre*—Him; *dekhe*—sees; *sei*—that person; *īśvara kari'*—as the Supreme Personality of Godhead; *kahe*—says; *aiche*—such; *mohana-vidyā*—hypnotism; *ye dekhe*—anyone who sees; *se mohe*—he becomes illusioned.

TRANSLATION

"Whoever sees Him accepts Him as the Supreme Personality of Godhead. Since He has some mystic power by which He hypnotizes people, everyone who sees Him is illusioned.

TEXT 119

সার্বভৌম ভট্টাচার্য—পণ্ডিত প্রবল।
শুনি' চৈতন্যের সঙ্গে হইল পাগল॥ ১১৯॥

sārvabhauma bhaṭṭācārya——paṇḍita prabala
śuni' caitanyera saṅge ha-ila pāgala

SYNONYMS

sārvabhauma bhaṭṭācārya—Sārvabhauma Bhaṭṭācārya; *paṇḍita prabala*—a learned scholar; *śuni'*—I have heard; *caitanyera saṅge*—in the association of Caitanya; *ha-ila pāgala*—has become a madman.

TRANSLATION

"Sārvabhauma Bhaṭṭācārya was a very learned scholar, but I have heard that he also has become a madman due to his association with this Caitanya.

TEXT 120

'সন্ন্যাসী'—নাম-মাত্র, মহা-ইন্দ্রজালী !
'কাশীপুরে' না বিকাবে তাঁর ভাবকালি ॥ ১২০ ॥

'sannyāsī'——nāma-mātra, mahā-indrajālī!
'kāśīpure' nā vikābe tāṅra bhāvakāli

SYNONYMS

sannyāsī—in the renounced order of life; *nāma-mātra*—in name only; *mahā-indrajālī*—first-class magician; *kāśīpure*—in Kāśī; *nā vikābe*—will not sell; *tāṅra*—His; *bhāvakāli*—sentimental activities.

TRANSLATION

"This Caitanya is a sannyāsī in name only. Actually He is a first-class magician. In any case, His sentimentalism cannot be very much in demand here in Kāśī.

TEXT 121

'বেদান্ত' শ্রবণ কর, না যাইহ তাঁর পাশ ।
উচ্ছৃঙ্খল-লোক-সঙ্গে দুইলোক-নাশ ॥" ১২১ ॥

'vedānta' śravaṇa kara, nā yāiha tāṅra pāśa
ucchṛṅkhala-loka-saṅge dui-loka-nāśa"

SYNONYMS

vedānta—the philosophy of Vedānta; *śravaṇa kara*—go on hearing; *nā*—do not; *yāiha*—go; *tāṅra pāśa*—near Him; *ucchṛṅkhala*—upstart; *loka*—people;

saṅge—in the association of; *dui-loka-nāśa*—destruction in this world and the next.

TRANSLATION

"Do not go to see Śrī Caitanya Mahāprabhu. Just continue hearing Vedānta. If you associate with upstarts, you will be lost in this world and in the next."

PURPORT

The word *ucchṛṅkhala,* meaning "whimsical," is significant in this verse. In *Bhagavad-gītā* (16.23), Lord Kṛṣṇa Himself says:

yaḥ śāstra-vidhim utsṛjya
vartate kāma-kārataḥ
na sa siddhim avāpnoti
na sukhaṁ na parāṁ gatim

If one acts whimsically and does not follow the śāstric principles, he will never attain perfection, happiness or the spiritual world.

TEXT 122

এত শুনি' সেই বিপ্র মহাদুঃখ পাইলা ।
'কৃষ্ণ' 'কৃষ্ণ' কহি' তথা হৈতে উঠি' গেলা ॥ ১২২ ॥

eta śuni' sei vipra mahā-duḥkha pāilā
'kṛṣṇa' 'kṛṣṇa' kahi' tathā haite uṭhi' gelā

SYNONYMS

eta śuni'—hearing this; *sei vipra*—that *brāhmaṇa; mahā-duḥkha pāilā*—became very much aggrieved; *kṛṣṇa kṛṣṇa kahi'*—uttering the holy name of Lord Kṛṣṇa; *tathā haite*—from there; *uṭhi' gelā*—got up and went away.

TRANSLATION

When the brāhmaṇa heard Prakāśānanda Sarasvatī speak like this about Śrī Caitanya Mahāprabhu, he became very grief-stricken. Chanting the holy name of Kṛṣṇa, he immediately left.

TEXT 123

প্রভুর দরশনে শুদ্ধ হঞাছে তাঁর মন ।
প্রভু-আগে দুঃখী হঞা কহে বিবরণ ॥ ১২৩ ॥

prabhura daraśane śuddha hañāche tāṅra mana
prabhu-āge duḥkhī hañā kahe vivaraṇa

SYNONYMS

prabhura daraśane—by seeing personally the Supreme Personality of Godhead; *śuddha*—purified; *hañāche*—was; *tāṅra mana*—his mind; *prabhu-āge*—before the Lord; *duḥkhī hañā*—being very much unhappy; *kahe vivaraṇa*—described the incidents.

TRANSLATION

The brāhmaṇa's mind was already purified by seeing the Supreme Personality of Godhead, Śrī Caitanya Mahāprabhu. He therefore went to Śrī Caitanya Mahāprabhu and described what took place before the Māyāvādī sannyāsī Prakāśānanda.

TEXT 124

শুনি' মহাপ্রভু তবে ঈষৎ হাসিলা ।
পুনরপি সেই বিপ্র প্রভুরে পুছিলা ॥ ১২৪ ॥

śuni' mahāprabhu tabe īṣat hāsilā
punarapi sei vipra prabhure puchilā

SYNONYMS

śuni'—hearing; *mahāprabhu*—Śrī Caitanya Mahāprabhu; *tabe*—then; *īṣat*—mildly; *hāsilā*—smiled; *punarapi*—again indeed; *sei*—that; *vipra*—*brāhmaṇa;* *prabhure puchilā*—inquired from Śrī Caitanya Mahāprabhu.

TRANSLATION

Hearing this, Śrī Caitanya Mahāprabhu mildly smiled. The brāhmaṇa then spoke again to the Lord.

TEXT 125

"তার আগে যবে আমি তোমার নাম লইল ।
সেহ তোমার নাম জানে,—আপনে কহিল ॥ ১২৫ ॥

"tāra āge yabe āmi tomāra nāma la-ila
seha tomāra nāma jāne,——āpane kahila

SYNONYMS

tāra āge—before him; *yabe*—when; *āmi*—I; *tomāra*—Your; *nāma*—name; *la-ila*—uttered; *seha*—he; *tomāra*—Your; *nāma*—name; *jāne*—knows; *āpane kahila*—he said himself.

TRANSLATION

The brāhmaṇa said, "As soon as I uttered Your name before him, he immediately confirmed the fact that he knew Your name.

TEXT 126

তোমার 'দোষ' কহিতে করে নামের উচ্চার ।
'চৈতন্য' 'চৈতন্য' করি' কহে তিনবার ॥ ১২৬ ॥

tomāra 'doṣa' kahite kare nāmera uccāra
'caitanya' 'caitanya' kari' kahe tina-bāra

SYNONYMS

tomāra doṣa—Your fault; *kahite*—describing; *kare*—does; *nāmera*—of the name; *uccāra*—utterances; *caitanya caitanya*—Caitanya, Caitanya; *kari'*—in that way; *kahe tina-bāra*—he uttered three times.

TRANSLATION

"While finding fault with You, he uttered Your name three times, saying, 'Caitanya, Caitanya, Caitanya.'

TEXT 127

তিনবারে 'কৃষ্ণনাম' না আইল তার মুখে ।
'অবজ্ঞা'তে নাম লয়, শুনি' পাই দুঃখে ॥ ১২৭ ॥

tina-bāre 'kṛṣṇa-nāma' nā āila tāra mukhe
'avajñā'te nāma laya, śuni' pāi duḥkhe

SYNONYMS

tina-bāre—three times; *kṛṣṇa-nāma*—the holy name of Kṛṣṇa; *nā āila*—did not come; *tāra mukhe*—in his mouth; *avajñā'te*—in contempt; *nāma laya*—takes Your name; *śuni'*—hearing; *pāi duḥkhe*—I was very much aggrieved.

TRANSLATION

"Although he spoke Your name three times, he did not utter the name of Kṛṣṇa. Because he uttered Your name in contempt, I was very much aggrieved.

PURPORT

Prakāśānanda Sarasvatī vilified and blasphemed Śrī Caitanya Mahāprabhu. Words like *brahma, caitanya, ātmā, paramātmā, jagadīśa, īśvara, virāṭ, vibhu, bhūmā, viśvarūpa* and *vyāpaka* all indirectly indicate Kṛṣṇa. However, the chanter of these names is not actually attracted to the Supreme Personality of Godhead Kṛṣṇa and His transcendental pastimes. One may get a little light from these names, but one cannot understand that the holy name of the Lord is identical with the Lord. One considers the Lord's names material due to a poor fund of knowledge. Māyāvādī philosophers and the *pañcopāsakas* cannot in the least understand the existence of the spiritual world and the blissful variegatedness there. They cannot understand the Absolute Truth and its spiritual varieties—name, form, qualities and pastimes. Consequently they conclude that Kṛṣṇa's transcendental activities are *māyā*. Due to this, one has to directly cultivate knowledge about the holy name of the Lord. Māyāvādī philosophers do not know this fact, and therefore they commit great offenses. One should not hear anything about Kṛṣṇa or devotional service from the mouths of Māyāvādī impersonalists.

TEXT 128

ইহার কারণ মোরে কহ কৃপা করি'।
তোমা দেখি' মুখ মোর বলে 'কৃষ্ণ' 'হরি"॥ ১২৮ ॥

ihāra kāraṇa more kaha kṛpā kari'
tomā dekhi' mukha mora bale 'kṛṣṇa' 'hari"

SYNONYMS

ihāra—of this; *kāraṇa*—cause; *more*—unto me; *kaha*—please speak; *kṛpā kari'*—by Your causeless mercy; *tomā dekhi'*—seeing You; *mukha*—mouth; *mora*—my; *bale*—says; *kṛṣṇa hari*—the holy names of Kṛṣṇa and Hari.

TRANSLATION

"Why could Prakāśānanda not utter the names of Kṛṣṇa and Hari? He chanted the name Caitanya thrice. As far as I am concerned, simply by seeing You I am moved to chant the holy names of Kṛṣṇa and Hari."

TEXT 129

প্রভু কহে,—"মায়াবাদী কৃষ্ণে অপরাধী ।
'ব্রহ্ম', 'আত্মা' 'চৈতন্য' কহে নিরবধি ॥ ১২৯ ॥

prabhu kahe,——"māyāvādī kṛṣṇe aparādhī
'brahma', 'ātmā' 'caitanya' kahe niravadhi

SYNONYMS

prabhu kahe—Śrī Caitanya Mahāprabhu said; *māyāvādī*—the impersonalists; *kṛṣṇe*—unto Kṛṣṇa; *aparādhī*—great offenders; *brahma—brahma; ātmā—ātmā; caitanya—caitanya; kahe*—say; *niravadhi*—without stopping.

TRANSLATION

Śrī Caitanya Mahāprabhu replied, "Māyāvādī impersonalists are great offenders unto Lord Kṛṣṇa; therefore they simply utter the words Brahman, ātmā and caitanya.

TEXT 130

অতএব তার মুখে না আইসে কৃষ্ণনাম ।
'কৃষ্ণনাম', 'কৃষ্ণস্বরূপ'—দুইত 'সমান' ॥ ১৩০ ॥

ataeva tāra mukhe nā āise kṛṣṇa-nāma
'kṛṣṇa-nāma', 'kṛṣṇa-svarūpa'——duita 'samāna'

SYNONYMS

ataeva—therefore; *tāra mukhe*—in their mouths; *nā*—not; *āise*—manifests; *kṛṣṇa-nāma*—the holy name of Kṛṣṇa; *kṛṣṇa-nāma*—the holy name of Kṛṣṇa; *kṛṣṇa-svarūpa*—the personality of the Lord; *duita samāna*—both identical.

TRANSLATION

"The holy name of Kṛṣṇa is not manifest in their mouths because they are offenders unto Kṛṣṇa, the Supreme Personality of Godhead, who is identical with His holy name.

TEXT 131

'নাম', 'বিগ্রহ', 'স্বরূপ' —তিন একরূপ ।
তিনে 'ভেদ' নাহি,—তিন 'চিদানন্দ-রূপ' ॥ ১৩১ ॥

'nāma', 'vigraha', 'svarūpa'——tina eka-rūpa
tine 'bheda' nāhi,——tina 'cid-ānanda-rūpa'

SYNONYMS

nāma—the name; *vigraha*—form; *sva-rūpa*—personality; *tina*—all three; *eka-rūpa*—one and the same; *tine*—between the three; *bheda nāhi*—there is no difference; *tina*—all three; *cit-ānanda-rūpa*—transcendentally blissful.

TRANSLATION

"The Lord's holy name, His form and His personality are all one and the same. There is no difference between them. Since all of them are absolute, they are transcendentally blissful.

TEXT 132

দেহ-দেহীর, নাম-নামীর কৃষ্ণে নাহি 'ভেদ'।
জীবের ধর্ম – নাম-দেহ-স্বরূপে 'বিভেদ' ॥ ১৩২ ॥

deha-dehīra, nāma-nāmīra kṛṣṇe nāhi 'bheda'
jīvera dharma——nāma-deha-svarūpe 'vibheda'

SYNONYMS

deha-dehīra—of the body and the owner of the body; *nāma-nāmīra*—of the name and the owner of the name; *kṛṣṇe*—in Kṛṣṇa; *nāhi bheda*—there is no difference; *jīvera dharma*—the situation of the conditioned soul; *nāma*—name; *deha*—body; *sva-rūpe*—original form; *vibheda*—different.

TRANSLATION

"There is no difference between Kṛṣṇa's body and Himself or between His name and Himself. As far as the conditioned soul is concerned, everything is different. One's name is different from the body, from one's original form and so on.

PURPORT

Śrī Caitanya Mahāprabhu is herein pointing out to the *brāhmaṇa* that Māyāvādī philosophers cannot understand that the living entity is equal in quality with the Supreme Personality of Godhead. Because they do not accept this, they think that the living entity has been falsely divided from the original Brahman due to being conditioned by *māyā*. Māyāvādīs believe that the Absolute Truth is ultimately impersonal. When an incarnation of God or God Himself comes, they think He is covered by *māyā.* In other words, Māyāvādī impersonalists think that the Lord's form is also a product of this material world. Due to a poor fund of knowledge, they cannot understand that Kṛṣṇa has no body separate from Himself. His body and Himself are both the same Absolute Truth. Not having perfect knowledge of Kṛṣṇa, such impersonalists certainly commit offenses at His lotus feet. Therefore they do not utter the original name of the Absolute Truth, Kṛṣṇa. In their impersonal way, they utter the name of impersonal Brahman, spirit soul. In other words, they indulge in indirect indications of the Absolute Truth. Even if they happen to utter the name of Govinda, Kṛṣṇa or Mādhava, they still cannot understand that these names are as good as Govinda, Kṛṣṇa or Mādhava the person. Because they are ultimately impersonalists, their uttering of the personal name has no potency. Actually they do not believe in Kṛṣṇa but consider all these names to be material vibrations. Not being able to appreciate the holy name of the Lord, they simply utter indirect names like Brahman, *ātmā* and *caitanya.*

It is a fact, however, that the name of Kṛṣṇa and Kṛṣṇa the person are both spiritual. Everything about Kṛṣṇa is transcendental, blissful and objective. For a conditioned soul, the body is different from the soul, and the name given by the father is also different from the soul. The conditioned living entity's identification with material objects keeps him from attaining his actual position. Although he is an eternal servant of Kṛṣṇa, he acts differently. The *svarūpa,* or actual identification of the living entity, is described by Śrī Caitanya Mahāprabhu as *jīvera 'svarūpa' haya——kṛṣṇera 'nitya-dāsa'.* The conditioned soul has forgotten the real activities of his original position. However, this is not the case with Kṛṣṇa. Kṛṣṇa's name and His person are identical. There is no such thing as *māyā* Kṛṣṇa because Kṛṣṇa is not a product of the material creation. There is no difference between Kṛṣṇa's body and His soul. Kṛṣṇa is simultaneously both soul and body. The distinction between body and soul applies to conditioned souls. The body of the conditioned soul is different from the soul, and the conditioned soul's name is different from his body. One may be named Mr. John, but if we call for Mr. John, Mr. John may never actually appear. However, if we utter the holy name of Kṛṣṇa, Kṛṣṇa is immediately present on our tongue. In the *Padma Purāṇa,* Kṛṣṇa says, *mad-bhaktā yatra gāyanti tatra tiṣṭhāmi nārada:* "O Nārada, I am present wherever My devotees are chanting." When the devotees chant the holy name of Kṛṣṇa—Hare Kṛṣṇa, Hare Kṛṣṇa, Kṛṣṇa Kṛṣṇa, Hare Hare/ Hare Rāma, Hare Rāma, Rāma Rāma, Hare Hare—Lord Kṛṣṇa is immediately present.

TEXT 133

নাম চিন্তামণিঃ কৃষ্ণশ্চৈতন্যরসবিগ্রহঃ ।
পূর্ণঃ শুদ্ধো নিত্যমুক্তোঽভিন্নত্বান্নামনামিনোঃ ॥ ১৩৩ ॥

nāma cintāmaṇiḥ kṛṣṇaś
caitanya-rasa-vigrahaḥ
pūrṇaḥ śuddho nitya-mukto
'bhinnatvān nāma-nāminoḥ

SYNONYMS

nāmaḥ—the holy name; *cintāmaṇiḥ*—transcendentally blissful giver of all spiritual benedictions; *kṛṣṇaḥ*—not different from Kṛṣṇa; *caitanya-rasa-vigrahaḥ*—the form of all transcendental mellows; *pūrṇaḥ*—complete; *śuddhaḥ*—pure, without material contamination; *nitya*—eternal; *muktaḥ*—liberated; *abhinna-tvāt*—due to not being different; *nāma*—of the holy name; *nāminoḥ*—and of the person who has the name.

TRANSLATION

"'The holy name of Kṛṣṇa is transcendentally blissful. It bestows all spiritual benedictions, for it is Kṛṣṇa Himself, the reservoir of all pleasure. Kṛṣṇa's name is complete, and it is the form of all transcendental mellows. It is not a material name under any condition, and it is no less powerful than Kṛṣṇa Himself. Since Kṛṣṇa's name is not contaminated by the material qualities, there is no question of its being involved with māyā. Kṛṣṇa's name is always liberated and spiritual; it is never conditioned by the laws of material nature. This is because the name of Kṛṣṇa and Kṛṣṇa Himself are identical.'

PURPORT

This is a quotation from *Padma Purāṇa.*

TEXT 134

অতএব কৃষ্ণের 'নাম', 'দেহ', 'বিলাস'।
প্রাকৃতেন্দ্রিয়-গ্রাহ্য নহে, হয় স্বপ্রকাশ ॥ ১৩৪ ॥

ataeva kṛṣṇera 'nāma', 'deha', 'vilāsa'
prākṛtendriya-grāhya nahe, haya sva-prakāśa

SYNONYMS

ataeva—therefore; *kṛṣṇera*—of Lord Kṛṣṇa; *nāma*—the holy name; *deha*—the spiritual body; *vilāsa*—the pastimes; *prākṛta-indriya*—by the dull senses made of matter; *grāhya*—perceptible; *nahe*—not; *haya*—are; *sva-prakāśa*—self-manifested.

TRANSLATION

"The holy name of Kṛṣṇa, His body and His pastimes cannot be understood by blunt material senses. They are manifest independently.

PURPORT

The transcendental body of Kṛṣṇa, His name, form, qualities, pastimes and entourage all constitute the Absolute Truth and are as good as Kṛṣṇa (*sac-cid-ānanda-vigraha*). As long as the living entity is conditioned by the three modes of material nature—(goodness, passion and ignorance)—the objects of his material senses—material form, taste, smell, sound and touch—will not help him understand spiritual knowledge and bliss. Rather, these are revealed to the pure devotee. One's material name, form and qualities are certainly different from one another. In the material world, there is no conception of absolute; however, when we come to Kṛṣṇa consciousness we find that there is no material difference between Kṛṣṇa's body and His names, activities and entourage.

TEXT 135

কৃষ্ণনাম, কৃষ্ণগুণ, কৃষ্ণলীলাবৃন্দ ।
কৃষ্ণের স্বরূপ-সম—সব চিদানন্দ ॥ ১৩৫ ॥

kṛṣṇa-nāma, kṛṣṇa-guṇa, kṛṣṇa-līlā-vṛnda
kṛṣṇera svarūpa-sama——saba cid-ānanda

SYNONYMS

kṛṣṇa-nāma—the holy name of Kṛṣṇa; *kṛṣṇa-guṇa*—the transcendental qualities of Kṛṣṇa; *kṛṣṇa-līlā-vṛnda*—the transcendental pastimes of Lord Kṛṣṇa; *kṛṣṇera sva-rūpa*—Kṛṣṇa's personality; *sama*—equal; *saba*—all; *cit-ānanda*—spiritual and full of bliss.

TRANSLATION

"The holy name of Kṛṣṇa, His transcendental qualities and pastimes as well as Lord Kṛṣṇa Himself are all equal. They are all spiritual and full of bliss.

TEXT 136

অতঃ শ্রীকৃষ্ণনামাদি ন ভবেদ্গ্রাহ্যমিন্দ্রিয়ৈঃ ।
সেবোন্মুখে হি জিহ্বাদৌ স্বয়মেব স্ফুরত্যদঃ ॥১৩৬॥

ataḥ śrī-kṛṣṇa-nāmādi
na bhaved grāhyam indriyaiḥ
sevonmukhe hi jihvādau
svayam eva sphuraty adaḥ

SYNONYMS

ataḥ—therefore (because Kṛṣṇa's name, form, quality are all on the absolute platform); *śrī-kṛṣṇa-nāma-ādi*—Lord Kṛṣṇa's name, form, quality, pastimes and so on; *na*—not; *bhavet*—can be; *grāhyam*—perceived; *indriyaiḥ*—by the blunt material senses; *sevā-unmukhe*—to one engaged in His service; *hi*—certainly; *jihvā-ādau*—beginning with the tongue; *svayam*—personally; *eva*—certainly; *sphurati*—become manifest; *adaḥ*—those (Kṛṣṇa's name, form, quality, and so on).

TRANSLATION

" 'Therefore material senses cannot appreciate Kṛṣṇa's holy name, form, qualities and pastimes. When a conditioned soul is awakened to Kṛṣṇa consciousness and renders service by using his tongue to chant the Lord's holy name and taste the remnants of the Lord's food, the tongue is purified, and one gradually comes to understand who Kṛṣṇa really is.'

PURPORT

This verse is recorded in *Bhakti-rasāmṛta-sindhu* (1.2.234).

TEXT 137

ব্রহ্মানন্দ হৈতে পূর্ণানন্দ লীলারস ।
ব্রহ্মজ্ঞানী আকর্ষিয়া করে আত্মবশ ॥ ১৩৭ ॥

brahmānanda haite pūrṇānanda līlā-rasa
brahma-jñānī ākarṣiyā kare ātma-vaśa

SYNONYMS

brahma-ānanda—the pleasure of self-realization; *haite*—from; *pūrṇa-ānanda*—complete pleasure; *līlā-rasa*—the mellows of the pastimes of the Lord; *brahma-jñānī*—those who are on the platform of Brahman understanding; *ākarṣiyā*—attracting; *kare*—make; *ātma-vaśa*—subordinate to Kṛṣṇa.

TRANSLATION

"The mellows of Lord Kṛṣṇa's pastimes, which are full of bliss, attract the jñānī from the pleasure of Brahman realization and conquer him.

PURPORT

When one understands that he belongs not to the material world but to the spiritual world, one is called liberated. Being situated in the spiritual world is certainly pleasurable, but those who realize the transcendental name, form, qualities and pastimes of Lord Kṛṣṇa enjoy transcendental bliss many times more than one who has simply realized the self. When one is situated on the platform of self-realization, he can certainly be easily attracted by Kṛṣṇa and become a servant of the Lord. This is explained in *Bhagavad-gītā:*

brahma-bhūtaḥ prasannātmā
na śocati na kāṅkṣati
samaḥ sarveṣu bhūteṣu
mad-bhaktiṁ labhate parām

"One who is thus transcendentally situated at once realizes the Supreme Brahman and becomes joyful. He never laments or desires to have anything; he is equally disposed to every living entity. In that state he attains pure devotional service unto Me." (Bg. 18.54)

When one becomes spiritually realized (*brahma-bhūta*), he becomes happy (*prasannātmā*), for he is relieved from material conceptions. One who has attained this platform is not agitated by material action and reaction. He sees everyone on the platform of spirit soul (*paṇḍitāḥ sama-darśinaḥ*). When one is completely realized, he can rise to the platform of pure devotional service (*mad-bhaktiṁ labhate parām*). When one comes to the platform of *bhakti,* devotional service, he automatically realizes who Kṛṣṇa is.

bhaktyā mām abhijānāti
yāvān yaś cāsmi tattvataḥ
tato māṁ tattvato jñātvā
viśate tad-anantaram

"One can understand the Supreme Personality as He is only by devotional service. And when one is in full consciousness of the Supreme Lord by such devotion, he can enter into the kingdom of God." (Bg. 18.55)

It is only on the *bhakti* platform that one can understand the Supreme Personality of Godhead Kṛṣṇa and His transcendental name, form, qualities, pastimes and entourage. Being thus qualified spiritually (*viśate tad-anantaram*), one is allowed to enter the spiritual kingdom of God and return home, back to Godhead.

TEXT 138

স্বসুখনিভৃতচেতাস্তদ্ব্যুদস্তান্যভাবো-
ঽপ্যজিতরুচিরলীলাকৃষ্টসারস্তদীয়ম্ ।

ব্যতনুত কৃপয়া যস্তত্ত্বদীপং পুরাণং
তমখিলবৃজিনঘ্নং ব্যাসসূনুং নতোঽস্মি ॥ ১৩৮ ॥

svasukha-nibhṛta-cetās tad vyudastānya-bhāvo
'py ajita-rucira-līlākṛṣṭa-sāras tadīyam
vyatanuta kṛpayā yas tattva-dīpaṁ purāṇaṁ
tam akhila-vṛjina-ghnaṁ vyāsa-sūnuṁ nato 'smi

SYNONYMS

sva-sukha—in happiness of the self; *nibhṛta*—solitary; *cetāḥ*—whose consciousness; *tat*—because of that; *vyudasta*—given up; *anya-bhāvaḥ*—any other type of consciousness; *api*—although; *ajita*—of Śrī Kṛṣṇa; *rucira*—pleasing; *līlā*—by the pastimes; *ākṛṣṭa*—attracted; *sāraḥ*—whose heart; *tadīyam*—consisting of the activities of the Lord; *vyatanuta*—spread, manifested; *kṛpayā*—mercifully; *yaḥ*—who; *tattva-dīpam*—the bright light of the Absolute Truth; *purāṇam*—the *Purāṇa* (*Śrīmad-Bhāgavatam*); *tam*—unto him; *akhila-vṛjina-ghnam*—defeating everything inauspicious; *vyāsa-sūnum*—the son of Vyāsadeva; *nataḥ asmi*—I offer my obeisances.

TRANSLATION

" 'Let me offer my respectful obeisances unto my spiritual master, the son of Vyāsadeva, Śukadeva Gosvāmī. It is he who defeats all inauspicious things within this universe. Although in the beginning he was absorbed in the happiness of Brahman realization and was living in a secluded place, giving up all other types of consciousness, he became attracted by the most melodious pastimes of Lord Śrī Kṛṣṇa. He therefore mercifully spoke the supreme Purāṇa, known as Śrīmad-Bhāgavatam, which is the bright light of the Absolute Truth and which describes the activities of Lord Kṛṣṇa.'

PURPORT

This verse was spoken by Sūta Gosvāmī in *Śrīmad-Bhāgavatam* (12.12.68).

TEXT 139

ব্রহ্মানন্দ হৈতে পূর্ণানন্দ কৃষ্ণগুণ ।
অতএব আকর্ষয়ে আত্মারামের মন ॥ ১৩৯ ॥

brahmānanda haite pūrṇānanda kṛṣṇa-guṇa
ataeva ākarṣaye ātmā-rāmera mana

SYNONYMS

brahma-ānanda—the pleasure of Brahman realization; *haite*—from; *pūrṇa-ānanda*—complete bliss; *kṛṣṇa-guṇa*—the qualities of Lord Kṛṣṇa; *ataeva*—

therefore; *ākarṣaye*—attract; *ātmā-rāmera mana*—the minds of self-realized persons.

TRANSLATION

"The transcendental qualities of Śrī Kṛṣṇa are completely blissful and relishable. Consequently Lord Kṛṣṇa's qualities attract even the minds of self-realized persons from the bliss of self-realization.

TEXT 140

আত্মারামাশ্চ মুনয়ো নির্গ্রন্থা অপ্যুরুক্রমে ।
কুর্বন্ত্যহৈতুকীং ভক্তিমিত্থম্ভূতগুণো হরিঃ ॥ ১৪০ ॥

ātmārāmāś ca munayo
nirgranthā apy urukrame
kurvanty ahaitukīṁ bhaktim
ittham-bhūta-guṇo hariḥ

SYNONYMS

ātma-ārāmaḥ—persons who take pleasure in being transcendentally situated in the service of the Lord; *ca*—also; *munayaḥ*—great saintly persons who have completely rejected material aspirations, fruitive activities, and so forth; *nirgranthāḥ*—without interest in any material desire; *api*—certainly; *urukrame*—unto the Supreme Personality of Godhead, Kṛṣṇa, whose activities are wonderful; *kurvanti*—do; *ahaitukīm*—causeless, or without material desires; *bhaktim*—devotional service; *ittham-bhūta*—so wonderful as to attract the attention of the self-satisfied; *guṇaḥ*—who has transcendental qualities; *hariḥ*—the Supreme Personality of Godhead.

TRANSLATION

" 'Those who are self-satisfied and unattracted by external material desires are also attracted to the loving service of Śrī Kṛṣṇa, whose qualities are transcendental and whose activities are wonderful. Hari, the Personality of Godhead, is called Kṛṣṇa because He has such transcendentally attractive features.'

TEXT 141

এই সব রহু—কৃষ্ণচরণ-সম্বন্ধে ।
আত্মারামের মন হরে তুলসীর গন্ধে ॥ ১৪১ ॥

ei saba rahu——kṛṣṇa-caraṇa-sambandhe
ātmārāmera mana hare tulasīra gandhe

SYNONYMS

ei saba rahu—apart from the pastimes of Lord Kṛṣṇa; *kṛṣṇa-caraṇa-sambandhe*—in relation to the lotus feet of Kṛṣṇa; *ātma-ārāmera*—of self-realized persons; *mana*—the mind; *hare*—attracts; *tulasīra gandhe*—the aroma of *tulasī* leaves.

TRANSLATION

"Apart from the pastimes of Lord Kṛṣṇa, when tulasī leaves are offered at the lotus feet of Śrī Kṛṣṇa, even the aroma of the leaves attracts the minds of self-realized persons.

TEXT 142

তস্যারবিন্দনয়নস্য পদারবিন্দ-
কিঞ্জল্কমিশ্রতুলসীমকরন্দবায়ুঃ।
অন্তর্গতঃ স্ববিবরেণ চকার তেষাং
সংক্ষোভমক্ষরজুষামপি চিত্ততন্বোঃ ॥ ১৪২ ॥

tasyāravinda-nayanasya padāravinda-
kiñjalka-miśra-tulasī-makaranda-vāyuḥ
antargataḥ svavivareṇa cakāra teṣāṁ
saṅkṣobham akṣara-juṣām api citta-tanvoḥ

SYNONYMS

tasya—of Him; *aravinda-nayanasya*—of the Supreme Personality of Godhead, whose eyes are like the petals of a lotus; *pada-aravinda*—of the lotus feet; *kiñjalka*—with saffron; *miśra*—mixed; *tulasī*—of *tulasī* leaves; *makaranda*—with the aroma; *vāyuḥ*—the air; *antargataḥ*—entered; *sva-vivareṇa*—through the nostrils; *cakāra*—created; *teṣām*—of them; *saṅkṣobham*—strong agitation; *akṣara-juṣām*—of the impersonally self-realized (Kumāras); *api*—also; *citta-tanvoḥ*—of the mind and body.

TRANSLATION

" 'When the breeze carrying the aroma of tulasī leaves and saffron from the lotus feet of the lotus-eyed Personality of Godhead entered through the nostrils into the hearts of those sages [the Kumāras], they experienced a

change in both body and mind, even though they were attached to impersonal Brahman understanding.'

PURPORT

This is a verse from *Śrīmad-Bhāgavatam* (3.15.43). Vidura and Maitreya discussed the pregnancy of Diti. Diti's pregnancy caused the demigods to be very much afraid, and the demigods went to see Lord Brahmā. Lord Brahmā explained the original incident involving the cursing of Jaya and Vijaya by the Catuḥsana Kumāras. Sometimes the Catuḥsana Kumāras went to Vaikuṇṭha to visit Nārāyaṇa, the Supreme Personality of Godhead, and once they were stopped from entering the palace at the seventh gate by two doorkeepers named Jaya and Vijaya. Due to their jealousy, Jaya and Vijaya would not allow the Kumāras entry, and consequently the Kumāras became angry and cursed Jaya and Vijaya, condemning them to take birth in a family of *asuras* in the material world. The omniscient Personality of Godhead could immediately understand the incident,.and He came with His eternal consort the goddess of fortune. The Catuḥsana Kumāras immediately offered their obeisances unto the Lord. Simply by seeing the Lord and smelling the aroma of *tulasī* and saffron from His lotus feet, the Kumāras became devotees and abandoned their long-cherished impersonalism. Thus the four Kumāras were turned into Vaiṣṇavas simply by smelling the aromatic *tulasī* mixed with saffron. Those who are actually on the platform of Brahman realization and who have not offended the lotus feet of Kṛṣṇa can immediately become Vaiṣṇavas simply by smelling the aroma of the Lord's lotus feet. However, those who are offenders or demons are never attracted to the Lord's personal feature, even though they may visit the Lord's temple many times. In Vṛndāvana we have seen many Māyāvādī *sannyāsīs* who do not even come to the temple of Govindajī, Gopīnātha or Madana-mohana because they think that such temples are *māyā*. Therefore they are called Māyāvādīs. Śrī Kṛṣṇa Caitanya Mahāprabhu therefore said that the Māyāvādīs are the greatest offenders.

TEXT 143

অতএব 'কৃষ্ণনাম' না আইসে তার মুখে ।
মায়াবাদি-গণ যাতে মহা বহির্মুখে ॥ ১৪৩ ॥

ataeva 'kṛṣṇa-nāma' nā āise tāra mukhe
māyāvādi-gaṇa yāte mahā bahirmukhe

SYNONYMS

ataeva—therefore; *kṛṣṇa-nāma*—the holy name of Kṛṣṇa; *nā*—does not; *āise*—come; *tāra mukhe*—in their mouths; *māyāvādi-gaṇa*—all the Māyāvādīs; *yāte*—because; *mahā bahiḥ-mukhe*—great offenders by dint of strong atheism.

TRANSLATION

"Because the Māyāvādīs are great offenders and atheistic philosophers, the holy name of Kṛṣṇa does not come from their mouths.

PURPORT

Because they are constantly blaspheming the Supreme Personality of Godhead by saying that He has no head, hands or legs, Māyāvādī philosophers remain offenders for many, many births, even though they have partially realized Brahman. However, if such impersonalists are not offenders at the lotus feet of the Lord, they immediately become devotees in the association of a devotee. In other words, if an impersonalist is not an offender, he can become a devotee if he gets a chance to associate with other devotees. If he is an offender, he cannot be converted even by the association of the Supreme Personality of Godhead. Śrī Kṛṣṇa Caitanya Mahāprabhu was very much afraid of this Māyāvādī offender; therefore He spoke as follows.

TEXT 144

ভাবকালি বেচিতে আমি আইলাঙ কাশীপুরে ।
গ্রাহক নাহি, না বিকায়, লঞা যাব ঘরে ॥ ১৪৪ ॥

bhāvakāli vecite āmi āilāṅa kāśīpure
grāhaka nāhi, nā vikāya, lañā yāba ghare

SYNONYMS

bhāvakāli—devotional sentiments; *vecite*—to sell; *āmi*—I; *āilāṅa*—came; *kāśīpure*—to the city of Kāśī; *grāhaka nāhi*—there is no customer; *nā vikāya*—do not sell; *lañā yāba ghare*—then I must take my commodity back home.

TRANSLATION

"I have come here to sell My emotional ecstatic sentiments in this city of Kāśī, but I cannot find any customers. If they are not sold, I must take them back home.

TEXT 145

ভারী বোঝা লঞা আইলাঙ, কেমনে লঞা যাব ?
অল্প-স্বল্প-মূল্য পাইলে, এথাই বেচিব ॥ ১৪৫ ॥

bhārī bojhā lañā āilāṅa, kemane lañā yāba?
alpa-svalpa-mūlya pāile, ethāi veciba

SYNONYMS

bhārī bojhā—heavy load; *lañā*—bearing; *āilāṅa*—I came; *kemane*—how; *lañā yāba*—shall I take it back; *alpa-svalpa-mūlya*—a fraction of the real price; *pāile*—if I get; *ethāi*—here; *veciba*—I shall sell.

TRANSLATION

"I have brought a heavy load to sell in this city. To take it back again is a very difficult job; therefore if I get but a fraction of the price, I shall sell it here in this city of Kāśī."

PURPORT

Śrī Caitanya Mahāprabhu was selling the transcendental holy name of the Lord. However, Kāśī was a city of Māyāvādīs (impersonalists), and such people will never chant the holy names of the Hare Kṛṣṇa *mahā-mantra.* Consequently Śrī Caitanya Mahāprabhu was feeling disappointed. How could He teach the Māyāvādīs the importance of chanting the Hare Kṛṣṇa *mahā-mantra?* The attraction for chanting the holy name of the Lord belongs absolutely to pure devotees, and there was no possibility of finding pure devotees at Kāśī. Consequently Śrī Caitanya Mahāprabhu's commodity was certainly very heavy. The Lord therefore suggested that even though there were no pure devotees in Kāśī, if someone was a little inclined to chant the Hare Kṛṣṇa *mantra,* He would deliver this big load, although the proper price was not paid.

Actually we experienced this when we came to preach the Hare Kṛṣṇa movement in the West. When we came to New York in 1965, we never expected that the Hare Kṛṣṇa *mahā-mantra* would be accepted in this country. Nonetheless, we invited people to our storefront to join in chanting the Hare Kṛṣṇa *mantra,* and the Lord's holy name is so attractive that simply by coming to our storefront in New York, fortunate young people became Kṛṣṇa conscious. Although this mission was started with insignificant capital, it is now going nicely. The spreading of the Hare Kṛṣṇa *mahā-mantra* in the West has become successful because the young people were not offenders. The youths who joined this movement were not very advanced as far as purity was concerned, nor were they very well educated in Vedic knowledge, but because they were not offenders, they could accept the importance of the Hare Kṛṣṇa movement. We are now very happy to see that this movement is advancing more and more in the Western countries. We therefore conclude that the so-called *mlecchas* and *yavanas* of the Western countries are more purified than offensive Māyāvādīs or atheistic impersonalists.

TEXT 146

এত বলি' সেই বিপ্রে আত্মসাথ করি'।
প্রাতে উঠি' মথুরা চলিলা গৌরহরি ॥ ১৪৬ ॥

eta bali' sei vipre ātmasātha kari'
prāte uṭhi mathurā calilā gaurahari

SYNONYMS

eta bali'—saying this; *sei vipre*—that *brāhmaṇa; ātmasātha kari'*—accepting as His devotee; *prāte uṭhi*—rising early in the morning; *mathurā calilā*—started for Mathurā; *gaurahari*—Śrī Caitanya Mahāprabhu.

TRANSLATION

After saying this, Śrī Caitanya Mahāprabhu accepted that brāhmaṇa as His devotee. The next morning, rising very early, the Lord started for Mathurā.

TEXT 147

সেই তিন সঙ্গে চলে, প্রভু নিষেধিল ।
দূর হৈতে তিনজনে ঘরে পাঠাইল ॥ ১৪৭ ॥

sei tina saṅge cale, prabhu niṣedhila
dūra haite tina-jane ghare pāṭhāila

SYNONYMS

sei tina—those three; *saṅge*—with Śrī Caitanya Mahāprabhu; *cale*—go; *prabhu*—Śrī Caitanya Mahāprabhu; *niṣedhila*—forbade; *dūra haite*—from a distance; *tina-jane*—the three persons; *ghare*—home; *pāṭhāila*—sent back.

TRANSLATION

When Śrī Caitanya Mahāprabhu started for Mathurā, all three devotees started to go with Him. However, the Lord forbade them to accompany Him, and from a distance He asked them to return home.

TEXT 148

প্রভুর বিরহে তিনে একত্র মিলিয়া ।
প্রভুগুণ গান করে প্রেমে মত্ত হঞা ॥ ১৪৮ ॥

prabhura virahe tine ekatra miliyā
prabhu-guṇa gāna kare preme matta hañā

SYNONYMS

prabhura virahe—because of separation from the Lord; *tine*—all three; *ekatra*—together; *miliyā*—meeting; *prabhu-guṇa*—the transcendental qualities of the Lord; *gāna kare*—chant; *preme*—with love; *matta hañā*—being mad.

TRANSLATION

Feeling separation from the Lord, the three used to meet and glorify the holy qualities of the Lord. Thus they were absorbed in ecstatic love.

TEXT 149

‘প্রয়াগে’ আসিয়া প্রভু কৈল বেণী-স্নান ।
‘মাধব’ দেখিয়া প্রেমে কৈল নৃত্যগান ॥ ১৪৯ ॥

'prayāge' āsiyā prabhu kaila veṇī-snāna
'mādhava' dekhiyā preme kaila nṛtya-gāna

SYNONYMS

prayāge—to Prayāga; *āsiyā*—coming; *prabhu*—Śrī Caitanya Mahāprabhu; *kaila*—did; *veṇī-snāna*—bathing in the confluence of the Ganges and Yamunā; *mādhava*—the predominating Deity there, Veṇī Mādhava; *dekhiyā*—seeing; *preme*—in ecstatic love; *kaila*—performed; *nṛtya-gāna*—dancing and chanting.

TRANSLATION

Śrī Caitanya Mahāprabhu then went to Prayāga, where He bathed at the confluence of the Ganges and the Yamunā. He then visited the temple of Veṇī Mādhava and chanted and danced there in ecstatic love.

PURPORT

The city of Prayāga is situated a few miles from the city of Allahabad. The name Prayāga is given due to successful sacrifices performed there. It is said: *prakṛṣṭaḥ yāgaḥ yāga-phalaṁ yasmāt.* If one performs sacrifices at Prayāga, he certainly gets immediate results without difficulty. Prayāga is also called Tīrtharāja, the king of all places of pilgrimage. This holy place is situated on the confluence of the Rivers Ganges and Yamunā. Every year a fair takes place there known as Māgha-melā, and every twelve years a Kumbha-melā is also held. In any case, many people come to bathe there every year. During Māgha-melā, people from the local district generally come, and during Kumbha-melā people come from all over India to live there and bathe in the Ganges and Yamunā. Whoever goes there immediately feels the place's spiritual influence. A fort located there was constructed by the Emperor Akbar about five hundred years ago, and near the fort is a place called Triveṇī. On the other side of Prayāga is an old place known as Pratiṣṭhāna-pura. It is also well known as Jhuṅsi. Many saintly people live there, and consequently it is very attractive from the spiritual point of view.

TEXT 150

যমুনা দেখিয়া প্রেমে পড়ে ঝাঁপ দিয়া ।
আস্তে-ব্যস্তে ভট্টাচার্য উঠায় ধরিয়া ॥ ১৫০ ॥

yamunā dekhiyā preme paḍe jhāṅpa diyā
āste-vyaste bhaṭṭācārya uṭhāya dhariyā

SYNONYMS

yamunā—the River Yamunā; *dekhiyā*—seeing; *preme*—in ecstatic love; *paḍe*—falls down; *jhāṅpa diyā*—jumping; *āste-vyaste*—in great haste; *bhaṭ-ṭācārya*—Balabhadra Bhaṭṭācārya; *uṭhāya*—raises; *dhariyā*—catching.

TRANSLATION

As soon as Śrī Caitanya Mahāprabhu saw the River Yamunā, He threw Himself in it. Balabhadra Bhaṭṭācārya hastily caught the Lord and very carefully raised Him up again.

TEXT 151

এইমত তিনদিন প্রয়াগে রহিলা ।
কৃষ্ণ-নাম-প্রেম দিয়া লোক নিস্তারিলা ॥ ১৫১ ॥

ei-mata tina-dina prayāge rahilā
kṛṣṇa-nāma-prema diyā loka nistārilā

SYNONYMS

ei-mata—in this way; *tina-dina*—for three days; *prayāge*—at Prayāga; *rahilā*—remained; *kṛṣṇa-nāma*—the holy name of Lord Kṛṣṇa; *prema*—and ecstatic love; *diyā*—delivering; *loka nistārilā*—delivered the people.

TRANSLATION

The Lord stayed at Prayāga for three days. He delivered the holy name of Kṛṣṇa and ecstatic love. Thus He delivered many people.

TEXT 152

'মথুরা' চলিতে পথে যথা রহি' যায় ।
কৃষ্ণ-নাম-প্রেম দিয়া লোকেরে নাচায় ॥ ১৫২ ॥

'mathurā' calite pathe yathā rahi' yāya
kṛṣṇa-nāma-prema diyā lokere nācāya

SYNONYMS

mathurā—to Mathurā; *calite*—going; *pathe*—on the road; *yathā*—wherever; *rahi'*—staying; *yāya*—goes; *kṛṣṇa-nāma-prema*—the holy name of Kṛṣṇa and His ecstatic love; *diyā*—delivering; *lokere nācāya*—made the people dance.

TRANSLATION

Wherever the Lord stopped to rest on the way to Mathurā, He delivered the holy name of Kṛṣṇa and ecstatic love of Kṛṣṇa. Thus He made the people dance.

TEXT 153

পূর্বে যেন 'দক্ষিণ' যাইতে লোক নিস্তারিলা।
'পশ্চিম'-দেশে তৈছে সব 'বৈষ্ণব' করিলা ॥ ১৫৩ ॥

pūrve yena 'dakṣiṇa' yāite loka nistārilā
'paścima'-deśe taiche saba 'vaiṣṇava' karilā

SYNONYMS

pūrve—formerly; *yena*—as; *dakṣiṇa*—South India; *yāite*—going to; *loka*—the people; *nistārilā*—He delivered; *paścima-deśe*—in the western countries; *taiche*—similarly; *saba*—all; *vaiṣṇava*—devotees; *karilā*—made.

TRANSLATION

When the Lord toured South India, He delivered many people, and when He traveled in the western sector, He similarly converted many people to Vaiṣṇavism.

PURPORT

Formerly Śrī Caitanya Mahāprabhu converted people when He toured southern and western India. Similarly, this Hare Kṛṣṇa movement is now delivering the people of the Western world wherever devotees are chanting the holy names. This is all being done by the Lord's mercy. Śrī Caitanya Mahāprabhu predicted that He would deliver people in every city and village of the world by giving them a chance to chant the Hare Kṛṣṇa *mahā-mantra.*

TEXT 154

পথে যাহাঁ যাহাঁ হয় যমুনা-দর্শন।
তাহাঁ ঝাঁপ দিয়া পড়ে প্রেমে অচেতন ॥ ১৫৪ ॥

pathe yāhāṅ yāhāṅ haya yamunā-darśana
tāhāṅ jhāṅpa diyā paḍe preme acetana

SYNONYMS

pathe—on the road; *yāhāṅ yāhāṅ*—wherever; *haya*—there is; *yamunā-darśana*—meeting with the Yamunā River; *tāhāṅ*—there; *jhāṅpa diyā paḍe*—jumps over and falls down; *preme acetana*—unconscious in the ecstasy of love.

TRANSLATION

While the Lord was going to Mathurā, He came across the River Yamunā several times, and as soon as He saw the River Yamunā, He would immediately jump in, falling unconscious in the water in the ecstasy of love of Kṛṣṇa.

TEXT 155

মথুরা-নিকটে আইলা—মথুরা দেখিয়া।
দণ্ডবৎ হঞা পড়ে প্রেমাবিষ্ট হঞা ॥ ১৫৫ ॥

mathurā-nikaṭe āilā——mathurā dekhiyā
daṇḍavat hañā paḍe premāviṣṭa hañā

SYNONYMS

mathurā-nikaṭe—near Mathurā; *āilā*—came; *mathurā dekhiyā*—seeing the city of Mathurā; *daṇḍavat hañā*—offering obeisances; *paḍe*—falls down; *prema-āviṣṭa hañā*—in the great ecstasy of love.

TRANSLATION

When He approached Mathurā and saw the city, He immediately fell to the ground and offered obeisances with great ecstatic love.

TEXT 156

মথুরা আসিয়া কৈলা 'বিশ্রান্তি-তীর্থে' স্নান।
'জন্মস্থানে' 'কেশব' দেখি' করিলা প্রণাম ॥ ১৫৬ ॥

mathurā āsiyā kailā 'viśrānti-tīrthe' snāna
'janma-sthāne' 'keśava' dekhi' karilā praṇāma

SYNONYMS

mathurā āsiyā—coming in to Mathurā; *kailā*—performed; *viśrānti-tīrthe*—at the bathing place known as Viśrāma-ghāṭa; *snāna*—bathing; *janma-sthāne*—at the place of Lord Kṛṣṇa's birth; *keśava*—the Deity named Keśava; *dekhi'*—seeing; *karilā praṇāma*—offered His respectful obeisances.

TRANSLATION

When Śrī Caitanya Mahāprabhu entered the city of Mathurā, He took His bath at Viśrāma-ghāṭa. He then visited the birthplace of Kṛṣṇa and saw the Deity named Keśavajī. He offered His respectful obeisances to this Deity.

PURPORT

At the present moment, the temple of Keśavajī is very much improved. At one time, Keśavajī-mandira was attacked by the emperor Aurangzeb, who constructed such a big mosque there that the temple of Keśavajī was insignificant in comparison. However, with the help of many rich Maḍwaris, the temple has improved, and a very large temple is now being constructed so that the mosque is now appearing diminished in comparison. Many archeological discoveries have been made there, and many people from foreign countries are beginning to appreciate Kṛṣṇa's birthplace. This Kṛṣṇa consciousness movement is attracting many foreigners to the Keśavajī temple, and now they will also be attracted by the Kṛṣṇa-Balarāma temple in Vṛndāvana.

TEXT 157

প্রেমানন্দে নাচে, গায়, সঘন হুঙ্কার ।
প্রভুর প্রেমাবেশ দেখি' লোকে চমৎকার ॥ ১৫৭ ॥

premānande nāce, gāya, saghana huṅkāra
prabhura premāveśa dekhi' loke camatkāra

SYNONYMS

prema-ānande—in ecstatic love; *nāce*—dances; *gāya*—chants; *saghana*—repeatedly; *huṅkāra*—tumultuous sound vibrations; *prabhura*—of Lord Śrī Caitanya Mahāprabhu; *prema-āveśa*—ecstatic love; *dekhi'*—seeing; *loke*—all people; *camatkāra*—astonished.

TRANSLATION

When Śrī Caitanya Mahāprabhu chanted, danced and made loud vibrations, all the people were astonished to see His ecstatic love.

TEXT 158

একবিপ্র পড়ে প্রভুর চরণ ধরিয়া ।
প্রভু-সঙ্গে নৃত্য করে প্রেমাবিষ্ট হঞা ॥ ১৫৮ ॥

eka-vipra paḍe prabhura caraṇa dhariyā
prabhu-saṅge nṛtya kare premāviṣṭa hañā

SYNONYMS

eka-vipra—one *brāhmaṇa; paḍe*—falls down; *prabhura*—of Śrī Caitanya Mahāprabhu; *caraṇa dhariyā*—catching the lotus feet; *prabhu-saṅge*—with Śrī Caitanya Mahāprabhu; *nṛtya kare*—he dances; *prema-āviṣṭa hañā*—being absorbed in ecstatic love.

TRANSLATION

One brāhmaṇa fell at the lotus feet of Śrī Caitanya Mahāprabhu and then began to dance with Him in ecstatic love.

TEXT 159

দুঁহে প্রেমে নৃত্য করি' করে কোলাকুলি ।
হরি কৃষ্ণ কহ দুঁহে বলে বাহু তুলি' ॥ ১৫৯ ॥

duṅhe preme nṛtya kari' kare kolākuli
hari kṛṣṇa kaha duṅhe bale bāhu tuli'

SYNONYMS

duṅhe—both of them; *preme*—in ecstatic love; *nṛtya kari'*—dancing; *kare*—do; *kolākuli*—embracing; *hari*—the holy name of Hari; *kṛṣṇa*—the holy name of Kṛṣṇa; *kaha*—go on chanting; *duṅhe*—both of them; *bale*—speak; *bāhu tuli'*—raising the arms.

TRANSLATION

Both of them danced in ecstatic love and embraced one another. Raising their arms, they said, "Chant the holy names of Hari and Kṛṣṇa!"

TEXT 160

লোক 'হরি' 'হরি' বলে, কোলাহল হৈল ।
'কেশব'-সেবক প্রভুকে মালা পরাইল ॥ ১৬০ ॥

loka 'hari' 'hari' bale, kolāhala haila
'keśava'-sevaka prabhuke mālā parāila

SYNONYMS

loka—all the people; *hari hari bale*—began to chant the holy names Hari, Hari; *kolāhala haila*—there was a great uproar; *keśava-sevaka*—the priest in the service of Lord Keśava; *prabhuke*—unto Śrī Caitanya Mahāprabhu; *mālā parāila*—offered a garland.

TRANSLATION

All the people then began to chant, "Hari! Hari!" and there was a great uproar. The priest in Lord Keśava's service offered Śrī Caitanya Mahāprabhu a garland.

TEXT 161

লোকে কহে প্রভু দেখি' হঞা বিস্ময়।
ঐছে হেন প্রেম 'লৌকিক' কভু নয়॥ ১৬১ ॥

loke kahe prabhu dekhi' hañā vismaya
aiche hena prema 'laukika' kabhu naya

SYNONYMS

loke kahe—the people said; *prabhu*—Śrī Caitanya Mahāprabhu; *dekhi'*—seeing; *hañā vismaya*—being struck with wonder; *aiche*—such; *hena*—similar; *prema*—love of Godhead; *laukika*—ordinary; *kabhu naya*—never is.

TRANSLATION

When the people saw Śrī Caitanya Mahāprabhu's dancing and chanting, they were struck with wonder, and they all said, "Such transcendental love is never an ordinary thing."

TEXT 162

যাঁহার দর্শনে লোকে প্রেমে মত্ত হঞা।
হাসে, কান্দে, নাচে, গায়, কৃষ্ণনাম লঞা॥ ১৬২ ॥

yāṅhāra darśane loke preme matta hañā
hāse, kānde, nāce, gāya, kṛṣṇa-nāma lañā

SYNONYMS

yāṅhāra darśane—by seeing whom; *loke*—people; *preme*—in love; *matta hañā*—becoming mad; *hāse*—laugh; *kānde*—cry; *nāce*—dance; *gāya*—chant; *kṛṣṇa-nāma lañā*—taking the holy name of Lord Kṛṣṇa.

TRANSLATION

The people said, "Simply by seeing Śrī Caitanya Mahāprabhu, everyone is maddened with love of Kṛṣṇa. Indeed, everyone is laughing, crying, dancing, chanting and taking the holy name of Kṛṣṇa.

TEXT 163

সর্বথা-নিশ্চিত—ইঁহো কৃষ্ণ-অবতার ।
মথুরা আইলা লোকের করিতে নিস্তার ॥ ১৬৩ ॥

sarvathā-niścita——iṅho kṛṣṇa-avatāra
mathurā āilā lokera karite nistāra

SYNONYMS

sarvathā—in every respect; *niścita*—ascertained; *iṅho*—He; *kṛṣṇa-avatāra*—incarnation of Lord Kṛṣṇa; *mathurā āilā*—has come to Mathurā; *lokera*—of the people; *karite*—to perform; *nistāra*—deliverance.

TRANSLATION

"Certainly Śrī Caitanya Mahāprabhu is in all respects the incarnation of Lord Kṛṣṇa. Now He has come to Mathurā to deliver everyone."

TEXT 164

তবে মহাপ্রভু সেই ব্রাহ্মণে লঞা ।
তাঁহারে পুছিলা কিছু নিভৃতে বসিয়া ॥ ১৬৪ ॥

tabe mahāprabhu sei brāhmaṇe lañā
tāṅhāre puchilā kichu nibhṛte vasiyā

SYNONYMS

tabe—after that; *mahāprabhu*—Śrī Caitanya Mahāprabhu; *sei*—that; *brāhmaṇe*—*brāhmaṇa;* *lañā*—taking; *tāṅhāre*—unto him; *puchilā*—inquired; *kichu*—something; *nibhṛte vasiyā*—sitting in a solitary place.

TRANSLATION

After this, Śrī Caitanya Mahāprabhu took aside the brāhmaṇa. Sitting in a solitary place, the Lord began to question him.

TEXT 165

'আর্য, সরল, তুমি – বৃদ্ধ ব্রাহ্মণ ।
কাহাঁ হৈতে পাইলে তুমি এই প্রেমধন ?' ১৬৫ ॥

'ārya, sarala, tumi——vṛddha brāhmaṇa
kāhāṅ haite pāile tumi ei prema-dhana?'

SYNONYMS

ārya—advanced in devotional service; *sarala*—simple; *tumi*—you; *vṛddha brāhmaṇa*—elderly *brāhmaṇa; kāhāṅ haite*—from where; *pāile tumi*—did you obtain; *ei*—this; *prema-dhana*—transcendental opulence of ecstatic love.

TRANSLATION

Śrī Caitanya Mahāprabhu said, "You are an elderly brāhmaṇa, you are sincere, and you are advanced in spiritual life. Wherefrom have you gotten this transcendental opulence of ecstatic love for Kṛṣṇa?"

TEXT 166

বিপ্র কহে,—'শ্রীপাদ শ্রীমাধবেন্দ্রপুরী ।
ভ্রমিতে ভ্রমিতে আইলা মথুরা-নগরী ॥ ১৬৬ ॥

vipra kahe,—'śrīpāda śrī-mādhavendra-purī
bhramite bhramite āilā mathurā-nagarī

SYNONYMS

vipra kahe—the *brāhmaṇa* said; *śrīpāda*—His Holiness; *śrī-mādhavendra-purī*—Śrī Mādhavendra Purī; *bhramite bhramite*—while touring; *āilā*—came; *mathurā-nagarī*—to the city of Mathurā.

TRANSLATION

The brāhmaṇa replied, "His Holiness Śrīla Mādhavendra Purī came to the city of Mathurā while he was on a tour.

TEXT 167

কৃপা করি' তেঁহো মোর নিলয়ে আইলা ।
মোরে শিষ্য করি' মোর হাতে 'ভিক্ষা' কৈলা ॥১৬৭॥

kṛpā kari' teṅho mora nilaye āilā
more śiṣya kari' mora hāte 'bhikṣā' kailā

SYNONYMS

kṛpā kari'—by his causeless mercy; *teṅho*—he; *mora nilaye*—to my humble place; *āilā*—came; *more*—me; *śiṣya kari'*—accepting as his disciple; *mora hāte*—from my hand; *bhikṣā kailā*—accepted lunch.

TRANSLATION

"While at Mathurā, Śrīpāda Mādhavendra Purī visited my house and accepted me as a disciple. He even took lunch at my home.

TEXT 168

গোপাল প্রকট করি' সেবা কৈল 'মহাশয়'।
অদ্যাপিহ তাঁহার সেবা 'গোবর্ধনে' হয় ॥ ১৬৮ ॥

gopāla prakaṭa kari' sevā kaila 'mahāśaya'
adyāpiha tāṅhāra sevā 'govardhane' haya

SYNONYMS

gopāla—the Deity Gopāla; *prakaṭa kari'*—installing; *sevā*—service; *kaila*—did; *mahāśaya*—that great personality; *adyāpiha*—still now; *tāṅhāra*—of that Deity Gopāla; *sevā*—the service; *govardhane*—on the Govardhana Hill; *haya*—is conducted.

TRANSLATION

"After installing the Deity Gopāla, Śrīla Mādhavendra Purī rendered Him service. That very Deity is still being worshiped at Govardhana Hill."

TEXT 169

শুনি' প্রভু কৈল তাঁর চরণ বন্দন।
ভয় পাঞা প্রভু-পায় পড়িলা ব্রাহ্মণ ॥ ১৬৯ ॥

śuni' prabhu kaila tāṅra caraṇa vandana
bhaya pāñā prabhu-pāya paḍilā brāhmaṇa

SYNONYMS

śuni'—after hearing; *prabhu*—Śrī Caitanya Mahāprabhu; *kaila*—did; *tāṅra*—of him; *caraṇa vandana*—worshiping the feet; *bhaya pāñā*—being afraid; *prabhu-pāya*—at the lotus feet of Śrī Caitanya Mahāprabhu; *paḍilā*—fell down; *brāhmaṇa*—the *brāhmaṇa.*

TRANSLATION

As soon as Caitanya Mahāprabhu heard about Mādhavendra Purī's relationship with the brāhmaṇa, He immediately offered obeisances at his feet. Becoming fearful, the brāhmaṇa also immediately fell at the Lord's feet.

TEXT 170

প্রভু কহে,—“তুমি ‘গুরু’, আমি ‘শিষ্য’-প্রায়।
‘গুরু’ হঞা ‘শিষ্যে’ নমস্কার না যুয়ায় ॥ ১৭০ ॥

prabhu kahe,——"tumi 'guru', āmi 'śiṣya'-prāya
'guru' hañā 'śiṣye' namaskāra nā yuyāya

SYNONYMS

prabhu kahe—Śrī Caitanya Mahāprabhu said; *tumi*—you; *guru*—My spiritual master; *āmi*—I; *śiṣya-prāya*—like your disciple; *guru hañā*—being the spiritual master; *śiṣye*—unto the disciple; *namaskāra*—obeisances; *nā yuyāya*—is not befitting.

TRANSLATION

Śrī Caitanya Mahāprabhu said, "You are on the platform of My spiritual master, and I am your disciple. Since you are My spiritual master, it is not befitting that you offer Me obeisances."

TEXT 171

শুনিয়া বিস্মিত বিপ্র কহে ভয় পাঞা।
ঐছে বাত্ কহ কেনে সন্ন্যাসী হঞা ॥ ১৭১ ॥

śuniyā vismita vipra kahe bhaya pāñā
aiche vāt kaha kene sannyāsī hañā

SYNONYMS

śuniyā—after hearing; *vismita*—astonished; *vipra*—the *brāhmaṇa; kahe*—said; *bhaya pāñā*—being afraid; *aiche vāt*—such a statement; *kaha*—You say; *kene*—why; *sannyāsī hañā*—although You are a *sannyāsī.*

TRANSLATION

Upon hearing this, the brāhmaṇa became afraid. He then said, "Why do You speak like this? You are a sannyāsī.

TEXT 172

কিন্তু তোমার প্রেম দেখি’ মনে অনুমানি।
মাধবেন্দ্র-পুরীর ‘সম্বন্ধ’ ধর—জানি ॥ ১৭২ ॥

kintu tomāra prema dekhi' mane anumāni
mādhavendra-purīra 'sambandha' dhara——jāni

SYNONYMS

kintu—still; *tomāra prema*—Your ecstatic love; *dekhi'*—after seeing; *mane*—in my mind; *anumāni*—I imagine; *mādhavendra-purīra*—of Śrī Mādhavendra Purī; *sambandha*—relationship; *dhara*—You have; *jāni*—I can understand.

TRANSLATION

"Upon seeing Your ecstatic love, I can just imagine that You must have some relationship with Mādhavendra Purī. This is my understanding.

TEXT 173

কৃষ্ণপ্রেমা তাঁহা, যাঁহা তাঁহার 'সম্বন্ধ' ।
তাহাঁ বিনা এই প্রেমার কাহাঁ নাহি গন্ধ ॥ ১৭৩ ॥

kṛṣṇa-premā tāṅhā, yāṅhā tāṅhāra 'sambandha'
tāhāṅ vinā ei premāra kāhāṅ nāhi gandha

SYNONYMS

kṛṣṇa-premā—love of Kṛṣṇa; *tāṅhā*—there; *yāṅhā*—where; *tāṅhāra*—his; *sambandha*—relationship; *tāhāṅ vinā*—without him; *ei premāra*—of this ecstatic love; *kāhāṅ nāhi gandha*—there is no possibility of even a scent.

TRANSLATION

"This kind of ecstatic love can be experienced only when one has a relationship with Mādhavendra Purī. Without him, even a scent of such transcendental ecstatic love is impossible."

TEXT 174

তবে ভট্টাচার্য তারে 'সম্বন্ধ' কহিল ।
শুনি' আনন্দিত বিপ্র নাচিতে লাগিল ॥ ১৭৪ ॥

tabe bhaṭṭācārya tāre 'sambandha' kahila
śuni' ānandita vipra nācite lāgila

SYNONYMS

tabe—thereafter; *bhaṭṭācārya*—Balabhadra Bhaṭṭācārya; *tāre*—unto the *brāhmaṇa; sambandha kahila*—explained the relationship; *śuni'*—after hearing; *ānandita*—being pleased; *vipra*—the *brāhmaṇa; nācite lāgila*—began to dance.

TRANSLATION

Balabhadra Bhaṭṭācārya then explained the relationship between Mādhavendra Purī and Śrī Caitanya Mahāprabhu. After hearing this, the brāhmaṇa became very pleased and began to dance.

TEXT 175

তবে বিপ্র প্রভুরে লঞা আইলা নিজ-ঘরে ।
আপন-ইচ্ছায় প্রভুর নানা সেবা করে ॥ ১৭৫ ॥

tabe vipra prabhure lañā āilā nija-ghare
āpana-icchāya prabhura nānā sevā kare

SYNONYMS

tabe—thereafter; *vipra*—the *brāhmaṇa; prabhure*—Śrī Caitanya Mahāprabhu; *lañā*—taking; *āilā*—came back; *nija-ghare*—to his home; *āpana-icchāya*—by his own will; *prabhura*—of Śrī Caitanya Mahāprabhu; *nānā*—various; *sevā*—services; *kare*—rendered.

TRANSLATION

The brāhmaṇa then took Śrī Caitanya Mahāprabhu to his home and, out of his own free will, began to serve the Lord in various ways.

TEXT 176

ভিক্ষা লাগি' ভট্টাচার্যে করাইলা রন্ধন ।
তবে মহাপ্রভু হাসি' বলিলা বচন ॥ ১৭৬ ॥

bhikṣā lāgi' bhaṭṭācārye karāilā randhana
tabe mahāprabhu hāsi' balilā vacana

SYNONYMS

bhikṣā lāgi'—for lunch; *bhaṭṭācārye*—Balabhadra Bhaṭṭācārya; *karāilā randhana*—made to cook; *tabe*—at that time; *mahāprabhu*—Śrī Caitanya Mahāprabhu; *hāsi'*—smiling; *balilā vacana*—said these words.

TRANSLATION

He asked Balabhadra Bhaṭṭācārya to cook Śrī Caitanya Mahāprabhu's lunch. At that time, the Lord, smiling, spoke as follows.

TEXT 177

“পুরী-গোসাঞি তোমার ঘরে কর্‌যাছেন ভিক্ষা ।
মোরে তুমি ভিক্ষা দেহ,—এই মোর ‘শিক্ষা’॥” ১৭৭॥

"purī-gosāñi tomāra ghare karyāchena bhikṣā
more tumi bhikṣā deha,——ei mora 'śikṣā' "

SYNONYMS

purī-gosāñi—Mādhavendra Purī; *tomāra ghare*—at your place; *karyāchena bhikṣā*—accepted lunch; *more*—for Me; *tumi bhikṣā deha*—better for you to cook; *ei*—that; *mora śikṣā*—My instruction.

TRANSLATION

Śrī Caitanya Mahāprabhu said, "Mādhavendra Purī has already taken lunch at your place. Therefore you may cook and give Me the food. That is My instruction."

TEXT 178

যদ্‌যদাচরতি শ্রেষ্ঠস্তত্তদেবেতরো জনঃ ।
স যৎ প্রমাণং কুরুতে লোকস্তদনুবর্ততে ॥ ১৭৮ ॥

yad yad ācarati śreṣṭhas
tat tad evetaro janaḥ
sa yat pramāṇaṁ kurute
lokas tad anuvartate

SYNONYMS

yat yat—however; *ācarati*—behaves; *śreṣṭaḥ*—the best man; *tat tat*—that; *eva*—certainly; *itaraḥ*—the lesser; *janaḥ*—men; *saḥ*—he; *yat*—which; *pramāṇam*—standard; *kurute*—shows; *lokaḥ*—the people; *tat*—that; *anuvartate*—follow.

TRANSLATION

"Whatever action is performed by a great man, common men follow. And whatever standards he sets by exemplary acts, all the world pursues."

PURPORT

This is a quotation from *Bhagavad-gītā* (3.21).

TEXT 179

যদ্যপি 'সনোড়িয়া' হয় সেইত ব্রাহ্মণ ।
সনোড়িয়া-ঘরে সন্ন্যাসী না করে ভোজন ॥ ১৭৯ ॥

yadyapi 'sanoḍiyā' haya seita brāhmaṇa
sanoḍiyā-ghare sannyāsī nā kare bhojana

SYNONYMS

yadyapi—although; *sanoḍiyā*—a priest of the Sanoḍiyā community; *haya*—was; *seita*—that; *brāhmaṇa*—*brāhmaṇa; sanoḍiyā-ghare*—in the house of a Sanoḍiyā (goldsmith); *sannyāsī*—a person in the renounced order of life; *nā kare bhojana*—does not accept food.

TRANSLATION

The brāhmaṇa belonged to the Sanoḍiyā brāhmaṇa community, and a sannyāsī does not accept food from such a brāhmaṇa.

PURPORT

In northwestern India, *vaiśyas* are divided in various subdivisions. Śrīla Bhaktivinoda Ṭhākura points out that they are divided as Āgaraoyālā, Kālaoyāra and Sānoyāḍa. Out of them, the Āgaraoyālās are supposed to be first-class *vaiśyas,* and the Kālaoyāras and Sānoyāḍas are considered lower due to their occupational degradation. The Kālaoyāras generally take wine and other intoxicants. Although they are *vaiśyas,* they are considered to belong to a lower class. The priests who guide the Kālaoyāras and the Sānoyāḍas are called Sanoḍiyā *brāhmaṇas.* Śrīla Bhaktivinoda Ṭhākura states that the word *sānoyāḍa* in Bengal indicates *suvarṇa-vaṇik.* In Bengal there are priests who guide the *suvarṇa-vaṇik* community, which is also considered a low class. There is little difference between the Sānoyāḍa and the *suvarṇa-vaṇik.* Generally the *suvarṇa-vaṇiks* are bankers dealing in gold and silver. In western India, the Āgaraoyālās also belong to the banking profession. This is the original business of the *suvarṇa-vaṇik* or Āgaraoyāla community. Historically, the Āgaraoyālās came from the up-country named Ayodha, and the *suvarṇa-vaṇik* community came from Ayodha. It appears that the *suvarṇa-vaṇiks* and the Āgaraoyālās belong to the same community. The Sanoḍiyā *brāhmaṇas* were the guides of the Kālaoyāra and Sānoyāḍa. They are therefore considered to be lower-class *brāhmaṇas,* and a *sannyāsī* is not allowed to take alms or food from them. However, Śrī Caitanya Mahāprabhu accepted lunch cooked by a Sanoḍiyā *brāhmaṇa* simply because he belonged to Mādhavendra Purī's community. Śrīla Mādhavendra Purī was the spiritual master of Īśvara Purī, who was the spiritual master of Śrī Caitanya Mahāprabhu. Thus a spiritual relationship is established on the spiritual platform without consideration of material inferiority or superiority.

TEXT 180

তথাপি পুরী দেখি' তাঁর 'বৈষ্ণব'-আচার।
'শিষ্য' করি' তাঁর ভিক্ষা কৈল অঙ্গীকার॥ ১৮০॥

tathāpi purī dekhi' tāṅra 'vaiṣṇava'-ācāra
'śiṣya' kari' tāṅra bhikṣā kaila aṅgīkāra

SYNONYMS

tathāpi—still; *purī*—Mādhavendra Purī; *dekhi'*—after seeing; *tāṅra*—of the *brāhmaṇa; vaiṣṇava-ācāra*—behavior like a Vaiṣṇava; *śiṣya kari'*—accepting him as his disciple; *tāṅra bhikṣā*—food offered by him; *kaila aṅgīkāra*—accepted.

TRANSLATION

Although the brāhmaṇa belonged to the Sanoḍiyā community, Śrīla Mādhavanedra Purī saw that he behaved like a Vaiṣṇava and therefore accepted him as his disciple. The food he cooked was also accepted by Mādhavendra Purī.

TEXT 181

মহাপ্রভু তাঁরে যদি 'ভিক্ষা' মাগিল।
দৈন্য করি' সেই বিপ্র কহিতে লাগিল॥ ১৮১॥

mahāprabhu tāṅre yadi 'bhikṣā' māgila
dainya kari' sei vipra kahite lāgila

SYNONYMS

mahāprabhu—Śrī Caitanya Mahāprabhu; *tāṅre*—from him; *yadi*—when; *bhikṣā māgila*—requested lunch; *dainya kari'*—out of humility; *sei vipra*—that *brāhmaṇa; kahite lāgila*—began to speak.

TRANSLATION

Therefore Śrī Caitanya Mahāprabhu willingly requested food from the brāhmaṇa, and the brāhmaṇa, feeling a natural humility, began to speak as follows.

TEXT 182

তোমারে 'ভিক্ষা' দিব—বড় ভাগ্য সে আমার।
তুমি—ঈশ্বর, নাহি তোমার বিধি-ব্যবহার॥ ১৮২॥

tomāre 'bhikṣā' diba——baḍa bhāgya se āmāra
tumi——īśvara, nāhi tomāra vidhi-vyavahāra

SYNONYMS

tomāre—unto You; *bhikṣā diba*—I shall offer food; *baḍa bhāgya*—great fortune; *se*—that; *āmāra*—my; *tumi*—You; *īśvara*—the Supreme Personality of Godhead; *nāhi*—there is not; *tomāra*—of You; *vidhi-vyavahāra*—regulative behavior.

TRANSLATION

"It is a great fortune for me to offer You food. You are the Supreme Lord, and, being in the transcendental position, You are not restricted in any way.

TEXT 183

'মূর্খ'-লোক করিবেক তোমার নিন্দন।
সহিতে না পারিমু সেই 'দুষ্টে'র বচন॥ ১৮৩॥

'mūrkha'-loka karibeka tomāra nindana
sahite nā pārimu sei 'duṣṭe'ra vacana

SYNONYMS

mūrkha-loka—foolish persons; *karibeka*—will do; *tomāra nindana*—blaspheming You; *sahite nā pārimu*—I shall not be able to tolerate; *sei*—those; *duṣṭera vacana*—words of mischievous persons.

TRANSLATION

"Foolish people will blaspheme You, but I shall not tolerate the words of such mischievous people."

PURPORT

Śrīla Bhaktisiddhānta Sarasvatī Ṭhākura remarks that although the *brāhmaṇa* did not belong to a superior community, he fearlessly chastised so-called caste *brāhmaṇas* because he was situated on the platform of pure devotional service. There are people who are opposed to Śrī Caitanya Mahāprabhu's accepting a Vaiṣṇava belonging to a lower caste. Such people do not consider *mahā-prasāda* transcendental, and therefore they are described here as *mūrkha* (foolish) and *duṣṭa* (mischievous). A pure devotee has the power to challenge such high-caste people, and his brave statements are not to be considered proud or puffed up. On the contrary, he is to be considered straightforward. Such a person does not like to flatter high-class *brāhmaṇas* who belong to the non-Vaiṣṇava community.

TEXT 184

প্রভু কহে,—শ্রুতি, স্মৃতি, যত ঋষিগণ ।
সবে 'এক'-মত নহে, ভিন্ন ভিন্ন ধর্ম ॥ ১৮৪ ॥

prabhu kahe,——śruti, smṛti, yata ṛṣi-gaṇa
sabe 'eka'-mata nahe, bhinna bhinna dharma

SYNONYMS

prabhu kahe—Lord Śrī Caitanya Mahāprabhu said; *śruti*—the *Vedas; smṛti*—the *Purāṇas; yata*—all; *ṛṣi-gaṇa*—great sages; *sabe*—all of them; *eka-mata nahe*—do not agree; *bhinna bhinna dharma*—different grades of religious principles.

TRANSLATION

Śrī Caitanya Mahāprabhu replied, "The Vedas, Purāṇas and great learned sages are not always in agreement with one another. Consequently there are different religious principles.

PURPORT

Unless one comes to the Absolute Truth, there is no possibility of agreement. *Nāsav ṛṣir yasya mataṁ na bhinnam:* it is said that a great learned scholar or sage cannot be exalted unless he disagrees. On the material platform, there is no possibility of agreement; therefore there are different kinds of religious systems. However, the Absolute Truth is one, and when one is situated in the Absolute Truth, there is no disagreement. On that absolute platform the Supreme Personality of Godhead is worshipable. As stated in *Bhagavad-gītā* (18.55): *bhaktyā mām abhijānāti yāvān yaś cāsmi tattvataḥ.* On the absolute platform, the worshipful Deity is one, and the process of worship is also one. That process is *bhakti.*

There are many different religions throughout the world because they are not all on the absolute platform of devotional service. As confirmed in *Bhagavad-gītā* (18.66): *sarva-dharmān parityajya mām ekaṁ śaraṇaṁ vraja.* The word *ekam* means "one," Kṛṣṇa. On this platform, there are no different religious systems. According to *Śrīmad-Bhāgavatam* (1.1.2): *dharmaḥ projjhita-kaitavo 'tra.* On the material platform, religious systems are different. *Śrīmad-Bhāgavatam* describes them from the very beginning as *dharmaḥ kaitavaḥ,* cheating religions. None of these religions are actually genuine. The genuine religious system is that which enables one to become a lover of the Supreme Personality of Godhead. In the words of *Śrīmad-Bhāgavatam* (1.2.6):

sa vai puṁsāṁ paro dharmo
yato bhaktir adhokṣaje

ahaituky apratihatā
yayātmā suprasīdati

"The supreme occupation [*dharma*] for all humanity is that by which men can attain to loving devotional service unto the transcendent Lord. Such devotional service must be unmotivated and uninterrupted in order to completely satisfy the self."

On this platform there is nothing but the service of the Lord. When a person has no ulterior motive, there is certainly oneness and agreement of principles. Since everyone has a different body and mind, different types of religions are needed. But when one is situated on the spiritual platform, there are no bodily and mental differences. Consequently on the absolute platform there is oneness in religion.

TEXT 185

ধর্ম-স্থাপন-হেতু সাধুর ব্যবহার ।
পুরী-গোসাঞির যে আচরণ, সেই ধর্ম সার ॥ ১৮৫ ॥

dharma-sthāpana-hetu sādhura vyavahāra
purī-gosāñira ye ācaraṇa, sei dharma sāra

SYNONYMS

dharma-sthāpana-hetu—to establish the principles of religion; *sādhura vyavahāra*—behavior of a devotee; *purī-gosāñira*—of Mādhavendra Purī; *ye ācaraṇa*—the behavior; *sei*—that; *dharma sāra*—the essence of all religion.

TRANSLATION

"A devotee's behavior establishes the true purpose of religious principles. The behavior of Mādhavendra Purī Gosvāmī is the essence of such religious principles."

PURPORT

Śrīla Bhaktisiddhānta Sarasvatī Ṭhākura gives the following commentary on this passage. A *sādhu* or an honest man is called a *mahājana* or a *mahātmā*. The *mahātmā* is thus described in *Bhagavad-gītā:*

mahātmānas tu māṁ pārtha
daivīṁ prakṛtim āśritāḥ
bhajanty ananya-manaso
jñātvā bhūtādim avyayam

"O son of Pṛthā, those who are not deluded, the great souls, are under the protection of the divine nature. They are fully engaged in devotional service because they know Me as the Supreme Personality of Godhead, original and inexhaustible." (Bg. 9.13)

In the material world, the word *mahātmā* is understood in different ways by different religionists. Mundaners also come up with their different angles of vision. For the conditioned soul busy in sense gratification, a *mahājana* is recognized according to the proportion of sense gratification he offers. For instance, a businessman may consider a certain banker to be a *mahājana,* and *karmīs* desiring material enjoyment may consider philosophers like Jaimini to be *mahājanas.* There are many *yogīs* who want to control the senses, and for them Patañjali Ṛṣi is a *mahājana.* For the *jñānīs,* the atheist Kapila, Vaśiṣṭha, Durvāsā, Dattātreya and other impersonalist philosophers are *mahājanas.* For the demons, Hiraṇyākṣa, Hiraṇyakaśipu, Rāvaṇa, Rāvaṇa's son Meghanāda, Jarāsandha and others are accepted as *mahājanas.* For materialistic anthropologists speculating on the evolution of the body, a person like Darwin is a *mahājana.* The scientists who are bewildered by Kṛṣṇa's external energy have no relationship with the Supreme Personality of Godhead, yet they are accepted by some as *mahājanas.* Similarly, philosophers, historians, literary men, public speakers and social and political leaders are sometimes accepted as *mahājanas.* Such *mahājanas* are respected by certain men who have been described in *Śrīmad-Bhāgavatam* (2.3.19):

śva-viḍ-varāhoṣṭra-kharaiḥ
saṁstutaḥ puruṣaḥ paśuḥ
na yat-karṇa-pathopeto
jātu nāma gadāgrajaḥ

"Men who are like dogs, hogs, camels and asses praise those men who never listen to the transcendental pastimes of Lord Śrī Kṛṣṇa, the deliverer from evils."

Thus on the material platform animalistic leaders are worshiped by animals. Sometimes physicians, psychiatrists and social workers try to mitigate bodily pain, distress and fear, but they have no knowledge of spiritual identity and are bereft of a relationship with God. Yet they are considered *mahājanas* by the illusioned. Self-deceived persons sometimes accept leaders or spiritual masters from a priestly order that has been officially appointed by the codes of material life. In this way, they are deceived by official priests. Sometimes people accept as *mahājanas* those who have been designated by Śrīla Vṛndāvana dāsa Ṭhākura as *ḍhaṅga-vipras* (imposter *brāhmaṇas*). Such imposters imitate the characteristics of Śrīla Haridāsa Ṭhākura, and they envy Haridāsa Ṭhākura, who was certainly a *mahājana.* They make great artificial endeavors, advertising themselves as great devotees of the Lord or as mystic hypnotists knowledgeable in witchcraft, hypnotism and miracles. Sometimes people accept demons like Pūtanā, Tṛṇāvarta,

Vatsa, Baka, Aghāsura and Dhenuka, Kālīya and Pralamba. Some people accept imitators and adversaries of the Supreme Personality of Godhead, such as Pauṇḍraka, Śṛgāla Vāsudeva, the spiritual master of the demons (Śukrācārya), or atheists like Cārvāka, King Vena, Sugata and Arhat. Such people have no faith in Śrī Caitanya Mahāprabhu as the Supreme Personality of Godhead. Rather, they accept godless cheaters who present themselves as incarnations of God and cheat foolish people within the material world by word jugglery. Thus many rascals are accepted as *mahājanas.*

In this material world a person may be famous as a *karma-vīra,* a successful fruitive worker, or one may be very successful in performing religious duties, or he may be known as a hero in mental speculation (*jñāna-vīra*), or he may be a very famous renunciant. In any case, *Śrīmad-Bhāgavatam* (3.23.56) gives the following opinion in this matter.

neha yat karma dharmāya
na virāgāya kalpate
na tīrtha-pada-sevāyai
jīvann api mṛto hi saḥ

"Anyone whose work is not meant to elevate him to religious life, anyone whose religious ritualistic performances do not raise him to renunciation, and anyone situated in renunciation that does not lead him to devotional service to the Supreme Personality of Godhead must be considered dead, although he is breathing."

The conclusion is that all pious activity, fruitive activity, religious principles and renunciation must ultimately lead to devotional service. There are different types of processes for rendering service. One may serve his country, people, society, the *varṇāśrama-dharma,* the sick, the poor, the rich, women, demigods and so on. All this comes under the heading of sense gratification, or enjoyment in the material world. It is most unfortunate that people are more or less attracted by such material activity and that the leaders of these activities are accepted as *mahājanas,* great ideal leaders. Actually they are only misleaders, but an ordinary man cannot understand how he is being misled.

Narottama dāsa Ṭhākura says: *sādhu-śāstra-guru-vākya, cittete kariyā aikya.* A *sādhu* is a great personality like Śrī Caitanya Mahāprabhu. The *śāstras* are the injunctions of revealed scriptures. Those who are devoid of devotional service sometimes mistake those who have mundane motives for *mahājanas.* The only motive must be *kṛṣṇa-bhakti,* devotional service to the Lord. Sometimes fruitive workers, dry philosophers, nondevotees, mystic *yogīs* and persons attached to material opulence, women and money are considered *mahājanas.* However, *Śrīmad-Bhāgavatam* (6.3.25) gives the following statements about such unauthorized *mahājanas:*

prāyeṇa veda tad idaṁ na mahājano 'yaṁ
devyā vimohita-matir bata māyayālam
trayyāṁ jaḍī-kṛta-matir madhu-puṣpitāyāṁ
vaitānike mahati karmaṇi yujyamānaḥ

In this material world, *karmīs* (fruitive actors) are accepted as *mahājanas* by foolish people who do not know the value of devotional service. Their mundane intelligence and mental speculative methods are under the control of the three modes of material nature. Consequently they cannot understand unalloyed devotional service. They are attracted by material activities, and they become worshipers of material nature. Thus they are known as fruitive actors. They even become entangled in material activities disguised as spiritual activities. In *Bhagavad-gītā,* such people are described as *veda-vāda-ratā.* They do not understand the real purpose of the *Vedas,* yet they think of themselves as Vedic authorities. People versed in Vedic knowledge must know Kṛṣṇa as the Supreme Personality of Godhead. *Vedaiś ca sarvair aham eva vedyaḥ.* (Bg. 15.15)

A man covered by illusion cannot understand the proper way; therefore Śrī Caitanya Mahāprabhu says: *dharma-sthāpana-hetu sādhura vyavahāra.* The behavior of a devotee is the criterion for all other behavior. Śrī Caitanya Mahāprabhu Himself followed the devotional principles and taught others to follow them. *Purī-gosāñira ye ācaraṇa, sei dharma sāra.* Śrī Caitanya Mahāprabhu personally followed the behavior of Mādhavendra Purī and advised others to follow his principles. Unfortunately, people have been attracted to the material body since time immemorial.

yasyātma-buddhiḥ kuṇape tridhātuke
sva-dhīḥ kalatrādiṣu bhauma ijya-dhīḥ
yat-tīrtha-buddhiḥ salile na karhicij
janeṣv abhijñeṣu sa eva go-kharaḥ

"A human being who identifies this body made of three elements with his self, who considers the by-products of the body to be his kinsmen, who considers the land of birth worshipable, and who goes to the place of pilgrimage simply to take a bath rather than meet men of transcendental knowledge there is to be considered like an ass or a cow." (*Bhāg.* 10.84.13) Those who accept the logic of *gaḍḍalikā-pravāha* and follow in the footsteps of pseudo-*mahājanas* are carried away by the waves of *māyā.* Bhaktivinoda Ṭhākura therefore warns:

miche māyāra vaśe, yāccha bhese',
khāccha hābuḍubu, bhāi
jīva kṛṣṇa-dāsa, e viśvāsa,
ka'rle ta' āra duḥkha nāi

"Don't be carried away by the waves of *māyā*. Just surrender to the lotus feet of Kṛṣṇa, and all miseries will end." Those who follow social customs and behavior forget to follow the path chalked out by the *mahājanas;* thus they are offenders at the feet of the *mahājanas*. Sometimes they consider such *mahājanas* very conservative, or they create their own *mahājanas*. In this way they ignore the principles of the *paramaparā* system. This is a great misfortune for everyone. If one does not follow in the footsteps of a real *mahājana,* one's plans for happiness will be frustrated. This is elaborately explained in *Madhya-līlā* (Chapter Twenty-five, verses 55, 56 and 58). It is there stated:

parama kāraṇa īśvare keha nāhi māne
sva-sva-mata sthāpe para-matera khaṇḍane

tāte chaya darśana haite 'tattva' nāhi jāni
'mahājana' yei kahe, sei 'satya' māni

śrī-kṛṣṇa-caitanya-vāṇī——amṛtera dhāra
tiṅho ye kahaye vastu, sei 'tattva'——sāra

People are so unfortunate that they do not accept the instructions of the Supreme Personality of Godhead. Instead, they want to be supported by so-called *mahājanas,* authorities. *Tāte chaya darśana haite 'tattva' nāhi jāni:* we cannot ascertain the real truth simply by following speculators. We have to follow the footsteps of the *mahājanas* in the disciplic succession. Then our attempt will be successful. *Śrī-kṛṣṇa-caitanya-vāṇī—amṛtera dhāra:* "Whatever is spoken by Śrī Caitanya Mahāprabhu is an incessant flow of nectar." Whoever accepts His words as reality can understand the essence of the Absolute Truth. No one can ascertain the Absolute Truth by following the philosophy of Sāṅkhya or Patañjali, for the followers of Sāṅkhya or Patañjali do not accept Lord Viṣṇu as the Supreme Personality of Godhead (*na te viduḥ svārtha-gatiṁ hi viṣṇum*). The ambition of such people is never fulfilled; therefore they are attracted by the external energy. Although mental speculators may be renowned all over the world as great authorities, actually they are not. Such leaders are themselves conservative and not at all liberal. However, if we preach this philosophy, people will consider Vaiṣṇavas very sectarian. Śrīla Mādhavendra Purī was a real *mahājana,* but misguided people cannot distinguish the real from the unreal. However, a person who is awakened to Kṛṣṇa consciousness can understand the real religious path chalked out by the Lord and His pure devotees. Śrī Mādhavendra Purī was a real *mahājana* because he understood the Absolute Truth properly and throughout his life behaved like a pure devotee. Śrī Caitanya Mahāprabhu approved the method of Śrī Mādhavendra Purī. Therefore, although from the material viewpoint the Sanoḍiyā *brāhmaṇa* was on a lower platform, Śrī Caitanya Mahāprabhu considered him situated on the highest platform of spiritual realization.

Śrīmad-Bhāgavatam (6.3.20) states that there are twelve *mahājanas:* Brahmā, Nārada, Śambhu, Kumāra, Kapila, Manu, Prahlāda, Janaka, Bhīṣma, Bali, Śukadeva and Yamarāja.

To select our *mahājanas* in the Gauḍīya-sampradāya, we have to follow in the footsteps of Śrī Caitanya Mahāprabhu and His representatives. His next representative is Śrī Svarūpa Dāmodara Gosvāmī, and the next are the six Gosvāmīs—Śrī Rūpa, Śrī Sanātana, Bhaṭṭa Raghunātha, Śrī Jīva, Gopāla Bhaṭṭa and Dāsa Raghunātha. The follower of Viṣṇusvāmī was Śrīdhara Svāmī, the most well known commentator on *Śrīmad-Bhāgavatam.* He was also a *mahājana.* Similarly, Caṇḍīdāsa, Vidyāpati and Jayadeva were all *mahājanas.* One who tries to imitate the *mahājanas* just to become an imitative spiritual master is certainly far away from following in the footsteps of the *mahājanas.* Sometimes people cannot actually understand how a *mahājana* follows other *mahājanas.* In this way people are inclined to fall from devotional service.

TEXT 186

তর্কোঽপ্রতিষ্ঠঃ শ্রুতয়ো বিভিন্না
নাসাবৃষির্যস্য মতং ন ভিন্নম্ ।
ধর্মস্য তত্ত্বং নিহিতং গুহায়াং
মহাজনো যেন গতঃ স পন্থাঃ ॥ ১৮৬ ॥

tarko 'pratiṣṭhaḥ śrutayo vibhinnā
nāsāv ṛṣir yasya mataṁ na bhinnam
dharmasya tattvaṁ nihitaṁ guhāyāṁ
mahājano yena gataḥ sa panthāḥ

SYNONYMS

tarkaḥ—dry argument; *apratiṣṭhaḥ*—not fixed; *śrutayaḥ—Vedas; vibhinnāḥ*—possessing different departments; *na*—not; *asau*—that; *ṛṣiḥ*—great sage; *yasya*—whose; *matam*—opinion; *na*—not; *bhinnam*—separate; *dharmasya*—of religious principles; *tattvam*—truth; *nihitam*—placed; *guhāyām*—in the heart of a realized person; *mahā-janaḥ*—self-realized predecessors; *yena*—by which way; *gataḥ*—acted; *saḥ*—that; *panthāḥ*—the pure unadulterated path.

TRANSLATION

Śrī Caitanya Mahāprabhu continued, " 'Dry arguments are inconclusive. A great personality whose opinion does not differ from others is not considered a great sage. Simply by studying the Vedas, which are variegated, one cannot come to the right path by which religious principles are understood. The solid truth of religious principles is hidden in the heart of an unadulterated self-

realized person. Consequently, as the śāstras confirm, one should accept whatever progressive path the mahājanas advocate.' "

PURPORT

This is a verse spoken by Yudhiṣṭhira Mahārāja in the *Mahābhārata, Vana-pārva* (313.117).

TEXT 187

তবে সেই বিপ্র প্রভুকে ভিক্ষা করাইল ।
মধুপুরীর লোক সব প্রভুকে দেখিতে আইল ॥১৮৭॥

tabe sei vipra prabhuke bhikṣā karāila
madhu-purīra loka saba prabhuke dekhite āila

SYNONYMS

tabe—after that; *sei vipra*—that *brāhmaṇa; prabhuke*—unto Lord Śrī Caitanya Mahāprabhu; *bhikṣā karāila*—gave lunch; *madhu-purīra*—of Mathurā; *loka*—people in general; *saba*—all; *prabhuke*—Śrī Caitanya Mahāprabhu; *dekhite āila*—came to see.

TRANSLATION

After this discussion, the brāhmaṇa gave lunch to Śrī Caitanya Mahāprabhu. Then all the people residing in Mathurā came to see the Lord.

TEXT 188

লক্ষ-সংখ্য লোক আইসে, নাহিক গণন ।
বাহির হঞা প্রভু দিল দরশন ॥ ১৮৮ ॥

lakṣa-saṅkhya loka āise, nāhika gaṇana
bāhira hañā prabhu dila daraśana

SYNONYMS

lakṣa-saṅkhya—numbering hundreds of thousands; *loka āise*—people came; *nāhika gaṇana*—there is no counting; *bāhira hañā*—coming out; *prabhu*—Śrī Caitanya Mahāprabhu; *dila daraśana*—gave audience.

TRANSLATION

People came by hundreds of thousands, and no one could count them. Therefore Śrī Caitanya Mahāprabhu came out of the house to give audience to the people.

TEXT 189

বাহু তুলি' বলে প্রভু 'হরিবোল'-ধ্বনি।
প্রেমে মত্ত নাচে লোক করি' হরিধ্বনি॥ ১৮৯॥

bāhu tuli' bale prabhu 'hari-bola'-dhvani
preme matta nāce loka kari' hari-dhvani

SYNONYMS

bāhu tuli'—raising the arms; *bale*—says; *prabhu*—Śrī Caitanya Mahāprabhu; *hari-bola-dhvani*—the transcendental sound vibration Hari bol; *preme*—in ecstasy; *matta*—maddened; *nāce*—dance; *loka*—the people; *kari' hari-dhvani*—making the transcendental vibration Hari.

TRANSLATION

When the people assembled, Śrī Caitanya Mahāprabhu raised His arms and said very loudly, "Hari bol!" The people responded to the Lord and became ecstatic. As if mad, they began to dance and vibrate the transcendental sound, "Hari!"

TEXT 190

যমুনার 'চব্বিশ ঘাটে' প্রভু কৈল স্নান।
সেই বিপ্র প্রভুকে দেখায় তীর্থস্থান॥ ১৯০॥

yamunāra 'cabbiśa ghāṭe' prabhu kaila snāna
sei vipra prabhuke dekhāya tīrtha-sthāna

SYNONYMS

yamunāra—of the River Yamunā; *cabbiśa ghāṭe*—in the twenty-four ghats, or bathing places; *prabhu*—Śrī Caitanya Mahāprabhu; *kaila*—performed; *snāna*—bathing; *sei vipra*—that *brāhmaṇa; prabhuke*—unto Śrī Caitanya Mahāprabhu; *dekhāya*—shows; *tīrtha-sthāna*—the holy places of pilgrimage.

TRANSLATION

Śrī Caitanya Mahāprabhu bathed in twenty-four ghats along the banks of the Yamunā, and the brāhmaṇa showed Him all the places of pilgrimage.

PURPORT

The twenty-four ghats (bathing places) along the Yamunā are (1) Avimukta, (2) Adhirūḍha, (3) Guhya-tīrtha, (4) Prayāga-tīrtha, (5) Kanakhala-tīrtha, (6) Tinduka,

(7) Sūrya-tīrtha, (8) Vaṭasvāmī, (9) Dhruva-ghāṭa, (10) Ṛṣi-tīrtha, (11) Mokṣa-tīrtha, (12) Bodha-tīrtha, (13) Gokarṇa, (14) Kṛṣṇagaṅgā, (15) Vaikuṇṭha, (16) Asi-kuṇḍa, (17) Catuḥ-sāmudrika-kūpa, (18) Akrūra-tīrtha, (19) Yājñika-vipra-sthāna, (20) Kubjā-kūpa, (21) Raṅga-sthala, (22) Mañca-sthala, (23) Mallayuddha-sthāna and (24) Daśāśvamedha.

TEXT 191

স্বয়ম্ভু, বিশ্রাম, দীর্ঘবিষ্ণু, ভূতেশ্বর।
মহাবিদ্যা, গোকর্ণাদি দেখিলা বিস্তর ॥ ১৯১ ॥

svayambhu, viśrāma, dīrgha-viṣṇu, bhūteśvara
mahāvidyā, gokarṇādi dekhilā vistara

SYNONYMS

svayambhu—Svayambhu; *viśrāma*—Viśrāma; *dīrgha-viṣṇu*—Dīrgha Viṣṇu; *bhūteśvara*—Bhūteśvara; *mahāvidyā*—Mahāvidyā; *gokarṇa*—Gokarṇa; *ādi*—and so on; *dekhilā*—saw; *vistara*—many.

TRANSLATION

Śrī Caitanya Mahāprabhu visited all the holy places on the banks of the Yamunā, including Svayambhu, Viśrāma-ghāṭa, Dīrgha Viṣṇu, Bhūteśvara, Mahāvidyā and Gokarṇa.

TEXT 192

'বন' দেখিবারে যদি প্রভুর মন হৈল।
সেইত ব্রাহ্মণে প্রভু সঙ্গেতে লইল ॥ ১৯২ ॥

'vana' dekhibāre yadi prabhura mana haila
sei ta brāhmaṇe prabhu saṅgete la-ila

SYNONYMS

vana—the forests; *dekhibāre*—to see; *yadi*—when; *prabhura*—of Śrī Caitanya Mahāprabhu; *mana*—mind; *haila*—was; *sei ta*—indeed that; *brāhmaṇe*—*brāhmaṇa; prabhu*—Śrī Caitanya Mahāprabhu; *saṅgete la-ila*—took along.

TRANSLATION

When Śrī Caitanya Mahāprabhu wanted to see the various forests of Vṛndāvana, He took the brāhmaṇa with Him.

TEXT 193

মধুবন, তাল, কুমুদ, বহুলা-বন গেলা ।
তাহাঁ তাহাঁ স্নান করি' প্রেমাবিষ্ট হৈলা ॥ ১৯৩ ॥

madhu-vana, tāla, kumuda, bahulā-vana gelā
tāhāṅ tāhāṅ snāna kari' premāviṣṭa hailā

SYNONYMS

madhu-vana—Madhuvana; *tāla*—Tālavana; *kumuda*—Kumudavana; *bahulā-vana*—Bahulāvana; *gelā*—He visited; *tāhāṅ tāhāṅ*—here and there; *snāna kari'*—taking bath; *prema-āviṣṭa hailā*—became overwhelmed by ecstatic love.

TRANSLATION

Śrī Caitanya Mahāprabhu visited the different forests, including Madhuvana, Tālavana, Kumudavana and Bahulāvana. Wherever He went, He took His bath with great ecstatic love.

PURPORT

The word *vana* means "forest." Vṛndāvana is the name given to the forest where Śrīmatī Vṛndādevī (Tulasīdevī) grows profusely. Actually it is not a forest as we ordinarily consider a forest because it is very thick with green vegetation. There are twelve such *vanas* in Vṛndāvana. Some are located on the western side of the Yamunā and others on the eastern side. The forests situated on the eastern side are Bhadravana, Bilvavana, Lauhavana, Bhāṇḍīravana and Mahāvana. On the western side are Madhuvana, Tālavana, Kumudavana, Bahulāvana, Kāmyavana, Khadiravana and Vṛndāvana. These are the twelve forests of the Vṛndāvana area.

TEXT 194

পথে গাভীঘটা চরে প্রভুরে দেখিয়া ।
প্রভুকে বেড়য় আসি' হুঙ্কার করিয়া ॥ ১৯৪ ॥

pathe gābhī-ghaṭā care prabhure dekhiyā
prabhuke beḍaya āsi' huṅkāra kariyā

SYNONYMS

pathe—on the road; *gābhī-ghaṭā*—groups of cows; *care*—graze; *prabhure dekhiyā*—after seeing Lord Śrī Caitanya Mahāprabhu; *prabhuke beḍaya*—they surrounded the Lord; *āsi'*—coming; *huṅ-kāra kariyā*—making a loud vibration.

TRANSLATION

When Śrī Caitanya Mahāprabhu passed through Vṛndāvana, herds of grazing cows saw Him pass and, immediately surrounding Him, began to moo very loudly.

TEXT 195

গাভী দেখি' স্তব্ধ প্রভু প্রেমের তরঙ্গে ।
বাৎসল্যে গাভী প্রভুর চাটে সব-অঙ্গে ॥ ১৯৫ ॥

gābhī dekhi' stabdha prabhu premera taraṅge
vātsalye gābhī prabhura cāṭe saba-aṅge

SYNONYMS

gābhī dekhi'—seeing the cows; *stabdha*—stunned; *prabhu*—Śrī Caitanya Mahāprabhu; *premera taraṅge*—in the waves of ecstatic love; *vātsalye*—in great affection; *gābhī*—all the cows; *prabhura*—of Śrī Caitanya Mahāprabhu; *cāṭe*—licked; *saba-aṅge*—all over the body.

TRANSLATION

Seeing the herds approach Him, the Lord was stunned with ecstatic love. The cows then began to lick His body in great affection.

TEXT 196

সুস্থ হঞা প্রভু করে অঙ্গ-কণ্ডূয়ন ।
প্রভু-সঙ্গে চলে, নাহি ছাড়ে ধেনুগণ ॥ ১৯৬ ॥

sustha hañā prabhu kare aṅga-kaṇḍūyana
prabhu-saṅge cale, nāhi chāḍe dhenu-gaṇa

SYNONYMS

sustha hañā—becoming patient; *prabhu*—Śrī Caitanya Mahāprabhu; *kare*—does; *aṅga*—of the body; *kaṇḍūyana*—scratching; *prabhu-saṅge*—with Śrī Caitanya Mahāprabhu; *cale*—go; *nāhi chāḍe*—do not give up; *dhenu-gaṇa*—all the cows.

TRANSLATION

Becoming pacified, Śrī Caitanya Mahāprabhu began to caress the cows, and the cows, being unable to give up His company, went with Him.

TEXT 197

কষ্টে-সৃষ্ট্যে ধেনু সব রাখিল গোয়াল ।
প্রভুকণ্ঠধ্বনি শুনি' আইসে মৃগীপাল ॥ ১৯৭ ॥

kaṣṭe-sṛṣṭye dhenu saba rākhila goyāla
prabhu-kaṇṭha-dhvani śuni' āise mṛgī-pāla

SYNONYMS

kaṣṭe-sṛṣṭye—with great difficulty; *dhenu*—the cows; *saba*—all; *rākhila*—kept back; *goyāla*—the cowherd men; *prabhu-kaṇṭha-dhvani*—the musical voice of Śrī Caitanya Mahāprabhu; *śuni'*—hearing; *āise*—came; *mṛgī-pāla*—flocks of deer.

TRANSLATION

It was with great difficulty that the cowherd men were able to keep the cows back. Then when the Lord chanted, all the deer heard His sweet voice and approached Him.

TEXT 198

মৃগ-মৃগী মুখ দেখি' প্রভু-অঙ্গ চাটে ।
ভয় নাহি করে, সঙ্গে যায় বাটে-বাটে ॥ ১৯৮ ॥

mṛga-mṛgī mukha dekhi' prabhu-aṅga cāṭe
bhaya nāhi kare, saṅge yāya vāṭe-vāṭe

SYNONYMS

mṛga-mṛgī—the deer, both male and female; *mukha dekhi'*—seeing His face; *prabhu-aṅga cāṭe*—began to lick the body of the Lord; *bhaya nāhi kare*—they were not at all afraid; *saṅge yāya*—go with Him; *vāṭe-vāṭe*—all along the road.

TRANSLATION

When the does and bucks came and saw the Lord's face, they began to lick His body. Not being at all afraid of Him, they accompanied Him along the path.

TEXT 199

শুক, পিক, ভৃঙ্গ প্রভুরে দেখি' 'পঞ্চম' গায় ।
শিখিগণ নৃত্য করি' প্রভু-আগে যায় ॥ ১৯৯ ॥

śuka, pika, bhṛṅga prabhure dekhi' 'pañcama' gāya
śikhi-gaṇa nṛtya kari' prabhu-āge yāya

SYNONYMS

śuka—parrots; *pika*—cuckoos; *bhṛṅga*—bumblebees; *prabhure*—Śrī Caitanya Mahāprabhu; *dekhi'*—seeing; *pañcama*—the fifth musical note; *gāya*—sing; *śikhi-gaṇa*—peacocks; *nṛtya*—dancing; *kari'*—performing; *prabhu-āge*—in front of Śrī Caitanya Mahāprabhu; *yāya*—go.

TRANSLATION

Bumblebees and birds like the parrot and cuckoo all began to sing loudly on the fifth note, and the peacocks began to dance in front of the Lord.

TEXT 200

প্রভু দেখি' বৃন্দাবনের বৃক্ষ-লতাগণে ।
অঙ্কুর-পুলক, মধু-অশ্রু বরিষণে ॥ ২০০ ॥

prabhu dekhi' vṛndāvanera vṛkṣa-latā-gaṇe
aṅkura pulaka, madhu-aśru variṣaṇe

SYNONYMS

prabhu—Śrī Caitanya Mahāprabhu; *dekhi'*—seeing; *vṛndāvane*—of Vṛndāvana; *vṛkṣa-latā-gaṇe*—the trees and creepers; *aṅkura*—twigs; *pulaka*—jubilant; *madhu-aśru*—tears in the form of honey; *variṣaṇe*—pour.

TRANSLATION

Upon seeing Śrī Caitanya Mahāprabhu, the trees and creepers of Vṛndāvana became jubilant. Their twigs stood up, and they began to shed tears of ecstasy in the form of honey.

TEXT 201

ফুল-ফল ভরি' ডাল পড়ে প্রভু-পায় ।
বন্ধু দেখি' বন্ধু যেন 'ভেট' লঞা যায় ॥ ২০১ ॥

phula-phala bhari' ḍāla paḍe prabhu-pāya
bandhu dekhi' bandhu yena 'bheṭa' lañā yāya

SYNONYMS

phula-phala bhari'—loaded with fruits and flowers; *ḍāla*—the branches; *paḍe*—fall down; *prabhu-pāya*—at the lotus feet of the Lord; *bandhu dekhi'*—

seeing one friend; *bandhu*—another friend; *yena*—as if; *bheṭa*—a presentation; *lañā*—taking; *yāya*—goes.

TRANSLATION

The trees and creepers, overloaded with fruits and flowers, fell down at the lotus feet of the Lord and greeted Him with various presentations as if they were friends.

TEXT 202

প্রভু দেখি' বৃন্দাবনের স্থাবর-জঙ্গম ।
আনন্দিত—বন্ধু যেন দেখে বন্ধুগণ ॥ ২০২ ॥

prabhu dekhi' vṛndāvanera sthāvara-jaṅgama
ānandita——bandhu yena dekhe bandhu-gaṇa

SYNONYMS

prabhu dekhi'—seeing the Lord; *vṛndāvanera*—of Vṛndāvana; *sthāvara-jaṅgama*—all living entities, moving and not moving; *ānandita*—very jubilant; *bandhu*—friend; *yena*—as if; *dekhe*—see; *bandhu-gaṇa*—friends.

TRANSLATION

Thus all the moving and nonmoving living entities of Vṛndāvana became very jubilant to see the Lord. It was as if friends were made happy by seeing another friend.

TEXT 203

তা-সবার প্রীতি দেখি' প্রভু ভাবাবেশে ।
সবা-সনে ক্রীড়া করে হঞা তার বশে ॥ ২০৩ ॥

tā-sabāra prīti dekhi' prabhu bhāvāveśe
sabā-sane krīḍā kare hañā tāra vaśe

SYNONYMS

tā-sabāra—of all of them; *prīti*—affection; *dekhi'*—seeing; *prabhu*—Śrī Caitanya Mahāprabhu; *bhāva-āveśe*—in ecstatic love; *sabā-sane*—with all of them; *krīḍā*—sporting; *kare*—performs; *hañā*—being; *tāra*—their; *vaśe*—under control.

TRANSLATION

Seeing their affection, the Lord was moved by ecstatic love. He began to sport with them exactly as a friend sports with another friend. Thus He voluntarily came under the control of His friends.

TEXT 204

প্রতি বৃক্ষ-লতা প্রভু করেন আলিঙ্গন ।
পুষ্পাদি ধ্যানে করেন কৃষ্ণে সমর্পণ ॥ ২০৪ ॥

prati vṛkṣa-latā prabhu karena āliṅgana
puṣpādi dhyāne karena kṛṣṇe samarpaṇa

SYNONYMS

prati—each and every; *vṛkṣa-latā*—tree and creeper; *prabhu*—Śrī Caitanya Mahāprabhu; *karena āliṅgana*—embraced; *puṣpa-ādi*—all the flowers and fruits; *dhyāne*—in meditation; *karena*—do; *kṛṣṇe*—unto Lord Kṛṣṇa; *samarpaṇa*—offering.

TRANSLATION

Śrī Caitanya Mahāprabhu began to embrace each and every tree and creeper, and they began to offer their fruits and flowers as if in meditation.

TEXT 205

অশ্রু-কম্প-পুলক-প্রেমে শরীর অস্থিরে ।
'কৃষ্ণ' বল, 'কৃষ্ণ' বল—বলে উচ্চৈঃস্বরে ॥ ২০৫॥

aśru-kampa-pulaka-preme śarīra asthire
'kṛṣṇa' bala, 'kṛṣṇa' bala——bale uccaiḥsvare

SYNONYMS

aśru—tears; *kampa*—trembling; *pulaka*—jubilation; *preme*—in ecstatic love; *śarīra*—the whole body; *asthire*—restless; *kṛṣṇa bala*—say Kṛṣṇa; *kṛṣṇa bala*—say Kṛṣṇa; *bale*—the Lord says; *uccaiḥ-svare*—very loudly.

TRANSLATION

The Lord's body was restless, and tears, trembling and jubilation were manifest. He said very loudly, "Chant Kṛṣṇa! Chant Kṛṣṇa!"

TEXT 206

স্থাবর-জঙ্গম মিলি' করে কৃষ্ণধ্বনি ।
প্রভুর গম্ভীর-স্বরে যেন প্রতিধ্বনি ॥ ২০৬ ॥

sthāvara-jaṅgama mili' kare kṛṣṇa-dhvani
prabhura gambhīra-svare yena prati-dhvani

SYNONYMS

sthāvara-jaṅgama—all living entities, nonmoving and moving; *mili'*—meeting together; *kare*—perform; *kṛṣṇa-dhvani*—vibration of the sound Hare Kṛṣṇa; *prabhura*—of Śrī Caitanya Mahāprabhu; *gambhīra-svare*—deep voice; *yena*—as if; *prati-dhvani*—responsive vibration.

TRANSLATION

All moving and nonmoving creatures then began to vibrate the transcendental sound of Hare Kṛṣṇa, as if they were echoing the deep sound of Caitanya Mahāprabhu.

TEXT 207

মৃগের গলা ধরি' প্রভু করেন রোদনে ।
মৃগের পুলক অঙ্গে, অশ্রু নয়নে ॥ ২০৭ ॥

mṛgera galā dhari' prabhu karena rodane
mṛgera pulaka aṅge, aśru nayane

SYNONYMS

mṛgera—of the deer; *galā dhari'*—catching the necks; *prabhu*—Śrī Caitanya Mahāprabhu; *karena*—does; *rodane*—crying; *mṛgera*—of the deer; *pulaka aṅge*—jubilation; *aśru*—tears; *nayane*—in the eyes.

TRANSLATION

The Lord then clasped the necks of the deer and began to cry. There was jubilation manifest in the bodies of the deer, and tears were in their eyes.

TEXT 208

বৃক্ষডালে শুক-শারী দিল দরশন ।
তাহা দেখি' প্রভুর কিছু শুনিতে হৈল মন ॥ ২০৮ ॥

vṛkṣa-ḍāle śuka-śārī dila daraśana
tāhā dekhi' prabhura kichu śunite haila mana

SYNONYMS

vṛkṣa-ḍāle—on a branch of a tree; *śuka-śārī*—male and female parrots; *dila*—gave; *daraśana*—appearance; *tāhā dekhi'*—seeing that; *prabhura*—of Śrī Caitanya Mahāprabhu; *kichu*—something; *śunite*—to hear; *haila*—there was; *mana*—mind.

TRANSLATION

When a male and female parrot appeared on the branches of a tree, the Lord saw them and wanted to hear them speak.

TEXT 209

শুক-শারিকা প্রভুর হাতে উড়ি' পড়ে ।
প্রভুকে শুনাঞা কৃষ্ণের গুণ-শ্লোক পড়ে ॥ ২০৯ ॥

śuka-śārikā prabhura hāte uḍi' paḍe
prabhuke śunāñā kṛṣṇera guṇa-śloka paḍe

SYNONYMS

śuka-śārikā—the parrots, male and female; *prabhura*—of Śrī Caitanya Mahāprabhu; *hāte*—on the hand; *uḍi'*—flying; *paḍe*—fall; *prabhuke*—Śrī Caitanya Mahāprabhu; *śunāñā*—causing to hear; *kṛṣṇera*—of Lord Kṛṣṇa; *guṇa-śloka paḍe*—chanted verses about the transcendental qualities.

TRANSLATION

Both parrots flew onto the hand of the Lord and began to chant the transcendental qualities of Kṛṣṇa, and the Lord listened to them.

TEXT 210

সৌন্দর্যং ললনালিধৈর্যদলনং লীলা রমাস্তম্ভিনী
বীর্যং কন্দুকিতাদ্রিবর্যমমলাঃ পারে-পরার্ধং গুণাঃ ।
শীলং সর্বজনানুরঞ্জনমহো যস্যায়মস্মৎপ্রভু-
র্বিশ্বং বিশ্বজনীনকীর্তিরবতাৎ কৃষ্ণো জগন্মোহনঃ ॥২১০॥

saundaryaṁ lalanāli-dhairya-dalanaṁ līlā ramā-stambhinī
vīryaṁ kandukitādri-varyam amalāḥ pāre-parārdhaṁ guṇāḥ
śīlaṁ sarva-janānurañjanam aho yasyāyam asmat-prabhur
viśvaṁ viśva-janīna-kīrtir avatāt kṛṣṇo jagan-mohanaḥ

SYNONYMS

saundaryam—the bodily beauty; *lalanā-āli*—of groups of *gopīs; dhairya*—the patience; *dalanam*—subduing; *līlā*—pastimes; *ramā*—the goddess of fortune; *stambhinī*—astounding; *vīryam*—strength; *kandukita*—making like a small ball for throwing; *adri-varyam*—the great mountain; *amalāḥ*—without a spot; *pāre-parārdham*—unlimited; *guṇāḥ*—qualities; *śīlam*—behavior; *sarva-jana*—all kinds of living entities; *anurañjanam*—satisfying; *aho*—oh; *yasya*—whose; *ayam*—this; *asmat-prabhuḥ*—our Lord; *viśvam*—the whole universe; *viśva-janīna*—for the benefit of everyone; *kīrtiḥ*—whose glorification; *avatāt*—may He maintain; *kṛṣṇaḥ*—Lord Kṛṣṇa; *jagat-mohanaḥ*—the attractor of the whole world.

TRANSLATION

The male parrot sang: "The glorification of Lord Kṛṣṇa, the Supreme Personality of Godhead, is beneficial to everyone in the universe. His beauty is victorious over the gopīs of Vṛndāvana, and it subdues their patience. His pastimes astound the goddess of fortune, and His bodily strength turns Govardhana Hill into a small toy like a ball. His spotless qualities are unlimited, and His behavior satisfies everyone. Lord Kṛṣṇa is attractive to everyone. Oh, may our Lord maintain the whole universe!"

PURPORT

This verse is found in the *Govinda-līlāmṛta* (13.29).

TEXT 211

শুক-মুখে শুনি' তবে কৃষ্ণের বর্ণন ।
শারিকা পড়য়ে তবে রাধিকা-বর্ণন ॥ ২১১ ॥

śuka-mukhe śuni' tabe kṛṣṇera varṇana
śārikā paḍaye tabe rādhikā-varṇana

SYNONYMS

śuka-mukhe—in the mouth of the male parrot; *śuni'*—hearing; *kṛṣṇera varṇana*—a description of Lord Kṛṣṇa; *śārikā*—female parrot; *paḍaye*—recites; *tabe*—then; *rādhikā-varṇana*—a description of Śrīmatī Rādhārāṇī.

TRANSLATION

After hearing this description of Lord Kṛṣṇa from the male parrot, the female parrot began to recite a description of Śrīmatī Rādhārāṇī.

TEXT 212

শ্রীরাধিকায়াঃ প্রিয়তা স্বরূপতা
সুশীলতা নর্তনগানচাতুরী ।
গুণালিসম্পৎ কবিতা চ রাজতে
জগন্মনোমোহন-চিত্তমোহিনী ॥ ২১২ ॥

śrī-rādhikāyāḥ priyatā surūpatā
suśīlatā nartana-gāna-cāturī
guṇāli-sampat kavitā ca rājate
jagan-mano-mohana-citta-mohinī

SYNONYMS

śrī-rādhikāyāḥ—of Śrīmatī Rādhārāṇī; *priyatā*—affection; *su-rūpatā*—exquisite beauty; *su-śīlatā*—good behavior; *nartana-gāna*—in chanting and dancing; *cāturī*—artistry; *guṇa-āli-sampat*—possession of such transcendental qualities; *kavitā*—poetry; *ca*—also; *rājate*—shine; *jagat-manaḥ-mohana*—of Kṛṣṇa, who attracts the mind of the whole universe; *citta-mohinī*—the attractor of the mind.

TRANSLATION

The female parrot said: "Śrīmatī Rādhārāṇī's affection, Her exquisite beauty and good behavior, Her artistic dancing and chanting and Her poetic compositions are all so attractive that they attract the mind of Kṛṣṇa, who attracts the mind of everyone in the universe."

PURPORT

This verse is found in the *Govinda-līlāmṛta* (13.30).

TEXT 213

পুনঃ শুক কহে,—কৃষ্ণ 'মদনমোহন'।
তবে আর শ্লোক শুক করিল পঠন ॥ ২১৩ ॥

punaḥ śuka kahe,——kṛṣṇa 'madana-mohana'
tabe āra śloka śuka karila paṭhana

SYNONYMS

punaḥ—again; *śuka*—the male parrot; *kahe*—says; *kṛṣṇa madana-mohana*—Kṛṣṇa is the conqueror of the mind of Cupid; *tabe*—thereafter; *āra*—another; *śloka*—verse; *śuka*—the male parrot; *karila paṭhana*—recited.

TRANSLATION

Thereafter the male parrot said,"Kṛṣṇa is the enchanter of the mind of Cupid." He then began to recite another verse.

TEXT 214

বংশীধারী জগন্নারী-চিত্তহারী স শারিকে।
বিহারী গোপনারীভির্জীয়ান্মদনমোহনঃ ॥ ২১৪ ॥

vaṁśī-dhārī jagan-nārī-
citta-hārī sa śārike
vihārī gopa-nārībhir
jīyān madana-mohanaḥ

SYNONYMS

vaṁśī-dhārī—the carrier of the flute; *jagat-nārī*—of all women of the universe; *citta-hārī*—the stealer of the hearts; *saḥ*—He; *śārike*—my dear *śārī; vihārī*—enjoyer; *gopa-nārībhiḥ*—with the *gopīs; jīyāt*—let Him be glorified; *madana*—of Cupid; *mohanaḥ*—the enchanter.

TRANSLATION

The parrot then said, "My dear śārī [female parrot], Śrī Kṛṣṇa carries a flute and enchants the hearts of all women throughout the universe. He is specifically the enjoyer of beautiful gopīs, and He is the enchanter of Cupid also. Let Him be glorified!"

PURPORT

This verse is also found in the *Govinda-līlāmṛta* (13.31).

TEXT 215

পুনঃ শারী কহে শুকে করি' পরিহাস ।
তাহা শুনি' প্রভুর হৈল বিস্ময়-প্রেমোল্লাস ॥ ২১৫ ॥

punaḥ śārī kahe śuke kari' parihāsa
tāhā śuni' prabhura haila vismaya-premollāsa

SYNONYMS

punaḥ—again; *śārī kahe*—the female parrot said; *śuke*—unto the male parrot; *kari' parihāsa*—jokingly; *tāhā śuni'*—hearing that; *prabhura*—of Śrī Caitanya Mahāprabhu; *haila*—there was; *vismaya*—wonderful; *prema-ullāsa*—awakening of ecstatic love.

TRANSLATION

Then the female parrot began to speak jokingly to śuka, and Śrī Caitanya Mahāprabhu was struck with wonderful ecstatic love to hear her speak.

TEXT 216

রাধা-সঙ্গে যদা ভাতি তদা 'মদনমোহনঃ' ।
অন্যথা বিশ্বমোহোঽপি স্বয়ং 'মদনমোহিতঃ' ॥২১৬॥

rādhā-saṅge yadā bhāti
tadā 'madana-mohanaḥ'
anyathā viśva-moho 'pi
svayaṁ 'madana-mohitaḥ'

SYNONYMS

rādhā-saṅge—with Śrīmatī Rādhārāṇī; *yadā*—when; *bhāti*—shines; *tadā*—at that time; *madana-mohanaḥ*—the enchanter of the mind of Cupid; *anyathā*—otherwise; *viśva-mohaḥ*—the enchanter of the whole universe; *api*—even though; *svayam*—personally; *madana-mohitaḥ*—enchanted by Cupid.

TRANSLATION

The parrot śārī said, "When Lord Śrī Kṛṣṇa is with Rādhārāṇī, He is the enchanter of Cupid; otherwise, when He is alone, He Himself is enchanted by erotic feelings even though He enchants the whole universe."

PURPORT

This is another verse from the *Govinda-līlāmṛta* (13.32).

TEXT 217

শুক-শারী উড়ি' পুনঃ গেল বৃক্ষডালে ।
ময়ূরের নৃত্য প্রভু দেখে কুতুহলে ॥ ২১৭ ॥

śuka-śārī uḍi' punaḥ gela vṛkṣa-ḍāle
mayūrera nṛtya prabhu dekhe kutūhale

SYNONYMS

śuka-śārī—the male and female parrots; *uḍi'*—flying; *punaḥ*—again; *gela*—went; *vṛkṣa-ḍāle*—to the branch of a tree; *mayūrera*—of the peacocks; *nṛtya*—dancing; *prabhu*—Śrī Caitanya Mahāprabhu; *dekhe*—sees; *kutūhale*—with curiosity.

TRANSLATION

Both parrots then flew onto a tree branch, and Śrī Caitanya Mahāprabhu began to watch the dancing of peacocks with curiosity.

TEXT 218

ময়ূরের কণ্ঠ দেখি' প্রভুর কৃষ্ণস্মৃতি হৈল ।
প্রেমাবেশে মহাপ্রভু ভূমিতে পড়িল ॥ ২১৮ ॥

mayūrera kaṇṭha dekhi' prabhura kṛṣṇa-smṛti haila
premāveśe mahāprabhu bhūmite paḍila

SYNONYMS

mayūrera—of the peacocks; *kaṇṭha*—necks; *dekhi'*—seeing; *prabhura*—of Śrī Caitanya Mahāprabhu; *kṛṣṇa-smṛti*—remembrance of Lord Kṛṣṇa; *haila*—there was; *prema-āveśe*—in ecstatic love; *mahāprabhu*—Śrī Caitanya Mahāprabhu; *bhūmite*—on the ground; *paḍila*—fell down.

TRANSLATION

When the Lord saw the bluish necks of the peacocks, His remembrance of Kṛṣṇa immediately awakened, and He fell to the ground in ecstatic love.

TEXT 219

প্রভুরে মূর্চ্ছিত দেখি' সেই ত ব্রাহ্মণ ।
ভট্টাচার্য-সঙ্গে করে প্রভুর সন্তর্পণ ॥ ২১৯ ॥

prabhure mūrcchita dekhi' sei ta brāhmaṇa
bhaṭṭācārya-saṅge kare prabhura santarpaṇa

SYNONYMS

prabhure—Śrī Caitanya Mahāprabhu; *mūrcchita*—unconscious; *dekhi'*—seeing; *sei ta brāhmaṇa*—indeed that *brāhmaṇa; bhaṭṭācārya-saṅge*—with Bhaṭṭācārya; *kare*—does; *prabhura*—of Śrī Caitanya Mahāprabhu; *santarpaṇa*—taking care.

TRANSLATION

When the brāhmaṇa saw that Śrī Caitanya Mahāprabhu was unconscious, he and Balabhadra Bhaṭṭācārya took care of Him.

TEXT 220

আস্তে-ব্যস্তে মহাপ্রভুর লঞা বহির্বাস ।
জলসেক করে অঙ্গে, বস্ত্রের বাতাস ॥ ২২০ ॥

āste-vyaste mahāprabhura lañā bahirvāsa
jala-seka kare aṅge, vastrera vātāsa

SYNONYMS

āste-vyaste—with great haste; *mahāprabhura*—of Śrī Caitanya Mahāprabhu; *lañā*—taking; *bahirvāsa*—covering cloth; *jala-seka kare*—sprinkle water; *aṅge*—on the body; *vastrera vātāsa*—fanning with the cloth.

TRANSLATION

They hastily sprinkled water over the Lord's body. Then they took up His cloth and began to fan Him with it.

TEXT 221

প্রভু-কর্ণে কৃষ্ণনাম কহে উচ্চ করি' ।
চেতন পাঞা প্রভু যা'ন গড়াগড়ি ॥ ২২১ ॥

prabhu-karṇe kṛṣṇa-nāma kahe ucca kari'
cetana pāñā prabhu yā'na gaḍāgaḍi

SYNONYMS

prabhu-karṇe—in the ear of Śrī Caitanya Mahāprabhu; *kṛṣṇa-nāma*—the holy name of Lord Kṛṣṇa; *kahe*—chant; *ucca kari'*—loudly; *cetana pāñā*—coming to consciousness; *prabhu*—Śrī Caitanya Mahāprabhu; *yā'na*—goes; *gaḍāgaḍi*—rolling on the ground.

TRANSLATION

They then began to chant the holy name of Kṛṣṇa into the Lord's ear. When the Lord regained consciousness, He began rolling on the ground.

TEXT 222

কণ্টক-দুর্গম বনে অঙ্গ ক্ষত হৈল ।
ভট্টাচার্য কোলে করি' প্রভুরে সুস্থ কৈল ॥ ২২২ ॥

kaṇṭaka-durgama vane aṅga kṣata haila
bhaṭṭācārya kole kari' prabhure sustha kaila

SYNONYMS

kaṇṭaka-durgama—difficult to traverse because of thorns; *vane*—in the forest; *aṅga*—the body; *kṣata haila*—became injured; *bhaṭṭācārya*—Balabhadra Bhaṭṭācārya; *kole kari'*—taking Him on his lap; *prabhure*—Śrī Caitanya Mahāprabhu; *sustha kaila*—pacified.

TRANSLATION

When the Lord rolled on the ground, sharp thorns injured His body. Taking Him on his lap, Balabhadra Bhaṭṭācārya pacified Him.

TEXT 223

কৃষ্ণাবেশে প্রভুর প্রেমে গরগর মন।
'বোল্' 'বোল্' করি' উঠি' করেন নর্তন ॥ ২২৩ ॥

kṛṣṇāveśe prabhura preme garagara mana
'bol' 'bol' kari' uṭhi' karena nartana

SYNONYMS

kṛṣṇa-āveśe—in ecstatic love of Kṛṣṇa; *prabhura*—of Śrī Caitanya Mahāprabhu; *preme*—by love; *garagara*—disturbed; *mana*—mind; *bol bol*—chant, chant; *kari'*—saying; *uṭhi'*—standing up; *karena nartana*—began to dance.

TRANSLATION

Śrī Caitanya Mahāprabhu's mind wandered in ecstatic love of Kṛṣṇa. He immediately stood up and said, "Chant! Chant!" Then He Himself began to dance.

TEXT 224

ভট্টাচার্য,সেই বিপ্র 'কৃষ্ণনাম' গায়।
নাচিতে নাচিতে পথে প্রভু চলি' যায় ॥ ২২৪ ॥

bhaṭṭācārya, sei vipra 'kṛṣṇa-nāma' gāya
nācite nācite pathe prabhu cali' yāya

SYNONYMS

bhaṭṭācārya—Bhaṭṭācārya; *sei vipra*—that *brāhmaṇa; kṛṣṇa-nāma gāya*—chant the holy name of Kṛṣṇa; *nācite nācite*—dancing and dancing; *pathe*—on the road; *prabhu*—Śrī Caitanya Mahāprabhu; *cali' yāya*—goes forward.

TRANSLATION

Being thus ordered by the Lord, both Balabhadra Bhaṭṭācārya and the brāhmaṇa began to chant the holy name of Kṛṣṇa. Then the Lord, dancing and dancing, proceeded along the path.

TEXT 225

প্রভুর প্রেমাবেশ দেখি' ব্রাহ্মণ -বিস্মিত।
প্রভুর রক্ষা লাগি' বিপ্র হইলা চিন্তিত ॥ ২২৫ ॥

prabhura premāveśa dekhi' brāhmaṇa——vismita
prabhura rakṣā lāgi' vipra ha-ilā cintita

SYNONYMS

prabhura—of Śrī Caitanya Mahāprabhu; *prema-āveśa*—ecstatic love; *dekhi'*—seeing; *brāhmaṇa*—the *brāhmaṇa; vismita*—astonished; *prabhura*—of Śrī Caitanya Mahāprabhu; *rakṣā lāgi'*—for the protection; *vipra*—the *brāhmaṇa; ha-ilā*—became; *cintita*—very anxious.

TRANSLATION

The brāhmaṇa was astounded to see the symptoms of ecstatic love exhibited by Śrī Caitanya Mahāprabhu. He then became anxious to give the Lord protection.

TEXT 226

নীলাচলে ছিলা যৈছে প্রেমাবেশ মন।
বৃন্দাবন যাইতে পথে হৈল শত-গুণ ॥ ২২৬ ॥

nīlācale chilā yaiche premāveśa mana
vṛndāvana yāite pathe haila śata-guṇa

SYNONYMS

nīlācale—at Jagannātha Purī; *chilā*—was; *yaiche*—as; *prema-āveśa mana*—always in a mentality of ecstatic love; *vṛndāvana*—to Vṛndāvana; *yāite*—going; *pathe*—on the road; *haila*—became; *śata-guṇa*—one hundred times.

TRANSLATION

Śrī Caitanya Mahāprabhu's mind was absorbed in ecstatic love at Jagannātha Purī, but when He passed along the road on the way to Vṛndāvana, that love increased a hundred times.

TEXT 227

সহস্রগুণ প্রেম বাড়ে মথুরা দরশনে।
লক্ষগুণ প্রেম বাড়ে, ভ্রমেন যবে বনে ॥ ২২৭ ॥

sahasra-guṇa prema bāḍe mathurā daraśane
lakṣa-guṇa prema bāḍe, bhramena yabe vane

SYNONYMS

sahasra-guṇa—one thousand times; *prema*—love; *bāḍe*—increased; *mathurā*—Mathurā; *daraśane*—upon seeing; *lakṣa-guṇa*—a hundred thousand times; *prema bāḍe*—love increases; *bhramena*—wanders; *yabe*—when; *vane*—in the forests of Vṛndāvana.

TRANSLATION

The Lord's ecstatic love increased a thousand times when He visited Mathurā, but it increased a hundred thousand times when He wandered in the forests of Vṛndāvana.

TEXTS 228-229

অন্য-দেশ প্রেম উছলে 'বৃন্দাবন'-নামে ।
সাক্ষাৎ ভ্রময়ে এবে সেই বৃন্দাবনে ॥ ২২৮ ॥
প্রেমে গরগর মন রাত্রি-দিবসে ।
স্নান-ভিক্ষাদি-নির্বাহ করেন অভ্যাসে ॥ ২২৯ ॥

anya-deśa prema uchale 'vṛndāvana'-nāme
sākṣāt bhramaye ebe sei vṛndāvane

preme garagara mana rātri-divase
snāna-bhikṣādi-nirvāha karena abhyāse

SYNONYMS

anya-deśa—in other countries; *prema*—love; *uchale*—increases; *vṛndāvana-nāme*—by the name of Vṛndāvana; *sākṣāt*—directly; *bhramaye*—travels; *ebe*—now; *sei vṛndāvane*—in that Vṛndāvana; *preme*—in ecstatic love; *garagara*—faltering; *mana*—mind; *rātri-divase*—day and night; *snāna-bhikṣā-ādi*—bathing and accepting food; *nirvāha*—accomplishing; *karena*—does; *abhyāse*—by habit.

TRANSLATION

When Śrī Caitanya Mahāprabhu was elsewhere, the very name of Vṛndāvana was sufficient to increase His ecstatic love. Now, when He was actually traveling in the Vṛndāvana forest, His mind was absorbed in great ecstatic love day and night. He ate and bathed simply out of habit.

TEXT 230

এইমত প্রেম—যাবৎ ভ্রমিল 'বার' বন ।
একত্র লিখিলুঁ, সর্বত্র না যায় বর্ণন ॥ ২৩০ ॥

ei-mata prema——yāvat bhramila 'bāra' vana
ekatra likhiluṅ, sarvatra nā yāya varṇana

SYNONYMS

ei-mata—in this way; *prema*—ecstatic love; *yāvat*—so long; *bhramila*—He traveled; *bāra vana*—through the twelve forests of Vṛndāvana; *ekatra*—in one place; *likhiluṅ*—I have written; *sarvatra*—everywhere; *nā yāya varṇana*—cannot be described.

TRANSLATION

Thus I have written a description of the ecstatic love Lord Caitanya manifested while He walked through the twelve forests of Vṛndāvana. To describe it all would be impossible.

TEXT 231

বৃন্দাবনে হৈল প্রভুর যতেক প্রেমের বিকার ।
কোটি-গ্রন্থে 'অনন্ত' লিখেন তাহার বিস্তার ॥ ২৩১ ॥

vṛndāvane haila prabhura yateka premera vikāra
koṭi-granthe 'ananta' likhena tāhāra vistāra

SYNONYMS

vṛndāvane—in Vṛndāvana; *haila*—there were; *prabhura*—of Śrī Caitanya Mahāprabhu; *yateka*—as many; *premera vikāra*—transformations of ecstasy; *koṭi-granthe*—in millions of books; *ananta*—Lord Ananta; *likhena*—writes; *tāhāra*—of them; *vistāra*—elaboration.

TRANSLATION

Lord Ananta writes millions of books elaborately describing the transformations of ecstatic love experienced by Śrī Caitanya Mahāprabhu in Vṛndāvana.

TEXT 232

তবু লিখিবারে নারে তার এক কণ ।
উদ্দেশ করিতে করি দিগ্‌দরশন ॥ ২৩২ ॥

tabu likhibāre nāre tāra eka kaṇa
uddeśa karite kari dig-daraśana

SYNONYMS

tabu—yet; *likhibāre*—to write; *nāre*—is not able; *tāra*—of that; *eka*—one; *kaṇa*—fragment; *uddeśa*—indication; *karite*—to make; *kari*—I perform; *dik-daraśana*—pointing out the direction.

TRANSLATION

Since Lord Ananta Himself cannot describe even a fragment of these pastimes, I am simply pointing out the direction.

TEXT 233

জগৎ ভাসিল চৈতন্যলীলার পাথারে ।
যাঁর যত শক্তি তত পাথারে সাঁতারে ॥ ২৩৩ ॥

jagat bhāsila caitanya-līlāra pāthāre
yāṅra yata śakti tata pāthāre sāṅtāre

SYNONYMS

jagat—the whole world; *bhāsila*—floated; *caitanya-līlāra*—of the pastimes of Śrī Caitanya Mahāprabhu; *pāthāre*—in the inundation; *yāṅra*—of whom; *yata*—as much; *śakti*—power; *tata*—that much; *pāthāre*—in the inundation; *sāṅtāre*—swims.

TRANSLATION

The whole world became merged in the inundation of the pastimes of Śrī Caitanya Mahāprabhu. One can swim in that water to the extent that he has the strength.

TEXT 234

শ্রীরূপ-রঘুনাথ-পদে যার আশ ।
চৈতন্যচরিতামৃত কহে কৃষ্ণদাস ॥ ২৩৪ ॥

śrī-rūpa-raghunātha-pade yāra āśa
caitanya-caritāmṛta kahe kṛṣṇadāsa

SYNONYMS

śrī-rūpa—Śrīla Rūpa Gosvāmī; *raghunātha*—Śrīla Raghunātha dāsa Gosvāmī; *pade*—at the lotus feet; *yāra*—whose; *āśa*—expectation; *caitanya-caritāmṛta*—the book named *Caitanya-caritāmṛta;* *kahe*—describes; *kṛṣṇadāsa*—Śrīla Kṛṣṇadāsa Kavirāja Gosvāmī.

TRANSLATION

Praying at the lotus feet of Śrī Rūpa and Śrī Raghunātha, always desiring their mercy, I, Kṛṣṇadāsa, narrate Śrī Caitanya-caritāmṛta, following in their footsteps.

Thus end the Bhaktivedanta purports to the Śrī Caitanya-caritāmṛta, Madhya-līlā, *Seventeenth Chapter, describing the Lord's traveling to Vṛndāvana.*

CHAPTER 18

Lord Śrī Caitanya Mahāprabhu's Visit to Śrī Vṛndāvana

The following summary of the Eighteenth Chapter is given by Śrīla Bhaktivinoda Ṭhākura in his *Amṛta-pravāha-bhāṣya.* In the village of Āriṭ-grāma, Śrī Caitanya Mahāprabhu discovered the transcendental lakes known as Rādhā-kuṇḍa and Śyāma-kuṇḍa. He then saw the Deity Harideva at Govardhana Village. Śrī Caitanya Mahāprabhu had no desire to climb Govardhana Hill because the hill is worshiped as Kṛṣṇa. The Gopāla Deity could understand the mind of Śrī Caitanya Mahāprabhu; therefore on the plea of being attacked by Muslims, Gopāla transferred Himself to the village of Gāṅṭhuli-grāma. Śrī Caitanya Mahāprabhu then went to Gāṅṭhuli-grāma to see Lord Gopāla. Some years later, Lord Gopāla also went to Mathurā to the temple of Viṭhṭhaleśvara and stayed there for one month just to give an audience to Śrīla Rūpa Gosvāmī.

After visiting Nandīśvara, Pāvana-sarovara, Śeṣaśāyī, Khelā-tīrtha, Bhāṇḍīravana, Bhadravana, Lohavana and Mahāvana, Śrī Caitanya Mahāprabhu went to Gokula and then finally returned to Mathurā. Seeing a great crowd in Mathurā, He moved His residence near Akrūra-ghāṭa, and from there He went every day to Vṛndāvana to see Kālīya-hrada, Dvādaśāditya-ghāṭa, Keśī-ghāṭa, Rāsa-sthalī, Cīra-ghāṭa and Āmli-talā. At Kālīya Lake, many people mistook a fisherman for Kṛṣṇa. When some respectable people came to see Śrī Caitanya Mahāprabhu, they expressed their opinion that when one takes *sannyāsa,* he becomes Nārāyaṇa. Their mistake was corrected by the Lord. In this way, their Kṛṣṇa consciousness was awakened, and they could understand that a *sannyāsī* is simply a living entity and not the Supreme Personality of Godhead.

When Śrī Caitanya Mahāprabhu took His bath at Akrūra-ghāṭa, He submerged Himself in the water for a long time. Balabhadra Bhaṭṭācārya decided to take Śrī Caitanya Mahāprabhu to Prayāga after visiting the holy place known as Soro-kṣetra. While stopping near a village on the way to Prayāga, Śrī Caitanya Mahāprabhu fainted in ecstatic love. Some Pāṭhāna soldiers who were passing through saw Śrī Caitanya Mahāprabhu and falsely concluded that the Lord's associates, Balabhadra Bhaṭṭācārya and others, had killed the Lord with a poison named *dhuturā* and were taking His wealth. Thus the soldiers arrested them. However, when Śrī Caitanya Mahāprabhu regained His senses, His associates were released. He talked with a person who was supposed to be a holy man in the party. From the Koran, Śrī Caitanya Mahāprabhu established devotional service to Kṛṣṇa. Thus the leader of the soldiers, named Vijalī Khān, surrendered to Śrī

Caitanya Mahāprabhu, and he and his party became devotees of Lord Kṛṣṇa. The same village today is known as the village of Pāṭhāna Vaiṣṇavas. After bathing in the Ganges at Soro, Śrī Caitanya Mahāprabhu arrived at Prayāga at the confluence of three rivers—the Ganges, Yamunā and Sarasvatī.

TEXT 1

বৃন্দাবনে স্থিরচরান্নন্দয়ন্ স্বাবলোকনৈঃ ।
আত্মানঞ্চ তদালোকাদ্গৌরাঙ্গঃ পরিতোঽভ্রমৎ ॥১॥

vṛndāvane sthira-carān
nandayan svāvalokanaiḥ
ātmānaṁ ca tad-ālokād
gaurāṅgaḥ parito 'bhramat

SYNONYMS

vṛndāvane—in Vṛndāvana; *sthira-carān*—to the living entities, both moving and not moving; *nandayan*—giving pleasure; *sva-avalokanaiḥ*—by His personal glances; *ātmānam*—to Himself; *ca*—also; *tat-ālokāt*—by seeing them; *gaurāṅgaḥ*—Śrī Caitanya Mahāprabhu; *paritaḥ*—all around; *abhramat*—traveled.

TRANSLATION

Śrī Caitanya Mahāprabhu traveled all over Vṛndāvana and pleased all living entities, moving and nonmoving, with His glances. The Lord took much personal pleasure in seeing everyone. In this way Lord Gaurāṅga traveled in Vṛndāvana.

TEXT 2

জয় জয় গৌরচন্দ্র জয় নিত্যানন্দ ।
জয়াদ্বৈতচন্দ্র জয় গৌরভক্তবৃন্দ ॥ ২ ॥

jaya jaya gauracandra jaya nityānanda
jayādvaita-candra jaya gaura-bhakta-vṛnda

SYNONYMS

jaya jaya—all glories; *gauracandra*—to Lord Gauracandra (Śrī Caitanya Mahāprabhu); *jaya*—all glories; *nityānanda*—to Lord Nityānanda Prabhu; *jaya*—all glories; *advaita-candra*—to Śrī Advaita Gosāñi; *jaya*—all glories; *gaura-bhakta-vṛnda*—to the devotees of Lord Caitanya.

TRANSLATION

All glories to Lord Gauracandra! All glories to Nityānanda Prabhu! All glories to Advaita Prabhu! And all glories to the devotees of Lord Caitanya headed by Śrīvāsa Ṭhākura!

TEXT 3

এইমত মহাপ্রভু নাচিতে নাচিতে।
'আরিট্'-গ্রামে আসি' 'বাহ্য' হৈল আচম্বিতে ॥ ৩ ॥

ei-mata mahāprabhu nācite nācite
'āriṭ'-grāme āsi' 'bāhya' haila ācambite

SYNONYMS

ei-mata—in this way; *mahāprabhu*—Śrī Caitanya Mahāprabhu; *nācite nācite*—dancing and dancing; *āriṭ-grāme*—in the village known as Āriṭ-grāma; *āsi'*—coming; *bāhya*—sense perception; *haila*—there was; *ācambite*—suddenly.

TRANSLATION

Śrī Caitanya Mahāprabhu danced in ecstasy, but when He arrived at Āriṭ-grāma, His sense perception was awakened.

PURPORT

Āriṭ-grāma is also called Ariṣṭa-grāma. Śrī Caitanya Mahāprabhu understood that in that village, Ariṣṭāsura was killed by Śrī Kṛṣṇa. While there, He inquired about Rādhā-kuṇḍa, but no one could tell Him where it was. The *brāhmaṇa* accompanying Him could also not ascertain its whereabouts. Śrī Caitanya Mahāprabhu could then understand that the holy places known as Rādhā-kuṇḍa and Śyāma-kuṇḍa were at that time lost to everyone's vision. He therefore discovered Rādhā-kuṇḍa and Śyāma-kuṇḍa, which were two reservoirs of water in two paddy fields. Although there was very little water, Śrī Caitanya Mahāprabhu was omniscient and could understand that formerly these two ponds were called Śrī Rādhā-kuṇḍa and Śyāma-kuṇḍa. In this way Rādhā-kuṇḍa and Śyāma-kuṇḍa were discovered.

TEXT 4

আরিটে রাধাকুণ্ড-বার্তা পুছে লোক-স্থানে।
কেহ নাহি কহে, সঙ্গের ব্রাহ্মণ না জানে ॥ ৪ ॥

āriṭe rādhā-kuṇḍa-vārtā puche loka-sthāne
keha nāhi kahe, saṅgera brāhmaṇa nā jāne

SYNONYMS

ārite—in the village known as Ārit-grāma; *rādhā-kuṇḍa-vārtā*—news of Rādhā-kuṇḍa; *puche*—inquires; *loka-sthāne*—from the local people; *keha*—anyone; *nāhi*—not; *kahe*—could say; *saṅgera*—the companion; *brāhmaṇa*—*brāhmaṇa;* *nā jāne*—does not know.

TRANSLATION

Śrī Caitanya Mahāprabhu asked the local people, "Where is Rādhā-kuṇḍa?" No one could inform Him, and the brāhmaṇa accompanying Him did not know either.

TEXT 5

তীর্থ 'লুপ্ত' জানি' প্রভু সর্বজ্ঞ ভগবান্ ।
দুই ধান্যক্ষেত্রে অল্পজলে কৈলা স্নান ॥ ৫ ॥

tīrtha 'lupta' jāni' prabhu sarvajña bhagavān
dui dhānya-kṣetre alpa-jale kailā snāna

SYNONYMS

tīrtha—holy place; *lupta*—lost; *jāni'*—knowing; *prabhu*—Śrī Caitanya Mahāprabhu; *sarva-jña*—omniscient; *bhagavān*—the Supreme Personality of Godhead; *dui*—two; *dhānya-kṣetre*—in paddy fields; *alpa-jale*—in not very deep water; *kailā snāna*—took a bath.

TRANSLATION

The Lord then understood that the holy place called Rādhā-kuṇḍa was no longer visible. However, being the omniscient Supreme Personality of Godhead, He discovered Rādhā-kuṇḍa and Śyāma-kuṇḍa in two paddy fields. There was only a little water, but He took His bath there.

TEXT 6

দেখি' সব গ্রাম্য-লোকের বিস্ময় হৈল মন ।
প্রেমে প্রভু করে রাধাকুণ্ডের স্তবন ॥ ৬ ॥

dekhi' saba grāmya-lokera vismaya haila mana
preme prabhu kare rādhā-kuṇḍera stavana

SYNONYMS

dekhi'—seeing; *saba grāmya-lokera*—of all the people of the village; *vismaya haila*—became astonished; *mana*—the minds; *preme*—in ecstatic love; *prabhu*—

Śrī Caitanya Mahāprabhu; *kare*—does; *rādhā-kuṇḍera*—of Rādhā-kuṇḍa; *stavana*—prayers.

TRANSLATION

When the people of the village saw Śrī Caitanya Mahāprabhu taking His bath in those two ponds in the middle of the paddy fields, they were very astonished. The Lord then offered His prayers to Śrī Rādhā-kuṇḍa.

TEXT 7

সব গোপী হৈতে রাধা কৃষ্ণের প্রেয়সী ।
তৈছে রাধাকুণ্ড প্রিয় 'প্রিয়ার সরসী' ॥ ৭ ॥

saba gopī haite rādhā kṛṣṇera preyasī
taiche rādhā-kuṇḍa priya 'priyāra sarasī'

SYNONYMS

saba—all; *gopī*—the *gopīs; haite*—from; *rādhā*—Rādhārāṇī; *kṛṣṇera*—of Lord Kṛṣṇa; *preyasī*—most beloved; *taiche*—similarly; *rādhā-kuṇḍa*—Rādhā-kuṇḍa; *priya*—very dear; *priyāra sarasī*—the lake of the most beloved Rādhārāṇī.

TRANSLATION

"Of all the gopīs, Rādhārāṇī is the dearmost. Similarly, the lake known as Rādhā-kuṇḍa is very dear to the Lord because it is very dear to Śrīmatī Rādhārāṇī.

TEXT 8

যথা রাধা প্রিয়া বিষ্ণোস্তস্যাঃ কুণ্ডং প্রিয়ং তথা ।
সর্বগোপীষু সৈবৈকা বিষ্ণোরত্যন্তবল্লভা ॥ ৮ ॥

yathā rādhā priyā viṣṇos
tasyāḥ kuṇḍaṁ priyaṁ tathā
sarva-gopīṣu saivaikā
viṣṇor atyanta-vallabhā

SYNONYMS

yathā—as; *rādhā*—Śrīmatī Rādhārāṇī; *priyā*—beloved; *viṣṇoḥ*—of Lord Kṛṣṇa; *tasyāḥ*—Her; *kuṇḍam*—lake; *priyam*—very dear; *tathā*—similarly; *sarva-gopīṣu*—

among all the *gopīs; sā*—She; *eva*—certainly; *ekā*—alone; *viṣṇoḥ*—of Lord Kṛṣṇa; *atyanta*—very much; *vallabhā*—dear.

TRANSLATION

" 'Śrīmatī Rādhārāṇī is most dear to Lord Kṛṣṇa, and Her lake known as Rādhā-kuṇḍa is also very dear to Him. Of all the gopīs, Śrīmatī Rādhārāṇī is certainly the most beloved.'

PURPORT

This is a verse from the *Padma Purāṇa.*

TEXT 9

**যেই কুণ্ডে নিত্য কৃষ্ণ রাধিকার সঙ্গে ।
জলে জলকেলি করে, তীরে রাস-রঙ্গে ॥ ৯ ॥**

yei kuṇḍe nitya kṛṣṇa rādhikāra saṅge
jale jala-keli kare, tīre rāsa-raṅge

SYNONYMS

yei kuṇḍe—in which lake; *nitya*—daily; *kṛṣṇa*—Lord Kṛṣṇa; *rādhikāra saṅge*—accompanied by Śrīmatī Rādhārāṇī; *jale*—in the water; *jala-keli*—sporting in the water; *kare*—performs; *tīre*—on the bank; *rāsa-raṅge*—His *rāsa* dance.

TRANSLATION

"In that lake, Lord Kṛṣṇa and Śrīmatī Rādhārāṇī used to sport daily in the water and have a rāsa dance on the bank.

TEXT 10

**সেই কুণ্ডে যেই একবার করে স্নান ।
তাঁরে রাধা-সম 'প্রেম' কৃষ্ণ করে দান ॥ ১০ ॥**

sei kuṇḍe yei eka-bāra kare snāna
tāṅre rādhā-sama 'prema' kṛṣṇa kare dāna

SYNONYMS

sei kuṇḍe—in that lake; *yei*—anyone who; *eka-bāra*—once; *kare snāna*—takes a bath; *tāṅre*—unto him; *rādhā-sama*—like Śrīmatī Rādhārāṇī; *prema*—ecstatic love; *kṛṣṇa*—Lord Kṛṣṇa; *kare dāna*—gives as charity.

TRANSLATION

"Indeed, Lord Kṛṣṇa gives ecstatic love like that of Śrīmatī Rādhārāṇī to whoever bathes in that lake even once in his life.

TEXT 11

কুণ্ডের 'মাধুরী'—যেন রাধার 'মধুরিমা'।
কুণ্ডের 'মহিমা'—যেন রাধার 'মহিমা' ॥ ১১ ॥

kuṇḍera 'mādhurī'——yena rādhāra 'madhurimā'
kuṇḍera 'mahimā'——yena rādhāra 'mahimā'

SYNONYMS

kuṇḍera—of the lake; *mādhurī*—sweetness; *yena*—as if; *rādhāra*—of Śrīmatī Rādhārāṇī; *madhurimā*—sweetness; *kuṇḍera*—of the lake; *mahimā*—glories; *yena*—as if; *rādhāra*—of Śrīmatī Rādhārāṇī; *mahimā*—glories.

TRANSLATION

"The attraction of Rādhā-kuṇḍa is as sweet as that of Śrīmatī Rādhārāṇī. Similarly, the glories of the kuṇḍa [lake] are as glorious as Śrīmatī Rādhārāṇī.

TEXT 12

শ্রীরাধেব হরেস্তদীয়সরসী প্রেষ্ঠাদ্ভুতৈঃ স্বৈর্গুণৈ-
র্যস্যাং শ্রীযুত-মাধবেন্দুরনিশং প্রীত্যা তয়া ক্রীড়তি।
প্রেমাস্মিন্ বত রাধিকেব লভতে যস্যাং সকৃৎ স্নানকৃৎ
তস্যা বৈ মহিমা তথা মধুরিমা কেনাস্তু বর্ণ্যঃ ক্ষিতৌ ॥১২॥

śrī-rādheva hares tadīya-sarasī preṣṭhādbhutaiḥ svair guṇair
yasyāṁ śrī-yuta-mādhavendur aniśaṁ prītyā tayā krīḍati
premāsmin bata rādhikeva labhate yasyāṁ sakṛt snāna-kṛt
tasyā vai mahimā tathā madhurimā kenāstu varṇyaḥ kṣitau

SYNONYMS

śrī-rādhā—Śrīmatī Rādhārāṇī; *iva*—like; *hareḥ*—of Kṛṣṇa; *tadīya*—Her; *sarasī*—lake; *preṣṭhā*—very dear; *adbhutaiḥ*—by wonderful; *svaiḥ*—own; *guṇaiḥ*—transcendental qualities; *yasyām*—in which; *śrī-yuta*—all-opulent; *mādhava*—Śrī Kṛṣṇa; *induḥ*—like the moon; *aniśam*—incessantly; *prītyā*—with great affection; *tayā*—in association with Śrīmatī Rādhārāṇī; *krīḍati*—performs pastimes; *premā*—

love; *asmin*—for Lord Kṛṣṇa; *bata*—certainly; *rādhikā iva*—exactly like Śrīmatī Rādhārāṇī; *labhate*—obtains; *yasyām*—in which; *sakṛt*—once; *snāna-kṛt*—one who takes a bath; *tasyāḥ*—of the lake; *vai*—certainly; *mahimā*—glories; *tathā*—as well as; *madhurimā*—sweetness; *kena*—by whom; *astu*—can be; *varṇyaḥ*—described; *kṣitau*—on this earth.

TRANSLATION

" 'Because of its wonderful transcendental qualities, Rādhā-kuṇḍa is as dear to Kṛṣṇa as Śrīmatī Rādhārāṇī. It was in that lake that the all-opulent Lord Śrī Kṛṣṇa performed His pastimes with Śrīmatī Rādhārāṇī with great pleasure and transcendental bliss. Whoever bathes just once in Rādhā-kuṇḍa attains Śrīmatī Rādhārāṇī's loving attraction for Śrī Kṛṣṇa. Who within this world can describe the glories and sweetness of Śrī Rādhā-kuṇḍa?' "

PURPORT

This verse is found in the *Govinda-līlāmṛta* (7.102).

TEXT 13

এইমত স্তুতি করে প্রেমাবিষ্ট হঞা ।
তীরে নৃত্য করে কুণ্ডলীলা সঙরিয়া ॥ ১৩ ॥

ei-mata stuti kare premāviṣṭa hañā
tīre nṛtya kare kuṇḍa-līlā saṅariyā

SYNONYMS

ei-mata—in this way; *stuti kare*—offers prayers; *prema-āviṣṭa*—overwhelmed by ecstatic love; *hañā*—becoming; *tīre*—on the bank; *nṛtya kare*—dances; *kuṇḍa-līlā*—pastimes of Rādhā-kuṇḍa; *saṅariyā*—remembering.

TRANSLATION

Śrī Caitanya Mahāprabhu thus offered prayers to Rādhā-kuṇḍa. Overwhelmed by ecstatic love, He danced on the bank, remembering the pastimes Lord Kṛṣṇa performed on the bank of Rādhā-kuṇḍa.

TEXT 14

কুণ্ডের মৃত্তিকা লঞা তিলক করিল ।
ভট্টাচার্য-দ্বারা মৃত্তিকা সঙ্গে করি' লৈল ॥ ১৪ ॥

kuṇḍera mṛttikā lañā tilaka karila
bhaṭṭācārya-dvārā mṛttikā saṅge kari' laila

SYNONYMS

kuṇḍera—of the lake; *mṛttikā*—earth; *lañā*—taking; *tilaka karila*—formed *tilaka; bhaṭṭācārya-dvārā*—with the help of Balabhadra Bhaṭṭācārya; *mṛttikā*—earth; *saṅge*—along; *kari'*—making; *laila*—took.

TRANSLATION

Śrī Caitanya Mahāprabhu then marked His body with tilaka made from the mud of Rādhā-kuṇḍa, and with the help of Balabhadra Bhaṭṭācārya, He collected some of the mud and took it with Him.

TEXT 15

তবে চলি' আইলা প্রভু 'সুমনঃ-সরোবর' ।
তাহাঁ 'গোবর্ধন' দেখি' হইলা বিহ্বল ॥ ১৫ ॥

tabe cali' āilā prabhu 'sumanaḥ-sarovara'
tāhāṅ 'govardhana' dekhi' ha-ilā vihvala

SYNONYMS

tabe—thereafter; *cali'*—traveling; *āilā*—came; *prabhu*—Śrī Caitanya Mahāprabhu; *sumanaḥ-sarovara*—to the lake known as Sumanaḥ; *tāhāṅ*—there; *govardhana*—Govardhana Hill; *dekhi'*—seeing; *ha-ilā vihvala*—became overwhelmed.

TRANSLATION

From Rādhā-kuṇḍa, Śrī Caitanya Mahāprabhu went to Sumanaḥ Lake. When He saw Govardhana Hill from there, He was overwhelmed by joy.

TEXT 16

গোবর্ধন দেখি' প্রভু হইলা দণ্ডবৎ ।
'এক শিলা' আলিঙ্গিয়া হইলা উন্মত্ত ॥ ১৬ ॥

govardhana dekhi' prabhu ha-ilā daṇḍavat
'eka śilā' āliṅgiyā ha-ilā unmatta

SYNONYMS

govardhana dekhi'—seeing Govardhana Hill; *prabhu*—Śrī Caitanya Mahāprabhu; *ha-ilā daṇḍavat*—offered obeisances like a straight rod; *eka śilā*—one piece of stone; *āliṅgiyā*—embracing; *ha-ilā*—became; *unmatta*—maddened.

TRANSLATION

When the Lord saw Govardhana Hill, He immediately offered obeisances, falling down on the ground like a rod. He embraced one piece of rock from Govardhana Hill and became mad.

TEXT 17

প্রেমে মত্ত চলি' আইলা গোবর্ধন-গ্রাম ।
'হরিদেব' দেখি' তাহাঁ হইলা প্রণাম ॥ ১৭ ॥

preme matta cali' āilā govardhana-grāma
'harideva' dekhi' tāhāṅ ha-ilā praṇāma

SYNONYMS

preme—in ecstatic love; *matta*—maddened; *cali'*—proceeding; *āilā*—came; *govardhana-grāma*—to the village known as Govardhana; *hari-deva*—the Deity named Harideva installed there; *dekhi'*—seeing; *tāhāṅ*—there; *ha-ilā praṇāma*—offered obeisances.

TRANSLATION

Mad with ecstatic love, the Lord came to the village known as Govardhana. It was there that He saw the Deity Harideva and offered His obeisances unto Him.

TEXT 18

'মথুরা'-পদ্মের পশ্চিমদলে যাঁর বাস ।
'হরিদেব' নারায়ণ—আদি পরকাশ ॥ ১৮ ॥

'mathurā'-padmera paścima-dale yāṅra vāsa
'harideva' nārāyaṇa——ādi parakāśa

SYNONYMS

mathurā-padmera—of the lotus flower of Mathurā; *paścima-dale*—on the western petal; *yāṅra*—whose; *vāsa*—residence; *hari-deva*—Lord Harideva; *nārāyaṇa*—incarnation of Nārāyaṇa; *ādi*—original; *parakāśa*—manifestation.

TRANSLATION

Harideva is an incarnation of Nārāyaṇa, and His residence is on the western petal of the lotus of Mathurā.

TEXT 19

হরিদেব-আগে নাচে প্রেমে মত্ত হঞা ।
সব লোক দেখিতে আইল আশ্চর্য শুনিয়া ॥ ১৯ ॥

harideva-āge nāce preme matta hañā
saba loka dekhite āila āścarya śuniyā

SYNONYMS

hari-deva-āge—in front of Harideva; *nāce*—dances; *preme*—in ecstatic love; *matta hañā*—becoming maddened; *saba loka*—all the people; *dekhite*—to see; *āila*—came; *āścarya*—wonderful; *śuniyā*—hearing.

TRANSLATION

Mad with ecstatic love, Śrī Caitanya Mahāprabhu began to dance before the Harideva Deity. Hearing of the Lord's wonderful activities, all the people came to see Him.

TEXT 20

প্রভু-প্রেম-সৌন্দর্য দেখি' লোকে চমৎকার ।
হরিদেবের ভৃত্য প্রভুর করিল সৎকার ॥ ২০ ॥

prabhu-prema-saundarya dekhi' loke camatkāra
haridevera bhṛtya prabhura karila satkāra

SYNONYMS

prabhu—of Śrī Caitanya Mahāprabhu; *prema-saundarya*—ecstatic love and beauty; *dekhi'*—seeing; *loke*—people; *camatkāra*—astonished; *hari-devera*—of Lord Harideva; *bhṛtya*—servants; *prabhura*—of Śrī Caitanya Mahāprabhu; *karila satkāra*—offered a good reception.

TRANSLATION

The people were astonished when they saw Śrī Caitanya Mahāprabhu's ecstatic love and personal beauty. The priests who served the Harideva Deity offered the Lord a good reception.

TEXT 21

ভট্টাচার্য 'ব্রহ্মকুণ্ডে' পাক যাঞা কৈল ।
ব্রহ্মকুণ্ডে স্নান করি' প্রভু ভিক্ষা কৈল ॥ ২১ ॥

bhaṭṭācārya 'brahma-kuṇḍe' pāka yāñā kaila
brahma-kuṇḍe snāna kari' prabhu bhikṣā kaila

SYNONYMS

bhaṭṭācārya—Balabhadra Bhaṭṭācārya; *brahma-kuṇḍe*—at the lake called Brahma-kuṇḍa; *pāka*—cooking; *yāñā*—going there; *kaila*—performed; *brahma-kuṇḍe*—at Brahma-kuṇḍa; *snāna kari'*—taking a bath; *prabhu*—Śrī Caitanya Mahāprabhu; *bhikṣā kaila*—accepted lunch.

TRANSLATION

At Brahma-kuṇḍa, Bhaṭṭācārya cooked food, and the Lord, after taking His bath at Brahma-kuṇḍa, accepted His lunch.

TEXT 22

সে-রাত্রি রহিলা হরিদেবের মন্দিরে।
রাত্রে মহাপ্রভু করে মনেতে বিচারে ॥ ২২ ॥

se-rātri rahilā haridevera mandire
rātre mahāprabhu kare manete vicāre

SYNONYMS

se-rātri—that night; *rahilā*—remained; *hari-devera*—of Harideva; *mandire*—in the temple; *rātre*—at night; *mahāprabhu*—Śrī Caitanya Mahāprabhu; *kare*—does; *manete*—in the mind; *vicāre*—consideration.

TRANSLATION

That night the Lord stayed at the temple of Harideva, and during the night He began to reflect.

TEXT 23

'গোবর্ধন-উপরে আমি কভু না চড়িব।
গোপাল-রায়ের দরশন কেমনে পাইব?' ২৩ ॥

'govardhana-upare āmi kabhu nā caḍiba
gopāla-rāyera daraśana kemane pāiba?'

SYNONYMS

govardhana-upare—upon the hill known as Govardhana; *āmi*—I; *kabhu*—at any time; *nā*—not; *caḍiba*—shall climb; *gopāla-rāyera*—of Lord Gopāla; *daraśana*—visit; *kemane*—how; *pāiba*—I shall get.

TRANSLATION

Śrī Caitanya Mahāprabhu thought, "Since I shall not at any time climb Govardhana Hill, how shall I be able to see Gopāla Rāya?"

TEXT 24

এত মনে করি' প্রভু মৌন করি' রহিলা ।
জানিয়া গোপাল কিছু ভঙ্গী উঠাইলা ॥ ২৪ ॥

eta mane kari' prabhu mauna kari' rahilā
jāniyā gopāla kichu bhaṅgī uṭhāilā

SYNONYMS

eta—so much; *mane kari'*—considering within the mind; *prabhu*—Śrī Caitanya Mahāprabhu; *mauna*—silent; *kari'*—becoming; *rahilā*—remained; *jāniyā*—knowing; *gopāla*—the Deity Gopāla; *kichu*—some; *bhaṅgī*—tricks; *uṭhāilā*—raised.

TRANSLATION

Thinking in this way, the Lord remained silent, and Lord Gopāla, knowing His contemplation, played a trick.

TEXT 25

অনারুরুক্ষবে শৈলং স্বস্মৈ ভক্তাভিমানিনে ।
অবরুহ্য গিরেঃ কৃষ্ণো গৌরায় স্বমদর্শয়ৎ ॥ ২৫ ॥

anārurukṣave śailaṁ
svasmai bhaktābhimānine
avaruhya gireḥ kṛṣṇo
gaurāya svam adarśayat

SYNONYMS

anārurukṣave—who was unwilling to climb up; *śailam*—the mountain; *svasmai*—unto Himself; *bhakta-abhimānine*—considering Himself a devotee of Lord Kṛṣṇa; *avaruhya*—getting down; *gireḥ*—from the hill; *kṛṣṇaḥ*—Lord Kṛṣṇa; *gaurāya*—unto Śrī Caitanya Mahāprabhu; *svam*—Himself; *adarśayat*—showed.

TRANSLATION

Coming down from Govardhana Hill, Lord Gopāla granted an interview to Lord Śrī Caitanya Mahāprabhu, who was unwilling to climb the hill, thinking Himself a devotee of Lord Kṛṣṇa.

TEXT 26

'অন্নকূট'-নামে গ্রামে গোপালের স্থিতি ।
রাজপুত-লোকের সেই গ্রামে বসতি ॥ ২৬ ॥

'annakūṭa'-nāme grāme gopālera sthiti
rāja-puta-lokera sei grāme vasati

SYNONYMS

annakūṭa-nāme—by the name Annakūṭa; *grāme*—in the village; *gopālera*—of Gopāla; *sthiti*—residence; *rāja-puta-lokera*—of people from Rajasthan; *sei grāme*—in that village; *vasati*—habitation.

TRANSLATION

Gopāla stayed in a village called Annakūṭa-grāma on Govardhana Hill. The villagers who lived in that village were mainly from Rajasthan.

PURPORT

The village named Annakūṭa-grāma is referred to in *Bhakti-ratnākara* (Fifth Wave):

gopa-gopī bhuñjāyena kautuka apāra
ei hetu 'āniyora' nāma se ihāra

annakūṭa-sthāna ei dekha śrīnivāsa
e-sthāna darśane haya pūrṇa abhilāṣa

"It is here that all the *gopīs* and the *gopas* enjoyed wonderful pastimes with Śrī Kṛṣṇa. Therefore this place is also called Āniyora. The Annakūṭa ceremony was celebrated here. O Śrīnivāsa, whoever sees this place has all his desires fulfilled." It is also stated:

kuṇḍera nikaṭa dekha niviḍa-kānana
ethāi 'gopāla' chilā hañā saṅgopana

"Look at the dense forest near the *kuṇḍa*. It was there that Gopāla was concealed." Also, the *Stavāvalī* (8.75) by Raghunātha dāsa Gosvāmī states:

vrajendra-varyārpita-bhogam uccair
dhṛtvā bṛhat-kāyam aghārir utkaḥ
vareṇa rādhāṁ chalayan vibhuṅkte
yatrānna-kūṭaṁ tad ahaṁ prapadye

TEXT 27

একজন আসি' রাত্রে গ্রামীকে বলিল ।
'তোমার গ্রাম মারিতে তুরুক-ধারী সাজিল ॥ ২৭ ॥

eka-jana āsi' rātre grāmīke balila
'tomāra grāma mārite turuka-dhārī sājila

SYNONYMS

eka-jana—one person; *āsi'*—coming; *rātre*—at night; *grāmīke*—to the inhabitants of the village; *balila*—said; *tomāra*—your; *grāma*—village; *mārite*—to attack; *turuka-dhārī*—Turkish Mohammedan soldiers; *sājila*—are prepared.

TRANSLATION

One person who came to the village informed the inhabitants, "The Turkish soldiers are now preparing to attack your village.

TEXT 28

আজি রাত্র্যে পলাহ, না রহিহ একজন ।
ঠাকুর লঞা ভাগ', আসিবে কালি যবন ॥' ২৮ ॥

āji rātrye palāha, nā rahiha eka-jana
ṭhākura lañā bhāga', āsibe kāli yavana'

SYNONYMS

āji rātrye—this night; *palāha*—go away; *nā rahiha*—do not remain; *eka-jana*—one person; *ṭhākura*—the Deity; *lañā*—taking; *bhāga'*—go away; *āsibe*—will come; *kāli*—tomorrow; *yavana*—the Mohammedan soldiers.

TRANSLATION

"Flee this village tonight, and do not allow one person to remain. Take the Deity with you and leave, for the Mohammedan soldiers will come tomorrow."

TEXT 29

শুনিয়া গ্রামের লোক চিন্তিত হইল ।
প্রথমে গোপাল লঞা গাঁঠুলি-গ্রামে খুইল ॥ ২৯ ॥

śuniyā grāmera loka cintita ha-ila
prathame gopāla lañā gāṅṭhuli-grāme khuila

SYNONYMS

śuniyā—hearing; *grāmera loka*—all the people in the village; *cintita ha-ila*—became very anxious; *prathame*—first; *gopāla lañā*—taking Gopāla; *gāṅṭhuli-grāme*—in the village known as Gāṅṭhuli; *khuila*—kept Him hidden.

TRANSLATION

Hearing this, all the villagers became very anxious. They first took Gopāla and moved Him to a village known as Gāṅṭhuli.

TEXT 30

বিপ্রগৃহে গোপালের নিভৃতে সেবন।
গ্রাম উজাড় হৈল, পলাইল সর্বজন ॥ ৩০ ॥

vipra-gṛhe gopālera nibhṛte sevana
grāma ujāḍa haila, palāila sarva-jana

SYNONYMS

vipra-gṛhe—in the house of a *brāhmaṇa; gopālera*—of Lord Gopāla; *nibhṛte*—very secretly; *sevana*—worship; *grāma*—the village; *ujāḍa haila*—became deserted; *palāila*—fled; *sarva-jana*—all the people.

TRANSLATION

The Gopāla Deity was kept in the house of a brāhmaṇa, and His worship was conducted secretly. Everyone fled, and thus the village of Annakūṭa was deserted.

TEXT 31

ঐছে ম্লেচ্ছভয়ে গোপাল ভাগে বারে-বারে।
মন্দির ছাড়ি' কুঞ্জে রহে, কিবা গ্রামান্তরে ॥ ৩১ ॥

aiche mleccha-bhaye gopāla bhāge bāre-bāre
mandira chāḍi' kuñje rahe, kibā grāmāntare

SYNONYMS

aiche—in that way; *mleccha-bhaye*—because of fear of the Mohammedans; *gopāla*—the Deity of Gopāla Rāya; *bhāge*—runs away; *bāre-bāre*—again and again; *mandira chāḍi'*—giving up the temple; *kuñje*—in the bush; *rahe*—remains; *kibā*—or; *grāma-antare*—in a different village.

TRANSLATION

Due to fear of the Mohammedans, the Gopāla Deity was moved from one place to another again and again. Thus giving up His temple, Lord Gopāla would sometimes live in a bush and sometimes in one village after another.

TEXT 32

প্রাতঃকালে প্রভু 'মানসগঙ্গা'য় করি' স্নান।
গোবর্ধন-পরিক্রমায় করিলা প্রয়াণ ॥ ৩২ ॥

prātaḥ-kāle prabhu 'mānasa-gaṅgā'ya kari' snāna
govardhana-parikramāya karilā prayāṇa

SYNONYMS

prātaḥ-kāle—in the morning; *prabhu*—Śrī Caitanya Mahāprabhu; *mānasa-gaṅgāya*—in the lake named Mānasa-gaṅgā; *kari'*—performing; *snāna*—bathing; *govardhana*—Govardhana Hill; *parikramāya*—in circumambulating; *karilā*—did; *prayāṇa*—starting.

TRANSLATION

In the morning, Śrī Caitanya Mahāprabhu took His bath in a lake called Mānasa-gaṅgā. He then circumambulated Govardhana Hill.

TEXT 33

গোবর্ধন দেখি' প্রভু প্রেমাবিষ্ট হঞা।
নাচিতে নাচিতে চলিলা শ্লোক পড়িয়া ॥ ৩৩ ॥

govardhana dekhi' prabhu premāviṣṭa hañā
nācite nācite calilā śloka paḍiyā

SYNONYMS

govardhana dekhi'—seeing Govardhana Hill; *prabhu*—Śrī Caitanya Mahāprabhu; *prema-āviṣṭa hañā*—becoming ecstatic in love; *nācite nācite*—dancing and dancing; *calilā*—departed; *śloka paḍiyā*—reciting the following verse.

TRANSLATION

Just by seeing Govardhana Hill, Śrī Caitanya Mahāprabhu became ecstatic with love of Kṛṣṇa. While dancing and dancing, He recited the following verse.

TEXT 34

হন্তায়মদ্রিরবলা হরিদাসবর্যো
যদ্রামকৃষ্ণচরণস্পরশপ্রমোদঃ ।
মানং তনোতি সহ-গোগণয়োস্তয়োর্যৎ
পানীয়-সূযবস-কন্দর-কন্দমূলৈঃ ॥ ৩৪ ॥

hantāyam adrir abalā hari-dāsa-varyo
yad rāma-kṛṣṇa-caraṇa-sparaśa-pramodaḥ
mānaṁ tanoti saha-go-gaṇayos tayor yat
pānīya-sūyavasa-kandara-kanda-mūlaiḥ

SYNONYMS

hanta—oh; *ayam*—this; *adriḥ*—hill; *abalāḥ*—O friends; *hari-dāsa-varyaḥ*—the best among the servants of the Lord; *yat*—because; *rāma-kṛṣṇa-caraṇa*—of the lotus feet of Lord Kṛṣṇa and Balarāma; *sparaśa*—by the touch; *pramodaḥ*—jubilant; *mānam*—respects; *tanoti*—offers; *saha*—with; *go-gaṇayoḥ*—cows, calves and cowherd boys; *tayoḥ*—to Them (Śrī Kṛṣṇa and Balarāma); *yat*—because; *pānīya*—drinking water; *sūyavasa*—very soft grass; *kandara*—caves; *kanda-mūlaiḥ*—and by roots.

TRANSLATION

"Of all the devotees, this Govardhana Hill is the best! O My friends, this hill supplies Kṛṣṇa and Balarāma, as well as Their calves, cows and cowherd friends, with all kinds of necessities—water for drinking, very soft grass, caves, fruits, flowers and vegetables. In this way the hill offers respect to the Lord. Being touched by the lotus feet of Kṛṣṇa and Balarāma, Govardhana Hill appears very jubilant."

PURPORT

This is a quotation from *Śrīmad-Bhāgavatam* (10.21.18). It was spoken by the *gopīs* when Lord Kṛṣṇa and Balarāma entered the forest in the autumn. The *gopīs* spoke among themselves and glorified Kṛṣṇa and Balarāma for Their pastimes.

TEXT 35

'গোবিন্দকুণ্ডাদি' তীর্থে প্রভু কৈলা স্নান ।
তাহাঁ শুনিলা—গোপাল গেল গাঁঠুলি গ্রাম ॥ ৩৫ ॥

'govinda-kuṇḍādi' tīrthe prabhu kailā snāna
tāhāṅ śunilā——gopāla gela gāṅṭhuli grāma

SYNONYMS

govinda-kuṇḍa-ādi—Govinda-kuṇḍa and others; *tīrthe*—in the holy places; *prabhu*—Śrī Caitanya Mahāprabhu; *kailā snāna*—performed bathing; *tāhāṅ*—there; *śunilā*—heard; *gopāla*—the Gopāla Deity; *gela*—has gone; *gāṅṭhuli*—Gāṅṭhuli; *grāma*—to the village.

TRANSLATION

Śrī Caitanya Mahāprabhu then took His bath in a lake called Govinda-kuṇḍa, and while He was there, He heard that the Deity Gopāla had already gone to Gāṅṭhuli-grāma.

TEXT 36

সেই গ্রামে গিয়া কৈল গোপাল-দরশন ।
প্রেমাবেশে প্রভু করে কীর্তন-নর্তন ॥ ৩৬ ॥

sei grāme giyā kaila gopāla-daraśana
premāveśe prabhu kare kīrtana-nartana

SYNONYMS

sei grāme—to that village; *giyā*—going; *kaila*—performed; *gopāla-daraśana*—seeing Lord Gopāla; *prema-āveśe*—in ecstatic love; *prabhu*—Śrī Caitanya Mahāprabhu; *kare*—performs; *kīrtana-nartana*—chanting and dancing.

TRANSLATION

Śrī Caitanya Mahāprabhu then went to the village of Gāṅṭhuli-grāma and saw the Lord Gopāla Deity. Overwhelmed by ecstatic love, He began to chant and dance.

TEXT 37

গোপালের সৌন্দর্য দেখি' প্রভুর আবেশ ।
এই শ্লোক পড়ি' নাচে, হৈল দিন-শেষ ॥ ৩৭ ॥

gopālera saundarya dekhi' prabhura āveśa
ei śloka paḍi' nāce, haila dina-śeṣa

SYNONYMS

gopālera—of Gopāla; *saundarya*—beauty; *dekhi'*—seeing; *prabhura*—of Śrī Caitanya Mahāprabhu; *āveśa*—ecstasy; *ei śloka paḍi'*—reciting the following verse; *nāce*—dances; *haila*—there was; *dina-śeṣa*—the end of the day.

TRANSLATION

As soon as the Lord saw the beauty of the Gopāla Deity, He was immediately overwhelmed by ecstatic love, and He recited the following verse. He then chanted and danced until the day ended.

PURPORT

Śrīla Bhaktisiddhānta Sarasvatī Ṭhākura gives the following information about Govinda-kuṇḍa. There is a village named Āniyora on Govardhana Hill, a little distance from the village of Paiṭhā. Govinda-kuṇḍa is situated near here, and there are two temples to Govinda and Baladeva there. According to some, Queen Padmāvatī excavated this lake. In the *Bhakti-ratnākara* (Fifth Wave), the following statement is found:

ei śrī-govinda-kuṇḍa-mahimā aneka
ethā indra kaila govindera abhiṣeka

"Govinda-kuṇḍa is exalted for its many spiritual activities. It was here that Indra was defeated by Lord Kṛṣṇa, and Indra offered his prayers and bathed Lord Govinda." In the book *Stavāvalī* (*Vraja-vilāsa-stava,* 74) the following verse is found:

nīcaiḥ prauḍha-bhayāt svayaṁ surapatiḥ pādau vidhṛtyeha yaiḥ
svar-gaṅgā-salilaiś cakāra surabhi-dvārābhiṣekotsavam
govindasya navaṁ gavām adhipatā rājye sphuṭaṁ kautukāt
tair yat prādurabhūt sadā sphuratu tad govinda-kuṇḍaṁ dṛśoḥ

In the *Mathurā-khaṇḍa* it is also stated:

yatrābhiṣikto bhagavān
maghonā yadu-vairiṇā
govinda-kuṇḍaṁ taj-jātaṁ
snāna-mātreṇa mokṣadam

"Simply by bathing in Govinda-kuṇḍa, one is awarded liberation. This lake was produced when Bhagavān Śrī Kṛṣṇa was bathed by Lord Indra."

Gāṅṭhuli-grāma is situated near the two villages Bilachu and Gopāla-pura. According to hearsay, Rādhā and Kṛṣṇa first met here. In the *Bhakti-ratnākara* (Fifth Wave), it is stated: *sakhī duṅha vastre gāṅṭhi dila saṅgopane.* It is also stated: *phāguyā laiyā keha gāṅṭhi khuli' dilā.* For this reason the village is known as Gāṅṭhuli.

TEXT 38

বামস্তামরসাক্ষস্য ভুজদণ্ডঃ স পাতু বঃ ।
ক্রীড়াকন্দুকতাং যেন নীতো গোবর্ধনো গিরিঃ ॥ ৩৮ ॥

vāmas tāmarasākṣasya
bhuja-daṇḍaḥ sa pātu vaḥ
krīḍā-kandukatāṁ yena
nīto govardhano giriḥ

SYNONYMS

vāmaḥ—the left; *tāmarasa-akṣasya*—of Kṛṣṇa, who has eyes like lotus petals; *bhuja-daṇḍaḥ*—arm; *saḥ*—that; *pātu*—let it protect; *vaḥ*—all of you; *krīḍā-kandukatām*—being like a toy; *yena*—by which; *nītaḥ*—attained; *govardhanaḥ*—named Govardhana; *giriḥ*—the hill.

TRANSLATION

Śrī Caitanya Mahāprabhu said, " 'May the left arm of Śrī Kṛṣṇa, whose eyes are like the petals of a lotus flower, always protect you. With His left arm He raised Govardhana Hill as if it were a toy.' "

PURPORT

This verse is found in *Bhakti-rasāmṛta-sindhu* (2.1.62).

TEXT 39

এইমত তিনদিন গোপালে দেখিলা ।
চতুর্থ-দিবসে গোপাল স্বমন্দিরে গেলা ॥ ৩৯ ॥

ei-mata tina-dina gopāle dekhilā
caturtha-divase gopāla svamandire gelā

SYNONYMS

ei-mata—in this way; *tina-dina*—for three days; *gopāle*—Gopāla; *dekhilā*—saw; *caturtha-divase*—on the fourth day; *gopāla*—the Deity Gopāla; *sva-mandire*—in His own temple; *gelā*—returned.

TRANSLATION

Śrī Caitanya Mahāprabhu saw the Gopāla Deity for three days. On the fourth day, the Deity returned to His own temple.

TEXT 40

গোপাল সঙ্গে চলি' আইলা নৃত্য-গীত করি ।
আনন্দ-কোলাহলে লোক বলে 'হরি' 'হরি' ॥ ৪০ ॥

gopāla saṅge cali' āilā nṛtya-gīta kari
ānanda-kolāhale loka bale 'hari' 'hari'

SYNONYMS

gopāla saṅge—with Gopāla; *cali'*—walking; *āilā*—came; *nṛtya-gīta kari*—chanting and dancing; *ānanda-kolāhale*—in great jubilation; *loka*—people; *bale*—say; *hari hari*—Hari, Hari.

TRANSLATION

Caitanya Mahāprabhu walked with the Deity of Gopāla, and He chanted and danced. A large and jubilant crowd of people also chanted the transcendental name of Kṛṣṇa, "Hari! Hari!"

TEXT 41

গোপাল মন্দিরে গেলা, প্রভু রহিলা তলে ।
প্রভুর বাঞ্ছা পূর্ণ সব করিল গোপালে ॥ ৪১ ॥

gopāla mandire gelā, prabhu rahilā tale
prabhura vāñchā pūrṇa saba karila gopāle

SYNONYMS

gopāla—the Deity Gopāla; *mandire gelā*—returned to His temple; *prabhu*—Śrī Caitanya Mahāprabhu; *rahilā tale*—remain at the bottom; *prabhura*—of Śrī Caitanya Mahāprabhu; *vāñchā*—desires; *pūrṇa*—satisfied; *saba*—all; *karila*—made; *gopāle*—the Deity Gopāla.

TRANSLATION

The Deity Gopāla then returned to His own temple, and Śrī Caitanya Mahāprabhu remained at the bottom of the hill. Thus all the desires of Śrī Caitanya Mahāprabhu were satisfied by the Deity Gopāla.

TEXT 42

এইমত গোপালের করুণ স্বভাব ।
যেই ভক্ত জনের দেখিতে হয় 'ভাব' ॥ ৪২ ॥

ei-mata gopālera karuṇa svabhāva
yei bhakta janera dekhite haya 'bhāva'

SYNONYMS

ei-mata—in this way; *gopālera*—of the Deity Gopāla; *karuṇa sva-bhāva*—kind behavior; *yei*—which; *bhakta janera*—of persons who are devotees; *dekhite*—to see; *haya*—there is; *bhāva*—ecstatic love.

TRANSLATION

This is the way of Lord Gopāla's kind behavior to His devotees. Seeing this, the devotees were overwhelmed by ecstatic love.

TEXT 43

দেখিতে উৎকণ্ঠা হয়, না চড়ে গোবর্ধনে।
কোন ছলে গোপাল আসি' উতরে আপনে ॥ ৪৩ ॥

dekhite utkaṇṭhā haya, nā caḍe govardhane
kona chale gopāla āsi' utare āpane

SYNONYMS

dekhite—to see; *utkaṇṭhā haya*—there was great anxiety; *nā caḍe*—does not go up; *govardhane*—on the hill known as Govardhana; *kona chale*—by some trick; *gopāla*—the Deity Gopāla; *āsi'*—coming; *utare*—descends; *āpane*—personally.

TRANSLATION

Śrī Caitanya Mahāprabhu was very anxious to see Gopāla, but He did not want to climb Govardhana Hill. Therefore by some trick the Deity Gopāla personally descended.

TEXT 44

কভু কুঞ্জে রহে, কভু রহে গ্রামান্তরে।
সেই ভক্ত, তাহাঁ আসি' দেখয়ে তাঁহারে ॥ ৪৪ ॥

kabhu kuñje rahe, kabhu rahe grāmāntare
sei bhakta, tāhāṅ āsi' dekhaye tāṅhāre

SYNONYMS

kabhu—sometimes; *kuñje*—in the bushes; *rahe*—remains; *kabhu*—sometimes; *rahe*—He stays; *grāma-antare*—in a different village; *sei bhakta*—that devotee; *tāhāṅ āsi'*—coming there; *dekhaye tāṅhāre*—sees Him.

TRANSLATION

In this way, giving some excuse, Gopāla sometimes remains in the bushes of the forest, and sometimes He stays in a village. One who is a devotee comes to see the Deity.

TEXT 45

পর্বতে না চড়ে দুই—রূপ-সনাতন ।
এইরূপে তাঁ-সবারে দিয়াছেন দরশন ॥ ৪৫ ॥

parvate nā caḍe dui——rūpa-sanātana
ei-rūpe tāṅ-sabāre diyāchena daraśana

SYNONYMS

parvate—on the hill; *nā caḍe*—do not ascend; *dui*—two; *rūpa-sanātana*—Rūpa Gosvāmī and Sanātana Gosvāmī; *ei-rūpe*—in this way; *tāṅ-sabāre*—unto them; *diyāchena*—has given; *daraśana*—interview.

TRANSLATION

The two brothers Rūpa and Sanātana did not climb the hill. To them also Lord Gopāla granted an interview.

TEXT 46

বৃদ্ধকালে রূপ-গোসাঞি না পারে যাইতে ।
বাঞ্ছা হৈল গোপালের সৌন্দর্য দেখিতে ॥ ৪৬ ॥

vṛddha-kāle rūpa-gosāñi nā pāre yāite
vāñchā haila gopālera saundarya dekhite

SYNONYMS

vṛddha-kāle—in ripe old age; *rūpa-gosāñi*—Rūpa Gosvāmī; *nā pāre*—is not able; *yāite*—to go; *vāñchā haila*—there was a desire; *gopālera*—of Gopāla; *saundarya dekhite*—to see the beauty.

TRANSLATION

In ripe old age, Śrīla Rūpa Gosvāmī could not go there, but he had a desire to see the beauty of Gopāla.

TEXT 47

ম্লেচ্ছভয়ে আইলা গোপাল মথুরা-নগরে ।
একমাস রহিল বিঠ্ঠলেশ্বর-ঘরে ॥ ৪৭ ॥

mleccha-bhaye āilā gopāla mathurā-nagare
eka-māsa rahila viṭhṭhaleśvara-ghare

SYNONYMS

mleccha-bhaye—because of fear of the Muslims; *āilā*—came; *gopāla*—the Deity Gopāla; *mathurā-nagare*—to the city of Mathurā; *eka-māsa*—one month; *rahila*—stayed; *viṭhṭhaleśvara-ghare*—in the temple of Viṭhṭhaleśvara.

TRANSLATION

Due to fear of the Mohammedans, Gopāla went to Mathurā, where He remained in the temple of Viṭhṭhaleśvara for one full month.

PURPORT

When the two brothers Śrīla Rūpa Gosvāmī and Sanātana Gosvāmī went to Vṛndāvana, they decided to live there. Following Śrī Caitanya Mahāprabhu's example, they did not climb the hill because they considered it nondifferent from Kṛṣṇa, the Supreme Personality of Godhead. On some pretext, the Gopāla Deity granted Śrī Caitanya Mahāprabhu an audience beneath the hill, and Gopāla similarly favored Śrīla Rūpa Gosvāmī and Sanātana Gosvāmī. During his ripe old age, when Rūpa Gosvāmī could not go to Govardhana Hill because of invalidity, Gopāla kindly went to Mathurā and remained at the temple of Viṭhṭhaleśvara for one month. It was then that Śrīla Rūpa Gosvāmī could see Gopāla's beauty to his heart's content.

TEXT 48

তবে রূপ গোসাঞি সব নিজগণ লঞা ।
একমাস দরশন কৈলা মথুরায় রহিয়া ॥ ৪৮ ॥

tabe rūpa gosāñi saba nija-gaṇa lañā
eka-māsa daraśana kailā mathurāya rahiyā

SYNONYMS

tabe—thereupon; *rūpa gosāñi*—Śrīla Rūpa Gosvāmī; *saba*—all; *nija-gaṇa lañā*—taking his associates with him; *eka-māsa*—for one month; *daraśana kailā*—saw the Deity; *mathurāya rahiyā*—staying at the city of Mathurā.

TRANSLATION

Śrīla Rūpa Gosvāmī and his associates stayed in Mathurā for one month and saw the Deity Gopāla.

PURPORT

The following description of the temple of Viṭhṭhaleśvara is given in *Bhakti-ratnākara* (Fifth Wave):

viṭhṭhalera sevā kṛṣṇa-caitanya-vigraha
tāhāra darśane haila parama āgraha

śrī-viṭhṭhalanātha——bhaṭṭa-vallabha-tanaya
karilā yateka prīti kahile nā haya

gāṭholi-grāme gopāla āilā 'chala' kari'
tāṅre dekhi' nṛtya-gīte magna gaurahari

śrī-dāsa-gosvāmī ādi parāmarśa kari'
śrī-viṭhṭhaleśvare kailā sevā-adhikārī

pitā śrī-vallabha-bhaṭṭa tāṅra adarśane
kata-dina mathurāya chilena nirjane

Śrī Vallabha Bhaṭṭa had two sons. The elder, Gopīnātha, was born in 1432 Śakābda Era, and the younger, Viṭhṭhalanātha, was born in 1437 and died in 1507. Viṭhṭhala had seven sons: Giridhara, Govinda, Bālakṛṣṇa, Gokuleśa, Raghunātha, Yadunātha and Ghanaśyāma. Viṭhṭhala completed many of his father's unfinished books, including his commentary on *Vedānta-sūtra,* the *Subodhinī* commentary on *Śrīmad-Bhāgavatam, Vidvan-maṇḍana, Śṛṅgāra-rasa-maṇḍana* and *Nyāsādeśa-vivaraṇa.* Śrī Caitanya Mahāprabhu went to Vṛndāvana before the birth of Viṭhṭhala. Śrīla Rūpa Gosvāmī was very old at the time Gopāla stayed at the house of Viṭhṭhalanātha.

TEXT 49

সঙ্গে গোপাল-ভট্ট, দাস-রঘুনাথ ।
রঘুনাথ-ভট্টগোসাঞি, আর লোকনাথ ॥ ৪৯ ॥

saṅge gopāla-bhaṭṭa, dāsa-raghunātha
raghunātha-bhaṭṭa-gosāñi, āra lokanātha

SYNONYMS

saṅge—with Rūpa Gosvāmī; *gopāla-bhaṭṭa*—Gopāla Bhaṭṭa; *dāsa-raghunātha*—Raghunātha dāsa Gosvāmī; *raghunātha-bhaṭṭa-gosāñi*—Raghunātha Bhaṭṭa Gosvāmī; *āra*—and; *lokanātha*—Lokanātha dāsa Gosvāmī.

TRANSLATION

When Rūpa Gosvāmī stayed at Mathurā, he was accompanied by Gopāla Bhaṭṭa Gosvāmī, Raghunātha dāsa Gosvāmī, Raghunātha Bhaṭṭa Gosvāmī and Lokanātha dāsa Gosvāmī.

PURPORT

Śrī Lokanātha Gosvāmī was a personal associate of Śrī Caitanya Mahāprabhu and a great devotee of the Lord. He was a resident of a village named Tālakhaḍi in the district of Yaśohara in Bengal. Previously he lived in Kācnāpāḍā. His father's name was Padmanābha, and his only younger brother was Pragalbha. Following the orders of Śrī Caitanya Mahāprabhu, Śrī Lokanātha went to Vṛndāvana to live. He established a temple named Gokulānanda. Śrīla Narottama dāsa Ṭhākura selected Lokanātha dāsa Gosvāmī to be his spiritual master, and he was his only disciple. Because Lokanātha dāsa Gosvāmī did not want his name mentioned in *Caitanya-caritāmṛta,* we do not often see it in this celebrated book. On the E.B.R. Railroad, the Yaśohara station is located in Bangladesh. From the railway station one has to go by bus to the village of Sonākhāli and from there to Khejurā. From there one has to walk, or, during the rainy season, go by boat to the village of Tālakhaḍi. In this village there are still descendants of Lokanātha Gosvāmī's younger brother.

TEXT 50

ভূগর্ভ-গোসাঞি, আর শ্রীজীব-গোসাঞি ।
শ্রীযাদব-আচার্য, আর গোবিন্দ গোসাঞি ॥ ৫০ ॥

bhūgarbha-gosāñi, āra śrī-jīva-gosāñi
śrī-yādava-ācārya, āra govinda gosāñi

SYNONYMS

bhūgarbha-gosāñi—Bhūgarbha Gosāñi; *āra*—and; *śrī-jīva-gosāñi*—Śrī Jīva Gosvāmī; *śrī-yādava-ācārya*—Śrī Yādava Ācārya; *āra*—and; *govinda gosāñi*—Govinda Gosvāmī.

TRANSLATION

Bhūgarbha Gosvāmī, Śrī Jīva Gosvāmī, Śrī Yādava Ācārya and Govinda Gosvāmī also accompanied Śrīla Rūpa Gosvāmī.

TEXT 51

শ্রীউদ্ধব-দাস, আর মাধব – দুইজন ।
শ্রীগোপাল-দাস, আর দাস-নারায়ণ ॥ ৫১ ॥

śrī-uddhava-dāsa, āra mādhava——dui-jana
śrī-gopāla-dāsa, āra dāsa-nārāyaṇa

SYNONYMS

śrī-uddhava-dāsa—Śrī Uddhava dāsa; *āra*—and; *mādhava*—Mādhava; *dui-jana*—two persons; *śrī-gopāla-dāsa*—Śrī Gopāla dāsa; *āra*—and; *dāsa-nārāyaṇa*—Nārāyaṇa dāsa.

TRANSLATION

He was also accompanied by Śrī Uddhava dāsa, Mādhava, Śrī Gopāla dāsa and Nārāyaṇa dāsa.

TEXT 52

'গোবিন্দ' ভক্ত, আর বাণী-কৃষ্ণদাস ।
পুণ্ডরীকাক্ষ, ঈশান, আর লঘু-হরিদাস ॥ ৫২ ॥

'govinda' bhakta, āra vāṇī-kṛṣṇadāsa
puṇḍarīkākṣa, īśāna, āra laghu-haridāsa

SYNONYMS

govinda—Govinda; *bhakta*—a great devotee; *āra*—and; *vāṇī-kṛṣṇadāsa*—Vāṇī Kṛṣṇadāsa; *puṇḍarīkākṣa*—Puṇḍarīkākṣa; *īśāna*—Īśāna; *āra*—and; *laghu-haridāsa*—Laghu Haridāsa.

TRANSLATION

The great devotee Govinda, Vāṇī Kṛṣṇadāsa, Puṇḍarīkākṣa, Īśāna and Laghu Haridāsa also accompanied him.

PURPORT

Laghu Haridāsa should not be confused with Junior Haridāsa, who committed suicide at Prayāga. Generally a devotee is called Haridāsa, and consequently there are many Haridāsas. The chief was Ṭhākura Haridāsa. There was also a Madhyama Haridāsa.

In *Bhakti-ratnākara* (Sixth Wave), there is a list of many of the chief devotees who accompanied Śrīla Rūpa Gosvāmī.

gosvāmī gopāla-bhaṭṭa ati dayāmaya
bhūgarbha, śrī-lokanātha——guṇera ālaya

śrī-mādhava, śrī-paramānanda-bhaṭṭācārya
śrī-madhu-paṇḍita——yāṅra caritra āścarya

premī kṛṣṇadāsa kṛṣṇadāsa brahmacārī
yādava ācārya, nārāyaṇa kṛpāvān
śrī-puṇḍarīkākṣa-gosāñi, govinda, īśāna

śrī-govinda vāṇī-kṛṣṇadāsa aty-udāra
śrī-uddhava——madhye-madhye gauḍe gati yāṅra

dvija-haridāsa kṛṣṇadāsa kavirāja
śrī-gopāla-dāsa yāṅra alaukika kāya
śrī-gopāla, mādhavādi yateka vaiṣṇava

"The following Vaiṣṇavas were present with Śrīla Rūpa Gosvāmī: the merciful Gopāla Bhaṭṭa Gosvāmī; Bhūgarbha Gosvāmī; Śrī Lokanātha dāsa Gosvāmī, a reservoir of good qualities; Śrī Mādhava; Śrī Paramānanda Bhaṭṭācārya; Śrī Madhu Paṇḍita, whose characteristics are all wonderful; Premī Kṛṣṇadāsa; Kṛṣṇadāsa Brahmacārī; Yādava Ācārya; the merciful Nārāyaṇa; Śrī Puṇḍarīkākṣa Gosvāmī; Govinda; Īśāna; Śrī Govinda; the magnanimous Vāṇī Kṛṣṇadāsa; Śrī Uddhava, who occasionally visited Bengal; Dvija Haridāsa; Kṛṣṇadāsa Kavirāja; Śrī Gopāla dāsa, whose body is completely spiritual; Śrī Gopāla; Mādhava; and many others."

TEXT 53

এই সব মুখ্যভক্ত লঞা নিজ-সঙ্গে ।
শ্রীগোপাল দরশন কৈলা বহু-রঙ্গে ॥ ৫৩ ॥

ei saba mukhya-bhakta lañā nija-saṅge
śrī-gopāla daraśana kailā bahu-raṅge

SYNONYMS

ei saba—all these; *mukhya-bhakta*—chief devotees; *lañā nija-saṅge*—taking with him personally; *śrī-gopāla daraśana*—visiting Lord Gopāla; *kailā bahu-raṅge*—performed in great jubilation.

TRANSLATION

It was with great jubilation that Rūpa Gosvāmī visited Lord Gopāla accompanied by all these devotees.

TEXT 54

একমাস রহি' গোপাল গেলা নিজ-স্থানে ।
শ্রীরূপ-গোসাঞি আইলা শ্রীবৃন্দাবনে ॥ ৫৪ ॥

eka-māsa rahi' gopāla gelā nija-sthāne
śrī-rūpa-gosāñi āilā śrī-vṛndāvane

SYNONYMS

eka-māsa rahi'—staying for one month; *gopāla*—the Deity Gopāla; *gelā*—went; *nija-sthāne*—to His own place; *śrī-rūpa-gosāñi*—Śrī Rūpa Gosvāmī; *āilā*—came back; *śrī-vṛndāvane*—to Vṛndāvana.

TRANSLATION

After staying at Mathurā for one month, the Deity Gopāla returned to His own place, and Śrī Rūpa Gosvāmī returned to Vṛndāvana.

TEXT 55

প্রস্তাবে কহিলুঁ গোপাল-কৃপার আখ্যান ।
তবে মহাপ্রভু গেলা 'শ্রীকাম্যবন' ॥ ৫৫ ॥

prastāve kahiluṅ gopāla-kṛpāra ākhyāna
tabe mahāprabhu gelā 'śrī-kāmyavana'

SYNONYMS

prastāve—in the course of the story; *kahiluṅ*—I have stated; *gopāla-kṛpāra*—of the mercy of Gopāla; *ākhyāna*—description; *tabe*—after this; *mahāprabhu*—Śrī Caitanya Mahāprabhu; *gelā*—went; *śrī-kāmya-vana*—to Śrī Kāmyavana.

TRANSLATION

In the course of this story, I have given a description of Lord Gopāla's mercy. After seeing the Gopāla Deity, Śrī Caitanya Mahāprabhu went to Śrī Kāmyavana.

PURPORT

Kāmyavana is mentioned in the *Ādi-varāha Purāṇa:*

caturthaṁ kāmyaka-vanaṁ
vanānāṁ vanam uttamam
tatra gatvā naro devi
mama loke mahīyate

In the *Bhakti-ratnākara* (Fifth Wave) it is also said:

ei kāmyavane kṛṣṇa-līlā manohara
karibe darśana sthāna kuṇḍa bahutara
kāmyavane yata tīrtha lekhā nāhi tāra

TEXT 56

প্রভুর গমন-রীতি পূর্বে যে লিখিল ।
সেইমত বৃন্দাবনে তাবৎ দেখিল ॥ ৫৬ ॥

prabhura gamana-rīti pūrve ye likhila
sei-mata vṛndāvane tāvat dekhila

SYNONYMS

prabhura—of Śrī Caitanya Mahāprabhu; *gamana-rīti*—method of touring; *pūrve*—formerly; *ye*—which; *likhila*—I have written; *sei-mata*—similarly; *vṛndāvane*—at Vṛndāvana; *tāvat dekhila*—saw all the places.

TRANSLATION

Śrī Caitanya Mahāprabhu's touring Vṛndāvana has been previously described. In the same ecstatic way, He traveled all over Vṛndāvana.

TEXT 57

তাহাঁ লীলাস্থলী দেখি' গেলা 'নন্দীশ্বর' ।
'নন্দীশ্বর' দেখি' প্রেমে হইলা বিহ্বল ॥ ৫৭ ॥

tāhāṅ līlā-sthalī dekhi' gelā 'nandīśvara'
'nandīśvara' dekhi' preme ha-ilā vihvala

SYNONYMS

tāhāṅ—at Kāmyavana; *līlā-sthalī*—all the places of pastimes; *dekhi'*—visiting; *gelā nandīśvara*—went to Nandīśvara; *nandīśvara dekhi'*—while seeing Nandīśvara; *preme ha-ilā vihvala*—became overwhelmed by ecstatic love.

TRANSLATION

After visiting the places of Kṛṣṇa's pastimes at Kāmyavana, Śrī Caitanya Mahāprabhu went to Nandīśvara. While there, He was overwhelmed with ecstatic love.

PURPORT

Nandīśvara is the house of Mahārāja Nanda.

TEXT 58

'পাবনাদি' সব কুণ্ডে স্নান করিয়া ।
লোকেরে পুছিল, পর্বত-উপরে যাঞা ॥ ৫৮ ॥

'pāvanādi' saba kuṇḍe snāna kariyā
lokere puchila, parvata-upare yāñā

SYNONYMS

pāvana-ādi—Pāvana and others; *saba kuṇḍe*—in every lake; *snāna kariyā*—taking a bath; *lokere puchila*—inquired from persons there; *parvata-upare yāñā*—going up a hill.

TRANSLATION

Śrī Caitanya Mahāprabhu bathed in all the celebrated lakes, beginning with Lake Pāvana. Thereafter He climbed a hill and spoke to the people.

PURPORT

The Pāvana-sarovara is described in the *Mathurā-māhātmya:*

pāvane sarasi snātvā
kṛṣṇaṁ nandīśvare girau
dṛṣṭvā nandaṁ yaśodāṁ ca
sarvābhīṣṭam avāpnuyāt

TEXT 59

কিছু দেবমূর্তি হয় পর্বত-উপরে ?
লোক কহে,—মূর্তি হয় গোফার ভিতরে ॥ ৫৯ ॥

kichu deva-mūrti haya parvata-upare?
loka kahe,——mūrti haya gophāra bhitare

SYNONYMS

kichu—any; *deva-mūrti*—deities; *haya*—are there; *parvata-upare*—on the top of the hill; *loka kahe*—people said; *mūrti haya*—there are deities; *gophāra bhitare*—within a cave.

TRANSLATION

Śrī Caitanya Mahāprabhu asked, "Are there any deities on top of this hill?" The local people replied, "There are deities on this hill, but they are located within a cave.

TEXT 60

দুইদিকে মাতা-পিতা পুষ্ট কলেবর ।
মধ্যে এক 'শিশু' হয় ত্রিভঙ্গ-সুন্দর ॥ ৬০ ॥

dui-dike mātā-pitā puṣṭa kalevara
madhye eka 'śiśu' haya tribhaṅga-sundara

SYNONYMS

dui-dike—on two sides; *mātā-pitā*—father and mother; *puṣṭa kalevara*—very well-built body; *madhye*—between them; *eka*—one; *śiśu*—child; *haya*—there is; *tri-bhaṅga*—curved in three places; *sundara*—very beautiful.

TRANSLATION

"There is a father and mother with well-built bodies, and between them is a very beautiful child who is curved in three places."

TEXT 61

শুনি' মহাপ্রভু মনে আনন্দ পাঞা ।
'তিন' মূর্তি দেখিলা সেই গোফা উঘাড়িয়া ॥ ৬১ ॥

śuni' mahāprabhu mane ānanda pāñā
'tina' mūrti dekhilā sei gophā ughāḍiyā

SYNONYMS

śuni'—hearing; *mahāprabhu*—Śrī Caitanya Mahāprabhu; *mane*—within the mind; *ānanda pāñā*—getting great pleasure; *tina mūrti*—the three deities; *dekhilā*—saw; *sei gophā ughāḍiyā*—by excavating the cave.

TRANSLATION

Hearing this, Śrī Caitanya Mahāprabhu became very happy. After excavating the cave, He saw the three deities.

TEXT 62

ব্রজেন্দ্র-ব্রজেশ্বরীর কৈল চরণ বন্দন ।
প্রেমাবেশে কৃষ্ণের কৈল সর্বাঙ্গ-স্পর্শন ॥ ৬২ ॥

vrajendra-vrajeśvarīra kaila caraṇa vandana
premāveśe kṛṣṇera kaila sarvāṅga-sparśana

SYNONYMS

vraja-indra—of the King of Vraja, Nanda Mahārāja; *vraja-īśvarīra*—and of the Queen of Vraja, mother Yaśodā; *kaila*—did; *caraṇa vandana*—worshiping the lotus feet; *prema-āveśe*—in ecstatic love; *kṛṣṇera*—of Lord Kṛṣṇa; *kaila*—did; *sarva-aṅga-sparśana*—touching the whole body.

TRANSLATION

Śrī Caitanya Mahāprabhu offered His respects to Nanda Mahārāja and mother Yaśodā, and with great ecstatic love He touched the body of Lord Kṛṣṇa.

TEXT 63

সব দিন প্রেমাবেশে নৃত্য-গীত কৈলা ।
তাহাঁ হৈতে মহাপ্রভু 'খদির-বন' আইলা ॥ ৬৩ ॥

saba dina premāveśe nṛtya-gīta kailā
tāhāṅ haite mahāprabhu 'khadira-vana' āilā

SYNONYMS

saba dina—all the days; *prema-āveśe*—in ecstatic love; *nṛtya-gīta kailā*—danced and chanted; *tāhāṅ haite*—from there; *mahāprabhu*—Śrī Caitanya Mahāprabhu; *khadira-vana āilā*—came to the place known as Khadiravana.

TRANSLATION

Every day the Lord chanted and danced in ecstatic love. Finally He went to Khadiravana.

PURPORT

Khadiravana is described in the *Bhakti-ratnākara* (Fifth Wave):

dekhaha khadira-vana vidita jagate
viṣṇu-loka-prāpti ethā gamana-mātrete

"Behold the forest named Khadiravana, renowned throughout the universe. If one comes to Khadiravana, he can immediately be elevated to Viṣṇuloka."

TEXT 64

লীলাস্থল দেখি' তাহাঁ গেলা 'শেষশায়ী' ।
'লক্ষ্মী' দেখি' এই শ্লোক পড়েন গোসাঞি ॥ ৬৪ ॥

līlā-sthala dekhi' tāhāṅ gelā 'śeṣaśāyī'
'lakṣmī' dekhi' ei śloka paḍena gosāñi

SYNONYMS

līlā-sthala dekhi'—seeing the places of pastimes; *tāhāṅ*—there; *gelā*—departed; *śeṣa-śāyī*—for seeing Śeṣaśāyī; *lakṣmī*—the goddess of fortune; *dekhi'*—seeing; *ei*—this; *śloka*—verse; *paḍena*—recites; *gosāñi*—Śrī Caitanya Mahāprabhu.

TRANSLATION

After seeing the places of Lord Kṛṣṇa's pastimes, Śrī Caitanya went to Śeṣaśāyī, where He saw Lakṣmī and recited the following verse.

TEXT 65

যত্তে সুজাতচরণাম্বুরুহং স্তনেষু
ভীতাঃ শনৈঃ প্রিয় দধিমহি কর্কশেষু ।
তেনাটবীমটসি তদ্ব্যথতে ন কিংস্বিৎ
কূর্পাদিভির্ভ্রমতি ধীর্ভবদায়ুষাং নঃ ॥ ৬৫ ॥

yat te sujāta-caraṇāmburuhaṁ staneṣu
bhītāḥ śanaiḥ priya dadhīmahi karkaśeṣu
tenāṭavīm aṭasi tad vyathate na kiṁ svit
kūrpādibhir bhramati dhīr bhavad-āyuṣāṁ naḥ

SYNONYMS

yat—which; *te*—Your; *sujāta*—very fine; *caraṇa-ambu-ruham*—lotus feet; *staneṣu*—on the breasts; *bhītāḥ*—being afraid; *śanaiḥ*—gently; *priya*—O dear one; *dadhīmahi*—we place; *karkaśeṣu*—rough; *tena*—with them; *aṭavīm*—the path; *aṭasi*—You roam; *tat*—they; *vyathate*—are distressed; *na*—not; *kim svit*—we wonder; *kūrpa-ādibhiḥ*—by small stones and so on; *bhramati*—flutters; *dhīḥ*—the mind; *bhavat-āyuṣām*—of those of whom Your Lordship is the very life; *naḥ*—of us.

TRANSLATION

"O dearly beloved! Your lotus feet are so soft that we place them gently on our breasts, fearing that Your feet will be hurt. Our life rests only in You. Our

minds, therefore, are filled with anxiety that Your tender feet might be wounded by pebbles as You roam about on the forest path."

PURPORT

This is a verse from *Śrīmad-Bhāgavatam* (10.31.19) spoken by the *gopīs* when Kṛṣṇa left them in the midst of the *rāsa-līlā.*

TEXT 66

তবে 'খেলা-তীর্থ' দেখি' 'ভাণ্ডীরবন' আইলা ।
যমুনা পার হঞা 'ভদ্র-বন' গেলা ॥ ৬৬ ॥

tabe 'khelā-tīrtha' dekhi' 'bhāṇḍīravana' āilā
yamunā pāra hañā 'bhadra-vana' gelā

SYNONYMS

tabe—thereafter; *khelā-tīrtha*—Khelā-tīrtha; *dekhi'*—seeing; *bhāṇḍīravana*—Bhāṇḍīravana; *āilā*—came to; *yamunā pāra hañā*—crossing the River Yamunā; *bhadra-vana*—to Bhadravana; *gelā*—went.

TRANSLATION

Afterwards, Śrī Caitanya Mahāprabhu saw Khelā-tīrtha and then went to Bhāṇḍīravana. Crossing the Yamunā River, He went to Bhadravana.

PURPORT

In the *Bhakti-ratnākara* it is said that Śrī Kṛṣṇa and Balarāma used to play at Khelā-tīrtha with the cowherd boys during the entire day. Mother Yaśodā had to call Them to take Their baths and eat Their lunch.

TEXT 67

'শ্রীবন' দেখি' পুনঃ গেলা 'লোহ-বন' ।
'মহাবন' গিয়া কৈলা জন্মস্থান-দরশন ॥ ৬৭ ॥

'śrīvana' dekhi' punaḥ gelā 'loha-vana'
'mahāvana' giyā kailā janma-sthāna-daraśana

SYNONYMS

śrī-vana—Śrīvana; *dekhi'*—seeing; *punaḥ*—again; *gelā*—went; *loha-vana*—to Lohavana; *mahā-vana*—to Mahāvana; *giyā*—going; *kailā*—performed; *janma-sthāna*—birth site; *daraśana*—seeing.

TRANSLATION

Śrī Caitanya Mahāprabhu then visited Śrīvana and Lohavana. He then went to Mahāvana and saw Gokula, the place of Lord Kṛṣṇa's early childhood pastimes.

PURPORT

Of Śrīvana (also called Bilvavana), the *Bhakti-ratnākara* states, *devatā-pūjita bilvavana śobhāmaya:* "The beautiful forest of Bilvavana is worshiped by all the demigods."

About Lohavana, *Bhakti-ratnākara* (Fifth Wave) states:

lohavane kṛṣṇera adbhuta go-cāraṇa
ethā loha-jaṅghāsure vadhe bhagavān

"At Lohavana, Lord Kṛṣṇa used to tend cows. The demon named Lohajaṅgha was killed at this place."

Mahāvana is described as follows in *Bhakti-ratnākara* (Fifth Wave):

dekha nanda-yaśodā-ālaya mahāvane
ei dekha śrī-kṛṣṇa-candrera janma sthala
śrī-gokula, mahāvana——dui 'eka' haya

"Behold the house of Nanda and Yaśodā in Mahāvana. See the birthplace of Lord Kṛṣṇa. Mahāvana and the birthplace of Lord Kṛṣṇa, Gokula, are one and the same."

TEXT 68

যমলার্জুনভঙ্গাদি দেখিল সেই স্থল ।
প্রেমাবেশে প্রভুর মন হৈল টলমল ॥ ৬৮ ॥

yamalārjuna-bhaṅgādi dekhila sei sthala
premāveśe prabhura mana haila ṭalamala

SYNONYMS

yamala-arjuna-bhaṅga—the place where the twin *arjuna* trees were broken; *ādi*—beginning with; *dekhila*—saw; *sei sthala*—that place; *prema-āveśe*—in great ecstasy; *prabhura*—of Śrī Caitanya Mahāprabhu; *mana*—mind; *haila*—became; *ṭalamala*—agitated.

TRANSLATION

Upon seeing the place where the twin arjuna trees were broken by Śrī Kṛṣṇa, Śrī Caitanya Mahāprabhu was moved to great ecstatic love.

TEXT 69

'গোকুল' দেখিয়া আইলা 'মথুরা'-নগরে ।
'জন্মস্থান' দেখি' রহে সেই বিপ্র-ঘরে ॥ ৬৯ ॥

'gokula' dekhiyā āilā 'mathurā'-nagare
'janma-sthāna' dekhi' rahe sei vipra-ghare

SYNONYMS

gokula dekhiyā—seeing Gokula; *āilā*—came; *mathurā-nagare*—in the city of Mathurā; *janma-sthāna*—the birthplace of Lord Kṛṣṇa; *dekhi'*—seeing; *rahe*—stays; *sei vipra-ghare*—in the house of the Sanoḍiyā *brāhmaṇa.*

TRANSLATION

After seeing Gokula, Śrī Caitanya Mahāprabhu returned to Mathurā, where He saw the birthplace of the Lord. While there, He stayed at the house of the Sanoḍiyā brāhmaṇa.

TEXT 70

লোকের সংঘট্ট দেখি মথুরা ছাড়িয়া ।
একান্তে 'অক্রুর-তীর্থে' রহিলা আসিয়া ॥ ৭০ ॥

lokera saṅghaṭṭa dekhi mathurā chāḍiyā
ekānte 'akrūra-tīrthe' rahilā āsiyā

SYNONYMS

lokera—of people; *saṅghaṭṭa*—crowd; *dekhi*—seeing; *mathurā*—the city of Mathurā; *chāḍiyā*—leaving; *ekānte*—in a solitary place; *akrūra-tīrthe*—at Akrūra-tīrtha; *rahilā*—stayed; *āsiyā*—coming.

TRANSLATION

Seeing a great crowd assemble at Mathurā, Śrī Caitanya Mahāprabhu left and went to Akrūra-tīrtha. He remained there in a solitary place.

PURPORT

Akrūra-tīrtha is also mentioned in the *Bhakti-ratnākara* (Fifth Wave):

dekha, śrīnivāsa, ei akrūra grāmete
śrī-kṛṣṇa-caitanya-prabhu chilena nibhṛte

"Śrīnivāsa, look at this village of Akrūra. Śrī Caitanya Mahāprabhu stayed there in a solitary place."

TEXT 71

আর দিন আইলা প্রভু দেখিতে 'বৃন্দাবন'।
'কালীয়-হ্রদে' স্নান কৈলা আর প্রস্কন্দন ॥ ৭১ ॥

āra dina āilā prabhu dekhite 'vṛndāvana'
'kālīya-hrade' snāna kailā āra praskandana

SYNONYMS

āra dina—the next day; *āilā*—came; *prabhu*—Śrī Caitanya Mahāprabhu; *dekhite*—to see; *vṛndāvana*—Vṛndāvana; *kālīya-hrade*—in the Kālīya Lake; *snāna kailā*—took a bath; *āra*—and; *praskandana*—at Praskandana.

TRANSLATION

The next day, Śrī Caitanya Mahāprabhu went to Vṛndāvana and took His bath at the Kālīya Lake and Praskandana.

PURPORT

Kālīya-hrada is mentioned in *Bhakti-ratnākara* (Fifth Wave):

e kālīya-tīrtha pāpa vināśaya
kālīya-tīrtha-sthāne bahu-kārya-siddhi haya

"When one takes a bath in Kālīya-hrada, he is freed from all sinful activities. One can also be successful in business by bathing in Kālīya-hrada."

TEXT 72

'দ্বাদশ-আদিত্য' হৈতে 'কেশীতীর্থে' আইলা।
রাস-স্থলী দেখি' প্রেমে মূর্চ্ছিত হইলা ॥ ৭২ ॥

'dvādaśa-āditya' haite 'keśī-tīrthe' āilā
rāsa-sthalī dekhi' preme mūrcchita ha-ilā

SYNONYMS

dvādaśa-āditya haite—from Dvādaśāditya; *keśī-tīrthe āilā*—came to Keśī-tīrtha; *rāsa-sthalī dekhi'*—visiting the place of the *rāsa* dance; *preme*—in ecstatic love; *mūrcchita ha-ilā*—became unconscious.

TRANSLATION

After seeing the holy place called Praskandana, Śrī Caitanya Mahāprabhu went to Dvādaśāditya. From there He went to Keśī-tīrtha, and when He saw

the place where the rāsa dance had taken place, He immediately lost consciousness due to ecstatic love.

TEXT 73

চেতন পাঞা পুনঃ গড়াগড়ি যায় ।
হাসে, কান্দে, নাচে, পড়ে, উচ্চৈঃস্বরে গায় ॥ ৭৩ ॥

cetana pāñā punaḥ gaḍāgaḍi yāya
hāse, kānde, nāce, paḍe, uccaiḥ-svare gāya

SYNONYMS

cetana pāñā—getting His senses back; *punaḥ*—again; *gaḍāgaḍi yāya*—rolls on the ground; *hāse*—laughs; *kānde*—cries; *nāce*—dances; *paḍe*—falls down; *uccaiḥ-svare gāya*—sings very loudly.

TRANSLATION

When the Lord regained His senses, He began to roll on the ground. He would sometimes laugh, cry, dance and fall down. He would also chant very loudly.

TEXT 74

এইরঙ্গে সেইদিন তথা গোঙাইলা ।
সন্ধ্যাকালে অক্রূরে আসি' ভিক্ষা নির্বাহিলা ॥ ৭৪ ॥

ei-raṅge sei-dina tathā goṅāilā
sandhyā-kāle akrūre āsi' bhikṣā nirvāhilā

SYNONYMS

ei-raṅge—in this amusement; *sei-dina*—that day; *tathā goṅāilā*—passed the day there; *sandhyā-kāle*—in the evening; *akrūre āsi'*—returning to Akrūra-tīrtha; *bhikṣā nirvāhilā*—took His meal.

TRANSLATION

Being thus transcendentally amused, Śrī Caitanya Mahāprabhu passed that day happily at Keśī-tīrtha. In the evening He returned to Akrūra-tīrtha, where He took His meal.

TEXT 75

প্রাতে বৃন্দাবনে কৈলা 'চীরঘাটে' স্নান ।
তেঁতুলী-তলাতে আসি' করিলা বিশ্রাম ॥ ৭৫ ॥

prāte vṛndāvane kailā 'cīra-ghāṭe' snāna
teṅtulī-talāte āsi' karilā viśrāma

SYNONYMS

prāte—in the morning; *vṛndāvane*—in Vṛndāvana; *kailā*—performed; *cīra-ghāṭe snāna*—bathing at Cīra-ghāṭa; *teṅtulī-talāte*—underneath the Teṅtulī tree; *āsi'*—coming; *karilā viśrāma*—took rest.

TRANSLATION

The next morning Śrī Caitanya Mahāprabhu returned to Vṛndāvana and took His bath at Cīra-ghāṭa. He then went to Teṅtulī-talā, where He took rest.

TEXT 76

কৃষ্ণলীলা-কালের সেই বৃক্ষ পুরাতন ।
তার তলে পিঁড়ি-বান্ধা পরম-চিক্কণ ॥ ৭৬ ॥

kṛṣṇa-līlā-kālera sei vṛkṣa purātana
tāra tale piṅḍi-bāndhā parama-cikkaṇa

SYNONYMS

kṛṣṇa-līlā-kālera—of the time of Lord Kṛṣṇa's presence; *sei vṛkṣa*—that tamarind tree; *purātana*—very old; *tāra tale*—underneath that tree; *piṅḍi-bāndhā*—a platform; *parama-cikkaṇa*—very shiny.

TRANSLATION

The tamarind tree named Teṅtulī-talā was very old, having been there since the time of Lord Kṛṣṇa's pastimes. Beneath the tree was a very shiny platform.

TEXT 77

নিকটে যমুনা বহে শীতল সমীর ।
বৃন্দাবন-শোভা দেখে যমুনার নীর ॥ ৭৭ ॥

nikaṭe yamunā vahe śītala samīra
vṛndāvana-śobhā dekhe yamunāra nīra

SYNONYMS

nikaṭe—near the Teṅtulī-talā, or Āmli-talā; *yamunā*—the Yamunā; *vahe*—flows; *śītala samīra*—very cool breeze; *vṛndāvana-śobhā*—the beauty of Vṛndāvana; *dekhe*—sees; *yamunāra*—of the River Yamunā; *nīra*—water.

TRANSLATION

Since the River Yamunā flowed near Teṅtulī-talā, a very cool breeze blew there. While there, the Lord saw the beauty of Vṛndāvana and the water of the River Yamunā.

TEXT 78

তেঁতুল-তলে বসি' করে নাম-সংকীর্তন ।
মধ্যাহ্ন করি' আসি' করে 'অক্রূরে' ভোজন ॥ ৭৮ ॥

teṅtula-tale vasi' kare nāma-saṅkīrtana
madhyāhna kari' āsi' kare 'akrūre' bhojana

SYNONYMS

teṅtula-tale—underneath the tamarind tree; *vasi'*—sitting down; *kare*—does; *nāma-saṅkīrtana*—chanting the holy name of the Lord; *madhyāhna kari'*—at noon; *āsi'*—coming back; *kare*—performs; *akrūre*—at Akrūra-tīrtha; *bhojana*—taking lunch.

TRANSLATION

Śrī Caitanya Mahāprabhu used to sit beneath the old tamarind tree and chant the holy name of the Lord. At noon He would return to Akrūra-tīrtha to take lunch.

TEXT 79

অক্রূরের লোক আইসে প্রভুরে দেখিতে ।
লোক-ভিড়ে স্বচ্ছন্দে নারে 'কীর্তন' করিতে ॥ ৭৯ ॥

akrūrera loka āise prabhure dekhite
loka-bhiḍe svacchande nāre 'kīrtana' karite

SYNONYMS

akrūrera loka—the people at Akrūra-tīrtha; *āise*—came; *prabhure*—Śrī Caitanya Mahāprabhu; *dekhite*—to see; *loka-bhiḍe*—because of such a crowd of people; *svacchande*—without disturbance; *nāre*—was not able; *kīrtana karite*—to perform *kīrtana.*

TRANSLATION

All the people who lived near Akrūra-tīrtha came to see Śrī Caitanya Mahāprabhu, and due to the large crowds, the Lord could not peacefully chant the holy name.

TEXT 80

বৃন্দাবনে আসি' প্রভু বসিয়া একান্ত ।
নামসংকীর্তন করে মধ্যাহ্ন-পর্যন্ত ॥ ৮০ ॥

vṛndāvane āsi' prabhu vasiyā ekānta
nāma-saṅkīrtana kare madhyāhna-paryanta

SYNONYMS

vṛndāvane āsi'—coming to Vṛndāvana; *prabhu*—Śrī Caitanya Mahāprabhu; *vasiyā*—sitting; *ekānta*—in a solitary place; *nāma-saṅkīrtana kare*—performs chanting of the holy name; *madhyāhna-paryanta*—until noon.

TRANSLATION

Therefore Śrī Caitanya Mahāprabhu would go to Vṛndāvana and sit in a solitary place. It was there that He chanted the holy name until noon.

TEXT 81

তৃতীয়-প্রহরে লোক পায় দরশন ।
সবারে উপদেশ করে 'নামসংকীর্তন' ॥ ৮১ ॥

tṛtīya-prahare loka pāya daraśana
sabāre upadeśa kare 'nāma-saṅkīrtana'

SYNONYMS

tṛtīya-prahare—in the afternoon; *loka*—people; *pāya daraśana*—get an interview; *sabāre*—unto everyone; *upadeśa kare*—instructs; *nāma-saṅkīrtana*—chanting of the holy name of the Lord.

TRANSLATION

In the afternoon, people were able to speak to Him. The Lord told everyone of the importance of chanting the holy name.

TEXT 82

হেনকালে আইল বৈষ্ণব 'কৃষ্ণদাস' নাম ।
রাজপুত-জাতি, গৃহস্থ, যমুনা-পারে গ্রাম ॥ ৮২ ॥

hena-kāle āila vaiṣṇava 'kṛṣṇadāsa' nāma
rājaputa-jāti,—gṛhastha, yamunā-pāre grāma

SYNONYMS

hena-kāle—at this time; *āila*—came; *vaiṣṇava*—a devotee; *kṛṣṇadāsa nāma*—of the name Kṛṣṇadāsa; *rājaputa-jāti*—belonging to the *kṣatriya* class; *gṛhastha*—householder; *yamunā-pāre grāma*—his residence on the other side of the Yamunā.

TRANSLATION

During this time, a Vaiṣṇava named Kṛṣṇadāsa came to see Śrī Caitanya Mahāprabhu. He was a householder belonging to the kṣatriya caste, and his house was located on the other side of the Yamunā.

TEXT 83

'কেশী' স্নান করি' সেই 'কালীয়দহ' যাইতে।
আম্‌লি-তলায় গোসাঞিরে দেখে আচম্বিতে ॥৮৩॥

'keśī' snāna kari' sei 'kālīya-daha' yāite
āmli-talāya gosāñire dekhe ācambite

SYNONYMS

keśī snāna kari'—after taking his bath at the place known as Keśī-tīrtha; *sei*—that person; *kālīya-daha yāite*—going to the Kālīya-daha; *āmli-talāya*—at the place known as Āmli-talā; *gosāñire*—Śrī Caitanya Mahāprabhu; *dekhe*—sees; *ācambite*—suddenly.

TRANSLATION

After bathing at Keśī-tīrtha, Kṛṣṇadāsa went toward Kālīya-daha and suddenly saw Śrī Caitanya Mahāprabhu sitting at Āmli-talā [Teṅtulī-talā].

TEXT 84

প্রভুর রূপ-প্রেম দেখি' হইল চমৎকার।
প্রেমাবেশে প্রভুরে করেন নমস্কার ॥ ৮৪ ॥

prabhura rūpa-prema dekhi' ha-ila camatkāra
premāveśe prabhure karena namaskāra

SYNONYMS

prabhura—of Śrī Caitanya Mahāprabhu; *rūpa-prema*—personal beauty and ecstatic love; *dekhi'*—seeing; *ha-ila camatkāra*—became astonished; *prema-āveśe*—in ecstatic love; *prabhure*—to Śrī Caitanya Mahāprabhu; *karena namaskāra*—offers obeisances.

TRANSLATION

Upon seeing the Lord's personal beauty and ecstatic love, Kṛṣṇadāsa was very astonished. Out of ecstatic love, he offered his respectful obeisances unto the Lord.

TEXT 85

প্রভু কহে,—কে তুমি, কাহাঁ তোমার ঘর ?
কৃষ্ণদাস কহে,– মুঞি গৃহস্থ পামর ॥ ৮৫ ॥

prabhu kahe,—ke tumi, kāhāṅ tomāra ghara?
kṛṣṇadāsa kahe,—mui gṛhastha pāmara

SYNONYMS

prabhu kahe—the Lord inquired; *ke tumi*—who are you; *kāhāṅ*—where; *tomāra*—your; *ghara*—residence; *kṛṣṇadāsa kahe*—Kṛṣṇadāsa replied; *mui*—I; *gṛhastha*—householder; *pāmara*—most fallen.

TRANSLATION

Śrī Caitanya Mahāprabhu asked Kṛṣṇadāsa, "Who are you? Where is your home?" Kṛṣṇadāsa replied, "I am a most fallen householder.

TEXT 86

রাজপুত-জাতি মুঞি, ও-পারে মোর ঘর ।
মোর ইচ্ছা হয় –'হঙ বৈষ্ণব-কিঙ্কর' ॥ ৮৬ ॥

rājaputa-jāti muñi, o-pāre mora ghara
mora icchā haya—'haṅa vaiṣṇava-kiṅkara'

SYNONYMS

rājaputa-jāti—belong to the Rājaputa caste; *muñi*—I; *o-pāre*—on the other side of the Yamunā; *mora ghara*—my residence; *mora icchā haya*—I wish; *haṅa*—to become; *vaiṣṇava-kiṅkara*—the servant of a Vaiṣṇava.

TRANSLATION

"I belong to the Rājaputa caste, and my home is just on the other side of the River Yamunā. However, I wish to be the servant of a Vaiṣṇava.

TEXT 87

কিন্তু আজি এক মুঞি 'স্বপ্ন' দেখিনু।
সেই স্বপ্ন পরতেক তোমা আসি' পাইনু ॥ ৮৭ ॥

kintu āji eka muñi 'svapna' dekhinu
sei svapna parateka tomā āsi' pāinu

SYNONYMS

kintu—but; *āji*—today; *eka*—one; *muñi*—I; *svapna*—dream; *dekhinu*—saw; *sei svapna*—that dream; *parateka*—according to; *tomā*—You; *āsi'*—coming; *pāinu*—I have gotten.

TRANSLATION

"Today I have had a dream, and according to that dream I have come here and found You."

TEXT 88

প্রভু তাঁরে কৃপা কৈলা আলিঙ্গন করি।
প্রেমে মত্ত হৈল সেই নাচে, বলে 'হরি' ॥ ৮৮ ॥

prabhu tāṅre kṛpā kailā āliṅgana kari
preme matta haila sei nāce, bale 'hari'

SYNONYMS

prabhu—Śrī Caitanya Mahāprabhu; *tāṅre*—unto him; *kṛpā kailā*—bestowed His mercy; *āliṅgana kari*—embracing; *preme*—in ecstatic love; *matta haila*—became mad; *sei*—that Kṛṣṇadāsa; *nāce*—dances; *bale*—chants; *hari*—the holy name of the Lord.

TRANSLATION

Śrī Caitanya Mahāprabhu then bestowed upon Kṛṣṇadāsa His causeless mercy by embracing him. Kṛṣṇadāsa became mad with ecstatic love and began to dance and chant the holy name of Hari.

TEXT 89

প্রভু-সঙ্গে মধ্যাহ্নে অক্রূর তীর্থে আইলা।
প্রভুর অবশিষ্টপাত্র-প্রসাদ পাইলা ॥ ৮৯ ॥

prabhu-saṅge madhyāhne akrūra tīrthe āilā
prabhura avaśiṣṭa-pātra-prasāda pāilā

SYNONYMS

prabhu-saṅge—with the Lord; *madhyāhne*—in the afternoon; *akrūra tīrthe*—to Akrūra-tīrtha; *āilā*—came; *prabhura*—of Śrī Caitanya Mahāprabhu; *avaśiṣṭa-pātra-prasāda*—remnants of food; *pāilā*—got.

TRANSLATION

Kṛṣṇadāsa returned to Akrūra-tīrtha with the Lord, and remnants of the Lord's food were given to him.

TEXT 90

প্রাতে প্রভু-সঙ্গে আইলা জলপাত্র লঞা ।
প্রভু-সঙ্গে রহে গৃহ-স্ত্রী-পুত্র ছাড়িয়া ॥ ৯০ ॥

prāte prabhu-saṅge āilā jala-pātra lañā
prabhu-saṅge rahe gṛha-strī-putra chāḍiyā

SYNONYMS

prāte—in the morning; *prabhu-saṅge*—with Śrī Caitanya Mahāprabhu; *āilā*—came; *jala-pātra lañā*—carrying a waterpot; *prabhu-saṅge rahe*—remains with Śrī Caitanya Mahāprabhu; *gṛha*—home; *strī*—wife; *putra*—children; *chāḍiyā*—leaving aside.

TRANSLATION

The next morning, Kṛṣṇadāsa went with Śrī Caitanya Mahāprabhu to Vṛndāvana and carried His waterpot. Kṛṣṇadāsa thus left his wife, home and children in order to remain with Śrī Caitanya Mahāprabhu.

TEXT 91

বৃন্দাবনে পুনঃ 'কৃষ্ণ' প্রকট হইল ।
যাহাঁ তাহাঁ লোক সব কহিতে লাগিল ॥ ৯১ ॥

vṛndāvane punaḥ 'kṛṣṇa' prakaṭa ha-ila
yāhāṅ tāhāṅ loka saba kahite lāgila

SYNONYMS

vṛndāvane—at Vṛndāvana; *punaḥ*—again; *kṛṣṇa*—Lord Śrī Kṛṣṇa; *prakaṭa haila*—became manifested; *yāhāṅ tāhāṅ*—everywhere; *loka*—people; *saba*—all; *kahite lāgila*—began to speak.

TRANSLATION

Everywhere the Lord went, all the people said, "Kṛṣṇa has again manifest at Vṛndāvana."

TEXT 92

একদিন অক্রূরেতে লোক প্রাতঃকালে।
বৃন্দাবন হৈতে আইসে করি' কোলাহলে ॥ ৯২ ॥

eka-dina akrūrete loka prātaḥ-kāle
vṛndāvana haite āise kari' kolāhale

SYNONYMS

eka-dina—one day; *akrūrete*—at Akrūra-tīrtha; *loka*—people; *prātaḥ-kāle*—in the morning; *vṛndāvana haite*—from Vṛndāvana; *āise*—came; *kari'*—making; *kolāhale*—tumult.

TRANSLATION

One morning many people came to Akrūra-tīrtha. As they came from Vṛndāvana, they made a tumultuous sound.

TEXT 93

প্রভু দেখি' করিল লোক চরণ বন্দন।
প্রভু কহে,—কাহাঁ হৈতে করিলা আগমন ? ৯৩ ॥

prabhu dekhi' karila loka caraṇa vandana
prabhu kahe,——kāhāṅ haite karilā āgamana?

SYNONYMS

prabhu dekhi'—seeing Lord Śrī Caitanya Mahāprabhu; *karila*—offered; *loka*—people; *caraṇa vandana*—respect unto His lotus feet; *prabhu kahe*—Śrī Caitanya Mahāprabhu said; *kāhāṅ haite*—from where; *karilā āgamana*—have you come.

TRANSLATION

Upon seeing Śrī Caitanya Mahāprabhu, all the people offered respects at His lotus feet. The Lord then asked them, "Where are you all coming from?"

TEXT 94

লোকে কহে,—কৃষ্ণ প্রকট কালীয়দহের জলে !
কালীয়-শিরে নৃত্য করে, ফণা-রত্ন জ্বলে ॥ ৯৪ ॥

loke kahe,——kṛṣṇa prakaṭa kālīya-dahera jale!
kālīya-śire nṛtya kare, phaṇā-ratna jvale

SYNONYMS

loke kahe—all the people replied; *kṛṣṇa prakaṭa*—Kṛṣṇa is again manifest; *kālīya-dahera jale*—in the water of Lake Kālīya; *kālīya-śire*—on the head of the serpent Kālīya; *nṛtya kare*—dances; *phaṇā-ratna jvale*—the jewels on the hoods blaze.

TRANSLATION

The people replied, "Kṛṣṇa has again manifest Himself on the waters of the Kālīya Lake. He dances on the hoods of the serpent Kālīya, and the jewels on those hoods are blazing.

TEXT 95

সাক্ষাৎ দেখিল লোক—নাহিক সংশয় ।
শুনি' হাসি' কহে প্রভু,—সব 'সত্য' হয় ॥ ৯৫ ॥

sākṣāt dekhila loka——nāhika saṁśaya
śuni' hāsi' kahe prabhu,——saba 'satya' haya

SYNONYMS

sākṣāt—directly; *dekhila loka*—all the people saw; *nāhika saṁśaya*—there is no doubt; *śuni'*—hearing; *hāsi'*—laughing; *kahe prabhu*—Śrī Caitanya Mahāprabhu said; *saba satya haya*—all that you have said is correct.

TRANSLATION

"Everyone has seen Lord Kṛṣṇa Himself. There is no doubt about it." Hearing this, Śrī Caitanya Mahāprabhu began to laugh. He then said, "Everything is correct."

TEXT 96

এইমত তিন-রাত্রি লোকের গমন ।
সবে আসি' কহে,— কৃষ্ণ পাইলুঁ দরশন ॥ ৯৬ ॥

ei-mata tina-rātri lokera gamana
sabe āsi' kahe,——kṛṣṇa pāiluṅ daraśana

SYNONYMS

ei-mata—in this way; *tina-rātri*—three nights; *lokera gamana*—people went; *sabe*—all; *āsi'*—coming; *kahe*—say; *kṛṣṇa pāiluṅ daraśana*—we have seen Lord Kṛṣṇa directly.

TRANSLATION

For three successive nights people went to Kālīya-daha to see Kṛṣṇa, and everyone returned saying, "Now we have seen Kṛṣṇa Himself."

TEXT 97

প্রভু-আগে কহে লোক,—শ্রীকৃষ্ণ দেখিল ।
'সরস্বতী' এই বাক্যে 'সত্য' কহাইল ॥ ৯৭ ॥

prabhu-āge kahe loka,——śrī-kṛṣṇa dekhila
'sarasvatī' ei vākye 'satya' kahāila

SYNONYMS

prabhu-āge—in front of Śrī Caitanya Mahāprabhu; *kahe loka*—all the people began to say; *śrī-kṛṣṇa dekhila*—that they have seen Lord Kṛṣṇa; *sarasvatī*—the goddess of learning; *ei vākye*—this statement; *satya*—true; *kahāila*—caused the people to speak.

TRANSLATION

Everyone came before Śrī Caitanya Mahāprabhu and said, "Now we have directly seen Lord Kṛṣṇa." Thus by the mercy of the goddess of learning they were made to speak the truth.

TEXT 98

মহাপ্রভু দেখি' 'সত্য' কৃষ্ণ-দরশন ।
নিজাজ্ঞানে সত্য ছাড়ি' 'অসত্যে সত্য-ভ্রম' ॥ ৯৮ ॥

mahāprabhu dekhi' 'satya' kṛṣṇa-daraśana
nijājñāne satya chāḍi' 'asatye satya-bhrama'

SYNONYMS

mahāprabhu dekhi'—by seeing Śrī Caitanya Mahāprabhu; *satya*—truly; *kṛṣṇa-daraśana*—seeing Kṛṣṇa; *nija-ajñāne*—by their personal lack of knowledge; *satya chāḍi'*—giving up the real truth; *asatye*—untruth; *satya-bhrama*—mistaking for the truth.

TRANSLATION

When the people saw Śrī Caitanya Mahāprabhu, they actually saw Kṛṣṇa, but because they were following their own imperfect knowledge, they accepted the wrong thing as Kṛṣṇa.

TEXT 99

ভট্টাচার্য তবে কহে প্রভুর চরণে ।
'আজ্ঞা দেহ', যাই' করি কৃষ্ণ দরশনে !' ৯৯ ॥

bhaṭṭācārya tabe kahe prabhura caraṇe
'ājñā deha', yāi' kari kṛṣṇa daraśane!'

SYNONYMS

bhaṭṭācārya—Balabhadra Bhaṭṭācārya; *tabe*—at that time; *kahe*—says; *prabhura caraṇe*—at the lotus feet of Śrī Caitanya Mahāprabhu; *ājñā deha'*—please give permission; *yāi'*—going; *kari kṛṣṇa daraśane*—I shall see Lord Kṛṣṇa directly.

TRANSLATION

At that time Balabhadra Bhaṭṭācārya placed a request at the lotus feet of Śrī Caitanya Mahāprabhu. He said, "Please give me permission to go see Lord Kṛṣṇa directly."

PURPORT

The puzzled people who visited Śrī Caitanya Mahāprabhu were actually seeing Lord Kṛṣṇa, but they were mistaken in thinking that Lord Kṛṣṇa had come to Kālīya Lake. They all said that they had seen Kṛṣṇa directly performing His pastimes on the hood of the serpent Kālīya and that the jewels on Kālīya's hoods were blazing brilliantly. Because they were speculating with their imperfect knowledge, they saw Śrī Caitanya Mahāprabhu as an ordinary human being and a boatman's light in the lake as Kṛṣṇa. One must see things as they are through the mercy of a spiritual master; otherwise if one tries to see Kṛṣṇa directly, he may mistake an ordinary man for Kṛṣṇa or Kṛṣṇa for an ordinary man. Everyone has to see Kṛṣṇa according to the verdict of Vedic literatures presented by the self-realized spiritual master. A sincere person is able to see Kṛṣṇa through the transparent via medium of Śrī Gurudeva, the spiritual master. Unless one is enlightened by the knowledge given by the spiritual master, he cannot see things as they are, even though he remains constantly with the spiritual master. This incident at Kālīya-daha is very instructive for those eager to advance in Kṛṣṇa consciousness.

TEXT 100

তবে তাঁরে কহে প্রভু চাপড় মারিয়া।
"মূর্খের বাক্যে 'মূর্খ' হৈলা পণ্ডিত হঞা ॥ ১০০ ॥

tabe tāṅre kahe prabhu cāpaḍa māriyā
"mūrkhera vākye 'mūrkha' hailā paṇḍita hañā

SYNONYMS

tabe—thereafter; *tāṅre*—unto Balabhadra Bhaṭṭācārya; *kahe*—says; *prabhu*—Śrī Caitanya Mahāprabhu; *cāpaḍa māriyā*—slapping; *mūrkhera vākye*—by the words of some rascals and fools; *mūrkha hailā*—you became a fool; *paṇḍita hañā*—being a learned scholar.

TRANSLATION

When Balabhadra Bhaṭṭācārya asked to see Kṛṣṇa at Kālīya-daha, Śrī Caitanya Mahāprabhu mercifully slapped him, saying, "You are a learned scholar, but you have become a fool influenced by the statements of other fools.

PURPORT

Māyā is so strong that even a person like Balabhadra Bhaṭṭācārya, who was constantly staying with Śrī Caitanya Mahāprabhu, was influenced by the words of fools. He wanted to see Kṛṣṇa directly by going to Kālīya-daha, but Śrī Caitanya Mahāprabhu, being the original spiritual master, would not allow His servant to fall into such foolishness. He therefore chastised him, slapping him just to bring him to a real sense of Kṛṣṇa consciousness.

TEXT 101

কৃষ্ণ কেনে দরশন দিবে কলিকালে ?
নিজ-ভ্রমে মূর্খ-লোক করে কোলাহলে ॥ ১০১ ॥

kṛṣṇa kene daraśana dibe kali-kāle?
nija-bhrame mūrkha-loka kare kolāhale

SYNONYMS

kṛṣṇa—Lord Kṛṣṇa; *kene*—why; *daraśana*—interview; *dibe*—would give; *kali-kāle*—in this age of Kali; *nija-bhrame*—by their own mistake; *mūrkha-loka*—foolish persons; *kare kolāhale*—make a chaotic tumult.

TRANSLATION

"Why will Kṛṣṇa appear in the age of Kali? Foolish people who are mistaken are simply causing agitation and making a tumult.

PURPORT

Śrī Caitanya Mahāprabhu's first statement (*kṛṣṇa kene daraśana dibe kali-kāle*) refers to the scriptures. According to scripture, Kṛṣṇa appears in Dvāpara-yuga, but He never appears as Himself in Kali-yuga. Rather, He appears in Kali-yuga in a covered form. As stated in *Śrīmad-Bhāgavatam* (11.5.32): *kṛṣṇa-varṇaṁ tviṣākṛṣṇaṁ sāṅgopāṅgāstra-pārṣadam.* Kṛṣṇa appears in the age of Kali in the garb of a devotee, Śrī Caitanya Mahāprabhu, who always associates with His internal soldiers—Śrī Advaita Prabhu, Śrī Nityānanda Prabhu, Śrīvāsa Prabhu and Gadādhara Prabhu. Although Balabhadra Bhaṭṭācārya was personally serving Lord Kṛṣṇa in His role as a devotee (Caitanya Mahāprabhu), he mistook Lord Kṛṣṇa for an ordinary man and an ordinary man for Lord Kṛṣṇa because he did not follow the rules set down by *śāstra* and *guru.*

TEXT 102

'বাতুল' না হইও, ঘরে রহত বসিয়া ।
'কৃষ্ণ' দরশন করিহ কালি রাত্র্যে যাঞা ॥" ১০২ ॥

'vātula' nā ha-io, ghare rahata vasiyā
'kṛṣṇa' daraśana kariha kāli rātrye yāñā"

SYNONYMS

vātula—mad; *nā ha-io*—do not become; *ghare*—at home; *rahata*—keep; *vasiyā*—sitting; *kṛṣṇa*—Lord Kṛṣṇa; *daraśana*—seeing; *kariha*—you may do; *kāli*—tomorrow; *rātrye*—at night; *yāñā*—going.

TRANSLATION

"Do not become mad. Simply sit down here, and tomorrow night you will go see Kṛṣṇa."

TEXT 103

প্রাতঃকালে ভব্য-লোক প্রভু-স্থানে আইলা।
'কৃষ্ণ দেখি' আইলা ?'—প্রভু তাঁহারে পুছিলা ॥১০৩ ॥

prātaḥ-kāle bhavya-loka prabhu-sthāne āilā
'kṛṣṇa dekhi' āilā?'——prabhu tāṅhāre puchilā

SYNONYMS

prātaḥ-kāle—the next morning; *bhavya-loka*—respectable gentlemen; *prabhu-sthāne*—at the place of Śrī Caitanya Mahāprabhu; *āilā*—came; *kṛṣṇa dekhi'*—seeing Lord Kṛṣṇa; *āilā*—have you come; *prabhu*—Śrī Caitanya Mahāprabhu; *tāṅhāre puchilā*—inquired from them.

TRANSLATION

The next morning some respectable gentlemen came to see Śrī Caitanya Mahāprabhu, and the Lord asked them, "Have you seen Kṛṣṇa?"

TEXT 104

লোক কহে,—রাত্র্যে কৈবর্ত্য নৌকাতে চড়িয়া।
কালীয়দহে মৎস্য মারে, দেউটী জ্বালিয়া ॥ ১০৪ ॥

loka kahe,——rātrye kaivartya naukāte caḍiyā
kālīya-dahe matsya māre, deuṭī jvāliyā

SYNONYMS

loka kahe—the sensible respectable persons said; *rātrye*—at night; *kaivartya*—a fisherman; *naukāte*—on a boat; *caḍiyā*—getting up; *kālīya-dahe*—in the lake of Kālīya; *matsya māre*—catches fish; *deuṭī jvāliyā*—lighting a torch.

TRANSLATION

These respectable gentlemen replied, "At night in the Kālīya Lake a fisherman lighting a torch in his boat catches many fish.

TEXT 105

দূর হৈতে তাহা দেখি' লোকের হয় 'ভ্রম'।
'কালীয়ের শরীরে কৃষ্ণ করিছে নর্তন' ! ১০৫ ॥

dūra haite tāhā dekhi' lokera haya 'bhrama'
'kālīyera śarīre kṛṣṇa kariche nartana'!

SYNONYMS

dūra haite—from a distant place; *tāhā dekhi'*—seeing that; *lokera*—of people in general; *haya*—there is; *bhrama*—mistake; *kālīyera*—of the snake Kālīya; *śarīre*—on the body; *kṛṣṇa*—Lord Kṛṣṇa; *kariche nartana*—is dancing.

TRANSLATION

"From a distance, people mistakenly think that they are seeing Kṛṣṇa dancing on the body of the Kālīya serpent.

TEXT 106

নৌকাতে কালীয়-জ্ঞান, দীপে রত্ন-জ্ঞানে !
জালিয়ারে মূঢ়-লোক 'কৃষ্ণ' করি' মানে ! ১০৬ ॥

naukāte kālīya-jñāna, dīpe ratna-jñāne!
jāliyāre mūḍha-loka 'kṛṣṇa' kari' māne!

SYNONYMS

naukāte—on the boat; *kālīya-jñāna*—knowledge as the Kālīya snake; *dīpe*—on the torch; *ratna-jñāne*—consideration as jewels; *jāliyāre*—the fisherman; *mūḍha-loka*—foolish men; *kṛṣṇa kari' māne*—accept as Kṛṣṇa.

TRANSLATION

"These fools think that the boat is the Kālīya serpent and the torchlight the jewels on his hoods. People also mistake the fisherman to be Kṛṣṇa.

TEXT 107

বৃন্দাবনে 'কৃষ্ণ' আইলা,—সেহ 'সত্য' হয় ।
কৃষ্ণেরে দেখিল লোক,—ইহা 'মিথ্যা' নয় ॥ ১০৭ ॥

vṛndāvane 'kṛṣṇa' āilā,——sei 'satya' haya
kṛṣṇere dekhila loka,——ihā 'mithyā' naya

SYNONYMS

vṛndāvane—to Vṛndāvana; *kṛṣṇa*—Lord Kṛṣṇa; *āilā*—has come back; *sei*—that; *satya haya*—is true; *kṛṣṇere*—Kṛṣṇa; *dekhila*—saw; *loka*—the people; *ihā mithyā naya*—this is not false.

TRANSLATION

"Actually Lord Kṛṣṇa has again returned to Vṛndāvana. That also is a truth, and people have seen Him.

TEXT 108

কিন্তু কাহোঁ 'কৃষ্ণ' দেখে, কাহোঁ 'ভ্রম' মানে।
স্থাণু-পুরুষে যৈছে বিপরীত-জ্ঞানে ॥ ১০৮ ॥

kintu kāhoṅ 'kṛṣṇa' dekhe, kāhoṅ 'bhrama' māne
sthāṇu-puruṣe yaiche viparīta-jñāne

SYNONYMS

kintu—but; *kāhoṅ*—where; *kṛṣṇa*—Kṛṣṇa; *dekhe*—one sees; *kāhoṅ*—where; *bhrama māne*—mistakes; *sthāṇu-puruṣe*—the dry tree and a person; *yaiche*—as; *viparīta-jñāne*—by understanding one to be the other.

TRANSLATION

"But where they are seeing Kṛṣṇa is their mistake. It is like considering a dry tree to be a person."

PURPORT

The word *sthāṇu* means "a dry tree without leaves." From a distance one may mistake such a tree for a person. This is called *sthāṇu-puruṣa.* Although Śrī Caitanya Mahāprabhu was living in Vṛndāvana, the inhabitants considered Him an ordinary human being, and they mistook the fisherman to be Kṛṣṇa. Every human being is prone to make such mistakes. Śrī Caitanya Mahāprabhu was mistaken for an ordinary *sannyāsī,* the fisherman was mistaken for Kṛṣṇa, and the torchlight was mistaken for bright jewels on Kālīya's hoods.

TEXT 109

প্রভু কহে,—'কাহাঁ পাইলা 'কৃষ্ণ দরশন ?'
লোক কহে,—'সন্ন্যাসী তুমি জঙ্গম-নারায়ণ ॥ ১০৯ ॥

prabhu kahe,—'kāhāṅ pāilā 'kṛṣṇa daraśana?'
loka kahe,—'sannyāsī tumi jaṅgama-nārāyaṇa

SYNONYMS

prabhu kahe—Śrī Caitanya Mahāprabhu further inquired; *kāhāṅ pāilā*—where have you gotten; *kṛṣṇa daraśana*—sight of Kṛṣṇa; *loka kahe*—the respectable persons replied; *sannyāsī tumi*—You are a *sannyāsī; jaṅgama-nārāyaṇa*—moving Nārāyaṇa.

TRANSLATION

Śrī Caitanya Mahāprabhu then asked them, "Where have you seen Kṛṣṇa directly?" The people replied, "You are a sannyāsī, a renunciant; therefore You are a moving Nārāyaṇa [jaṅgama-nārāyaṇa]."

PURPORT

This is the viewpoint of Māyāvāda philosophy. Māyāvāda philosophy supports the impersonalist view that Nārāyaṇa, the Supreme Personality of Godhead, has no form. One can imagine impersonal Brahman in any form—as Viṣṇu, Lord Śiva, Vivasvān, Gaṇeśa or Devī Durgā. According to the Māyāvāda philosophy, when one becomes a *sannyāsī,* he is to be considered a moving Nārāyaṇa. Māyāvāda philosophy holds that the real Nārāyaṇa does not move because, being impersonal, He has no legs. Thus according to Māyāvāda philosophy, whoever becomes a *sannyāsī* declares himself Nārāyaṇa. Foolish people accept such ordinary human beings as the Supreme Personality of Godhead. This is called *vivarta-vāda.*

In this regard, Śrīla Bhaktisiddhānta Sarasvatī Ṭhākura comments that *jaṅgama-nārāyaṇa* means that the impersonal Brahman takes a shape and moves here and there in the form of a Māyāvādī *sannyāsī.* The Māyāvāda philosophy confirms this. *Daṇḍa-grahaṇa-mātreṇa naro nārāyaṇo bhavet:* "Simply by accepting the *daṇḍa* of the order of *sannyāsa,* one is immediately transformed into Nārāyaṇa." Therefore Māyāvādī *sannyāsīs* address themselves by saying, *oṁ namo nārāyaṇāya.* In this way one Nārāyaṇa worships another Nārāyaṇa.

Actually an ordinary human being cannot become Nārāyaṇa. Even the chief Māyāvādī *sannyāsī,* Śrī Saṅkarācārya, says, *nārāyaṇaḥ paro 'vyaktāt:* "Nārāyaṇa is not a creation of this material world. Nārāyaṇa is above the material creation." Due to their poor fund of knowledge, Māyāvādī *sannyāsīs* think that Nārāyaṇa, the Absolute Truth, takes birth as a human being and that when He realizes this, He becomes Nārāyaṇa again. They never consider why Nārāyaṇa, the Supreme Personality of Godhead, accepts an inferior position as a human being and then again becomes Nārāyaṇa when He is perfect. Why should Nārāyaṇa be imperfect? Why should He appear as a human being? Śrī Caitanya Mahāprabhu very nicely explained these points while at Vṛndāvana.

TEXT 110

বৃন্দাবনে হইলা তুমি কৃষ্ণ-অবতার ।
তোমা দেখি' সর্বলোক হইল নিস্তার ॥ ১১০ ॥

vṛndāvane ha-ilā tumi kṛṣṇa-avatāra
tomā dekhi' sarva-loka ha-ila nistāra

SYNONYMS

vṛndāvane—at Vṛndāvana; *ha-ilā*—became; *tumi*—You; *kṛṣṇa-avatāra*—incarnation of Kṛṣṇa; *tomā dekhi'*—by seeing You; *sarva-loka*—all people; *ha-ila nistāra*—become liberated.

TRANSLATION

The people then said, "You have appeared in Vṛndāvana as an incarnation of Kṛṣṇa. Just by seeing You, everyone is now liberated."

TEXT 111

প্রভু কহে,—'বিষ্ণু' 'বিষ্ণু', ইহা না কহিবা !
জীবাধমে 'কৃষ্ণ'-জ্ঞান কভু না করিবা ! ১১১ ॥

prabhu kahe,——'viṣṇu' 'viṣṇu', ihā nā kahibā!
jīvādhame 'kṛṣṇa'-jñāna kabhu nā karibā!

SYNONYMS

prabhu kahe—Śrī Caitanya Mahāprabhu replied; *viṣṇu viṣṇu*—O Viṣṇu, Viṣṇu; *ihā*—this; *nā kahibā*—do not speak; *jīva-adhame*—fallen conditioned souls; *kṛṣṇa-jñāna*—accepting as Lord Kṛṣṇa; *kabhu*—ever; *nā karibā*—do not do.

TRANSLATION

Śrī Caitanya Mahāprabhu immediately exclaimed, "Viṣṇu! Viṣṇu! Do not call Me the Supreme Personality of Godhead. A jīva cannot become Kṛṣṇa at any time. Do not even say such a thing!

PURPORT

Śrī Caitanya Mahāprabhu immediately stated that a living being, however exalted he may be, should never be compared to the Supreme Personality of Godhead. All of Śrī Caitanya Mahāprabhu's preaching protests the monistic philosophy of the Māyāvāda school. The central point of Kṛṣṇa consciousness is that the *jīva,* the living entity, can never be accepted as Kṛṣṇa or Viṣṇu. This viewpoint is elaborated in the following verses.

TEXT 112

সন্ন্যাসী—চিৎকণ জীব, কিরণ-কণ-সম ।
ষড়ৈশ্বর্যপূর্ণ কৃষ্ণ হয় সূর্যোপম ॥ ১১২ ॥

sannyāsī——cit-kaṇa jīva, kiraṇa-kaṇa-sama
ṣaḍ-aiśvarya-pūrṇa kṛṣṇa haya sūryopama

SYNONYMS

sannyāsī—a person in the renounced order of life; *cit-kaṇa jīva*—a small fragmental living being; *kiraṇa*—of sunshine; *kaṇa*—small particle; *sama*—like; *ṣaṭ-aiśvarya-pūrṇa*—full in six opulences; *kṛṣṇa*—Lord Kṛṣṇa; *haya*—is; *sūrya-upama*—compared to the sun.

TRANSLATION

"A sannyāsī in the renounced order is certainly part and parcel of the complete whole, just as a shining molecular particle of sunshine is part and parcel of the sun itself. Kṛṣṇa is like the sun, full of six opulences, but the living entity is only a fragment of the complete whole.

TEXT 113

জীব, ঈশ্বর-তত্ত্ব—কভু নহে 'সম'।
জ্বলদগ্নিরাশি যৈছে স্ফুলিঙ্গের 'কণ' ॥ ১১৩ ॥

jīva, īśvara-tattva——kabhu nahe 'sama'
jvalad-agni-rāśi yaiche sphuliṅgera 'kaṇa'

SYNONYMS

jīva—a living being; *īśvara-tattva*—and the Supreme Personality of Godhead; *kabhu*—at any time; *nahe*—not; *sama*—equal; *jvalat-agni-rāśi*—large flame; *yaiche*—as; *sphuliṅgera*—of a spark; *kaṇa*—fragmental portion.

TRANSLATION

"A living entity and the Absolute Personality of Godhead are never to be considered equal, just as a fragmental spark can never be considered the original flame.

PURPORT

Māyāvādī *sannyāsīs* consider themselves Brahman, and they superficially speak of themselves as Nārāyaṇa. The monistic disciples of the Māyāvāda school (known as *smārta-brāhmaṇas*) are generally householder *brāhmaṇas* who accept the Māyāvādī *sannyāsīs* as Nārāyaṇa incarnate; therefore they offer their obeisances to them. Śrī Caitanya Mahāprabhu immediately protested this unauthorized system, specifically mentioning that a *sannyāsī* (*cit-kaṇa jīva*) is nothing but a fragmental portion of the Supreme. In other words, he is nothing more than an ordinary living being. He is never Nārāyaṇa, just as a molecular portion of sunshine is never the sun itself. The living entity is nothing but a fragmental part of the Absolute Truth; therefore at no stage of perfection can a living entity become the Supreme Personality of Godhead. This Māyāvāda viewpoint is always condemned by the Vaiṣṇava school. Śrī Caitanya Mahāprabhu Himself protested this philosophy. When the Māyāvādīs accept *sannyāsa* and consider themselves Nārāyaṇa, they become so puffed up that they do not even enter the temple of Nārāyaṇa to offer respects, for they falsely think themselves Nārāyaṇa Himself. Although Māyāvādī *sannyāsīs* may offer respects to other *sannyāsīs* and address them as Nārāyaṇa, they do not go to a Nārāyaṇa temple and offer respects. These Māyāvādī *sannyāsīs* are always condemned and are described as demons. The *Vedas* clearly state that living entities are subordinate parts and parcels of the supreme. *Eko bahūnāṁ yo vidadhāti kāmān:* the Supreme Being, Kṛṣṇa, maintains all living entities.

TEXT 114

হ্লাদিন্যা সংবিদাশ্লিষ্টঃ সচ্চিদানন্দ ঈশ্বরঃ ।
স্বাবিদ্যা-সংবৃতো জীবঃ সংক্লেশনিকরাকরঃ ॥ ১১৪ ॥

hlādinyā saṁvid-āśliṣṭaḥ
sac-cid-ānanda īśvaraḥ
svāvidyā-saṁvṛto jīvaḥ
saṅkleśa-nikarākaraḥ

SYNONYMS

hlādinyā—by the *hlādinī* potency; *saṁvit*—by the *samvit* potency; *āśliṣṭaḥ*—surrounded; *sat-cit-ānandaḥ*—always transcendentally blissful; *īśvaraḥ*—the supreme controller; *sva*—own; *avidyā*—by ignorance; *saṁvṛtaḥ*—surrounded; *jīvaḥ*—the living entity; *saṅkleśa*—of the threefold miseries; *nikara*—of the multitude; *ākaraḥ*—the mine.

TRANSLATION

" 'The Supreme Personality of Godhead, the supreme controller, is always full of transcendental bliss and is accompanied by the potencies known as hlādinī and samvit. The conditioned soul, however, is always covered by ignorance and embarrassed by the threefold miseries of life. Thus he is a treasure-house of all kinds of tribulations.'

PURPORT

This quotation of Viṣṇusvāmī is cited in Śrīdhara Svāmī's *Bhāvārtha-dīpikā* commentary on *Śrīmad-Bhāgavatam* (1.7.6).

TEXT 115

যেই মূঢ় কহে,—জীব ঈশ্বর হয় 'সম'।
সেইত 'পাষণ্ডী' হয়, দণ্ডে তারে যম ॥ ১১৫ ॥

yei mūḍha kahe,——jīva īśvara haya 'sama'
seita 'pāṣaṇḍī' haya, daṇḍe tāre yama

SYNONYMS

yei mūḍha—any foolish person who; *kahe*—says; *jīva*—the living entity; *īśvara*—the supreme controller; *haya*—are; *sama*—equal; *seita*—he; *pāṣandī haya*—is a first-class atheist; *daṇḍe*—punishes; *tāre*—him; *yama*—the superintendent of death, Yamarāja.

TRANSLATION

"A foolish person who says that the Supreme Personality of Godhead is the same as the living entity is an atheist, and he becomes subject to punishment by the superintendent of death, Yamarāja.

PURPORT

Śrīla Bhaktisiddhānta Sarasvatī Ṭhākura says that the word *pāsaṇḍī* refers to one who considers the living entity under the control of the illusory energy to be equal with the Supreme Personality of Godhead, who is transcendental to all material qualities. Another kind of *pāṣaṇḍī* is one who does not believe in the spirit soul, the superior potency of the Lord, and therefore does not distinguish between spirit and matter. While describing one of the offenses against chanting the holy names, an offense called *śruti-śāstra-nindana* (blaspheming the Vedic literature), Jīva Gosvāmī states in his *Bhakti-sandarbha: yathā pāṣaṇda-mārgeṇa dattātreyarṣabha-devopāsakānāṁ pāṣaṇḍīnām.* Worshipers of impersonalists like Dattātreya are also *pāṣaṇḍīs.* Concerning the offense of *ahaṁ-mama-buddhi,* or *dehātma-buddhi* (considering the body to be the self), Jīva Gosvāmī states: *deva-draviṇādi-nimittaka-'pāṣaṇḍa'-śabdena ca daśāparādhā eva lakṣyante, pāṣaṇḍamayatvāt teṣām.* "Those who are overly absorbed in the conception of the body and the bodily necessities are also called *pāṣaṇḍīs.*" Elsewhere in *Bhakti-sandarbha* it is stated:

uddiśya devatā eva
juhoti ca dadāti ca
sa pāṣaṇḍīti vijñeyaḥ
svatantro vāpi karmasu

"A *pāṣaṇḍī* is one who considers the demigods and the Supreme Personality of Godhead to be one; therefore a *pāṣaṇḍī* worships any kind of demigod as the

Supreme Personality of Godhead." One who disobeys the orders of the spiritual master is also considered a *pāṣaṇḍī.* The word *pāṣaṇḍī* has been described in many places in *Śrīmad-Bhāgavatam,* including 4.2.28, 30, 32; 5.6.9 and 12.2.13, 43.

On the whole, a *pāṣaṇḍī* is a nondevotee who does not accept the Vedic conclusions. In the *Hari-bhakti-vilāsa* (1.117) there is a verse quoted from *Padma Purāṇa* describing the *pāṣaṇḍī.* Śrī Caitanya Mahāprabhu quotes this verse as the following text.

TEXT 116

যস্তু নারায়ণং দেবং ব্রহ্মরুদ্রাদিদৈবতৈঃ ।
সমত্বেনৈব বীক্ষেত স পাষণ্ডী ভবেদ্ধ্রুবম্ ॥ ১১৬ ॥

yas tu nārāyaṇaṁ devaṁ
brahma-rudrādi-daivataiḥ
samatvenaiva vīkṣeta
sa pāṣaṇḍī bhaved dhruvam

SYNONYMS

yaḥ—any person who; *tu*—however; *nārāyaṇam*—the Supreme Personality of Godhead, the master of such demigods as Brahmā and Śiva; *devam*—the Lord; *brahma*—Lord Brahmā; *rudra*—Lord Śiva; *ādi*—and others; *daivataiḥ*—with such demigods; *samatvena*—on an equal level; *eva*—certainly; *vīkṣeta*—observes; *saḥ*—such a person; *pāṣaṇḍī*—*pāṣaṇḍī; bhavet*—must be; *dhruvam*—certainly.

TRANSLATION

" 'A person who considers demigods like Brahmā and Śiva to be on an equal level with Nārāyaṇa is to be considered an offender and a pāṣaṇḍī.' "

TEXT 117

লোক কহে,—তোমাতে কভু নহে 'জীব'-মতি ।
কৃষ্ণের সদৃশ তোমার আকৃতি-প্রকৃতি ॥ ১১৭ ॥

loka kahe,——tomāte kabhu nahe 'jīva'-mati
kṛṣṇera sadṛśa tomāra ākṛti-prakṛti

SYNONYMS

loka kahe—the people said; *tomāte*—unto You; *kabhu*—at any time; *nahe*—there is not; *jīva-mati*—considering an ordinary living being; *kṛṣṇera sadṛśa*—like Lord Kṛṣṇa; *tomāra*—Your; *ākṛti*—bodily features; *prakṛti*—characteristics.

TRANSLATION

After Śrī Caitanya Mahāprabhu explained the difference between an ordinary living being and the Supreme Personality of Godhead, the people said, "No one considers You an ordinary human being. You are like Kṛṣṇa in every respect, in both bodily features and characteristics.

TEXT 118

'আকৃত্যে' তোমারে দেখি 'ব্রজেন্দ্র-নন্দন' ।
দেহকান্তি পীতাম্বর কৈল আচ্ছাদন ॥ ১১৮ ॥

'ākṛtye' tomāre dekhi 'vrajendra-nandana'
deha-kānti pītāmbara kaila ācchādana

SYNONYMS

ākṛtye—by bodily features; *tomāre*—You; *dekhi*—we see; *vrajendra-nandana*—directly the son of Mahārāja Nanda; *deha-kānti*—the luster of the body; *pīta-ambara*—golden covering; *kaila ācchādana*—covered.

TRANSLATION

"By Your bodily features we can see that You are none other than the son of Nanda Mahārāja, although the golden luster of Your body has covered Your original complexion.

TEXT 119

মৃগমদ বস্ত্রে বান্ধে, তবু না লুকায় ।
'ঈশ্বর-স্বভাব' তোমার ঢাকা নাহি যায় ॥ ১১৯ ॥

mṛga-mada vastre bāndhe, tabu nā lukāya
'īśvara-svabhāva' tomāra ṭākā nāhi yāya

SYNONYMS

mṛga-mada—deer musk; *vastre*—in cloth; *bāndhe*—wraps; *tabu*—still; *nā*—not; *lukāya*—is concealed; *īśvara-svabhāva*—characteristics as the Supreme Personality of Godhead; *tomāra*—of You; *ṭākā nāhi yāya*—are not concealed.

TRANSLATION

"As the aroma of deer musk cannot be concealed by wrapping it in a cloth, Your characteristics as the Supreme Personality of Godhead cannot be concealed by any means.

TEXT 120

অলৌকিক 'প্রকৃতি' তোমার—বুদ্ধি-অগোচর ।
তোমা দেখি' কৃষ্ণপ্রেমে জগৎ পাগল ॥ ১২০ ॥

alaukika 'prakṛti' tomāra——buddhi-agocara
tomā dekhi' kṛṣṇa-preme jagat pāgala

SYNONYMS

alaukika—uncommon; *prakṛti*—characteristics; *tomāra*—Your; *buddhi-agocara*—beyond our imagination; *tomā dekhi'*—by seeing You; *kṛṣṇa-preme*—in ecstatic love for Kṛṣṇa; *jagat*—the whole world; *pāgala*—mad.

TRANSLATION

"Indeed, Your characteristics are uncommon and beyond the imagination of an ordinary living being. Simply by seeing You, the entire universe becomes mad with ecstatic love for Kṛṣṇa.

TEXTS 121-122

স্ত্রী-বাল-বৃদ্ধ, আর 'চণ্ডাল', 'যবন' ।
যেই তোমার একবার পায় দরশন ॥ ১২১ ॥
কৃষ্ণনাম লয়, নাচে হঞা উন্মত্ত ।
আচার্য হইল সেই, তারিল জগত ॥ ১২২ ॥

strī-bāla-vṛddha, āra 'caṇḍāla', 'yavana'
yei tomāra eka-bāra pāya daraśana

kṛṣṇa-nāma laya, nāce hañā unmatta
ācārya ha-ila sei, tārila jagata

SYNONYMS

strī—women; *bāla*—children; *vṛddha*—old men; *āra*—and; *caṇḍāla*—the lowest of men; *yavana*—persons who eat meat; *yei*—anyone who; *tomāra*—Your; *eka-bāra*—once; *pāya daraśana*—gets the sight; *kṛṣṇa-nāma*—the holy name of Kṛṣṇa; *laya*—chants; *nāce*—dances; *hañā unmatta*—like a madman; *ācārya ha-ila*—becomes a spiritual master; *sei*—that man; *tārila jagata*—delivers the whole world.

The Maṇikarṇikā-ghāṭa, where Śrī Caitanya Mahāprabhu bathed after arriving in Vārāṇasī (Benares). (*p.41*)

The Viśrāma-ghāṭa, where Caitanya Mahāprabhu bathed after falling unconscious upon seeing Mathurā. (*p.86*)

The holy places of Bhūteśvara (left) and Mahāvidyā (right), situated on the banks of the Yamunā River and visited by Śrī Caitanya Mahāprabhu. (*p.108*)

The sacred lakes of Śrī Śyāma-kuṇḍa (above) and Śrī Rādhā-kuṇḍa (below), which are very dear to Lord Kṛṣṇa. Śrī Caitanya Mahāprabhu discovered them during His tour of Vṛndāvana. (*p.132*)

Govardhana Hill, the famous site of Lord Kṛṣṇa's pastimes, where Śrī Caitanya Mahāprabhu became mad with ecstatic love of Godhead. (*p.138*)

Varṣāṇa, the most sacred site where Śrīmatī Rādhārāṇī, the queen of Vṛndāvana and the greatest devotee of Lord Kṛṣṇa, made Her appearance in this world.

Nandīśvara, the site where Śrī Kṛṣṇa, the Supreme Personality of Godhead, performed His childhood pastimes as the son of Yaśodāmātā and Nanda Mahārāja. Upon visiting this site, Śrī Caitanya Mahāprabhu became overwhelmed with ecstatic love.

Sevā-kuñja, the site of the *rāsa* dance, where Śrī Kṛṣṇa expanded Himself into many forms in order to satisfy the *gopīs,* the most exalted devotees of the Supreme Personality of Godhead.

LEFT: The *samādhi* tomb of Śrīla Lokanātha dāsa Gosvāmī, the spiritual master of Narottama dāsa Ṭhākura. On the order of Śrī Caitanya Mahāprabhu, Lokanātha dāsa Gosvāmī went to Vṛndāvana to construct the temple of Śrī Śrī Rādhā-Gokulānanda, one of the seven major temples of Vṛndāvana.
RIGHT: The main gate to the Rādhā-Gokulānanda temple.

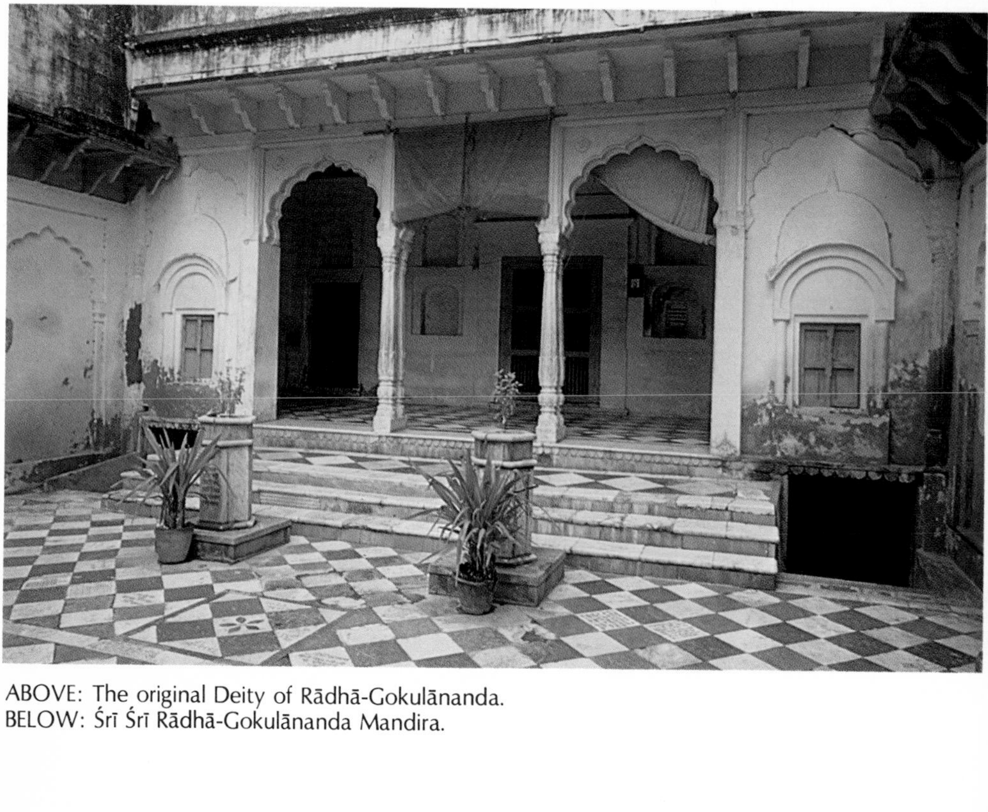

ABOVE: The original Deity of Rādhā-Gokulānanda.
BELOW: Śrī Śrī Rādhā-Gokulānanda Mandira.

'he temple and courtyard of Śrī Śrī Rādhā-Śyāmasundara, established in Vṛndāvana by Śrīla Śyāmā-
ıanda Gosvāmī, an intimate student of Śrīla Jīva Gosvāmī. In his later years, Śyāmānanda Gosvāmī
esided in Orissa, where he made innumerable disciples.

Śrī Śrī Rādhā-Śyāmasundara, the beloved Deities of Śrīla Syāmānanda Gosvāmī.

TRANSLATION

"If even women, children, old men, meat-eaters or members of the lowest caste can see You even once, they immediately chant the holy name of Kṛṣṇa, dance like madmen and become spiritual masters capable of delivering the whole world.

TEXT 123

দর্শনের কার্য আছুক, যে তোমার 'নাম' শুনে ।
সেই কৃষ্ণপ্রেমে মত্ত, তারে ত্রিভুবনে ॥ ১২৩ ॥

darśanera kārya āchuka, ye tomāra 'nāma' śune
sei kṛṣṇa-preme matta, tāre tribhuvane

SYNONYMS

darśanera kārya āchuka—aside from seeing You; *ye*—anyone who; *tomāra*—Your; *nāma*—holy name; *śune*—hears; *sei*—that man; *kṛṣṇa-preme*—in ecstatic love of Kṛṣṇa; *matta*—maddened; *tāre*—delivers; *tri-bhuvane*—the three worlds.

TRANSLATION

"Apart from seeing You, whoever listens to Your holy name is made mad with ecstatic love for Kṛṣṇa and is able to deliver the three worlds.

TEXT 124

তোমার নাম শুনি' হয় শ্বপচ 'পাবন' ।
অলৌকিক শক্তি তোমার না যায় কথন ॥ ১২৪ ॥

tomāra nāma śuni' haya śvapaca 'pāvana'
alaukika śakti tomāra nā yāya kathana

SYNONYMS

tomāra—Your; *nāma*—holy name; *śuni'*—hearing; *haya*—become; *śvapaca*—dog-eaters, the lowest of men; *pāvana*—saintly persons; *alaukika*—uncommon; *śakti*—potency; *tomāra*—Your; *nā*—not; *yāya kathana*—can be described.

TRANSLATION

"Simply by hearing Your holy name, dog-eaters become holy saints. Your uncommon potencies cannot be described in words.

TEXT 125

যন্নামধেয়-শ্রবণানুকীর্তনাদ্
যৎপ্রহ্বণাদ্‌যৎস্মরণাদপি ক্বচিৎ।
শ্বাদোঽপি সদ্যঃ সবনায় কল্পতে
কুতঃ পুনস্তে ভগবন্নু দর্শনাৎ ॥ ১২৫ ॥

yan-nāmadheya-śravaṇānukīrtanād
yat-prahvaṇād yat-smaraṇād api kvacit
śvādo 'pi sadyaḥ savanāya kalpate
kutaḥ punas te bhagavan nu darśanāt

SYNONYMS

yat—of whom; *nāmadheya*—of the name; *śravaṇa*—from hearing; *anukīrtanāt*—and thereafter from chanting; *yat*—to whom; *prahvaṇāt*—from offering respects; *yat*—of whom; *smaraṇāt*—from simply remembering; *api*—also; *kvacit*—sometimes; *śva-adaḥ*—a dog-eater; *api*—even; *sadyaḥ*—immediately; *savanāya*—for performing Vedic sacrifices; *kalpate*—becomes eligible; *kutaḥ*—what to speak; *punaḥ*—again; *te*—of You; *bhagavan*—O Supreme Personality of Godhead; *nu*—certainly; *darśanāt*—from seeing.

TRANSLATION

" 'To say nothing of the spiritual advancement of persons who see the Supreme Person face to face, even a person born in a family of dog-eaters becomes immediately eligible to perform Vedic sacrifices if he once utters the holy name of the Supreme Personality of Godhead, or chants about Him, hears about His pastimes, offers Him obeisances or even remembers Him.'

PURPORT

This is a quotation from *Śrīmad-Bhāgavatam* (3.33.6). According to this verse, it doesn't matter what position a person holds. One may be the lowest of the low—a *caṇḍāla,* or dog-eater—but if he takes to chanting and hearing the holy name of the Lord, he is immediately eligible to perform Vedic sacrifices. This is especially true in this age of Kali.

harer nāma harer nāma
harer nāmaiva kevalam
kalau nāsty eva nāsty eva
nāsty eva gatir anyathā
(*Bṛhan-nāradīya Purāṇa,* 38.126)

A person born in a *brāhmaṇa* family cannot perform Vedic sacrifices until he is properly purified and has attained his sacred thread. However, according to this verse, it is understood that even a lowborn person can immediately perform sacrifices if he sincerely chants and hears the holy name of the Lord. Sometimes envious people ask how Europeans and Americans in this Kṛṣṇa consciousness movement can become *brāhmaṇas* and perform sacrifices. They do not know that the Europeans and Americans have already been purified by chanting the holy name of the Lord—Hare Kṛṣṇa, Hare Kṛṣṇa, Kṛṣṇa Kṛṣṇa, Hare Hare/Hare Rāma, Hare Rāma, Rāma Rāma, Hare Hare. This is the proof. *Śvādo 'pi sadyaḥ savanāya kalpate.* One may be born in a family of dog-eaters, but he can perform sacrifices simply by chanting the *mahā-mantra.*

Those who find fault in the Western Vaiṣṇavas should consider this statement from *Śrīmad-Bhāgavatam* and the commentary on this verse by Śrīla Jīva Gosvāmī. In this regard, Śrīla Jīva Gosvāmī has stated that to become a *brāhmaṇa,* one has to wait for purification and undergo the sacred thread ceremony, but a chanter of the holy name does not have to wait for the sacred thread ceremony. We do not allow devotees to perform sacrifices until they are properly initiated in the sacred thread ceremony. Yet according to this verse, an offenseless chanter of the holy name is already fit to perform a fire ceremony, even though he is not doubly initiated by the sacred thread ceremony. This is the verdict given by Lord Kapiladeva in His instructions to His mother, Devahūti. It was Lord Kapiladeva who instructed Devahūti in pure Sāṅkhya philosophy.

TEXT 126

এইত' মহিমা—তোমার 'তটস্থ'-লক্ষণ ।
'স্বরূপ'-লক্ষণে তুমি—'ব্রজেন্দ্রনন্দন' ॥ ১২৬ ॥

eita' mahimā——tomāra 'taṭastha'-lakṣaṇa
'svarūpa'-lakṣaṇe tumi——'vrajendra-nandana'

SYNONYMS

eita'—all these; *mahimā*—glories; *tomāra*—Your; *taṭastha-lakṣaṇa*—marginal characteristics; *sva-rūpa*—original; *lakṣaṇe*—by characteristics; *tumi*—You; *vrajendra-nandana*—the son of Mahārāja Nanda.

TRANSLATION

"These glories of Yours are only marginal. Originally You are the son of Mahārāja Nanda."

PURPORT

The original characteristics of a substance are called *svarūpa,* and the subsequent corollaries are called *taṭastha-lakṣaṇa,* or marginal characteristics. The glories of the Lord's marginal characteristics prove Him to be the original Supreme Personality of Godhead, the son of Mahārāja Nanda. As soon as one understands this, one accepts Śrī Caitanya Mahāprabhu as the Supreme Personality of Godhead, Lord Śrī Kṛṣṇa.

TEXT 127

সেই সব লোকে প্রভু প্রসাদ করিল ।
কৃষ্ণপ্রেমে মত্ত লোক নিজ-ঘরে গেল ॥ ১২৭ ॥

sei saba loke prabhu prasāda karila
kṛṣṇa-preme matta loka nija-ghare gela

SYNONYMS

sei saba loke—unto all those persons; *prabhu*—Śrī Caitanya Mahāprabhu; *prasāda karila*—bestowed His causeless mercy; *kṛṣṇa-preme*—in ecstatic love of Kṛṣṇa; *matta*—maddened; *loka*—persons; *nija-ghare gela*—returned to their own homes.

TRANSLATION

Śrī Caitanya Mahāprabhu then bestowed His causeless mercy upon all the people there, and everyone became ecstatic with love of God. Finally they all returned to their homes.

TEXT 128

এইমত কতদিন 'অক্রূরে' রহিলা ।
কৃষ্ণ-নাম-প্রেম দিয়া লোক নিস্তারিলা ॥ ১২৮ ॥

ei-mata kata-dina 'akrūre' rahilā
kṛṣṇa-nāma-prema diyā loka nistārilā

SYNONYMS

ei-mata—in this way; *kata-dina*—for some days; *akrūre rahilā*—stayed at Akrūra-tīrtha; *kṛṣṇa-nāma*—the holy name of Kṛṣṇa; *prema*—ecstatic love; *diyā*—distributing; *loka*—everyone; *nistārilā*—delivered.

TRANSLATION

Śrī Caitanya Mahāprabhu remained for some days in Akrūra-tīrtha. He delivered everyone there simply by distributing the holy name of Kṛṣṇa and ecstatic love for the Lord.

TEXT 129

মাধবপুরীর শিষ্য সেইত ব্রাহ্মণ ।
মথুরার ঘরে-ঘরে করা'ন নিমন্ত্রণ ॥ ১২৯ ॥

mādhava-purīra śiṣya seita brāhmaṇa
mathurāra ghare-ghare karā'na nimantraṇa

SYNONYMS

mādhava-purīra—of Mādhavendra Purī; *śiṣya*—disciple; *seita*—that; *brāhmaṇa*—*brāhmaṇa; mathurāra*—of Mathurā City; *ghare-ghare*—home to home; *karā'na*—causes to make; *nimantraṇa*—invitation.

TRANSLATION

The brāhmaṇa disciple of Mādhavendra Purī went from house to house in Mathurā and inspired other brāhmaṇas to invite Caitanya Mahāprabhu to their homes.

TEXT 130

মথুরার যত লোক ব্রাহ্মণ সজ্জন ।
ভট্টাচার্য-স্থানে আসি' করে নিমন্ত্রণ ॥ ১৩০ ॥

mathurāra yata loka brāhmaṇa sajjana
bhaṭṭācārya-sthāne āsi' kare nimantraṇa

SYNONYMS

mathurāra—of Mathurā; *yata*—all; *loka*—people; *brāhmaṇa sat-jana*—gentlemen and *brāhmaṇas; bhaṭṭācārya-sthāne*—unto Balabhadra Bhaṭṭācārya; *āsi'*—coming; *kare nimantraṇa*—offer invitations.

TRANSLATION

Thus all the respectable people of Mathurā, headed by the brāhmaṇas, came to Balabhadra Bhaṭṭācārya and extended invitations to the Lord.

TEXT 131

একদিন 'দশ' 'বিশ' আইসে নিমন্ত্রণ ।
ভট্টাচার্য একের মাত্র করেন গ্রহণ ॥ ১৩১ ॥

eka-dina 'daśa' 'biśa' āise nimantraṇa
bhaṭṭācārya ekera mātra karena grahaṇa

SYNONYMS

eka-dina—in one day; *daśa biśa*—ten to twenty; *āise*—come; *nimantraṇa*—the invitations; *bhaṭṭācārya*—Balabhadra Bhaṭṭācārya; *ekera*—of one of them; *mātra*—only; *karena grahaṇa*—accepts.

TRANSLATION

In one day, ten to twenty invitations were received, but Balabhadra Bhaṭṭācārya would accept only one of them.

TEXT 132

অবসর না পায় লোক নিমন্ত্রণ দিতে ।
সেই বিপ্রে সাধে লোক নিমন্ত্রণ নিতে ॥ ১৩২ ॥

avasara nā pāya loka nimantraṇa dite
sei vipre sādhe loka nimantraṇa nite

SYNONYMS

avasara nā pāya—do not get the opportunity; *loka*—people; *nimantraṇa dite*—to offer invitations; *sei vipre*—unto that *brāhmaṇa; sādhe*—request; *loka*—people; *nimantraṇa nite*—to accept the invitation.

TRANSLATION

Since everyone did not get an opportunity to offer invitations to Śrī Caitanya Mahāprabhu personally, they requested the Sanoḍiyā brāhmaṇa to ask the Lord to accept their invitations.

TEXT 133

কান্যকুব্জ-দাক্ষিণাত্যের বৈদিক ব্রাহ্মণ ।
দৈন্য করি, করে মহাপ্রভুর নিমন্ত্রণ ॥ ১৩৩ ॥

kānyakubja-dākṣiṇātyera vaidika brāhmaṇa
dainya kari, kare mahāprabhura nimantraṇa

SYNONYMS

kānyakubja—*brāhmaṇas* from Kānyakubja; *dākṣiṇātyera*—certain *brāhmaṇas* from South India; *vaidika*—followers of the Vedic religion; *brāhmaṇa*—*brāhmaṇas; dainya kari*—with great humility; *kare*—do; *mahāprabhura*—of Śrī Caitanya Mahāprabhu; *nimantraṇa*—invitation.

TRANSLATION

The brāhmaṇas from different places, such as Kānyakubja and South India, who were all strict followers of the Vedic religion, offered invitations to Śrī Caitanya Mahāprabhu with great humility.

TEXT 134

প্রাতঃকালে অক্রূরে আসি' রন্ধন করিয়া ।
প্রভুরে ভিক্ষা দেন শালগ্রামে সমর্পিয়া ॥ ১৩৪ ॥

prātaḥ-kāle akrūre āsi' randhana kariyā
prabhure bhikṣā dena śālagrāme samarpiyā

SYNONYMS

prātaḥ-kāle—in the morning; *akrūre*—to Akrūra-tīrtha; *āsi'*—coming; *randhana kariyā*—cooking; *prabhure*—unto Śrī Caitanya Mahāprabhu; *bhikṣā dena*—offer lunch; *śālagrāme samarpiyā*—after offering to the *śālagrāma-śilā.*

TRANSLATION

In the morning they would come to Akrūra-tīrtha and cook food. After offering it to the śālagrāma-śilā, they offered it to Śrī Caitanya Mahāprabhu.

PURPORT

There are *brāhmaṇas* known as *pañca-gauḍa-brāhmaṇas* who come from five places in northern India, and there are *brāhmaṇas* known as *pañca-dākṣiṇātya-brāhmaṇas* who come from five places in southern India. In northern India the places are Kānyakubja, Sārasvata, Gauḍa, Maithila and Utkala. In southern India the places are Āndhra, Karṇāta, Gurjara, Drāviḍa and Mahārāṣṭra. The *brāhmaṇas* from these places are considered to be very strict followers of the Vedic principles, and they are accepted as pure *brāhmaṇas.* They strictly observe Vedic principles and are not polluted by tantric misdeeds. All of these *brāhmaṇas* respectfully invited Caitanya Mahāprabhu for lunch.

TEXT 135

একদিন সেই অক্রূর-ঘাটের উপরে ।
বসি' মহাপ্রভু কিছু করেন বিচারে ॥ ১৩৫ ॥

eka-dina sei akrūra-ghāṭera upare
vasi' mahāprabhu kichu karena vicāre

SYNONYMS

eka-dina—once upon a time; *sei*—that; *akrūra-ghāṭera*—of the Akrūra bathing ghat; *upare*—on the bank; *vasi'*—sitting; *mahāprabhu*—Śrī Caitanya Mahāprabhu; *kichu*—some; *karena*—does; *vicāre*—consideration.

TRANSLATION

One day Śrī Caitanya Mahāprabhu sat at the bathing ghat of Akrūra-tīrtha and thought the following thoughts.

PURPORT

Akrūra-tīrtha is located on the road between Vṛndāvana and Mathurā. When Kṛṣṇa and Balarāma were being taken to Mathurā by Akrūra, the Lord rested at this place and took His bath in the Yamunā. When Kṛṣṇa and Balarāma took Their baths, Akrūra saw the entire world of Vaikuṇṭha within the water. The inhabitants of Vṛndāvana also saw the Vaikuṇṭha planets within the water.

TEXT 136

এই ঘাটে অক্রূর বৈকুণ্ঠ দেখিল ।
ব্রজবাসী লোক 'গোলোক' দর্শন কৈল ॥ ১৩৬ ॥

ei ghāṭe akrūra vaikuṇṭha dekhila
vrajavāsī loka 'goloka' darśana kaila

SYNONYMS

ei ghāṭe—in this bathing place; *akrūra*—Akrūra; *vaikuṇṭha dekhila*—saw the spiritual world; *vrajavāsī loka*—the inhabitants of Vṛndāvana; *goloka darśana kaila*—saw Goloka.

TRANSLATION

Śrī Caitanya Mahāprabhu thought, "At this bathing place, Akrūra saw Vaikuṇṭha, the spiritual world, and all the inhabitants of Vraja saw Goloka Vṛndāvana."

TEXT 137

এত বলি' ঝাঁপ দিলা জলের উপরে ।
ডুবিয়া রহিলা প্রভু জলের ভিতরে ॥ ১৩৭ ॥

eta bali' jhāṅpa dilā jalera upare
ḍubiyā rahilā prabhu jalera bhitare

SYNONYMS

eta bali'—saying this; *jhāṅpa dilā*—jumped; *jalera upare*—above the water; *ḍubiyā*—sinking; *rahilā*—remained; *prabhu*—Śrī Caitanya Mahāprabhu; *jalera bhitare*—within the water.

TRANSLATION

While considering how Akrūra remained within the water, Śrī Caitanya Mahāprabhu immediately jumped in and stayed under water for some time.

TEXT 138

দেখি' কৃষ্ণদাস কান্দি' ফুকার করিল ।
ভট্টাচার্য শীঘ্র আসি' প্রভুরে উঠাইল ॥ ১৩৮ ॥

dekhi' kṛṣṇadāsa kāndi' phukāra karila
bhaṭṭācārya śīghra āsi' prabhure uṭhāila

SYNONYMS

dekhi'—seeing; *kṛṣṇadāsa*—Kṛṣṇadāsa; *kāndi'*—crying; *phu-kāra karila*—called loudly; *bhaṭṭācārya*—Balabhadra Bhaṭṭācārya; *śīghra*—hastily; *āsi'*—coming; *prabhure uṭhāila*—raised Śrī Caitanya Mahāprabhu.

TRANSLATION

When Kṛṣṇadāsa saw that Caitanya Mahāprabhu was drowning, he cried and shouted very loudly. Balabhadra Bhaṭṭācārya immediately came and pulled the Lord out.

TEXT 139

তবে ভট্টাচার্য সেই ব্রাহ্মণে লঞা ।
যুক্তি করিলা কিছু নিভৃতে বসিয়া ॥ ১৩৯ ॥

tabe bhaṭṭācārya sei brāhmaṇe lañā
yukti karilā kichu nibhṛte vasiyā

SYNONYMS

tabe—thereafter; *bhaṭṭācārya*—Bhaṭṭācārya; *sei brāhmaṇe*—the Sanoḍiyā *brāhmaṇa; lañā*—taking; *yukti karilā*—consulted; *kichu*—something; *nibhṛte vasiyā*—sitting in a solitary place.

TRANSLATION

After this, Balabhadra Bhaṭṭācārya took the Sanoḍiyā brāhmaṇa to a secluded place and consulted with him.

TEXT 140

আজি আমি আছিলাঙ উঠাইলুঁ প্রভুরে ।
বৃন্দাবনে ডুবেন যদি, কে উঠাবে তাঁরে ? ১৪০ ॥

āji āmi āchilāṅa uṭhāiluṅ prabhure
vṛndāvane ḍubena yadi, ke uṭhābe tāṅre?

SYNONYMS

āji—today; *āmi*—I; *āchilāṅa*—was present; *uṭhāiluṅ*—raised; *prabhure*—Śrī Caitanya Mahāprabhu; *vṛndāvane*—in Vṛndāvana; *ḍubena yadi*—if He drowns; *ke uṭhābe tāṅre*—who will raise Him.

TRANSLATION

Balabhadra Bhaṭṭācārya said, "Since I was present today, it was possible for me to pull the Lord up. However, if He starts to drown at Vṛndāvana, who will help Him?

TEXT 141

লোকের সংঘট্ট, আর নিমন্ত্রণের জঞ্জাল ।
নিরন্তর আবেশ প্রভুর না দেখিয়ে ভাল ॥ ১৪১ ॥

lokera saṅghaṭṭa, āra nimantraṇera jañjāla
nirantara āveśa prabhura nā dekhiye bhāla

SYNONYMS

lokera saṅghaṭṭa—crowds of people; *āra*—and; *nimantraṇera jañjāla*—the disturbance of invitations; *nirantara*—always; *āveśa*—ecstatic love; *prabhura*—of Śrī Caitanya Mahāprabhu; *nā dekhiye bhāla*—I do not see any good in this.

TRANSLATION

"Now there is a crowd of people here, and these invitations are causing much disturbance. In addition, the Lord is always ecstatic and emotional. I do not find the situation here very good.

TEXT 142

বৃন্দাবন হৈতে যদি প্রভুরে কাড়িয়ে ।
তবে মঙ্গল হয়,—এই ভাল যুক্তি হয়ে ॥ ১৪২ ॥

vṛndāvana haite yadi prabhure kāḍiye
tabe maṅgala haya,——ei bhāla yukti haye

SYNONYMS

vṛndāvana haite—from Vṛndāvana; *yadi*—if; *prabhure*—Śrī Caitanya Mahāprabhu; *kāḍiye*—I take away; *tabe*—then; *maṅgala haya*—there is auspiciousness; *ei*—this; *bhāla*—good; *yukti*—plan; *haye*—is.

TRANSLATION

"It would be good if we could get Śrī Caitanya Mahāprabhu out of Vṛndāvana. That is my final conclusion."

TEXT 143

বিপ্র কহে,—প্রয়াগে প্রভু লঞা যাই ।
গঙ্গাতীর-পথে যাই, তবে সুখ পাই ॥ ১৪৩ ॥

vipra kahe,——prayāge prabhu lañā yāi
gaṅgā-tīra-pathe yāi, tabe sukha pāi

SYNONYMS

vipra kahe—the *brāhmaṇa* said; *prayāge*—to Prayāga; *prabhu*—Śrī Caitanya Mahāprabhu; *lañā*—taking; *yāi*—let us go; *gaṅgā-tīra-pathe*—on the bank of the Ganges; *yāi*—let us go; *tabe*—then; *sukha pāi*—we shall get pleasure.

TRANSLATION

The Sanoḍiyā brāhmaṇa said, "Let us take Him to Prayāga and go along the banks of the Ganges. It will be very pleasurable to go that way.

TEXT 144

'সোরোক্ষেত্রে, আগে যাঞা করি' গঙ্গাস্নান ।
সেই পথে প্রভু লঞা করিয়ে পয়ান ॥ ১৪৪ ॥

'soro-kṣetre, āge yāñā kari' gaṅgā-snāna
sei pathe prabhu lañā kariye payāna

SYNONYMS

soro-kṣetre—to the holy place named Soro-kṣetra; *āge*—first, beyond; *yāñā*—going; *kari' gaṅgā-snāna*—having taken bath in the Ganges; *sei pathe*—that way; *prabhu lañā*—taking Lord Śrī Caitanya Mahāprabhu; *kariye payāna*—let us go.

TRANSLATION

"After going to the holy place named Soro-kṣetra, and taking bath in the Ganges, let us take Śrī Caitanya Mahāprabhu that way and go.

TEXT 145

মাঘ-মাস লাগিল, এবে যদি যাইয়ে ।
মকরে প্রয়াগ-স্নান কত দিন পাইয়ে ॥ ১৪৫ ॥

māgha-māsa lāgila, ebe yadi yāiye
makare prayāga-snāna kata dina pāiye

SYNONYMS

māgha-māsa lāgila—the month of Māgha has begun; *ebe*—now; *yadi*—if; *yāiye*—we go; *makare*—during the Makara-saṅkrānti; *prayāga-snāna*—bathing at Prayāga; *kata dina*—for a few days; *pāiye*—we shall get.

TRANSLATION

"It is now the beginning of the month of Māgha. If we go to Prayāga at this time, we shall have an opportunity to bathe for a few days during Makara-saṅkrānti."

PURPORT

Bathing during the month of Māgha at Māgha-melā still takes place. This has been a very old *melā* (assembly) from time immemorial. It is said that the Lord in the form of Mohinī took a bucket of nectar and kept it at Prayāga. Consequently Māgha-melā has been observed, and there is an assembly of holy men there every year. Every twelfth year there is a Kumbha-melā, a great festival, and all the holy men from all over India assemble there. The *brāhmaṇa* wanted to take advantage of the Māgha-melā and bathe there.

Bathing at the confluence of the Ganges and Yamunā near the fort at Allahabad, Prayāga, is mentioned in revealed scriptures:

māghe māsi gamiṣyanti
gaṅgā-yāmuna-saṅgamam

gavāṁ śata-sahasrasya
samyag dattaṁ ca yat-phalam
prayāge māgha-māse vai
tryahaṁ snātasya tat-phalam

"If one goes to Prayāga and bathes at the confluence of the Ganges and Yamunā in the month of Māgha, he attains the result of giving hundreds and thousands of cows in charity. Simply by bathing for three days there, he attains the results of such a pious activity." Because of this, the Sanoḍiyā *brāhmaṇa* was very eager to go to Prayāga and bathe. Generally *karmīs* (fruitive laborers) take advantage of bathing there during the month of Māgha, thinking that they will be rewarded in the future. Those who are situated in devotional service do not very strictly follow this *karma-kāṇḍīya* process.

TEXT 146

আপনার দুঃখ কিছু করি' নিবেদন ।
'মকর-পঁচসি প্রয়াগে' করিহ সূচন ॥ ১৪৬ ॥

āpanāra duḥkha kichu kari' nivedana
'makara-pañcasi prayāge' kariha sūcana

SYNONYMS

āpanāra—personal; *duḥkha*—unhappiness; *kichu*—some; *kari'*—doing; *nivedana*—submission; *makara-pañcasi*—the full-moon day in the month of Māgha; *prayāge*—to Prayāga; *kariha sūcana*—kindly inform.

TRANSLATION

The Sanoḍiyā brāhmaṇa continued, "Kindly submit to Śrī Caitanya Mahāprabhu the unhappiness you are feeling within yourself. Then propose that we all go to Prayāga on the full-moon day of the month of Māgha.

TEXT 147

গঙ্গাতীর-পথে সুখ জানাইহ তাঁরে ।
ভট্টাচার্য আসি' তবে কহিল প্রভুরে ॥ ১৪৭ ॥

gaṅgā-tīra-pathe sukha jānāiha tāṅre
bhaṭṭācārya āsi' tabe kahila prabhure

SYNONYMS

gaṅgā-tīra—on the bank of the Ganges; *pathe*—on the path; *sukha*—happiness; *jānāiha*—kindly let know; *tāṅre*—Śrī Caitanya Mahāprabhu; *bhaṭṭācārya*—Balabhadra Bhaṭṭācārya; *āsi'*—coming; *tabe*—thereafter; *kahila prabhure*—informed Śrī Caitanya Mahāprabhu.

TRANSLATION

"Tell the Lord of the happiness you will feel in traveling via the banks of the Ganges." Balabhadra Bhaṭṭācārya therefore submitted this prayer to Śrī Caitanya Mahāprabhu.

TEXT 148

"সহিতে না পারি আমি লোকের গড়বড়ি ।
নিমন্ত্রণ লাগি' লোক করে হুড়াহুড়ি ॥ ১৪৮ ॥

"sahite nā pāri āmi lokera gaḍabaḍi
nimantraṇa lāgi' loka kare huḍāhuḍi

SYNONYMS

sahite nā pāri—cannot tolerate; *āmi*—I; *lokera*—of people; *gaḍabaḍi*—disturbance; *nimantraṇa*—invitations; *lāgi'*—for; *loka*—people; *kare*—do; *huḍāhuḍi*—hurrying.

TRANSLATION

Balabhadra Bhaṭṭācārya told the Lord, "I can no longer tolerate the disturbance of the crowd. People are coming one after another to offer invitations.

TEXT 149

প্রাতঃকালে আইসে লোক, তোমারে না পায় ।
তোমারে না পাঞা লোক মোর মাথা খায় ॥ ১৪৯ ॥

prātaḥ-kāle āise loka, tomāre nā pāya
tomāre nā pāñā loka mora māthā khāya

SYNONYMS

prātaḥ-kāle—in the morning; *āise*—come; *loka*—people; *tomāre*—You; *nā pāya*—cannot see; *tomāre nā pāñā*—not getting You; *loka*—people; *mora māthā khāya*—tax my brain.

TRANSLATION

"Early in the morning people come here, and not seeing You present, they simply tax my brain.

TEXT 150

তবে সুখ হয় যবে গঙ্গাপথে যাইয়ে ।
এবে যদি যাই, 'মকরে' গঙ্গাস্নান পাইয়ে ॥ ১৫০ ॥

tabe sukha haya yabe gaṅgā-pathe yāiye
ebe yadi yāi, 'makare' gaṅgā-snāna pāiye

SYNONYMS

tabe—then; *sukha haya*—it will be great happiness for me; *yabe*—when; *gaṅgā-pathe*—on the path of the Ganges; *yāiye*—we go; *ebe yadi yāi*—if we go just now; *makare*—during Makara-saṅkrānti; *gaṅgā-snāna pāiye*—we can take bath in the Ganges.

TRANSLATION

"I will be very happy if we all leave and take the path by the banks of the Ganges. Then we can have the opportunity to bathe in the Ganges in Prayāga during Makara-saṅkrānti.

PURPORT

There are two great occasions for bathing in the Ganges during Māgha-melā. One is on the day of the dark moon, and the other is on the day of the full moon during the month of Māgha.

TEXT 151

উদ্বিগ্ন হইল প্রাণ, সহিতে না পারি ।
প্রভুর যে আজ্ঞা হয়, সেই শিরে ধরি ॥" ১৫১ ॥

udvigna ha-ila prāṇa, sahite nā pāri
prabhura ye ājñā haya, sei śire dhari"

SYNONYMS

udvigna—agitated; *ha-ila*—has become; *prāṇa*—my mind; *sahite*—to bear; *nā pāri*—I am unable; *prabhura*—of Śrī Caitanya Mahāprabhu; *ye*—what; *ājñā*—order; *haya*—there is; *sei śire dhari*—I accept that.

TRANSLATION

"My mind has become very agitated, and I cannot bear this anxiety. May everything rest on the permission of Your Lordship. I will accept whatever You want to do."

TEXT 152

যদ্যপি বৃন্দাবন-ত্যাগে নাহি প্রভুর মন ।
ভক্ত-ইচ্ছা পূরিতে কহে মধুর বচন ॥ ১৫২ ॥

yadyapi vṛndāvana-tyāge nāhi prabhura mana
bhakta-icchā pūrite kahe madhura vacana

SYNONYMS

yadyapi—although; *vṛndāvana-tyāge*—to leave Vṛndāvana; *nāhi prabhura mana*—was not the desire of the Lord; *bhakta*—of the devotee; *icchā*—desire; *pūrite*—to fulfill; *kahe*—says; *madhura vacana*—sweet words.

TRANSLATION

Although Śrī Caitanya Mahāprabhu had no desire to leave Vṛndāvana, He began to speak sweet words just to fulfill the desire of His devotee.

TEXT 153

"তুমি আমায় আনি' দেখাইলা বৃন্দাবন ।
এই 'ঋণ' আমি নারিব করিতে শোধন ॥ ১৫৩ ॥

"tumi āmāya āni' dekhāilā vṛndāvana
ei 'ṛṇa' āmi nāriba karite śodhana

SYNONYMS

tumi—you; *āmāya*—Me; *āni'*—bringing; *dekhāilā*—showed; *vṛndāvana*—the holy place named Vṛndāvana; *ei ṛṇa*—this debt; *āmi nāriba*—I shall not be able; *karite śodhana*—to repay.

TRANSLATION

Śrī Caitanya Mahāprabhu said, "You have brought Me here to show Me Vṛndāvana. I am very much indebted to you, and I shall not be able to repay this debt.

TEXT 154

যে তোমার ইচ্ছা, আমি সেইত করিব।
যাহাঁ লঞা যাহ তুমি, তাহাঁই যাইব ॥" ১৫৪ ॥

ye tomāra icchā, āmi seita kariba
yāhāṅ lañā yāha tumi, tāhāṅi yāiba"

SYNONYMS

ye tomāra icchā—whatever You like; *āmi*—I; *seita kariba*—must act accordingly; *yāhāṅ*—wherever; *lañā yāha*—take; *tumi*—you; *tāhāṅi yāiba*—I shall go there.

TRANSLATION

"Whatever you desire, I must do. Wherever you take Me, I shall go."

TEXT 155

প্রাতঃকালে মহাপ্রভু প্রাতঃস্নান কৈল।
'বৃন্দাবন ছাড়িব' জানি' প্রেমাবেশ হৈল ॥ ১৫৫ ॥

prātaḥ-kāle mahāprabhu prātaḥ-snāna kaila
'vṛndāvana chāḍiba' jāni' premāveśa haila

SYNONYMS

prātaḥ-kāle—in the morning; *mahāprabhu*—Śrī Caitanya Mahāprabhu; *prātaḥ-snāna kaila*—took His morning bath; *vṛndāvana chāḍiba*—I shall have to leave Vṛndāvana; *jāni'*—knowing; *prema-āveśa haila*—became ecstatic in love.

TRANSLATION

The next morning, Śrī Caitanya Mahāprabhu got up early. After taking His bath, He became ecstatic with love, knowing that He now had to leave Vṛndāvana.

TEXT 156

বাহ্য বিকার নাহি, প্রেমাবিষ্ট মন।
ভট্টাচার্য কহে,—চল, যাই মহাবন ॥ ১৫৬ ॥

bāhya vikāra nāhi, premāviṣṭa mana
bhaṭṭācārya kahe,——cala, yāi mahāvana

SYNONYMS

bāhya—external; *vikāra*—symptoms; *nāhi*—there were not; *prema-āviṣṭa mana*—the mind was full of ecstatic love; *bhaṭṭācārya kahe*—Bhaṭṭācārya said; *cala*—let us go; *yāi mahāvana*—let us go to Mahāvana.

TRANSLATION

Although the Lord did not exhibit any external symptoms, His mind was filled with ecstatic love. At that time, Balabhadra Bhaṭṭācārya said, "Let us go to Mahāvana [Gokula]."

TEXT 157

এত বলি' মহাপ্রভুরে নৌকায় বসাঞা ।
পার করি' ভট্টাচার্য চলিলা লঞা ॥ ১৫৭ ॥

eta bali' mahāprabhure naukāya vasāñā
pāra kari' bhaṭṭācārya calilā lañā

SYNONYMS

eta bali'—saying this; *mahāprabhure*—Śrī Caitanya Mahāprabhu; *naukāya*—on a boat; *vasāñā*—making sit down; *pāra kari'*—crossing the river; *bhaṭṭācārya*—Balabhadra Bhaṭṭācārya; *calilā*—went; *lañā*—taking.

TRANSLATION

Saying this, Balabhadra Bhaṭṭācārya made Śrī Caitanya Mahāprabhu sit aboard a boat. After they crossed the river, he took the Lord with him.

TEXT 158

প্রেমী কৃষ্ণদাস, আর সেইত ব্রাহ্মণ ।
গঙ্গাতীর-পথে যাইবার বিজ্ঞ দুইজন ॥ ১৫৮ ॥

premī kṛṣṇadāsa, āra seita brāhmaṇa
gaṅgā-tīra-pathe yāibāra vijña dui-jana

SYNONYMS

premī kṛṣṇadāsa—the devotee Rājaputa Kṛṣṇadāsa; *āra*—and; *seita brāhmaṇa*—that Sanoḍiyā *brāhmaṇa; gaṅgā-tīra-pathe*—on the path by the bank of the Ganges; *yāibāra*—to go; *vijña*—experienced; *dui-jana*—two persons.

TRANSLATION

Both Rājaputa Kṛṣṇadāsa and the Sanoḍiyā brāhmaṇa knew the path along the Ganges bank very well.

TEXT 159

যাইতে এক বৃক্ষতলে প্রভু সবা লঞা ।
বসিলা, সবার পথ-শ্রান্তি দেখিয়া ॥ ১৫৯ ॥

yāite eka vṛkṣa-tale prabhu sabā lañā
vasilā, sabāra patha-śrānti dekhiyā

SYNONYMS

yāite—while passing; *eka*—one; *vṛkṣa-tale*—underneath a tree; *prabhu*—Śrī Caitanya Mahāprabhu; *sabā lañā*—taking all of them; *vasilā*—sat down; *sabāra*—of all of them; *patha-śrānti*—fatigue because of walking; *dekhiyā*—understanding.

TRANSLATION

While walking, Śrī Caitanya Mahāprabhu, understanding that the others were fatigued, took them all beneath a tree and sat down.

TEXT 160

সেই বৃক্ষ-নিকটে চরে বহু গাভীগণ ।
তাহা দেখি' মহাপ্রভুর উল্লসিত মন ॥ ১৬০ ॥

sei vṛkṣa-nikaṭe care bahu gābhī-gaṇa
tāhā dekhi' mahāprabhura ullasita mana

SYNONYMS

sei—that; *vṛkṣa-nikaṭe*—near the tree; *care*—were grazing; *bahu*—many; *gābhī-gaṇa*—cows; *tāhā*—that; *dekhi'*—seeing; *mahāprabhura*—of Śrī Caitanya Mahāprabhu; *ullasita mana*—the mind became very pleased.

TRANSLATION

There were many cows grazing near that tree, and the Lord was very pleased to see them.

TEXT 161

আচম্বিতে এক গোপ বংশী বাজাইল ।
শুনি' মহাপ্রভুর মহা-প্রেমাবেশ হৈল ॥ ১৬১ ॥

ācambite eka gopa vaṁśī bājāila
śuni' mahāprabhura mahā-premāveśa haila

SYNONYMS

ācambite—suddenly; *eka gopa*—one cowherd boy; *vaṁśī*—flute; *bājāila*—blew; *śuni'*—hearing; *mahāprabhura*—of Śrī Caitanya Mahāprabhu; *mahā-prema-āveśa*—absorption in great ecstatic love; *haila*—there was.

TRANSLATION

Suddenly a cowherd boy blew on his flute, and immediately the Lord was struck with ecstatic love.

TEXT 162

অচেতন হঞা প্রভু ভূমিতে পড়িলা ।
মুখে ফেনা পড়ে, নাসায় শ্বাস রুদ্ধ হৈলা ॥ ১৬২ ॥

acetana hañā prabhu bhūmite paḍilā
mukhe phenā paḍe, nāsāya śvāsa ruddha hailā

SYNONYMS

acetana—unconscious; *hañā*—becoming; *prabhu*—Śrī Caitanya Mahāprabhu; *bhūmite paḍilā*—fell on the ground; *mukhe*—at the mouth; *phenā paḍe*—there was foam; *nāsāya*—in the nostrils; *śvāsa*—breath; *ruddha hailā*—stopped.

TRANSLATION

Filled with ecstatic love, the Lord fell unconscious to the ground. He foamed about the mouth, and His breathing stopped.

TEXT 163

হেনকালে তাহাঁ আশোয়ার দশ আইলা ।
ম্লেচ্ছ-পাঠান ঘোড়া হৈতে উত্তরিলা ॥ ১৬৩ ॥

hena-kāle tāhāṅ āśoyāra daśa āilā
mleccha-pāṭhāna ghoḍā haite uttarilā

SYNONYMS

hena-kāle—just at this time; *tāhāṅ*—there; *āśoyāra*—soldiers; *daśa*—ten; *āilā*—came; *mleccha*—Mohammedans; *pāṭhāna*—the race of Pāṭhānas; *ghoḍā*—horses; *haite*—from; *uttarilā*—got down.

TRANSLATION

While the Lord was unconscious, ten cavalry soldiers belonging to the Mohammedan Pāṭhāna military order rode up and dismounted.

TEXT 164

প্রভুরে দেখিয়া ম্লেচ্ছ করয়ে বিচার ।
এই যতি-পাশ ছিল সুবর্ণ অপার ॥ ১৬৪ ॥

prabhure dekhiyā mleccha karaye vicāra
ei yati-pāśa chila suvarṇa apāra

SYNONYMS

prabhure—Śrī Caitanya Mahāprabhu; *dekhiyā*—seeing; *mleccha*—the Mohammedans; *karaye vicāra*—considered; *ei yati-pāśa*—within the possession of this *sannyāsī; chila*—there was; *suvarṇa apāra*—a large quantity of gold.

TRANSLATION

Seeing the Lord unconscious, the soldiers thought, "This sannyāsī must have possessed a large quantity of gold.

TEXT 165

এই চারি বাটোয়ার ধুতুরা খাওয়াঞা ।
মারি' ডারিয়াছে, যতির সব ধন লঞা ॥ ১৬৫ ॥

ei cāri bāṭoyāra dhuturā khāoyāñā
māri' ḍāriyāche, yatira saba dhana lañā

SYNONYMS

ei—these; *cāri*—four; *bāṭoyāra*—rogues; *dhuturā*—*dhuturā; khāoyāñā*—making Him eat; *māri' ḍāriyāche*—killed; *yatira*—of the *sannyāsī; saba*—all; *dhana*—wealth; *lañā*—taking away.

TRANSLATION

"These four rogues here must have taken away that sannyāsī's riches after killing Him by making Him take the poison dhuturā."

TEXT 166

তবে সেই পাঠান চারি-জনেরে বাঁধিল ।
কাটিতে চাহে, গৌড়িয়া সব কাঁপিতে লাগিল ॥১৬৬॥

tabe sei pāṭhāna cāri-janere bāṅdhila
kāṭite cāhe, gauḍiyā saba kāṅpite lāgila

SYNONYMS

tabe—then; *sei pāṭhāna*—the Pāṭhāna soldiers; *cāri-janere*—the four persons; *bāṅdhila*—arrested; *kāṭite cāhe*—wanted to kill them; *gauḍiyā*—the Bengalis; *saba*—all; *kāṅpite lāgila*—began to tremble.

TRANSLATION

Thinking this, the Pāṭhāna soldiers arrested the four persons and decided to kill them. Because of this, the two Bengalis began to tremble.

PURPORT

The four persons were Balabhadra Bhaṭṭācārya, his assistant *brāhmaṇa,* Rājaputa Kṛṣṇadāsa and the Sanoḍiyā *brāhmaṇa* devotee of Mādhavendra Purī.

TEXT 167

কৃষ্ণদাস—রাজপুত, নির্ভয় সে বড় ।
সেই বিপ্র –নির্ভয়, সে—মুখে বড় দড় ॥ ১৬৭ ॥

kṛṣṇadāsa——rājaputa, nirbhaya se baḍa
sei vipra——nirbhaya, se——mukhe baḍa daḍa

SYNONYMS

kṛṣṇadāsa—Kṛṣṇadāsa; *rājaputa*—belonging to the Rājaputa race; *nirbhaya*—fearless; *se*—he; *baḍa*—very; *sei vipra*—the Sanoḍiyā *brāhmaṇa; nirbhaya*—also fearless; *se*—he; *mukhe*—in the mouth; *baḍa daḍa*—very brave.

TRANSLATION

The devotee Kṛṣṇadāsa, who belonged to the Rājaputa race, was very fearless. The Sanoḍiyā brāhmaṇa was also fearless, and he spoke very bravely.

TEXT 168

বিপ্র কহে,—পাঠান, তোমার পাৎসার দোহাই ।
চল তুমি আমি সিক্‌দার-পাশ যাই ॥ ১৬৮ ॥

vipra kahe,——pāṭhāna, tomāra pātsāra dohāi
cala tumi āmi sikdāra-pāśa yāi

SYNONYMS

vipra kahe—the *brāhmaṇa* said; *pāṭhāna*—you Pāṭhāna soldiers; *tomāra*—your; *pātsāra*—king; *dohāi*—under the protection of; *cala*—let us go; *tumi*—you; *āmi*—we; *sikdāra-pāśa*—to the commander; *yāi*—let us go.

TRANSLATION

The brāhmaṇa said, "You Pāṭhāna soldiers are all under the protection of your king. Let us go to your commander and get his decision.

TEXT 169

এই যতি – আমার গুরু, আমি—মাথুর ব্রাহ্মণ ।
পাৎসার আগে আছে মোর 'শত জন' ॥ ১৬৯ ॥

ei yati——āmāra guru, āmi——māthura brāhmaṇa
pātsāra āge āche mora 'śata jana'

SYNONYMS

ei yati—this *sannyāsī; āmāra guru*—my spiritual master; *āmi*—I; *māthura brāhmaṇa*—a *brāhmaṇa* from Mathurā; *pātsāra āge*—in the service of the Mohammedan king; *āche*—there are; *mora*—my; *śata jana*—one hundred persons.

TRANSLATION

"This sannyāsī is my spiritual master, and I am from Mathurā. I am a brāhmaṇa, and I know many people who are in the service of the Mohammedan king.

TEXT 170

এই যতি ব্যাধিতে কভু হয়েন মূর্চ্ছিত ।
অবঁহি চেতন পাইবে, হইবে সম্বিত ॥ ১৭০ ॥

ei yati vyādhite kabhu hayena mūrcchita
abaṅhi cetana pāibe, ha-ibe samvita

SYNONYMS

ei yati—this *sannyāsī; vyādhite*—under the influence of disease; *kabhu*—sometimes; *hayena mūrcchita*—becomes unconscious; *abaṅhi*—very soon; *cetana*—consciousness; *pāibe*—will get back; *ha-ibe samvita*—will come to His proper senses.

TRANSLATION

"This sannyāsī sometimes falls unconscious due to the influence of a disease. Please sit down here, and you will see that He will very soon regain consciousness and His normal condition.

TEXT 171

ক্ষণেক ইহাঁ বৈস, বান্ধি' রাখহ সবারে ।
ইঁহাকে পুছিয়া, তবে মারিহ সবারে ॥ ১৭১ ॥

kṣaṇeka ihāṅ vaisa, bāndhi' rākhaha sabāre
iṅhāke puchiyā, tabe māriha sabāre

SYNONYMS

kṣaṇeka—for some time; *ihāṅ vaisa*—sit down here; *bāndhi'*—arresting; *rākhaha*—keep; *sabāre*—all of us; *iṅhāke puchiyā*—after questioning Him; *tabe*—then; *māriha sabāre*—you can kill all of us.

TRANSLATION

"Sit down here for a while and keep us all under arrest. When the sannyāsī regains his senses, you can question Him. Then, if you like, you can kill us all."

TEXT 172

পাঠান কহে,—তুমি পশ্চিমা মাথুর দুইজন ।
'গৌড়িয়া' ঠক্ এই কাঁপে দুইজন ॥ ১৭২ ॥

pāṭhāna kahe,——tumi paścimā māthura dui-jana
'gauḍiyā' ṭhak ei kāṅpe dui-jana

SYNONYMS

pāṭhāna kahe—the soldiers said; *tumi*—you; *paścimā*—western Indians; *māthura*—belonging to the district of Mathurā; *dui-jana*—two of you; *gauḍiyā*—Bengalis; *ṭhak*—rogues; *ei*—these; *kāṅpe*—are trembling; *dui-jana*—two persons.

TRANSLATION

The Pāṭhāna soldiers said, "You are all rogues. Two of you belong to the district of Mathurā, and the other two, who are trembling, belong to Bengal."

TEXT 173

**কৃষ্ণদাস কহে,–আমার ঘর এই গ্রামে ।
দুইশত তুর্কী আছে, শতেক কামানে ॥ ১৭৩ ॥**

kṛṣṇadāsa kahe,——āmāra ghara ei grāme
dui-śata turkī āche, śateka kāmāne

SYNONYMS

kṛṣṇadāsa kahe—Rājaputa Kṛṣṇadāsa said; *āmāra ghara*—my home; *ei grāme*—in this village; *dui-śata turkī*—two hundred Turks; *āche*—I have; *śateka kāmāne*—one hundred cannons.

TRANSLATION

Rājaputa Kṛṣṇadāsa said, "I have my home here, and I also have about two hundred Turkish soldiers and about one hundred cannons.

TEXT 174

**এখনি আসিবে সব, আমি যদি ফুকারি ।
ঘোড়া-পিড়া লুটি' লবে তোমা-সবা মারি' ॥ ১৭৪ ॥**

ekhani āsibe saba, āmi yadi phukāri
ghoḍā-piḍā luṭi' labe tomā-sabā māri'

SYNONYMS

ekhani—immediately; *āsibe saba*—all of them will come; *āmi*—I; *yadi*—if; *phu-kāri*—call loudly; *ghoḍā-piḍā*—horses and their saddles; *luṭi'*—plundering; *labe*—will take; *tomā-sabā māri'*—after killing all of you.

TRANSLATION

"If I call loudly, they will come immediately to kill you and plunder your horses and saddles.

TEXT 175

**গৌড়িয়া—'বাটপাড়' নহে, তুমি—'বাটপাড়' ।
তীর্থবাসী লুঠ', আর চাহ' মারিবার ॥ ১৭৫ ॥**

gauḍiyā——'bāṭapāḍa' nahe, tumi——'bāṭapāḍa'
tīrtha-vāsī luṭha', āra cāha' māribāra

SYNONYMS

gauḍiyā—the Bengalis; *bāṭapāḍa nahe*—are not rogues; *tumi*—you; *bāṭapāḍa*—rogues; *tīrtha-vāsī*—persons visiting places of pilgrimage; *luṭha'*—you plunder; *āra*—and; *cāha'*—you want; *māribāra*—to kill.

TRANSLATION

"The Bengali pilgrims are not rogues. You are rogues, for you want to kill the pilgrims and plunder them."

TEXT 176

শুনিয়া পাঠান মনে সঙ্কোচ হইল ।
হেনকালে মহাপ্রভু 'চৈতন্য' পাইল ॥ ১৭৬ ॥

śuniyā pāṭhāna mane saṅkoca ha-ila
hena-kāle mahāprabhu 'caitanya' pāila

SYNONYMS

śuniyā—hearing; *pāṭhāna*—the Mohammedan soldiers; *mane*—in the mind; *saṅkoca ha-ila*—there was a little hesitation; *hena-kāle*—at this time; *mahāprabhu*—Śrī Caitanya Mahāprabhu; *caitanya pāila*—came to his senses.

TRANSLATION

Upon hearing this challenge, the Pāṭhāna soldiers became hesitant. Then suddenly Śrī Caitanya Mahāprabhu regained consciousness.

TEXT 177

হুঙ্কার করিয়া উঠে, বলে 'হরি' 'হরি' ।
প্রেমাবেশে নৃত্য করে ঊর্ধ্ববাহু করি' ॥ ১৭৭ ॥

huṅkāra kariyā uṭhe, bale 'hari' 'hari'
premāveśe nṛtya kare ūrdhva-bāhu kari'

SYNONYMS

huṅ-kāra kariyā—resounded very loudly; *uṭhe*—stands up; *bale hari hari*—chants Hari, Hari; *prema-āveśe*—in ecstatic love; *nṛtya kare*—dances; *ūrdhva-bāhu kari'*—raising his arms upward.

TRANSLATION

Coming to His senses, the Lord very loudly began chanting the holy name, "Hari! Hari!" The Lord raised His arms upward and began to dance in ecstatic love.

TEXT 178

প্রেমাবেশে প্রভু যবে করেন চিৎকার ।
ম্লেচ্ছের হৃদয়ে যেন লাগে শেলধার ॥ ১৭৮ ॥

premāveśe prabhu yabe karena citkāra
mlecchera hṛdaye yena lāge śeladhāra

SYNONYMS

prema-āveśe—in ecstatic love; *prabhu*—Śrī Caitanya Mahāprabhu; *yabe*—when; *karena citkāra*—loudly shouts; *mlecchera hṛdaye*—in the hearts of the Mohammedan soldiers; *yena*—as if; *lāge*—strikes; *śela-dhāra*—a thunderbolt.

TRANSLATION

When the Lord shouted very loudly in ecstatic love, it appeared to the Mohammedan soldiers that their hearts were struck by thunderbolts.

TEXT 179

ভয় পাঞা ম্লেচ্ছ ছাড়ি' দিল চারিজন ।
প্রভু না দেখিল নিজ-গণের বন্ধন ॥ ১৭৯ ॥

bhaya pāñā mleccha chāḍi' dila cāri-jana
prabhu nā dekhila nija-gaṇera bandhana

SYNONYMS

bhaya pāñā—being afraid; *mleccha*—the Mohammedans; *chāḍi' dila*—released; *cāri-jana*—the four persons; *prabhu*—Śrī Caitanya Mahāprabhu; *nā dekhila*—did not see; *nija-gaṇera*—of His personal associates; *bandhana*—the arrest.

TRANSLATION

Seized by fear, all the Pāṭhāna soldiers immediately released the four persons. Thus Śrī Caitanya Mahāprabhu did not see His personal associates arrested.

TEXT 180

ভট্টাচার্য আসি' প্রভুরে ধরি' বসাইল ।
ম্লেচ্ছগণ দেখি' মহাপ্রভুর 'বাহ্য' হৈল ॥ ১৮০ ॥

bhaṭṭācārya āsi' prabhure dhari' vasāila
mleccha-gaṇa dekhi' mahāprabhura 'bāhya' haila

SYNONYMS

bhaṭṭācārya—Bhaṭṭācārya; *āsi'*—immediately coming near; *prabhure*—Śrī Caitanya Mahāprabhu; *dhari'*—taking; *vasāila*—made to sit; *mleccha-gaṇa dekhi'*—seeing the Mohammedan soldiers; *mahāprabhura*—of Śrī Caitanya Mahāprabhu; *bāhya*—external consciousness; *haila*—there was.

TRANSLATION

At that time, Balabhadra Bhaṭṭācārya went to Śrī Caitanya Mahāprabhu and made Him sit down. Seeing the Mohammedan soldiers, the Lord regained His normal senses.

TEXT 181

ম্লেচ্ছগণ আসি' প্রভুর বন্দিল চরণ ।
প্রভু-আগে কহে,—এই ঠক্ চারিজন ॥ ১৮১ ॥

mleccha-gaṇa āsi' prabhura vandila caraṇa
prabhu-āge kahe,——ei ṭhak cāri-jana

SYNONYMS

mleccha-gaṇa—the Mohammedan soldiers; *āsi'*—after coming there; *prabhura*—of Śrī Caitanya Mahāprabhu; *vandila caraṇa*—worshiped the lotus feet; *prabhu-āge kahe*—said before the Lord; *ei ṭhak cāri-jana*—these four persons are rogues.

TRANSLATION

All the Mohammedan soldiers then came before the Lord, worshiped His lotus feet and said, "Here are four rogues.

TEXT 182

এই চারি মিলি' তোমায় ধুতুরা খাওয়াঞা ।
তোমার ধন লৈল তোমায় পাগল করিয়া ॥ ১৮২ ॥

ei cāri mili' tomāya dhuturā khāoyāñā
tomāra dhana laila tomāya pāgala kariyā

SYNONYMS

ei cāri mili'—four rogues together; *tomāya*—You; *dhuturā khāoyāñā*—making to drink poison; *tomāra*—Your; *dhana*—wealth; *laila*—took away; *tomāya*—You; *pāgala*—intoxicated; *kariyā*—making.

TRANSLATION

"These rogues have made You take dhuturā. Having made You mad, they have taken all Your possessions."

TEXT 183

প্রভু কহেন,—ঠক্ নহে, মোর 'সঙ্গী' জন ।
ভিক্ষুক সন্ন্যাসী, মোর নাহি কিছু ধন ॥ ১৮৩ ॥

prabhu kahena,——ṭhak nahe, mora 'saṅgī' jana
bhikṣuka sannyāsī, mora nāhi kichu dhana

SYNONYMS

prabhu kahena—Śrī Caitanya Mahāprabhu replied; *ṭhak nahe*—they are not rogues; *mora saṅgī jana*—My associates; *bhikṣuka*—beggar; *sannyāsī*—*sannyāsī;* *mora*—My; *nāhi*—are not; *kichu*—any; *dhana*—riches.

TRANSLATION

Śrī Caitanya Mahāprabhu said, "These are not rogues. They are My associates. Being a sannyāsī beggar, I do not possess anything.

TEXT 184

মৃগী-ব্যাধিতে আমি কভু হই অচেতন ।
এই চারি দয়া করি' করেন পালন ॥ ১৮৪ ॥

mṛgī-vyādhite āmi kabhu ha-i acetana
ei cāri dayā kari' karena pālana

SYNONYMS

mṛgī-vyādhite—due to epilepsy; *āmi*—I; *kabhu*—sometimes; *ha-i*—become; *acetana*—unconscious; *ei cāri*—these four men; *dayā kari'*—being merciful; *karena pālana*—maintain Me.

TRANSLATION

"Due to epilepsy, I sometimes fall unconscious. Out of their mercy, these four men maintain Me."

TEXT 185

সেই ম্লেচ্ছ-মধ্যে এক পরম গম্ভীর ।
কাল বস্ত্র পরে সেই,— লোকে কহে 'পীর' ॥ ১৮৫ ॥

sei mleccha-madhye eka parama gambhīra
kāla vastra pare sei,——loke kahe 'pīra'

SYNONYMS

sei mleccha-madhye—among those Mohammedans; *eka*—one; *parama gambhīra*—very grave; *kāla vastra*—black garments; *pare sei*—he wears; *loke*—people; *kahe*—call; *pīra*—a saintly person.

TRANSLATION

Among the Mohammedans was a grave person who was wearing a black dress. People called him a saintly person.

TEXT 186

চিত্ত আর্দ্র হৈল তাঁর প্রভুরে দেখিয়া ।
'নির্বিশেষ-ব্রহ্ম' স্থাপে স্বশাস্ত্র উঠাঞা ॥ ১৮৬ ॥

citta ārdra haila tāṅra prabhure dekhiyā
'nirviśeṣa-brahma' sthāpe svaśāstra uṭhāñā

SYNONYMS

citta—heart; *ārdra*—softened; *haila*—became; *tāṅra*—his; *prabhure dekhiyā*—seeing Lord Caitanya Mahāprabhu; *nirviśeṣa-brahma*—impersonal Brahman; *sthāpe*—wanted to establish; *sva-śāstra uṭhāñā*—raising his scripture.

TRANSLATION

The heart of that saintly person softened upon seeing Śrī Caitanya Mahāprabhu. He wanted to talk to Him and establish impersonal Brahman on the basis of his own scripture, the Koran.

TEXT 187

'অদ্বৈত-ব্রহ্মবাদ' সেই করিল স্থাপন ।
তার শাস্ত্রযুক্ত্যে তারে প্রভু কৈলা খণ্ডন ॥ ১৮৭ ॥

'advaita-brahma-vāda' sei karila sthāpana
tāra śāstra-yuktye tāre prabhu kailā khaṇḍana

SYNONYMS

advaita-brahma-vāda—the impersonal Brahman conception; *sei*—that saintly person; *karila sthāpana*—established; *tāra śāstra-yuktye*—on the logic of his scripture; *tāre*—unto him; *prabhu*—Śrī Caitanya Mahāprabhu; *kailā*—did; *khaṇḍana*—refutation.

TRANSLATION

When that person established the impersonal Brahman conception of the Absolute Truth on the basis of the Koran, Śrī Caitanya Mahāprabhu refuted his argument.

TEXT 188

যেই যেই কহিল, প্রভু সকলি খণ্ডিল ।
উত্তর না আইসে মুখে, মহাস্তব্ধ হৈল ॥ ১৮৮ ॥

yei yei kahila, prabhu sakali khaṇḍila
uttara nā āise mukhe, mahā-stabdha haila

SYNONYMS

yei yei kahila—whatever he spoke; *prabhu*—Śrī Caitanya Mahāprabhu; *sakali khaṇḍila*—refuted everything; *uttara*—answer; *nā āise*—could not come; *mukhe*—in his mouth; *mahā-stabdha haila*—he became greatly stunned.

TRANSLATION

Whatever arguments he put forward, the Lord refuted them all. Finally the person became stunned and could not speak.

TEXT 189

প্রভু কহে,—তোমার শাস্ত্র স্থাপে 'নির্বিশেষে' ।
তাহা খণ্ডি' 'সবিশেষ' স্থাপিয়াছে শেষে ॥ ১৮৯ ॥

prabhu kahe,——tomāra śāstra sthāpe 'nirviśeṣe'
tāhā khaṇḍi' 'saviśeṣa' sthāpiyāche śeṣe

SYNONYMS

prabhu kahe—Śrī Caitanya Mahāprabhu continued to speak; *tomāra śāstra*—your scripture (the Koran); *sthāpe*—establishes; *nirviśeṣe*—impersonalism; *tāhā khaṇḍi'*—refuting that; *sa-viśeṣa*—personal God; *sthāpiyāche*—established; *śeṣe*—at the end.

TRANSLATION

Śrī Caitanya Mahāprabhu said, "The Koran has certainly established impersonalism, but at the end it refutes that impersonalism and establishes the personal God.

TEXT 190

তোমার শাস্ত্রে কহে শেষে 'একই ঈশ্বর' ।
'সর্বৈশ্বর্যপূর্ণ তেঁহো—শ্যাম-কলেবর ॥ ১৯০ ॥

tomāra śāstre kahe śeṣe 'eka-i īśvara'
'sarvaiśvarya-pūrṇa teṅho——śyāma-kalevara

SYNONYMS

tomāra śāstre—in your scripture; *kahe*—it says; *śeṣe*—at the end; *eka-i īśvara*—there is one God; *sarva-aiśvarya-pūrṇa*—full of all opulence; *teṅho*—He; *śyāma-kalevara*—bodily complexion is blackish.

TRANSLATION

"The Koran accepts the fact that ultimately there is only one God. He is full of opulence, and His bodily complexion is blackish.

PURPORT

The revealed scripture of the Mohammedans is the Koran. There is one Mohammedan *sampradāya* known as the Sufis. The Sufis accept impersonalism, believing in the oneness of the living entity with the Absolute Truth. Their supreme slogan is *"analahak."* The Sufi *sampradāya* was certainly derived from Śaṅkarācārya's impersonalists.

TEXT 191

সচ্চিদানন্দ-দেহ, পূর্ণব্রহ্ম-স্বরূপ ।
'সর্বাত্মা', 'সর্বজ্ঞ', নিত্য সর্বাদি-স্বরূপ ॥ ১৯১ ॥

sac-cid-ānanda-deha, pūrṇa-brahma-svarūpa
'sarvātmā', 'sarvajña', nitya sarvādi-svarūpa

SYNONYMS

sat-cit-ānanda-deha—transcendental, blissful, spiritual body; *pūrṇa-brahma-svarūpa*—the identification of the Absolute Truth; *sarva-ātmā*—all-pervading; *sarva-jña*—omniscient; *nitya*—eternal; *sarva-ādi*—the origin of everything; *svarūpa*—the real form of the Lord.

TRANSLATION

"According to the Koran, the Lord has a supreme, blissful, transcendental body. He is the Absolute Truth, the all-pervading, omniscient and eternal being. He is the origin of everything.

TEXT 192

সৃষ্টি, স্থিতি, প্রলয় তাঁহা হৈতে হয় ।
স্থূল-সূক্ষ্ম-জগতের তেঁহো সমাশ্রয় ॥ ১৯২ ॥

sṛṣṭi, sthiti, pralaya tāṅhā haite haya
sthūla-sūkṣma-jagatera teṅho samāśraya

SYNONYMS

sṛṣṭi—creation; *sthiti*—maintenance; *pralaya*—dissolution; *tāṅhā*—Him; *haite*—from; *haya*—becomes possible; *sthūla*—gross; *sūkṣma*—subtle; *jagatera*—of the cosmic manifestation; *teṅho*—He; *samāśraya*—the only shelter.

TRANSLATION

"Creation, maintenance and dissolution come from Him. He is the original shelter of all gross and subtle cosmic manifestations.

TEXT 193

'সর্ব-শ্রেষ্ঠ, সর্বারাধ্য, কারণের কারণ ।
তাঁর ভক্ত্যে হয় জীবের সংসার-তারণ ॥১৯৩ ॥

'sarva-śreṣṭha, sarvārādhya, kāraṇera kāraṇa
tāṅra bhaktye haya jīvera saṁsāra-tāraṇa

SYNONYMS

sarva-śreṣṭha—the Supreme Truth; *sarva-ārādhya*—worshipable by everyone; *kāraṇera kāraṇa*—the cause of all causes; *tāṅra*—His; *bhaktye*—by devotional service; *haya*—becomes; *jīvera*—of the living entity; *saṁsāra-tāraṇa*—deliverance from material existence.

TRANSLATION

"The Lord is the Supreme Truth worshipable by everyone. He is the cause of all causes. By engaging in His devotional service, the living entity is relieved from material existence.

TEXT 194

তাঁর সেবা বিনা জীবের না যায় 'সংসার'।
তাঁহার চরণে প্রীতি—'পুরুষার্থ-সার' ॥ ১৯৪ ॥

tāṅra sevā vinā jīvera nā yāya 'saṁsāra'
tāṅhāra caraṇe prīti——'puruṣārtha-sāra'

SYNONYMS

tāṅra—His; *sevā*—service; *vinā*—without; *jīvera*—of the conditioned soul; *nā*—not; *yāya*—finishes; *saṁsāra*—material bondage; *tāṅhāra*—His; *caraṇe*—at the lotus feet; *prīti*—love; *puruṣārtha-sāra*—the ultimate goal of life.

TRANSLATION

"No conditioned soul can get out of material bondage without serving the Supreme Personality of Godhead. Love at His lotus feet is the ultimate goal of life.

PURPORT

According to the Mohammedan scripture, without *evādat,* offering prayers at a mosque or elsewhere five times daily (*namāja*), one cannot be successful in life. Śrī Caitanya Mahāprabhu pointed out that in the revealed scripture of the Mohammedans, love of Godhead is the ultimate goal. *Karma-yoga* and *jñāna-yoga* are certainly described in the Koran, but ultimately the Koran states that the ultimate goal is the offering of prayers to the Supreme Person (*evādat*).

TEXT 195

মোক্ষাদি আনন্দ যার নহে এক 'কণ'।
পূর্ণানন্দ-প্রাপ্তি তাঁর চরণ-সেবন ॥ ১৯৫ ॥

mokṣādi ānanda yāra nahe eka 'kaṇa'
pūrṇānanda-prāpti tāṅra caraṇa-sevana

SYNONYMS

mokṣa-ādi—liberation and so on; *ānanda*—transcendental bliss; *yāra*—whose; *nahe*—not; *eka*—even; *kaṇa*—a fragment; *pūrṇa-ānanda-prāpti*—attainment of completely blissful life; *tāṅra caraṇa-sevana*—service to His lotus feet.

TRANSLATION

"The happiness of liberation, whereby one merges into the Lord's existence, cannot even be compared to a fragment of the transcendental bliss obtained by service unto the Lord's lotus feet.

TEXT 196

'কর্ম', 'জ্ঞান', 'যোগ' আগে করিয়া স্থাপন ।
সব খণ্ডি' স্থাপে 'ঈশ্বর', 'তাঁহার সেবন' ॥ ১৯৬ ॥

'karma', 'jñāna', 'yoga' āge kariyā sthāpana
saba khaṇḍi' sthāpe 'īśvara', 'tāṅhāra sevana'

SYNONYMS

karma—fruitive activities; *jñāna*—speculative knowledge; *yoga*—mystic power; *āge*—in the beginning; *kariyā sthāpana*—establishing; *saba khaṇḍi'*—refuting everything; *sthāpe*—establishes; *īśvara*—the Personality of Godhead; *tāṅhāra sevana*—His service.

TRANSLATION

"In the Koran there are descriptions of fruitive activity, speculative knowledge, mystic power and union with the Supreme, but ultimately everything is refuted as the Lord's personal feature and His devotional service is established.

TEXT 197

তোমার পণ্ডিত-সবার নাহি শাস্ত্র-জ্ঞান ।
পূর্বাপর-বিধি-মধ্যে 'পর'—বলবান্ ॥ ১৯৭ ॥

tomāra paṇḍita-sabāra nāhi śāstra-jñāna
pūrvāpara-vidhi-madhye 'para'——balavān

SYNONYMS

tomāra paṇḍita-sabāra—of the learned scholars of your community; *nāhi*—there is not; *śāstra-jñāna*—knowledge of revealed scripture; *pūrva-āpara*—former and latter; *vidhi*—regulative principles; *madhye*—among; *para*—the conclusion at the end; *balavān*—most powerful.

TRANSLATION

"The scholars of the Koran are not very advanced in knowledge. Although there are many methods prescribed, they do not know that the ultimate conclusion should be considered the most powerful.

TEXT 198

নিজ-শাস্ত্র দেখি' তুমি বিচার করিয়া ।
কি লিখিয়াছে শেষে কহ নির্ণয় করিয়া ॥ ১৯৮ ॥

nija-śāstra dekhi' tumi vicāra kariyā
ki likhiyāche śeṣe kaha nirṇaya kariyā

SYNONYMS

nija-śāstra—your own scripture; *dekhi'*—seeing; *tumi*—you; *vicāra kariyā*—deliberating; *ki likhiyāche*—what was written; *śeṣe*—at the end; *kaha*—say; *nirṇaya kariyā*—ascertaining.

TRANSLATION

"Seeing your own Koran and deliberating over what is written there, what is your conclusion?"

TEXT 199

ম্লেচ্ছ কহে,—যেই কহ, সেই 'সত্য' হয় ।
শাস্ত্রে লিখিয়াছে, কেহ লইতে না পারয় ॥ ১৯৯ ॥

mleccha kahe,——yei kaha, sei 'satya' haya
śāstre likhiyāche, keha la-ite nā pāraya

SYNONYMS

mleccha kahe—the Mohammedan replied; *yei kaha*—what You say; *sei*—that; *satya haya*—is true; *śāstre*—in the Koran; *likhiyāche*—it has been written; *keha*—anyone; *la-ite*—to take; *nā pāraya*—is not able.

TRANSLATION

The saintly Mohammedan replied, "All that You have said is true. This has certainly been written in the Koran, but our scholars can neither understand nor accept it.

TEXT 200

'নির্বিশেষ-গোসাঞি' লঞা করেন ব্যাখ্যান ।
'সাকার-গোসাঞি'—সেব্য, কারো নাহি জ্ঞান॥২০০

'nirviśeṣa-gosāñi' lañā karena vyākhyāna
'sākāra-gosāñi'——sevya, kāro nāhi jñāna

SYNONYMS

nirviśeṣa-gosāñi—the Supreme Personality of Godhead as impersonal; *lañā*—taking; *karena vyākhyāna*—they describe; *sa-ākāra-gosāñi*—the personal feature of the Lord; *sevya*—worshipable; *kāro nāhi jñāna*—no one has this knowledge.

TRANSLATION

"Usually they describe the Lord's impersonal aspect, but they hardly know that the Lord's personal feature is worshipable. They are undoubtedly lacking this knowledge.

PURPORT

The saintly Mohammedan admitted that those who were supposedly conversant in the teachings of the Koran could not ultimately understand the essence of the Koran. Because of this, they accepted only the Lord's impersonal feature. Generally they recite and explain this portion only. Although the transcendental body of the Lord is worshipable, most of them are unaware of this.

TEXT 201

সেইত 'গোসাঞি' তুমি—সাক্ষাৎ 'ঈশ্বর'।
মোরে কৃপা কর, মুঞি—অযোগ্য পামর ॥ ২০১ ॥

seita 'gosāñi' tumi——sākṣāt 'īśvara'
more kṛpā kara, muñi——ayogya pāmara

SYNONYMS

seita—that; *gosāñi*—Personality of Godhead; *tumi*—You; *sākṣāt*—directly; *īśvara*—the Personality of Godhead; *more*—upon me; *kṛpā kara*—kindly be merciful; *muñi*—I; *ayogya pāmara*—very fallen and unfit.

TRANSLATION

"Since You are that very same Supreme Personality of Godhead Himself, please be merciful upon me. I am fallen and unfit.

TEXT 202

অনেক দেখিনু মুঞি ম্লেচ্ছ-শাস্ত্র হৈতে।
'সাধ্য-সাধন-বস্তু' নারি নির্ধারিতে ॥ ২০২ ॥

aneka dekhinu muñi mleccha-śāstra haite
'sādhya-sādhana-vastu' nāri nirdhārite

SYNONYMS

aneka—many; *dekhinu*—have studied; *muñi*—I; *mleccha-śāstra*—Mohammedan scripture; *haite*—from; *sādhya*—the ultimate goal of life; *sādhana*—how to approach it; *vastu*—matter; *nāri nirdhārite*—I cannot decide conclusively.

TRANSLATION

"I have studied the Mohammedan scripture very extensively, but from it I cannot conclusively decide what the ultimate goal of life is or how I can approach it.

TEXT 203

তোমা দেখি' জিহ্বা মোর বলে 'কৃষ্ণনাম'।
'আমি—বড় জ্ঞানী'—এই গেল অভিমান ॥ ২০৩ ॥

tomā dekhi' jihvā mora bale 'kṛṣṇa-nāma'
'āmi——baḍa jñānī'——ei gela ābhimāna

SYNONYMS

tomā dekhi'—by seeing You; *jihvā*—tongue; *mora*—my; *bale kṛṣṇa-nāma*—chants the Hare Kṛṣṇa *mantra;* *āmi*—I; *baḍa jñānī*—very learned scholar; *ei*—this; *gela ābhimāna*—false prestige has gone away.

TRANSLATION

"Now that I have seen You, my tongue is chanting the Hare Kṛṣṇa mahā-mantra. The false prestige I felt from being a learned scholar is now gone."

TEXT 204

কৃপা করি' বল মোরে 'সাধ্য-সাধনে'।
এত বলি' পড়ে মহাপ্রভুর চরণে ॥ ২০৪ ॥

kṛpā kari' bala more 'sādhya-sādhane'
eta bali' paḍe mahāprabhura caraṇe

SYNONYMS

kṛpā kari'—by Your causeless mercy; *bala*—speak; *more*—to me; *sādhya-sādhane*—the ultimate object of life and the process to achieve it; *eta bali'*—saying this; *paḍe*—falls down; *mahāprabhura caraṇe*—at the lotus feet of Śrī Caitanya Mahāprabhu.

TRANSLATION

Saying this, the saintly Mohammedan fell at the lotus feet of Śrī Caitanya Mahāprabhu and requested Him to speak of life's ultimate goal and the process by which it could be obtained.

TEXT 205

প্রভু কহে,—উঠ, কৃষ্ণনাম তুমি লইলা।
কোটি-জন্মের পাপ গেল, 'পবিত্র' হইলা ॥ ২০৫ ॥

prabhu kahe,——uṭha, kṛṣṇa-nāma tumi la-ilā
koṭi-janmera pāpa gela, 'pavitra' ha-ilā

SYNONYMS

prabhu kahe—Śrī Caitanya Mahāprabhu said; *uṭha*—please get up; *kṛṣṇa-nāma*—the holy name of Kṛṣṇa; *tumi*—you; *la-ilā*—have taken; *koṭi-janmera*—of many millions of births; *pāpa gela*—your sinful reactions have gone; *pavitra ha-ilā*—you have become pure.

TRANSLATION

Śrī Caitanya Mahāprabhu said, "Please get up. You have chanted the holy name of Kṛṣṇa; therefore the sinful reactions you have accrued for many millions of lives are now gone. You are now pure."

TEXT 206

'কৃষ্ণ' কহ, 'কৃষ্ণ' কহ,—কৈলা উপদেশ।
সবে 'কৃষ্ণ' কহে, সবার হৈল প্রেমাবেশ ॥ ২০৬ ॥

'kṛṣṇa' kaha, 'kṛṣṇa' kaha,——kailā upadeśa
sabe 'kṛṣṇa' kahe, sabāra haila premāveśa

SYNONYMS

kṛṣṇa kaha—just chant "Kṛṣṇa"; *kṛṣṇa kaha*—just chant "Kṛṣṇa"; *kailā upadeśa*—Śrī Caitanya Mahāprabhu instructed; *sabe*—all; *kṛṣṇa kahe*—chant the holy name of Kṛṣṇa; *sabāra*—of all of them; *haila*—there was; *prema-āveśa*—ecstatic love.

TRANSLATION

Śrī Caitanya Mahāprabhu then told all the Mohammedans there, "Chant the holy name of Kṛṣṇa! Chant the holy name of Kṛṣṇa!" As they all began to chant, they were overwhelmed by ecstatic love.

TEXT 207

'রামদাস' বলি' প্রভু তাঁর কৈল নাম ।
আর এক পাঠান, তাঁর নাম—'বিজুলী-খাঁন' ॥ ২০৭ ॥

'rāmadāsa' bali' prabhu tāṅra kaila nāma
āra eka pāṭhāna, tāṅra nāma——'vijulī-khāṅna'

SYNONYMS

rāmadāsa bali'—of the name Rāmadāsa; *prabhu*—Śrī Caitanya Mahāprabhu; *tāṅra*—his; *kaila*—made; *nāma*—name; *āra eka pāṭhāna*—another Mohammedan; *tāṅra nāma*—his name; *vijulī-khāṅna*—Vijulī Khān.

TRANSLATION

In this way Śrī Caitanya Mahāprabhu indirectly initiated the saintly Mohammedan by advising him to chant the holy name of Kṛṣṇa. The Mohammedan's name was changed to Rāmadāsa. There was also another Pāṭhāna Moslem present whose name was Vijulī Khān.

PURPORT

After being initiated, the devotees in the Kṛṣṇa consciousness movement change their names. Whenever a person in the Western world becomes interested in this Kṛṣṇa consciousness movement, he is initiated by this process. In India we are falsely accused of converting *mlecchas* and *yavanas* into the Hindu religion. In India there are many Māyāvādī *sannyāsīs* known as *jagad-guru,* although they have hardly visited the whole world. Some are not even sufficiently educated, yet they make accusations against our movement and accuse us of destroying the principles of the Hindu religion by accepting Mohammedans and *yavanas* as Vaiṣṇavas. Such people are simply envious. We are not spoiling the Hindu system of religion but are simply following in the footsteps of Śrī Caitanya Mahāprabhu by traveling all over the world and accepting those who are interested in understanding Kṛṣṇa as Kṛṣṇadāsa or Rāmadāsa. By the process of a bona fide initiation, their names are changed.

TEXT 208

অল্প বয়স তাঁর, রাজার কুমার ।
'রামদাস' আদি পাঠান—চাকর তাঁহার ॥ ২০৮ ॥

alpa vayasa tāṅra, rājāra kumāra
'rāmadāsa' ādi pāṭhāna——cākara tāṅhāra

SYNONYMS

alpa vayasa tāṅra—his age is very young; *rājāra kumāra*—son of the king; *rāmadāsa*—Rāmadāsa; *ādi*—heading the list; *pāṭhāna*—the Mohammedans; *cākara tāṅhāra*—servants of him.

TRANSLATION

Vijulī Khān was very young, and he was the son of the king. All the other Mohammedans, Pāṭhānas, headed by Rāmadāsa, were his servants.

TEXT 209

'কৃষ্ণ' বলি' পড়ে সেই মহাপ্রভুর পায় ।
প্রভু শ্রীচরণ দিল তাঁহার মাথায় ॥ ২০৯ ॥

'kṛṣṇa' bali' paḍe sei mahāprabhura pāya
prabhu śrī-caraṇa dila tāṅhāra māthāya

SYNONYMS

kṛṣṇa bali'—chanting the holy name of Kṛṣṇa; *paḍe*—falls down; *sei*—that Vijulī Khān; *mahāprabhura pāya*—at the lotus feet of Śrī Caitanya Mahāprabhu; *prabhu*—Śrī Caitanya Mahāprabhu; *śrī-caraṇa dila*—placed His foot; *tāṅhāra māthāya*—on his head.

TRANSLATION

Vijulī Khān also fell down at the lotus feet of Śrī Caitanya Mahāprabhu, and the Lord placed His foot on his head.

TEXT 210

তাঁ-সবারে কৃপা করি' প্রভু ত' চলিলা ।
সেইত পাঠান সব 'বৈরাগী' হইলা ॥ ২১০ ॥

tāṅ-sabāre kṛpā kari' prabhu ta' calilā
seita pāṭhāna saba 'vairāgī' ha-ilā

SYNONYMS

tāṅ-sabāre—to all of them; *kṛpā kari'*—bestowing mercy; *prabhu*—Śrī Caitanya Mahāprabhu; *ta'*—indeed; *calilā*—departed; *seita*—they; *pāṭhāna*—the Mohammedans of the Pāṭhāna community; *saba*—all; *vairāgī ha-ilā*—became mendicants.

TRANSLATION

Bestowing His mercy upon them in this way, Śrī Caitanya Mahāprabhu left. All the Pāṭhāna Mohammedans then became mendicants.

TEXT 211

পাঠান-বৈষ্ণব বলি' হৈল তাঁর খ্যাতি ।
সর্বত্র গাহিয়া বুলে মহাপ্রভুর কীর্তি ॥ ২১১ ॥

pāṭhāna-vaiṣṇava bali' haila tāṅra khyāti
sarvatra gāhiyā bule mahāprabhura kīrti

SYNONYMS

pāṭhāna-vaiṣṇava bali'—known as Pāṭhāna Vaiṣṇavas; *haila*—became; *tāṅra*—their; *khyāti*—reputation; *sarvatra*—everywhere; *gāhiyā bule*—travel while chanting; *mahāprabhura*—of Śrī Caitanya Mahāprabhu; *kīrti*—glorious activities.

TRANSLATION

Later these very Pāṭhānas became celebrated as the Pāṭhāna Vaiṣṇavas. They toured all over the country and chanted the glorious activities of Śrī Caitanya Mahāprabhu.

TEXT 212

সেই বিজুলী-খাঁন হৈল 'মহাভাগবত' ।
সর্বতীর্থে হৈল তাঁর পরম-মহত্ত্ব ॥ ২১২ ॥

sei vijulī-khāṅna haila 'mahā-bhāgavata'
sarva-tīrthe haila tāṅra parama-mahattva

SYNONYMS

sei—that; *vijulī-khāṅna*—Vijulī Khān; *haila*—became; *mahā-bhāgavata*—most advanced devotee; *sarva-tīrthe*—in all places of pilgrimage; *haila*—became; *tāṅra*—his; *parama*—great; *mahattva*—importance.

TRANSLATION

Vijulī Khān became a greatly advanced devotee, and his importance was celebrated at every holy place of pilgrimage.

TEXT 213

ঐছে লীলা করে প্রভু শ্রীকৃষ্ণচৈতন্য ।
'পশ্চিমে' আসিয়া কৈল যবনাদি ধন্য ॥ ২১৩ ॥

aiche līlā kare prabhu śrī-kṛṣṇa-caitanya
'paścime' āsiyā kaila yavanādi dhanya

SYNONYMS

aiche—in that way; *līlā*—pastimes; *kare*—performed; *prabhu*—the Lord; *śrī-kṛṣṇa-caitanya*—Śrī Caitanya Mahāprabhu; *paścime*—to the western part of India; *āsiyā*—coming; *kaila*—made; *yavana-ādi*—meat-eaters and others; *dhanya*—fortunate.

TRANSLATION

In this way Lord Śrī Caitanya Mahāprabhu performed His pastimes. Coming to the western part of India, He bestowed good fortune upon the yavanas and mlecchas.

PURPORT

The word *yavana* means "meat-eater." Anyone from a meat-eating community is called a *yavana.* One who does not strictly observe the Vedic regulative principles is called a *mleccha.* These words do not refer to any particular man. Even if a person is born in a *brāhmaṇa, kṣatriya, vaiśya* or *śūdra* family, he is a *mleccha* or *yavana* if he does not strictly follow the regulative principles or if he eats meat.

TEXT 214

সোরোক্ষেত্রে আসি' প্রভু কৈলা গঙ্গাস্নান ।
গঙ্গাতীর-পথে কৈলা প্রয়াগে প্রয়াণ ॥ ২১৪ ॥

soro-kṣetre āsi' prabhu kailā gaṅgā-snāna
gaṅgā-tīra-pathe kailā prayāge prayāṇa

SYNONYMS

soro-kṣetre—to Soro-kṣetra; *āsi'*—coming; *prabhu*—Śrī Caitanya Mahāprabhu; *kailā*—did; *gaṅgā-snāna*—bathing in the Ganges; *gaṅgā-tīra-pathe*—on the path on the bank of the Ganges; *kailā*—did; *prayāge prayāṇa*—departure for Prayāga.

TRANSLATION

Śrī Caitanya Mahāprabhu next went to a holy place of pilgrimage called Soro-kṣetra. He took His bath in the Ganges there and started for Prayāga on the path along the banks of the Ganges.

TEXT 215

সেই বিপ্রে, কৃষ্ণদাসে, প্রভু বিদায় দিলা ।
যোড়-হাতে দুইজন কহিতে লাগিলা ॥ ২১৫ ॥

sei vipre, kṛṣṇadāse, prabhu vidāya dilā
yoḍa-hāte dui-jana kahite lāgilā

SYNONYMS

sei vipre—to the Sanoḍiyā *brāhmaṇa; kṛṣṇadāse*—and the Rājaputa Kṛṣṇadāsa; *prabhu*—Śrī Caitanya Mahāprabhu; *vidāya dilā*—asked to go back; *yoḍa-hāte*—with folded hands; *dui-jana*—two persons; *kahite lāgilā*—began to say.

TRANSLATION

At Soro-kṣetra, the Lord requested the Sanoḍiyā brāhmaṇa and Rājaputa Kṛṣṇadāsa to return home, but with folded hands they began to speak as follows.

TEXT 216

প্রয়াগ-পর্যন্ত দুঁহে তোমা-সঙ্গে যাব ।
তোমার চরণ-সঙ্গ পুনঃ কাহাঁ পাব ? ২১৬ ॥

prayāga-paryanta duṅhe tomā-saṅge yāba
tomāra caraṇa-saṅga punaḥ kāhāṅ pāba?

SYNONYMS

prayāga-paryanta—up to Prayāga; *duṅhe*—both of us; *tomā-saṅge*—with You; *yāba*—shall go; *tomāra*—Your; *caraṇa-saṅga*—association of the lotus feet; *punaḥ*—again; *kāhāṅ*—where; *pāba*—shall we get.

TRANSLATION

They prayed, "Let us go to Prayāga with You. If we do not go, when shall we again get the association of Your lotus feet?

TEXT 217

ম্লেচ্ছদেশ, কেহ কাহাঁ করয়ে উৎপাত ।
ভট্টাচার্য—পণ্ডিত, কহিতে না জানেন বাত্ ॥ ২১৭ ॥

mleccha-deśa, keha kāhāṅ karaye utpāta
bhaṭṭācārya——paṇḍita, kahite nā jānena vāt

SYNONYMS

mleccha-deśa—this is a country occupied by the Mohammedans; *keha*—anyone; *kāhāṅ*—anywhere; *karaye utpāta*—can create a disturbance; *bhaṭṭācārya*—Balabhadra Bhaṭṭācārya; *paṇḍita*—learned scholar; *kahite*—to speak; *nā jānena*—does not know; *vāt*—language.

TRANSLATION

"This country is mainly occupied by Mohammedans. At any place someone can create a disturbance, and although Your companion Balabhadra Bhaṭṭācārya is a learned scholar, he does not know how to speak the local language."

TEXT 218

শুনি' মহাপ্রভু ঈষৎ হাসিতে লাগিলা ।
সেই দুইজন প্রভুর সঙ্গে চলি' আইলা ॥ ২১৮ ॥

śuni' mahāprabhu īṣat hāsite lāgilā
sei dui-jana prabhura saṅge cali' āilā

SYNONYMS

śuni'—hearing; *mahāprabhu*—Śrī Caitanya Mahāprabhu; *īṣat*—mildly; *hāsite lāgilā*—began to smile; *sei*—those; *dui-jana*—two persons; *prabhura saṅge*—with Śrī Caitanya Mahāprabhu; *cali' āilā*—came.

TRANSLATION

Hearing this, Śrī Caitanya Mahāprabhu accepted their proposal by smiling mildly. Thus those two persons continued to accompany Him.

TEXT 219

যেই যেই জন প্রভুর পাইল দরশন ।
সেই প্রেমে মত্ত হয়, করে কৃষ্ণ-সংকীর্তন ॥ ২১৯ ॥

yei yei jana prabhura pāila daraśana
sei preme matta haya, kare kṛṣṇa-saṅkīrtana

SYNONYMS

yei yei—anyone who; *jana*—person; *prabhura*—of Śrī Caitanya Mahāprabhu; *pāila daraśana*—got the sight; *sei*—that person; *preme*—with ecstatic love; *matta haya*—becomes overwhelmed; *kare*—performs; *kṛṣṇa-saṅkīrtana*—chanting of the holy name of Kṛṣṇa.

TRANSLATION

Whoever got to see Śrī Caitanya Mahāprabhu would feel himself overwhelmed with ecstatic love and would begin to chant the Hare Kṛṣṇa mantra.

TEXT 220

তাঁর সঙ্গে অন্যোন্যে, তাঁর সঙ্গে আন।
এইমত 'বৈষ্ণব' কৈলা সব দেশ-গ্রাম ॥ ২২০ ॥

tāṅra saṅge anyonye, tāṅra saṅge āna
ei-mata 'vaiṣṇava' kailā saba deśa-grāma

SYNONYMS

tāṅra saṅge—with Him; *anyonye*—other; *tāṅra saṅge*—and with him; *āna*—another; *ei-mata*—in this way; *vaiṣṇava*—Vaiṣṇava; *kailā*—made; *saba*—all; *deśa-grāma*—villages and towns.

TRANSLATION

Whoever met Śrī Caitanya Mahāprabhu became a Vaiṣṇava, and whoever met that Vaiṣṇava also became a Vaiṣṇava. In this way, all the towns and villages one after the other became Vaiṣṇava.

TEXT 221

দক্ষিণ যাইতে যৈছে শক্তি প্রকাশিলা।
সেইমত পশ্চিম দেশ, প্রেমে ভাসাইলা ॥ ২২১ ॥

dakṣiṇa yāite yaiche śakti prakāśilā
sei-mata paścima deśa, preme bhāsāilā

SYNONYMS

dakṣiṇa yāite—while touring in the southern part of India; *yaiche*—as; *śakti prakāśilā*—manifested His spiritual energy; *sei-mata*—in that way; *paścima deśa*—the western part of India; *preme bhāsāilā*—inundated with love of Kṛṣṇa.

TRANSLATION

Just as the Lord inundated South India on His tour there, He also inundated the western part of the country with love of Godhead.

PURPORT

According to some opinions, Śrī Caitanya Mahāprabhu visited Kurukṣetra while going to Prayāga from Vṛndāvana. There is a temple of Bhadra-kālī in Kurukṣetra, and near that temple there is a temple containing the Deity of Śrī Caitanya Mahāprabhu.

TEXT 222

এইমত চলি' প্রভু 'প্রয়াগ' আইলা।
দশ-দিন ত্রিবেণীতে মকর-স্নান কৈলা ॥ ২২২ ॥

ei-mata cali' prabhu 'prayāga' āilā
daśa-dina triveṇīte makara-snāna kailā

SYNONYMS

ei-mata—in this way; *cali'*—walking; *prabhu*—Śrī Caitanya Mahāprabhu; *prayāga*—the holy place named Prayāga; *āilā*—reached; *daśa-dina*—ten days; *triveṇīte*—at the confluence of the Rivers Ganges and Yamunā; *makara-snāna kailā*—bathed during the festival of Makara, or Māgha-melā.

TRANSLATION

Śrī Caitanya Mahāprabhu finally arrived at Prayāga and for ten successive days bathed in the confluence of the Rivers Yamunā and Ganges during the festival of Makara-saṅkrānti [Māgha-melā].

PURPORT

Actually the word *triveṇī* indicates the confluence of three rivers—namely the Ganges, Yamunā and Sarasvatī. Presently the Sarasvatī River is not visible, but the River Ganges and the River Yamunā merge at Allahabad.

TEXT 223

বৃন্দাবন-গমন, প্রভু-চরিত্র অনন্ত ।
'সহস্র-বদন' যাঁর নাহি পা'ন অন্ত ॥ ২২৩ ॥

vṛndāvana-gamana, prabhu-caritra ananta
'sahasra-vadana' yāṅra nāhi pā'na anta

SYNONYMS

vṛndāvana-gamana—going to Vṛndāvana; *prabhu-caritra*—pastimes of Śrī Caitanya Mahāprabhu; *ananta*—unlimited; *sahasra-vadana*—Lord Śeṣa, who has thousands of hoods; *yāṅra*—whose; *nāhi*—does not; *pā'na*—get; *anta*—limit.

TRANSLATION

Śrī Caitanya Mahāprabhu's visit to Vṛndāvana and His activities there are unlimited. Even Lord Śeṣa, who has thousands of hoods, cannot reach the end of His activities.

TEXT 224

তাহা কে কহিতে পারে ক্ষুদ্র জীব হঞা ।
দিগ্‌-দরশন কৈলুঁ মুঞি সূত্র করিয়া ॥ ২২৪ ॥

tāhā ke kahite pāre kṣudra jīva hañā
dig-daraśana kailuṅ muñi sūtra kariyā

SYNONYMS

tāhā—that; *ke kahite pāre*—who can describe; *kṣudra*—very little; *jīva hañā*—being a conditioned soul; *dik-daraśana kailuṅ*—have simply made an indication; *muñi*—I; *sūtra kariyā*—in codes.

TRANSLATION

What ordinary living being can describe the pastimes of Śrī Caitanya Mahāprabhu? I have only indicated the general direction in the form of codes.

TEXT 225

অলৌকিক-লীলা প্রভুর অলৌকিক-রীতি ।
শুনিলেও ভাগ্যহীনের না হয় প্রতীতি ॥ ২২৫ ॥

alaukika-līlā prabhura alaukika-rīti
śunileo bhāgya-hīnera nā haya pratīti

SYNONYMS

alaukika-līlā—uncommon pastimes; *prabhura*—of Śrī Caitanya Mahāprabhu; *alaukika-rīti*—uncommon method; *śunileo*—even though one hears; *bhāgya-hīnera*—of one who is unfortunate; *nā haya pratīti*—there is no belief.

TRANSLATION

The pastimes and methods of Śrī Caitanya Mahāprabhu are uncommon. Unfortunate is he who cannot believe even after hearing all these things.

TEXT 226

আদ্যোপান্ত চৈতন্যলীলা—'অলৌকিক' জান'।
শ্রদ্ধা করি' শুন ইহা, 'সত্য' করি' মান' ॥ ২২৬ ॥

ādyopānta caitanya-līlā——'alaukika' jāna'
śraddhā kari' śuna ihā, 'satya' kari' māna'

SYNONYMS

ādya-upānta—from beginning to end; *caitanya-līlā*—the pastimes of Śrī Caitanya Mahāprabhu; *alaukika jāna'*—everyone should know as uncommon; *śraddhā kari'*—with faith; *śuna ihā*—hear this; *satya kari' māna'*—accepting it as true and correct.

TRANSLATION

From beginning to end the pastimes of Śrī Caitanya Mahāprabhu are uncommon. Just hear them with faith and accept them as true and correct.

TEXT 227

যেই তর্ক করে ইহাঁ, সেই—'মূর্খরাজ'।
আপনার মুণ্ডে সে আপনি পাড়ে বাজ ॥ ২২৭ ॥

yei tarka kare ihāṅ, sei——'mūrkha-rāja'
āpanāra muṇḍe se āpani pāḍe vāja

SYNONYMS

yei tarka kare—one who simply argues; *ihāṅ*—in this matter; *sei*—that person; *mūrkha-rāja*—a great fool; *āpanāra muṇḍe*—on his own head; *se*—that person; *āpani*—himself; *pāḍe vāja*—strikes with a thunderbolt.

TRANSLATION

Whoever argues about this is a great fool. He intentionally and personally brings a thunderbolt down upon his head.

TEXT 228

চৈতন্য-চরিত্র এই—'অমৃতের সিন্ধু'।
জগৎ আনন্দে ভাসায় যার একবিন্দু ॥ ২২৮ ॥

caitanya-caritra ei——'amṛtera sindhu'
jagat ānande bhāsāya yāra eka-bindu

SYNONYMS

caitanya-caritra—pastimes of Śrī Caitanya Mahāprabhu; *ei*—these; *amṛtera sindhu*—ocean of nectar; *jagat*—the whole world; *ānande*—with bliss; *bhāsāya*—inundates; *yāra*—of which; *eka-bindu*—one drop.

TRANSLATION

The pastimes of Śrī Caitanya Mahāprabhu are an ocean of nectar. Even a drop of this ocean can inundate the whole world with transcendental bliss.

TEXT 229

শ্রীরূপ-রঘুনাথ-পদে যার আশ।
চৈতন্যচরিতামৃত কহে কৃষ্ণদাস ॥ ২২৯ ॥

śrī-rūpa-raghunātha-pade yāra āśa
caitanya-caritāmṛta kahe kṛṣṇadāsa

SYNONYMS

śrī-rūpa—Śrī Rūpa Gosvāmī; *raghunātha*—Śrīla Raghunātha dāsa Gosvāmī; *pade*—at the lotus feet; *yāra*—whose; *āśa*—expectation; *caitanya-caritāmṛta*—the book named *Caitanya-caritāmṛta; kahe*—describes; *kṛṣṇadāsa*—Śrīla Kṛṣṇadāsa Kavirāja Gosvāmī.

TRANSLATION

Praying at the lotus feet of Śrī Rūpa and Śrī Raghunātha, always desiring their mercy, I, Kṛṣṇadāsa, narrate Śrī Caitanya-caritāmṛta, following in their footsteps.

Thus end the Bhaktivedanta purports of the Śrī Caitanya-caritāmṛta, Madhya-līlā, *Eighteenth Chapter, describing the Lord's visit to Śrī Vṛndāvana and His conversion of the Mohammedan soldiers on the way to Prayāga.*

CHAPTER 19

Lord Śrī Caitanya Mahāprabhu Instructs Śrīla Rūpa Gosvāmī

A summary of this chapter is given by Śrīla Bhaktivinoda Ṭhākura in his *Amṛta-pravāha-bhāṣya.* Meeting Śrī Caitanya Mahāprabhu in a village called Rāmakeli, two brothers, Rūpa and Sanātana, began to devise means to get out of their government service. Both brothers appointed some *brāhmaṇas* to perform *puraścaraṇa* ceremonies and chant the holy name of Kṛṣṇa. Śrīla Rūpa Gosvāmī deposited ten thousand gold coins with a grocer, and the balance he brought in two boats to a place called Bāklā Candradvīpa. There he divided this money among the *brāhmaṇas,* Vaiṣṇavas and his relatives, and a portion he kept for emergency measures and personal needs. He was informed that Śrī Caitanya Mahāprabhu was going to Vṛndāvana from Jagannātha Purī through the forest of Madhya Pradesh; therefore he sent two people to Jagannātha Purī to find out when the Lord would leave for Vṛndāvana. In this way Rūpa Gosvāmī retired, but Sanātana Gosvāmī told the Nawab that he was sick and could not attend to his work. Giving this excuse, he sat home and studied *Śrīmad-Bhāgavatam* with learned *brāhmaṇa* scholars. The Nawab Hussain Shah first sent his personal physician to see what the real facts were; then he personally came to see why Sanātana was not attending to official business. Knowing that he wanted to resign his post, the Nawab had him arrested and imprisoned. The Nawab then went off to attack Orissa.

When Śrī Caitanya Mahāprabhu started for Vṛndāvana through the forest of Madhya Pradesh (Jhārikhaṇḍa), Rūpa Gosvāmī left home and sent news to Sanātana that he was leaving home with his younger brother (Anupama Mallika) to meet Śrī Caitanya Mahāprabhu. Śrīla Rūpa Gosvāmī finally reached Prayāga and met with Śrī Caitanya Mahāprabhu for ten successive days. During this time, Vallabha Bhaṭṭa extended an invitation to the Lord with great respect. Śrī Caitanya Mahāprabhu introduced Śrīla Rūpa Gosvāmī to Vallabha Bhaṭṭa. After this, a *brāhmaṇa* scholar named Raghupati Upādhyāya arrived and discussed Kṛṣṇa consciousness with the Lord. Kavirāja Gosvāmī then extensively describes the living condition of Śrī Rūpa and Sanātana at Vṛndāvana. During the ten days at Prayāga, Śrīla Rūpa Gosvāmī was instructed by the Lord, who gave him the basic principles of the *Bhakti-rasāmṛta-sindhu.* The Lord then sent Śrīla Rūpa Gosvāmī to Vṛndāvana. The Lord Himself returned to Vārāṇasī and stayed at the home of Candraśekhara.

TEXT 1

বৃন্দাবনীয়াং রসকেলিবার্তাং
কালেন লুপ্তাং নিজশক্তিমুৎকঃ ।
সঞ্চার্য রূপে ব্যতনোৎ পুনঃ স
প্রভুর্বিধৌ প্রাগিব লোকসৃষ্টিম্ ॥ ১ ॥

vṛndāvanīyāṁ rasa-keli-vārtāṁ
kālena luptāṁ nija-śaktim utkaḥ
sañcārya rūpe vyatanot punaḥ sa
prabhur vidhau prāg iva loka-sṛṣṭim

SYNONYMS

vṛndāvanīyām—related to Vṛndāvana; *rasa-keli-vārtām*—talks about the pastimes of Śrī Kṛṣṇa; *kālena*—with the course of time; *luptām*—lost; *nija-śaktim*—His personal potency; *utkaḥ*—being eager; *sañcārya*—infusing; *rūpe*—to Rūpa Gosvāmī; *vyatanot*—manifested; *punaḥ*—again; *saḥ*—He; *prabhuḥ*—Śrī Caitanya Mahāprabhu; *vidhau*—unto Lord Brahmā; *prāk iva*—as formerly; *loka-sṛṣṭim*—the creation of this cosmic manifestation.

TRANSLATION

Before the creation of this cosmic manifestation, the Lord enlightened the heart of Lord Brahmā with the details of the creation and manifested the Vedic knowledge. In exactly the same way, the Lord, being anxious to revive the Vṛndāvana pastimes of Lord Kṛṣṇa, impregnated the heart of Rūpa Gosvāmī with spiritual potency. By this potency, Śrīla Rūpa Gosvāmī could revive the activities of Kṛṣṇa in Vṛndāvana, activities almost lost to memory. In this way, He spread Kṛṣṇa consciousness throughout the world.

TEXT 2

জয় জয় শ্রীচৈতন্য জয় নিত্যানন্দ ।
জয়াদ্বৈতচন্দ্র জয় গৌরভক্তবৃন্দ ॥ ২ ॥

jaya jaya śrī-caitanya jaya nityānanda
jayādvaita-candra jaya gaura-bhakta-vṛnda

SYNONYMS

jaya jaya śrī-caitanya—all glories to Śrī Caitanya Mahāprabhu; *jaya nityānanda*—all glories to Lord Nityānanda; *jaya advaita-candra*—all glories to Advaita Prabhu; *jaya gaura-bhakta-vṛnda*—all glories to the devotees of the Lord.

TRANSLATION

All glories to Lord Śrī Caitanya Mahāprabhu! All glories to Lord Nityānanda! All glories to Advaitacandra! And all glories to all the devotees of the Lord!

TEXT 3

শ্রীরূপ-সনাতন রহে রামকেলি-গ্রামে ।
প্রভুরে মিলিয়া গেলা আপন-ভবনে ॥ ৩ ॥

śrī-rūpa-sanātana rahe rāmakeli-grāme
prabhure miliyā gelā āpana-bhavane

SYNONYMS

śrī-rūpa-sanātana—the brothers named Rūpa and Sanātana; *rahe*—stayed; *rāmakeli-grāme*—in Rāmakeli; *prabhure*—Śrī Caitanya Mahāprabhu; *miliyā*—meeting; *gelā*—went back; *āpana-bhavane*—to their own homes.

TRANSLATION

After meeting Śrī Caitanya Mahāprabhu in the village of Rāmakeli, the brothers Rūpa and Sanātana returned to their homes.

TEXT 4

দুইভাই বিষয়-ত্যাগের উপায় সৃজিল ।
বহুধন দিয়া দুই ব্রাহ্মণে বরিল ॥ ৪ ॥

dui-bhāi viṣaya-tyāgera upāya sṛjila
bhau-dhana diyā dui brāhmaṇe varila

SYNONYMS

dui-bhāi—the two brothers; *viṣaya-tyāgera*—of giving up material activities; *upāya sṛjila*—discovered a means; *bahu-dhana*—much money; *diyā*—paying; *dui brāhmaṇe*—two *brāhmaṇas; varila*—appointed.

TRANSLATION

The two brothers devised a means whereby they could give up their material activities. For this purpose, they appointed two brāhmaṇas and paid them a large amount of money.

TEXT 5

কৃষ্ণমন্ত্রে করাইল দুই পুরশ্চরণ ।
অচিরাৎ পাইবারে চৈতন্য-চরণ ॥ ৫ ॥

kṛṣṇa-mantre karāila dui puraścaraṇa
acirāt pāibāre caitanya-caraṇa

SYNONYMS

kṛṣṇa-mantre—in the holy *mantra* Hare Kṛṣṇa; *karāila*—caused to perform; *dui*—two; *puraścaraṇa*—religious ceremonies; *acirāt*—without delay; *pāibāre*—to get; *caitanya-caraṇa*—the shelter of the lotus feet of Śrī Caitanya Mahāprabhu.

TRANSLATION

The brāhmaṇas performed religious ceremonies and chanted the holy name of Kṛṣṇa so that the two brothers might attain shelter at the lotus feet of Śrī Caitanya Mahāprabhu very soon.

PURPORT

A *puraścaraṇa* is a ritualistic ceremony performed under the guidance of an expert spiritual master or a *brāhmaṇa.* It is performed for the fulfillment of certain desires. One rises early in the morning, chants the Hare Kṛṣṇa *mantra,* performs *arcana* by the *ārati* ceremony and worships the Deities. These activities are described in the Fifteenth Chapter, verse 108.

TEXT 6

শ্রীরূপ-গোসাঞি তবে নৌকাতে ভরিয়া।
আপনার ঘরে আইলা বহুধন লঞা ॥ ৬ ॥

śrī-rūpa-gosāñi tabe naukāte bhariyā
āpanāra ghare āilā bahu-dhana lañā

SYNONYMS

śrī-rūpa-gosāñi—Śrī Rūpa Gosvāmī; *tabe*—thereafter; *naukāte bhariyā*—filling boats; *āpanāra ghare*—to his own house; *āilā*—returned; *bahu-dhana lañā*—taking large amounts of riches.

TRANSLATION

At this time, Śrī Rūpa Gosvāmī returned home, taking with him large quantities of riches loaded in boats.

TEXT 7

ব্রাহ্মণ-বৈষ্ণবে দিলা তার অর্ধ-ধনে।
এক চৌঠি ধন দিলা কুটুম্ব-ভরণে ॥ ৭ ॥

brāhmaṇa-vaiṣṇave dilā tāra ardha-dhane
eka cauṭhi dhana dilā kuṭumba-bharaṇe

SYNONYMS

brāhmaṇa-vaiṣṇave—to the *brāhmaṇas* and Vaiṣṇavas; *dilā*—gave as charity; *tāra*—of the riches; *ardha-dhane*—fifty percent; *eka cauṭhi dhana*—one-fourth of the riches; *dilā*—gave; *kuṭumba-bharaṇe*—to satisfy the relatives.

TRANSLATION

Śrīla Rūpa Gosvāmī divided the wealth that he brought back home. He gave fifty percent in charity to brāhmaṇas and Vaiṣṇavas and twenty-five percent to his relatives.

PURPORT

This is a practical example of how one should divide his money and retire from household life. Fifty percent of one's money should be distributed to qualified and pure devotees of the Lord. Twenty-five percent may be given to family members, and twenty-five percent may be kept for personal use in case of emergency.

TEXT 8

দণ্ডবন্ধ লাগি' চৌঠি সঞ্চয় করিলা ।
ভাল-ভাল বিপ্র-স্থানে স্থাপ্য রাখিলা ॥ ৮ ॥

daṇḍa-bandha lāgi' cauṭhi sañcaya karilā
bhāla-bhāla vipra-sthāne sthāpya rākhilā

SYNONYMS

daṇḍa-bandha lāgi'—in case of legal implications; *cauṭhi*—one-fourth; *sañcaya karilā*—he collected; *bhāla-bhāla*—very respectable; *vipra-sthāne*—in the custody of a *brāhmaṇa; sthāpya rākhilā*—kept deposited.

TRANSLATION

He kept one-fourth of his wealth with a respectable brāhmaṇa. He kept this for his personal safety because he was expecting some legal complications.

TEXT 9

গৌড়ে রাখিল মুদ্রা দশ-হাজারে ।
সনাতন ব্যয় করে, রাখে মুদি-ঘরে ॥ ৯ ॥

gauḍe rākhila mudrā daśa-hājāre
sanātana vyaya kare, rākhe mudi-ghare

SYNONYMS

gauḍe—in Bengal; *rākhila*—kept; *mudrā*—coins; *daśa-hājāre*—ten thousand; *sanātana*—his elder brother; *vyaya kare*—spent; *rākhe*—deposited; *mudi-ghare*—in the place of a local grocer.

TRANSLATION

He deposited ten thousand coins, which were later spent by Śrī Sanātana Gosvāmī, in the custody of a local Bengali grocer.

TEXT 10

শ্রীরূপ শুনিল প্রভুর নীলাদ্রি-গমন ।
বনপথে যাবেন প্রভু শ্রীবৃন্দাবন ॥ ১০ ॥

śrī-rūpa śunila prabhura nīlādri-gamana
vana-pathe yābena prabhu śrī-vṛndāvana

SYNONYMS

śrī-rūpa—Śrīla Rūpa Gosvāmī; *śunila*—heard; *prabhura*—of Śrī Caitanya Mahāprabhu; *nīlādri-gamana*—departure for Jagannātha Purī; *vana-pathe*—on the path through the forest; *yābena*—will go; *prabhu*—Śrī Caitanya Mahāprabhu; *śrī-vṛndāvana*—to Vṛndāvana.

TRANSLATION

Śrī Rūpa Gosvāmī heard that Śrī Caitanya Mahāprabhu had returned to Jagannātha Purī and was preparing to go to Vṛndāvana through the forest.

TEXT 11

রূপ-গোসাঞি নীলাচলে পাঠাইল দুইজন ।
প্রভু যবে বৃন্দাবন করেন গমন ॥ ১১ ॥

rūpa-gosāñi nīlācale pāṭhāila dui-jana
prabhu yabe vṛndāvana karena gamana

SYNONYMS

rūpa-gosāñi—Rūpa Gosvāmī; *nīlācale*—to Jagannātha Purī; *pāṭhāila*—sent; *dui-jana*—two persons; *prabhu*—Śrī Caitanya Mahāprabhu; *yabe*—when; *vṛndāvana*—to Vṛndāvana; *karena*—makes; *gamana*—departure.

TRANSLATION

Śrī Rūpa Gosvāmī sent two people to Jagannātha Purī to find out when Śrī Caitanya Mahāprabhu would depart for Vṛndāvana.

TEXT 12

শীঘ্র আসি' মোরে তাঁর দিবা সমাচার।
শুনিয়া তদনুরূপ করিব ব্যবহার ॥ ১২ ॥

śīghra āsi' more tāṅra dibā samācāra
śuniyā tad-anurūpa kariba vyavahāra

SYNONYMS

śīghra āsi'—very hastily returning; *more*—unto me; *tāṅra*—His; *dibā*—give; *samācāra*—news; *śuniyā*—hearing; *tat-anurūpa*—accordingly; *kariba*—I shall make; *vyavahāra*—arrangements.

TRANSLATION

Śrī Rūpa Gosvāmī told the two men, "You are to return quickly and let me know when He will depart. Then I shall make the proper arrangements."

TEXT 13

এথা সনাতন-গোসাঞি ভাবে মনে মন।
রাজা মোরে প্রীতি করে, সে—মোর বন্ধন ॥ ১৩ ॥

ethā sanātana-gosāñi bhāve mane mana
rājā more prīti kare, se——mora bandhana

SYNONYMS

ethā—here (in Gauḍa-deśa); *sanātana-gosāñi*—the elder brother, Sanātana Gosvāmī; *bhāve*—considers; *mane mana*—in the mind; *rājā*—the Nawab; *more*—me; *prīti kare*—loves very much; *se*—that; *mora*—my; *bandhana*—great obligation.

TRANSLATION

While Sanātana Gosvāmī was at Gauḍa-deśa, he was thinking, "The Nawab is very pleased with me. I certainly have an obligation.

TEXT 14

কোন মতে রাজা যদি মোরে ক্রুদ্ধ হয়।
তবে অব্যাহতি হয়, করিলুঁ নিশ্চয় ॥ ১৪ ॥

kona mate rājā yadi more kruddha haya
tabe avyāhati haya, kariluṅ niścaya

SYNONYMS

kona mate—somehow or other; *rājā*—the Nawab; *yadi*—if; *more*—upon me; *kruddha haya*—becomes angry; *tabe*—then; *avyāhati*—escape; *haya*—there is; *kariluṅ niścaya*—I have decided.

TRANSLATION

"Somehow or other, if the Nawab becomes angry with me, I shall be greatly relieved. That is my conclusion."

TEXT 15

অস্বাস্থ্যের ছদ্ম করি' রহে নিজ-ঘরে ।
রাজকার্য ছাড়িলা, না যায় রাজদ্বারে ॥ ১৫ ॥

asvāsthyera chadma kari' rahe nija-ghare
rāja-kārya chāḍilā, nā yāya rāja-dvāre

SYNONYMS

asvāsthyera—of not being well; *chadma*—pretext; *kari'*—making; *rahe*—remains; *nija-ghare*—at home; *rāja-kārya*—government service; *chāḍilā*—relinquished; *nā yāya*—did not go; *rāja-dvāre*—to the court of the Nawab.

TRANSLATION

On the pretext of bad health, Sanātana Gosvāmī remained home. Thus he gave up government service and did not go to the royal court.

TEXT 16

লোভী কায়স্থগণ রাজকার্য করে ।
আপনে স্বগৃহে করে শাস্ত্রের বিচারে ॥ ১৬ ॥

lobhī kāyastha-gaṇa rāja-kārya kare
āpane svagṛhe kare śāstrera vicāre

SYNONYMS

lobhī—greedy; *kāyastha-gaṇa*—persons engaged in secretarial and clerical work; *rāja-kārya kare*—executed the government service; *āpane*—personally; *sva-gṛhe*—at home; *kare*—did; *śāstrera vicāre*—discussion of the revealed scriptures.

TRANSLATION

The greedy masters of his clerical and secretarial staff performed the government duties while Sanātana personally remained home and discussed revealed scriptures.

PURPORT

Sanātana Gosvāmī was the minister in charge of the government secretariat, and his assistants—the undersecretaries and clerks—all belonged to the *kāyastha* community. Formerly the *kāyasthas* belonged to the clerical and secretarial staff of the government, and later if one served in such a post, he was called a *kāyastha.* Eventually if a person could not identify himself as a *brāhmaṇa, kṣatriya, vaiśya* or *śūdra,* he used to intoduce himself as a *kāyastha* to get a wealthy and honorable position. In Bengal it is said that if one cannot give the identity of his caste, he calls himself a *kāyastha.* On the whole, the *kāyastha* community is a mixture of all castes, and it especially includes those engaged in clerical or secretarial work. Materially such people are always busy occupying responsible government posts.

When Sanātana Gosvāmī was relaxing and feeling inclined to retire from government service, many *kāyasthas* on his secretarial staff were very eager to occupy his post. In this regard, Śrīla Bhaktivinoda Ṭhākura states that when Sanātana Gosvāmī was a government minister and the *kāyasthas* who assisted him saw that he was reluctant to continue, they became very expert in their duties. Sanātana Gosvāmī was a *brāhmaṇa* belonging to the Sārasvata *brāhmaṇa* community. It is said that when he resigned, an underworker named Purandara Khān, who was a *kāyastha,* occupied his post.

TEXT 17

ভট্টাচার্য পণ্ডিত বিশ ত্রিশ লঞা ।
ভাগবত বিচার করেন সভাতে বসিয়া ॥ ১৭ ॥

bhaṭṭācārya paṇḍita biśa triśa lañā
bhāgavata vicāra karena sabhāte vasiyā

SYNONYMS

bhaṭṭācārya paṇḍita—learned scholars known as *bhaṭṭācāryas; biśa triśa*—twenty or thirty; *lañā*—taking with him; *bhāgavata vicāra*—discussion of *Śrīmad-Bhāgavatam; karena*—does; *sabhāte vasiyā*—sitting in an assembly.

TRANSLATION

Śrī Sanātana Gosvāmī used to discuss Śrīmad-Bhāgavatam in an assembly of twenty or thirty learned brāhmaṇa scholars.

PURPORT

Śrīla Bhaktisiddhānta Sarasvatī Ṭhākura gives the following commentary on the words *bhāgavata vicāra.* As confirmed in the *Muṇḍaka Upaniṣad* (1.1.4,5), there are two kinds of educational systems:

dve vidye veditavya iti, ha sma yad brahma-vido vadanti—parā caivāparā ca. tatrāparā ṛg-vedo yajur-vedaḥ sāma-vedo 'tharva-vedaḥ śikṣā kalpo vyākaraṇaṁ niruktaṁ chando jyotiṣam iti. atha parā yayā tad-akṣaram adhigamyate.

"There are two kinds of educational systems. One deals with transcendental knowledge [*parā vidyā*] and the other with material knowledge [*aparā vidyā*]. All the *Vedas—Ṛg Veda, Yajur Veda, Sāma Veda, Atharva Veda* and their corollaries known as *śikṣā, kalpa, vyākaraṇa, nirukta, chanda* and *jyotiṣa*—belong to the inferior system of material knowledge [*aparā vidyā*]. By *parā vidyā,* one can understand the *akṣara,* Brahman or the Absolute Truth." As far as Vedic literature is concerned, *Vedānta-sūtra* is accepted as the *parā vidyā. Śrīmad-Bhāgavatam* is an explanation of that *parā vidyā.* Those who aspire for liberation (*mukti* or *mokṣa*) and introduce themselves as *vaidāntika* are also equal to those groups aspiring to improve religion (*dharma*), economic development (*artha*) and sense gratification (*kāma*). *Dharma, artha, kāma* and *mokṣa* are called *catur-varga.* They are all within the system of inferior material knowledge. Any literature giving information about the spiritual world, spiritual life, spiritual identity and the spirit soul is called *parā vidyā. Śrīmad-Bhāgavatam* does not have anything to do with the materialistic way of life; it gives transcendental information to educate people in the superior system of *parā vidyā.* Sanātana Gosvāmī was engaged in discussing the *bhāgavata-vidyā,* which means he discussed transcendental superior knowledge. Those who are *karmīs, jñānīs* or *yogīs* are not actually fit to discuss *Śrīmad-Bhāgavatam.* Only Vaiṣṇavas or pure devotees are fit to discuss that literature. As stated in *Śrīmad-Bhāgavatam* itself (12.13.18):

śrīmad-bhāgavataṁ purāṇam amalaṁ yad vaiṣṇavānāṁ priyaṁ
yasmin pāramahaṁsyam ekam amalaṁ jñānaṁ paraṁ gīyate
yatra jñāna-virāga-bhakti-sahitaṁ naiṣkarmyam āviṣkṛtaṁ
tac chṛṇvan supaṭhan vicāraṇa-paro bhaktyā vimucyen naraḥ

Although *Śrīmad-Bhāgavatam* is counted among the *Purāṇas,* it is called the spotless *Purāṇa.* Because it does not discuss anything material, it is liked by transcendental Vaiṣṇava devotees. The subject matter found in *Śrīmad-Bhāgavatam* is meant for *paramahaṁsas.* As it is said: *paramo-nirmatsarāṇām.* A *paramahaṁsa* is one who does not live in the material world and who does not envy others. In *Śrīmad-Bhāgavatam,* devotional service is discussed to arouse the living entity to the transcendental position of *jñāna* (knowledge) and *vairāgya* (renunciation). As stated in *Śrīmad-Bhāgavatam* (1.2.12):

tac chraddadhānāḥ munayo
jñāna-vairāgya-yuktayā
paśyanty ātmani cātmānaṁ
bhaktyā śruta-gṛhītayā

"That Absolute Truth is realized by the seriously inquisitive student or sage who is well equipped with knowledge and who has become detached by rendering devotional service and hearing the *Vedānta-śruti.*"

This is not sentiment. Knowledge and renunciation can be obtained through devotional service (*bhaktyā śruta-gṛhītayā*), that is, by arousing one's dormant devotional consciousness, Kṛṣṇa consciousness. When Kṛṣṇa consciousness is aroused, it relieves one from fruitive activity, activity for economic improvement and material enjoyment. This relief is technically called *naiṣkarma,* and when one is relieved, he is no longer interested in working hard for sense gratification. *Śrīmad-Bhāgavatam* is Śrīla Vyāsadeva's last mature contribution, and one should read and hear it in an assembly of realized souls while engaging in devotional service. At such a time one can be liberated from all material bondage. This was the course taken by Sanātana Gosvāmī, who retired from government service to study *Śrīmad-Bhāgavatam* with learned scholars.

TEXT 18

আর দিন গৌড়েশ্বর, সঙ্গে একজন ।
আচম্বিতে গোসাঞি-সভাতে কৈল আগমন ॥ ১৮ ॥

āra dina gauḍeśvara, saṅge eka-jana
ācambite gosāñi-sabhāte kaila āgamana

SYNONYMS

āra dina—one day; *gauḍeśvara*—the Nawab of Bengal; *saṅge*—with; *eka-jana*—one other person; *ācambite*—suddenly; *gosāñi-sabhāte*—in the assembly of Sanātana Gosvāmī; *kaila āgamana*—came.

TRANSLATION

While Sanātana Gosvāmī was studying Śrīmad-Bhāgavatam in the assembly of learned brāhmaṇas, one day the Nawab of Bengal and another person suddenly appeared.

PURPORT

The full name of the Nawab of Bengal (Hussain Shah) was Ālāuddīna Saiyada Husena Sāha Seripha Makkā, and he ruled Bengal for twenty-three years, from 1420 to 1443 Śakābda Era. Sanātana Gosvāmī was studying *Śrīmad-Bhāgavatam* with the scholars in the year 1424.

TEXT 19

পাৎসাহ দেখিয়া সবে সম্ভ্রমে উঠিলা ।
সম্ভ্রমে আসন দিয়া রাজারে বসাইলা ॥ ১৯ ॥

pātsāha dekhiyā sabe sambhrame uṭhilā
sambhrame āsana diyā rājāre vasāilā

SYNONYMS

pātsāha dekhiyā—seeing the Nawab; *sabe*—all of them; *sambhrame*—in great respect; *uṭhilā*—stood up; *sambhrame*—with great respect; *āsana diyā*—giving a sitting place; *rājāre*—the King; *vasāilā*—made to sit.

TRANSLATION

As soon as all the brāhmaṇas and Sanātana Gosvāmī saw the Nawab appear, they all stood up and respectfully gave him a sitting place to honor him.

PURPORT

Although Nawab Hussain Shah was a *mleccha-yavana,* he was nonetheless the governor of the country, and the learned scholars and Sanātana Gosvāmī offered him all the respect due a king or a governor. When a person occupies an exalted executive post, one should consider that he has acquired the grace of the Lord. In *Bhagavad-gītā* it is said:

yad yad vibhūtimat sattvaṁ
śrīmad ūrjitam eva vā
tat tad evāvagaccha tvaṁ
mama tejo 'ṁśa-saṁbhavam

"Know that all beautiful, glorious and mighty creations spring from but a spark of My splendor." (Bg. 10.41)

Whenever we see something exalted, we must consider it part of the power of the Supreme Personality of Godhead. A powerful man (*vibhūtimat sattvam*) is one who has obtained the grace of the Lord or has derived some power from Him. In *Bhagavad-gītā* (7.10) Kṛṣṇa says, *tejas tejasvinām aham:* "I am the power of the powerful." The learned *brāhmaṇa* scholars showed respect to Nawab Hussain Shah because he represented a fraction of Kṛṣṇa's power.

TEXT 20

রাজা কহে,—তোমার স্থানে বৈদ্য পাঠাইলুঁ ।
বৈদ্য কহে,—ব্যাধি নাহি, সুস্থ যে দেখিলুঁ ॥ ২০ ॥

rājā kahe,——tomāra sthāne vaidya pāṭhāiluṅ
vaidya kahe,——vyādhi nāhi, sustha ye dekhiluṅ

SYNONYMS

rājā kahe—the Nawab said; *tomāra sthāne*—to your place; *vaidya*—a physician; *pāṭhāiluṅ*—I sent; *vaidya kahe*—the physician said; *vyādhi nāhi*—there is no disease; *su-stha*—completely healthy; *ye*—that; *dekhiluṅ*—I have seen.

TRANSLATION

The Nawab said, "I sent my physician to you, and he has reported that you are not diseased. As far as he could see, you are completely healthy.

TEXT 21

আমার যে কিছু কার্য, সব তোমা লঞা ।
কার্য ছাড়ি' রহিলা তুমি ঘরেতে বসিয়া ॥ ২১ ॥

āmāra ye kichu kārya, saba tomā lañā
kārya chāḍi' rahilā tumi gharete vasiyā

SYNONYMS

āmāra—my; *ye kichu*—whatever; *kārya*—business; *saba*—everything; *tomā*—you; *lañā*—with; *kārya chāḍi'*—giving up your duties; *rahilā*—remained; *tumi*—you; *gharete*—at home; *vasiyā*—sitting.

TRANSLATION

"I am depending on you to carry out so many of my activities, but you have given up your governmental duties to sit here at home.

TEXT 22

মোর যত কার্য-কাম, সব কৈলা নাশ ।
কি তোমার হৃদয়ে আছে, কহ মোর পাশ ॥ ২২ ॥

mora yata kārya-kāma, saba kailā nāśa
ki tomāra hṛdaye āche, kaha mora pāśa

SYNONYMS

mora—my; *yata*—all; *kārya-kāma*—occupational duties; *saba*—everything; *kailā nāśa*—you have spoiled; *ki*—what; *tomāra*—your; *hṛdaye*—within the heart; *āche*—there is; *kaha*—kindly tell; *mora pāśa*—to me.

TRANSLATION

"You have spoiled all my activities. What is your intention? Please tell me frankly."

TEXT 23

সনাতন কহে,—নহে আমা হৈতে কাম।
আর একজন দিয়া কর সমাধান ॥ ২৩ ॥

sanātana kahe,——nahe āmā haite kāma
āra eka-jana diyā kara samādhāna

SYNONYMS

sanātana kahe—Sanātana Gosvāmī replied; *nahe*—not; *āmā*—me; *haite*—from; *kāma*—execution of the duty; *āra eka-jana*—someone else; *diyā*—by means of; *kara samādhāna*—execute the management.

TRANSLATION

Sanātana Gosvāmī replied, "You can no longer expect any service from me. Please arrange for someone else to tend to the management."

TEXT 24

তবে ক্রুদ্ধ হঞা রাজা কহে আরবার।
তোমার 'বড় ভাই' করে দস্যুব্যবহার ॥ ২৪ ॥

tabe kruddha hañā rājā kahe āra-bāra
tomāra 'baḍa bhāi' kare dasyu-vyavahāra

SYNONYMS

tabe—at that time; *kruddha hañā*—becoming angry; *rājā kahe*—the Nawab said; *āra-bāra*—again; *tomāra baḍa bhāi*—your elder brother; *kare*—does; *dasyu-vyavahāra*—the activity of a plunderer.

TRANSLATION

Becoming angry with Sanātana Gosvāmī, the Nawab said, "Your elder brother is acting just like a plunderer.

TEXT 25

জীব-বহু মারি' কৈল চাক্‌লা সব নাশ।
এথা তুমি কৈলা মোর সর্ব কার্য নাশ ॥ ২৫ ॥

jīva-bahu māri' kaila cāklā saba nāśa
ethā tumi kailā mora sarva kārya nāśa

SYNONYMS

jīva—living entities; *bahu*—many; *māri'*—killing; *kaila*—did; *cāklā*—the province of Bengal; *saba*—all; *nāśa*—destruction; *ethā*—here; *tumi*—you; *kailā*—did; *mora*—my; *sarva*—all; *kārya*—plans; *nāśa*—destruction.

TRANSLATION

"By killing many living entities, your elder brother has destroyed all Bengal. Now here you are destroying all my plans."

TEXT 26

সনাতন কহে,—তুমি স্বতন্ত্র গৌড়েশ্বর ।
যে যেই দোষ করে, দেহ' তার ফল ॥ ২৬ ॥

sanātana kahe,——tumi svatantra gauḍeśvara
ye yei doṣa kare, deha' tāra phala

SYNONYMS

sanātana kahe—Sanātana Gosvāmī said; *tumi*—you; *svatantra*—independent; *gauḍa-īśvara*—the ruler of Bengal; *ye yei*—whatever; *doṣa*—faults; *kare*—one commits; *deha'*—you award; *tāra phala*—the results of that.

TRANSLATION

Sanātana Gosvāmī said, "You are the supreme ruler of Bengal and are completely independent. Whenever someone commits a fault, you punish him accordingly."

TEXT 27

এত শুনি' গৌড়েশ্বর উঠি' ঘরে গেলা ।
পলাইব বলি' সনাতনেরে বান্ধিলা ॥ ২৭ ॥

eta śuni' gauḍeśvara uṭhi' ghare gelā
palāiba bali' sanātanere bāndhilā

SYNONYMS

eta śuni'—hearing this; *gauḍa-īśvara*—the Nawab of Bengal; *uṭhi'*—standing up; *ghare gelā*—went back home; *palāiba*—I shall run away; *bali'*—because of this; *sanātanere bāndhilā*—he arrested Sanātana.

TRANSLATION

Hearing this, the Nawab of Bengal stood up and returned to his home. He ordered the arrest of Sanātana Gosvāmī so that he would not be able to leave.

PURPORT

It is said that the relationship between the Nawab of Bengal and Sanātana Gosvāmī was very intimate. The Nawab used to consider Sanātana Gosvāmī his younger brother, and when Sanātana Gosvāmī showed a very strong intention to resign, the Nawab, feeling familial affection, essentially said, "I am your elder brother, but I do not look after the state management. My only business is attacking other states with my soldiers and fighting everywhere as a plunderer. Because I am a meateater [*yavana*], I am used to hunting all kinds of living beings. In this way I am destroying all kinds of living entities in Bengal. While engaged in this destructive business, I am hoping that you will tend to the administration of the state. Since I, your elder brother, am engaged in such a destructive business, you, being my younger brother, should look after the state management. If you do not, how will things continue?" This talk was based on a family relationship, and Sanātana Gosvāmī also replied in an intimate and joking way. Essentially he told the Nawab, "My dear brother, you are the independent ruler of Bengal. You can act in whatever way you like, and if someone commits fault, you can punish him accordingly." In other words, Sanātana Gosvāmī was saying that since the Nawab was accustomed to acting like a plunderer, he should go ahead and take action. Since Sanātana was not showing much enthusiasm in performing his duty, the Nawab should dismiss him from his service. The Nawab could understand the intention of Sanātana Gosvāmī's statement. He therefore left in an angry mood and ordered Sanātana Gosvāmī's arrest.

TEXT 28

হেনকালে গেল রাজা উড়িয়া মারিতে ।
সনাতনে কহে,—তুমি চল মোর সাথে ॥ ২৮ ॥

hena-kāle gela rājā uḍiyā mārite
sanātane kahe,——tumi cala mora sāthe

SYNONYMS

hena-kāle—at this time; *gela*—went; *rājā*—the King; *uḍiyā mārite*—to attack the Orissa province; *sanātane kahe*—he said to Sanātana Gosvāmī; *tumi cala*—you come; *mora sāthe*—along with me.

TRANSLATION

At this time, the Nawab was going to attack the province of Orissa, and he told Sanātana Gosvāmī, "Come along with me."

PURPORT

Hussain Shah attacked the province of Orissa in 1424 Śakābda Era. At that time he conquered the feudal princes of neighboring Orissa.

TEXT 29

তেঁহো কহে,—যাবে তুমি দেবতায় দুঃখ দিতে ।
মোর শক্তি নাহি, তোমার সঙ্গে যাইতে ॥ ২৯ ॥

teṅho kahe,——yābe tumi devatāya duḥkha dite
mora śakti nāhi, tomāra saṅge yāite

SYNONYMS

teṅho kahe—Sanātana Gosvāmī replied; *yābe*—will go; *tumi*—you; *devatāya*—to the Supreme Personality of Godhead; *duḥkha dite*—to give unhappiness; *mora śakti*—my power; *nāhi*—there is not; *tomāra saṅge*—in company with you; *yāite*—to go.

TRANSLATION

Sanātana Gosvāmī replied, "You are going to Orissa to give pain to the Supreme Personality of Godhead. For this reason I am powerless to go with you."

TEXT 30

তবে তাঁরে বান্ধি' রাখি' করিলা গমন ।
এথা নীলাচল হৈতে প্রভু চলিলা বৃন্দাবন ॥ ৩০ ॥

tabe tāṅre bāndhi' rākhi' karilā gamana
ethā nīlācala haite prabhu calilā vṛndāvana

SYNONYMS

tabe—thereafter; *tāṅre*—him; *bāndhi'*—arresting; *rākhi'*—keeping; *karilā gamana*—he went away; *ethā*—at this time; *nīlācala haite*—from Jagannātha Purī; *prabhu*—Śrī Caitanya Mahāprabhu; *calilā vṛndāvana*—departed for Vṛndāvana.

TRANSLATION

The Nawab again arrested Sanātana Gosvāmī and kept him in prison. At this time, Śrī Caitanya Mahāprabhu departed for Vṛndāvana from Jagannātha Purī.

TEXT 31

তবে সেই দুই চর রূপ-ঠাঞি আইল ।
'বৃন্দাবন চলিলা প্রভু'—আসিয়া কহিল ॥ ৩১ ॥

tabe sei dui cara rūpa-ṭhāñi āila
'vṛndāvana calilā prabhu'——āsiyā kahila

SYNONYMS

tabe—at that time; *sei*—those; *dui*—two; *cara*—messengers; *rūpa-ṭhāñi*—to the presence of Rūpa Gosvāmī; *āila*—came back; *vṛndāvana calilā prabhu*—Śrī Caitanya Mahāprabhu has departed for Vṛndāvana; *āsiyā*—coming; *kahila*—they informed.

TRANSLATION

The two persons who went to Jagannātha Purī to inquire about the Lord's departure returned and informed Rūpa Gosvāmī that the Lord had already departed for Vṛndāvana.

TEXT 32

শুনিয়া শ্রীরূপ লিখিল সনাতন-ঠাঞি ।
'বৃন্দাবন চলিলা শ্রীচৈতন্য-গোসাঞি ॥ ৩২ ॥

śuniyā śrī-rūpa likhila sanātana-ṭhāñi
'vṛndāvana calilā śrī-caitanya-gosāñi

SYNONYMS

śuniyā—hearing; *śrī-rūpa*—Śrī Rūpa Gosvāmī; *likhila*—wrote; *sanātana-ṭhāñi*—to Sanātana Gosvāmī; *vṛndāvana*—to Vṛndāvana; *calilā*—has gone; *śrī-caitanya-gosāñi*—Śrī Caitanya Mahāprabhu.

TRANSLATION

Upon receiving this message from his two messengers, Rūpa Gosvāmī immediately wrote a letter to Sanātana Gosvāmī saying that Śrī Caitanya Mahāprabhu had departed for Vṛndāvana.

TEXT 33

আমি-দুইভাই চলিলাঙ তাঁহারে মিলিতে।
তুমি যৈছে তৈছে ছুটি' আইস তাহাঁ হৈতে ॥ ৩৩ ॥

āmi-dui-bhāi calilāṅa tāṅhāre milite
tumi yaiche taiche chuṭi' āisa tāhāṅ haite

SYNONYMS

āmi-dui-bhāi—we two brothers; *calilāṅa*—have gone; *tāṅhāre milite*—to meet Him; *tumi*—you; *yaiche taiche*—somehow or other; *chuṭi'*—getting free; *āisa*—come; *tāhāṅ haite*—from there.

TRANSLATION

In his letter to Sanātana Gosvāmī, Śrīla Rūpa Gosvāmī wrote, "We two brothers are starting out to go see Śrī Caitanya Mahāprabhu. You must also somehow or other get released and come meet us."

PURPORT

The two brothers herein mentioned are Rūpa Gosvāmī and his younger brother, Anupama Mallika. Rūpa Gosvāmī was informing Sanātana Gosvāmī that he should join him and his younger brother.

TEXT 34

দশসহস্র মুদ্রা তথা আছে মুদি-স্থানে।
তাহা দিয়া কর শীঘ্র আত্ম-বিমোচনে ॥ ৩৪ ॥

daśa-sahasra mudrā tathā āche mudi-sthāne
tāhā diyā kara śīghra ātma-vimocane

SYNONYMS

daśa-sahasra mudrā—ten thousand coins; *tāthā*—there; *āche*—there are; *mudi-sthāne*—in the grocer's place; *tāhā diyā*—with this amount; *kara*—get; *śīghra*—as soon as possible; *ātma-vimocane*—release from the internment.

TRANSLATION

Rūpa Gosvāmī further informed Śrīla Sanātana Gosvāmī: "I have left a deposit of ten thousand coins with the grocer. Use that money to get out of prison.

TEXT 35

যেছে তৈছে ছুটি' তুমি আইস বৃন্দাবন ।'
এত লিখি' দুইভাই করিলা গমন ॥ ৩৫ ॥

yaiche taiche chuṭi' tumi āisa vṛndāvana'
eta likhi' dui-bhāi karilā gamana

SYNONYMS

yaiche taiche—somehow or other; *chuṭi'*—getting released; *tumi*—you; *āisa*—come; *vṛndāvana*—to Vṛndāvana; *eta likhi'*—writing this; *dui-bhāi*—the two brothers, namely Rūpa Gosvāmī and his younger brother Anupama; *karilā gamana*—departed.

TRANSLATION

"Somehow or other get yourself released and come to Vṛndāvana." After writing this, the two brothers [Rūpa Gosvāmī and Anupama] went to see Śrī Caitanya Mahāprabhu.

TEXT 36

অনুপম মল্লিক, তাঁর নাম—'শ্রীবল্লভ' ।
রূপ-গোসাঞির ছোটভাই—পরম-বৈষ্ণব ॥ ৩৬ ॥

anupama mallika, tāṅra nāma——'śrī-vallabha'
rūpa-gosāñira choṭa-bhāi——parama-vaiṣṇava

SYNONYMS

anupama mallika—Anupama Mallika; *tāṅra nāma*—his name; *śrī-vallabha*—Śrī Vallabha; *rūpa-gosāñira*—of Rūpa Gosvāmī; *choṭa-bhāi*—younger brother; *parama-vaiṣṇava*—great devotee.

TRANSLATION

Rūpa Gosvāmī's younger brother was a great devotee whose actual name was Śrī Vallabha, but he was given the name Anupama Mallika.

TEXT 37

তাঁহা লঞা রূপ-গোসাঞি প্রয়াগে আইলা ।
মহাপ্রভু তাহাঁ শুনি' আনন্দিত হৈলা ॥ ৩৭ ॥

tāṅhā lañā rūpa-gosāñi prayāge āilā
mahāprabhu tāhāṅ śuni' ānandita hailā

SYNONYMS

tāṅhā lañā—taking him along; *rūpa-gosāñi*—Śrī Rūpa Gosvāmī; *prayāge*—to Prayāga; *āilā*—came; *mahāprabhu*—Śrī Caitanya Mahāprabhu; *tāhāṅ*—there; *śuni'*—hearing; *ānandita hailā*—were very much pleased.

TRANSLATION

Śrī Rūpa Gosvāmī and Anupama Mallika went to Prayāga, and they were very pleased to hear news that Śrī Caitanya Mahāprabhu was there.

TEXT 38

প্রভু চলিয়াছেন বিন্দুমাধব-দরশনে ।
লক্ষ লক্ষ লোক আইসে প্রভুর মিলনে ॥ ৩৮ ॥

prabhu caliyāchena bindu-mādhava-daraśane
lakṣa lakṣa loka āise prabhura milane

SYNONYMS

prabhu—Śrī Caitanya Mahāprabhu; *caliyāchena*—was going; *bindu-mādhava-daraśane*—to see Lord Bindu Mādhava; *lakṣa lakṣa loka*—many hundreds of thousands of people; *āise*—came; *prabhura*—with Śrī Caitanya Mahāprabhu; *milane*—for meeting.

TRANSLATION

At Prayāga, Śrī Caitanya Mahāprabhu went to see the temple of Bindu Mādhava, and many hundreds of thousands of people followed Him just to meet Him.

TEXT 39

কেহ কান্দে, কেহ হাসে, কেহ নাচে, গায় ।
'কৃষ্ণ' 'কৃষ্ণ' বলি' কেহ গড়াগড়ি যায় ॥ ৩৯ ॥

keha kānde, keha hāse, keha nāce, gāya
'kṛṣṇa' 'kṛṣṇa' bali' keha gaḍāgaḍi yāya

SYNONYMS

keha kānde—some cried; *keha hāse*—some laughed; *keha nāce*—some danced; *gāya*—chanted; *kṛṣṇa kṛṣṇa bali'*—saying Kṛṣṇa, Kṛṣṇa; *keha*—some; *gaḍāgaḍi yāya*—rolled on the ground.

TRANSLATION

Some of the people following the Lord were crying. Some were laughing, some dancing and some chanting. Indeed, some of them were rolling on the ground, exclaiming, "Kṛṣṇa! Kṛṣṇa!"

TEXT 40

গঙ্গা-যমুনা প্রয়াগ নারিল ডুবাইতে ।
প্রভু ডুবাইল কৃষ্ণপ্রেমের বন্যাতে ॥ ৪০ ॥

gaṅgā-yamunā prayāga nārila ḍubāite
prabhu ḍubāila kṛṣṇa-premera vanyāte

SYNONYMS

gaṅgā-yamunā—the River Ganges and River Yamunā; *prayāga*—Prayāga; *nārila*—were not able; *ḍubāite*—to flood; *prabhu*—Śrī Caitanya Mahāprabhu; *ḍubāila*—flooded; *kṛṣṇa-premera*—of ecstatic love of Kṛṣṇa; *vanyāte*—in an inundation.

TRANSLATION

Prayāga is located at the confluence of two rivers—the Ganges and the Yamunā. Although these rivers were not able to flood Prayāga with water, Śrī Caitanya Mahāprabhu inundated the whole area with waves of ecstatic love for Kṛṣṇa.

TEXT 41

ভিড় দেখি' দুই ভাই রহিলা নির্জনে ।
প্রভুর আবেশ হৈল মাধব-দরশনে ॥ ৪১ ॥

bhiḍa dekhi' dui bhāi rahilā nirjane
prabhura āveśa haila mādhava-daraśane

SYNONYMS

bhiḍa dekhi'—seeing the crowd; *dui bhāi*—the two brothers; *rahilā*—remained; *nirjane*—in a secluded place; *prabhura*—of Śrī Caitanya Mahāprabhu; *āveśa*—ecstasy; *haila*—there was; *mādhava-daraśane*—by seeing the Deity, Bindu Mādhava.

TRANSLATION

Seeing the great crowd, the two brothers remained standing in a secluded place. They could see that Śrī Caitanya Mahāprabhu was ecstatic to see Lord Bindu Mādhava.

TEXT 42

প্রেমাবেশে নাচে প্রভু হরিধ্বনি করি' ।
ঊর্ধ্ববাহু করি' বলে– বল 'হরি' 'হরি' ॥ ৪২ ॥

premāveśe nāce prabhu hari-dhvani kari'
ūrdhva bāhu kari' bale——bala 'hari' 'hari'

SYNONYMS

prema-āveśe—in ecstatic love; *nāce*—danced; *prabhu*—Śrī Caitanya Mahāprabhu; *hari-dhvani kari'*—vibrating the holy name of Hari; *ūrdhva*—raised; *bāhu*—the arms; *kari'*—making; *bale*—says; *bala hari hari*—chant Hari, Hari.

TRANSLATION

The Lord was loudly chanting the holy name of Hari. Dancing in ecstatic love and raising His arms, He asked everyone to chant "Hari! Hari!"

TEXT 43

প্রভুর মহিমা দেখি' লোকে চমৎকার ।
প্রয়াগে প্রভুর লীলা নারি বর্ণিবার ॥ ৪৩ ॥

prabhura mahimā dekhi' loke camatkāra
prayāge prabhura līlā nāri varṇibāra

SYNONYMS

prabhura—of Śrī Caitanya Mahāprabhu; *mahimā*—the greatness; *dekhi'*—seeing; *loke*—in all people; *camatkāra*—astonishment; *prayāge*—at Prayāga; *prabhura*—of Śrī Caitanya Mahāprabhu; *līlā*—the pastimes; *nāri*—I am not able; *varṇibāra*—to describe.

TRANSLATION

Everyone was astounded to see the greatness of Śrī Caitanya Mahāprabhu. Indeed, I cannot properly describe the pastimes of the Lord at Prayāga.

TEXT 44

দাক্ষিণাত্য-বিপ্র-সনে আছে পরিচয় ।
সেই বিপ্র নিমন্ত্রিয়া নিল নিজালয় ॥ ৪৪ ॥

dākṣiṇātya-vipra-sane āche paricaya
sei vipra nimantriyā nila nijālaya

SYNONYMS

dākṣiṇātya—Deccan; *vipra-sane*—with a *brāhmaṇa; āche*—there was; *paricaya*—acquaintance; *sei*—that; *vipra*—*brāhmaṇa; nimantriyā*—inviting; *nila*—brought; *nija-ālaya*—to his own place.

TRANSLATION

Śrī Caitanya Mahāprabhu had made an acquaintance with a brāhmaṇa from Deccan [in South India], and that brāhmaṇa invited Him for meals and took Him to his place.

TEXT 45

বিপ্র-গৃহে আসি' প্রভু নিভৃতে বসিলা ।
শ্রীরূপ-বল্লভ দুঁহে আসিয়া মিলিলা ॥ ৪৫ ॥

vipra-gṛhe āsi' prabhu nibhṛte vasilā
śrī-rūpa-vallabha duṅhe āsiyā mililā

SYNONYMS

vipra-gṛhe—to the house of that *brāhmaṇa; āsi'*—coming; *prabhu*—Śrī Caitanya Mahāprabhu; *nibhṛte*—in a solitary place; *vasilā*—sat down; *śrī-rūpa-vallabha*—the two brothers Rūpa Gosvāmī and Śrī Vallabha; *duṅhe*—both of them; *āsiyā*—coming; *mililā*—met Him.

TRANSLATION

While Śrī Caitanya Mahāprabhu was sitting in a solitary place in the home of that Deccan brāhmaṇa, Rūpa Gosvāmī and Śrī Vallabha [Anupama Mallika] came to meet Him.

TEXT 46

দুইগুচ্ছ তৃণ দুঁহে দশনে ধরিয়া ।
প্রভু দেখি' দূরে পড়ে দণ্ডবৎ হঞা ॥ ৪৬ ॥

dui-guccha tṛṇa duṅhe daśane dhariyā
prabhu dekhi' dūre paḍe daṇḍavat hañā

SYNONYMS

dui-guccha—two bunches; *tṛṇa*—straw; *duṅhe*—both of them; *daśane dhariyā*—holding in the teeth; *prabhu dekhi'*—seeing the Lord; *dūre*—in a distant place; *paḍe*—fell down; *daṇḍa-vat*—like rods; *hañā*—becoming.

TRANSLATION

Seeing the Lord from a distance, the two brothers put two clumps of straw between their teeth and immediately fell down on the ground like rods, offering Him obeisances.

TEXT 47

নানা শ্লোক পড়ি' উঠে, পড়ে বার বার ।
প্রভু দেখি' প্রেমাবেশ হইল দুঁহার ॥ ৪৭ ॥

nānā śloka paḍi' uṭhe, paḍe bāra bāra
prabhu dekhi' premāveśa ha-ila duṅhara

SYNONYMS

nānā—various; *śloka*—verses; *paḍi'*—reciting; *uṭhe*—stood up; *paḍe*—fell down; *bāra bāra*—again and again; *prabhu dekhi'*—seeing the Lord; *prema-āveśa*—ecstatic emotion; *ha-ila*—there was; *duṅhāra*—of both of them.

TRANSLATION

Both brothers were overwhelmed with ecstatic emotion, and reciting various Sanskrit verses, they stood up and fell down again and again.

TEXT 48

শ্রীরূপে দেখিয়া প্রভুর প্রসন্ন হৈল মন ।
'উঠ, উঠ, রূপ, আইস', বলিলা বচন ॥ ৪৮ ॥

śrī-rūpe dekhiyā prabhura prasanna haila mana
'uṭha, uṭha, rūpa, āisa', balilā vacana

SYNONYMS

śrī-rūpe dekhiyā—seeing Śrīla Rūpa Gosvāmī; *prabhura*—of Śrī Caitanya Mahāprabhu; *prasanna*—very pleased; *haila*—was; *mana*—mind; *uṭha*—please stand up; *uṭha*—please stand up; *rūpa*—My dear Rūpa; *āisa*—come; *balilā*—He said; *vacana*—the words.

TRANSLATION

Śrī Caitanya Mahāprabhu was very pleased to see Śrīla Rūpa Gosvāmī, and He told him, "Stand up! Stand up! My dear Rūpa, come here."

TEXT 49

কৃষ্ণের করুণা কিছু না যায় বর্ণনে ।
বিষয়কূপ হৈতে কাড়িল তোমা দুইজনে ॥ ৪৯ ॥

kṛṣṇera karuṇā kichu nā yāya varṇane
viṣaya-kūpa haite kāḍila tomā dui-jane

SYNONYMS

kṛṣṇera—of Lord Kṛṣṇa; *karuṇā*—the mercy; *kichu*—any; *nā*—not; *yāya*—is possible; *varṇane*—to describe; *viṣaya-kūpa haite*—from the well of material enjoyment; *kāḍila*—delivered; *tomā*—you; *dui-jane*—both.

TRANSLATION

Śrī Caitanya Mahāprabhu then said, "It is not possible to describe Kṛṣṇa's mercy, for He has delivered you both from the well of material enjoyment.

TEXT 50

ন মেঽভক্তশ্চতুর্বেদী মদ্ভক্তঃ শ্বপচঃ প্রিয়ঃ ।
তস্মৈ দেয়ং ততো গ্রাহ্যং স চ পূজ্যো যথা হ্যহম্ ॥৫০॥

na me 'bhaktaś catur-vedī
mad-bhaktaḥ śvapacaḥ priyaḥ
tasmai deyaṁ tato grāhyaṁ
sa ca pūjyo yathā hy aham

SYNONYMS

na—not; *me*—My; *abhaktaḥ*—devoid of pure devotional service; *catuḥ-vedī*—a scholar in the four *Vedas; mat-bhaktaḥ*—My devotee; *śva-pacaḥ*—even from a family of dog-eaters; *priyaḥ*—very dear; *tasmai*—to him (a pure devotee, even though born in a very low family); *deyam*—should be given; *tataḥ*—from him; *grāhyam*—should be accepted (remnants of food); *saḥ*—that person; *ca*—also; *pūjyaḥ*—worshipable; *yathā*—as much as; *hi*—certainly; *aham*—I.

TRANSLATION

"'Even though a person is a very learned scholar of the Sanskrit Vedic literatures, he is not accepted as My devotee unless he is pure in devotional

service. Even though a person is born in a family of dog-eaters, he is very dear to Me if he is a pure devotee who has no motive to enjoy fruitive activities or mental speculation. Indeed, all respects should be given to him, and whatever he offers should be accepted. Such devotees are as worshipable as I am.' "

PURPORT

This verse is included in the *Hari-bhakti-vilāsa* (10.127) compiled by Sanātana Gosvāmī.

TEXT 51

এই শ্লোক পড়ি' দুঁহারে কৈলা আলিঙ্গন ।
কৃপাতে দুঁহার মাথায় ধরিলা চরণ ॥ ৫১ ॥

ei śloka paḍi' duṅhāre kailā āliṅgana
kṛpāte duṅhāra māthāya dharilā caraṇa

SYNONYMS

ei śloka—this verse; *paḍi'*—reciting; *duṅhāre*—the two brothers; *kailā āliṅgana*—embraced; *kṛpāte*—out of causeless mercy; *duṅhāra*—of both of them; *māthāya*—on the heads; *dharilā*—placed; *caraṇa*—His feet.

TRANSLATION

After reciting this verse, Śrī Caitanya Mahāprabhu embraced both brothers, and out of His causeless mercy He placed His feet on their heads.

TEXT 52

প্রভু-কৃপা পাঞা দুঁহে দুই হাত যুড়ি' ।
দীন হঞা স্তুতি করে বিনয় আচরি' ॥ ৫২ ॥

prabhu-kṛpā pāñā duṅhe dui hāta yuḍi'
dīna hañā stuti kare vinaya ācari'

SYNONYMS

prabhu-kṛpā—the Lord's mercy; *pāñā*—getting; *duṅhe*—both of them; *dui*—two; *hāta*—hands; *yuḍi'*—folding; *dīna hañā*—most humbly; *stuti kare*—offer prayers; *vinaya ācari'*—with submission.

TRANSLATION

After receiving the Lord's causeless mercy, the brothers folded their hands and in great humility offered the following prayers unto the Lord.

TEXT 53

নমো মহাবদান্যায় কৃষ্ণপ্রেমপ্রদায় তে ।
কৃষ্ণায় কৃষ্ণচৈতন্যনাম্নে গৌরত্বিষে নমঃ ॥ ৫৩ ॥

namo mahā-vadānyāya
kṛṣṇa-prema-pradāya te
kṛṣṇāya kṛṣṇa-caitanya-
nāmne gaura-tviṣe namaḥ

SYNONYMS

namaḥ—obeisances; *mahā-vadānyāya*—who is most munificent and charitably disposed; *kṛṣṇa-prema*—love of Kṛṣṇa; *pradāya*—who can give; *te*—unto You; *kṛṣṇāya*—the original Personality of Godhead; *kṛṣṇa-caitanya-nāmne*—under the name Kṛṣṇa Caitanya; *gaura-tviṣe*—whose complexion is the golden complexion of Śrīmatī Rādhārāṇī; *namaḥ*—obeisances.

TRANSLATION

"O most munificent incarnation! You are Kṛṣṇa Himself appearing as Śrī Kṛṣṇa Caitanya Mahāprabhu. You have assumed the golden color of Śrīmatī Rādhārāṇī, and You are widely distributing pure love of Kṛṣṇa. We offer our respectful obeisances unto You.

TEXT 54

যোঽজ্ঞানমত্তং ভুবনং দয়ালুরুল্লাঘয়ন্নপ্যকরোৎ প্রমত্তম্ ।
স্বপ্রেমসম্পৎসুধয়াদ্ভুতেহং শ্রীকৃষ্ণচৈতন্যমমুং প্রপদ্যে ॥ ৫৪ ॥

yo 'jñāna-mattaṁ bhuvanaṁ dayālur
ullāghayann apy akarot pramattam
sva-prema-sampat-sudhayādbhutehaṁ
śrī-kṛṣṇa-caitanyam amuṁ prapadye

SYNONYMS

yaḥ—that Personality of Godhead who; *ajñāna-mattam*—maddened by ignorance or foolishly passing time in *karma, jñāna, yoga* and Māyāvāda philosophy; *bhuvanam*—the entire three worlds; *dayāluḥ*—so merciful; *ullāghayan*—subduing such processes as *karma, jñāna* and *yoga; api*—despite; *akarot*—made; *pramattam*—maddened; *sva-prema-sampat-sudhayā*—by the nectar of His personal devotional service, which is an invaluable treasure of bliss; *adbhuta-īham*—whose activities are wonderful; *śrī-kṛṣṇa-caitanyam*—unto Lord Śrī Caitanya Mahāprabhu; *amum*—that; *prapadye*—I surrender.

TRANSLATION

"We offer our respectful obeisances unto that merciful Supreme Personality of Godhead who has converted all three worlds, which were maddened by ignorance, and saved them from their diseased condition by making them mad with the nectar from the treasure-house of love of God. Let us take full shelter of that Personality of Godhead, Śrī Kṛṣṇa Caitanya, whose activities are wonderful."

PURPORT

This verse is found in the *Govinda-līlāmṛta* (1.2).

TEXT 55

তবে মহাপ্রভু তাঁরে নিকটে বসাইলা ।
'সনাতনের বার্তা কহ'—তাঁহারে পুছিলা ॥ ৫৫ ॥

tabe mahāprabhu tāṅre nikaṭe vasāilā
'sanātanera vārtā kaha'——tāṅhāre puchilā

SYNONYMS

tabe—thereafter; *mahāprabhu*—Śrī Caitanya Mahāprabhu; *tāṅre*—them; *nikaṭe*—near Him; *vasāilā*—sat down; *sanātanera vārtā*—news of Sanātana; *kaha* —please tell; *tāṅhāre*—them; *puchilā*—questioned.

TRANSLATION

After this, Śrī Caitanya Mahāprabhu sat them down by His side and asked them, "What news do you have of Sanātana?"

TEXT 56

রূপ কহেন,—তেঁহো বন্দী হয় রাজ-ঘরে ।
তুমি যদি উদ্ধার', তবে হইবে উদ্ধারে ॥ ৫৬ ॥

rūpa kahena,——teṅho bandī haya rāja-ghare
tumi yadi uddhāra', tabe ha-ibe uddhāre

SYNONYMS

rūpa kahena—Rūpa Gosvāmī said; *teṅho*—he; *bandī*—arrested; *haya*—is; *rāja-ghare*—in the court of the government; *tumi*—You; *yadi*—if; *uddhāra'*—kindly rescue; *tabe*—then; *ha-ibe*—he will be; *uddhāre*—relieved from that entanglement.

TRANSLATION

Rūpa Gosvāmī replied, "Sanātana has now been arrested by the government of Hussain Shah. If You kindly save him, he can be liberated from that entanglement."

TEXT 57

প্রভু কহে,—সনাতনের হঞাছে মোচন।
অচিরাৎ আমা-সহ হইবে মিলন ॥ ৫৭ ॥

prabhu kahe,——sanātanera hañāche mocana
acirāt āmā-saha ha-ibe milana

SYNONYMS

prabhu kahe—Śrī Caitanya Mahāprabhu said; *sanātanera*—of Sanātana Gosvāmī; *hañāche*—there has been; *mocana*—release; *acirāt*—very soon; *āmā-saha*—with Me; *ha-ibe milana*—there will be meeting.

TRANSLATION

Śrī Caitanya Mahāprabhu immediately replied, "Sanātana has already been released from his confinement, and he will very soon meet with Me."

TEXT 58

মধ্যাহ্ন করিতে বিপ্র প্রভুরে কহিলা।
রূপ-গোসাঞি সে-দিবস তথাঞি রহিলা ॥ ৫৮ ॥

madhyāhna karite vipra prabhure kahilā
rūpa-gosāñi se-divasa tathāñi rahilā

SYNONYMS

madhyāhna karite—to accept lunch; *vipra*—the *brāhmaṇa* of Deccan; *prabhure*—Śrī Caitanya Mahāprabhu; *kahilā*—requested; *rūpa-gosāñi*—Rūpa Gosvāmī; *se-divasa*—that day; *tathāñi*—there; *rahilā*—remained.

TRANSLATION

Śrī Caitanya Mahāprabhu was then requested by the brāhmaṇa to accept His lunch. Rūpa Gosvāmī also remained there that day.

TEXT 59

ভট্টাচার্য দুই ভাইয়ে নিমন্ত্রণ কৈল ।
প্রভুর শেষ প্রসাদ-পাত্র দুইভাই পাইল ॥ ৫৯ ॥

bhaṭṭācārya dui bhāiye nimantraṇa kaila
prabhura śeṣa prasāda-pātra dui-bhāi pāila

SYNONYMS

bhaṭṭācārya—Balabhadra Bhaṭṭācārya; *dui bhāiye*—the two brothers; *nimantraṇa kaila*—invited to take lunch; *prabhura śeṣa prasāda-pātra*—the remnants of the plate of food offered to Śrī Caitanya Mahāprabhu; *dui-bhāi pāila*—the two brothers obtained.

TRANSLATION

Balabhadra Bhaṭṭācārya invited the two brothers to take lunch also. The remnants of food from the plate of Śrī Caitanya Mahāprabhu were offered to them.

TEXT 60

ত্রিবেণী-উপর প্রভুর বাসা-ঘর স্থান ।
দুই ভাই বাসা কৈল প্রভু-সন্নিধান ॥ ৬০ ॥

triveṇī-upara prabhura vāsā-ghara sthāna
dui bhāi vāsā kaila prabhu-sannidhāna

SYNONYMS

tri-veṇī-upara—on the bank of the confluence of the Yamunā and Ganges; *prabhura*—of Śrī Caitanya Mahāprabhu; *vāsā-ghara*—of the residential house; *sthāna*—the place; *dui bhāi*—the two brothers; *vāsā kaila*—resided; *prabhu-sannidhāna*—near Śrī Caitanya Mahāprabhu.

TRANSLATION

Śrī Caitanya Mahāprabhu selected His residence beside the confluence of the Ganges and Yamunā at a place called Triveṇī. The two brothers—Rūpa Gosvāmī and Śrī Vallabha—selected their residence near the Lord's.

TEXT 61

সে-কালে বল্লভ-ভট্ট রহে আড়াইল-গ্রামে ।
মহাপ্রভু আইলা শুনি' আইল তাঁর স্থানে ॥ ৬১ ॥

se-kāle vallabha-bhaṭṭa rahe āḍāila-grāme
mahāprabhu āilā śuni' āila tāṅra sthāne

SYNONYMS

se-kāle—at that time; *vallabha-bhaṭṭa*—Vallabha Bhaṭṭa; *rahe*—resided; *āḍāila-grāme*—in the village known as Āḍāila; *mahāprabhu*—Śrī Caitanya Mahāprabhu; *āilā*—has come; *śuni'*—hearing; *āila*—came; *tāṅra sthāne*—to His place.

TRANSLATION

At that time, Śrī Vallabha Bhaṭṭa was staying at Āḍāila-grāma, and when he heard that Śrī Caitanya Mahāprabhu had arrived, he went to His place to see Him.

PURPORT

Vallabha Bhaṭṭa was a great learned scholar of Vaiṣṇavism. In the beginning he was very much devoted to Śrī Caitanya Mahāprabhu, but since he thought that he could not receive proper respect from Him, he later joined the Viṣṇusvāmī sect and became *ācārya* of that sect. His sect is celebrated as the Vallabhācārya-sampradāya. This *sampradāya* has had great influence in Vṛndāvana near Gokula and in Bombay. Vallabha Bhaṭṭa wrote many books, including a commentary on *Śrīmad-Bhāgavatam* called *Subodhinī-ṭīkā,* and notes on the *Vedānta-sūtra,* in the form of an *Anubhāṣya.* He also wrote a combination of sixteen short works called *Ṣoḍaśa-grantha.* Āḍāila-grāma, where he was staying, was near the confluence of the Rivers Ganges and Yamunā on the other side of the Yamunā about one mile from the river. The village there is called Aḍelī-grāma, or Āḍāila-grāma. A temple of Lord Viṣṇu there still belongs to the Vallabha-sampradāya.

Vallabha Bhaṭṭa was originally from a place in southern India called Trailaṅga. There is a railway station there called Niḍāḍābhalu. Sixteen miles from that station is a village called Kāṅkaḍabāḍa, or Kākuṅrapāḍhu. A learned *brāhmaṇa* named Lakṣmaṇa Dīkṣita used to live there, and Vallabha Bhaṭṭa was his son. There are five sections of the *brāhmaṇa* community of Āndhra Pradesh known as *bella-nāṭī, vegī-nāṭī, muraki-nāṭī, telagu-nāṭī* and *kāśala-nāṭī.* Out of these five brahminical communities, Vallabhācārya took his birth in the community of *bella-nāṭī* in the year 1400 Śakābda Era. According to some people, Vallabha Bhaṭṭācārya's father took *sannyāsa* before Vallabha's birth, and he returned home to take Vallabhācārya as his son. According to the opinion of others, Vallabhācārya was born in 1400 Śakābda Era on the Ekādaśī day of the dark moon in the month of Caitra, and he took his birth in a *brāhmaṇa* family surnamed Khambhaṁpāṭībāru. According to this account, his father's name was Lakṣmaṇa Bhaṭṭa Dīkṣita, and he was born in Campakāraṇya. In someone else's opinion, Vallabhācārya appeared near the village named Cāṅpā-jhāra-grāma, which is near a railway station named Rājima in Madhya Pradesh.

After studying for eleven years at Vārāṇasī, Vallabhācārya returned home. On his return, he heard that his father had departed from the material world. Keeping his brother and mother at home, he went to the banks of the River Tuṅgabhadrā in a village called Vidyānagara, and it was there that he enlightened Kṛṣṇadeva, the grandson of King Bukkarāja. After that, he traveled throughout India thrice on trips lasting six years. Thus he passed eighteen years and became victorious in his discussions of revealed scripture. When he was thirty years old, he married Mahālakṣmī, who belonged to the same *brāhmaṇa* community. Near Govardhana Hill he established a Deity in the valley. Finally he came to Āḍāila, which is on the other side of Prayāga.

Vallabhācārya had two sons, Gopīnātha and Viṭhṭhaleśvara, and in his old age he accepted the renounced order. In 1452 Śakābda Era, he passed away from the material world at Vārāṇasī. His book known as *Ṣoḍaśa-grantha* and his commentaries on *Vedānta-sūtra* (*Anubhāṣya*) and *Śrīmad-Bhāgavatam* (*Subodhinī*) are very famous. He has written many other books besides.

TEXT 62

তেঁহো দণ্ডবৎ কৈল, প্রভু কৈলা আলিঙ্গন ।
দুই জনে কৃষ্ণকথা হৈল কতক্ষণ ॥ ৬২ ॥

teṅho daṇḍavat kaila, prabhu kailā āliṅgana
dui jane kṛṣṇa-kathā haila kata-kṣaṇa

SYNONYMS

teṅho—he; *daṇḍavat*—obeisances; *kaila*—made; *prabhu*—Śrī Caitanya Mahāprabhu; *kailā*—did; *āliṅgana*—embracing; *dui jane*—between the two of them; *kṛṣṇa-kathā*—topics about Lord Kṛṣṇa; *haila*—there were; *kata-kṣaṇa*—for some time.

TRANSLATION

Vallabha Bhaṭṭācārya offered Śrī Caitanya Mahāprabhu his obeisances, and the Lord embraced him. After that, they discussed topics about Kṛṣṇa for some time.

TEXT 63

কৃষ্ণকথায় প্রভুর মহাপ্রেম উথলিল ।
ভট্টের সঙ্কোচে প্রভু সম্বরণ কৈল ॥ ৬৩ ॥

kṛṣṇa-kathāya prabhura mahā-prema uthalila
bhaṭṭera saṅkoce prabhu samvaraṇa kaila

SYNONYMS

kṛṣṇa-kathāya—in the discussion on Kṛṣṇa; *prabhura*—of Śrī Caitanya Mahāprabhu; *mahā-prema*—great love; *uthalila*—arose; *bhaṭṭera*—of Bhaṭṭācārya; *saṅkoce*—due to shyness; *prabhu*—Śrī Caitanya Mahāprabhu; *samvaraṇa kaila*—restrained Himself.

TRANSLATION

Śrī Caitanya Mahāprabhu felt great ecstatic love when they began discussing Kṛṣṇa, but the Lord checked His feelings because He felt shy before Vallabha Bhaṭṭa.

TEXT 64

অন্তরে গর-গর প্রেম, নহে সম্বরণ ।
দেখি' চমৎকার হৈল বল্লভ-ভট্টের মন ॥ ৬৪ ॥

antare gara-gara prema, nahe samvaraṇa
dekhi' camatkāra haila vallabha-bhaṭṭera mana

SYNONYMS

antare—inside; *gara-gara*—raged; *prema*—ecstatic love; *nahe*—there was not; *samvaraṇa*—checking; *dekhi'*—detecting; *camatkāra*—astonishment; *haila*—there was; *vallabha-bhaṭṭera mana*—on the mind of Vallabha Bhaṭṭa.

TRANSLATION

Although the Lord restrained Himself externally, ecstatic love raged within. There was no checking that. Vallabha Bhaṭṭa was astonished to detect this.

TEXT 65

তবে ভট্ট মহাপ্রভুরে নিমন্ত্রণ কৈলা ।
মহাপ্রভু দুইভাই তাঁহারে মিলাইলা ॥ ৬৫ ॥

tabe bhaṭṭa mahāprabhure nimantraṇa kailā
mahāprabhu dui-bhāi tāṅhāre milāilā

SYNONYMS

tabe—then; *bhaṭṭa*—Vallabha Bhaṭṭa; *mahāprabhure*—Śrī Caitanya Mahāprabhu; *nimantraṇa kailā*—invited; *mahāprabhu*—Śrī Caitanya

Mahāprabhu; *dui-bhāi*—the two brothers Rūpa and Vallabha; *tāṅhāre*—to him; *milāilā*—introduced.

TRANSLATION

Thereafter, Vallabha Bhaṭṭa invited Śrī Caitanya Mahāprabhu for lunch, and the Lord introduced the brothers Rūpa and Vallabha to him.

TEXT 66

দুইভাই দূর হৈতে ভূমিতে পড়িয়া।
ভট্টে দণ্ডবৎ কৈলা অতি দীন হঞা ॥ ৬৬ ॥

dui-bhāi dūra haite bhūmite paḍiyā
bhaṭṭe daṇḍavat kailā ati dīna hañā

SYNONYMS

dui-bhāi—the two brothers; *dūra haite*—from a distance; *bhūmite*—on the ground; *paḍiyā*—falling flat; *bhaṭṭe*—to Vallabha Bhaṭṭa; *daṇḍavat kailā*—offered obeisances; *ati dīna hañā*—being very humble.

TRANSLATION

From a distance, the brothers Rūpa Gosvāmī and Śrī Vallabha fell on the ground and offered obeisances to Vallabha Bhaṭṭa with great humility.

TEXT 67

ভট্ট মিলিবারে যায়, দুঁহে পলায় দূরে।
'অস্পৃশ্য পামর মুঞি, না ছুঁইহ মোরে ॥' ৬৭ ॥

bhaṭṭa milibāre yāya, duṅhe palāya dūre
'aspṛśya pāmara muñi, nā chuṅiha more'

SYNONYMS

bhaṭṭa—Vallabha Bhaṭṭa; *milibāre*—to meet; *yāya*—goes; *duṅhe*—the two brothers; *palāya*—ran away; *dūre*—to a distant place; *aspṛśya*—untouchable; *pāmara*—most fallen; *muñi*—I; *nā chuṅiha*—do not touch; *more*—me.

TRANSLATION

When Vallabha Bhaṭṭācārya walked toward them, they ran away to a more distant place. Rūpa Gosvāmī said, "I am untouchable and most sinful. Please do not touch me."

TEXT 68

ভট্টের বিস্ময় হৈল, প্রভুর হর্ষ মন।
ভট্টেরে কহিলা প্রভু তাঁর বিবরণ॥ ৬৮॥

bhaṭṭera vismaya haila, prabhura harṣa mana
bhaṭṭere kahilā prabhu tāṅra vivaraṇa

SYNONYMS

bhaṭṭera—of Vallabha Bhaṭṭācārya; *vismaya haila*—there was surprise; *prabhura*—of Śrī Caitanya Mahāprabhu; *harṣa*—very happy; *mana*—the mind; *bhaṭṭere kahilā*—said to Vallabha Bhaṭṭācārya; *prabhu*—Śrī Caitanya Mahāprabhu; *tāṅra vivaraṇa*—description of Rūpa Gosvāmī.

TRANSLATION

Vallabha Bhaṭṭācārya was very surprised at this. Śrī Caitanya Mahāprabhu, however, was very pleased, and He therefore spoke to him this description of Rūpa Gosvāmī.

TEXT 69

'ইঁহো না স্পর্শিহ, ইঁহো জাতি অতি-হীন!
বৈদিক, যাজ্ঞিক তুমি কুলীন প্রবীণ!' ৬৯॥

'iṅho nā sparśiha, iṅho jāti ati-hīna!
vaidika, yājñika tumi kulīna pravīṇa!'

SYNONYMS

iṅho—him; *nā sparśiha*—do not touch; *iṅho*—He; *jāti*—caste; *ati-hīna*—very low; *vaidika*—a follower of Vedic principles; *yājñika*—a performer of many sacrifices; *tumi*—you; *kulīna*—aristocratic *brāhmaṇa; pravīṇa*—an experienced person.

TRANSLATION

Śrī Caitanya Mahāprabhu said, "Don't touch him, for he belongs to a very low caste. You are a follower of Vedic principles and are a well experienced performer of many sacrifices. You also belong to the aristocracy."

PURPORT

Generally *brāhmaṇas* are puffed up with false prestige because they belong to the aristocracy and perform many Vedic sacrifices. In South India especially, this fastidious position is most prominent. At any rate, this was the case five hundred years ago. Śrī Caitanya Mahāprabhu actually started a revolution against this brahminical system by inaugurating the chanting of the Hare Kṛṣṇa *mantra*. By this chanting, one can be delivered regardless of caste, creed, color or social position. Whoever chants the Hare Kṛṣṇa *mahā-mantra* is immediately purified due to the transcendental position of devotional service. Śrī Caitanya Mahāprabhu is here hinting to Vallabha Bhaṭṭācārya that an exalted *brāhmaṇa* who makes sacrifices and follows Vedic principles should not neglect a person who is engaged in devotional service by chanting the holy name of the Lord.

Actually Rūpa Gosvāmī did not belong to a lower caste. He was from a highly aristocratic *brāhmaṇa* family, but due to his association with the Mohammedan Nawab, he was considered fallen and excommunicated from *brāhmaṇa* society. However, due to his advanced devotional service, Śrī Caitanya Mahāprabhu accepted him as a *gosvāmī*. Vallabha Bhaṭṭācārya knew all this. One who is a devotee is above caste and creed, yet Vallabha Bhaṭṭācārya felt himself prestigious.

The present head of the Vallabha Bhaṭṭācārya *sampradāya* of Bombay is named Dīkṣita Mahārāja. He is very friendly to our movement, and whenever we meet him, this learned *brāhmaṇa* scholar highly praises the activities of the Hare Kṛṣṇa movement. He is a life member of our Society, and although he is a learned scholar in the brahminical caste tradition, he accepts our Society and considers its members bona fide devotees of Lord Viṣṇu.

TEXT 70

দুঁহার মুখে নিরন্তর কৃষ্ণনাম শুনি'।
ভট্ট কহে, প্রভুর কিছু ইঙ্গিত-ভঙ্গী জানি' ॥ ৭০ ॥

duṅhāra mukhe nirantara kṛṣṇa-nāma śuni'
bhaṭṭa kahe, prabhura kichu iṅgita-bhaṅgī jāni'

SYNONYMS

duṅhāra mukhe—in the mouths of both Rūpa Gosvāmī and his brother Vallabha; *nirantara*—continuously; *kṛṣṇa-nāma śuni'*—hearing the chanting of the holy name of Kṛṣṇa; *bhaṭṭa kahe*—Vallabha Bhaṭṭācārya said; *prabhura*—of Lord Śrī Caitanya Mahāprabhu; *kichu*—some; *iṅgita*—indications; *bhaṅgī*—hints; *jāni'*—understanding.

TRANSLATION

Hearing the holy name constantly vibrated by the two brothers, Vallabha Bhaṭṭācārya could understand the hints of Śrī Caitanya Mahāprabhu.

TEXT 71

'দুঁহার মুখে কৃষ্ণনাম করিছে নর্তন।
এই-দুই 'অধম' নহে, হয় 'সর্বোত্তম' ॥ ৭১ ॥

'duṅhāra mukhe kṛṣṇa-nāma kariche nartana
ei-dui 'adhama' nahe, haya 'sarvottama'

SYNONYMS

duṅhāra mukhe—in the mouths of both; *kṛṣṇa-nāma*—the holy name of Lord Kṛṣṇa; *kariche*—is doing; *nartana*—dancing; *ei-dui*—both of them; *adhama nahe*—not fallen; *haya*—are; *sarva-uttama*—the most exalted.

TRANSLATION

Vallabha Bhaṭṭācārya admitted, "Since these two are constantly chanting the holy name of Kṛṣṇa, how can they be untouchable? On the contrary, they are most exalted."

PURPORT

Vallabha Bhaṭṭācārya's admission of the brothers' exalted position should serve as a lesson to one who is falsely proud of his position as a *brāhmaṇa.* Sometimes so-called *brāhmaṇas* do not recognize our European and American disciples as devotees or *brāhmaṇas,* and some *brāhmaṇas* are so proud that they do not allow them to enter temples. Śrī Caitanya Mahāprabhu herein gives a great lesson. Although Vallabha Bhaṭṭācārya was a great authority on brahmanism and a learned scholar, he admitted that those who chant the Lord's holy name are bona fide *brāhmaṇas* and Vaiṣṇavas and are therefore exalted.

TEXT 72

অহো বত শ্বপচোঽতো গরীয়ান্
যজ্জিহ্বাগ্রে বর্ততে নাম তুভ্যম্।
তেপুস্তপস্তে জুহুবুঃ সস্নুরার্যা
ব্রহ্মানূচুর্নাম গৃণন্তি যে তে ॥ ৭২ ॥

aho bata śva-paco 'to garīyān
yaj-jihvāgre vartate nāma tubhyam
tepus tapas te juhuvuḥ sasnur āryā
brahmānūcur nāma gṛṇanti ye te

SYNONYMS

aho bata—how wonderful it is; *śva-pacaḥ*—dog-eaters; *ataḥ*—than the initiated *brāhmaṇa; garīyān*—more glorious; *yat*—of whom; *jihvā-agre*—on the tongue; *vartate*—remains; *nāma*—the holy name; *tubhyam*—of You, my Lord; *tepuḥ*—have performed; *tapaḥ*—austerity; *te*—they; *juhuvuḥ*—have performed sacrifices; *sasnuḥ*—have bathed in all holy places; *āryāḥ*—really belonging to the Āryan race; *brahma*—all the *Vedas; anūcuḥ*—have studied; *nāma*—the holy name; *gṛṇanti*—chant; *ye*—who; *te*—they.

TRANSLATION

Vallabha Bhaṭṭācārya then recited the following verse: " 'My dear Lord, one who always keeps Your holy name on his tongue becomes greater than an initiated brāhmaṇa. Although he may be born in a family of dog-eaters and may therefore, by material calculation, be the lowest among men, he is still glorious. This is the wonderful effect of chanting the holy name of the Lord. It is therefore concluded that one who chants the holy name of the Lord should be understood to have performed all kinds of austerities and great sacrifices mentioned in the Vedas. He has already taken his bath in all the holy places of pilgrimage. He has studied all the Vedas, and he is actually an Āryan.' "

PURPORT

This verse is quoted from *Śrīmad-Bhāgavatam* (3.33.7).

TEXT 73

শুনি' মহাপ্রভু তাঁরে বহু প্রশংশিলা ।
প্রেমাবিষ্ট হঞা শ্লোক পড়িতে লাগিলা ॥ ৭৩ ॥

śuni' mahāprabhu tāṅre bahu praśaṁśilā
premāviṣṭa hañā śloka paḍite lāgilā

SYNONYMS

śuni'—hearing; *mahāprabhu*—Śrī Caitanya Mahāprabhu; *tāṅre*—him; *bahu*—very much; *praśaṁśilā*—praised; *prema-āviṣṭa hañā*—becoming ecstatic in love of Godhead; *śloka*—verses; *paḍite lāgilā*—began to recite.

TRANSLATION

Śrī Caitanya Mahāprabhu was very pleased to hear Vallabha Bhaṭṭa quoting from śāstra about the position of a devotee. The Lord praised him personally,

and, feeling ecstatic love of Godhead, began to quote many verses from śāstra.

TEXT 74

শুচিঃ সদ্ভক্তিদীপ্তাগ্নিদগ্ধদুর্জাতিকল্মষঃ ।
শ্বপাকোঽপি বুধৈঃ শ্লাঘ্যো ন বেদজ্ঞোঽপি নাস্তিকঃ ॥৭৪॥

śuciḥ sad-bhakti-dīptāgni-
dagdha-durjāti-kalmaṣaḥ
śvapāko 'pi budhaiḥ ślāgyo
na vedajño 'pi nāstikaḥ

SYNONYMS

śuciḥ—a *brāhmaṇa* purified internally and externally; *sat-bhakti*—of devotional service without motives; *dīpta-agni*—by the blazing fire; *dagdha*—burnt to ashes; *durjāti*—such as birth in a low family; *kalmaṣaḥ*—whose sinful reactions; *śva-pākaḥ api*—even though born in a family of dog-eaters; *budhaiḥ*—by learned scholars; *ślāgyaḥ*—recognized; *na*—not; *veda-jñaḥ api*—even though completely conversant in Vedic knowledge; *nāstikaḥ*—an atheist.

TRANSLATION

Śrī Caitanya Mahāprabhu said, " 'A person who has the pure characteristics of a brāhmaṇa due to devotional service, which is like a blazing fire burning to ashes all the sinful reactions of past lives, is certainly saved from the consequences of sinful acts, such as taking birth in a lower family. Even though he may be born in a family of dog-eaters, he is recognized by learned scholars. However, although a person may be a learned scholar in Vedic knowledge, he is not recognized if he is an atheist.

PURPORT

This verse and the next are quoted from the *Hari-bhakti-sudhodaya* (3.11,12), a transcendental literature extracted from the *Purāṇas.*

TEXT 75

ভগবদ্ভক্তিহীনস্য জাতিঃ শাস্ত্রং জপস্তপঃ ।
অপ্রাণস্যেব দেহস্য মণ্ডনং লোকরঞ্জনম্ ॥ ৭৫ ॥

bhagavad-bhakti-hīnasya
jātiḥ śāstraṁ japas tapaḥ

aprāṇasyeva dehasya
maṇḍanaṁ loka-rañjanam

SYNONYMS

bhagavat-bhakti-hīnasya—of a person devoid of devotional service to the Supreme Personality of Godhead; *jātiḥ*—birth in a high caste; *śāstram*—knowledge in revealed scriptures; *japaḥ*—pronunciation of *mantras; tapaḥ*—austerities and penances; *aprāṇasya*—which is dead; *iva*—like; *dehasya*—of a body; *maṇḍanam*—decoration; *loka*—to the whims of people in general; *rañjanam*—simply pleasing.

TRANSLATION

" 'For a person devoid of devotional service, birth in a great family or nation, knowledge of revealed scripture, performance of austerities and penance, and chanting of Vedic mantras are all like ornaments on a dead body. Such ornaments simply serve the concocted pleasures of the general populace.' "

TEXT 76

প্রভুর প্রেমাবেশ, আর প্রভাব ভক্তিসার ।
সৌন্দর্যাদি দেখি' ভট্টের হৈল চমৎকার ॥ ৭৬ ॥

prabhura premāveśa, āra prabhāva bhakti-sāra
saundaryādi dekhi' bhaṭṭera haila camatkāra

SYNONYMS

prabhura—of Śrī Caitanya Mahāprabhu; *prema-āveśa*—ecstasy in love of Godhead; *āra*—and; *prabhāva*—the influence; *bhakti-sāra*—the essence of devotional service; *saundarya-ādi*—personal beauty and other qualities; *dekhi'*—seeing; *bhaṭṭera*—of Vallabha Bhaṭṭācārya; *haila*—there was; *camatkāra*—astonishment.

TRANSLATION

When he saw the Lord's ecstatic love, Vallabha Bhaṭṭācārya was certainly very astonished. He was also astonished by the Lord's knowledge of the essence of devotional service, as well as by His personal beauty and influence.

TEXT 77

সগণে প্রভুরে ভট্ট নৌকাতে চড়াঞা ।
ভিক্ষা দিতে নিজ-ঘরে চলিলা লঞা ॥ ৭৭ ॥

sagaṇe prabhure bhaṭṭa naukāte caḍāñā
bhikṣā dite nija-ghare calilā lañā

SYNONYMS

sa-gaṇe—with His associates; *prabhure*—Śrī Caitanya Mahāprabhu; *bhaṭṭa*—Vallabha Bhaṭṭācārya; *naukāte*—a boat; *caḍāñā*—putting aboard; *bhikṣā dite*—to offer lunch; *nija-ghare*—to his own place; *calilā*—departed; *lañā*—taking.

TRANSLATION

Vallabha Bhaṭṭācārya then put Śrī Caitanya Mahāprabhu and His associates aboard a boat and took them to his own place to offer them lunch.

TEXT 78

যমুনার জল দেখি' চিক্কণ শ্যামল ।
প্রেমাবেশে মহাপ্রভু হইলা বিহ্বল ॥ ৭৮ ॥

yamunāra jala dekhi' cikkaṇa śyāmala
premāveśe mahāprabhu ha-ilā vihvala

SYNONYMS

yamunāra—of the River Yamunā; *jala*—the water; *dekhi'*—seeing; *cikkaṇa*—glossy; *śyāmala*—blackish; *prema-āveśe*—in ecstatic love; *mahāprabhu*—Śrī Caitanya Mahāprabhu; *ha-ilā*—became; *vihvala*—bewildered.

TRANSLATION

While crossing the River Yamunā, Śrī Caitanya Mahāprabhu saw the glossy black water and was immediately bewildered with ecstatic love.

TEXT 79

হুঙ্কার করি' যমুনার জলে দিলা ঝাঁপ ।
প্রভু দেখি' সবার মনে হৈল ভয়-কাঁপ ॥ ৭৯ ॥

huṅkāra kari' yamunāra jale dilā jhāṅpa
prabhu dekhi' sabāra mane haila bhaya-kāṅpa

SYNONYMS

huṅkāra kari'—making a loud sound; *yamunāra jale*—in the water of the River Yamunā; *dilā*—gave; *jhāṅpa*—a plunge; *prabhu dekhi'*—seeing Lord Śrī Caitanya

Mahāprabhu; *sabāra*—of everyone; *mane*—in the mind; *haila*—there was; *bhaya-kāṅpa*—fear and trembling.

TRANSLATION

Indeed, as soon as Śrī Caitanya Mahāprabhu saw the River Yamunā, He immediately made a great sound and jumped into the water. Everyone was filled with fear and trembling to see this.

TEXT 80

আস্তে-ব্যস্তে সবে ধরি' প্রভুরে উঠাইল ।
নৌকার উপরে প্রভু নাচিতে লাগিল ॥ ৮০ ॥

āste-vyaste sabe dhari' prabhure uṭhāila
naukāra upare prabhu nācite lāgila

SYNONYMS

āste-vyaste—with great haste; *sabe*—all of them; *dhari'*—catching; *prabhure*—Śrī Caitanya Mahāprabhu; *uṭhāila*—raised; *naukāra*—of the boat; *upare*—on top; *prabhu*—Śrī Caitanya Mahāprabhu; *nācite lāgila*—began to dance.

TRANSLATION

They all hastily grabbed Śrī Caitanya Mahāprabhu and pulled Him out of the water. Once on the boat's platform, the Lord began to dance.

TEXT 81

মহাপ্রভুর ভরে নৌকা করে টলমল ।
ডুবিতে লাগিল নৌকা, ঝলকে ভরে জল ॥ ৮১ ॥

mahāprabhura bhare naukā kare ṭalamala
ḍubite lāgila naukā, jhalake bhare jala

SYNONYMS

mahāprabhura—of Śrī Caitanya Mahāprabhu; *bhare*—because of the weight; *naukā*—the boat; *kare*—does; *ṭalamala*—tilting; *ḍubite*—to sink; *lāgila*—began; *naukā*—the boat; *jhalake*—in gushes; *bhare*—fills; *jala*—water.

TRANSLATION

Due to the Lord's heavy weight, the boat began to tilt. It began filling up with water and was on the verge of sinking.

TEXT 82

যদ্যপি ভট্টের আগে প্রভুর ধৈর্য হৈল মন।
দুর্বার উদ্ভট প্রেম নহে সম্বরণ ॥ ৮২ ॥

yadyapi bhaṭṭera āge prabhura dhairya haila mana
durvāra udbhaṭa prema nahe saṁvaraṇa

SYNONYMS

yadyapi—although; *bhaṭṭera*—of Vallabhācārya; *āge*—in front; *prabhura*—of Śrī Caitanya Mahāprabhu; *dhairya*—patient; *haila*—was; *mana*—the mind; *durvāra*—difficult to stop; *udbhaṭa*—wonderful; *prema*—ecstatic love; *nahe*—there is not; *saṁvaraṇa*—checking.

TRANSLATION

Śrī Caitanya Mahāprabhu tried to restrain Himself as far as possible before Vallabhācārya, but although He tried to keep calm, His ecstatic love could not be checked.

TEXT 83

দেশ-পাত্র দেখি' মহাপ্রভু ধৈর্য হইল।
আড়াইলের ঘাটে নৌকা আসি' উত্তরিল ॥ ৮৩ ॥

deśa-pātra dekhi' mahāprabhu dhairya ha-ila
āḍāilera ghāṭe naukā āsi' uttarila

SYNONYMS

deśa-pātra dekhi'—seeing the circumstances; *mahāprabhu*—Śrī Caitanya Mahāprabhu; *dhairya ha-ila*—became calm; *āḍāilera ghāṭe*—at the shore of the village Āḍāila; *naukā*—the boat; *āsi'*—coming; *uttarila*—landed.

TRANSLATION

Seeing the circumstances, Śrī Caitanya Mahāprabhu finally became calm so that the boat was able to reach the shore of Āḍāila and land there.

TEXT 84

ভয়ে ভট্ট সঙ্গে রহে, মধ্যাহ্ন করাঞা।
নিজ-গৃহে আনিলা প্রভুরে সঙ্গেতে লঞা ॥ ৮৪ ॥

bhaye bhaṭṭa saṅge rahe, madhyāhna karāñā
nija-gṛhe ānilā prabhure saṅgete lañā

SYNONYMS

bhaye—with fear; *bhaṭṭa*—Vallabha Bhaṭṭācārya; *saṅge*—in Śrī Caitanya Mahāprabhu's association; *rahe*—remains; *madhyāhna karāñā*—after arranging for His bath; *nija-gṛhe*—to his own home; *ānilā*—brought; *prabhure*—Śrī Caitanya Mahāprabhu; *saṅgete*—in company; *lañā*—taking.

TRANSLATION

Fearing for the Lord's welfare, Vallabha Bhaṭṭācārya stayed in His association. After arranging for the Lord's bath, he took Him to his own house.

TEXT 85

আনন্দিত হঞা ভট্ট দিল দিব্যাসন ।
আপনে করিল প্রভুর পাদপ্রক্ষালন ॥ ৮৫ ॥

ānandita hañā bhaṭṭa dila divyāsana
āpane karila prabhura pāda-prakṣālana

SYNONYMS

ānandita hañā—becoming pleased; *bhaṭṭa*—Vallabha Bhaṭṭācārya; *dila*—gave; *divya-āsana*—a nice sitting place; *āpane*—personally; *karila*—did; *prabhura*—of Śrī Caitanya Mahāprabhu; *pāda-prakṣālana*—washing of the feet.

TRANSLATION

When Śrī Caitanya Mahāprabhu arrived at his home, Vallabha Bhaṭṭācārya, being greatly pleased, offered the Lord a nice sitting place and personally washed His feet.

TEXT 86

সবংশে সেই জল মস্তকে ধরিল ।
নূতন কৌপীন-বহির্বাস পরাইল ॥ ৮৬ ॥

savaṁśe sei jala mastake dharila
nūtana kaupīna-bahirvāsa parāila

SYNONYMS

sa-vaṁśe—with all the family members; *sei*—that; *jala*—water; *mastake*—on the head; *dharila*—sprinkled; *nūtana*—fresh; *kaupīna*—underwear; *bahirvāsa*—external covering; *parāila*—put on.

TRANSLATION

Vallabha Bhaṭṭācārya and his whole family then sprinkled that water over their heads. They then offered the Lord new underwear and outer garments.

TEXT 87

গন্ধ-পুষ্প-ধূপ-দীপে মহাপূজা কৈল ।
ভট্টাচার্যে মান্য করি' পাক করাইল ॥ ৮৭ ॥

gandha-puṣpa-dhūpa-dīpe mahā-pūjā kaila
bhaṭṭācārye mānya kari' pāka karāila

SYNONYMS

gandha—scents; *puṣpa*—flowers; *dhūpa*—incense; *dīpe*—by lamps; *mahā-pūjā kaila*—he worshiped the Lord with great pomp; *bhaṭṭācārye*—to Balabhadra Bhaṭṭācārya; *mānya kari'*—offering respect; *pāka karāila*—engaging in cooking.

TRANSLATION

Vallabhācārya worshiped the Lord with great pomp, offering scents, incense, flowers and lamps, and with great respect he induced Balabhadra Bhaṭṭa [the Lord's cook] to cook.

TEXT 88

ভিক্ষা করাইল প্রভুরে সস্নেহ যতনে ।
রূপগোসাঞি দুইভাইয়ে করাইল ভোজনে ॥ ৮৮ ॥

bhikṣā karāila prabhure sasneha yatane
rūpa-gosāñi dui-bhāiye karāila bhojane

SYNONYMS

bhikṣā karāila—made take His lunch; *prabhure*—Śrī Caitanya Mahāprabhu; *sa-sneha*—with affection; *yatane*—with great care; *rūpa-gosāñi*—Śrīla Rūpa Gosvāmī; *dui-bhāiye*—the two brothers; *karāila bhojane*—made eat.

TRANSLATION

Thus Śrī Caitanya Mahāprabhu was offered lunch with great care and affection. The brothers Rūpa Gosvāmī and Śrī Vallabha were also offered food.

TEXT 89

ভট্টাচার্য শ্রীরূপে দেওয়াইল 'অবশেষ'।
তবে সেই প্রসাদ কৃষ্ণদাস পাইল শেষ ॥ ৮৯ ॥

bhaṭṭācārya śrī-rūpe deoyāila 'avaśeṣa'
tabe sei prasāda kṛṣṇadāsa pāila śeṣa

SYNONYMS

bhaṭṭācārya—Vallabha Bhaṭṭācārya; *śrī-rūpe*—to Śrīla Rūpa Gosvāmī; *deoyāila*—offered; *avaśeṣa*—the remnants; *tabe*—thereafter; *sei*—those; *prasāda*—remnants of food; *kṛṣṇadāsa*—Kṛṣṇadāsa; *pāila*—got; *śeṣa*—the balance.

TRANSLATION

Vallabha Bhaṭṭācārya first offered the remnants of the Lord's food to Śrīla Rūpa Gosvāmī and then to Kṛṣṇadāsa.

TEXT 90

মুখবাস দিয়া প্রভুরে করাইল শয়ন।
আপনে ভট্ট করেন প্রভুর পাদ-সম্বাহন ॥ ৯০ ॥

mukha-vāsa diyā prabhure karāila śayana
āpane bhaṭṭa karena prabhura pāda-samvāhana

SYNONYMS

mukha-vāsa—spices; *diyā*—offering; *prabhure*—Śrī Caitanya Mahāprabhu; *karāila*—made to do; *śayana*—resting; *āpane*—personally; *bhaṭṭa*—Śrīla Vallabha Bhaṭṭa; *karena*—does; *prabhura*—of Śrī Caitanya Mahāprabhu; *pāda-samvāhana*—massaging the leg.

TRANSLATION

The Lord was then given spices to purify His mouth. Afterwards He was made to rest, and Vallabha Bhaṭṭācārya personally massaged His legs.

TEXT 91

প্রভু পাঠাইল তাঁরে করিতে ভোজনে ।
ভোজন করি' আইলা তেঁহো প্রভুর চরণে ॥ ৯১ ॥

prabhu pāṭhāila tāṅre karite bhojane
bhojana kari' āilā teṅho prabhura caraṇe

SYNONYMS

prabhu—Śrī Caitanya Mahāprabhu; *pāṭhāila*—sent; *tāṅre*—him (Vallabha Bhaṭṭācārya); *karite bhojane*—to take his lunch; *bhojana kari'*—after taking lunch; *āilā*—came; *teṅho*—he; *prabhura caraṇe*—to the lotus feet of Śrī Caitanya Mahāprabhu.

TRANSLATION

While Vallabha Bhaṭṭācārya was massaging Him, the Lord asked him to go take prasāda. After taking prasāda, he returned to the lotus feet of the Lord.

TEXT 92

হেনকালে আইলা রঘুপতি উপাধ্যায় ।
তিরুহিতা পণ্ডিত, বড় বৈষ্ণব, মহাশয় ॥ ৯২ ॥

hena-kāle āilā raghupati upādhyāya
tiruhitā paṇḍita, baḍa vaiṣṇava, mahāśaya

SYNONYMS

hena-kāle—at this time; *āilā*—arrived; *raghupati upādhyāya*—a *brāhmaṇa* named Raghupati Upādhyāya; *tiruhitā*—belonging to the Tiruhitā state; *paṇḍita*—a very learned scholar; *baḍa*—great; *vaiṣṇava*—devotee; *mahāśaya*—respectable gentleman.

TRANSLATION

At that time there arrived Raghupati Upādhyāya, who belonged to the Tiruhitā district. He was a very learned scholar, a great devotee and a respectable gentleman.

PURPORT

Tiruhitā, or Tirhuṭiyā, is a combination of four districts in Behar: Sāraṇa, Campāraṇa, Majaḥphara-pura and Dvārabhāṅgā. The people of this state are called Tiruṭiyā.

TEXT 93

আসি' তেঁহো কৈল প্রভুর চরণ বন্দন ।
'কৃষ্ণে মতি রহু' বলি' প্রভুর বচন ॥ ৯৩ ॥

āsi' teṅho kaila prabhura caraṇa vandana
'kṛṣṇe mati rahu' bali' prabhura vacana

SYNONYMS

āsi'—coming; *teṅho*—he; *kaila*—did; *prabhura*—of Śrī Caitanya Mahāprabhu; *caraṇa vandana*—worshiping the lotus feet; *kṛṣṇe mati rahu*—just remain always Kṛṣṇa conscious; *bali'*—saying; *prabhura vacana*—the blessings of Śrī Caitanya Mahāprabhu.

TRANSLATION

Raghupati Upādhyāya first offered his respects to Śrī Caitanya Mahāprabhu, and the Lord gave him His blessings, saying, "Always stay in Kṛṣṇa consciousness."

TEXT 94

শুনি' আনন্দিত হৈল উপাধ্যায়ের মন ।
প্রভু তাঁরে কহিল,—'কহ কৃষ্ণের বর্ণন' ॥ ৯৪ ॥

śuni' ānandita haila upādhyāyera mana
prabhu tāṅre kahila,——'kaha kṛṣṇera varṇana'

SYNONYMS

śuni'—hearing; *ānandita*—very pleased; *haila*—became; *upādhyāyera mana*—the mind of Upādhyāya; *prabhu*—Śrī Caitanya Mahāprabhu; *tāṅre*—to him; *kahila*—spoke; *kaha kṛṣṇera varṇana*—just try to describe Kṛṣṇa.

TRANSLATION

Raghupati Upādhyāya was very pleased to hear the Lord's blessings. The Lord then asked him to describe Kṛṣṇa.

TEXT 95

নিজ-কৃত কৃষ্ণলীলা-শ্লোক পড়িল ।
শুনি' মহাপ্রভুর মহা প্রেমাবেশ হৈল ॥ ৯৫ ॥

nija-kṛta kṛṣṇa-līlā-śloka paḍila
śuni' mahāprabhura mahā premāveśa haila

SYNONYMS

nija-kṛta—personally composed; *kṛṣṇa-līlā*—on pastimes of Kṛṣṇa; *śloka*—verses; *paḍila*—recited; *śuni'*—hearing; *mahāprabhura*—of Śrī Caitanya Mahāprabhu; *mahā*—great; *prema-āveśa*—ecstatic love; *haila*—there was.

TRANSLATION

When Raghupati Upādhyāya was requested to describe Kṛṣṇa, he began to recite some verses he had personally composed about Kṛṣṇa's pastimes. Hearing those verses, Śrī Caitanya Mahāprabhu was overwhelmed with ecstatic love.

TEXT 96

শ্রুতিমপরে স্মৃতিমিতরে ভারতমন্যে ভজন্তু ভব-ভীতাঃ ।
অহমিহ নন্দং বন্দে যস্যালিন্দে পরং ব্রহ্ম ॥ ৯৬ ॥

śrutim apare smṛtim itare
bhāratam anye bhajantu bhava-bhītāḥ
aham iha nandaṁ vande
yasyālinde paraṁ brahma

SYNONYMS

śrutim—Vedic literature; *apare*—someone; *smṛtim*—corollary to the Vedic literature; *itare*—others; *bhāratam*—*Mahābhārata; anye*—still others; *bhajantu*—let them worship; *bhava-bhītāḥ*—those who are afraid of material existence; *aham*—I; *iha*—here; *nandam*—Mahārāja Nanda; *vande*—worship; *yasya*—whose; *alinde*—in the courtyard; *param brahma*—the Supreme Brahman, Absolute Truth.

TRANSLATION

Raghupati Upādhyāya recited: "Those who are afraid of material existence worship Vedic literature. Some worship smṛti, the corollaries to Vedic literature, and others worship the Mahābhārata. As far as I am concerned, I worship Mahārāja Nanda, the father of Kṛṣṇa, in whose courtyard the Supreme Personality of Godhead, the Absolute Truth, is playing."

PURPORT

This verse recited by Raghupati Upādhyāya was later included in Śrī Rūpa Gosvāmī's *Padyāvalī* (126).

TEXT 97

'আগে কহ'—প্রভু-বাক্যে উপাধ্যায় কহিল ।
রঘুপতি উপাধ্যায় নমস্কার কৈল ॥ ৯৭ ॥

'āge kaha'—prabhu-vākye upādhyāya kahila
raghupati upādhyāya namaskāra kaila

SYNONYMS

āge kaha—please speak further; *prabhu-vākye*—on the request of Śrī Caitanya Mahāprabhu; *upādhyāya*—Raghupati Upādhyāya; *kahila*—said; *raghupati upādhyāya*—Raghupati Upādhyāya; *namaskāra kaila*—offered Śrī Caitanya Mahāprabhu obeisances.

TRANSLATION

When Raghupati Upādhyāya was requested by the Lord to recite more, he immediately offered his respects to the Lord and granted His request.

TEXT 98

কং প্রতি কথয়িতুমীশে সম্প্রতি কো বা প্রতীতিমায়াতু ।
গোপতি-তনয়াকুঞ্জে গোপবধূটী-বিটং ব্রহ্ম ॥ ৯৮ ॥

kaṁ prati kathayitum īśe
samprati ko vā pratītim āyātu
go-pati-tanayā-kuñje
gopa-vadhūṭī-viṭaṁ brahma

SYNONYMS

kam prati—unto whom; *kathayitum*—to speak; *īśe*—am I able; *samprati*—now; *kaḥ*—who; *vā*—or; *pratītim*—belief; *āyātu*—would do; *go-pati*—of the sun-god; *tanayā*—of the daughter (the Yamunā); *kuñje*—in the bushes on the bank; *gopa-vadhūṭī*—of the cowherd girls; *viṭam*—the hunter; *brahma*—the Supreme Personality of Godhead.

TRANSLATION

"To whom can I speak who will believe me when I say that Kṛṣṇa, the Supreme Personality of Godhead, is hunting the gopīs in the bushes by the banks of the River Yamunā? In this way the Lord demonstrates His pastimes."

PURPORT

This verse was also later included in *Padyāvalī* (98).

TEXT 99

প্রভু কহেন,—কহ, তেঁহো পড়ে কৃষ্ণলীলা।
প্রেমাবেশে প্রভুর দেহ-মন আলুয়াইলা ॥ ৯৯ ॥

prabhu kahena,——kaha, teṅho paḍe kṛṣṇa-līlā
premāveśe prabhura deha-mana āyuyāilā

SYNONYMS

prabhu kahena—Śrī Caitanya Mahāprabhu said; *kaha*—please go on speaking; *teṅho*—he; *paḍe*—recites; *kṛṣṇa-līlā*—the pastimes of Lord Kṛṣṇa; *prema-āveśe*—in great ecstasy of love; *prabhura*—of Śrī Caitanya Mahāprabhu; *deha-mana*—body and mind; *āyuyāilā*—became slackened.

TRANSLATION

Śrī Caitanya Mahāprabhu requested Raghupati Upādhyāya to continue speaking about the pastimes of Śrī Kṛṣṇa. Thus the Lord was absorbed in ecstatic love, and His mind and body slackened.

PURPORT

Our minds and bodies are always engaged in material activities. When they are activated on the spiritual platform, they slacken on the material platform.

TEXT 100

প্রেম দেখি' উপাধ্যায়ের হৈল চমৎকার।
'মনুষ্য নহে, ইঁহো—কৃষ্ণ'— করিল নির্ধার ॥ ১০০ ॥

prema dekhi' upādhyāyera haila camatkāra
'manuṣya nahe, iṅho——kṛṣṇa'——karila nirdhāra

SYNONYMS

prema dekhi'—seeing His ecstatic love; *upādhyāyera*—of Raghupati Upādhyāya; *haila*—there was; *camatkāra*—wonder; *manuṣya nahe*—not a human being; *iṅho*—He; *kṛṣṇa*—Lord Kṛṣṇa Himself; *karila nirdhāra*—made assessment.

TRANSLATION

When Raghupati Upādhyāya saw Śrī Caitanya Mahāprabhu's ecstatic symptoms, he decided that the Lord was not a human being but Kṛṣṇa Himself.

TEXT 101

প্রভু কহে,— উপাধ্যায়, শ্রেষ্ঠ মান' কায় ?
'শ্যামমেব পরং রূপং'—কহে উপাধ্যায় ॥ ১০১ ॥

prabhu kahe,——upādhyāya, śreṣṭha māna' kāya?
'śyāmam eva paraṁ rūpaṁ'——kahe upādhyāya

SYNONYMS

prabhu kahe—Śrī Caitanya Mahāprabhu inquired; *upādhyāya*—My dear Upādhyāya; *śreṣṭha*—the supermost; *māna'*—you consider; *kāya*—what; *śyāmam*—Śyāmasundara, Kṛṣṇa; *eva*—certainly; *param rūpam*—the supreme form; *kahe*—replied; *upādhyāya*—Raghupati Upādhyāya.

TRANSLATION

Śrī Caitanya Mahāprabhu asked Raghupati Upādhyāya, "According to your decision, who is the foremost being?" Raghupati Upādhyāya replied, "Lord Śyāmasundara is the supreme form."

TEXT 102

শ্যাম-রূপের বাসস্থান শ্রেষ্ঠ মান' কায় ?
'পুরী মধুপুরী বরা'—কহে উপাধ্যায় ॥ ১০২ ॥

śyāma-rūpera vāsa-sthāna śreṣṭha māna' kāya?
'purī madhu-purī varā'——kahe upādhyāya

SYNONYMS

śyāma-rūpera—of the supreme form, Śyāmasundara; *vāsa-sthāna*—residence; *śreṣṭha*—the supreme; *māna'*—you accept; *kāya*—which; *purī*—the city; *madhu-purī*—Mathurā; *varā*—best; *kahe*—said; *upādhyāya*—Raghupati Upādhyāya.

TRANSLATION

"Of all Kṛṣṇa's abodes, which do you think is the best?" Raghupati Upādhyāya said, "Madhu-purī, or Mathurā-dhāma, is certainly the best."

PURPORT

Lord Kṛṣṇa has many forms, as stated in *Brahma-saṁhitā* (5.33): *advaitam acyutam anādim ananta-rūpam.* Śrī Caitanya Mahāprabhu asked Raghupati Upādhyāya which form was the best of Lord Kṛṣṇa's millions of forms, and he immediately replied that the supreme form was the Śyāmasundara form. In that form, Kṛṣṇa stands curved in three places and holds His flute. The Śyāmasundara form is also described in *Brahma-saṁhitā* (5.38):

premāñjana-cchurita-bhakti-vilocanena
santaḥ sadaiva hṛdayeṣu vilokayanti
yaṁ śyāmasundaram acintya-guṇa-svarūpaṁ
govindam ādi-puruṣaṁ tam ahaṁ bhajāmi

"I worship the primeval Lord, Govinda, who is always seen by the devotee whose eyes are anointed with the pulp of love. He is seen in His eternal form of Śyāmasundara situated within the heart of the devotee."

Those who are filled with ecstatic love for Kṛṣṇa always see the form of Śyāmasundara within their hearts. Raghupati Upādhyāya confirms that the Absolute Truth, the Supreme Personality of Godhead, has many incarnations—Nārāyaṇa, Nṛsiṁha, Varāha and others—but Kṛṣṇa is distinguished as the supermost. According to *Śrīmad-Bhāgavatam: kṛṣṇas tu bhagavān svayam.* "Kṛṣṇa is the original Personality of Godhead." Kṛṣṇa means Śyāmasundara, who plays His flute in Vṛndāvana. Of all forms, this form is the best of all. Kṛṣṇa lives sometimes in Mathurā and sometimes in Dvārakā, but Mathurā is considered the better place. This is also confirmed by Rūpa Gosvāmī in his *Upadeśāmṛta* (9): *vaikuṇṭhāj janito varā madhu-purī.* "Madhu-purī, or Mathurā, is far superior to the Vaikuṇṭhalokas in the spiritual world."

TEXT 103

বাল্য, পৌগণ্ড, কৈশোরে, শ্রেষ্ঠ মান' কায় ?
'বয়ঃ কৈশোরকং ধ্যেয়ং'—**কহে উপাধ্যায় ॥ ১০৩ ॥**

bālya, paugaṇḍa, kaiśore, śreṣṭha māna' kāya?
'vayaḥ kaiśorakaṁ dhyeyaṁ'——kahe upādhyāya

SYNONYMS

bālya—childhood; *paugaṇḍa*—the boyhood age before youth; *kaiśore*—the beginning of youth; *śreṣṭha*—best; *māna'*—you think; *kāya*—which; *vayaḥ*—the age; *kaiśorakam*—*kaiśora* or fresh youth; *dhyeyam*—most worshipable; *kahe*—said; *upādhyāya*—Raghupati Upādhyāya.

TRANSLATION

Śrī Caitanya Mahāprabhu asked, "Of the three ages of Kṛṣṇa known as childhood, boyhood and fresh youth, which do you consider best?" Raghupati Upādhyāya replied, "Fresh youth is the best age."

TEXT 104

রসগণ-মধ্যে তুমি শ্রেষ্ঠ মান' কায় ?
'আদ্য এব পরো রসঃ'—কহে উপাধ্যায় ॥ ১০৪ ॥

rasa-gaṇa-madhye tumi śreṣṭha māna' kāya?
'ādya eva paro rasaḥ'——kahe upādhyāya

SYNONYMS

rasa-gaṇa-madhye—among all the mellows; *tumi*—you; *śreṣṭha*—as supreme; *māna'*—accept; *kāya*—which one; *ādyaḥ*—conjugal love; *eva*—certainly; *paraḥ rasaḥ*—the best of all mellows; *kahe*—replied; *upādhyāya*—Raghupati Upādhyāya.

TRANSLATION

When Śrī Caitanya Mahāprabhu asked, "Among all the mellows, which do you consider best?" Raghupati Upādhyāya replied, "The mellow of conjugal love is supermost."

TEXT 105

প্রভু কহে,—ভাল তত্ত্ব শিখাইলা মোরে ।
এত বলি' শ্লোক পড়ে গদ্‌গদ-স্বরে ॥ ১০৫ ॥

prabhu kahe,——bhāla tattva śikhāilā more
eta bali' śloka paḍe gadgada-svare

SYNONYMS

prabhu—Śrī Caitanya Mahāprabhu; *kahe*—said; *bhāla*—good; *tattva*—conclusions; *śikhāilā more*—you have taught Me; *eta bali'*—saying this; *śloka paḍe*—Śrī Caitanya Mahāprabhu recited the full verse; *gadgada-svare*—in a faltering voice.

TRANSLATION

Śrī Caitanya Mahāprabhu then said, "You have certainly given first-class conclusions." After saying this, He began to recite the full verse with a faltering voice.

TEXT 106

শ্যামমেব পরং রূপং পুরী মধুপুরী বরা।
বয়ঃ কৈশোরকং ধ্যেয়মাদ্য এব পরো রসঃ ॥ ১০৬ ॥

śyāmam eva paraṁ rūpaṁ
purī madhu-purī varā
vayaḥ kaiśorakaṁ dhyeyam
ādya eva paro rasaḥ

SYNONYMS

śyāmam—the form of Śyāmasundara; *eva*—certainly; *param*—supreme; *rūpam*—form; *purī*—the place; *madhu-purī*—Mathurā; *varā*—best; *vayaḥ*—the age; *kaiśorakam*—fresh youth; *dhyeyam*—always to be meditated on; *ādyaḥ*—the original transcendental mellow, or conjugal love; *eva*—certainly; *paraḥ*—the supreme; *rasaḥ*—mellow.

TRANSLATION

" 'The form of Śyāmasundara is the supreme form, the city of Mathurā is the supreme abode, Lord Kṛṣṇa's fresh youth should always be meditated upon, and the mellow of conjugal love is the supreme mellow.' "

PURPORT

This verse is found in *Padyāvalī* (82).

TEXT 107

প্রেমাবেশে প্রভু তাঁরে কৈলা আলিঙ্গন।
প্রেম মত্ত হঞা তেঁহো করেন নর্তন ॥ ১০৭ ॥

premāveśe prabhu tāṅre kailā āliṅgana
prema matta hañā teṅho karena nartana

SYNONYMS

prema-āveśe—in ecstatic love; *prabhu*—Śrī Caitanya Mahāprabhu; *tāṅre*—him; *kailā*—did; *āliṅgana*—embracing; *prema matta hañā*—being overwhelmed by ecstatic love; *teṅho*—he; *karena nartana*—began to dance.

TRANSLATION

Śrī Caitanya Mahāprabhu then embraced Raghupati Upādhyāya in ecstatic love. Raghupati Upādhyāya also was overwhelmed by love, and he began to dance.

TEXT 108

দেখি' বল্লভ-ভট্ট মনে চমৎকার হৈল ।
দুই পুত্র আনি' প্রভুর চরণে পাড়িল ॥ ১০৮ ॥

dekhi' vallabha-bhaṭṭa mane camatkāra haila
dui putra āni' prabhura caraṇe pāḍila

SYNONYMS

dekhi'—seeing; *vallabha-bhaṭṭa*—of Vallabha Bhaṭṭācārya; *mane*—in the mind; *camatkāra haila*—there was astonishment; *dui putra āni'*—bringing his two sons; *prabhura caraṇe pāḍila*—made them lie at the lotus feet of Śrī Caitanya Mahāprabhu.

TRANSLATION

Vallabha Bhaṭṭācārya was struck with wonder to see Śrī Caitanya Mahāprabhu and Raghupati Upādhyāya dance. He even brought forward his two sons and made them fall down at the Lord's lotus feet.

PURPORT

The two sons of Vallabhācārya were Gopīnātha and Viṭhṭhaleśvara. When Śrī Caitanya Mahāprabhu visited Prayāga in the year 1434 or 1435 Śakābda Era, Viṭhṭhaleśvara was not yet born. In this regard, one should see *Madhya-līlā* 18.47.

TEXT 109

প্রভু দেখিবারে গ্রামের সব-লোক আইল ।
প্রভু-দরশনে সবে 'কৃষ্ণভক্ত' হইল ॥ ১০৯ ॥

prabhu dekhibāre grāmera saba-loka āila
prabhu-daraśane sabe 'kṛṣṇa-bhakta' ha-ila

SYNONYMS

prabhu dekhibāre—to see Śrī Caitanya Mahāprabhu; *grāmera*—of the village; *saba-loka*—all the people; *āila*—came; *prabhu-daraśane*—simply by seeing Śrī Caitanya Mahāprabhu; *sabe*—all of them; *kṛṣṇa-bhakta ha-ila*—became devotees of Lord Kṛṣṇa.

TRANSLATION

Upon hearing that Śrī Caitanya Mahāprabhu had arrived, all the villagers went to see Him. Simply by seeing Him, they all became devotees of Kṛṣṇa.

TEXT 110

ব্রাহ্মণসকল করেন প্রভুর নিমন্ত্রণ।
বল্লভ-ভট্ট তাঁ-সবারে করেন নিবারণ ॥ ১১০ ॥

brāhmaṇa-sakala karena prabhura nimantraṇa
vallabha-bhaṭṭa tāṅ-sabāre karena nivāraṇa

SYNONYMS

brāhmaṇa-sakala—all the *brāhmaṇas* of that village; *karena*—make; *prabhura*—of Śrī Caitanya Mahāprabhu; *nimantraṇa*—invitations; *vallabha-bhaṭṭa*—Vallabha Bhaṭṭācārya; *tāṅ-sabāre*—all of them; *karena*—does; *nivāraṇa*—forbidding.

TRANSLATION

All the brāhmaṇas of the village were anxious to extend invitations to the Lord, but Vallabha Bhaṭṭācārya forbade them to do so.

TEXT 111

'প্রেমোন্মাদে পড়ে গোসাঞি মধ্য-যমুনাতে।
প্রয়াগে চালাইব, ইহাঁ না দিব রহিতে ॥ ১১১ ॥

'premonmāde paḍe gosāñi madhya-yamunāte
prayāge cālāiba, ihāṅ nā diba rahite

SYNONYMS

prema-unmāde—in the madness of ecstatic love; *paḍe*—fell down; *gosāñi*—Śrī Caitanya Mahāprabhu; *madhya-yamunāte*—in the River Yamunā; *prayāge cālāiba*—I shall again take Him to Prayāga; *ihāṅ*—here; *nā*—not; *diba*—I shall allow Him; *rahite*—to stay.

TRANSLATION

Vallabha Bhaṭṭa then decided not to keep Śrī Caitanya Mahāprabhu at Āḍāila because the Lord had jumped into the River Yamunā in ecstatic love. Therefore he decided to bring Him to Prayāga.

TEXT 112

যাঁর ইচ্ছা, প্রয়াগে যাঞা করিবে নিমন্ত্রণ'।
এত বলি' প্রভু লঞা করিল গমন ॥ ১১২ ॥

yāṅra icchā, prayāge yāñā karibe nimantraṇa'
eta bali' prabhu lañā karila gamana

SYNONYMS

yāṅra—of whom; *icchā*—there is a desire; *prayāge yāñā*—going to Prayāga; *karibe*—may do; *nimantraṇa*—invitations; *eta bali'*—saying this; *prabhu lañā*—with Śrī Caitanya Mahāprabhu; *karila gamana*—he departed for Prayāga.

TRANSLATION

Vallabha Bhaṭṭa said, "If anyone likes, he can go to Prayāga and extend invitations to the Lord." In this way he took the Lord with him and departed for Prayāga.

TEXT 113

গঙ্গা-পথে মহাপ্রভুরে নৌকাতে বসাঞা ।
প্রয়াগে আইলা ভট্ট গোসাঞিরে লঞা ॥ ১১৩ ॥

gaṅgā-pathe mahāprabhure naukāte vasāñā
prayāge āilā bhaṭṭa gosāñire lañā

SYNONYMS

gaṅgā-pathe—on the Ganges; *mahāprabhure*—Śrī Caitanya Mahāprabhu; *naukāte vasāñā*—making to sit down on the boat; *prayāge āilā*—went to Prayāga; *bhaṭṭa*—Vallabha Bhaṭṭa; *gosāñire lañā*—with Śrī Caitanya Mahāprabhu.

TRANSLATION

Vallabha Bhaṭṭācārya avoided the River Yamunā. Putting the Lord on a boat in the River Ganges, he went with Him to Prayāga.

TEXT 114

লোক-ভিড়-ভয়ে প্রভু 'দশাশ্বমেধে' যাঞা ।
রূপ-গোসাঞিরে শিক্ষা করা'ন শক্তি সঞ্চারিয়া ॥ ১১৪ ॥

loka-bhiḍa-bhaye prabhu 'daśāśvamedhe' yāñā
rūpa-gosāñire śikṣā karā'na śakti sañcāriyā

SYNONYMS

loka-bhiḍa-bhaye—from fear of the great crowd of people; *prabhu*—Śrī Caitanya Mahāprabhu; *daśāśvamedhe*—to Daśāśvamedha-ghāṭa; *yāñā*—going;

rūpa-gosāñire—Rūpa Gosvāmī; *śikṣā karā'na*—teaches; *śakti sañcāriyā*—endowing him with potency.

TRANSLATION

Due to the great crowds in Prayāga, Śrī Caitanya Mahāprabhu went to a place called Daśāśvamedha-ghāṭa. It was there that the Lord instructed Śrī Rūpa Gosvāmī and empowered him in the philosophy of devotional service.

PURPORT

Parāsya śaktir vividhaiva śrūyate. The Supreme Lord has multi-potencies, which the Lord bestows on His fortunate devotees. The Lord has a special potency by which He spreads the Kṛṣṇa consciousness movement. This is also explained in *Caitanya-caritāmṛta* (*Antya* 7.11). *Kṛṣṇa-śakti vinā nahe tāra pravartana:* "One cannot spread the holy name of Kṛṣṇa without being specifically empowered by Lord Kṛṣṇa." A devotee who receives this power from the Lord must be considered very fortunate. The Kṛṣṇa consciousness movement is spreading to enlighten people about their real position, their original relationship with Kṛṣṇa. One requires Kṛṣṇa's special power in order to be able to do this. People forget their relationship with Kṛṣṇa and work under the spell of *māyā* life after life, transmigrating from one body to another. This is the process of material existence. The Supreme Lord Śrī Kṛṣṇa personally descends to teach people that their position in the material world is a mistaken one. The Lord again comes as Śrī Caitanya Mahāprabhu to induce people to take to Kṛṣṇa consciousness. The Lord also empowers a special devotee to teach people their constitutional position.

TEXT 115

কৃষ্ণতত্ত্ব-ভক্তিতত্ত্ব-রসতত্ত্ব-প্রান্ত ।
সব শিখাইল প্রভু ভাগবত-সিদ্ধান্ত ॥ ১১৫ ॥

kṛṣṇatattva-bhaktitattva-rasatattva-prānta
saba śikhāila prabhu bhāgavata-siddhānta

SYNONYMS

kṛṣṇa-tattva—of the truth about Lord Kṛṣṇa; *bhakti-tattva*—of the truth about devotional service; *rasa-tattva*—of the truth about transcendental mellows; *prānta*—the ultimate limit; *saba*—all; *śikhāila*—taught; *prabhu*—Śrī Caitanya Mahāprabhu; *bhāgavata-siddhānta*—the conclusions of *Śrīmad-Bhāgavatam.*

TRANSLATION

Śrī Caitanya Mahāprabhu taught Śrīla Rūpa Gosvāmī the ultimate limit of the truth about Lord Kṛṣṇa, the truth about devotional service and the truth

about transcendental mellows, consummating in conjugal love between Rādhā and Kṛṣṇa. Finally He told Rūpa Gosvāmī about the ultimate conclusions of Śrīmad-Bhāgavatam.

TEXT 116

রামানন্দ-পাশে যত সিদ্ধান্ত শুনিলা ।
রূপে কৃপা করি' তাহা সব সঞ্চারিলা ॥ ১১৬ ॥

rāmānanda-pāśe yata siddhānta śunilā
rūpe kṛpā kari' tāhā saba sañcārilā

SYNONYMS

rāmānanda-pāśe—from Rāmānanda Rāya; *yata*—all; *siddhānta*—the ultimate conclusions; *śunilā*—he heard; *rūpe*—unto Śrī Rūpa Gosvāmī; *kṛpā kari'*—showing His causeless mercy; *tāhā saba*—all those; *sañcārilā*—infused.

TRANSLATION

Śrī Caitanya Mahāprabhu taught Rūpa Gosvāmī all the conclusions He had heard from Rāmānanda Rāya and duly empowered him so that he could understand them.

TEXT 117

শ্রীরূপ-হৃদয়ে প্রভু শক্তি সঞ্চারিলা ।
সর্বতত্ত্ব-নিরূপণে 'প্রবীণ' করিলা ॥ ১১৭ ॥

śrī-rūpa-hṛdaye prabhu śakti sañcārilā
sarva-tattva-nirūpaṇe 'pravīṇa' karilā

SYNONYMS

śrī-rūpa-hṛdaye—in the heart of Śrīla Rūpa Gosvāmī; *prabhu*—Lord Śrī Caitanya Mahāprabhu; *śakti sañcārilā*—infused spiritual strength; *sarva-tattva*—all conclusive truths; *nirūpaṇe*—in ascertaining; *pravīṇa karilā*—made him fully experienced.

TRANSLATION

By entering the heart of Rūpa Gosvāmī, Śrī Caitanya Mahāprabhu empowered him to ascertain properly the conclusions of all truths. He made him an experienced devotee whose decisions correctly agreed with the verdicts of the disciplic succession. Thus Śrī Rūpa Gosvāmī was personally empowered by Śrī Caitanya Mahāprabhu.

PURPORT

The principles of devotional service are only apparently under the jurisdiction of material activity. To be rightly guided, one must be personally guided by Śrī Caitanya Mahāprabhu. This was the case with Śrīla Rūpa Gosvāmī, Sanātana Gosvāmī and other *ācāryas.*

TEXT 118

শিবানন্দ-সেনের পুত্র 'কবিকর্ণপূর'।
'রূপের মিলন' স্ব-গ্রন্থে লিখিয়াছেন প্রচুর ॥ ১১৮ ॥

śivānanda-senera putra 'kavi-karṇapūra'
'rūpera milana' sva-granthe likhiyāchena pracura

SYNONYMS

śivānanda-senera—of Śivānanda Sena; *putra*—the son; *kavi-karṇapūra*—Kavi-karṇapūra; *rūpera milana*—meeting Rūpa Gosvāmī; *sva-granthe*—in his own book; *likhiyāchena pracura*—has written profusely.

TRANSLATION

In his book Caitanya-candrodaya, Kavi-karṇapūra, the son of Śivānanda Sena, has elaborately described the meeting between Śrī Rūpa Gosvāmī and Śrī Caitanya Mahāprabhu.

TEXT 119

কালেন বৃন্দাবনকেলিবার্তা
লুপ্তেতি তাং খ্যাপয়িতুং বিশিষ্য ।
কৃপামৃতেনাভিষিষেচ দেব-
স্তত্রৈব রূপঞ্চ সনাতনঞ্চ ॥ ১১৯ ॥

kālena vṛndāvana-keli-vārtā
lupteti tāṁ khyāpayituṁ viśiṣya
kṛpāmṛtenābhiṣiṣeca devas
tatraiva rūpaṁ ca sanātanaṁ ca

SYNONYMS

kālena—in the course of time; *vṛndāvana-keli-vārtā*—topics concerning the transcendental mellows of the pastimes of Lord Kṛṣṇa in Vṛndāvana; *luptā*—almost lost; *iti*—thus; *tām*—all those; *khyāpayitum*—to enunciate; *viśiṣya*—making specific; *kṛpā-amṛtena*—with the nectar of mercy; *abhiṣiṣeca*—sprinkled;

devaḥ—the Lord; *tatra*—there; *eva*—indeed; *rūpam*—Śrīla Rūpa Gosvāmī; *ca*—and; *sanātanam*—Sanātana Gosvāmī; *ca*—as well as.

TRANSLATION

"In the course of time, the transcendental news of Kṛṣṇa's pastimes in Vṛndāvana was almost lost. To enunciate explicitly those transcendental pastimes, Śrī Caitanya Mahāprabhu, at Prayāga, empowered Śrīla Rūpa Gosvāmī and Sanātana Gosvāmī with the nectar of His mercy to carry out this work in Vṛndāvana.

PURPORT

This verse and the following two verses are from Act Nine (38,29,30) of *Caitanya-candrodaya* by Śrī Kavi-karṇapūra.

TEXT 120

যঃ প্রাগেব প্রিয়গুণগণৈর্গাঢ়বদ্ধোঽপি মুক্তো
গেহাধ্যাসাদ্রস ইব পরো মূর্ত এবাপ্যমূর্তঃ।
প্রেমালাপৈর্দৃঢ়তরপরিষ্বঙ্গরঙ্গৈঃ প্রয়াগে
তং শ্রীরূপং সমমনুপমেনানুজগ্রাহ দেবঃ ॥ ১২০ ॥

yaḥ prāg eva priya-guṇa-gaṇair gāḍha-baddho 'pi mukto
gehādhyāsād rasa iva paro mūrta evāpy amūrtaḥ
premālāpair dṛḍhatara-pariṣvaṅga-raṅgaiḥ prayāge
taṁ śrī-rūpaṁ samam anupamenānujagrāha devaḥ

SYNONYMS

yaḥ—who; *prāk eva*—previously; *priya-guṇa-gaṇaiḥ*—by the desirable transcendental qualities of Śrī Caitanya Mahāprabhu; *gāḍha*—deeply; *baddhaḥ*—attached; *api*—although; *muktaḥ*—liberated; *geha-adhyāsāt*—from the bondage of family life; *rasaḥ*—transcendental mellows; *iva*—like; *paraḥ*—transcendental; *mūrtaḥ*—personal form; *eva*—certainly; *api*—although; *amūrtaḥ*—without having a material form; *prema-ālāpaiḥ*—by discussions of transcendental love of the Supreme; *dṛḍhatara*—firm; *pariṣvaṅga*—of embracing; *raṅgaiḥ*—with great pleasure; *prayāge*—at Prayāga; *tam*—to him; *śrī-rūpam*—Rūpa Gosvāmī; *samam*—with; *anupamena*—Anupama; *anujagrāha*—showed mercy; *devaḥ*—the Supreme Personality of Godhead.

TRANSLATION

"From the very beginning, Śrīla Rūpa Gosvāmī was deeply attracted by the transcendental qualities of Śrī Caitanya Mahāprabhu. Thus he was perma-

nently relieved from family life. Śrīla Rūpa Gosvāmī and his younger brother, Vallabha, were blessed by Śrī Caitanya Mahāprabhu. Although the Lord was transcendentally situated in His transcendental eternal form, at Prayāga He told Rūpa Gosvāmī about transcendental ecstatic love of Kṛṣṇa. The Lord then embraced him very fondly and bestowed all His mercy upon him.

TEXT 121

প্রিয়স্বরূপে দয়িতস্বরূপে প্রেমস্বরূপে সহজাভিরূপে ।
নিজানুরূপে প্রভুরেকরূপে ততান রূপে স্ববিলাসরূপে ॥১২১॥

priya-svarūpe dayita-svarūpe
prema-svarūpe sahajābhirūpe
nijānurūpe prabhur eka-rūpe
tatāna rūpe svavilāsa-rūpe

SYNONYMS

priya-svarūpe—unto the person whose dear friend was Śrīla Svarūpa Dāmodara Gosvāmī; *dayita-svarūpe*—who was very dear to Him (Śrī Caitanya Mahāprabhu); *prema-svarūpe*—unto the replica of His personal ecstatic love; *sahaja-abhirūpe*—who was naturally very beautiful; *nija-anurūpe*—who exactly followed the principles of Śrī Caitanya Mahāprabhu; *prabhuḥ*—Śrī Caitanya Mahāprabhu; *eka-rūpe*—to the one; *tatāna*—explained; *rūpe*—unto Rūpa Gosvāmī; *sva-vilāsa-rūpe*—who describes the pastimes of Lord Kṛṣṇa.

TRANSLATION

"Indeed, Śrīla Rūpa Gosvāmī, whose dear friend was Svarūpa Dāmodara, was the exact replica of Śrī Caitanya Mahāprabhu, and he was very, very dear to the Lord. Being the embodiment of Śrī Caitanya Mahāprabhu's ecstatic love, Rūpa Gosvāmī was naturally very beautiful. He very carefully followed the principles enunciated by the Lord, and he was a competent person to explain properly the pastimes of Lord Kṛṣṇa. Śrī Caitanya Mahāprabhu expanded His mercy to Śrīla Rūpa Gosvāmī just so he could render service by writing transcendental literatures."

TEXT 122

এইমত কর্ণপূর লিখে স্থানে-স্থানে ।
প্রভু কৃপা কৈলা যৈছে রূপ-সনাতনে ॥ ১২২ ॥

ei-mata karṇapūra likhe sthāne-sthāne
prabhu kṛpā kailā yaiche rūpa-sanātane

SYNONYMS

ei-mata—in this way; *karṇa-pūra*—the poet known as Kavi-karṇapūra; *likhe*—writes; *sthāne-sthāne*—in various places; *prabhu*—Śrī Caitanya Mahāprabhu; *kṛpā kailā*—showed His mercy; *yaiche*—how; *rūpa-sanātane*—to Śrīla Rūpa Gosvāmī and Śrīla Sanātana Gosvāmī.

TRANSLATION

The characteristics of Śrīla Rūpa Gosvāmī have thus been described in various places by the poet Kavi-karṇapūra. An account has also been given of how Śrī Caitanya Mahāprabhu bestowed His causeless mercy upon Śrīla Rūpa Gosvāmī and Śrīla Sanātana Gosvāmī.

TEXT 123

মহাপ্রভুর যত বড় বড় ভক্ত মাত্র ।
রূপ-সনাতন—সবার কৃপা-গৌরব-পাত্র ॥ ১২৩ ॥

mahāprabhura yata baḍa baḍa bhakta mātra
rūpa-sanātana——sabāra kṛpā-gaurava-pātra

SYNONYMS

mahāprabhura—of Śrī Caitanya Mahāprabhu; *yata*—all; *baḍa baḍa*—great, great; *bhakta*—devotees; *mātra*—up to; *rūpa-sanātana*—Śrīla Rūpa Gosvāmī and Śrīla Sanātana Gosvāmī; *sabāra*—of everyone; *kṛpā*—of the mercy; *gaurava*—and honor; *pātra*—objects.

TRANSLATION

Śrīla Rūpa Gosvāmī and Sanātana Gosvāmī were the objects of love and honor for all the great stalwart devotees of Śrī Caitanya Mahāprabhu.

TEXT 124

কেহ যদি দেশে যায় দেখি' বৃন্দাবন ।
তাঁরে প্রশ্ন করেন প্রভুর পারিষদগণ ॥ ১২৪ ॥

keha yadi deśe yāya dekhi' vṛndāvana
tāṅre praśna karena prabhura pāriṣada-gaṇa

SYNONYMS

keha—someone; *yadi*—if; *deśe*—to his country; *yāya*—goes; *dekhi'*—after seeing; *vṛndāvana*—Vṛndāvana; *tāṅre*—unto that person; *praśna karena*—put questions; *prabhura*—of Śrī Caitanya Mahāprabhu; *pāriṣada-gaṇa*—personal associates.

TRANSLATION

If someone returned to his country after seeing Vṛndāvana, the associates of the Lord would ask him questions.

TEXT 125

"কহ,—তাহাঁ কৈছে রহে রূপ-সনাতন ?
কৈছে রহে, কৈছে বৈরাগ্য, কৈছে ভোজন ? ১২৫ ॥

"kaha,——tāhāṅ kaiche rahe rūpa-sanātana?
kaiche rahe, kaiche vairāgya, kaiche bhojana?

SYNONYMS

kaha—please describe; *tāhāṅ*—there; *kaiche*—how; *rahe*—remain; *rūpa*—Rūpa Gosvāmī; *sanātana*—Sanātana Gosvāmī; *kaiche rahe*—how do they live; *kaiche vairāgya*—how do they practice renunciation; *kaiche bhojana*—how do they eat.

TRANSLATION

They would ask those returning from Vṛndāvana, "How are Rūpa and Sanātana doing in Vṛndāvana? What are their activities in the renounced order? How do they manage to eat?" These were the questions asked.

TEXT 126

কৈছে অষ্টপ্রহর করেন শ্রীকৃষ্ণ-ভজন ?"
তবে প্রশংসিয়া কহে সেই ভক্তগণ ॥ ১২৬ ॥

kaiche aṣṭa-prahara karena śrī-kṛṣṇa-bhajana?"
tabe praśaṁsiyā kahe sei bhakta-gaṇa

SYNONYMS

kaiche—how; *aṣṭa-prahara*—twenty-four hours; *karena*—do; *śrī-kṛṣṇa-bhajana*—worshiping of Lord Kṛṣṇa; *tabe*—at that time; *praśaṁsiyā*—praising; *kahe*—described; *sei bhakta-gaṇa*—those devotees.

TRANSLATION

The Lord's associates would also ask, "How is it that Rūpa and Sanātana are engaging in devotional service twenty-four hours daily?" At that time the person who had returned from Vṛndāvana would praise Śrīla Rūpa and Sanātana Gosvāmī.

TEXT 127

"অনিকেত দুঁহে, বনে যত বৃক্ষগণ ।
এক এক বৃক্ষের তলে এক এক রাত্রি শয়ন ॥ ১২৭ ॥

"aniketa duṅhe, vane yata vṛkṣa-gaṇa
eka eka vṛkṣera tale eka eka rātri śayana

SYNONYMS

aniketa—without a residence; *duṅhe*—both of them; *vane*—in the forest; *yata vṛkṣa-gaṇa*—as many trees as there are; *eka eka vṛkṣera*—of one tree after another; *tale*—at the base; *eka eka rātri*—one night after another; *śayana*—lying down to sleep.

TRANSLATION

"The brothers actually have no fixed residence. They reside beneath trees—one night under one tree and the next night under another.

TEXT 128

'বিপ্রগৃহে' স্থূলভিক্ষা, কাহাঁ মাধুকরী ।
শুষ্ক রুটী-চানা চিবায় ভোগ পরিহরি' ॥ ১২৮ ॥

'vipra-gṛhe' sthūla-bhikṣā, kāhāṅ mādhu-karī
śuṣka ruṭī-cānā civāya bhoga parihari'

SYNONYMS

vipra-gṛhe—in the house of a *brāhmaṇa; sthūla-bhikṣā*—full meals; *kāhāṅ*—sometimes; *mādhu-karī*—begging little by little like honeybees; *śuṣka*—dry; *ruṭī*—bread; *cānā*—chick-peas; *civāya*—chew; *bhoga parihari'*—giving up all kinds of material enjoyment.

TRANSLATION

"Śrīla Rūpa and Sanātana Gosvāmī beg a little food from the houses of brāhmaṇas. Giving up all kinds of material enjoyment, they only take some dry bread and fried chick-peas.

TEXT 129

করোঁয়া-মাত্র হাতে, কাঁথা ছিঁড়া, বহির্বাস।
কৃষ্ণকথা, কৃষ্ণনাম, নর্তন-উল্লাস ॥ ১২৯ ॥

karoṅyā-mātra hāte, kāṅthā chiṅḍā, bahirvāsa
kṛṣṇa-kathā, kṛṣṇa-nāma, nartana-ullāsa

SYNONYMS

karoṅyā—the waterpot of a *sannyāsī; mātra*—only; *hāte*—in the hand; *kāṅthā chiṅḍā*—torn quilt; *bahirvāsa*—outer garments; *kṛṣṇa-kathā*—discussion of Kṛṣṇa's pastimes; *kṛṣṇa-nāma*—chanting the holy name of Lord Kṛṣṇa; *nartana-ullāsa*—dancing in jubilation.

TRANSLATION

"They carry only waterpots, and they wear torn quilts. They always chant the holy names of Kṛṣṇa and discuss His pastimes. In great jubilation, they also dance.

TEXT 130

অষ্টপ্রহর কৃষ্ণভজন, চারি দণ্ড শয়নে।
নাম-সঙ্কীর্তনে সেহ নহে কোন দিনে ॥ ১৩০ ॥

aṣṭa-prahara kṛṣṇa-bhajana, cāri daṇḍa śayane
nāma-saṅkīrtane seha nahe kona dine

SYNONYMS

aṣṭa-prahara—twenty-four hours; *kṛṣṇa-bhajana*—worshiping Lord Kṛṣṇa; *cāri daṇḍa*—four *daṇḍas* (one *daṇḍa* equals twenty-four minutes); *śayane*—for sleeping; *nāma-saṅkīrtane*—because of chanting the holy name of the Lord; *seha*—that much time; *nahe*—not; *kona dine*—some days.

TRANSLATION

"They engage almost twenty-four hours daily in rendering service to the Lord. They usually sleep only an hour and a half, and some days, when they continuously chant the Lord's holy name, they do not sleep at all.

TEXT 131

কভু ভক্তিরসশাস্ত্র করয়ে লিখন ।
চৈতন্যকথা শুনে, করে চৈতন্য-চিন্তন ॥" ১৩১ ॥

kabhu bhakti-rasa-śāstra karaye likhana
caitanya-kathā śune, kare caitanya-cintana"

SYNONYMS

kabhu—sometimes; *bhakti-rasa-śāstra*—transcendental literature about the mellows of devotional service; *karaye likhana*—write; *caitanya-kathā*—talks about the pastimes of Śrī Caitanya Mahāprabhu; *śune*—they hear; *kare*—do; *caitanya-cintana*—thinking of Lord Caitanya.

TRANSLATION

"Sometimes they write transcendental literatures about devotional service, and sometimes they hear about Śrī Caitanya Mahāprabhu and spend their time thinking about the Lord."

TEXT 132

এইকথা শুনি' মহান্তের মহাসুখ হয় ।
চৈতন্যের কৃপা যাঁহে, তাঁহে কি বিস্ময় ? ১৩২ ॥

ei-kathā śuni' mahāntera mahā-sukha haya
caitanyera kṛpā yāṅhe, tāṅhe ki vismaya?

SYNONYMS

ei-kathā śuni'—hearing this news; *mahāntera*—of all the devotees; *mahā-sukha*—great pleasure; *haya*—was; *caitanyera*—of Lord Caitanya Mahāprabhu; *kṛpā*—mercy; *yāṅhe*—on whom; *tāṅhe*—in him; *ki*—what; *vismaya*—wonderful.

TRANSLATION

When the personal associates of Śrī Caitanya Mahāprabhu would hear of the activities of Rūpa and Sanātana Gosvāmīs, they would say, "What is wonderful for a person who has been granted the Lord's mercy?"

PURPORT

Śrīla Rūpa Gosvāmī and Sanātana Gosvāmī had no fixed residence. They stayed beneath a tree for one day only and wrote huge volumes of transcendental literature. They not only wrote books but chanted, danced, discussed Kṛṣṇa and remembered Śrī Caitanya Mahāprabhu's pastimes. Thus they executed devotional service.

In Vṛndāvana there are *prākṛta-sahajiyās* who say that writing books or even touching books is taboo. For them, devotional service means being relieved from these activities. Whenever they are asked to hear a recitation of Vedic literature, they refuse, saying, "What business do we have reading or hearing transcendental literatures? They are meant for neophytes." They pose themselves to be too elevated to exert energy for reading, writing and hearing. However, pure devotees under the guidance of Śrīla Rūpa Gosvāmī reject this *sahajiyā* philosophy. It is certainly not good to write literature for money or reputation, but to write books and publish them for the enlightenment of the general populace is real service to the Lord. That was Śrīla Bhaktisiddhānta Sarasvatī's opinion, and he specifically told his disciples to write books. He actually preferred to publish books rather than establish temples. Temple construction is meant for the general populace and neophyte devotees, but the business of advanced and empowered devotees is to write books, publish them and distribute them widely. According to Bhaktisiddhānta Sarasvatī Ṭhākura, distributing literature is like playing on a great *mṛdaṅga*. Consequently we always request members of the International Society for Krishna Consciousness to publish as many books as possible and distribute them widely throughout the world. By thus following in the footsteps of Śrīla Rūpa Gosvāmī, one can become a *rūpānuga* devotee.

TEXT 133

চৈতন্যের কৃপা রূপ লিখিয়াছেন আপনে ।
রসামৃতসিন্ধু-গ্রন্থের মঙ্গলাচরণে ॥ ১৩৩ ॥

caitanyera kṛpā rūpa likhiyāchena āpane
rasāmṛta-sindhu-granthera maṅgalācaraṇe

SYNONYMS

caitanyera—of Lord Śrī Caitanya Mahāprabhu; *kṛpā*—the mercy; *rūpa*—Śrīla Rūpa Gosvāmī; *likhiyāchena*—has written; *āpane*—personally; *rasāmṛta-sindhu-granthera*—of the book known as *Bhakti-rasāmṛta-sindhu; maṅgala-ācaraṇe*—in the auspicious introduction.

TRANSLATION

Śrīla Rūpa Gosvāmī has personally spoken about the mercy of Śrī Caitanya Mahāprabhu in his auspicious introduction to his book Bhakti-rasāmṛta-sindhu [1.1.2].

TEXT 134

হৃদি যস্য প্রেরণয়া প্রবর্তিতোহহং বরাকরূপোহপি ।
তস্য হরেঃ পদকমলং বন্দে চৈতন্যদেবস্য ॥ ১৩৪ ॥

hṛdi yasya preraṇayā
pravartito 'haṁ varāka-rūpo 'pi
tasya hareḥ pada-kamalaṁ
vande caitanya-devasya

SYNONYMS

hṛdi—within the heart; *yasya*—of whom (the Supreme Personality of Godhead, who gives His pure devotees intelligence with which to spread the Kṛṣṇa consciousness movement); *preraṇayā*—by the inspiration; *pravartitaḥ*—engaged; *aham*—I; *varāka*—insignificant and low; *rūpaḥ*—Rūpa Gosvāmī; *api*—although; *tasya*—of Him; *hareḥ*—who is Lord Hari, the Supreme Personality of Godhead; *pada-kamalam*—to the lotus feet; *vande*—let me offer my prayers; *caitanya-devasya*—of Śrī Caitanya Mahāprabhu.

TRANSLATION

"Although I am the lowest of men and have no knowledge, the inspiration to write transcendental literatures about devotional service has been mercifully bestowed upon me. Therefore I am offering my obeisances at the lotus feet of Śrī Caitanya Mahāprabhu, the Supreme Personality of Godhead, who has given me the chance to write these books."

TEXT 135

এইমত দশদিন প্রয়াগে রহিয়া ।
শ্রীরূপে শিক্ষা দিল শক্তি সঞ্চারিয়া ॥ ১৩৫ ॥

ei-mata daśa-dina prayāge rahiyā
śrī-rūpe śikṣā dila śakti sañcāriyā

SYNONYMS

ei-mata—in this way; *daśa-dina*—for ten days; *prayāge*—at Prayāga; *rahiyā*—staying; *śrī-rūpe*—to Śrīla Rūpa Gosvāmī; *śikṣā*—instructions; *dila*—imparted; *śakti sañcāriyā*—bestowing upon him the necessary potency.

TRANSLATION

For ten days Śrī Caitanya Mahāprabhu stayed at Prayāga and instructed Rūpa Gosvāmī, empowering him with the necessary potency.

PURPORT

This is a confirmation of the statement *kṛṣṇa-śakti vinā nahe tāra pravartana.* Unless one is specifically empowered by the Supreme Personality of Godhead, he cannot spread the Kṛṣṇa consciousness movement. An empowered devotee sees and feels himself to be the lowest of men, for he knows that whatever he does is due to the inspiration given by the Lord in the heart. This is also confirmed in *Bhagavad-gītā:*

teṣāṁ satata-yuktānāṁ
bhajatāṁ prīti-pūrvakam
dadāmi buddhi-yogaṁ taṁ
yena mām upayānti te

"To those who are constantly devoted and worship Me with love, I give the understanding by which they can come to Me." (Bg. 10.10)

To be empowered by the Supreme Personality of Godhead, one has to qualify himself. This means that one must engage twenty-four hours daily in the loving devotional service of the Lord. The material position of a devotee doesn't matter because devotional service is not dependent on material considerations. In his earlier life, Śrīla Rūpa Gosvāmī was a government officer and a *gṛhastha.* He was not even a *brahmacārī* or *sannyāsī.* He associated with *mlecchas* and *yavanas,* but because he was always eager to serve, he was a qualified recipient for the Lord's mercy. A sincere devotee can therefore be empowered by the Lord regardless of his situation. In the preceding verse from *Bhakti-rasāmṛta-sindhu,* Śrīla Rūpa Gosvāmī has described how he was personally empowered by the Lord. He further states in *Bhakti-rasāmṛta-sindhu* (1.2.187):

īhā yasya harer dāsye
karmaṇā manasā girā
nikhilāsv apy avasthāsu
jīvan-muktaḥ sa ucyate

"A person acting in the service of Kṛṣṇa with his body, mind and words is a liberated person even in the material world, although he may be engaged in many so-called material activities."

To keep oneself free from material contamination and attain the Lord's favor, one must be sincerely anxious to render service to the Lord. This is the only qualification necessary. As soon as one is favored by the mercy of the spiritual master and the Lord, one is immediately given all the power necessary to write books and propagate the Kṛṣṇa consciousness movement without being hampered by material considerations.

TEXT 136

প্রভু কহে,—শুন, রূপ, ভক্তিরসের লক্ষণ ।
সূত্ররূপে কহি, বিস্তার না যায় বর্ণন ॥ ১৩৬ ॥

prabhu kahe,——śuna, rūpa, bhakti-rasera lakṣaṇa
sūtra-rūpe kahi, vistāra nā yāya varṇana

SYNONYMS

prabhu kahe—Śrī Caitanya Mahāprabhu spoke; *śuna*—please listen; *rūpa*—My dear Rūpa; *bhakti-rasera*—of the transcendental mellows in devotional service; *lakṣaṇa*—the symptoms; *sūtra-rūpe*—in the form of a synopsis; *kahi*—I shall explain; *vistāra*—the whole breadth; *nā*—not; *yāya*—is possible; *varṇana*—description.

TRANSLATION

Śrī Caitanya Mahāprabhu said, "My dear Rūpa, please listen to Me. It is not possible to describe devotional service completely; therefore I am just trying to give you a synopsis of the symptoms of devotional service.

TEXT 137

পারাপার-শূন্য গভীর ভক্তিরস-সিন্ধু ।
তোমায় চাখাইতে তার কহি এক 'বিন্দু' ॥ ১৩৭ ॥

pārāpāra-śūnya gabhīra bhakti-rasa-sindhu
tomāya cākhāite tāra kahi eka 'bindu'

SYNONYMS

pāra-apāra—the length and breadth; *śūnya*—without; *gabhīra*—deep; *bhakti-rasa*—of the mellows in devotional service; *sindhu*—the ocean; *tomāya*—to you; *cākhāite*—to give a taste; *tāra*—of this ocean; *kahi*—I shall speak; *eka*—one; *bindu*—drop.

TRANSLATION

"The ocean of the transcendental mellow of devotional service is so big that no one can estimate its length and breadth. However, just to help you taste it, I am describing but one drop.

TEXT 138

এইত ব্রহ্মাণ্ড ভরি' অনন্ত জীবগণ ।
চৌরাশী-লক্ষ যোনিতে করয়ে ভ্রমণ ॥ ১৩৮ ॥

eita brahmāṇḍa bhari' ananta jīva-gaṇa
caurāśī-lakṣa yonite karaye bhramaṇa

SYNONYMS

ei-ta—in this way; *brahmāṇḍa*—the whole universe; *bhari'*—filling; *ananta*—unlimited; *jīva-gaṇa*—living entities; *caurāśī-lakṣa*—8,400,000; *yonite*—in species of life; *karaye*—do; *bhramaṇa*—wandering.

TRANSLATION

"In this universe there are limitless living entities in 8,400,000 species, and all are wandering within this universe.

PURPORT

This is a challenge to so-called scientists and philosophers who presume that there are living entities on this planet only. So-called scientists are going to the moon, and they say that there is no life there. This does not tally with Śrī Caitanya Mahāprabhu's version. He says that everywhere within the universe there are unlimited numbers of living entities in 8,400,000 different forms. In *Bhagavad-gītā* (2.24) we find that the living entities are *sarva-gataḥ,* which means that they can go anywhere. This indicates that there are living entities everywhere. They exist on land, in water, in air, in fire and in ether. Thus there are living entities in all types of material elements. Since the entire material universe is composed of five elements—earth, water, fire, air and ether—why should there be living entities on one planet and not others? Such a foolish version can never be accepted by Vedic students. From the Vedic literatures we understand that there are living entities on each and every planet, regardless of whether the planet is composed of earth, water, fire or ether. These living entities may not have the same forms that are found on this planet earth, but they have different forms composed of different elements. Even on this earth we can see that the forms of land animals are different from the forms of aquatics. According to the circumstance, living conditions differ, but undoubtedly there are living entities everywhere. Why should we deny the existence of living entities on this or that planet? Those who have claimed to have gone to the moon have not gone there, or else their imperfect vision cannot actually perceive the particular type of living entities there.

Living entities are described as *ananta,* or unlimited; nonetheless, they are said to belong to 8,400,000 species. As stated in the *Viṣṇu Purāṇa:*

jalajā nava-lakṣāṇi
sthāvarā lakṣa-viṁśati
kṛmayo rudra-saṅkhyakāḥ
pakṣiṇāṁ daśa-lakṣaṇam

triṁśal-lakṣāṇi paśavaḥ
catur-lakṣāṇi mānuṣāḥ

"There are 900,000 species living in the water. There are also 2,000,000 nonmoving living entities (*sthāvara*) such as trees and plants. There are also 1,100,000 species of insects and reptiles, and there are 1,000,000 species of birds. As far as quadrupeds are concerned there are 3,000,000 varieties, and there are 400,000 human species." Some of these species may exist on one planet and not on another, but in any case within all the planets of the universe—and even in the sun—there are living entities. This is the verdict of Vedic literatures. As *Bhagavad-gītā* (2.20) confirms:

na jāyate mriyate vā kadācin
nāyaṁ bhūtvā bhavitā vā na bhūyaḥ
ajo nityaḥ śāśvato 'yaṁ purāṇo
na hanyate hanyamāne śarīre

"For the soul there is never birth nor death. Nor, having once been, does he ever cease to be. He is unborn, eternal, ever-existing, undying and primeval. He is not slain when the body is slain."

Since the living entities are never annihilated, they simply transmigrate from one life form to another. Thus there is an evolution of forms according to the degree of developed consciousness. One experiences different degrees of consciousness in different forms. A dog's consciousness is different from a man's. Even within a species we find that a father's consciousness is different from his son's and that a child's consciousness is different from a youth's. Just as we find different forms, we find different states of consciousness. When we see different states of consciousness, we may take it for granted that the bodies are different. In other words, different types of bodies depend on different states of consciousness. This is also confirmed in *Bhagavad-gītā* (8.6): *yaṁ yaṁ vāpi smaran bhāvam.* One's consciousness at the time of death determines a type of body of the living entity. This is the process of transmigration of the soul. A variety of bodies is already there; we change from one body to another in terms of our consciousness.

TEXT 139

কেশাগ্র-শতেক-ভাগ পুনঃ শতাংশ করি ।
তার সম সূক্ষ্ম জীবের 'স্বরূপ' বিচারি ॥ ১৩৯ ॥

keśāgra-śateka-bhāga punaḥ śatāṁśa kari
tāra sama sūkṣma jīvera 'svarūpa' vicāri

SYNONYMS

keśa-agra—from the tip of a hair; *śata-eka*—one hundred; *bhāga*—divisions; *punaḥ*—again; *śata-aṁśa*—one hundred divisions; *kari*—making; *tāra sama*—equal to that; *sūkṣma*—very fine; *jīvera*—of the living entity; *sva-rūpa*—the actual form; *vicāri*—I consider.

TRANSLATION

"The length and breadth of the living entity is described as one ten-thousandth part of the tip of a hair. This is the original subtle nature of the living entity.

TEXT 140

কেশাগ্রশতভাগস্য শতাংশসদৃশাত্মকঃ ।
জীবঃ সূক্ষ্মস্বরূপোঽয়ং সংখ্যাতীতো হি চিৎকণঃ ॥ ১৪০ ॥

keśāgra-śata-bhāgasya
śatāṁśa-sadṛśātmakaḥ
jīvaḥ sūkṣma-svarūpo 'yaṁ
saṅkhyātīto hi cit-kaṇaḥ

SYNONYMS

keśa-agra—of the tip of a hair; *śata-bhāgasya*—of one hundredth; *śata-aṁśa*—a hundredth part; *sadṛśa*—equal to; *ātmakaḥ*—whose nature; *jīvaḥ*—the living entity; *sūkṣma*—very fine; *sva-rūpaḥ*—identification; *ayam*—this; *saṅkhya-atītaḥ*—numbering beyond calculation; *hi*—certainly; *cit-kaṇaḥ*—spiritual particle.

TRANSLATION

" 'If we divide the tip of a hair into a hundred parts and then take one of these parts and divide it again into a hundred parts, that very fine division is the size of but one of the numberless living entities. They are all cit-kaṇa, particles of spirit, not matter.'

PURPORT

This is quoted from the commentary on the portion of *Śrīmad-Bhāgavatam* wherein the *Vedas* personified offer their obeisances unto the Supreme Personality of Godhead. This is confirmed in *Bhagavad-gītā* (15.7). *Mamaivāṁśo jīva-loke jīva-bhūtaḥ sanātanaḥ:* "The living entities in this conditioned world are My eternal, fragmental parts."

Lord Śrī Kṛṣṇa personally identifies Himself with the minute living entities. Lord Kṛṣṇa is the supreme spirit, the Supersoul, and the living entities are His very minute parts and parcels. Of course, we cannot divide the tip of a hair into such fine particles, but spiritually such small particles can exist. Spiritual strength is so powerful that a mere atomic portion of spirit can be the biggest brain in the material world. The same spiritual spark is within an ant and within the body of Brahmā. According to his *karma,* material activities, the spiritual spark attains a certain type of body. Material activities are carried out in goodness, passion and ignorance or a combination of these. According to the mixture of the modes of material nature, the living entity is awarded a particular type of body. This is the conclusion.

TEXT 141

বালাগ্রশতভাগস্য শতধা কল্পিতস্য চ ।
ভাগো জীবঃ স বিজ্ঞেয় ইতি চাহ পরা শ্রুতিঃ ॥ ১৪১ ॥

bālāgra-śata-bhāgasya
śatadhā kalpitasya ca
bhāgo jīvaḥ sa vijñeya
iti cāha parā śrutiḥ

SYNONYMS

bāla-agra—the tip of a hair; *śata-bhāgasya*—of one hundredth; *śata-dhā*—into one hundred parts; *kalpitasya*—divided; *ca*—and; *bhāgaḥ*—minute portion; *jīvaḥ*—the living entity; *saḥ*—that; *vijñeyaḥ*—to be understood; *iti*—thus; *ca*—and; *āha*—have said; *parā*—chief; *śrutiḥ*—Vedic *mantras.*

TRANSLATION

" 'If we divide the tip of a hair into one hundred parts and then take one part and divide this into another one hundred parts, that ten-thousandth part is the dimension of the living entity. This is the verdict of the chief Vedic mantras.'

PURPORT

The first three *padas* of this verse from the *Pañcadaśī Citradīpa* (81) are taken from the *Śvetāśvatara Upaniṣad* (5.9).

TEXT 142

সূক্ষ্মাণামপ্যহং জীবঃ ॥ ১৪২ ॥

sūkṣmāṇām apy ahaṁ jīvaḥ

SYNONYMS

sūkṣmāṇām—of the minute particles; *api*—certainly; *aham*—I; *jīvaḥ*—the living entity.

TRANSLATION

" 'Among minute particles, I am the living entity.'

PURPORT

The living entity is one with and different from the Supreme Personality of Godhead. As spirit soul, the living entity is one in quality with the Supreme Lord; however, the Supreme Lord is bigger than the biggest, and the living entity is the smallest of the small. This quote is the third *pada* of a verse from *Śrīmad-Bhāgavatam* (11.16.11).

TEXT 143

অপরিমিতা ধ্রুবাস্তনুভৃতো যদি সর্বগতা-
স্তর্হি ন শাস্যতেতি নিয়মো ধ্রুব নেতরথা ।
অজনি চ যন্ময়ং তদবিমুচ্য নিয়ন্তৃ ভবেৎ
সমমনুজানতাং যদমতং মতদুষ্টতয়া ॥ ১৪৩ ॥

aparimitā dhruvās tanu-bhṛto yadi sarva-gatās
tarhi na śāsyateti niyamo dhruva netarathā
ajani ca yan-mayaṁ tad avimucya niyantṛ bhavet
samam anujānatāṁ yad amataṁ mata-duṣṭatayā

SYNONYMS

aparimitāḥ—unlimited in number; *dhruvāḥ*—eternals; *tanu-bhṛtaḥ*—who have accepted material bodies; *yadi*—if; *sarva-gatāḥ*—all-pervading; *tarhi*—then; *na*—not; *śāsyatā*—controllable; *iti*—thus; *niyamaḥ*—regulation; *dhruva*—O Supreme Truth; *na*—not; *itarathā*—in another manner; *ajani*—have been born; *ca*—and; *yat-mayam*—consisting of which; *tat*—that; *avimucya*—without giving up; *niyantṛ*—controller; *bhavet*—may become; *samam*—equal in all respects; *anujānatām*—of those who follow this philosophical calculation; *yat*—that; *amatam*—not conclusive; *mata-duṣṭatayā*—by faulty calculations.

TRANSLATION

" 'O Lord, although the living entities who have accepted material bodies are spiritual and unlimited in number, if they were all-pervading there would be no question of their being under Your control. If they are accepted,

however, as particles of the eternally existing spiritual entity—as part of You, who are the supreme spirit whole—we must conclude that they are always under Your control. If the living entities are simply satisfied with being identical with You as spiritual particles, then they will be happy being controllers of so many things. The conclusion that the living entities and the Supreme Personality of Godhead are one and the same is a faulty conclusion. It is not a fact.'

PURPORT

This verse, which is also from *Śrīmad-Bhāgavatam* (10.87.30), was spoken by the personified *Vedas.*

TEXT 144

তার মধ্যে 'স্থাবর', 'জঙ্গম'—দুই ভেদ ।
জঙ্গমে তির্যক্-জল-স্থলচর-বিভেদ ॥ ১৪৪ ॥

tāra madhye 'sthāvara', 'jaṅgama'——dui bheda
jaṅgame tiryak-jala-sthalacara-vibheda

SYNONYMS

tāra madhye—among the living entities who are conditioned within the material world; *sthāvara*—immovable; *jaṅgama*—movable; *dui bheda*—two divisions; *jaṅgame*—among the living entities who can move; *tiryak*—the living entities who can move in the air (the birds); *jala*—or living entities who can move within the water; *sthala-cara*—living entities who can move on land; *vibheda*—three divisions.

TRANSLATION

"The unlimited living entities can be divided into two divisions—those that can move and those that cannot move. Among living entities that can move, there are birds, aquatics and animals.

PURPORT

Śrī Caitanya Mahāprabhu is giving clear instructions on how the living entities live under different conditions. There are trees, plants and stones that cannot move, but still they must be considered living entities, or spiritual sparks. The soul is present in bodies like those of trees, plants and stones. They are all living entities. Among moving living entities such as birds, aquatics and animals, the same spiritual spark is there. As stated herein, there are living entities that can fly, swim and walk. We must also conclude that there are living entities that can move within fire and ether. Living entities have different material bodies composed of earth, water, air, fire and ether. The words *tāra madhye* mean "within this universe." The entire material universe is composed of five material elements. It is not true that living entities reside only within this planet and not within others. Such a conclusion is completely contradictory to the *Vedas.* As stated in *Bhagavad-gītā* (2.24):

acchedyo 'yam adāhyo 'yam
akledyo 'śoṣya eva ca
nityaḥ sarva-gataḥ sthāṇur
acalo 'yaṁ sanātanaḥ

"This individual soul is unbreakable and insoluble, and can be neither burned nor dried. He is everlasting, all-pervading, unchangeable, immovable and eternally the same."

The soul has nothing to do with the material elements. Any material element can be cut to pieces, especially earth. As far as the living entity is concerned, however, it can neither be burned nor cut to pieces. It can therefore live within fire. We can conclude that there are also living entities within the sun. Why should living entities be denied this planet or that planet? According to the *Vedas,* the living entities can live anywhere and everywhere—on land, in water, in air and in fire. Whatever the condition, the living entity is unchangeable (*sthāṇu*). From the statements of Śrī Caitanya Mahāprabhu and *Bhagavad-gītā,* we are to conclude that living entities are everywhere throughout the universes. They are distributed as trees, plants, aquatics, birds, human beings and so on.

TEXT 145

তার মধ্যে মনুষ্য-জাতি অতি অল্পতর ।
তার মধ্যে ম্লেচ্ছ, পুলিন্দ, বৌদ্ধ, শবর ॥ ১৪৫ ॥

tāra madhye manuṣya-jāti ati alpatara
tāra madhye mleccha, pulinda, bauddha, śabara

SYNONYMS

tāra madhye—among all such living entities; *manuṣya-jāti*—entities born as human beings; *ati*—very; *alpatara*—small in quantity; *tāra madhye*—among the small quantity of human beings; *mleccha*—uncivilized men who cannot follow the Vedic principles; *pulinda*—unregulated; *bauddha*—followers of Buddhist philosophy; *śabara*—the lowest of men (the hunter class).

TRANSLATION

"Although the living entities known as human beings are very small in quantity, that division may be still further subdivided, for there are many uncultured human beings like mlecchas, pulindas, bauddhas and śabaras.

TEXT 146

বেদনিষ্ঠ-মধ্যে অর্ধেক বেদ 'মুখে' মানে ।
বেদনিষিদ্ধ পাপ করে, ধর্ম নাহি গণে ॥ ১৪৬ ॥

veda-niṣṭha-madhye ardheka veda 'mukhe' māne
veda-niṣiddha pāpa kare, dharma nāhi gaṇe

SYNONYMS

veda-niṣṭha-madhye—among persons who are followers of the *Vedas; ardheka*—almost half; *veda*—Vedic scriptures; *mukhe*—in the mouth; *māne*—accept; *veda-niṣiddha*—forbidden in the *Vedas; pāpa*—sins; *kare*—perform; *dharma*—religious principles; *nāhi*—not; *gaṇe*—count.

TRANSLATION

"Among human beings, those who are followers of the Vedic principles are considered civilized. Among these, almost half simply give lip service while committing all kinds of sinful activities against these principles. Such people do not care for the regulative principles.

PURPORT

The word *veda* means "knowledge." Supreme knowledge consists of understanding the Supreme Personality of Godhead and our relationship with Him and acting according to that relationship. Action in accordance with the Vedic principles is called religion. Religion means following the orders of the Supreme Personality of Godhead. The Vedic principles are the injunctions given by the Supreme Personality of Godhead. Āryans are civilized human beings who have been following the Vedic principles since time immemorial. No one can trace out the history of the Vedic principles set forth so that man might understand the Supreme Being. Literature or knowledge that seeks the Supreme Being can be accepted as a bona fide religious system, but there are many different types of religious systems according to the place, the disciples and the people's capacity to understand.

The highest type of religious system is described in *Śrīmad-Bhāgavatam* (1.2.6) thus: *sa vai puṁsāṁ paro dharmo yato bhaktir adhokṣaje*. The highest form of religion is that by which one becomes fully conscious of the existence of God, His form, name, qualities, pastimes, abode and all-pervasive features. When everything is completely known, that is the perfection of Vedic knowledge. The fulfillment of Vedic knowledge is systematic knowledge of the characteristics of God. This is confirmed in *Bhagavad-gītā* (15.15): *vedaiś ca sarvair aham eva vedyaḥ*. The aim of Vedic knowledge is to understand God. Those who are actually following Vedic knowledge and searching after God cannot commit sinful activities against the Supreme Lord's order. However, in this age of Kali, although men profess to belong to so many different kinds of religion, most of them commit sinful activities against the orders of the Vedic scriptures. Śrī Caitanya Mahāprabhu therefore says herein: *veda-niṣiddha pāpa kare, dharma nāhi gaṇe*. In this age, men may profess a religion, but they actually do not follow the principles. Instead, they commit all kinds of sin.

TEXT 147

ধর্মাচারি-মধ্যে বহুত 'কর্মনিষ্ঠ' ।
কোটি-কর্মনিষ্ঠ-মধ্যে এক 'জ্ঞানী' শ্রেষ্ঠ ॥ ১৪৭ ॥

dharmācāri-madhye bahuta 'karma-niṣṭha'
koṭi-karma-niṣṭha-madhye eka 'jñānī' śreṣṭha

SYNONYMS

dharma-ācāri-madhye—among persons who actually follow the Vedic principles or religious system; *bahuta*—many of them; *karma-niṣṭha*—attracted to fruitive activities; *koṭi-karma-niṣṭha-madhye*—among millions of such performers of fruitive activities according to Vedic principles; *eka*—one; *jñānī*—wise man; *śreṣṭha*—the chief.

TRANSLATION

"Among the followers of Vedic knowledge, most are following the process of fruitive activity and distinguishing between good and bad work. Out of many such sincere fruitive actors, there may be one who is actually wise.

PURPORT

Śrīla Bhaktisiddhānta Sarasvatī Ṭhākura states that the word *karma-niṣṭha* refers to one who aspires to enjoy the results of his good work and pious activity. Some followers of Vedic principles offer everything to the Absolute Truth and do not aspire to enjoy the results of their pious actions. These are also considered among the *karma-niṣṭhas*. Sometimes we see pious men earn money with great hardship and then spend the money for some pious cause by opening public charities, schools and hospitals. Whether one earns money for himself or for the public benefit, he is called a *karma-niṣṭha.* Out of millions of *karma-niṣṭhas* there may be one who is wise. Those who try to avoid fruitive activity and who become silent in order to merge into the spiritual existence of the Absolute Truth are generally known as *jñānīs,* wise men. They are not interested in fruitive activity but in merging into the Supreme. In either case, both are interested in personal benefit. The *karmīs* are directly interested in personal benefit within the material world, and the *jñānīs* are interested in merging into the existence of the Supreme. The *jñānīs* maintain that fruitive activity is imperfect. For them, perfection is the cessation of work and the merging into the supreme existence. That is their goal in life. The *jñānī* wants to extinguish the distinction between knowledge, the knower and the aim of knowledge. This philosophy is called monism, or oneness, and is characterized by spiritual silence.

TEXT 148

কোটিজ্ঞানি-মধ্যে হয় একজন ‘মুক্ত’ ।
কোটিমুক্ত-মধ্যে ‘দুর্লভ’ এক কৃষ্ণভক্ত ॥ ১৪৮ ॥

koṭi-jñāni-madhye haya eka-jana ‘mukta’
koṭi-mukta-madhye ‘durlabha’ eka kṛṣṇa-bhakta

SYNONYMS

koṭi-jñāni-madhye—out of many millions of such wise men; *haya*—there is; *eka-jana*—one person; *mukta*—actually liberated; *koṭi-mukta-madhye*—out of many millions of such liberated persons; *durlabha*—very rare; *eka*—one; *kṛṣṇa-bhakta*—pure devotee of Lord Kṛṣṇa.

TRANSLATION

"Out of many millions of such wise men, one may actually become liberated [mukta], and out of many millions of such liberated persons, a pure devotee of Lord Kṛṣṇa is very difficult to find.

PURPORT

In *Śrīmad-Bhāgavatam* it is said that due to their poor fund of knowledge, the *jñānīs* are not actually liberated. They simply think that they are liberated. The perfection of knowledge culminates when one comes to the platform of knowing the Supreme Personality of Godhead. *Brahmeti paramātmeti bhagavān iti śabdyate.* The Absolute Truth (*satya-vastu*) is described as Brahman, Paramātmā and Bhagavān. Knowledge of impersonal Brahman and the Supersoul is imperfect until one comes to the platform of knowing the Supreme Personality of Godhead. It is therefore clearly said in this verse: *koṭi-mukta-madhye 'durlabha' eka kṛṣṇa-bhakta.* Those who search after the knowledge of impersonal Brahman or localized Paramātmā are certainly accepted as liberated, but due to their imperfect knowledge they are described in *Śrīmad-Bhāgavatam* as *vimukta-māninaḥ.* Since their knowledge is imperfect, their conception of liberation is imperfect. Perfect knowledge is possible when one knows the Supreme Personality of Godhead. This is supported in *Bhagavad-gītā* (5.29):

bhoktāraṁ yajña-tapasāṁ
sarva-loka-maheśvaram
suhṛdaṁ sarva-bhūtānāṁ
jñātvā māṁ śāntim ṛcchati

"The sages, knowing Me as the ultimate purpose of all sacrifices and austerities, the Supreme Lord of all planets and demigods and the benefactor and well-wisher of all living entities, attain peace from the pangs of material miseries."

Research is going on for the *karmīs, jñānīs* and *yogīs,* but until the search is complete, no one can attain peace. Therefore *Bhagavad-gītā* says, *jñātvā māṁ śāntim ṛcchati:* one can actually attain peace when he knows Kṛṣṇa. This is described in the next verse.

TEXT 149

কৃষ্ণভক্ত—নিষ্কাম, অতএব 'শান্ত'।
ভুক্তি-মুক্তি-সিদ্ধি-কামী—সকলি 'অশান্ত' ॥ ১৪৯ ॥

kṛṣṇa-bhakta——niṣkāma, ataeva 'śānta'
bhukti-mukti-siddhi-kāmī——sakali 'aśānta'

SYNONYMS

kṛṣṇa-bhakta—a devotee of Lord Kṛṣṇa; *niṣkāma*—actually desireless; *ataeva*—therefore; *śānta*—peaceful; *bhukti*—of material enjoyment; *mukti*—of liberation from material activities; *siddhi*—of perfection in yogic performance; *kāmī*—those who are desirous; *sakali*—all of them; *aśānta*—not peaceful.

TRANSLATION

"Because a devotee of Lord Kṛṣṇa is desireless, he is peaceful. Fruitive workers desire material enjoyment, jñānīs desire liberation, and yogīs desire material opulence; therefore they are all lusty and cannot be peaceful.

PURPORT

The devotee of Lord Kṛṣṇa has no desire other than serving Kṛṣṇa. Even so-called liberated people are full of desires. Fruitive actors desire better living accommodations, and *jñānīs* want to be one with the Supreme. *Yogīs* desire material opulence, yogic perfections and magic. All of these are lusty (*kāmī*). Because they desire something, they cannot have peace.

The peace formula is given by Kṛṣṇa in *Bhagavad-gītā:*

bhoktāraṁ yajña-tapasāṁ
sarva-loka-maheśvaram
suhṛdaṁ sarva-bhūtānāṁ
jñātvā māṁ śāntim ṛcchati

If one can understand that the only supreme enjoyer is Kṛṣṇa, one will perform all kinds of sacrifices, penances and austerities in order to attain Kṛṣṇa's devotional service. Kṛṣṇa is the Supreme Being, the proprietor of all the material worlds; therefore throughout the entire universe He is the only enjoyer and beneficiary. He is the only friend who can actually do good to all living entities (*suhṛdaṁ sarva-bhūtānām*). If one understands Kṛṣṇa, he immediately becomes desireless (*niṣkāma*) because a *kṛṣṇa-bhakta* knows that his friend and protector in all respects is Kṛṣṇa, who is able to do anything for His devotee. Kṛṣṇa says, *kaunteya pratijānīhi na me bhaktaḥ praṇaśyati:* "O son of Kuntī, declare it boldly that My devotee never perishes." Since Kṛṣṇa gives this assurance, the devotee lives in Kṛṣṇa and has no desire for personal benefit. The background for the devotee is the all-good Himself. Why should the devotee aspire for something good for himself? His only business is to please the Supreme by rendering service as much as possible. A *kṛṣṇa-bhakta* has no desire for his own personal benefit. He is completely protected by the Supreme. *Avaśya rakṣibe kṛṣṇa viśvāsa pālana.* Bhaktivinoda Ṭhākura says that he is desireless because Kṛṣṇa will give him protection in all circumstances. It is not that he expects any assistance from Kṛṣṇa; he simply depends on Kṛṣṇa just as a child depends on his parents. The child does not know how to expect service from his parents, but he is always protected nevertheless. This is called *niṣkāma* (desirelessness).

Although *karmīs, jñānīs* and *yogīs* fulfill their desires by performing various activities, they are never satisfied. A *karmī* may work very hard to acquire a million dollars, but as soon as he gets a million dollars he desires another million. For the *karmīs,* there is no end of desire. The more the *karmī* gets, the more he desires. The *jñānīs* cannot be desireless because their intelligence is unsound. They want to merge into the Brahman effulgence, but even though they may be raised to that platform, they cannot be satisfied there. There are many *jñānīs* or *sannyāsīs* who give up the world as false, but after taking *sannyāsa* they return to the world to engage in politics or philanthropy or to open schools and hospitals. This means that they could not attain the real Brahman (*brahma satyam*). They have to come down to the material platform to engage in philanthropic activity. Thus they again cultivate desires, and when these desires are exhausted, they desire something different. Therefore the *jñānī* cannot be *niṣkāma,* desireless. Nor can the *yogīs* be desireless, for they desire yogic perfections in order to exhibit some magical feats and gain popularity. People gather around these *yogīs,* and the *yogīs* desire more and more adulation. Because they misuse their mystic power, they fall down again onto the material platform. It is not possible for them to become *niṣkāma,* desireless.

The conclusion is that only the devotees who are simply satisfied in serving the Lord can actually become desireless. Therefore it is written: *kṛṣṇa-bhakta niṣkāma.* Since the *kṛṣṇa-bhakta,* the devotee of Kṛṣṇa, is satisfied with Kṛṣṇa, there is no possibility of falldown.

TEXT 150

মুক্তানামপি সিদ্ধানাং নারায়ণপরায়ণঃ ।
সুদুর্লভঃ প্রশান্তাত্মা কোটিষ্বপি মহামুনে ॥ ১৫০ ॥

muktānām api siddhānāṁ
nārāyaṇa-parāyaṇaḥ
sudurlabhaḥ praśāntātmā
koṭiṣv api mahā-mune

SYNONYMS

muktānām—of persons liberated or freed from the bondage of ignorance; *api*—even; *siddhānām*—of persons who have achieved perfection; *nārāyaṇa*—of the Supreme Personality of Godhead; *parāyaṇaḥ*—the devotee; *su-durlabhaḥ*—very rare; *praśānta-ātmā*—completely satisfied, desireless; *koṭiṣu*—among many millions; *api*—certainly; *mahā-mune*—O great sage.

TRANSLATION

" 'O great sage, out of many millions of materially liberated people who are free from ignorance, and out of many millions of siddhas who have nearly attained perfection, there is hardly one pure devotee of Nārāyaṇa. Only such a devotee is actually completely satisfied and peaceful.'

PURPORT

This verse is quoted from *Śrīmad-Bhāgavatam* (6.14.5). The *nārāyaṇa-parāyaṇa,* the devotee of Lord Nārāyaṇa, is the only blissful person. One who becomes a *nārāyaṇa-parāyaṇa* is already liberated from material bondage. He already possesses all the perfections of *yoga.* Unless one comes to the platform of *nārāyaṇa-parāyaṇa* and passes over the platform of *bhukti-mukti-siddhi,* he cannot be fully satisfied. That is the pure devotional stage.

anyābhilāṣitā-śūnyaṁ
jñāna-karmādy-anāvṛtam
ānukūlyena kṛṣṇānu-
śīlanaṁ bhaktir uttamā

One who has no other desire but Kṛṣṇa and who is not influenced by the process of *jñāna-mārga* (cultivation of knowledge) actually becomes free from ignorance. A first-class person is one who is not influenced by *karma* (fruitive activity) or *yoga* (mystic power). He simply depends on Kṛṣṇa and is satisfied in his devotional service. According to *Śrīmad-Bhāgavatam* (6.17.28): *nārāyaṇa-parāḥ sarve na kutaścana bibhyati.* Such a person is never afraid of anything. For him, heaven and hell are the same. Not knowing the situation of a *nārāyaṇa-parāyaṇa,* rascals become envious. By the grace of Nārāyaṇa, a devotee is situated in the most opulent position in the material world. Rascals are envious of Nārāyaṇa and His devotee, but the devotee knows how to please another devotee of Nārāyaṇa because he knows that by pleasing Nārāyaṇa's representative, one directly pleases Lord Nārāyaṇa. Therefore a devotee offers the best facilities to his spiritual master because he knows that by pleasing Nārāyaṇa's representative, he can please Lord Nārāyaṇa. Outsiders who have no knowledge of Nārāyaṇa are envious both of Nārāyaṇa and of His devotee. Consequently when they see that Nārāyaṇa's devotee is opulently situated, they become envious. But when the devotee of Nārāyaṇa asks such foolish people to come live with him in the same comfortable situation, they do not agree because they cannot give up illicit sex, meat eating, intoxication and gambling. Therefore the materialist refuses the company of a *nārāyaṇa-parāyaṇa,* although he is envious of the devotee's material situation. In Western countries when ordinary men—storekeepers and workers—see our devotees living and eating sumptuously and yet not working, they become very anxious to know where they get the money. Such people become envious and ask, "How is it possible to live so comfortably without working? How is it you have so many cars, bright faces and nice clothes?" Not knowing that Kṛṣṇa looks after His devotees, such people become surprised, and some become envious.

TEXT 151

ব্রহ্মাণ্ড ভ্রমিতে কোন ভাগ্যবান্ জীব ।
গুরু-কৃষ্ণ-প্রসাদে পায় ভক্তিলতা-বীজ ॥ ১৫১ ॥

brahmāṇḍa bhramite kona bhāgyavān jīva
guru-kṛṣṇa-prasāde pāya bhakti-latā-bīja

SYNONYMS

brahmāṇḍa bhramite—wandering in this universe; *kona*—some; *bhāgyavān*—most fortunate; *jīva*—living being; *guru*—of the spiritual master; *kṛṣṇa*—of Kṛṣṇa; *prasāde*—by the mercy; *pāya*—gets; *bhakti-latā*—of the creeper of devotional service; *bīja*—the seed.

TRANSLATION

"According to their karma, all living entities are wandering throughout the entire universe. Some of them are being elevated to the upper planetary systems, and some are going down into the lower planetary systems. Out of many millions of wandering living entities, one who is very fortunate gets an opportunity to associate with a bona fide spiritual master by the grace of Kṛṣṇa. By the mercy of both Kṛṣṇa and the spiritual master, such a person receives the seed of the creeper of devotional service.

PURPORT

When we speak of *brahmāṇḍa,* we refer to the whole universe, or to the cluster of many millions of universes. In all universes, there are innumerable planets and innumerable living entities upon those planets in the air and in the water. There are millions and trillions of living entities everywhere, and they are engaged by *māyā* in suffering and enjoying the results of their fruitive activity life after life. This is the position of the materially conditioned living entities. Out of many of these living entities, if one is actually fortunate (*bhāgyavān*), he comes in contact with a bona fide spiritual master by Kṛṣṇa's mercy.

Kṛṣṇa is situated in everyone's heart, and if one desires something, Kṛṣṇa fulfills one's desire. If the living entity by chance or fortune comes in contact with the Kṛṣṇa consciousness movement and wishes to associate with that movement, Kṛṣṇa, who is situated in everyone's heart, gives him the chance to meet a bona fide spiritual master. This is called *guru-kṛṣṇa-prasāda.* Kṛṣṇa is prepared to bestow His mercy upon all living entities, and as soon as a living entity desires the Lord's mercy, the Lord immediately gives him an opportunity to meet a bona fide spiritual master. Such a person is fortified by both Kṛṣṇa and the spiritual master. He is helped from within by Kṛṣṇa and from without by the spiritual master. Both are prepared to help the sincere living being become free from this material bondage.

How one can become this fortunate can be seen in the life of Śrīla Nārada Muni. In his previous life he was born of a maidservant. Although he was not born into a prestigious position, his mother was fortunately engaged in rendering service to some Vaiṣṇavas. When these Vaiṣṇavas were resting during the Cāturmāsya period, the boy Nārada took the opportunity to engage in their service. Taking compassion upon the boy, the Vaiṣṇavas offered him the remnants of their food.

By serving them and obeying their orders, the boy became the object of sympathy for the Vaiṣṇavas, and, by the Vaiṣṇavas' unknown mercy, he gradually became a pure devotee. In the next life he was Nārada Muni, the most exalted of Vaiṣṇavas and the most important *guru* and *ācārya* of Vaiṣṇavas.

Following in the footsteps of Nārada Muni, this Kṛṣṇa consciousness movement is rendering service to humanity by giving everyone a chance to come in contact with Kṛṣṇa. If one is fortunate, he becomes intimately related with this movement. Then, by the grace of Kṛṣṇa, one's life becomes successful. Everyone has dormant *kṛṣṇa-bhakti*—love for Kṛṣṇa—and in the association of good devotees, that love is revealed. As stated in *Caitanya-caritāmṛta* (*Madhya* 22.107):

nitya-siddha-kṛṣṇa-prema 'sādhya' kabhu naya
śravaṇādi-śuddha-citte karaye udaya

Dormant devotional service to Kṛṣṇa is within everyone. Simply by associating with devotees, hearing their good instructions and chanting the Hare Kṛṣṇa *mantra,* dormant love for Kṛṣṇa is awakened. In this way one acquires the seed of devotional service. *Guru-kṛṣṇa-prasāde pāya bhakti-latā-bīja.*

TEXT 152

মালী হঞা করে সেই বীজ আরোপণ ।
শ্রবণ-কীর্তন-জলে করয়ে সেচন ॥ ১৫২ ॥

mālī hañā kare sei bīja āropaṇa
śravaṇa-kīrtana-jale karaye secana

SYNONYMS

mālī hañā—becoming a gardener; *kare*—does; *sei*—that; *bīja*—seed of devotional service; *āropaṇa*—sowing; *śravaṇa*—of hearing; *kīrtana*—of chanting; *jale*—with the water; *karaye*—does; *secana*—sprinkling.

TRANSLATION

"When a person receives the seed of devotional service, he should take care of it by becoming a gardener and sowing the seed in his heart. If he waters the seed gradually by the process of śravaṇa and kīrtana [hearing and chanting], the seed will begin to sprout.

PURPORT

To live with devotees or to live in a temple means to associate with the *śravaṇa-kīrtana* process. Sometimes neophyte devotees think that they can continue the *śravaṇa-kīrtana* process without worshiping the Deity, but the execution of *śravaṇa-kīrtana* is meant for highly developed devotees like Haridāsa Ṭhākura, who engaged in the *śravaṇa-kīrtana* process without worshiping the Deity. However, one should not falsely imitate Haridāsa Ṭhākura and abandon Deity worship just to try to engage in *śravaṇa-kīrtana*. This is not possible for neophyte devotees.

The word *guru-prasāda* indicates that the spiritual master is very merciful in bestowing the boon of devotional service upon the disciple. That is the best possible gift the spiritual master has to offer. Those with a background of pious life are eligible to receive life's supreme benefit, and to bestow this benefit, the Supreme Personality of Godhead sends His representative to impart His mercy. Endowed with the mercy of the Supreme Personality of Godhead, the spiritual master distributes the mercy to those who are elevated and pious. Thus the spiritual master trains his disciples to render devotional service unto the Supreme Personality of Godhead. This is called *guru-kṛpā*. It is *kṛṣṇa-prasāda*, Kṛṣṇa's mercy, that He sends a bona fide spiritual master to the deserving disciple. By the mercy of Kṛṣṇa, one meets the bona fide spiritual master, and by the mercy of the spiritual master, the disciple is fully trained in the devotional service of the Lord.

Bhakti-latā-bīja means "the seed of devotional service." Everything has an original cause, or seed. For any idea, program, plan or device, there is first of all the contemplation of the plan, and that is called *bīja*, or the seed. The methods, rules and regulations by which one is perfectly trained in devotional service constitute the *bhakti-latā-bīja*, or seed of devotional service. This *bhakti-latā-bīja* is received from the spiritual master by the grace of Kṛṣṇa. Other seeds are called *anyābhilāṣa-bīja*, *karma-bīja* and *jñāna-bīja*. If one is not fortunate enough to receive the *bhakti-latā-bīja* from the spiritual master, he instead cultivates the seeds of *karma-bīja*, *jñāna-bīja*, or political and social or philanthropic *bīja*. However, *bhakti-latā-bīja* is different from these other *bījas*. *Bhakti-latā-bīja* can be received only through the mercy of the spiritual master. Therefore one has to satisfy the spiritual master to get *bhakti-latā-bīja* (*yasya prasādād bhagavat-prasādaḥ*). *Bhakti-latā-bīja* is the origin of devotional service. Unless one satisfies the spiritual master, he gets the *bīja*, or root cause, of *karma*, *jñāna* and *yoga* without the benefit of devotional service. However, one who is faithful to his spiritual master gets the *bhakti-latā-bīja*. This *bhakti-latā-bīja* is received when one is initiated by the bona fide spiritual master. After receiving the spiritual master's mercy, one must repeat his instructions, and this is called *śravaṇa-kīrtana*—hearing and chanting. One who has not properly heard from the spiritual master or who does not follow the regulative principles is not fit for chanting (*kīrtana*). This is explained in *Bhagavad-gītā* (2.41): *vyavasāyātmikā buddhir ekeha kuru-nandana*. One who has not listened carefully to the instructions of the spiritual master is unfit to chant or preach the cult of devotional service. One has to water the *bhakti-latā-bīja* after receiving instructions from the spiritual master.

TEXT 153

উপজিয়া বাড়ে লতা 'ব্রহ্মাণ্ড' ভেদি' যায় ।
'বিরজা', 'ব্রহ্মলোক' ভেদি' 'পরব্যোম' পায় ॥১৫৩॥

upajiyā bāḍe latā 'brahmāṇḍa' bhedi' yāya
'virajā', 'brahma-loka' bhedi' 'para-vyoma' pāya

SYNONYMS

upajiyā—being cultivated; *bāḍe*—increases; *latā*—the creeper of devotional service; *brahmāṇḍa*—the whole universe; *bhedi'*—penetrating; *yāya*—goes; *virajā*—the river between the spiritual world and the material world; *brahma-loka*—the Brahman effulgence; *bhedi'*—penetrating; *para-vyoma*—the spiritual sky; *pāya*—attains.

TRANSLATION

"As one waters the bhakti-latā-bīja, the seed sprouts, and the creeper gradually increases to the point where it penetrates the walls of this universe and goes beyond the Virajā River between the spiritual world and the material world. It attains brahma-loka, the Brahman effulgence, and, penetrating through that stratum, it reaches the spiritual sky and the spiritual planet Goloka Vṛndāvana.

PURPORT

A creeper generally takes shelter of a big tree, but the *bhakti-latā,* being the creeper of spiritual energy, cannot take shelter of any material planet, for there is no tree on any material planet that the *bhakti-latā* creeper can utilize for shelter. In other words, devotional service cannot be utilized for any material purpose. Devotional service is meant only for the Supreme Personality of Godhead. Sometimes men with a poor fund of knowledge maintain that *bhakti* can be applied to material things also. In other words, they say that devotional service can be rendered to one's country or to the demigods, but this is not a fact. Devotional service is especially meant for the Supreme Personality of Godhead, and it is beyond this material range. There is a river, or causal ocean, between the spiritual and material natures, and this river is free from the influence of the three modes of material nature; therefore it is called Virajā. The word *vi* means *vigata* (completely eradicated), and *rajaḥ* means "the influence of the material world." On this platform, a living entity is completely free from material entanglement. For the *jñānīs* who want to merge into the Brahman effulgence, there is *brahma-loka. Bhakti-latā,* however, has no shelter in the material world, nor has it shelter in *brahma-loka,* although *brahma-loka* is beyond the material world. The *bhakti-latā* increases until it reaches the spiritual sky, where Goloka Vṛndāvana is situated.

TEXT 154

তবে যায় তদুপরি 'গোলোক-বৃন্দাবন'।
'কৃষ্ণচরণ'-কল্পবৃক্ষে করে আরোহণ ॥ ১৫৪ ॥

tabe yāya tad-upari 'goloka-vṛndāvana'
'kṛṣṇa-caraṇa'-kalpa-vṛkṣe kare ārohaṇa

SYNONYMS

tabe—thereafter; *yāya*—goes; *tat-upari*—to the top of that (the spiritual sky); *goloka-vṛndāvana*—to the planet known as Goloka Vṛndāvana where Kṛṣṇa lives; *kṛṣṇa-caraṇa*—of the lotus feet of Lord Kṛṣṇa; *kalpa-vṛkṣe*—on the desire tree; *kare ārohaṇa*—climbs.

TRANSLATION

"Being situated in one's heart and being watered by śravaṇa-kīrtana, the bhakti creeper grows more and more. In this way it attains the shelter of the desire tree of the lotus feet of Kṛṣṇa, who is eternally situated in the planet known as Goloka Vṛndāvana in the topmost region of the spiritual sky.

PURPORT

In *Brahma-saṁhitā* (5.37) it is said:

ānanda-cinmaya-rasa-pratibhāvitābhis
tābhir ya eva nija-rūpatayā kalābhiḥ
goloka eva nivasaty akhilātma-bhūto
govindam ādi-puruṣaṁ tam ahaṁ bhajāmi

"I worship Govinda, the primeval Lord. He resides in His own realm, Goloka, with Rādhā, who resembles His own spiritual figure and who embodies the ecstatic potency [*hlādinī*]. Their companions are Her confidantes, who embody extensions of Her bodily form and who are imbued and permeated with ever-blissful spiritual *rasa.*" In the spiritual world, the Supreme Personality of Godhead, Kṛṣṇa, has expanded Himself in His spiritual potency. He has His eternal form of bliss and knowledge (*sac-cid-ānanda-vigraha*). Everything in the Goloka Vṛndāvana planet is a spiritual expansion of *sac-cid-ānanda.* Everyone there is of the same potency—*ānanda-cinmaya-rasa.* The relationship between the Supreme Personality of Godhead and His servitor is *cinmaya-rasa.* Kṛṣṇa and His entourage and paraphernalia are of the same *cinmaya* potency. When the *cinmaya-rasa* potency goes through the material potency, it becomes all-pervading. Although the Supreme

Personality of Godhead exists on His own planet Goloka Vṛndāvana, He is present everywhere. *Aṇḍāntara-stha-paramāṇu-cayāntara-stham.* He is present within all universes, although they are innumerable. He is present within the atom. *Īśvaraḥ sarva-bhūtānāṁ hṛd-deśe 'rjuna tiṣṭhati:* He is also present within the heart of all living entities. This is His all-pervasive potency.

Goloka Vṛndāvana is the highest planet in the spiritual world. In order to go to the spiritual world after penetrating the cover of the material universe, one must penetrate *brahma-loka,* the spiritual effulgence. Then one can come to the Goloka Vṛndāvana planet. There are also other planets in the spiritual world called Vaikuṇṭha planets, and on these planets Lord Nārāyaṇa is worshiped with awe and veneration. On these planets the *śānta-rasa* is prevalent, and some of the devotees are also connected with the Supreme Personality of Godhead in the *dāsya-rasa,* the mellow of servitorship. As far as the mellow of fraternity is concerned, the Vaikuṇṭha *rasa* is represented by *gaurava-sakhya,* friendship in awe and veneration. The other fraternity *rasa* is exhibited as *viśrambha* (friendship in equality), and this is found in the Goloka Vṛndāvana planet. Above that is service to the Lord in *vātsalya-rasa* (paternal love), and above all is the relationship with the Lord in the *mādhurya-rasa* (conjugal love). These five *rasas* are fully exhibited in the spiritual world in one's relationship with the Lord. Therefore in the spiritual world the *bhakti-latā* creeper finds its resting place at the lotus feet of Kṛṣṇa.

TEXT 155

তাহাঁ বিস্তারিত হঞা ফলে প্রেম-ফল ।
ইহাঁ মালী সেচে নিত্য শ্রবণাদি জল ॥ ১৫৫ ॥

tāhāṅ vistārita hañā phale prema-phala
ihāṅ mālī sece nitya śravaṇādi jala

SYNONYMS

tāhāṅ—there in the spiritual world (in the Goloka Vṛndāvana planet); *vistārita*—expanded; *hañā*—becoming; *phale*—produces; *prema-phala*—the fruit known as love of Godhead; *ihāṅ*—in the material world, where the devotee is still present; *mālī*—exactly like a gardener; *sece*—sprinkles; *nitya*—regularly, without fail; *śravaṇa-ādi jala*—the water of *śravaṇa, kīrtana* and so on.

TRANSLATION

"The creeper greatly expands in the Goloka Vṛndāvana planet, and there it produces the fruit of love for Kṛṣṇa. Although remaining in the material world, the gardener regularly sprinkles the creeper with the water of hearing and chanting.

PURPORT

In Goloka Vṛndāvana the devotees have very intimate relationships with the Supreme Personality of Godhead. The devotee engages in the Lord's service in great ecstatic love. Such love was exhibited personally by Śrī Caitanya Mahāprabhu in His teachings to the people of the material world. The fruit of the devotional creeper is pure desire to serve and please the senses of the Supreme Personality of Godhead. *Kṛṣṇendriya-prīti-icchā dhare 'prema' nāma.* (Cc. *Ādi.* 4.165) In the spiritual world one has no desire other than to please the senses of the Supreme Personality of Godhead. The conditioned soul within the material world can neither understand nor appreciate how the devotee in the material world can render confidential service to the Lord out of feelings of ecstatic love and always engage in pleasing the Supreme Lord's senses. Although seen within this material world, the pure devotee always engages in the confidential service of the Lord. An ordinary neophyte devotee cannot realize this; therefore it is said, *vaiṣṇavera kriyā-mudrā vijñāneha nā bujhaya.* The activities of a pure Vaiṣṇava cannot be understood even by a learned scholar in the material world.

Every living entity is wandering within this universe in different species and on different planetary systems according to his fruitive activities. Out of many millions of living entities, one may be fortunate enough to receive the seed of *bhakti-latā,* the creeper of devotional service. By the grace of the spiritual master and Kṛṣṇa, one nourishes the *bhakti-latā* by regularly sprinkling it with the water of *śravaṇa-kīrtana,* hearing and chanting. In this way the seed of *bhakti-latā* sprouts and grows up and up through the whole universe until it penetrates the covering of the material universe and reaches the spiritual world. The *bhakti-latā* continues to grow until it reaches the topmost planetary system, Goloka Vṛndāvana, where Kṛṣṇa lives. There the creeper takes shelter at the lotus feet of the Lord, and that is its final destination. At that time the creeper begins to grow the fruits of ecstatic love of God. It is the duty of the devotee who nourishes the creeper to be very careful. It is said that the watering of the creeper must continue: *ihāṅ mālī sece nitya śravaṇādi jala.* It is not that at a certain stage one can stop chanting and hearing and become a mature devotee. If one stops, one certainly falls down from devotional service. Although one may be very exalted in devotional service, he should not give up the watering process of *śravaṇa-kīrtana.* If one gives up that process, it is due to an offense. This is described in the following verse.

TEXT 156

যদি বৈষ্ণব-অপরাধ উঠে হাতী মাতা।
উপাড়ে বা ছিণ্ডে, তার শুখি' যায় পাতা ॥ ১৫৬ ॥

yadi vaiṣṇava-aparādha uṭhe hātī mātā
upāḍe vā chiṇḍe, tāra śukhi' yāya pātā

SYNONYMS

yadi—if; *vaiṣṇava-aparādha*—an offense at the feet of a Vaiṣṇava; *uṭhe*—arises; *hātī*—an elephant; *mātā*—mad; *upāḍe*—uproots; *vā*—or; *chiṇḍe*—breaks; *tāra*—of the creeper; *śukhi'*—shriveling up; *yāya*—goes; *pātā*—the leaf.

TRANSLATION

"If the devotee commits an offense at the feet of a Vaiṣṇava while cultivating the creeper of devotional service in the material world, his offense is compared to a mad elephant that uproots the creeper and breaks it. In this way the leaves of the creeper are dried up.

PURPORT

One's devotional attitude increases in the association of a Vaiṣṇava.

tāṅdera caraṇa sevi bhakta-sane vāsa
janame janame haya, ei abhilāṣa

By his personal example, Narottama dāsa Ṭhākura stresses that a devotee must always remember to please his predecessor *ācārya.* The Gosvāmīs are represented by one's spiritual master. One cannot be an *ācārya* (spiritual master) without following strictly in the disciplic succession of the *ācāryas.* One who is actually serious in advancing in devotional service should desire only to satisfy the previous *ācāryas. Ei chaya gosāñi yāra, mui tāra dāsa.* One should always think of oneself as a servant of the servant of the *ācāryas,* and thinking this, one should live in the society of Vaiṣṇavas. However, if one thinks that he has become very mature and can live separate from the association of Vaiṣṇavas and thus gives up all the regulative principles due to offending a Vaiṣṇava, one's position becomes very dangerous. Offenses against the holy name are explained in *Ādi-līlā* (Chapter Eight, verse 24). Giving up the regulative principles and living according to one's whims are compared to a mad elephant, which by force uproots the *bhakti-latā* and breaks it to pieces. In this way the *bhakti-latā* shrivels up. Such an offense is especially created when one disobeys the instructions of the spiritual master. This is called *guru-avajñā.* The devotee must therefore be very careful not to commit offenses against the spiritual master. As soon as one is deviated from the spiritual master, the uprooting of the *bhakti-latā* begins, and gradually all the leaves dry up.

TEXT 157

তাতে মালী যত্ন করি' করে আবরণ ।
অপরাধ-হস্তীর যৈছে না হয় উদ্গম ॥ ১৫৭ ॥

tāte mālī yatna kari' kare āvaraṇa
aparādha-hastīra yaiche nā haya udgama

SYNONYMS

tāte—therefore; *mālī*—the gardener devotee; *yatna kari'*—with great attention; *kare*—makes; *āvaraṇa*—protective fencing; *aparādha*—of offenses; *hastīra*—of the elephant; *yaiche*—so that; *nā*—not; *haya*—there is; *udgama*—birth.

TRANSLATION

"The gardener must defend the creeper by fencing it all around so that the powerful elephant of offenses may not enter.

PURPORT

While the *bhakti-latā* creeper is growing, the devotee must protect it by fencing it all around. The neophyte devotee must be protected by being surrounded by pure devotees. In this way he will not give the maddened elephant a chance to uproot his *bhakti-latā* creeper. When one associates with nondevotees, the maddened elephant is set loose. Śrī Caitanya Mahāprabhu has said: *asat-saṅga-tyāga,*——*ei vaiṣṇava-ācāra.* The first business of a Vaiṣṇava is to give up the company of nondevotees. A so-called mature devotee, however, commits a great offense by giving up the company of pure devotees. The living entity is a social animal, and if one gives up the society of pure devotees, he must associate with nondevotees (*asat-saṅga*). By contacting nondevotees and engaging in nondevotional activities, a so-called mature devotee will fall victim to the mad elephant offense. Whatever growth has taken place is quickly uprooted by such an offense. One should therefore be very careful to defend the creeper by fencing it in—that is, by following the regulative principles and associating with pure devotees.

If one thinks that there are many pseudo devotees or nondevotees in the Kṛṣṇa Consciousness Society, one can keep direct company with the spiritual master, and if there is any doubt, one should consult the spiritual master. However, unless one follows the spiritual master's instructions and the regulative principles governing chanting and hearing the holy name of the Lord, one cannot become a pure devotee. By one's mental concoctions, one falls down. By associating with nondevotees, one breaks the regulative principles and is thereby lost. In the *Upadeśāmṛta* of Śrīla Rūpa Gosvāmī, it is said:

atyāhāraḥ prayāsaś ca
prajalpo niyamāgrahaḥ
jana-saṅgaś ca laulyaṁ ca
ṣaḍbhir bhaktir vinaśyati

"One's devotional service is spoiled when he becomes too entangled in the following six activities: (1) eating more than necessary or collecting more funds than required, (2) overendeavoring for mundane things that are very difficult to attain, (3) talking unnecessarily about mundane subject matters, (4) practicing the scriptural rules and regulations only for the sake of following them and not for the sake of spiritual advancement, or rejecting the rules and regulations of the scriptures and working independently or whimsically, (5) associating with worldly-minded persons who are not interested in Kṛṣṇa consciousness, and (6) being greedy for mundane achievements."

TEXT 158

কিন্তু যদি লতার অঙ্গে উঠে 'উপশাখা'।
ভুক্তি-মুক্তি-বাঞ্ছা, যত অসংখ্য তার লেখা ॥ ১৫৮ ॥

kintu yadi latāra saṅge uṭhe 'upaśākhā'
bhukti-mukti-vāñchā, yata asaṅkhya tāra lekhā

SYNONYMS

kintu—but; *yadi*—if; *latāra*—the creeper of devotional service; *saṅge*—with; *uṭhe*—arise; *upaśākhā*—unwanted creepers; *bhukti*—for material enjoyment; *mukti*—for liberation from the material world; *vāñchā*—the desires; *yata*—as many as there are; *asaṅkhya*—unlimited; *tāra*—of those unwanted creepers; *lekhā*—the writing.

TRANSLATION

"Sometimes unwanted creepers, such as the creepers of desires for material enjoyment and liberation from the material world, grow along with the creeper of devotional service. The varieties of such unwanted creepers are unlimited.

TEXT 159

'নিষিদ্ধাচার', 'কুটীনাটী', 'জীবহিংসন'।
'লাভ', 'পূজা', 'প্রতিষ্ঠাদি' যত উপশাখাগণ ॥ ১৫৯ ॥

'niṣiddhācāra', 'kuṭīnāṭī', 'jīva-hiṁsana'
'lābha', 'pūjā', 'pratiṣṭhādi' yata upaśākhā-gaṇa

SYNONYMS

niṣiddha-ācāra—behavior not to be exhibited by a person desiring to become perfect; *kuṭīnāṭī*—diplomacy; *jīva-hiṁsana*—unnecessarily killing animals or the soul; *lābha*—profit according to material calculations; *pūjā*—adoration achieved by satisfying mundane people; *pratiṣṭha-ādi*—becoming an important man in material calculations, and so on; *yata*—all these; *upaśākhā-gaṇa*—unnecessary creepers.

TRANSLATION

"Some unnecessary creepers growing with the bhakti creeper are the creepers of behavior unacceptable for those trying to attain perfection, diplomatic behavior, animal killing, mundane profiteering, mundane adoration and mundane importance. All these are unwanted creepers.

PURPORT

There is a certain pattern of behavior prescribed for those actually trying to become perfect. In our Kṛṣṇa consciousness movement we advise our students not to eat meat, not to gamble, not to engage in illicit sex and not to indulge in intoxication. People who indulge in these activities can never become perfect; therefore these regulative principles are for those interested in becoming perfect and going back to Godhead. *Kuṭīnāṭī,* or diplomatic behavior, cannot satisfy the *ātmā,* the soul. It cannot even satisfy the body or the mind. The culprit mind is always suspicious; therefore our dealings should always be straightforward and approved by Vedic authorities. If we treat people diplomatically or duplicitously, our spiritual advancement is obstructed. *Jīva-hiṁsana* refers to the killing of animals or to envy of other living entities. The killing of poor animals is undoubtedly due to envy of those animals. The human form is meant for the understanding of Kṛṣṇa consciousness (*athāto brahma-jijñāsā*), for inquiring about the Supreme Brahman. In the human form, everyone has a chance to understand the Supreme Brahman. The so-called leaders of human society do not know the real aim of human life and are therefore busy with economic development. This is misleading. Every state and every society is busy trying to improve the quality of eating, sleeping, mating and defending. This human form of life is meant for more than these four animal principles. Eating, sleeping, mating and defending are problems found in the animal kingdom, and the animals have solved their problems without difficulty. Why should human society be so busy trying to solve these problems? The difficulty is that people are not educated to understand this simple philosophy. They think that advancement of civilization means increasing sense gratification.

There are many religious propagandists who do not know how the ultimate problems of life can be solved, and they also try to educate people in a form of sense gratification. This is also *jīva-hiṁsana.* Real knowledge is not given, and religionists mislead the general populace. As far as material profits are concerned, one should know that whatever material profit one has must be abandoned at the time of death. Unfortunately people do not know that there is life after death; therefore mundane people waste their time amassing material profit which has to be left behind at the time of death. Such profit has no eternal benefit. Similarly, adoration by mundane people is valueless because after death one has to accept another body. Material adoration and title are decorations that cannot be carried over to the next body. In the next life, everything is forgotten.

All these obstructions have been described in this verse as unwanted creepers. They simply present obstacles for the real creeper, *bhakti-latā-bīja.* One should be very careful to avoid all these unwanted things. Sometimes these unwanted creepers look exactly like the *bhakti-latā* creeper. They appear to be of the same size and the same species when they are packed together with the *bhakti-latā* creeper, but in spite of this, the creepers are called *upaśākhā.* A pure devotee can distinguish between the *bhakti-latā* creeper and a mundane creeper, and he is very alert to distinguish them and keep them separate.

TEXT 160

সেকজল পাঞা উপশাখা বাড়ি' যায় ।
স্তব্ধ হঞা মূলশাখা বাড়িতে না পায় ॥ ১৬০ ॥

seka-jala pāñā upaśākhā bāḍi' yāya
stabdha hañā mūla-śākhā bāḍite nā pāya

SYNONYMS

seka-jala—sprinkling water; *pāñā*—getting; *upaśākhā*—the unwanted creepers; *bāḍi' yāya*—grow luxuriantly; *stabdha hañā*—becoming stopped; *mūla-śākhā*—the chief creeper; *bāḍite*—to increase; *nā pāya*—is not able.

TRANSLATION

"If one does not distinguish between the bhakti-latā creeper and the other creepers, the sprinkling of water is misused because the other creepers are nourished while the bhakti-latā creeper is curtailed.

PURPORT

If one chants the Hare Kṛṣṇa *mantra* while committing offenses, these unwanted creepers will grow. One should not take advantage of chanting the Hare Kṛṣṇa *mantra* for some material profit. As mentioned in verse 159:

'niṣiddhācāra', 'kuṭīnāṭī', 'jīva-hiṁsana'
'lābha', 'pūjā', 'pratiṣṭhādi' yata upaśākhā-gaṇa

The unwanted creepers have been described by Śrīla Bhaktisiddhānta Sarasvatī Ṭhākura. He states that if one hears and chants without trying to give up offenses, one becomes materially attached to sense gratification. One may also desire freedom from material bondage like the Māyāvādīs, or one may become attached to the *yoga-siddhis* and desire wonderful yogic powers. If one is attached to wonderful material activities, one is called *siddhi-lobhī,* greedy for material perfection. One may also be victimized by diplomatic or crooked behavior, or one may associate with women for illicit sex. Others may make a show of devotional service like the *prākṛta-sahajiyās,* or one may try to support his philosophy by joining some caste or identifying himself with a certain dynasty, claiming a monopoly on spiritual advancement. Thus with the support of family tradition, one may become a pseudo *guru* or so-called spiritual master. One may become attached to the four sinful activities—illicit sex, intoxication, gambling and meat eating, or one may consider a Vaiṣṇava to belong to a mundane caste or creed. One may think, "This is a Hindu Vaiṣṇava, and this is a European Vaiṣṇava. A European Vaiṣṇava is not allowed to enter the temples." In other words, one may consider Vaiṣṇavas in terms of birth, thinking one a *brāhmaṇa* Vaiṣṇava, a *śūdra* Vaiṣṇava, a *mleccha* Vaiṣṇava and so on. One may also try to carry out a professional business while chanting the Hare Kṛṣṇa *mantra* or reading *Śrīmad-Bhāgavatam,* or one may try to increase his monetary strength by illegal means. One may also try to be a cheap Vaiṣṇava by chanting in a secluded place for material adoration, or one may desire mundane reputation by making compromises with nondevotees, compromising one's philosophy or spiritual life, or one may become a supporter of a hereditary caste system. All these are pitfalls of personal sense gratification. Just to cheat some innocent people, one makes a show of advanced spiritual life and becomes known as a *sādhu, mahātmā* or religious person. All this means that the so-called devotee has become victimized by all these unwanted creepers and that the real creeper of *bhakti-latā-bīja* has been stunted.

TEXT 161

প্রথমেই উপশাখার করয়ে ছেদন ।
তবে মূলশাখা বাড়ি' যায় বৃন্দাবন ॥ ১৬১ ॥

prathamei upaśākhāra karaye chedana
tabe mūla-śākhā bāḍi' yāya vṛndāvana

SYNONYMS

prathamei—from the very beginning; *upaśākhāra*—of the unwanted creepers; *karaye*—does; *chedana*—the cutting away; *tabe*—then only; *mūla-śākhā*—the chief creeper; *bāḍi'*—increasing; *yāya*—goes; *vṛndāvana*—to the lotus feet of Lord Śrī Kṛṣṇa in Vṛndāvana.

TRANSLATION

"As soon as an intelligent devotee sees an unwanted creeper growing beside the original creeper, he must cut it down instantly. Then the real creeper of bhakti-latā-bīja grows nicely, returns home, back to Godhead, and seeks shelter under the lotus feet of Kṛṣṇa.

PURPORT

If one is misled by unwanted creepers and is victimized, he cannot make progress back to Godhead. Rather, he remains within the material world and engages in activities having nothing to do with pure devotional service. Such a person may be elevated to the higher planetary systems, but because he remains within the material world, he is subjected to the threefold material miseries.

TEXT 162

'প্রেমফল' পাকি' পড়ে, মালী আস্বাদয়।
লতা অবলম্বি' মালী 'কল্পবৃক্ষ' পায়॥ ১৬২ ॥

'prema-phala' pāki' paḍe, mālī āsvādaya
latā avalambi' mālī 'kalpa-vṛkṣa' pāya

SYNONYMS

prema-phala—the fruit of love of God; *pāki'*—becoming mature; *paḍe*—falls down; *mālī*—the gardener; *āsvādaya*—tastes; *latā avalambi'*—taking advantage of the growing *bhakti-latā; mālī*—the gardener; *kalpa-vṛkṣa pāya*—reaches the desire tree in Goloka Vṛndāvana.

TRANSLATION

"When the fruit of devotional service becomes ripe and falls down, the gardener tastes the fruit and thus takes advantage of the creeper and reaches the desire tree of the lotus feet of Kṛṣṇa in Goloka Vṛndāvana.

TEXT 163

তাহাঁ সেই কল্পবৃক্ষের করয়ে সেবন।
সুখে প্রেমফল-রস করে আস্বাদন॥ ১৬৩ ॥

tāhāṅ sei kalpa-vṛkṣera karaye sevana
sukhe prema-phala-rasa kare āsvādana

SYNONYMS

tāhāṅ—there (in Goloka Vṛndāvana); *sei kalpa-vṛkṣera*—of the lotus feet of Kṛṣṇa, which are compared to a desire tree; *karaye sevana*—engages in the service; *sukhe*—in transcendental bliss; *prema-phala-rasa*—the juice of the fruit of devotional service; *kare*—does; *āsvādana*—tasting.

TRANSLATION

"There the devotee serves the lotus feet of the Lord, which are compared to a wish-fulfilling tree. With great bliss he tastes the juice of the fruit of love and becomes eternally happy.

PURPORT

The word *tāhāṅ* indicates that in the spiritual world one can taste the juice of the fruit of devotional service and thus become blissful.

TEXT 164

এইত পরম-ফল 'পরম-পুরুষার্থ' ।
যাঁর আগে তৃণ-তুল্য চারি পুরুষার্থ ॥ ১৬৪ ॥

eita parama-phala 'parama-puruṣārtha'
yāṅra āge tṛṇa-tulya cāri puruṣārtha

SYNONYMS

eita—this; *parama-phala*—the supreme goal of life; *parama*—supreme; *puruṣa-artha*—interest of the living being; *yāṅra āge*—in the presence of which; *tṛṇa-tulya*—very insignificant; *cāri*—four; *puruṣa-artha*—the different types of human interests.

TRANSLATION

"To taste the fruit of devotional service at Goloka Vṛndāvana is the highest perfection of life, and in the presence of such perfection, the four material perfections—religion, economic development, sense gratification and liberation—are very insignificant achievements.

PURPORT

The highest achievement attained by the *jñānīs* or impersonalists is becoming one with the Supreme, generally known as *mokṣa,* liberation. The highest achievements of the *yogīs* are the eight material perfections such as *aṇimā, laghimā* and *prāpti.* Yet these are nothing compared to the eternal bliss of the devotee who returns back to Godhead and tastes the fruit of devotional service to the lotus feet of the Lord. The material perfections up to the point of liberation are very insignificant in comparison; therefore the pure devotee is never interested in such things. His only interest is in perfecting his devotional service to the Lord. The pleasure of the impersonalist monist philosophers is condemned in the following verse, which is also found in Śrīla Rūpa Gosvāmī's *Lalita-mādhava.*

TEXT 165

ঋদ্ধা সিদ্ধিব্রজ-বিজয়িতা সত্যধর্মা সমাধি-
র্ব্রহ্মানন্দো গুরুরপি চমৎকারয়ত্যেব তাবৎ ।
যাবৎ প্রেম্ণাং মধুরিপু-বশীকার-সিদ্ধৌষধীনাং
গন্ধোঽপ্যন্তঃকরণসরণী-পান্থতাং ন প্রযাতি ॥ ১৬৫ ॥

ṛddhā siddhi-vraja-vijayitā satya-dharmā samādhir
brahmānando gurur api camatkārayaty eva tāvat
yāvat premṇāṁ madhu-ripu-vaśīkāra-siddhauṣadhīnāṁ
gandho 'py antaḥ-karaṇa-saraṇī-pānthatāṁ na prayāti

SYNONYMS

ṛddhā—excellent; *siddhi-vraja*—of the groups of material perfections of the *yogīs* (*aṇimā, laghimā, prāpti* and so on); *vijayitā*—the victory; *satya-dharmā*—the religious principles of perfection (*satya, śama, titikṣā* and so on); *samādhiḥ*—the yogic perfection of meditation; *brahma-ānandaḥ*—the spiritually blissful life of the monist; *guruḥ*—very high in material considerations; *api*—although; *camatkārayati*—they appear very important; *eva*—only; *tāvat*—that long; *yāvat*—as long as; *premṇām*—of love of Kṛṣṇa; *madhu-ripu*—of Kṛṣṇa, the enemy of the Madhu demon; *vaśīkāra*—in the controlling; *siddha-auṣadhīnām*—which is like perfect herbs that can control snakes; *gandhaḥ*—a light fragrance; *api*—even; *antaḥ-karaṇa-saraṇī-pānthatām*—a traveler on the path of the heart; *na prayāti*—does not become.

TRANSLATION

"As long as there is not the slightest fragrance of pure love of Kṛṣṇa, which is the perfected medicinal herb for controlling Lord Kṛṣṇa within the heart, the opulences of material perfection—known as the siddhis, the brahminical perfections [satya, śama, titikṣā and so on], the trance of the yogīs and the monistic bliss of Brahman—all seem wonderful for men.

PURPORT

There are different types of material perfection known as *siddhi-vraja,* brahminical qualifications, yogic trance and merging into the Supreme. All these are certainly very attractive for a mundane person, but their brilliance exists only as long as one does not take to devotional service. Devotional service can control the Supreme Personality of Godhead, who is the supreme controller of all universal affairs. The five *rasas* (mellows) in the transcendental world are practiced by the inhabitants of Goloka Vṛndāvana in neutrality, servitorship, friendship, paternal affection and conjugal love. All these please the Lord so much that He is controlled by the devotees. For instance, mother Yaśodā was so advanced in devotional service that Kṛṣṇa agreed to be controlled by her stick. In other words, the five principal mellows are so great and glorious that they are able to control the Supreme Personality of Godhead. In the material world, however, the so-called *siddhis,* or perfections, manifest their brightness only as long as one is not interested in devotional service. In other words, the perfection of the *karmīs, jñānīs, yogīs* and others remains attractive only as long as one does not come to the point of devotional service, which is so great and significant that it can control the supreme controller, Kṛṣṇa.

TEXT 166

‘শুদ্ধভক্তি’ হৈতে হয় ‘প্রেমা’ উৎপন্ন ।
অতএব শুদ্ধভক্তির কহিয়ে ‘লক্ষণ’ ॥ ১৬৬ ॥

‘śuddha-bhakti’ haite haya ‘premā’ utpanna
ataeva śuddha-bhaktira kahiye ‘lakṣaṇa’

SYNONYMS

śuddha-bhakti—pure devotional service without material contaminations; *haite*—from; *haya*—is; *premā*—love of the Supreme Personality of Godhead; *utpanna*—produced; *ataeva*—therefore; *śuddha-bhaktira*—of pure devotional service; *kahiye*—let me explain; *lakṣaṇa*—the symptoms.

TRANSLATION

"When one is situated in pure devotional service, he develops love of Godhead; therefore let me describe some of the symptoms of pure devotional service.

PURPORT

In *Bhagavad-gītā* (18.55) it is said: *bhaktyā mām abhijānāti yāvān yaś cāsmi tattvataḥ.* One cannot understand the Supreme Personality of Godhead in truth unless he takes to devotional service.

TEXT 167

অন্যাভিলাষিতা-শূন্যং জ্ঞান-কর্মাদ্যনাবৃতম্ ।
আনুকূল্যেন কৃষ্ণানুশীলনং ভক্তিরুত্তমা ॥ ১৬৭ ॥

anyābhilāṣitā-śūnyaṁ
jñāna-karmādy-anāvṛtam
ānukūlyena kṛṣṇānu-
śīlanaṁ bhaktir uttamā

SYNONYMS

anya-abhilāṣitā-śūnyam—without desires other than those for the service of Lord Kṛṣṇa, or without material desires (such as those for meat-eating, illicit sex, gambling and addiction to intoxicants); *jñāna*—by the knowledge of the philosophy of the monist Māyāvādīs;* *karma*—by fruitive activities; *ādi*—by artificially practicing detachment, by the mechanical practice of *yoga,* by studying the Sāṅkhya philosophy, and so on; *anāvṛtam*—uncovered; *ānukūlyena*— favorable; *kṛṣṇa-anuśīlanam*—cultivation of service in relationship to Kṛṣṇa; *bhaktiḥ uttamā*—first-class devotional service.

TRANSLATION

"When first-class devotional service develops, one must be devoid of all material desires, knowledge obtained by monistic philosophy, and fruitive action. The devotee must constantly serve Kṛṣṇa favorably, as Kṛṣṇa desires.

PURPORT

This verse is also found in Śrīla Rūpa Gosvāmī's *Bhakti-rasāmṛta-sindhu* (1.1.11). As we can understand from *Bhagavad-gītā* (9.34 and 18.65), the Supreme Personality of Godhead wants everyone to think of Him always (*man-manā bhava mad-bhaktaḥ*). Everyone should become His devotee, not the devotee of a demigod. Everyone should engage in devotional service or *arcana* Deity worship in the temple. *Man-manā bhava mad-bhakto mad-yājī māṁ namaskuru.* Everyone should offer obeisances, from moment to moment, to the Supreme Personality of Godhead. These are the desires of the Supreme Lord, and one who fulfills His desires favorably is actually a pure devotee. Kṛṣṇa wants everyone to surrender unto Him, and devotional service means preaching this gospel all over the world. The Lord says openly in *Bhagavad-gītā* (18.69): *na ca tasmān manuṣyeṣu kaścin me priya-kṛttamaḥ.* One should preach the gospel of *Bhagavad-gītā* for the benefit

*Here *jñāna* does not refer to perfect knowledge in devotional service. One has to learn the path of devotional service with full knowledge of the *Vedas* (*bhaktyā śruta-gṛhītayā—Bhāg.* 1.2.12).

of all. *Bhagavad-gītā* is spoken by the Lord so that human society can be perfectly organized from all angles of vision—politically, socially, economically, philosophically and religiously. From any point of view, human society can be reformed by the Kṛṣṇa consciousness movement; therefore one who spreads this philosophy of Kṛṣṇa consciousness for the benefit of all conditioned souls in the universe is perfect in pure devotional service.

The criterion is that a devotee must know what Kṛṣṇa wants him to do. This can be achieved through the medium of the spiritual master who is a bona fide representative of Kṛṣṇa. Śrīla Rūpa Gosvāmī advises, *ādau gurv-āśrayam.* One who is serious in wanting to render pure devotional service to the Lord must take shelter of the spiritual master who comes in the disciplic succession from Kṛṣṇa. *Evaṁ paramparā-prāptam imaṁ rājarṣayo viduḥ.* Without accepting a bona fide spiritual master coming in the disciplic succession, one cannot find out the real purpose of devotional service. Therefore one has to accept the shelter of a bona fide spiritual master and agree to be directed by him. The first business of a pure devotee is to satisfy his spiritual master, whose only business is to spread Kṛṣṇa consciousness. *Yasya prasādād bhagavat-prasādaḥ:* if one can satisfy the spiritual master, Kṛṣṇa is automatically satisfied. This is the success of devotional service. This is the meaning of the word *ānukūlyena*—that is, favorable devotional service to the Lord. A pure devotee has no plans other than those for the Lord's service. He is not interested in attaining success in mundane activities. He simply wants success in the progress of devotional service. For a devotee, there cannot be worship of others or demigod worship. A pure devotee does not engage himself in such pseudo-devotional service. He is interested only in satisfying Kṛṣṇa. If one lives only for the satisfaction of Kṛṣṇa, he does not have to accept this order or that order. One's only business should be to satisfy Kṛṣṇa. This process is completely manifest in the activities of the Kṛṣṇa consciousness movement. It has been actually proved that the entire world can accept devotional service without failure. One simply has to follow the instructions of the representative of Kṛṣṇa.

TEXT 168

অন্য-বাঞ্ছা, অন্য-পূজা ছাড়ি' 'জ্ঞান', 'কর্ম' ।
আনুকূল্যে সর্বেন্দ্রিয়ে কৃষ্ণানুশীলন ॥ ১৬৮ ॥

anya-vāñchā, anya-pūjā chāḍi' 'jñāna', 'karma'
ānukūlye sarvendriye kṛṣṇānuśīlana

SYNONYMS

anya-vāñchā—other desires; *anya-pūjā*—other types of worship; *chāḍi'*—giving up; *jñāna*—material knowledge; *karma*—material activities; *ānukūlye*—

favorably; *sarva-indriye*—with all the senses; *kṛṣṇa-anuśīlana*—cultivation of Kṛṣṇa consciousness.

TRANSLATION

"A pure devotee must not cherish any other desire than to serve Kṛṣṇa. He should not offer worship to the demigods or to mundane personalities. He should not cultivate artificial knowledge, which is devoid of Kṛṣṇa consciousness, and he should not engage himself in anything other than Kṛṣṇa conscious activities. One must engage all one's purified senses in the service of the Lord. This is the favorable execution of Kṛṣṇa conscious activities.

TEXT 169

এই 'শুদ্ধভক্তি'—ইহা হৈতে 'প্রেমা' হয়।
পঞ্চরাত্রে, ভাগবতে এই লক্ষণ কয় ॥ ১৬৯ ॥

ei 'śuddha-bhakti'——ihā haite 'premā' haya
pañcarātre, bhāgavate ei lakṣaṇa kaya

SYNONYMS

ei—this; *śuddha-bhakti*—pure devotional service; *ihā haite*—from which; *premā*—unalloyed love of Kṛṣṇa; *haya*—there is; *pañcarātre*—in the Vedic literature known as the *Pañcarātras; bhāgavate*—also in the *Śrīmad-Bhāgavatam; ei*—these; *lakṣaṇa*—symptoms; *kaya*—are described.

TRANSLATION

"These activities are called śuddha-bhakti, pure devotional service. If one renders such pure devotional service, he develops his original love for Kṛṣṇa in due course of time. In Vedic literatures like the Pañcarātras and Śrīmad-Bhāgavatam, these symptoms are described.

PURPORT

One has to develop his devotional service under the directions of a pure devotee, the spiritual master, and in accordance with the Vedic directions given in the *Pañcarātra* and *Bhāgavatam* systems. The *Pañcarātra* system includes methods of temple worship, and the *Bhāgavatam* system includes the spreading of Kṛṣṇa conscious philosophy through the recitation of *Śrīmad-Bhāgavatam* and the discussion of philosophy with people who are interested. Through discussion, one can create an interest and understanding of the *Pañcarātra* and *Bhāgavatam* systems.

TEXT 170

সর্বোপাধিবিনির্মুক্তং তৎপরত্বেন নির্মলম্ ।
হৃষীকেণ হৃষীকেশ-সেবনং ভক্তিরুচ্যতে ॥ ১৭০ ॥

sarvopādhi-vinirmuktaṁ
tat-paratvena nirmalam
hṛṣīkeṇa hṛṣīkeśa-
sevanaṁ bhaktir ucyate

SYNONYMS

sarva-upādhi-vinirmuktam—free from all kinds of material designations, or free from all desires except the desire to render service to the Supreme Personality of Godhead; *tat-paratvena*—by the sole purpose of serving the Supreme Personality of Godhead; *nirmalam*—uncontaminated by the effects of speculative philosophical research or fruitive activity; *hṛṣīkeṇa*—by purified senses freed from all designations; *hṛṣīkeśa*—of the master of the senses; *sevanam*—the service to satisfy the senses; *bhaktiḥ*—devotional service; *ucyate*—is called.

TRANSLATION

" 'Bhakti, or devotional service, means engaging all our senses in the service of the Lord, the Supreme Personality of Godhead, the master of all the senses. When the spirit soul renders service unto the Supreme, there are two side effects. One is freed from all material designations, and, simply by being employed in the service of the Lord, one's senses are purified.'

PURPORT

This verse quoted from the *Nārada-pañcarātra* is found in *Bhakti-rasāmṛta-sindhu* (1.1.12).

TEXT 171

মদ্‌গুণশ্রুতিমাত্রেণ ময়ি সর্বগুহাশয়ে ।
মনোগতিরবিচ্ছিন্না যথা গঙ্গাম্ভসোঽম্বুধৌ ॥ ১৭১ ॥

mad-guṇa-śruti-mātreṇa
mayi sarva-guhāśaye
manogatir avicchinnā
yathā gaṅgāmbhaso 'mbudhau

SYNONYMS

mat—of Me; *guṇa*—of the qualities; *śruti-mātreṇa*—only by hearing; *mayi*—to Me; *sarva-guhā*—in all hearts; *āśaye*—who am situated; *manaḥ-gatiḥ*—the movement of the mind; *avicchinnā*—unobstructed; *yathā*—just as; *gaṅgā-ambhasaḥ*—of the celestial waters of the Ganges; *ambudhau*—to the ocean.

TRANSLATION

" 'Just as the celestial waters of the Ganges flow unobstructed into the ocean, so when My devotees simply hear of Me, their minds come to Me. I reside in the hearts of all.

PURPORT

This verse and the following three verses quoted from *Śrīmad-Bhāgavatam* (3.29.11-14), were spoken by Lord Kṛṣṇa in the form of Kapiladeva.

TEXT 172

লক্ষণং ভক্তিযোগস্য নির্গুণস্য হ্যুদাহৃতম্ ।
অহৈতুক্যব্যবহিতা যা ভক্তিঃ পুরুষোত্তমে ॥ ১৭২ ॥

lakṣaṇaṁ bhakti-yogasya
nirguṇasya hy udāhṛtam
ahaituky avyavahitā
yā bhaktiḥ puruṣottame

SYNONYMS

lakṣaṇam—the symptom; *bhakti-yogasya*—of devotional service; *nirguṇasya*—beyond the three modes of nature; *hi*—certainly; *udāhṛtam*—is cited; *ahaitukī*—causeless; *avyavahitā*—uninterrupted; *yā*—which; *bhaktiḥ*—devotional service; *puruṣottame*—to the Supreme Personality of Godhead.

TRANSLATION

" 'These are the characteristics of transcendental loving service to Puruṣottama, the Supreme Personality of Godhead: it is causeless, and it cannot be obstructed in any way.

TEXT 173

সালোক্যসার্ষ্টিসামীপ্য-সারূপ্যৈকত্বমপ্যুত ।
দীয়মানং ন গৃহ্ণন্তি বিনা মৎসেবনং জনাঃ ॥ ১৭৩ ॥

sālokya-sārṣṭi-sāmīpya-
sārūpyaikatvam apy uta
dīyamānaṁ na gṛhṇanti
vinā mat-sevanaṁ janāḥ

SYNONYMS

sālokya—being on the same planet as Me; *sārṣṭi*—having opulence equal to Mine; *sāmīpya*—having direct association with Me; *sārūpya*—having the same form as Me; *ekatvam*—oneness with Me; *api*—even; *uta*—or; *dīyamānam*—being given; *na*—not; *gṛhṇanti*—accept; *vinā*—without; *mat-sevanam*—My service; *janāḥ*—the devotees.

TRANSLATION

" 'My devotees do not accept sāloka, sārṣṭi, sārūpya, sāmīpya or oneness with Me—even if I offer these liberations—in preference to serving Me.

TEXT 174

স এব ভক্তিযোগাখ্য আত্যন্তিক উদাহৃতঃ ।
যেনাতিব্রজ্য ত্রিগুণং মদ্ভাবায়োপপদ্যতে ॥ ১৭৪ ॥

sa eva bhakti-yogākhya
ātyantika udāhṛtaḥ
yenātivrajya triguṇaṁ
mad-bhāvāyopapadyate

SYNONYMS

saḥ—that (having the above symptoms); *eva*—certainly; *bhakti-yoga-ākhyaḥ*—called *bhakti-yoga; ātyantikaḥ*—the ultimate goal of life; *udāhṛtaḥ*—described as; *yena*—by which; *ativrajya*—transcending; *tri-guṇam*—the three modes of material nature; *mat-bhāvāya*—for direct touch with Me, the Supreme Personality of Godhead, and My nature; *upapadyate*—one becomes qualified.

TRANSLATION

" 'Bhakti-yoga, as described above, is the ultimate goal of life. By rendering devotional service to the Supreme Personality of Godhead, one transcends the modes of material nature and attains the spiritual position on the platform of direct devotional service.'

TEXT 175

ভুক্তি-মুক্তি আদি-বাঞ্ছা যদি মনে হয় ।
সাধন করিলে প্রেম উৎপন্ন না হয় ॥ ১৭৫ ॥

bhukti-mukti ādi-vāñchā yadi mane haya
sādhana karile prema utpanna nā haya

SYNONYMS

bhukti—material enjoyment; *mukti*—to become liberated from material bondage; *ādi*—and so on; *vāñchā*—desires; *yadi*—if; *mane*—in the mind; *haya*—are; *sādhana karile*—even executing devotional service according to the regulative routine; *prema*—real love of Kṛṣṇa; *utpanna*—awakened; *nā*—not; *haya*—is.

TRANSLATION

"If one is infected with the desire for material enjoyment or material liberation, he cannot rise to the platform of pure loving service unto the Lord, even though he may superficially render devotional service according to the routine regulative principles.

PURPORT

Śrīla Bhaktisiddhānta Sarasvatī Ṭhākura mentions that if one maintains within his heart the desire to enjoy the result of good work, or, being embarrassed by the material world, the desire to get out of material entanglement, one will never be able to attain the transcendental mellows of devotional service. In other words, one must not desire material profit when rendering devotional service. Even if one follows all the sixty-four regulative principles, he cannot attain pure devotional service with a contaminated heart.

TEXT 176

ভুক্তি-মুক্তি-স্পৃহা যাবৎ পিশাচী হৃদি বর্ততে।
তাবদ্ভক্তিসুখস্যাত্র কথমভ্যুদয়ো ভবেৎ ॥ ১৭৬ ॥

bhukti-mukti-spṛhā yāvat
piśācī hṛdi vartate
tāvad bhakti-sukhasyātra
katham abhyudayo bhavet

SYNONYMS

bhukti—for material enjoyment; *mukti*—and for liberation from material existence; *spṛhā*—desire; *yāvat*—as long as; *piśācī*—the witches; *hṛdi*—within the heart; *vartate*—remain; *tāvat*—that long; *bhakti*—of devotional service; *sukhasya*—of the happiness; *atra*—here; *katham*—how; *abhyudayaḥ*—awakening; *bhavet*—can there be.

TRANSLATION

"The material desire to enjoy the material world and the desire to become liberated from material bondage are considered to be two witches, and they haunt one like ghosts. As long as these witches remain within the heart, how can one feel transcendental bliss? As long as these two witches remain in the heart, there is no possibility of enjoying the transcendental bliss of devotional service.

PURPORT

This verse is found in *Bhakti-rasāmṛta-sindhu* (1.2.22).

TEXT 177

সাধনভক্তি হৈতে হয় 'রতি'র উদয়।
রতি গাঢ় হৈলে তার 'প্রেম' নাম কয়॥ ১৭৭॥

sādhana-bhakti haite haya 'rati'ra udaya
rati gāḍha haile tāra 'prema' nāma kaya

SYNONYMS

sādhana-bhakti—the process of regularly rendering devotional service; *haite*—from; *haya*—there is; *ratira*—of attachment; *udaya*—the awakening; *rati*—such attachment; *gāḍha haile*—becoming thick; *tāra*—of this; *prema*—love of Godhead; *nāma*—the name; *kaya*—is said.

TRANSLATION

"By regularly rendering devotional service, one gradually becomes attached to the Supreme Personality of Godhead. When that attachment is intensified, it becomes love of Godhead.

PURPORT

Bhakti-rasāmṛta-sindhu (1.2.2) gives the following information about *sādhana-bhakti:*

kṛti-sādhyā bhavet sādhya-
bhāvā sā sādhanābhidhā
nitya-siddhasya bhāvasya
prākaṭyaṁ hṛdi sādhyatā

The process of devotional service—beginning with chanting and hearing—is called *sādhana-bhakti.* This includes the regulative principles that are intended to awaken one to devotional service. Devotional service is always dormant in everyone's heart, and by the offenseless chanting of the holy names of the Lord, one's original dormant Kṛṣṇa consciousness is awakened. This awakening to Kṛṣṇa consciousness is the beginning of *sādhana-bhakti.* This can be divided into many different parts, including faith, association with devotees, initiation by the spiritual master, engagement in devotional service under the instructions of a spiritual master, steadiness in devotional service and the awakening of a taste for devotional service. In this way, one can become attached to Kṛṣṇa and His service, and when this attachment is intensified, it results in ecstatic love for Kṛṣṇa. The word *rati* is explained in the *Bhakti-rasāmṛta-sindhu* (1.3.41) as follows:

vyaktaṁ masṛṇatevāntar-
lakṣyate rati-lakṣaṇam
mumukṣu-prabhṛtīnāṁ ced
bhaved eṣā ratir na hi

"When a tenderness of the heart is manifest, there is *rati,* or attachment. Those who are interested in being liberated from material bondage must manifest this tenderness called *rati.*" This attachment is not like material attachment. When one is liberated from material contamination, the awakening of attachment for Kṛṣṇa's service is called *rati.* In the material world there is attachment for material enjoyment, but this is not *rati.* Transcendental *rati* can be awakened only on the spiritual platform. Ecstatic love for Kṛṣṇa (*prema*) is described in the *Bhakti-rasāmṛta-sindhu* (1.41) as follows:

samyaṅ masṛṇita-svānto
mamatvātiśayāṅkitaḥ
bhāvaḥ sa eva sāndrātmā
budhaiḥ premā nigadyate

"When the heart is completely softened and devoid of all material desires and when one's emotional feelings become very strong, one becomes very much attached to Kṛṣṇa. Such purified emotion is known as pure love."

TEXT 178

প্রেম বৃদ্ধিক্রমে নাম –স্নেহ,.মান, প্রণয় ।
রাগ, অনুরাগ, ভাব, মহাভাব হয় ॥ ১৭৮ ॥

prema vṛddhi-krame nāma——sneha, māna, praṇaya
rāga, anurāga, bhāva, mahābhāva haya

SYNONYMS

prema—ecstatic love for God; *vṛddhi-krame*—in terms of progressive increase; *nāma*—named; *sneha*—affection; *māna*—abhorrence; *praṇaya*—love; *rāga*—attachment; *anurāga*—further attachment; *bhāva*—ecstasy; *mahā-bhāva*—great ecstasy; *haya*—are.

TRANSLATION

"The basic aspects of prema, when gradually increasing to different states, are affection, abhorrence, love, attachment, further attachment, ecstasy and great ecstasy.

PURPORT

In *Bhakti-rasāmṛta-sindhu,* (3.2.84) *sneha* (affection) is described as follows:

sāndraś citta-dravaṁ kurvan
premā 'sneha' itīryate
kṣaṇikasyāpi neha syād
viśleṣasya sahiṣṇutā

"That aspect of *prema* in which the melting of the heart for the lover is concentrated is called *sneha,* or affection. The symptom of such affection is that the lover cannot for a moment remain without the association of the beloved." A description of *māna* can be found in *Madhya-līlā* (Chapter Two, verse 66). Similarly, a description of *praṇaya* is also there. As far as *rāga* is concerned, *Bhakti-rasāmṛta-sindhu* says (3.2.87) says:

snehaḥ sa rāgo yena syāt
sukhaṁ duḥkham api sphuṭam
tat-sambandha-lave 'py atra
prītiḥ prāṇa-vyayair api

"That stage at which affection for the beloved converts unhappiness into happiness is called *rāga,* or attachment. When one has such attachment for Kṛṣṇa, he can give up his own life to satisfy his beloved Kṛṣṇa." *Anurāga, bhāva* and *mahābhāva* are described in the Sixth Chapter of *Madhya-līlā,* verse 13. The purport to that verse explains *adhirūḍha-mahābhāva.*

TEXT 179

যৈছে বীজ, ইক্ষু, রস, গুড়, খণ্ড-সার।
শর্করা, সিতা, মিছরি, উত্তম-মিছরি আর ॥ ১৭৯ ॥

yaiche bīja, ikṣu, rasa, guḍa, khaṇḍa-sāra
śarkarā, sitā, michari, uttama-michari āra

SYNONYMS

yaiche—just like; *bīja*—the seed; *ikṣu*—the sugarcane plant; *rasa*—the juice; *guḍa*—molasses; *khaṇḍa-sāra*—dry molasses; *śarkarā*—sugar; *sitā*—candy; *michari*—rock candy; *uttama-michari*—lozenges; *āra*—and.

TRANSLATION

"The gradual development of love may be compared to different states of sugar. First there is the seed of the sugarcane, then sugarcane and then the juice extracted from the cane. When this juice is boiled, it forms a liquid molasses, then a solid molasses, then sugar, candy, rock candy and finally lozenges.

TEXT 180

এই সব কৃষ্ণভক্তি-রসের স্থায়িভাব ।
স্থায়িভাবে মিলে যদি বিভাব, অনুভাব ॥ ১৮০ ॥

ei saba kṛṣṇa-bhakti-rasera sthāyibhāva
sthāyibhāve mile yadi vibhāva, anubhāva

SYNONYMS

ei saba—all these; *kṛṣṇa-bhakti*—of devotional service to Kṛṣṇa; *rasera*—of the mellows; *sthāyi-bhāva*—continuous existence; *sthāyi-bhāve*—in this continuous existence; *mile*—one meets; *yadi*—if; *vibhāva*—special ecstasy; *anubhāva*—subecstasy.

TRANSLATION

"All these stages combined are called sthāyibhāva, or continuous love of Godhead in devotional service. In addition to these stages, there are vibhāva and anubhāva.

PURPORT

Attachment for Kṛṣṇa never wanes; it increases more and more as one attains different stages. All the stages together are called *sthāyibhāva,* or continuous existence. The nine forms of devotional service are *śravaṇaṁ kīrtanaṁ viṣṇoḥ smaraṇaṁ pāda-sevanam arcanaṁ vandanaṁ dāsyaṁ sakhyam ātma-nivedanam.* When continuous love of Godhead is mixed with the processes of devotional service, it is called *vibhāva, anubhāva, sāttvika* and *vyabhicārī*. The devotee thus enjoys a variety of transcendental bliss. In his *Amṛta-pravāha-bhāṣya,* Śrīla Bhaktivinoda Ṭhākura states that *anubhāva* can be divided into thirteen categories: (1) dancing, (2) rolling on the ground, (3) singing, (4) yelling, (5) jumping, (6) making loud noises, (7) yawning, (8) heavy breathing, (9) not caring for public opinion, (10) discharging saliva, (11) roaring laughter, (12) unsteadiness and (13) hiccupping. These are the symptoms of *anubhāva*. Thus the transcendental mellows are experienced in different stages. Similarly, there are many other forms of expression that have been analytically studied by the Gosvāmīs. In *Bhakti-rasāmṛta-sindhu,* Rūpa Gosvāmī gives each and every symptom a particular name.

TEXT 181

সাত্ত্বিক-ব্যভিচারি-ভাবের মিলনে ।
কৃষ্ণভক্তি-রস হয় অমৃত আস্বাদনে ॥ ১৮১ ॥

sāttvika-vyabhicāri-bhāvera milane
kṛṣṇa-bhakti-rasa haya amṛta āsvādane

SYNONYMS

sāttvika-vyabhicāri-bhāvera—of *sāttvika* and *vyabhicārī* with *sthāyibhāva; milane*—by mixing; *kṛṣṇa-bhakti-rasa*—the transcendental mellows of devotional service to the Lord; *haya*—become; *amṛta*—nectarean; *āsvādane*—in tasting.

TRANSLATION

"When the higher standard of ecstatic love is mixed with the symptoms of sāttvika and vyabhicārī, the devotee relishes the transcendental bliss of loving Kṛṣṇa in a variety of nectarean tastes.

TEXT 182

যৈছে দধি, সিতা, ঘৃত, মরীচ, কর্পূর ।
মিলনে 'রসালা' হয় অমৃত মধুর ॥ ১৮২ ॥

yaiche dadhi, sitā, ghṛta, marīca, karpūra
milane 'rasālā' haya amṛta madhura

SYNONYMS

yaiche—just as; *dadhi*—yogurt; *sitā*—sugar candy; *ghṛta*—clarified butter; *marīca*—black pepper; *karpūra*—camphor; *milane*—in mixing together; *rasālā*—very tasteful; *haya*—becomes; *amṛta*—nectarean; *madhura*—and sweet.

TRANSLATION

"These tastes are like a combination of yogurt, sugar candy, ghee [clarified butter], black pepper and camphor and are as palatable as sweet nectar.

TEXTS 183-184

ভক্তভেদে রতি-ভেদ পঞ্চ পরকার ।
শান্তরতি, দাস্যরতি, সখ্যরতি আর ॥ ১৮৩ ॥
বাৎসল্যরতি, মধুররতি,—এ পঞ্চ বিভেদ ।
রতিভেদে কৃষ্ণভক্তিরসে পঞ্চ ভেদ ॥ ১৮৪ ॥

bhakta-bhede rati-bheda pañca parakāra
śānta-rati, dāsya-rati, sakhya-rati āra

vātsalya-rati, madhura-rati,——ei pañca vibheda
rati-bhede kṛṣṇa-bhakti-rase pañca bheda

SYNONYMS

bhakta-bhede—according to varieties of devotees; *rati-bheda*—the different attachments; *pañca parakāra*—five categories; *śānti-rati*—neutral appreciation; *dāsya-rati*—attachment in a service attitude; *sakhya-rati*—attachment by friendly appreciation; *āra*—also; *vātsalya-rati*—attachment by paternal affection; *madhura-rati*—attachment by conjugal love; *ei*—these; *pañca*—five; *vibheda*—divisions; *rati-bhede*—by attachment on different platforms; *kṛṣṇa-bhakti-rase*—in mellows derived from devotional service to Kṛṣṇa; *pañca*—five; *bheda*—varieties.

TRANSLATION

"According to the devotee, attachment falls within the five categories of śānta-rati, dāsya-rati, sakhya-rati, vātsalya-rati and madhura-rati. These five categories arise from the devotees' different attachments to the Supreme Personality of Godhead. The transcendental mellows derived from devotional service are also of five varieties.

PURPORT

Śānta-rati is described in *Bhakti-rasāmṛta-sindhu* (2.5.16, 17, 18) as follows:

mānase nirvikalpatvaṁ
śama ity abhidhīyate

"When one is completely free from all doubts and material attachments, he attains the neutral position called *śānta.*".

vihāya viṣayonmukhyaṁ
nijānanda-sthitir yataḥ
ātmanaḥ kathyate so 'tra
svabhāvaḥ śama ity asau

prāyaḥ śama-pradhānanāṁ
mamatā-gandha-varjitā
paramātmatayā kṛṣṇe
jātā śānta-ratir matā

The *śānta-rati* realization of Kṛṣṇa is in the neutral stage between the conception of impersonalism and personalism. This means that one is not very strongly attached to the personal feature of the Lord. An appreciation of the greatness of the Lord is called *śānta-rati.* This is attachment not to the personal feature but to the impersonal feature. Generally, one in this stage is attached to the Paramātmā feature of the Supreme Personality of Godhead.

īśvaraḥ sarva-bhūtānāṁ
hṛd-deśe 'rjuna tiṣṭhati
bhrāmayan sarva-bhūtāni
yantrārūḍhāni māyayā

"The Supreme Lord is situated in everyone's heart, O Arjuna, and is directing the wanderings of all living entities, who are seated as on a machine, made of the material energy." (Bg. 18.61)

On the strength of this statement from *Bhagavad-gītā,* we can understand that in the *śānta-rasa,* a devotee sees the Lord's representation everywhere. *Dāsya-rati* is explained in the *Bhakti-rasāmṛta-sindhu* (2.5.27) thus:

svasmād bhavanti ye nyūnās
te 'nugrāhyā harer matāḥ
ārādhyatvātmikā teṣāṁ
ratiḥ prītir itīritā
tatrāsaktikṛd anyatra
prīti-saṁhāriṇī hy asau

When the Supreme Lord in His localized aspect is appreciated and a great devotee understands his subordinate position, not only does he surrender to the Supreme Personality of Godhead, but, due to his subordinate position, he wishes to render some service and thus become favored by the Supreme Personality of Godhead. A devotee in the *śānta-rati* is not very much willing to render service to the Lord, but a devotee in the *dāsya-rati* voluntarily wants to render service. Due to this attitude, the devotee in the *dāsya-rati* realizes the Supreme Personality of Godhead more fully than a devotee in the *śānta-rati.* He considers the Lord to be a worshipable object, and this means that his attachment for the Lord increases. On the *dāsya-rati* platform a devotee is attached to rendering service to the Lord, and he is detached from material activities. The *śānta-rati* is neither material nor spiritual, but the *dāsya-rati* is actually on the spiritual platform. There is no attachment for material things on the spiritual platform. A devotee in *dāsya-rati* has no attachment for anything but Kṛṣṇa's service.

Sakhya-rati is described in *Bhakti-rasāmṛta-sindhu* (2.5.30) as follows:

ye syus tulyā mukundasya
te sakhāyaḥ satāṁ matāḥ
sāmyād viśrambha-rūpaiṣāṁ
ratiḥ sakhyam ihocyate

According to the opinion of advanced devotees and learned scholars, a devotee in *sakhya-rati* feels equal to the Supreme Personality of Godhead. This is a relationship in friendship. Due to having a friendly relationship with the Lord, not only is one free from material attachment, but one believes in equal dealings with the Supreme Personality of Godhead. This is called *sakhya-rati.* The *sakhya-rati* devotee is so advanced that he treats the Lord on an equal level and even exchanges joking words. Although one is never equal to the Supreme Personality of Godhead, the *sakhya-rati* devotee feels equal to the Lord, and he does not feel guilty because of this. Actually it is offensive to consider oneself equal to the Lord. The Māyāvādīs consider themselves equal to the Lord, but such feelings entail bereavement because they are material. The *sakhya-rati,* however, is a feeling experienced in the mind by a pure devotee, and he is eternally related with the Supreme Personality of Godhead in that feeling.

Vātsalya-rati is described as follows in the *Bhakti-rasāmṛta-sindhu* (2.5.33):

guravo ye harer asya
te pūjyā iti viśrutāḥ
anugrahamayī teṣāṁ
ratir vātsalyam ucyate
idaṁ lālana-bhavyāśīś
cibuka-sparśanādi-kṛt

When a living entity is situated on the platform of *vātsalya-rati,* he thinks of the Supreme Personality of Godhead in His childhood feature. In this feature, the Lord has to be protected by the devotee, and at this time the devotee takes the position of being worshiped by the Supreme Personality of Godhead. The feelings of paternal love are called *vātsalya-rati.* When the devotee is situated on this platform, he wants to maintain the Lord like a son, and he desires all good fortune for the Lord. He offers blessings to the Lord by touching His feet and head.

Madhura-rati, or attachment in conjugal love, is described as follows:

mitho harer mṛgākṣyāś ca
sambhogasyādi-kāraṇam
madhurāpara-paryāyā
priyatākhyoditā ratiḥ
asyāṁ kaṭākṣa-bhrūkṣepa-
priya-vāṇī-smitādayaḥ

The conjugal relationship is experienced between the Supreme Personality of Godhead and the young damsels of Vrajabhūmi, and due to their conjugal love they continuously exist in eight kinds of remembrances called *madhura-rati.* This intimate relationship brought about by conjugal love produces movements of the eyebrows, glancing, sweet words and exchanges of joking words.

TEXT 185

শান্ত, দাস্য, সখ্য, বাৎসল্য, মধুর-রস নাম ।
কৃষ্ণভক্তি-রস-মধ্যে এ পঞ্চ প্রধান ॥ ১৮৫ ॥

śānta, dāsya, sakhya, vātsalya, madhura-rasa nāma
kṛṣṇa-bhakti-rasa-madhye e pañca pradhāna

SYNONYMS

śānta—neutrality; *dāsya*—servitude; *sakhya*—friendship; *vātsalya*—paternal affection; *madhura-rasa*—conjugal love; *nāma*—different names; *kṛṣṇa-bhakti*—of devotional service to the Supreme Personality of Godhead; *rasa*—the mellows; *madhye*—among; *e*—these; *pañca*—five; *pradhāna*—chief.

TRANSLATION

"The chief transcendental mellows experienced with the Supreme Personality of Godhead are five—śānta, dāsya, sakhya, vātsalya and madhura.

TEXT 186

হাস্যোঽদ্ভুতস্তথা বীরঃ করুণো রৌদ্র ইত্যপি ।
ভয়ানকঃ স বীভৎস ইতি গৌণশ্চ সপ্তধা ॥ ১৮৬ ॥

hāsyo 'dbhutas tathā vīraḥ
karuṇo raudra ity api
bhayānakaḥ sa bībhatsa
iti gauṇaś ca saptadhā

SYNONYMS

hāsyaḥ—laughter; *adbhutaḥ*—wonder; *tathā*—then; *vīraḥ*—chivalry; *karuṇaḥ*—compassion; *raudraḥ*—anger; *iti*—thus; *api*—also; *bhayānakaḥ*—fear; *saḥ*—that; *bībhatsaḥ*—disaster; *iti*—thus; *gauṇaḥ*—indirect; *ca*—also; *sapta-dhā*—seven kinds.

TRANSLATION

"Besides the five direct mellows, there are seven indirect mellows, known as laughter, wonder, chivalry, compassion, anger, disaster and fear.

PURPORT

This verse is found in *Bhakti-rasāmṛta-sindhu* (2.5.116).

TEXT 187

হাস্য, অদ্ভুত, বীর, করুণ, রৌদ্র, বীভৎস, ভয় ।
পঞ্চবিধ-ভক্তে গৌণ সপ্তরস হয় ॥ ১৮৭ ॥

hāsya, adbhuta, vīra, karuṇa, raudra, bībhatsa, bhaya
pañca-vidha-bhakte gauṇa sapta-rasa haya

SYNONYMS

hāsya—laughter; *adbhuta*—wonder; *vīra*—chivalry; *karuṇa*—pathetic feeling; *raudra*—anger; *bībhatsa*—disaster; *bhaya*—fearfulness; *pañca-vidha-bhakte*—in five kinds of devotees; *gauṇa*—indirect; *sapta-rasa*—seven kinds of mellows; *haya*—there are.

TRANSLATION

"In addition to the five direct mellows, there are seven indirect mellows, known as laughter, wonder, chivalry, compassion, anger, disaster and fear.

PURPORT

Śānta-bhakti-rasa is described in *Bhakti-rasāmṛta-sindhu* (3.1.4, 5, 6) as follows:

vakṣyamāṇair vibhāvādyaiḥ
śamināṁ svādyatāṁ gataḥ
sthāyī śānti-ratir dhīraiḥ
śānta-bhakti-rasaḥ smṛtaḥ

prāyaḥ svasukha-jātīyaṁ
sukhaṁ syād atra yogināṁ
kintv ātma-saukhyam aghanaṁ
ghanaṁ tv īśam ayaṁ sukham
tatrāpīśa-svarūpānubhavasyaivoru-hetutā
dāsādi-van-mano-jñatva-līlāder na tathā matā

When *śānta-rati* (neutral attraction) is continuously existent and mixed with ecstatic emotion, and when the devotee relishes that neutral position, it is called *śānta-bhakti-rasa. Śānta-bhakti-rasa* devotees generally relish the impersonal feature of the Supreme Personality of Godhead. Since their taste of transcendental bliss is incomplete, it is called *aghana,* or not concentrated. A comparison is made between ordinary milk and concentrated milk. When the same devotee goes beyond the impersonal and tastes the service of the Supreme Personality of Godhead in His original form as *sac-cid-ānanda-vigraha,* the taste is called concentrated (*ghana*) transcendental bliss. Sometimes the devotees in the *śānta-rasa* relish transcendental bliss after meeting the Supreme Personality of Godhead, but this is not comparable to the transcendental bliss relished by the devotees situated in *dāsya-rasa,* the transcendental mellow in which one renders service to the Supreme Personality of Godhead.

Dāsya-rasa, or *dāsya-bhakti-rasa,* is described in *Bhakti-rasāmṛta-sindhu* (3.2.4,5) as follows:

ātmocitair vibhāvādyaiḥ
prītir āsvādanīyatām
nītā cetasi bhaktānāṁ
prīti-bhakti-raso mataḥ

anugrāhyasya dāsatvāl
lālyatvād apy ayaṁ dvidhā
bhidyate sambhrama-prīto
gaurava-prīta ity api

When according to the desires of the spirit soul the living entity develops love for the Supreme Personality of Godhead, this beginning of love is called *dāsya-bhakti-rasa. Dāsya-bhakti-rasa* is divided into two categories called *sambhrama-dāsya* and *gaurava-dāsya.* In the *sambhrama-dāsya,* the devotee renders respectful service to the Supreme Personality of Godhead, but in the more advanced *gaurava-dāsya,* his service takes the form of giving protection to the Lord.

Sakhya-bhakti-rasa is described as follows in *Bhakti-rasāmṛta sindhu* (3.3.1):

sthāyibhāvo vibhāvādyaiḥ
sakhyam ātmocitair iha

nītaś citte satāṁ puṣṭiṁ
rasaḥ preyānudīryate

"According to one's original consciousness, ecstatic emotions are exhibited as continuously existing in eternity. When this stage of Kṛṣṇa consciousness is mature, it is called *preyo-rasa* or *sakhya-bhakti-rasa.*"

Vātsalya-bhakti-rasa is described in *Bhakti-rasāmṛta-sindhu* (3.4.1) as follows:

vibhāvādyais tu vātsalyaṁ
sthāyī puṣṭim upāgataḥ
eṣa vatsala-nāmātra
prokto bhakti-raso budhaiḥ

"When eternally existing love of Godhead transforms into paternal love and is mixed with corresponding emotions, that stage of spiritual existence is described by learned devotees as *vātsalya-bhakti-rasa.*"

Madhura-bhakti-rasa is described in *Bhakti-rasāmṛta-sindhu* (3.5.1) as follows:

ātmocitair vibhāvādyaiḥ
puṣṭiṁ nītā satāṁ hṛdi
madhurākhyo bhaved bhaktir
aso 'sau madhurā ratiḥ

"If in accordance with one's own natural development in Kṛṣṇa consciousness one's attraction leans toward conjugal love within the heart, that is called attachment in conjugal love, or *madhura-rasa.*"

Similarly, *hāsya, adbhuta, vīra, karuṇa, raudra, bhaya* and *bībhatsa*—the seven indirect mellows—are explained in *Bhakti-rasāmṛta-sindhu.* The *hāsya-bhakti-rasa,* laughing devotion, is explained as follows (B.r.s. 4.1.6):

vakṣyamāṇair vibhāvādyaiḥ
puṣṭiṁ hāsa-ratir gatā
hāsya-bhakti-raso nāma
budhair eṣa nigadyate

"When through devotional service a laughing attachment to Kṛṣṇa is developed, it is called *hāsya-bhakti-rasa* by learned scholars."

Similarly, *adbhuta-rasa* is described in *Bhakti-rasāmṛta-sindhu* (4.2.1):

ātmocitair vibhāvādyaiḥ
svādyatvaṁ bhakta-cetasi
sā vismaya-ratir nītād-
bhuto-bhakti-raso bhavet

"When one's general attachment is fixed in wonder, it is called *adbhuta-bhakti-rasa.*"

Vīra-bhakti-rasa is described (B.r.s. 4.3.1):

saivotsāha-ratiḥ sthāyī
vibhāvādyair nijocitaḥ
ānīyamānā svādyatvaṁ
vīra-bhakti-raso bhavet
yuddha-dāna-dayā-dharmaiś
caturdhā-vīra ucyate

"When attachment to Kṛṣṇa mixes with the bellicose tendency, the charitable tendency or the merciful tendency in the heart of the devotee, such devotion is called *vīra-bhakti-rasa.*"

Karuṇa-bhakti-rasa is described as follows (B.r.s. 4.4.1):

ātmocitair vibhāvādyair
nītā puṣṭiṁ satāṁ hṛdi
bhavec choka-ratir bhakti-
raso hi karuṇābhidhaḥ

"When one's devotional attitude and attachment for Kṛṣṇa is mixed with lamentation, it is called *karuṇa-bhakti-rasa.*"

Similarly, *raudra-bhakti-rasa* is described as follows (B.r.s. 4.5.1):

nītā krodha-ratiḥ puṣṭiṁ
vibhāvādyair nijocitaiḥ
hṛdi bhakta-janasyāsau
raudra-bhakti-raso bhavet

"When devotion is mixed with anger in the heart of the devotee, the taste is called *raudra-bhakti-rasa.*"

Bhayānaka-bhakti-rasa is described as follows (B.r.s. 4.6.1):

vakṣyamāṇair vibhāvādyaiḥ
puṣṭiṁ bhaya-ratir gatā
bhayānakābhidho bhakti-
raso dhīrair udīryate

"When devotion is mixed with fear, it is called *bhayānaka-bhakti-rasa.*"

Bībhatsa-bhakti-rasa is described as follows (B.r.s. 4.7.1):

puṣṭiṁ nija-vibhāvādyair
jugupsā-ratir āgatā
asau bhakti-raso dhīrair
bībhatsākhya itīryate

"When one's attachment for Kṛṣṇa develops in an abominable way, and the devotee enjoys it, that is called *bībhatsa-bhakti-rasa.*"

In conclusion, when a pure devotee is situated in any of the five principal mellows (*śānta, dāsya, sakhya, vātsalya* and *madhura*), and the mellow is mixed with the seven indirect *bhakti-rasas* (*hāsya, adbhuta, vīra, karuṇa, raudra, bhayānaka* and *bībhatsa*), the indirect mellows become prominent.

TEXT 188

পঞ্চরস 'স্থায়ী' ব্যাপী রহে ভক্ত-মনে ।
সপ্ত গৌণ 'আগন্তুক' পাইয়ে কারণে ॥ ১৮৮ ॥

pañca-rasa 'sthāyī' vyāpī rahe bhakta-mane
sapta gauṇa 'āgantuka' pāiye kāraṇe

SYNONYMS

pañca-rasa—five direct transcendental mellows; *sthāyī*—permanently existing; *vyāpī*—expanded; *rahe*—remain situated; *bhakta-mane*—in the heart of a devotee; *sapta gauṇa*—seven indirect mellows; *āgantuka*—accidental; *pāiye*—appearing; *kāraṇe*—under certain conditions.

TRANSLATION

"The five direct transcendental mellows of devotional service are permanently situated in the heart of the devotee, whereas the seven indirect emotions appear suddenly under certain conditions and appear more powerful.

TEXT 189

শান্তভক্ত – নব-যোগেন্দ্র, সনকাদি আর ।
দাস্যভাব-ভক্ত—সর্বত্র সেবক অপার ॥ ১৮৯ ॥

śānta-bhakta——nava-yogendra, sanakādi āra
dāsya-bhāva-bhakta——sarvatra sevaka apāra

SYNONYMS

śānta-bhakta—the neutral devotees; *nava*—nine; *yogendra*—saintly persons; *sanaka-ādi āra*—and the four Kumāras, headed by Sanaka; *dāsya-bhāva-bhakta*—

devotees in *dāsya-rasa; sarvatra sevaka apāra*—similar innumerable servants everywhere.

TRANSLATION

"Examples of śānta-bhaktas are the nine Yogendras and the four Kumāras. Examples of devotees in dāsya-bhakti are innumerable, for such devotees exist everywhere.

PURPORT

The nine Yogendras are Kavi, Havi, Antarīkṣa, Prabuddha, Pippalāyana, Āvirhotra, Draviḍa (Drumila), Camasa and Karabhājana. The four Kumāras are Sanaka, Sanandana, Sanat-kumāra and Sanātana. The servant devotees in Gokula are Raktaka, Citraka, Patraka and so on. In Dvārakā there are servants like Dāruka, and in the Lord's pastimes in the material world there are servants like Hanumān.

TEXT 190

সখ্য-ভক্ত—শ্রীদামাদি, পুরে ভীমার্জুন ।
বাৎসল্য-ভক্ত—মাতা পিতা, যত গুরুজন ॥ ১৯০ ॥

sakhya-bhakta——śrīdāmādi, pure bhīmārjuna
vātsalya-bhakta——mātā pitā, yata guru-jana

SYNONYMS

sakhya-bhakta—devotees in fraternity; *śrīdāmā-ādi*—of Śrīdāmā and others; *pure*—in Dvārakā; *bhīma-arjuna*—Bhīma and Arjuna; *vātsalya-bhakta*—devotees in parental love; *mātā pitā*—the mother and father; *yata guru-jana*—all other similarly superior persons.

TRANSLATION

"In Vṛndāvana, examples of devotees in fraternity are Śrīdāmā and Sudāmā; in Dvārakā the Lord's friends are Bhīma and Arjuna; in Vṛndāvana the devotees in parental love are mother Yaśodā and father Nanda Mahārāja, and in Dvārakā the Lord's parents are Vasudeva and Devakī. There are also other superior persons who are devotees in parental love.

TEXT 191

মধুর-রসে ভক্তমুখ্য—ব্রজে গোপীগণ ।
মহিষীগণ, লক্ষ্মীগণ, অসংখ্য গণন ॥ ১৯১ ॥

madhura-rase bhakta-mukhya——vraje gopī-gaṇa
mahiṣī-gaṇa, lakṣmī-gaṇa, asaṅkhya gaṇana

SYNONYMS

madhura-rase—in the mellow of conjugal love; *bhakta-mukhya*—the chief devotees; *vraje*—in Vṛndāvana; *gopī-gaṇa*—the *gopīs; mahiṣī-gaṇa*—the queens in Dvārakā; *lakṣmī-gaṇa*—the goddesses of fortune in Vaikuṇṭha; *asaṅkhya gaṇana*—of innumerable reckoning.

TRANSLATION

"The chief devotees in conjugal love are the gopīs in Vṛndāvana, the queens in Dvārakā and the goddesses of fortune in Vaikuṇṭha. These devotees are innumerable.

TEXT 192

পুনঃ কৃষ্ণরতি হয় দুইত প্রকার ।
ঐশ্বর্যজ্ঞানমিশ্রা, কেবলা-ভেদ আর ॥ ১৯২ ॥

punaḥ kṛṣṇa-rati haya duita prakāra
aiśvarya-jñāna-miśrā, kevalā-bheda āra

SYNONYMS

punaḥ—again; *kṛṣṇa-rati*—attachment for Kṛṣṇa; *haya*—becomes; *duita*—twofold; *prakāra*—varieties; *aiśvarya-jñāna-miśrā*—knowledge of Kṛṣṇa mixed with a reverential attitude; *kevalā*—pure attachment; *bheda*—division; *āra*—other.

TRANSLATION

"Attachment for Kṛṣṇa is divided into two categories. One is attachment with awe and reverence, and the other is pure attachment without reverence.

TEXT 193

গোকুলে 'কেবলা' রতি ঐশ্বর্যজ্ঞানহীন ।
পুরীদ্বয়ে, বৈকুণ্ঠাদ্যে ঐশ্বর্য-প্রবীণ ॥ ১৯৩ ॥

gokule 'kevalā' rati——aiśvarya-jñāna-hīna
purī-dvaye, vaikuṇṭhādye——aiśvarya-pravīṇa

SYNONYMS

gokule—in Gokula Vṛndāvana; *kevalā rati*—flawless attachment; *aiśvarya-jñāna-hīna*—without reverential considerations; *purī-dvaye*—in two *purīs,* namely Mathurā Purī and Dvārakā Purī; *vaikuṇṭha-ādye*—in the Vaikuṇṭha planets; *aiśvarya-pravīṇa*—prominence of awe and reverence.

TRANSLATION

"Pure attachment without reverence is found in Goloka Vṛndāvana. Attachment in which awe and reverence are prominent is found in the two cities Mathurā and Dvārakā and in Vaikuṇṭha.

TEXT 194

ঐশ্বর্যজ্ঞানপ্রাধান্যে সঙ্কুচিত প্রীতি ।
দেখিয়া না মানে ঐশ্বর্য—কেবলার রীতি ॥ ১৯৪ ॥

aiśvarya-jñāna-prādhānye saṅkucita prīti
dekhiyā nā māne aiśvarya——kevalāra rīti

SYNONYMS

aiśvarya-jñāna-prādhānye—in the predominance of awe and veneration; *saṅkucita*—crippled; *prīti*—love; *dekhiyā*—seeing; *nā māne*—does not care; *aiśvarya*—opulence; *kevalāra rīti*—that is the symptom of pure devotional service.

TRANSLATION

"When opulence is very prominent, love of Godhead is somewhat crippled. According to kevalā devotion, however, even though the devotee sees the unlimited potency of Kṛṣṇa, he considers himself equal with Him.

TEXT 195

শান্ত-দাস্য-রসে ঐশ্বর্য কাহাঁ উদ্দীপন ।
বাৎসল্য-সখ্য-মধুরে ত' করে সঙ্কোচন ॥ ১৯৫ ॥

śānta-dāsya-rase aiśvarya kāhāṅ uddīpana
vātsalya-sakhya-madhure ta' kare saṅkocana

SYNONYMS

śānta-dāsya-rase—in the transcendental mellows of neutrality and servitude; *aiśvarya*—opulence; *kāhāṅ*—somewhere; *uddīpana*—manifested; *vātsalya-*

sakhya-madhure—in fraternal love, paternity and conjugal love; *ta'*—certainly; *kare*—does; *saṅkocana*—minimizing.

TRANSLATION

"On the transcendental platform of neutrality and service, sometimes the opulence of the Lord is prominent. However, in the transcendental mellows of fraternal, paternal and conjugal love, the opulence is minimized.

TEXT 196

বসুদেব-দেবকীর কৃষ্ণ চরণ বন্দিল।
ঐশ্বর্যজ্ঞানে দুঁহার মনে ভয় হৈল ॥ ১৯৬ ॥

vasudeva-devakīra kṛṣṇa caraṇa vandila
aiśvarya-jñāne duṅhāra mane bhaya haila

SYNONYMS

vasudeva-devakīra—of Vasudeva and Devakī; *kṛṣṇa*—Lord Kṛṣṇa; *caraṇa*—to the lotus feet; *vandila*—offered prayers; *aiśvarya-jñāne*—because of knowledge of the opulence; *duṅhāra*—of both of them; *mane*—in the minds; *bhaya haila*—there was fear.

TRANSLATION

"When Kṛṣṇa offered prayers at the lotus feet of His mother and father, Vasudeva and Devakī, they both felt awe, reverence and fear due to knowledge of His opulences.

TEXT 197

দেবকী বসুদেবশ্চ বিজ্ঞায় জগদীশ্বরৌ।
কৃতসংবন্দনৌ পুত্রৌ সস্বজাতে ন শঙ্কিতৌ ॥ ১৯৭ ॥

devakī vasudevaś ca
vijñāya jagad-īśvarau
kṛta-saṁvandanau putrau
sasvajāte na śaṅkitau

SYNONYMS

devakī—Devakī; *vasudevaḥ*—Vasudeva; *ca*—and; *vijñāya*—understanding; *jagat-īśvarau*—the two Lords of the universe; *kṛta-saṁvandanau*—having paid obeisances; *putrau*—the two sons Kṛṣṇa and Balarāma; *sasvajāte*—embraced; *na*—not; *śaṅkitau*—being frightened.

TRANSLATION

" 'When Devakī and Vasudeva understood that their two sons Kṛṣṇa and Balarāma, who had paid obeisances to them, were the Supreme Personality of Godhead, they became fearful and did not embrace Them.'

PURPORT

This verse quoted from *Śrīmad-Bhāgavatam* (10.44.51) refers to the killing of Kaṁsa by Kṛṣṇa and Balarāma. Vasudeva and Devakī saw their son kill the powerful demon Kaṁsa, and after this they were immediately released from their shackles. Balarāma and Kṛṣṇa then offered respects to Devakī and Vasudeva. Both father and mother wanted to embrace their sons, but they understood that Kṛṣṇa and Balarāma were the Supreme Personality of Godhead, and they therefore hesitated to embrace Them. Their parental love for Kṛṣṇa and Balarāma was therefore hampered and decreased by awe and reverence.

TEXT 198

কৃষ্ণের বিশ্বরূপ দেখি' অর্জুনের হৈল ভয়।
সখ্যভাবে ধার্ষ্ট্য ক্ষমাপয় করিয়া বিনয়॥ ১৯৮ ॥

kṛṣṇera viśva-rūpa dekhi' arjunera haila bhaya
sakhya-bhāve dhārṣṭya kṣamāpaya kariyā vinaya

SYNONYMS

kṛṣṇera—of Lord Kṛṣṇa; *viśva-rūpa*—the universal form; *dekhi'*—seeing; *arjunera*—of Arjuna; *haila bhaya*—there was fear; *sakhya-bhāve*—as a friend; *dhārṣṭya*—impudence; *kṣamāpaya*—begs pardon for; *kariyā*—showing; *vinaya*—submission.

TRANSLATION

"When Kṛṣṇa manifested His universal form, Arjuna became reverent and fearful, and he begged forgiveness for his past impudence toward Kṛṣṇa as a friend.

TEXTS 199-200

সখেতি মত্বা প্রসভং যদুক্তং
হে কৃষ্ণ হে যাদব হে সখেতি।
অজানতা মহিমানং তবেদং
ময়া প্রমাদাৎ প্রণয়েন বাপি ॥ ১৯৯ ॥

যচ্চাবহাসার্থমসৎকৃতোঽসি
বিহার-শয্যাসন-ভোজনেষু ।
একোঽথ বাপ্যচ্যুত তৎসমক্ষং
তৎ ক্ষাময়ে ত্বামহমপ্রমেয়ম্ ॥ ২০০ ॥

sakheti matvā prasabhaṁ yad uktaṁ
he kṛṣṇa he yādava he sakheti
ajānatā mahimānaṁ tavedaṁ
mayā pramādāt praṇayena vāpi

yac cāvahāsārtham asat-kṛto 'si
vihāra-śayyāsana-bhojaneṣu
eko 'thavāpy acyuta tat-samakṣaṁ
tat kṣāmaye tvām aham aprameyam

SYNONYMS

sakhā—friend; *iti*—thus; *matvā*—thinking; *prasabham*—forcibly; *yat*—that which; *uktam*—was said; *he kṛṣṇa*—O Kṛṣṇa; *he yādava*—O descendant of Yadu; *he sakhā*—O my dear friend; *iti*—thus; *ajānatā*—without knowing; *mahimānam*—greatness; *tava*—Your; *idam*—this; *mayā*—by me; *pramādāt*—out of ignorance; *praṇayena*—out of affection; *vā*—or; *api*—certainly; *yat*—whatever; *ca*—and; *avahāsa-artham*—for the matter of joking; *asat-kṛtaḥ*—insulted; *asi*—You are; *vihāra*—while enjoying; *śayyā-āsana*—sitting or lying on the bed; *bhojaneṣu*—while eating together; *ekaḥ*—alone; *athavā*—or; *api*—certainly; *acyuta*—O my dear Kṛṣṇa; *tat-samakṣam*—in the presence of others; *tat*—all those; *kṣāmaye*—ask pardon; *tvām*—unto You; *aham*—I; *aprameyam*—who are unlimited.

TRANSLATION

"'I have in the past addressed You as "O Kṛṣṇa," "O Yādava," "O my friend" without knowing Your glories. Please forgive whatever I have done in madness or in love. I have dishonored You many times while we were relaxing, lying on the same bed or eating together, sometimes alone and sometimes in front of many friends. Please excuse me for all my offenses.'

PURPORT

This is a quotation from *Bhagavad-gītā* (11.41-42). In this verse, Arjuna is addressing Kṛṣṇa, who was exhibiting His universal form on the Battlefield of Kurukṣetra.

TEXT 201

কৃষ্ণ যদি রুক্মিণীরে কৈলা পরিহাস ।
'কৃষ্ণ ছাড়িবেন'—জানি' রুক্মিণীর হৈল ত্রাস ॥২০১॥

kṛṣṇa yadi rukmiṇīre kailā parihāsa
'kṛṣṇa chāḍibena'——jāni' rukmiṇīra haila trāsa

SYNONYMS

kṛṣṇa—Lord Kṛṣṇa; *yadi*—although; *rukmiṇīre*—unto Rukmiṇī, the first queen; *kailā*—did; *parihāsa*—joking; *kṛṣṇa*—Lord Kṛṣṇa; *chāḍibena*—will give me up; *jāni'*—thinking; *rukmiṇīra*—of Rukmiṇī; *haila*—there was; *trāsa*—shock.

TRANSLATION

"Although Kṛṣṇa was joking with Queen Rukmiṇī, she was thinking that He was going to give up her company, and she was therefore shocked.

TEXT 202

তস্যাঃ সুদুঃখভয়-শোক-বিনষ্ট-বুদ্ধে-
র্হস্তাচ্ছ্লথদ্বলয়তো ব্যজনং পপাত ।
দেহশ্চ বিক্লবধিয়ঃ সহসৈব মুহ্যন্
রম্ভেব বাতবিহতা প্রবিকীর্য কেশান্ ॥ ২০২ ॥

tasyāḥ suduḥkha-bhaya-śoka-vinaṣṭa-buddher
hastāc chlathad-valayato vyajanaṁ papāta
dehaś ca viklava-dhiyaḥ sahasaiva muhyan
rambheva vāta-vihatā pravikīrya keśān

SYNONYMS

tasyāḥ—of her; *su-duḥkha-bhaya*—due to great distress and fear; *śoka*—and lamentation; *vinaṣṭa*—lost; *buddheḥ*—whose intelligence; *hastāt*—from the hand; *ślathat*—being loose; *valayataḥ*—bangles; *vyajanam*—the fan; *papāta*—fell down; *dehaḥ*—body; *ca*—also; *viklava*—paralyzed by fear; *dhiyaḥ*—whose understanding; *sahasā eva*—suddenly; *muhyan*—fainting; *rambhā iva*—like a banana tree; *vāta-vihatā*—dashed by a high wind; *pravikīrya*—scattering; *keśān*—the hair.

TRANSLATION

" 'While Kṛṣṇa was joking with Rukmiṇī in Dvārakā, she was full of distress, fear and lamentation. She had also lost her intelligence. She dropped her hand

bangles and the fan she was using to fan the Lord. Her hair became disarrayed, and she fainted and fell suddenly, appearing like a banana tree knocked down by high winds.'

PURPORT

This verse from *Śrīmad-Bhāgavatam* (10.60.24) refers to Kṛṣṇa's speaking to Rukmiṇī in His bedroom. Just to test her sincerity, He began to joke with her, presenting Himself as poor, incapable and unfit to be her lover. Not understanding that He was joking, Rukmiṇī took Him seriously and thought that He wanted to leave her company. This misunderstanding made her very unhappy, and her whole body was affected. Her fan and bangles fell to the floor, and she also fell down like a banana tree knocked down by high winds.

TEXT 203

'কেবলা'র শুদ্ধপ্রেম 'ঐশ্বর্য' না জানে ।
ঐশ্বর্য দেখিলেও নিজ-সম্বন্ধ সে মানে ॥ ২০৩ ॥

'kevalā'ra śuddha-prema 'aiśvarya' nā jāne
aiśvarya dekhileo nija-sambandha se māne

SYNONYMS

kevalāra—of unmixed attraction for Kṛṣṇa; *śuddha-prema*—unalloyed love; *aiśvarya*—opulence; *nā jāne*—does not know; *aiśvarya*—opulence; *dekhileo*—in spite of experiencing; *nija-sambandha*—one's own relationship with Kṛṣṇa; *se māne*—he takes very seriously.

TRANSLATION

"In the stage of kevalā [unalloyed devotion] a devotee does not consider the unlimited opulence of Kṛṣṇa, even though he experiences it. He takes seriously only his own relationship with Kṛṣṇa.

PURPORT

When a devotee reaches the stage of pure unalloyed devotion, especially in friendship with Kṛṣṇa, he forgets the Lord's opulences, although he sees them, and he considers himself equal to Kṛṣṇa. There is no question of actually comparing oneself to Kṛṣṇa, but because the devotee is so advanced in Kṛṣṇa consciousness, he is able to behave with Kṛṣṇa as he would with an ordinary man.

TEXT 204

ত্রয্যা চোপনিষদ্ভিশ্চ সাংখ্যযোগৈশ্চ সাত্বতৈঃ ।
উপগীয়মানমাহাত্ম্যং হরিং সাঽমন্যতাত্মজম্ ॥ ২০৪ ॥

trayyā copaniṣadbhiś ca
sāṅkhya-yogaiś ca sātvataiḥ
upagīyamāna-māhātmyaṁ
hariṁ sā 'manyatātmajam

SYNONYMS

trayyā—by followers of three *Vedas* who perform great sacrifices (like the demigod Indra); *ca*—also; *upaniṣadbhiḥ*—by the followers of the *Upaniṣads,* the most exalted portion of Vedic knowledge (as Brahman); *ca*—also; *sāṅkhya*—by the philosophers who analytically study the universe (as the *puruṣa*); *yogaiḥ*—by mystic *yogīs* (as the Paramātmā situated everywhere); *ca*—and; *sātvataiḥ*—by devotees who follow the method of worship mentioned in the *Pañcarātra* and other Vedic literature (as Bhagavān); *upagīyamāna*—being sung; *māhātmyam*—whose glories; *harim*—unto the Supreme Personality of Godhead; *sā*—she (mother Yaśodā); *amanyata*—considered; *ātma-jam*—as her own son, born of her body.

TRANSLATION

" 'When mother Yaśodā saw all the universes within Kṛṣṇa's mouth, she was astonished for the time being. The Lord is worshiped like Indra and other demigods by the followers of the three Vedas, who offer Him sacrifices. He is worshiped as impersonal Brahman by saintly persons who understand His greatness through studying the Upaniṣads, as the puruṣa by great philosophers who analytically study the universe, as the all-pervading Supersoul by great yogīs, and as the Supreme Personality of Godhead by devotees. Nevertheless, mother Yaśodā considered the Lord her own son.'

PURPORT

This verse is quoted from *Śrīmad-Bhāgavatam* (10.8.45). Those who are spiritually advanced forget Kṛṣṇa's opulence by the mercy of *yogamāyā*. For instance, mother Yaśodā considered Kṛṣṇa an ordinary child.

TEXT 205

তং মত্বাত্মজমব্যক্তং মর্ত্যলিঙ্গমধোক্ষজম্ ।
গোপিকোলূখলে দাম্না ববন্ধ প্রাকৃতং যথা ॥ ২০৫ ॥

taṁ matvātmajam avyaktaṁ
martya-liṅgam adhokṣajam
gopikolūkhale dāmnā
babandha prākṛtaṁ yathā

SYNONYMS

tam—Him (Kṛṣṇa); *matvā*—considering; *ātmajam*—own son; *avyaktam*—unmanifested; *martya-liṅgam*—manifested as if perishable; *adhokṣajam*—beyond the perception of the senses; *gopikā*—mother Yaśodā; *ulūkhale*—to the mortar; *dāmnā*—with rope; *babandha*—bound; *prākṛtam*—an ordinary child; *yathā*—like.

TRANSLATION

" 'Although Kṛṣṇa is beyond sense perception and is unmanifest to human beings, he takes up the guise of a human being with a material body. Thus mother Yaśodā thought Him to be her son, and she bound Lord Kṛṣṇa with rope to a wooden mortar, as if He were an ordinary child.'

PURPORT

This verse from *Śrīmad-Bhāgavatam* (10.9.14) is in reference to Lord Kṛṣṇa's exhibiting Himself like an ordinary child before mother Yaśodā. He was playing like a naughty boy stealing butter and breaking butter pots. Mother Yaśodā became disturbed and wanted to bind the Lord to a mortar used for pounding spices. In other words, she considered the Supreme Personality of Godhead an ordinary child.

TEXT 206

উবাহ কৃষ্ণো ভগবান্ শ্রীদামানং পরাজিতঃ ।
বৃষভং ভদ্রসেনস্তু প্রলম্বো রোহিণীসুতম্ ॥ ২০৬ ॥

uvāha kṛṣṇo bhagavān
śrīdāmānaṁ parājitaḥ
vṛṣabhaṁ bhadrasenas tu
pralambo rohiṇī-sutam

SYNONYMS

uvāha—carried; *kṛṣṇaḥ*—Lord Kṛṣṇa; *bhagavān*—the Supreme Personality of Godhead; *śrīdāmānam*—Śrīdāmā; *parājitaḥ*—being defeated; *vṛṣabham*—Vṛṣabha; *bhadrasenaḥ*—Bhadrasena; *tu*—and; *pralambaḥ*—Pralamba; *rohiṇī-sutam*—Balarāma.

TRANSLATION

" 'When Kṛṣṇa was defeated by Śrīdāmā, He had to carry him on His shoulders. Similarly, Bhadrasena carried Vṛṣabha, and Pralamba carried Balarāma, the son of Rohiṇī.'

PURPORT

This verse is from *Śrīmad-Bhāgavatam* (10.18.24). When all the cowherd boys were playing in the forest of Vṛndāvana, the demon Pralambāsura appeared to kidnap Kṛṣṇa and Balarāma. The *asura* appeared disguised in the form of a cowherd boy, but Kṛṣṇa could understand his trick. Kṛṣṇa therefore divided all the cowherd boys into two parties. One party belonged to Balarāma, and the other party belonged to Kṛṣṇa Himself. Ultimately Kṛṣṇa was defeated in this play, and according to the wager, the defeated party had to carry the victorious party on their shoulders. Kṛṣṇa had to carry Śrīdāmā on His shoulders, and Bhadrasena had to carry Vṛṣabha. The demon Pralambāsura had to carry Balarāma, and when Balarāma mounted his shoulders, the demon ran far away. Finally the demon began to expand his body to a gigantic size, and Balarāma understood that he intended to kill Him. Balarāma immediately struck the demon's head with His strong fist, and the demon fell down dead as if he were a snake whose head had been smashed.

TEXTS 207-209

সা চ মেনে তদাত্মানং বরিষ্ঠাং সর্বযোষিতাম্ ।
হিত্বা গোপীঃ কামযানা মামসৌ ভজতে প্রিয়ঃ ॥২০৭॥
ততো গত্বা বনোদ্দেশং দৃপ্তা কেশবমব্রবীৎ ।
ন পারয়েঽহং চলিতুং নয় মাং যত্র তে মনঃ ॥ ২০৮ ॥
এবমুক্তঃ প্রিয়ামাহ স্কন্ধমারুহ্যতামিতি ।
ততশ্চান্তর্দধে কৃষ্ণঃ সা বধূরন্বতপ্যত ॥ ২০৯ ॥

sā ca mene tadātmānaṁ
variṣṭhāṁ sarva-yoṣitām
hitvā gopīḥ kāmayānā
mām asau bhajate priyaḥ

tato gatvā vanoddeśaṁ
dṛptā keśavam abravīt
na pāraye 'haṁ calituṁ
naya māṁ yatra te manaḥ

evam uktaḥ priyām āha
skandham āruhyatām iti
tataś cāntardadhe kṛṣṇaḥ
sā vadhūr anvatapyata

SYNONYMS

sā—Śrīmatī Rādhārāṇī; *ca*—also; *mene*—considered; *tadā*—at that time; *ātmānam*—Herself; *variṣṭhām*—the most glorious; *sarva-yoṣitām*—among all the *gopīs; hitvā*—giving up; *gopīḥ*—all the other *gopīs; kāmayānāḥ*—who were desiring the company of Kṛṣṇa; *mām*—Me; *asau*—that Śrī Kṛṣṇa; *bhajate*—worships; *priyaḥ*—the most dear; *tataḥ*—thereafter; *gatvā*—going; *vana-uddeśam*—to the deep forest; *dṛptā*—being very proud; *keśavam*—unto Kṛṣṇa; *abravīt*—said; *na pāraye*—am unable; *aham*—I; *calitum*—to walk; *naya*—just carry; *mām*—Me; *yatra*—wherever; *te*—Your; *manaḥ*—mind; *evam uktaḥ*—thus being ordered by Śrīmatī Rādhārāṇī; *priyām*—to this most dear *gopī; āha*—said; *skandham*—My shoulders; *āruhyatām*—please get on; *iti*—thus; *tataḥ*—thereafter; *ca*—also; *antardadhe*—disappeared; *kṛṣṇaḥ*—Lord Kṛṣṇa; *sā*—Śrīmatī Rādhārāṇī; *vadhūḥ*—the *gopī; anvatapyata*—began to lament.

TRANSLATION

" ' "My dearmost Kṛṣṇa, You are worshiping Me and giving up the company of all the other gopīs who wanted to enjoy themselves with You." Thinking like this, Śrīmatī Rādhārāṇī considered Herself Kṛṣṇa's most beloved gopī. She had become proud and had left the rāsa-līlā with Kṛṣṇa. In the deep forest She said, "My dear Kṛṣṇa, I cannot walk any more. You can take Me wherever You like." When Śrīmatī Rādhārāṇī petitioned Kṛṣṇa in this way, Kṛṣṇa said, "Just get up upon My shoulders." As soon as Śrīmatī Rādhārāṇī began to do so, He disappeared. Śrīmatī Rādhārāṇī then began to grieve over Her request and Kṛṣṇa's disappearance.'

PURPORT

These three verses are quoted from *Śrīmad-Bhāgavatam* (10.30.37-39).

TEXT 210

পতিসুতান্বয়ভ্রাতৃবান্ধবা-
নতিবিলঙ্ঘ্য তেঽন্ত্যচ্যুতাগতাঃ ।
গতিবিদস্তবোদ্গীতমোহিতাঃ
কিতব যোষিতঃ কস্ত্যজেন্নিশি ॥ ২১০ ॥

pati-sutānvaya-bhrātṛ-bāndhavān
ativilaṅghya te 'nty acyutāgatāḥ
gatividas tavodgīta-mohitāḥ
kitava yoṣitaḥ kas tyajen niśi

SYNONYMS

pati—husbands; *suta*—sons; *anvaya*—family; *bhrātṛ*—brothers; *bāndhavān*—friends; *ativilaṅghya*—without caring for; *te*—Your; *anti*—dear shelter; *acyuta*—O infallible one; *āgatāḥ*—have come; *gati-vidaḥ*—who know everything of our activities; *tava*—of You; *udgīta*—by the singing flute; *mohitāḥ*—being attracted; *kitava*—O great cheater; *yoṣitaḥ*—beautiful women; *kaḥ*—who; *tyajet*—would give up; *niśi*—in the dead of night.

TRANSLATION

"'Dear Kṛṣṇa, neglecting the order of our husbands and sons, family, brothers and friends and leaving their company, we gopīs have come to You. You know everything about our desires. We have only come because we are attracted by Your supremely musical flute. However, You are a great cheater. Who else would give up the company of young girls like us in the dead of night?'

PURPORT

This verse, quoted from *Śrīmad-Bhāgavatam* (10.31.16), describes how the *gopīs* exposed themselves for Kṛṣṇa's enjoyment in the dead of night. The *gopīs* approached Kṛṣṇa to enjoy themselves with Him in the *rāsa* dance. Kṛṣṇa knew this very well, but He was superficially trying to avoid them. He is therefore addressed by the *gopīs* as *kitava,* a great cheater, because He first attracted them to come dance with Him, and yet when they actually came, neglecting the orders of their friends and relatives, He tried to avoid them by giving them good instructions. These cunning instructions were too much for the *gopīs* to tolerate; they therefore had a right to address Kṛṣṇa as *kitava,* a great cheater. They were all young girls, and they had come to Him to be enjoyed. How could He avoid them? The *gopīs* therefore expressed great disappointment in this verse. They came voluntarily, but Kṛṣṇa was so cunning that He wanted to avoid their company. The *gopīs'* lamentation was certainly very appropriate, and in this way Kṛṣṇa tested their sincerity.

TEXT 211

শান্তরসে—'স্বরূপবুদ্ধ্যে কৃষ্ণৈকনিষ্ঠতা'।
"শমো মন্নিষ্ঠতা বুদ্ধেঃ" ইতি শ্রীমুখ-গাথা ॥ ২১১ ॥

śānta-rase——'svarūpa-buddhye kṛṣṇaika-niṣṭhatā'
"śamo man-niṣṭhatā buddheḥ" iti śrī-mukha-gāthā

SYNONYMS

śānta-rase—on the stage of *śānta-rasa,* or neutrality; *svarūpa-buddhye*—by self-realization; *kṛṣṇa-eka-niṣṭhatā*—fully devoted to the lotus feet of Kṛṣṇa;

śamaḥ—equilibrium; *mat*—to Me; *niṣṭhatā*—the quality of attachment; *buddheḥ*—of the mind; *iti*—thus; *śrī-mukha*—from the mouth of the Supreme Lord; *gāthā*—a verse.

TRANSLATION

"When one is fully attached to Kṛṣṇa's lotus feet, one attains the śamatā stage. The word śamatā is derived from the word śama; therefore śānta-rasa, the position of neutrality, means being fully attached to the lotus feet of Kṛṣṇa. This is the verdict from the mouth of the Supreme Personality of Godhead Himself. This state is called self-realization.

PURPORT

The word *śama* is explained by the Supreme Personality of Godhead in the following verse.

TEXT 212

শমো মন্নিষ্ঠতা বুদ্ধেরিতি শ্রীভগবদ্বচঃ ।
তন্নিষ্ঠা দুর্ঘটা বুদ্ধেরেতাং শান্তরতিং বিনা ॥ ২১২ ॥

śamo man-niṣṭhatā buddher
iti śrī-bhagavad-vacaḥ
tan-niṣṭhā durghaṭā buddher
etāṁ śānta-ratiṁ vinā

SYNONYMS

śamaḥ—equality or neutrality; *mat-niṣṭhatā*—being fixed in My lotus feet; *buddheḥ*—of the intelligence; *iti*—thus; *śrī-bhagavat-vacaḥ*—words of the Supreme Personality of Godhead; *tat-niṣṭhā*—attachment or attraction for Him; *durghaṭā*—very difficult to achieve; *buddheḥ*—of intelligence; *etām*—thus; *śānta-ratim*—attachment on the platform of *śānta-rasa; vinā*—without.

TRANSLATION

"These are the words of the Supreme Personality of Godhead: 'When one's intelligence is fully attached to My lotus feet but one does not render practical service, one has attained the stage called śānta-rati, or śama. Without śānta-rati, attachment to Kṛṣṇa is very difficult to achieve.'

PURPORT

This verse is found in *Bhakti-rasāmṛta-sindhu* (3.1.47).

TEXT 213

শমো মন্নিষ্ঠতা বুদ্ধের্দম ইন্দ্রিয়সংযমঃ ।
তিতিক্ষা দুঃখসংমর্ষো জিহ্বোপস্থজয়ো ধৃতিঃ ॥ ২১৩ ॥

śamo man-niṣṭhatā buddher
dama indriya-saṁyamaḥ
titikṣā duḥkha-sammarṣo
jihvopastha-jayo dhṛtiḥ

SYNONYMS

śamaḥ—neutrality; *mat-niṣṭhatā*—attachment for Me; *buddheḥ*—of intelligence; *damaḥ*—self-control; *indriya-saṁyamaḥ*—controlling the activities of the senses; *titikṣā*—tolerance; *duḥkha*—of unhappiness; *sammarṣaḥ*—endurance; *jihvā*—tongue; *upastha*—and the urge of the genitals; *jayaḥ*—conquering; *dhṛtiḥ*—control.

TRANSLATION

" 'The word śama or śānta-rasa indicates that one is attached to the lotus feet of Kṛṣṇa. Dama means controlling the senses and not being deviated from the Lord's service. Endurance of unhappiness is titikṣā, and dhṛti means controlling the tongue and the genitals.'

PURPORT

This verse is from *Śrīmad-Bhāgavatam* (11.19.36). The conditioned soul under the clutches of *māyā,* the material energy, is very much agitated by the urges of the tongue and the genitals. Control of the urges of the tongue, the belly and the genitals (which are situated in a straight line) is called *dhṛti.* Śrīla Bhaktivinoda Ṭhākura says, *tāra madhye jihvā ati, lobhamaya sudurmati.* Among the senses, the tongue is the most formidable enemy of the conditioned soul. Urged by the tongue, one commits many sinful activities. Although Kṛṣṇa has given human beings nice food, people still commit sins by killing poor animals for the satisfaction of the tongue. Not being able to control the tongue, the conditioned soul eats more than he needs. Of course, everyone must eat to keep the body fit for the Lord's service, but when one cannot control the senses, he falls victim to the dictations of the tongue and the belly. Naturally, genital agitation follows, and one seeks illicit sex. However, if one is fixed at the lotus feet of Kṛṣṇa, he can control the tongue. Bhaktivinoda Ṭhākura further states, *kṛṣṇa baḍa dayāmaya, karibāre jihvā jaya, sva-prasāda-anna dilā bhāi:* in order to conquer the tongue, Kṛṣṇa has been very merciful and has given us nice food that has been offered to Him. When a person is attached to Kṛṣṇa's lotus feet, he does not eat anything not offered to Kṛṣṇa. *Sei annāmṛta khāo, rādhā-kṛṣṇa-guṇa gāo, preme ḍāka caitanya-nitāi.* Since a devotee only eats *prasāda,* he conquers the dictations of the tongue, belly and genitals. One can control the dictates of the senses when situated in the position of *śānta-rasa.* Then one's advancement in Kṛṣṇa consciousness is assured.

TEXT 214

কৃষ্ণ বিনা তৃষ্ণা-ত্যাগ—তার কার্য মানি ।
অতএব 'শান্ত' কৃষ্ণভক্ত এক জানি ॥ ২১৪ ॥

kṛṣṇa vinā tṛṣṇā-tyāga——tāra kārya māni
ataeva 'śānta' kṛṣṇa-bhakta eka jāni

SYNONYMS

kṛṣṇa vinā—without Kṛṣṇa; *tṛṣṇā-tyāga*—giving up all desires; *tāra*—of *śānta-rasa; kārya*—the business; *māni*—I accept; *ataeva*—therefore; *śānta*—the position of equilibrium; *kṛṣṇa-bhakta*—a devotee of Kṛṣṇa; *eka*—only; *jāni*—I know.

TRANSLATION

"Giving up all desires not connected with Kṛṣṇa is the business of one who is in the śānta-rasa. Only a devotee of Kṛṣṇa can be situated on that platform. He is thus called a śānta-rasa-bhakta.

PURPORT

In this position, one is freed from all material enjoyment. When one is not agitated or disturbed, he can immediately realize his relationship with Kṛṣṇa. A *śānta-rasa* devotee is therefore always fixed in realization. This instruction was given by the Lord Himself to Uddhava. The beginning of pure devotional service is called *anyābhilāṣitā-śūnya.* When one is situated on the platform of neutrality, he is freed from the material platform and fully situated in spiritual life. The word *dama* used in verse 213 means *indriya-saṁyama*—curbing one's senses. The word *dama* can also mean curbing one's enemies. A king has to take steps to curb the criminal activities of his citizens. Great *rājarṣis,* devotee kings, used to control undesirable elements in their states, and this also may be called *dama.* However, *dama* here refers to the conditioned soul who must control his senses. Real *dama* means controlling the undesirable activities of the senses.

TEXT 215

স্বর্গ, মোক্ষ কৃষ্ণভক্ত 'নরক' করি' মানে ।
কৃষ্ণনিষ্ঠা, তৃষ্ণা-ত্যাগ—শান্তের 'দুই' গুণে ॥ ২১৫ ॥

svarga, mokṣa kṛṣṇa-bhakta 'naraka' kari' māne
kṛṣṇa-niṣṭhā, tṛṣṇā-tyāga——śāntera 'dui' guṇe

SYNONYMS

svarga—the heavenly kingdom; *mokṣa*—liberation from material bondage; *kṛṣṇa-bhakta*—a devotee of Lord Kṛṣṇa; *naraka kari' māne*—considers as good as hell; *kṛṣṇa-niṣṭhā*—being fixed at the lotus feet of Kṛṣṇa; *tṛṣṇa-tyāga*—giving up all material desires; *śāntera*—of one on the neutrality platform; *dui guṇe*—two transcendental qualities.

TRANSLATION

"When a devotee is situated on the platform of śānta-rasa, he desires neither elevation to the heavenly planets nor liberation. These are the results of karma and jñāna, and the devotee considers them no better than hell. A person situated on the śānta-rasa platform manifests the two transcendental qualities of detachment from all material desire and full attachment to Kṛṣṇa.

TEXT 216

নারায়ণপরাঃ সর্বে ন কুতশ্চন বিভ্যতি।
স্বর্গাপবর্গনরকেষ্বপি তুল্যার্থদর্শিনঃ ॥ ২১৬ ॥

nārāyaṇa-parāḥ sarve
na kutaścana bibhyati
svargāpavarga-narakeṣv
api tulyārtha-darśinaḥ

SYNONYMS

nārāyaṇa-parāḥ—persons who are attached to the Supreme Personality of Godhead; *sarve*—all; *na*—not; *kutaścana*—from any quarter; *bibhyati*—are afraid; *svarga*—in heavenly planets; *apavarga*—in liberation; *narakeṣu*—or in hell; *api*—although; *tulya-artha*—results as equal; *darśinaḥ*—who see.

TRANSLATION

" 'A person who is devoted to the Supreme Personality of Godhead, Nārāyaṇa, is not afraid of anything. Elevation to the heavenly kingdom, condemnation to hell and liberation from material bondage all appear the same to a devotee.'

PURPORT

This verse is quoted from *Śrīmad-Bhāgavatam* (6.17.28). Elevation to the heavenly planets, liberation from material bondage, and condemnation to hell are all equal to the devotee. The devotee's only desire is to be attached to the lotus feet of Kṛṣṇa and to engage in His transcendental loving service.

TEXT 217

এই দুই গুণ ব্যাপে সব ভক্তজনে।
আকাশের 'শব্দ'-গুণ যেন ভূতগণে ॥ ২১৭ ॥

ei dui guṇa vyāpe saba bhakta-jane
ākāśera 'śabda'-guṇa yena bhūta-gaṇe

SYNONYMS

ei dui—these two; *guṇa*—transcendental qualities; *vyāpe*—expand; *saba bhakta-jane*—in the lives of all devotees; *ākāśera*—of the sky; *śabda-guṇa*—the quality of sound; *yena*—like; *bhūta-gaṇe*—other material elements.

TRANSLATION

"These two qualities of the śānta stage spread through the lives of all devotees. They are like the quality of sound in the sky. Sound vibration is found in all material elements.

PURPORT

The qualities of *śānta-rasa* are present in all kinds of devotees, whether they are in the *dāsya-rasa, sakhya-rasa, vātsalya-rasa* or *madhura-rasa*. The example of sound is given herein. Sound not only exists in the sky, or ether, but it is also present in air, fire, water and earth. This is a scientific explanation of devotional service. Just as sound is present in all material elements, *śānta-rasa* is present in all devotees, whether they are on the platform of *dāsya-rasa, sakhya-rasa, vātsalya-rasa* or *madhura-rasa*.

TEXT 218

শান্তের স্বভাব—কৃষ্ণে মমতা-গন্ধহীন।
'পরংব্রহ্ম'-'পরমাত্মা'-জ্ঞান প্রবীণ ॥ ২১৮ ॥

śāntera svabhāva——kṛṣṇe mamatā-gandha-hīna
'paraṁ-brahma'-'paramātmā'-jñāna pravīṇa

SYNONYMS

śāntera sva-bhāva—the characteristic of *śānta-rasa; kṛṣṇe*—in Kṛṣṇa; *mamatā-gandha-hīna*—not even the smallest quantity of intimacy; *param-brahma*—impersonal Brahman; *paramātmā*—the localized situation of the Lord; *jñāna*—knowledge; *pravīṇa*—prominence.

TRANSLATION

"It is the nature of śānta-rasa that not even the smallest intimacy exists. Rather, knowledge of impersonal Brahman and localized Paramātmā is prominent.

PURPORT

Because of an impersonal impression of the Supreme Personality of Godhead, a devotee in the *śānta-rasa* relationship worships the impersonal Brahman or localized aspect of the Absolute Truth (Paramātmā). He does not develop a personal relationship with the Supreme Personality of Godhead, Śrī Kṛṣṇa.

TEXT 219

কেবল 'স্বরূপ-জ্ঞান' হয় শান্ত-রসে ।
'পূর্ণৈশ্বর্যপ্রভু-জ্ঞান' অধিক হয় দাস্যে ॥ ২১৯ ॥

kevala 'svarūpa-jñāna' haya śānta-rase
'pūrṇaiśvarya-prabhu-jñāna' adhika haya dāsye

SYNONYMS

kevala—only; *svarūpa-jñāna*—knowledge of the constitutional position of one's self; *haya*—there is; *śānta-rase*—in the mellow of neutrality; *pūrṇa-aiśvarya-prabhu-jñāna*—knowledge of the full opulences of the Supreme Personality of Godhead; *adhika*—greater; *haya*—becomes; *dāsye*—in the transcendental mellow of servitude.

TRANSLATION

"On the platform of śānta-rasa, one only realizes his constitutional position. However, when one is raised to the platform of dāsya-rasa, he better understands the full opulence of the Supreme Personality of Godhead.

TEXT 220

ঈশ্বরজ্ঞান, সম্ভ্রম-গৌরব প্রচুর ।
'সেবা' করি' কৃষ্ণে সুখ দেন নিরন্তর ॥ ২২০ ॥

īśvara-jñāna, sambhrama-gaurava pracura
'sevā' kari' kṛṣṇe sukha dena nirantara

SYNONYMS

īśvara-jñāna—knowledge of the supreme controller; *sambhrama-gaurava*—awe and veneration; *pracura*—abundant; *sevā*—service; *kari'*—performing; *kṛṣṇe*—unto Lord Kṛṣṇa; *sukha*—happiness; *dena*—gives; *nirantara*—constantly.

TRANSLATION

"On the dāsya-rasa platform, knowledge of the Supreme Personality of Godhead is revealed with awe and veneration. By rendering service unto Lord Kṛṣṇa, the devotee in dāsya-rasa gives constant happiness to the Lord.

TEXT 221

শান্তের গুণ দাস্যে আছে, অধিক—'সেবন'।
অতএব দাস্যরসের এই 'দুই' গুণ ॥ ২২১ ॥

śāntera guṇa dāsye āche, adhika——'sevana'
ataeva dāsya-rasera ei 'dui' guṇa

SYNONYMS

śāntera—of the platform of *śānta-rasa; guṇa*—the qualities; *dāsye*—on the platform of servitude; *āche*—are; *adhika*—additional; *sevana*—serving; *ataeva*—therefore; *dāsya-rasera*—of the platform of *dāsya-rasa; ei dui guṇa*—these two qualities (namely *śānta* and *dāsya*).

TRANSLATION

"The qualities of śānta-rasa are also present in dāsya-rasa, but service is added. Thus the dāsya-rasa platform contains the qualities of both śānta-rasa and dāsya-rasa.

TEXT 222

শান্তের গুণ, দাস্যের সেবন—সখ্যে দুই হয়।
দাস্যের'সম্ভ্রম-গৌরব'-সেবা, সখ্যে 'বিশ্বাস'-ময় ॥২২২॥

śāntera guṇa, dāsyera sevana——sakhye dui haya
dāsyera 'sambhrama-gaurava'-sevā, sakhye 'viśvāsa'-maya

SYNONYMS

śāntera guṇa—qualities of *śānta-rasa; dāsyera sevana*—the service of the *dāsya-rasa; sakhye*—on the platform of fraternity; *dui*—two qualities; *haya*—there are; *dāsyera*—of the *dāsya* platform; *sambhrama-gaurava*—with awe and veneration; *sevā*—service; *sakhye*—on the platform of fraternity; *viśvāsa-maya*—spread with confidence.

TRANSLATION

"The qualities of śānta-rasa and the service of dāsya-rasa are both present on the platform of sakhya-rasa. On the platform of fraternity, the qualities of dāsya-rasa are mixed with the confidence of fraternity instead of awe and veneration.

TEXT 223

কান্ধে চড়ে, কান্ধে চড়ায়, করে ক্রীড়া-রণ।
কৃষ্ণে সেবে, কৃষ্ণে করায় আপন-সেবন! ২২৩ ॥

kāndhe caḍe, kāndhe caḍāya, kare krīḍā-raṇa
kṛṣṇe seve, kṛṣṇe karāya āpana-sevana!

SYNONYMS

kāndhe—on the shoulders; *caḍe*—gets up; *kāndhe caḍāya*—sometimes takes on his own shoulders; *kare*—performs; *krīḍā-raṇa*—mock fighting; *kṛṣṇe seve*—serves Kṛṣṇa; *kṛṣṇe*—from Kṛṣṇa; *karāya*—causes; *āpana-sevana*—his own service.

TRANSLATION

"On the sakhya-rasa platform, the devotee sometimes offers the Lord service and sometimes makes Kṛṣṇa serve him in exchange. In their mock fighting, the cowherd boys would sometimes climb on Kṛṣṇa's shoulders, and sometimes they would make Kṛṣṇa climb on their shoulders.

TEXT 224

বিশ্রম্ভ-প্রধান সখ্য—গৌরব-সম্ভ্রম-হীন।
অতএব সখ্য-রসের 'তিন' গুণ—চিহ্ন ॥ ২২৪ ॥

viśrambha-pradhāna sakhya——gaurava-sambhrama-hīna
ataeva sakhya-rasera 'tina' guṇa——cihna

SYNONYMS

viśrambha-pradhāna sakhya—on the platform of fraternity, in which confidence is prominent; *gaurava-sambhrama*—awe and veneration; *hīna*—without; *ataeva*—therefore; *sakhya-rasera*—of the platform of fraternity; *tina guṇa*—three qualities, namely *śānta, dāsya* and *sakhya; cihna*—the symptom.

TRANSLATION

"Since the platform of fraternity is predominated by confidential service, awe and veneration are absent. Therefore sakhya-rasa is characterized by three qualities.

TEXT 225

'মমতা' অধিক, কৃষ্ণে আত্মসম জ্ঞান ।
অতএব সখ্যরসের বশ ভগবান্ ॥ ২২৫ ॥

'mamatā' adhika, kṛṣṇe ātma-sama jñāna
ataeva sakhya-rasera vaśa bhagavān

SYNONYMS

mamatā—intimacy; *adhika*—increase; *kṛṣṇe*—with Kṛṣṇa; *ātma-sama jñāna*—the notion of equality; *ataeva*—therefore; *sakhya-rasera*—by the mellow of fraternity; *vaśa*—subjected; *bhagavān*—the Supreme Personality of Godhead.

TRANSLATION

"On the platform of sakhya-rasa, the Supreme Personality of Godhead is obliged to the devotees who are intimate with Kṛṣṇa and think themselves equal to Him.

TEXT 226

বাৎসল্যে শান্তের গুণ, দাস্যের সেবন ।
সেই সেই সেবনের ইহাঁ নাম—'পালন' ॥ ২২৬ ॥

vātsalye śāntera guṇa, dāsyera sevana
sei sei sevanera ihāṅ nāma——'pālana'

SYNONYMS

vātsalye—on the platform of parental love; *śāntera guṇa*—the qualities of *śānta-rasa; dāsyera sevana*—the service of *dāsya-rasa; sei sei sevanera*—the service of *śānta-rasa, dāsya-rasa* and *sakhya-rasa; ihāṅ*—on this platform; *nāma*—named; *pālana*—maintenance.

TRANSLATION

"On the platform of parental love, the qualities of śānta-rasa, dāsya-rasa and sakhya-rasa are transformed into a form of service called maintenance.

TEXT 227

সখ্যের গুণ—'অসঙ্কোচ', 'অগৌরব' সার ।
মমতাধিক্যে তাড়ন-ভৎর্সন-ব্যবহার ॥ ২২৭ ॥

sakhyera guṇa——'asaṅkoca', 'agaurava' sāra
mamatādhikye tāḍana-bhartsana-vyavahāra

SYNONYMS

sakhyera guṇa—the quality of fraternity; *asaṅkoca*—without any formality; *agaurava*—without any veneration; *sāra*—the essence; *mamatā-adhikye*—on account of greater intimacy; *tāḍana*—of chastisement; *bhartsana*—of rebuking; *vyavahāra*—behavior.

TRANSLATION

"The essence of fraternal love is intimacy devoid of the formality and veneration found in the dāsya-rasa. Due to a greater sense of intimacy, the devotee functioning in paternal love chastises and rebukes the Lord in an ordinary way.

TEXT 228

আপনারে 'পালক' জ্ঞান, কৃষ্ণে 'পাল্য'-জ্ঞান ।
'চারি' গুণে বাৎসল্য রস—অমৃত-সমান ॥ ২২৮ ॥

āpanāre 'pālaka' jñāna, kṛṣṇe 'pālya'-jñāna
'cāri' guṇe vātsalya rasa——amṛta-samāna

SYNONYMS

āpanāre—unto himself; *pālaka jñāna*—the notion of a caretaker; *kṛṣṇe*—in Lord Kṛṣṇa; *pālya*—as object of protection; *jñāna*—notion; *cāri*—four; *guṇe*—in qualities; *vātsalya rasa*—the mellow of parental love; *amṛta-samāna*—like nectar.

TRANSLATION

"On the platform of paternal love, the devotee considers himself the Lord's maintainer. Thus the Lord is the object of maintenance, like a son, and therefore this mellow is full of the four qualities of śānta-rasa, dāsya-rasa, fraternity and parental love. This is more transcendental nectar.

PURPORT

In his *Amṛta-pravāha-bhāṣya,* Śrīla Bhaktivinoda Ṭhākura gives us a short summary of this complicated description of the different *rasas.* He states that by becoming firmly fixed in the Lord's service, one is devoid of all material desires. There are two transcendental qualities on the *śānta-rasa* platform. In all the material elements, sound vibration is found. Similarly, *śānta-rasa* is spread over all the other transcendental mellows, which are known as *dāsya-rasa, sakhya-rasa, vāt-*

salya-rasa and *madhura-rasa.* Although there is attachment for Kṛṣṇa in awe and veneration in the *śānta-rasa* along with two valuable transcendental qualities—attachment for Kṛṣṇa and detachment from material desires—nonetheless the sense of intimacy is lacking. Therefore in the *śānta-rasa,* attachment for impersonal Brahman and localized Paramātmā is prominent. The sense of intimacy is lacking. By that intimacy one thinks of Kṛṣṇa as one's only shelter and only friend. In the *śānta-rasa* one accepts Kṛṣṇa as the impersonal Param Brahma or the localized Paramātmā. This is based on the speculative knowledge of the *jñānī.* However, when this knowledge is further developed, one is convinced that Paramātmā, the Supreme Lord, is master and that the living entity is His eternal servant. One then attains the platform of *dāsya-rasa.* In *dāsya-rasa* the Lord is accepted with awe and veneration. However, although in the *śānta-rasa* there is no active service, in the *dāsya-rasa* active service is prominant. Thus in the *dāsya-rasa,* the qualities of *śānta-rasa* and service are predominantly visible. Similarly, when this same *rasa* is developed into fraternity (*sakhya-rasa*), a friendly intimacy is added. There is no awe or veneration in the *sakhya-rasa.*The *sakhya-rasa* is invested with three qualities—*śānta, dāsya,* and *sakhya.* Similarly, on the platform of parental love, the qualities of *śānta-rasa* and *dāsya-rasa* are fully developed in another form—the sense of maintaining the Lord. Therefore on the platform of parental love there exists a combination of four transcendental qualities—*śānta, dāsya, sakhya,* and the qualities of paternity, which put the devotee in the position of a maintainer. Thus on the platform of parental love the four qualities of transcendental love are present.

TEXT 229

সে অমৃতানন্দে ভক্ত সহ ডুবেন আপনে ।
'কৃষ্ণ—ভক্তবশ' গুণ কহে ঐশ্বর্য-জ্ঞানিগণে ॥ ২২৯ ॥

se amṛtānande bhakta saha ḍubena āpane
'kṛṣṇa——bhakta-vaśa' guṇa kahe aiśvarya-jñāni-gaṇe

SYNONYMS

se—that Lord Kṛṣṇa; *amṛta-ānande*—in spiritual happiness; *bhakta*—the devotee; *saha*—with; *ḍubena*—plunges; *āpane*—Himself; *kṛṣṇa*—Kṛṣṇa; *bhakta-vaśa*—of being subjugated by the devotee; *guṇa*—the quality; *kahe*—say; *aiśvarya-jñāni-gaṇe*—learned scholars knowing the opulence of Kṛṣṇa.

TRANSLATION

"The exchange of spiritual happiness between Kṛṣṇa and His devotee, in which Kṛṣṇa is controlled by His devotee, is compared to an ocean of nectar into which the devotee and Kṛṣṇa plunge. This is the verdict of learned scholars who appreciate Kṛṣṇa's opulence.

TEXT 230

ইতীদৃক্স্বলীলাভিরানন্দকুণ্ডে
স্বঘোষং নিমজ্জন্তমাখ্যাপয়ন্তম্।
তদীয়েশিতজ্ঞেষু ভক্তৈর্জিতত্বং
পুনঃ প্রেমতাস্তং শতাবৃত্তি বন্দে ॥ ২৩০ ॥

itīdṛk-svalīlābhir ānanda-kuṇḍe
svaghoṣaṁ nimajjantam ākhyāpayantam
tadīyeśita-jñeṣu bhaktair jitatvaṁ
punaḥ prematās taṁ śatāvṛtti vande

SYNONYMS

iti—thus; *īdṛk-sva-līlābhiḥ*—by this Dāmodara in His transcendental pastimes; *ānanda-kuṇḍe*—in the ocean of transcendental bliss; *sva-ghoṣam*—His personal associates; *nimajjantam*—plunging; *ākhyāpayantam*—declaring; *tadīya*—of the Supreme Personality of Godhead; *īśita-jñeṣu*—among learned scholars expert in the knowledge of the opulences; *bhaktaiḥ*—by the devotees; *jitatvam*—the subjugation; *punaḥ*—again; *prematāḥ*—with love; *tam*—unto Him; *śata-āvṛtti*—hundreds of times; *vande*—I offer my respectful obeisances.

TRANSLATION

" 'Again let me offer my respectful obeisances unto the Supreme Personality of Godhead. O my Lord, I offer my obeisances hundreds and thousands of times with all affection because by Your personal pastimes You plunge the gopīs into an ocean of nectar. Appreciating Your opulence, devotees generally declare that You are always subjugated by their feelings.'

PURPORT

This verse is from the *Dāmodarāṣṭaka* in the *Padma Purāṇa.* Attachment for Kṛṣṇa in *śānta-rasa,* rendering service to the Lord in *dāsya-rasa,* rendering relaxed service in fraternity, and serving in parental love with feelings of maintenance all combine on the platform of conjugal love when the devotee wants to serve the Lord by offering Him his personal body. Thus the qualities of the other *rasas* combine to form the nectar of conjugal love. On this platform, all the different feelings of a devotee are amalgamated.

TEXT 231

মধুর-রসে—কৃষ্ণনিষ্ঠা, সেবা অতিশয়।
সখ্যের অসঙ্কোচ, লালন-মমতাধিক্য হয় ॥ ২৩১ ॥

madhura-rase——kṛṣṇa-niṣṭhā, sevā atiśaya
sakhyera asaṅkoca, lālana-mamatādhikya haya

SYNONYMS

madhura-rase—on the platform of conjugal love; *kṛṣṇa-niṣṭhā*—attachment for Kṛṣṇa; *sevā atiśaya*—an improved rendering service; *sakhyera*—of the platform of fraternity; *asaṅkoca*—relaxation; *lālana*—maintenance; *mamatā-adhikya*—increase of intimacy; *haya*—there is.

TRANSLATION

"On the platform of conjugal love, attachment for Kṛṣṇa, rendering service unto Him, the relaxed feelings of fraternity and the feelings of maintenance all increase in intimacy.

TEXT 232

কান্তভাবে নিজাঙ্গ দিয়া করেন সেবন ।
অতএব মধুর-রসের হয় 'পঞ্চ' গুণ ॥ ২৩২ ॥

kānta-bhāve nijāṅga diyā karena sevana
ataeva madhura-rasera haya 'pañca' guṇa

SYNONYMS

kānta-bhāve—on the platform of conjugal love; *nija-aṅga*—own body; *diyā*—offering; *karena*—executes; *sevana*—service; *ataeva*—therefore; *madhura-rasera*—of the mellow of conjugal love; *haya*—there are; *pañca guṇa*—five kinds of transcendental qualities.

TRANSLATION

"On the platform of conjugal love, the devotee offers his body in the service of the Lord. Thus on this platform all five transcendental qualities are present.

TEXT 233

আকাশাদি গুণ যেন পর পর ভূতে ।
এক-দুই-তিন-চারি ক্রমে পঞ্চ পৃথিবীতে ॥ ২৩৩ ॥

ākāśādi guṇa yena para para bhūte
eka-dui-tina-cāri krame pañca pṛthivīte

SYNONYMS

ākāśa-ādi—beginning with the sky; *guṇa*—qualities; *yena*—as; *para para*—one after another; *bhūte*—in the material elements; *eka*—one; *dui*—two; *tina*—three; *cāri*—four; *krame*—in this way; *pañca*—all five qualities; *pṛthivīte*—in earth.

TRANSLATION

"All the material qualities evolve one after another in the material elements, beginning from ether. By gradual evolution, first one quality develops, then two qualities develop, then three and four, until all five qualities are found in earth.

TEXT 234

এইমত মধুরে সব ভাব-সমাহার ।
অতএব আস্বাদাধিক্যে করে চমৎকার ॥ ২৩৪ ॥

ei-mata madhure saba bhāva-samāhāra
ataeva āsvādādhikye kare camatkāra

SYNONYMS

ei-mata—in this way; *madhure*—on the platform of conjugal love; *saba*—all; *bhāva-samāhāra*—amalgamation of the feelings; *ataeva*—therefore; *āsvāda-adhikye*—from the increase of tasting by the devotees; *kare camatkāra*—is certainly wonderful.

TRANSLATION

"Similarly, on the platform of conjugal love, all the feelings of the devotees are amalgamated. The intensified taste is certainly wonderful."

TEXT 235

এই ভক্তিরসের করিলাঙ, দিগ্‌দরশন ।
ইহার বিস্তার মনে করিহ ভাবন ॥ ২৩৫ ॥

ei bhakti-rasera karilāṅa, dig-daraśana
ihāra vistāra mane kariha bhāvana

SYNONYMS

ei—this; *bhakti-rasera*—of the feelings of devotional service; *karilāṅa*—I have described; *dik-daraśana*—general survey; *ihāra*—of this; *vistāra*—expansion; *mane*—within the mind; *kariha*—you should do; *bhāvana*—consideration.

TRANSLATION

Śrī Caitanya Mahāprabhu then concluded: "I have simply given a general survey describing the mellows of devotional service. You can consider how to adjust and expand this.

TEXT 236

ভাবিতে ভাবিতে কৃষ্ণ স্ফুরয়ে অন্তরে ।
কৃষ্ণকৃপায় অজ্ঞ পায় রসসিন্ধু-পারে ॥ ২৩৬ ॥

bhāvite bhāvite kṛṣṇa sphuraye antare
kṛṣṇa-kṛpāya ajña pāya rasa-sindhu-pāre

SYNONYMS

bhāvite bhāvite—in this way when one is strictly in thought; *kṛṣṇa*—Lord Kṛṣṇa; *sphuraye antare*—manifests within; *kṛṣṇa-kṛpāya*—by the mercy of Kṛṣṇa; *ajña*—one not expert in knowledge; *pāya*—reaches; *rasa-sindhu-pāre*—the shore of the ocean of transcendental mellows.

TRANSLATION

"When one thinks of Kṛṣṇa constantly, love for Him is manifest within the heart. Even though one may be ignorant, one can reach the shore of the ocean of transcendental love by Lord Kṛṣṇa's mercy."

TEXT 237

এত বলি' প্রভু তাঁরে কৈলা আলিঙ্গন ।
বারাণসী চলিবারে প্রভুর হৈল মন ॥ ২৩৭ ॥

eta bali' prabhu tāṅre kailā āliṅgana
vārāṇasī calibāre prabhura haila mana

SYNONYMS

eta bali'—saying this; *prabhu*—Śrī Caitanya Mahāprabhu; *tāṅre*—unto Rūpa Gosvāmī; *kailā*—did; *āliṅgana*—embracing; *vārāṇasī*—toward Benares; *calibāre*—to go; *prabhura*—of Lord Śrī Caitanya Mahāprabhu; *haila*—was; *mana*—the mind.

TRANSLATION

After saying this, Śrī Caitanya Mahāprabhu embraced Śrīla Rūpa Gosvāmī. The Lord then decided to go to the city of Benares.

TEXT 238

প্রভাতে উঠিয়া যবে করিলা গমন।
তবে তাঁর পদে রূপ করে নিবেদন ॥ ২৩৮ ॥

prabhāte uṭhiyā yabe karilā gamana
tabe tāṅra pade rūpa kare nivedana

SYNONYMS

prabhāte—in the morning; *uṭhiyā*—getting up; *yabe*—when; *karilā*—made; *gamana*—departure; *tabe*—at that time; *tāṅra*—His; *pade*—at the lotus feet; *rūpa*—Śrīla Rūpa Gosvāmī; *kare*—does; *nivedana*—submission.

TRANSLATION

The next morning, when Śrī Caitanya Mahāprabhu arose and prepared to leave for Vārāṇasī [Benares], Śrīla Rūpa Gosvāmī made the following statement at the Lord's lotus feet.

TEXT 239

'আজ্ঞা হয়, আসি মুঞি শ্রীচরণ-সঙ্গে।
সহিতে না পারি মুঞি বিরহ-তরঙ্গে ॥' ২৩৯ ॥

'ājñā haya, āsi muñi śrī-caraṇa-saṅge
sahite nā pāri muñi viraha-taraṅge'

SYNONYMS

ājñā haya—if there is permission; *āsi*—may come; *muñi*—I; *śrī-caraṇa-saṅge*—with Your Lordship; *sahite*—to tolerate; *nā pāri*—not able; *muñi*—I; *viraha-taraṅge*—the waves of separation.

TRANSLATION

"If You give me permission, I shall go with Your Lordship. It is not possible for me to tolerate the waves of separation."

TEXT 240

প্রভু কহে,—তোমার কর্তব্য, আমার বচন।
নিকটে আসিয়াছ তুমি, যাহ বৃন্দাবন ॥ ২৪০ ॥

prabhu kahe,——tomāra kartavya, āmāra vacana
nikaṭe āsiyācha tumi, yāha vṛndāvana

SYNONYMS

prabhu kahe—Śrī Caitanya Mahāprabhu replied; *tomāra kartavya*—your duty; *āmāra vacana*—My order; *nikaṭe āsiyācha*—have come near; *tumi*—you; *yāha*—go; *vṛndāvana*—to Vṛndāvana.

TRANSLATION

Śrī Caitanya Mahāprabhu replied, "Your duty is to carry out My order. You have come near Vṛndāvana. Now you should go there.

TEXT 241

বৃন্দাবন হৈতে তুমি গৌড়দেশ দিয়া ।
আমারে মিলিবা নীলাচলেতে আসিয়া ॥ ২৪১ ॥

vṛndāvana haite tumi gauḍa-deśa diyā
āmāre milibā nīlācalete āsiyā

SYNONYMS

vṛndāvana haite—from Vṛndāvana; *tumi*—you; *gauḍa-deśa diyā*—by way of Bengal; *āmāre*—Me; *milibā*—will meet; *nīlācalete*—at Jagannātha Purī; *āsiyā*—coming.

TRANSLATION

"Later, you can go from Vṛndāvana to Jagannātha Purī through Bengal [Gauḍa-deśa]. There you will meet Me again."

TEXT 242

তাঁরে আলিঙ্গিয়া প্রভু নৌকাতে চড়িলা ।
মূর্চ্ছিত হঞা তেঁহো তাহাঞি পড়িলা ॥ ২৪২ ॥

tāṅre āliṅgiyā prabhu naukāte caḍilā
mūrcchita hañā teṅho tāhāñi paḍilā

SYNONYMS

tāṅre—him; *āliṅgiyā*—embracing; *prabhu*—Śrī Caitanya Mahāprabhu; *naukāte*—in a boat; *caḍilā*—got aboard; *mūrcchita hañā*—fainting; *teṅho*—he (Śrīla Rūpa Gosvāmī); *tāhāñi*—on the spot; *paḍilā*—fell.

TRANSLATION

After embracing Rūpa Gosvāmī, Śrī Caitanya Mahāprabhu got into a boat. Rūpa Gosvāmī fainted and fell down on the spot.

TEXT 243

দাক্ষিণাত্য-বিপ্র তাঁরে ঘরে লঞা গেলা ।
তবে দুই ভাই বৃন্দাবনেরে চলিলা ॥ ২৪৩ ॥

dākṣiṇātya-vipra tāṅre ghare lañā gelā
tabe dui bhāi vṛndāvanere calilā

SYNONYMS

dākṣiṇātya-vipra—the *brāhmaṇa* from Deccan; *tāṅre*—him (Rūpa Gosvāmī); *ghare lañā*—taking to his home; *gelā*—went; *tabe*—thereafter; *dui bhāi*—the two brothers; *vṛndāvanere*—toward Vṛndāvana; *calilā*—departed.

TRANSLATION

The brāhmaṇa from Deccan took Rūpa Gosvāmī to his home, and thereafter the two brothers departed for Vṛndāvana.

TEXT 244

মহাপ্রভু চলি' চলি' আইলা বারাণসী ।
চন্দ্রশেখর মিলিলা গ্রামের বাহিরে আসি' ॥ ২৪৪ ॥

mahāprabhu cali' cali' āilā vārāṇasī
candraśekhara mililā grāmera bāhire āsi'

SYNONYMS

mahāprabhu—Śrī Caitanya Mahāprabhu; *cali' cali'*—walking and walking; *āilā*—arrived; *vārāṇasī*—at Vārāṇasī; *candraśekhara*—Candraśekhara; *mililā*—He met; *grāmera*—of the village; *bāhire*—outside; *āsi'*—coming.

TRANSLATION

After walking and walking, Śrī Caitanya Mahāprabhu finally arrived at Vārāṇasī, where He met Candraśekhara, who was coming out of the city.

TEXT 245

রাত্রে তেঁহো স্বপ্ন দেখে,—প্রভু আইলা ঘরে ।
প্রাতঃকালে আসি' রহে গ্রামের বাহিরে ॥ ২৪৫ ॥

rātre teṅho svapna dekhe,—prabhu āilā ghare
prātaḥ-kāle āsi' rahe grāmera bāhire

SYNONYMS

rātre—at night; *teṅho*—he (Candraśekhara); *svapna*—a dream; *dekhe*—saw; *prabhu*—Śrī Caitanya Mahāprabhu; *āilā*—has come; *ghare*—to his home; *prātaḥ-kāle*—in the morning; *āsi'*—coming; *rahe*—he remained; *grāmera bāhire*—outside the city.

TRANSLATION

In a dream Candraśekhara had seen that Lord Śrī Caitanya Mahāprabhu had come to his home; therefore in the morning Candraśekhara went outside the city to receive the Lord.

TEXT 246

আচম্বিতে প্রভু দেখি' চরণে পড়িলা।
আনন্দিত হঞা নিজ-গৃহে লঞা গেলা ॥ ২৪৬ ॥

ācambite prabhu dekhi' caraṇe paḍilā
ānandita hañā nija-gṛhe lañā gelā

SYNONYMS

ācambite—suddenly; *prabhu*—Śrī Caitanya Mahāprabhu; *dekhi'*—seeing; *caraṇe*—at His feet; *paḍilā*—he fell; *ānandita hañā*—becoming very glad; *nija-gṛhe*—to his own place; *lañā*—taking; *gelā*—went.

TRANSLATION

While Candraśekhara was waiting outside the city, he suddenly saw Śrī Caitanya Mahāprabhu arrive, and he fell down at the Lord's feet. Being very happy, he took the Lord to his home.

TEXT 247

তপনমিশ্র শুনি' আসি' প্রভুরে মিলিলা।
ইষ্টগোষ্ঠী করি' প্রভুর নিমন্ত্রণ কৈলা ॥ ২৪৭ ॥

tapana-miśra śuni' āsi' prabhure mililā
iṣṭa-goṣṭhī kari' prabhura nimantraṇa kailā

SYNONYMS

tapana-miśra—Tapana Miśra; *śuni'*—hearing; *āsi'*—coming; *prabhure mililā*—met the Lord; *iṣṭa-goṣṭhī kari'*—conversing; *prabhura*—to Lord Śrī Caitanya Mahāprabhu; *nimantraṇa*—invitation; *kailā*—made.

TRANSLATION

Tapana Miśra also heard news of the Lord's arrival in Vārāṇasī, and he went to Candraśekhara's house to meet Him. After talking, he invited the Lord to take lunch at his place.

TEXT 248

নিজ ঘরে লঞা প্রভুরে ভিক্ষা করাইল ।
ভট্টাচার্যে চন্দ্রশেখর নিমন্ত্রণ কৈল ॥ ২৪৮ ॥

nija ghare lañā prabhure bhikṣā karāila
bhaṭṭācārye candraśekhara nimantraṇa kaila

SYNONYMS

nija ghare—to his own place; *lañā*—taking; *prabhure*—to the Lord; *bhikṣā karāila*—offered lunch; *bhaṭṭācārye*—unto Balabhadra Bhaṭṭācārya; *candra-śekhara*—Candraśekhara; *nimantraṇa*—invitation; *kaila*—made.

TRANSLATION

Tapana Miśra took Caitanya Mahāprabhu to his own house and gave Him lunch. Candraśekhara invited Balabhadra Bhaṭṭācārya to take lunch at his home.

TEXT 249

ভিক্ষা করাঞা মিশ্র কহে প্রভু-পায় ধরি' ।
এক ভিক্ষা মাগি, মোরে দেহ' কৃপা করি' ॥ ২৪৯ ॥

bhikṣā karāñā miśra kahe prabhu-pāya dhari'
eka bhikṣā māgi, more deha' kṛpā kari'

SYNONYMS

bhikṣā karāñā—after offering the lunch; *miśra*—Tapana Miśra; *kahe*—said; *prabhu*—of Lord Śrī Caitanya Mahāprabhu; *pāya*—the lotus feet; *dhari'*—touching; *eka bhikṣā*—one favor; *māgi*—I beg; *more*—unto Me; *deha'*—kindly deliver; *kṛpā kari'*—by Your causeless mercy.

TRANSLATION

After offering lunch to Śrī Caitanya Mahāprabhu, Tapana Miśra begged a favor from the Lord and requested Him to reward him mercy.

TEXT 250

যাবৎ তোমার হয় কাশীপুরে স্থিতি।
মোর ঘর বিনা ভিক্ষা না করিবা কতি॥ ২৫০ ॥

yāvat tomāra haya kāśī-pure sthiti
mora ghara vinā bhikṣā nā karibā kati

SYNONYMS

yāvat—as long as; *tomāra*—Your; *haya*—there is; *kāśī-pure*—at Vārāṇasī; *sthiti*—stay; *mora ghara*—my place; *vinā*—except; *bhikṣā*—lunch; *nā karibā*—kindly do not take; *kati*—anywhere.

TRANSLATION

Tapana Miśra said, "As long as Your Lordship stays in Vārāṇasī, please do not accept an invitation from anyone but me."

TEXT 251

প্রভু জানেন—দিন পাঁচ-সাত সে রহিব।
সন্ন্যাসীর সঙ্গে ভিক্ষা কাহাঁ না করিব॥ ২৫১ ॥

prabhu jānena——dina pāṅca-sāta se rahiba
sannyāsīra saṅge bhikṣā kāhāṅ nā kariba

SYNONYMS

prabhu—Śrī Caitanya Mahāprabhu; *jānena*—knows; *dina*—days; *pāṅca-sāta*—five days or at the most a week; *se*—that; *rahiba*—I shall stay; *sannyāsīra saṅge*—with other Māyāvādī *sannyāsīs; bhikṣā*—lunch; *kāhāṅ*—at any time; *nā kariba*—I shall not take.

TRANSLATION

It was known to Śrī Caitanya Mahāprabhu that He would remain there only five or seven days. He would not accept any invitation that involved Māyāvādī sannyāsīs.

TEXT 252

এত জানি' তাঁর ভিক্ষা কৈলা অঙ্গীকার।
বাসা-নিষ্ঠা কৈলা চন্দ্রশেখরের ঘর॥ ২৫২ ॥

eta jāni' tāṅra bhikṣā kailā aṅgīkāra
vāsā-niṣṭhā kailā candraśekharera ghara

SYNONYMS

eta jāni'—on this understanding; *tāṅra*—his; *bhikṣā*—lunch; *kailā aṅgīkāra*—He accepted; *vāsā-niṣṭhā*—residence; *kailā*—made; *candraśekharera ghara*—the house of Candraśekhara.

TRANSLATION

With this understanding, Śrī Caitanya Mahāprabhu agreed to accept lunch at the place of Tapana Miśra. The Lord made His residence at the home of Candraśekhara.

TEXT 253

মহারাষ্ট্রীয় বিপ্র আসি' তাঁহারে মিলিলা ।
প্রভু তাঁরে স্নেহ করি' কৃপা প্রকাশিলা ॥ ২৫৩ ॥

mahārāṣṭrīya vipra āsi' tāṅhāre mililā
prabhu tāṅre sneha kari' kṛpā prakāśilā

SYNONYMS

mahārāṣṭrīya vipra—the Mahārāṣṭrīya *brāhmaṇa; āsi'*—coming; *tāṅhāre*—him; *mililā*—met; *prabhu*—Śrī Caitanya Mahāprabhu; *tāṅre*—to him; *sneha kari'*—showing His affection; *kṛpā prakāśilā*—distributed His mercy.

TRANSLATION

The Mahārāṣṭrīya brāhmaṇa came, and the Lord met him. Out of affection, the Lord bestowed His mercy upon him.

TEXT 254

মহাপ্রভু আইলা শুনি' শিষ্ট শিষ্ট জন ।
ব্রাহ্মণ, ক্ষত্রিয় আসি' করেন দরশন ॥ ২৫৪ ॥

mahāprabhu āilā śuni' śiṣṭa śiṣṭa jana
brāhmaṇa, kṣatriya āsi' karena daraśana

SYNONYMS

mahāprabhu āilā—Śrī Caitanya Mahāprabhu has arrived; *śuni'*—hearing; *śiṣṭa śiṣṭa jana*—all respectable persons; *brāhmaṇa*—belonging to the *brāhmaṇa* community; *kṣatriya*—belonging to the *kṣatriya* community; *āsi'*—coming; *karena daraśana*—see.

TRANSLATION

Hearing that Śrī Caitanya Mahāprabhu had come, all the respectable members of the brāhmaṇa and kṣatriya communities came to see Him.

TEXT 255

শ্রীরূপ-উপরে প্রভুর যত কৃপা হৈল ।
অত্যন্ত বিস্তার-কথা সংক্ষেপে কহিল ॥ ২৫৫ ॥

śrī-rūpa-upare prabhura yata kṛpā haila
atyanta vistāra-kathā saṅkṣepe kahila

SYNONYMS

śrī-rūpa-upare—upon Śrī Rūpa Gosvāmī; *prabhura*—of Śrī Caitanya Mahāprabhu; *yata*—as much; *kṛpā*—mercy; *haila*—there was; *atyanta*—very much; *vistāra-kathā*—elaborate topic; *saṅkṣepe*—in brief; *kahila*—I have described.

TRANSLATION

Much mercy was thus bestowed upon Śrī Rūpa Gosvāmī, and I have briefly described all those topics.

TEXT 256

শ্রদ্ধা করি' এই কথা শুনে যেই জনে ।
প্রেমভক্তি পায় সেই চৈতন্য-চরণে ॥ ২৫৬ ॥

śraddhā kari' ei kathā śune ye jane
prema-bhakti pāya sei caitanya-caraṇe

SYNONYMS

śraddhā kari'—with faith; *ei kathā*—this description; *śune*—hears; *yei jane*—any person who; *prema-bhakti*—love of Godhead; *pāya*—achieves; *sei*—that person; *caitanya-caraṇe*—at the lotus feet of Śrī Caitanya Mahāprabhu.

TRANSLATION

Whoever hears this narration with faith and love certainly develops love of God at the lotus feet of Śrī Caitanya Mahāprabhu.

TEXT 257

শ্রীরূপ-রঘুনাথ-পদে যার আশ ।
চৈতন্যচরিতামৃত কহে কৃষ্ণদাস ॥ ২৫৭ ॥

śrī-rūpa-raghunātha-pade yāra āśa
caitanya-caritāmṛta kahe kṛṣṇadāsa

SYNONYMS

śrī-rūpa—Śrīla Rūpa Gosvāmī; *raghunātha*—Śrīla Raghunātha dāsa Gosvāmī; *pade*—at the lotus feet; *yāra*—whose; *āśa*—expectation; *caitanya-caritāmṛta*—the book named *Caitanya-caritāmṛta; kahe*—describes; *kṛṣṇadāsa*—Śrīla Kṛṣṇadāsa Kavirāja Gosvāmī.

TRANSLATION

Praying at the lotus feet of Śrī Rūpa and Śrī Raghunātha, always desiring their mercy, I, Kṛṣṇadāsa, narrate Śrī Caitanya-caritāmṛta, following in their footsteps.

Thus end the Bhaktivedanta purports to the Śrī Caitanya-caritāmṛta, Madhya-līlā, *Nineteenth Chapter, describing the Lord's instructions to Śrīla Rūpa Gosvāmī at Prayāga in the science of devotional service.*

References

The statements of *Śrī Caitanya-caritāmṛta* are all confirmed by standard Vedic authorities. The following authentic scriptures are quoted in this book on the pages listed. Numerals in bold type refer the reader to *Śrī Caitanya-caritāmṛta's* translations. Numerals in regular type are references to its purports.

Ādi-varāha Purāṇa, 158.

Amṛta-pravāha-bhāṣya (Bhaktivinoda Ṭhākura), 129, 245, 392-393.

Bhagavad-gītā, 16, 49, 50, 55, 64, 74, **95,** 99, 100, 103, 316, 318, 319, 320, 326, 328, 349, 350, 362, 375

Bhakti-rasāmṛta-sindhu (Rūpa Gosvāmī), 48, 49, 73, 315, 316, 352, 356, 360, 361-364, 365, 366, 367, 383

Bhakti-ratnākara (Narahari Cakravartī), 142, 148, 157, 158, 162, 164, 165, 166

Bhakti-sandarbha (Jīva Gosvāmī), 189

Bhāvārtha-dīpikā (Śrīdhara Svāmī), 40, 188

Brahma-saṁhitā, 26, 48, 298, 336

Bṛhan-nāradīya Purāṇa, 194

Caitanya-bhāgavata (Vṛndāvana dāsa Ṭhākura), 54

Caitanya-candrodaya (Kavi-karṇapūra), **307-**308

Govinda-līlāmṛta (Kṛṣṇadāsa Kavirāja), **117-120, 273**

Hari-bhakti-sudhodaya, **284**

Hari-bhakti-vilāsa (Sanātana Gosvāmī), 190, **270-271**

Kāśī-khaṇḍa, 41

Mahābhārata, 106

Mathurā-khaṇḍa, 148

Mathurā-māhātmya, 60

Glossary

A

Ācārya—one who teaches by his example.
Adbhuta-rasa—the indirect relationship of wonder.
Aghana—transcendental bliss that is incomplete, or not concentrated.
Ananta—unlimited.
Aṇimā-siddhi—mystic power by which one can become so small that he can enter into stone.
Anubhāva—bodily symptoms manifested by a devotee in ecstatic love for Kṛṣṇa.
Anukara—imitating.
Anusara—trying to follow in the footsteps.
Aparā vidyā—material knowledge.
Arcana—Deity worship.
Artha—economic development.
Āryans—civilized human beings who follow the Vedic principles.
Asat-saṅga—the association of nondevotees.
Ātmā—the soul.
Avyakta—the unmanifested material energy.

B

Bhāgavatam system—spreading of Kṛṣṇa consciousness philosophy by recitation and discussion of *Śrīmad-Bhāgavatam.*
Bhāvuka—sentimental; can also mean advanced in the knowledge of spiritual *rasas.*
Bhāva—preliminary stage of love of God.
Bhakta-latā-bīja—the seed of devotional service.
Bhakti—devotional service; engaging all the senses in the service of the master of the senses, Kṛṣṇa.
Bhakta—a devotee.
Bhāgyavān—most fortunate.
Bhāgavata-vidyā—transcendental superior knowledge.
Bhayānaka-rasa—the indirect relationship of fear.
Bībhatsa-rasa—the indirect relationship of abomination.
Brahma-bhūta—the stage of spiritual realization when one becomes happy as a result of being relieved from material conceptions.
Brahmāṇḍa—the universe.

C

Caṇḍāla—dog-eater.
Cit-kaṇa—a particle of spirit.

D

Dama—controlling the senses and not being deviated from the Lord's service.

Dāsya-rasa—one of the direct relationships, servitude; condition when the living entity develops love of God according to the desires of the spirit soul.

Dāsya-rati—*dāsya-rasa;* the platform on which a devotee is attached to rendering service to Kṛṣṇa.

Dharma—religion; actual *dharma* is devotional service to Kṛṣṇa, the supreme occupation for all humanity.

Dharmaḥ kaitavaḥ—cheating religions.

Dhṛti—controlling the tongue and the genitals.

E

Evādat—offering prayers to the Supreme Person (Arabic).

G

Garuḍa—the eagle carrier of Lord Viṣṇu.

Gaurava-dāsya—condition when the devotee takes the form of giving protection to the Lord; category of *dāsya-rasa.*

Gaurava-sakhya—the mellow friendship in awe and veneration.

Ghana—transcendental bliss that is complete, or concentrated.

Guru—spiritual master.

Guru-avajña—disobeying the instructions of the spiritual master.

Guru-kṛpā—the mercy of the spiritual master.

H

Hari—the name of Kṛṣṇa which means He who takes away all miseries.

Hari bol—"Chant the holy name of Hari."

Hāsya-rasa—the indirect relationship of laughing.

Hlādinī—the ecstatic potency of the Lord.

I

Indriya-saṁyama—curbing one's senses.

J

Jaṅgama-nārāyaṇa—moving Nārāyaṇa.

Jīva—the living entity.

Jīva-hiṁsana—animal killing or envy of other living beings.
Jñāna—knowledge.
Jñāna-mārga—the cultivation of knowledge.
Jñānīs—mental speculative philosophers.

K

Kāma—sense gratification.
Karma—fruitive work and the resultant reactions.
Karma-vīra—a successful fruitive worker.
Karmīs—fruitive workers.
Karma-niṣṭha—one who aspires to enjoy the results of his pious activities.
Karuṇa-rasa—the indirect relationship of compassion.
Kevalā—devotional platform of seeing the unlimited potency of Kṛṣṇa, but still considering oneself equal with Him.
Kīrtana—congregational chanting of the holy names of the Lord.
Kitava—a great cheater.
Kleśa-ghnī—description of devotional service indicating that it reduces or nullifies all kinds of suffering.
Kṛṣṇa-bhakta—a devotee of Kṛṣṇa.
Kumbha-melā—a fair held every twelve years at Prayāga for spiritual upliftment; attended by people from all over India.
Kuṭīnāṭī—diplomatic behavior.
Kṛṣṇa-ākarṣiṇī—description of devotional service indicating that it gradually attracts Kṛṣṇa toward the devotee.

L

Laghimā-siddhi—mystic perfection of entering into the sun planet by using the rays of the sunshine.
Loka-pratāraka—a pretender.

M

Madhura-rasa—attachment in conjugal love when in accordance with one's own natural development in Kṛṣṇa consciousness one's attraction leans towards conjugal love within the heart.
Mādhurya-rati—madhura-rasa; devotional service to Kṛṣṇa in the mood of conjugal love.
Māgha-melā—a yearly fair held during the month of Māgha at Prayāga for spiritual upliftment.
Mahābhāva—stage of love of Kṛṣṇa when ecstatic symptoms become most bright.
Mahājana—one who understands the Absolute Truth and throughout his life behaves likes a pure devotee.

Mahā-mantra—the great chanting for deliverance: Hare Kṛṣṇa, Hare Kṛṣṇa, Kṛṣṇa Kṛṣṇa, Hare Hare/ Hare Rāma, Hare Rāma, Rāma Rāma, Hare Hare.

Mahātmā—great soul.

Mahā-vadānya-avatāra—Caitanya Mahāprabhu, the most munificent incarnation.

Majīda—a mosque.

Māna—when the lover feels novel sweetness by exchanging hearty loving words but wishes to hide his feelings by crooked means.

Māyā—illusion; the external energy of Kṛṣṇa.

Mleccha—one who does not strictly follow regulative principles.

Mokṣa—liberation.

Mṛdaṅga—a double-headed drum used in *kīrtana*.

Mukti—liberation.

N

Naiṣkarma—*akarma;* action for which one suffers no reaction because it is performed in Kṛṣṇa consciousness.

Nārāyaṇa-parāyaṇa—a devotee of Lord Nārāyaṇa.

Nitya-siddha—devotee who is eternally on the transcendental platform.

P

Pañcarātra system—method of temple worship.

Paramahaṁsa—one who does not live in the material world and who does not envy others.

Paramparā—disciplic succession.

Parā-vidyā—transcendental knowledge.

Pāṣaṇḍī—a nondevotee who does not accept the Vedic conclusions; an atheist.

Prākṛta-sahjiyās—materialistic so-called devotees who imagine that they are advanced in confidential love of Kṛṣṇa.

Praṇaya—that mellow of love when there is a possibility to receive direct honor, but it is avoided.

Prāpti-siddhi—mystic perfection of aquisition by which the *yogī* can reach his hand anywhere and obtain whatever he likes.

Prasannātmā—joyfulness attained when one is relieved from material conceptions.

Prema—pure love of Kṛṣṇa, symptomized by a heart completely softened and devoid of material desires, and by strong emotional feelings.

Prema-vataḥ—one who has great love for the spiritual master.

Puraścaraṇa—a preliminary ritualistic performance for the fulfillment of certain desires.

Puruṣa—Viṣṇu, the incarnation of the Lord for material creation; the male or controlling principle.

R

Rāga—attachment for Kṛṣṇa, at which stage the beloved converts unhappiness into happiness.
Raudra-rasa—one of the indirect relationships, anger.
Rājarṣi—a devotee king.
Rasas—mellows of devotional service. *See also: śānta-, dāsya-, sakhya-, vātsalya-, madhura-rasas.*
Rūpānuga—one who follows in the footsteps of Rūpa Gosvāmī.

S

Sac-cid-ānanda-vigraha—Kṛṣṇa's eternal form of bliss and knowledge.
Sādhaka—neophyte devotees who are advancing toward the perfectional platform.
Sādhava-bhakti—awakening to devotional service by following regulative principles.
Sādhana-siddha—devotee who is elevated to the transcendental platform by the execution of devotional service.
Sādhu—an honest man.
Sakhya-rasa—the direct relationship of friendship.
Sakhya-rati—*sakhya-rasa;* relationship with Kṛṣṇa on the platform of friendship.
Śālagrāma-śilā—a stone Deity incarnation of Viṣṇu.
Sāloka—liberation of living on the same planet as the Lord.
Śamatā—stage when one is fully attached to Kṛṣṇa's lotus feet.
Sambhrama-dāsya—one of the indirect relationships, respect.
Sāmīpya—liberation of having the Lord's personal association.
Śānta-rasa—the direct relationship of neutral love.
Śānta-rati—*śānta-rasa;* neutral position of realization of Kṛṣṇa.
Sārṣṭi—liberation of having equal opulences with the Supreme Lord.
Sārūpya—liberation of having the same bodily features as the Lord.
Śāstras—revealed scriptures.
Sāttvika—endowed with the quality of goodness.
Siddhi-lobhī—one who is greedy for material perfection.
Siddhi-vraja—opulences of material perfection.
Smārta-brāhmaṇas—*brāhmaṇas* who are disciples of the Māyāvāda school.
Sneha—affection for Kṛṣṇa, at which stage the lover cannot be without the beloved.
Snigdha—very peaceful.
Śravaṇa—hearing.
Śruti-śāstra-nindana—offense of blaspheming the Vedic literature.
Sthānu—unchangeable.
Stāṃi-puruṣa—mistaking a dry tree without leaves for a person.
Sthāyibhāva—continuous love of Godhead in devotional service.
Śubhadā—description of devotional service indicating that it bestows all good fortune.

Śuddha-bhakti—pure devotional service.

Śūdra-mahājana—a person born in a low family but raised to the platform of *brāhmaṇa* by initiation.

Su-snigdha—affectionate.

Svarūpa—original characteristics of a substance; for the *jīva*, service of Kṛṣṇa.

T

Titikṣā—tolerance; endurance of unhappiness.

Tulasī—a pure devotee in the form of a tree, the leaves of which are always offered to Kṛṣṇa.

Triveṇī—confluence of three sacred rivers at Prayāga.

U

Ucchṛṅkhala—whimsical.

V

Vaikuṇṭha—(lit., without anxiety) the spiritual sky.

Vairāgya—renunciation.

Vātsalya-rasa—the direct relationship of parental love.

Vātsalya-rati—*vātsalya-rasa;* the platform on which the devotee thinks of Kṛṣṇa in His childhood feature.

Veda—knowledge.

Veda-vāda-ratā—*karmīs* who become entangled in material activities disguised as spiritual activities.

Vibhāva—the cause or basis for relishing transcendental mellow.

Vīra-rasa—one of the indirect relationships, chivalry.

Virajā River—the river between the material and spiritual natures.

Viśrambha—the mellow of friendship in equality.

Vivarta-vāda—the Māyāvādī interpretation of Vedānta that the Supreme Lord becomes changed when He expands.

Y

Yavana—meat-eater.

Yogamāyā—Kṛṣṇa's internal energy.

Yoga-siddhis—mystic perfections.

Yogīs—those who practive the eight-fold mystic *yoga* process to gain mystic *siddhis* or Paramātmā realization.

Bengali Pronunciation Guide

BENGALI DIACRITICAL EQUIVALENTS AND PRONUNCIATION

Vowels

অ a   আ ā   ই i   ঈ ī   উ u   ঊ ū   ঋ ṛ

ৠ ṝ   এ e   ঐ ai   ও o   ঔ au

ং ṁ *(anusvāra)*   ঁ ṅ *(candra-bindu)*   ঃ ḥ *(visarga)*

Consonants

Gutterals:	ক ka	খ kha	গ ga	ঘ gha	ঙ ṅa
Palatals:	চ ca	ছ cha	জ ja	ঝ jha	ঞ ña
Cerebrals:	ট ṭa	ঠ ṭha	ড ḍa	ঢ ḍha	ণ ṇa
Dentals:	ত ta	থ tha	দ da	ধ dha	ন na
Labials:	প pa	ফ pha	ব ba	ভ bha	ম ma
Semivowels:	য ya	র ra	ল la	ব va	
Sibilants:	শ śa	ষ ṣa	স sa	হ ha	

Vowel Symbols

The vowels are written as follows after a consonant:

া ā   ি i   ী ī   ু u   ূ ū   ৃ ṛ   ৄ ṝ   ে e   ৈ ai   ো o   ৌ au

For example: কা kā   কি ki   কী kī   কু ku   কূ kū   কৃ kṛ

কৄ kṝ   কে ke   কৈ kai   কো ko   কৌ kau

The letter *a* is implied after a consonant with no vowel symbol.

The symbol *virāma* (্) indicates that there is no final vowel. ক্ k

The letters above should be pronounced as follows:

a –like the *o* in h*o*t; sometimes like the *o* in go; final *a* is usually silent.
ā –like the *a* in f*a*r.
i, ī –like the *ee* in m*ee*t.
u, ū –like the *u* in r*u*le.
ṛ –like the *ri* in *ri*m.
ṝ –like the *ree* in *ree*d.
e –like the *ai* in p*ai*n; rarely like *e* in b*e*t.
ai –like the *oi* in b*oi*l.
o –like the *o* in g*o*.
au –like the *ow* in *ow*l.
ṁ –*(anusvāra)* like the *ng* in so*ng*.
ḥ –*(visarga)* a final *h* sound like in Ah.
ṅ –*(candra-bindu)* a nasal *n* sound like in the French word *bon*.
k –like the *k* in *k*ite.
kh –like the *kh* in Ec*kh*art.
g –like the *g* in *g*ot.
gh –like the *gh* in bi*g-h*ouse.
ṅ –like the *n* in ba*n*k.
c –like the *ch* in *ch*alk.
ch –like the *chh* in mu*ch-h*aste.
j –like the *j* in *j*oy.
jh –like the *geh* in colle*ge-h*all.
ñ –like the *n* in bu*n*ch.
ṭ –like the *t* in *t*alk.
ṭh –like the *th* in ho*t-h*ouse.
ḍ –like the *d* in *d*awn.
ḍh –like the *dh* in goo*d-h*ouse.
ṇ –like the *n* in *gn*aw.
t–as in *t*alk but with the tongue against the the teeth.
th–as in ho*t-h*ouse but with the tongue against the teeth.
d–as in *d*awn but with the tongue against the teeth.
dh–as in goo*d-h*ouse but with the tongue against the teeth.
n–as in *n*or but with the tongue against the teeth.
p –like the *p* in *p*ine.
ph –like the *ph* in *ph*ilosopher.
b –like the *b* in *b*ird.
bh –like the *bh* in ru*b-h*ard.
m –like the *m* in *m*other.
y –like the *j* in *j*aw. য
y –like the *y* in *y*ear. য়
r –like the *r* in *r*un.
l –like the *l* in *l*aw.
v –like the *b* in *b*ird or like the *w* in d*w*arf.
ś, ṣ –like the *sh* in *sh*op.
s –like the *s* in *s*un.
h–like the *h* in *h*ome.

This is a general guide to Bengali pronunciation. The Bengali transliterations in this book accurately show the original Bengali spelling of the text. One should note, however, that in Bengali, as in English, spelling is not always a true indication of how a word is pronounced. Tape recordings of His Divine Grace A. C. Bhaktivedanta Swami Prabhupāda chanting the original Bengali verses are available from the International Society for Krishna Consciousness, 3764 Watseka Ave., Los Angeles, California 90034.

Index of Bengali and Sanskrit Verses

This index constitutes a complete alphabetical listing of the first and third line of each four-line verse and both lines of each two-line verse in *Śrī Caitanya-caritāmṛta.* In the first column the transliteration is given, and in the second and third columns respectively the chapter-verse references and page number for each verse are to be found.

B

C

D

E

G

H

I

J

K

U

General Index

Numerals in bold type indicate references to *Śrī Caitanya-caritāmṛta's* verses. Numerals in regular type are references to its purports.

A

Absolute Truth
according to Māyāvāda philosophy, 69-70
constituents of, 72
explained by Prakāśānanda Sarasvatī, 55-56
has many incarnations, 298
living entity always fragmental part of, 188
three features of, 327-328
Vedānta ultimate conclusion of, 50
See also: Kṛṣṇa, Supreme Lord

Acchedyo 'yam adāhyo 'yam
verses quoted, 324

Āḍāila-grāma
Vallabha Bhaṭṭa stayed at, 276-277

Ādau gurv-āśrayam
quoted, 350

Ādi-varāha Purāṇa
quoted on Kāmyavana, 158

Advaitam acyutam anādim ananta-rūpam
quoted, 298

Āgaraoyālās
as same community as *svarṇa-vaṇiks,* 96

Ahaṁ-mama-buddhi
quoted, 189

Akrūra
saw Vaikuṇṭha under water, 200

Akrūra-tīrtha
Caitanya stayed at, **166**
location of, 200

Allahabad
See: Prayāga

Amṛta-pravāha-bhāṣya
description of *rasas* summarized in, 392-393
summary of Chapter Nineteen in, 245
summary of Chapter Eighteen in, 129

Ānanda-cinmaya-rasa-pratibhāvitā-bhis
verses quoted, 336

Ananta
writes millions of books on Caitanya, **126**

Anger
absent in Vṛndāvana, **20**
as indirect mellow, **365**

Animals
induced to chant Hare Kṛṣṇa, **2, 15-21, 23**
killing of as weed to devotional creeper, 342
live in friendship with humans in Vṛndāvana, **20**
of Vṛndāvana greet Caitanya, **110-121**

Annakūṭa-grāma
Bhakti-ratnākara quoted on, 142
Gopāla Deity stayed at, **142**

Anubhāva
thirteen categories of, 360

Anugrahyasya dāsatvāl
quoted, 366

Anupama Mallika
as younger brother of Rūpa Gosvāmī, 263, **264**

Anyābhilāṣitā-śūnya
as beginning of pure devotional service, 385

Anyābhilāṣitā-śūnyaṁ jñāna
verses quoted, 331

Aprārabdha-phalaṁ pāpaṁ
quoted, 49

Ariṣṭa-grāma
Ariṣṭāsura killed at, 131

Arjuna
as devotee in fraternity, **370**
begs forgiveness for offenses, **374-375**

Āryan
description of, 325
one who chants holy name is an, **283**

Asat-saṅga-tyāga-ei vaiṣṇava-ācāra
quoted, 340

C

E

H

O

Offenses
against holy name, 189-**190**
against holy name by Māyāvādīs, **67-68**
at feet of Vaiṣṇava, **339**
of Arjuna against Kṛṣṇa, **374-375**
of Māyāvādīs, 78-**79**
Oṁ namo nārāyaṇa
quoted, 185
Opulences
cripple love of God, **372**
of Kṛṣṇa not considered in *kevalā* stage, **377**
of Kṛṣṇa understood in *dāsya-rasa,* **388**
of Vṛndāvana appreciated by Brahmā, 21
sometimes prominent in mellows, **373**
Orissa
attacked by Nawab Hussain Shah, 260
toured by Caitanya, **27**

P

Padmanābha
as father of Lokanātha dāsa Gosvāmī, 155
Padma Purāṇa
quoted on holy name, 71
quoted on Kṛṣṇa's presence, 70
quoted on sin, 49
verses quoted, **134**
Padyāvalī
quoted on supreme form of Kṛṣṇa, **300**
verses of Raghupati Upādhyāya in quoted, **294-295**
Pañcadaśī Citradīpa
quoted on size of soul, **321**
Pañca-dākṣiṇātya-brāhmaṇas
as pure *brāhmaṇas,* 199
Pañca-gauḍa brāhmaṇas
as pure *brāhmaṇas,* 199
Paṇḍitāḥ sama-darśinaḥ
quoted, 74
Paramahaṁsas
Bhāgavatam meant for, 254
Parama-kāraṇa īśvare keha nāhi māne
verses quoted, 104
Paramātmā
realization in *śānta-rasa,* **388**
those in *śānta-rati* attached to, 362
See also: Supersoul
Paramparā
hearing Caitanya through, 27
Parāsya śaktir vividhaiva śrūyate
quoted, 304
Pāṣaṇḍī
explained, 189-**190**
Pastimes of Caitanya
whoever argues about is a fool, **242**
Pastimes of Kṛṣṇa
jñānī attracted by mellows of, **73**
Raghupati Upādhyāya composed verses about, **294**
revived by Rūpa Gosvāmī, **246**
Rūpa and Sanātana empowered to enunciate, **307, 308**
Patañjali Ṛṣi
considered *mahājana* by *yogīs,* 101
Pāṭhāna Vaiṣṇava
toured and glorified Caitanya, **234**
Pāvana Lake
Caitanya bathed in, **160**
Pāvane sarasi snātvā
verses quoted, 160
Peace
formula for in *Gītā,* 329
Phāguyā laiyā keha gāṅṭhi
quoted, 148
Prabhodhānanda Sarasvatī
identification of, 55
Prahlāda Mahārāja
as *mahājana,* 105
Pragalbha
as younger brother of Lokanātha dāsa Gosvāmī, 155
Prakāśānanda Sarasvatī
blasphemes against Caitanya, **61-64,** 67
discussed *Vedānta-sūtra* with Caitanya, 45
explains impersonalism, 55
meets with a *brāhmaṇa,* **56-64**
taught Vedānta philosophy, **54**

R

T

U

W

Y

The Author

His Divine Grace A. C. Bhaktivedanta Swami Prabhupāda appeared in this world in 1896 in Calcutta, India. He first met his spiritual master, Śrīla Bhaktisiddhānta Sarasvatī Gosvāmī, in Calcutta in 1922. Bhaktisiddhānta Sarasvatī, a prominent devotional scholar and the founder of sixty-four Gauḍīya Maṭhas (Vedic Institutes), liked this educated young man and convinced him to dedicate his life to teaching Vedic knowledge. Śrīla Prabhupāda became his student, and eleven years later (1933) at Allahabad he became his formally initiated disciple.

At their first meeting, in 1922, Śrīla Bhaktisiddhānta Sarasvatī Ṭhākura requested Śrīla Prabhupāda to broadcast Vedic knowledge through the English language. In the years that followed, Śrīla Prabhupāda wrote a commentary on the *Bhagavad-gītā,* assisted the Gauḍīya Maṭha in its work and, in 1944, without assistance, started an English fortnightly magazine, edited it, typed the manuscripts and checked the galley proofs. He even distributed the individual copies freely and struggled to maintain the publication. Once begun, the magazine never stopped; it is now being continued by his disciples in the West.

Recognizing Śrīla Prabhupāda's philosophical learning and devotion, the Gauḍīya Vaiṣṇava Society honored him in 1947 with the title "Bhaktivedanta." In 1950, at the age of fifty-four, Śrīla Prabhupāda retired from married life, and four years later he adopted the *vānaprastha* (retired) order to devote more time to his studies and writing. Śrīla Prabhupāda traveled to the holy city of Vṛndāvana, where he lived in very humble circumstances in the historic medieval temple of Rādhā-Dāmodara. There he engaged for several years in deep study and writing. He accepted the renounced order of life (*sannyāsa*) in 1959. At Rādhā-Dāmodara, Śrīla Prabhupāda began work on his life's masterpiece: a multivolume translation and commentary on the eighteen thousand verse *Śrīmad-Bhāgavatam* (*Bhāgavata Purāṇa*). He also wrote *Easy Journey to Other Planets.*

After publishing three volumes of *Bhāgavatam,* Śrīla Prabhupāda came to the United States, in 1965, to fulfill the mission of his spiritual master. Since that time, His Divine Grace has written over forty volumes of authoritative translations, commentaries and summary studies of the philosophical and religious classics of India.

In 1965, when he first arrived by freighter in New York City, Śrīla Prabhupāda was practically penniless. It was after almost a year of great difficulty that he established the International Society for Krishna Consciousness in July of 1966. Under his careful guidance, the Society has grown within a decade to a worldwide confederation of almost one hundred *āśramas,* schools, temples, institutes and farm communities.

In 1968, Śrīla Prabhupāda created New Vṛndāvana, an experimental Vedic community in the hills of West Virginia. Inspired by the success of New Vṛndāvana, now a thriving farm community of more than one thousand acres, his students have since founded several similar communities in the United States and abroad.

In 1972, His Divine Grace introduced the Vedic system of primary and secondary education in the West by founding the *Gurukula* school in Dallas, Texas. The school began with 3 children in 1972, and by the beginning of 1975 the enrollment had-grown to 150.

Śrīla Prabhupāda has also inspired the construction of a large international center at Śrīdhāma Māyāpur in West Bengal, India, which is also the site for a planned Institute of Vedic Studies. A similar project is the magnificent Kṛṣṇa-Balarāma Temple and International Guest House in Vṛndāvana, India. These are centers where Westerners can live to gain firsthand experience of Vedic culture.

Śrīla Prabhupāda's most significant contribution, however, is his books. Highly respected by the academic community for their authoritativeness, depth and clarity, they are used as standard textbooks in numerous college courses. His writings have been translated into eleven languages. The Bhaktivedanta Book Trust, established in 1972 exclusively to publish the works of His Divine Grace, has thus become the world's largest publisher of books in the field of Indian religion and philosophy. Its latest project is the publishing of Śrīla Prabhupāda's most recent work: a seventeen-volume translation and commentary—completed by Śrīla Prabhupāda in only eighteen months—on the Bengali religious classic *Śrī Caitanya-caritāmṛta*.

In the past ten years, in spite of his advanced age, Śrīla Prabhupāda has circled the globe twelve times on lecture tours that have taken him to six continents. In spite of such a vigorous schedule, Śrīla Prabhupāda continues to write prolifically. His writings constitute a veritable library of Vedic philosophy, religion, literature and culture.